The NIV Standard Lesson Commentary 1994-95

D1551838

International Sunday School Lessons

published by

Standard Publishing

Eugene H. Wigginton, *Publisher*

Richard C. McKinley, *Director of Curriculum Development*

James I. Fehl, *Senior Editor*　　　　　　Hela M. Campbell, *Office Editor*

Jonathan Underwood, *NIV Editor*

First Annual Volume

STANDARD PUBLISHING
Cincinnati, Ohio

© 1994

The STANDARD PUBLISHING Company

division of STANDEX INTERNATIONAL Corporation

8121 Hamilton Avenue, Cincinnati, Ohio 45231

Printed in U.S.A.

In This Volume

Autumn Quarter, 1994
Theme: From the Conquest to the Kingdom

Writers

Lesson Development............................*Orrin Root*
Verbal Illustrations..................*Charles R. Boatman*
Discovery Learning ....*Mark Taylor*

What Do You Think? ....*Kenton K. Smith*
Reproducible Activities ....*Jonathan Underwood*

Winter Quarter, 1994-95
Theme: Jesus the Fulfillment
(The Gospel of Matthew)

Writers

Lesson Development.............*Carl Bridges, Jr.* (1-4)
David Morely (5, 6)
R. Edwin Groover (7)
Robert Lowery (8)
David Engart (9)
J. Lee Magness (10-13)
Verbal Illustrations.................*Woodrow W. Phillips*

Discovery Learning ....*Greg Bowman* (1-4)
Dennis Glenn (5, 6)
Eleanor Daniel (7-9)
Jonathon Stedman (10-13)
What Do You Think? ....*Joe Sutherland*
Reproducible Activities ....*Linda Ford*

Spring Quarter, 1995
Theme: Christian Living in Community

Writers

Lesson Development.........*John D. Castelein* (1, 2)
Roger W. Thomas (3, 4)
Johnny Pressley (5-9)
Edwin V. Hayden (10-13)
Verbal Illustrations...................*James G. VanBuren*

Discovery Learning ....*Sue Sutherland*
What Do You Think? ....*Kenton K. Smith*
Reproducible Activities...................*Phil Haas* (1-4)
Michael D. McCann (5-9)
Jonathan Underwood (10-13)

Summer Quarter, 1995
Theme: A Nation Turns to God

Writers

Lesson Development.......................*John W. Wade*
Verbal Illustrations....................*Richard W. Baynes*
Johnny Pressley (5-9)
Discovery Learning ....*Michael D. McCann*

What Do You Think? ....*David Baynes* (1-4)
R. David Roberts (5-13)
Reproducible Activities....................*Mark Plunkett*

Lessons based on International Sunday School Lessons

The Complete Picture

Of what value to Christians is a knowledge of the Old Testament? Isn't it just ancient history? One of the values of these writings is precisely that—they relate to the history of an ancient people, Israel. More specifically, however, they contain the record of God's working through that people to accomplish his purpose.

In time, God's purpose was brought to light in the life, death, and resurrection of Jesus and in the establishment of the church. An understanding of the historical background of these events, along with the prophecies regarding them, helps to establish the certainty of one's faith in Jesus Christ as Lord and Savior.

The Autumn and Summer quarters this year are courses of Old Testament history. It can be seen that the latter quarter takes up the story where the former leaves off. All of the Old Testament historical studies in this lesson cycle are in chronological sequence in order to give a clear and comprehensive view of Israel's history.

The New Testament is emphasized in this lesson cycle, also. The Winter quarter examines the life of Jesus, focusing on his fulfillment of the Old Testament promises. Paul's letters to the Corinthians, the subject of the Spring quarter, provide guidance for the church today, as they did for the church in Corinth in the first century.

International Sunday School Lesson Cycle
September, 1992—August, 1998

YEAR	AUTUMN QUARTER (Sept., Oct., Nov.)	WINTER QUARTER (Dec., Jan., Feb.)	SPRING QUARTER (Mar., Apr., May)	SUMMER QUARTER (June, July, Aug.)
1992-1993	Old Testament Personalities (Old Testament Survey)	Good News for All (Old Testament Survey)	Believing in Christ (John)	Following God's Purpose (Ephesians, Philippians, Colossians, Philemon)
1993-1994	The Story of Beginnings (Genesis)	The Story of Jesus (Luke)	Good News for God's People (Romans) Set Free by God's Grace (Galatians)	God Redeems a People (Exodus, Leviticus, Numbers, Deuteronomy)
1994-1995	From the Conquest to the Kingdom (Joshua, Judges, 1 and 2 Samuel, 1 Kings)	Jesus the Fulfillment (Matthew)	Christians Living in Community (1 and 2 Corinthians)	A Nation Turns From God (1 and 2 Kings, Amos, Hosea, Micah, Isaiah)
1995-1996	The Story of Christian Beginnings (Acts)	God's Promise of Deliverance (Isaiah) God's Love for All People (Jonah, Ruth)	Teachings of Jesus (Matthew, Mark, Luke)	A Practical Religion (James) God Is With Us (Psalms)
1996-1997	God's People Face Judgment (2 Kings, Jeremiah, Lamentations, Ezekiel, Habakkuk)	New Testament Personalities	Hope for the Future (1 and 2 Thessalonians, Revelation)	Guidance for Ministry (1 and 2 Timothy, Titus) A Call to Faithfulness (Hebrews)
1997-1998	God Leads a People Home (Major Prophets, Minor Prophets, Nehemiah)	God's People in a Troubled World (1 and 2 Peter, 1, 2, 3 John, Jude)	The Gospel of Action (Mark)	Wisdom for Living (Job, Proverbs, Ecclesiastes)

Index of Printed Texts, 1994-95

The printed texts for 1994-95 are arranged here in the order in which they appear in the Bible. Opposite each reference is the page number on which the passage begins in this volume.

Introducing *The NIV Standard Lesson Commentary*

At last! Here is a user-friendly Uniform Lesson commentary based on the *New International Version* Scripture text. Teachers familiar with the *Standard Lesson Commentary* will immediately feel at home with this volume. Many features here are the same as in that popular resource (based on the King James Version). Whether or not you have used the *Standard Lesson Commentary* before, however, you will quickly find *The NIV Standard Lesson Commentary* a helpful companion in preparing your Sunday school lessons.

LESSON DEVELOPMENT

The first page of each lesson clearly identifies the title, Scripture, current unit, and lesson aims for the session. A thumb tab identifies the date the lesson will be taught so that it is quickly found. The date is repeated on each page at the top outside corner.

The first item in the lesson development is a brief rationale for the lesson: **"Why Teach This Lesson?"** Tying the lesson theme to contemporary life, this section puts application at the forefront of your preparation. Then comes the lesson treatment itself, following a three-point structure: introduction, exposition, and conclusion. The **introduction** provides background and other useful information to set the stage, tie the current lessons with earlier ones, and generally give you a handle on the context for the current lesson.

What follows is a **verse-by-verse Scripture exposition.** The text is printed in the *New International Version,* usually one verse at a time. Bold type sets the text off from commentary so you can read it easily, even if you just want to read through the passage without comment at first. The commentary is interspersed so you can relate the comments to the specific Scripture passage it illuminates.

The **conclusion** leans heavily toward **application,** giving specific examples of how the principles of the lesson Scripture can be put to practice in real life.

Verbal illustrations, usually two in each lesson, help to illuminate the concepts of the lesson. These are usually found in the exposition section, providing yet another tool for you to illustrate the point of the Scripture. These are set off in block quotes so they can be easily found or easily jumped over if you choose not to use them.

MARGINAL NOTES

Many of the most helpful features of this lesson commentary are found in the margins. Occasionally the text suggests some interesting point for discussion. These issues are raised under the heading of **"What Do You Think?"** The question is raised, sometimes from more than one perspective. The Scripture in the main section is relevant, and other Scriptures may also be suggested. No answers are given, however, because these are questions without pat answers. These will encourage your students to wrestle with the big issues without being trite.

"Visuals" are pictured in the margins, also. These are reproductions of the classroom visuals available from Standard Publishing each quarter to help your students visualize the points being made. Again, these appear in the margin alongside the Scripture or other part of the lesson where they are most appropriate.

Daily Bible readings, points to remember, and even prayer ideas are included in the margin near the end of each lesson.

DISCOVERY LEARNING

For teachers who like to involve their students in the learning process, a page of **Discovery Learning** is included in each lesson. These alternate lesson plans are designed to get the students busy in Bible study and application to discover for themselves the timeless truths of the Scriptures. Each one has an activity to begin the lesson, a Bible Study activity, and an application activity.

The last page of each lesson is a **reproducible page.** These, too, are designed to involve the students in discovery learning. They provide optional activities that may be introduced at different points in the lesson. Marginal "Option" notes frequently call your attention to an activity on this page. Or start with the whole page and build your lesson plan around it, using the other resources in this book.

OPTIONS

This is a lesson planner with lots of options! No matter what style you prefer—lecture, discussion, activities—you'll find resources to plan a great lesson. If you like variety, this will help you design a lesson unique to the personality of you and your class. Or, if you like a ready-made plan you can take with minimal preparation time, you'll find that, too. It's all here.

We'd Like Your Input!

We consider ourselves your partners in teaching the Word of God. Therefore we want to make the NIV Standard Lesson Commentary as helpful as possible to you. To help us do this, please rate the following features of the commentary as to their usefulness to you.

Lesson Feature	Very Helpful	Somewhat Helpful	Seldom Helpful	Not Helpful
1. "Why Teach This Lesson?"				
2. "Introduction to the Lesson"				
3. "Lesson Aims"				
4. "Key Verse"				
5. Explanation of the Scripture				
6. "How to Say It"				
7. "What Do You Think?"				
8. Verbal illustrations				
9. "Prayer"				
10. "Thought to Remember"				
11. "Daily Bible Readings"				
12. "Discovery Learning" lesson plan				
13. Reproducible student page				
14. Reproductions of the visual aids				
15. "Index of Printed Texts"				
16. Introductory Articles				

17. Would you prefer to have the lesson Scripture printed all together in one block even though that means there would be less space for other lesson material?

❑ Strongly prefer, ❑ Slightly prefer, ❑ No, ❑ Undecided

18. Would you prefer to have the commentary printed in larger type even though that would mean less space for lesson content?

❑ Strongly prefer, ❑ Slightly prefer, ❑ No, ❑ Undecided

19. Please list other suggestions you have for improving future editions of The NIV Standard Lesson Commentary. (Continue on the back of this page if necessary).

THANK YOU!

We appreciate your help. Now please cut or tear this page carefully from your book, fold as indicated on the reverse side, tape the loose edges, and drop in a mail box. We will consider every response and attempt to refine The NIV Standard Lesson Commentary *for 1995-96 to be even more useful than this edition.*

Autumn Quarter, 1994

Theme: From the Conquest to the Kingdom

Special Features

Lessons

Unit 1. The Conquest of the Land

Unit 2. The Rule of the Judges

Unit 3. The Beginning of the Kingdom

Unit 4. The Kingdom Under David and Solomon

About these lessons

This study focuses on the history of the people of Israel from their conquest of the promised land to the later years of Solomon's reign. Significant achievements and failures of the people and of their first three kings are noted.

Sep 4

Sep 11

Sep 18

Sep 25

Oct 2

Oct 9

Oct 16

Oct 23

Oct 30

Nov 6

Nov 13

Nov 20

Nov 27

Experiments in Government

by Orrin Root

When we see the many kinds of governments in the world, it is almost a shock to read that "the powers that be are ordained of God" (Romans 13:1, KJV). Is God experimenting with all those governments to see what kind will work the best? No, God does not experiment in order to learn. He already knows. But within limits he lets us experiment so that we may learn.

When God called the people of Israel from Egypt to be his own, he gave them a law. If all of them would live by it, they would be governed in the ideal way. But those people were not prepared for the responsibility of ordering their lives by the law. God made Moses a virtual dictator, and backed him by such evidence of divine power that resistance was overwhelmed.

When Joshua took Moses' place, the people seemed to have learned their lesson. With few aberrations they followed the new leader and lived by the law while they conquered the promised land and settled down in it.

Then it was time for each person to accept his own responsibility, but the people failed miserably. Through greed and malice and laziness and love of pleasure, they disobeyed God's law. Thus they became weak and spineless, easy prey for bandit gangs or national armies of pagans who invaded the land. Through the time of the judges they showed that only with powerful leadership would they behave as they ought.

Since strong leadership seemed to be needed, the people asked for a king. God knew that was not the answer, but he let them experiment and learn. Kings are only human. They too can be motivated by greed, malice, laziness, and love of pleasure.

Would Israel—would any nation—ever learn the infallible way to national stability, prosperity, and happiness? It is for each person to do right by preference, not by compulsion—and to look to God's Word to see what is right.

In past lessons we have read of Moses' troubled dictatorship that was able to succeed because it was supported and directed by the Almighty. In the lessons before us we shall see the times of Joshua and the judges and the first three kings of Israel. Our studies of the next three months are divided into four units as follows:

SEPTEMBER

UNIT ONE: THE CONQUEST OF THE LAND

Lesson 1. From the camp of Israel east of the Jordan, Joshua sent two daring spies across the flooded river to learn what they could about Jericho. They found that the city walls were strong, but the people were frightened.

Lesson 2. The river was a raging torrent overflowing its banks. But God said it was time to go, so the people loaded their donkeys and shouldered their packs and marched toward the swollen stream. As the first feet splashed into the shallows, the flow swiftly receded. Far upstream the water piled up in a heap, leaving an empty river bed for the people to cross.

Lesson 3. Defenders on the walls of Jericho watched and wondered as day after day the Hebrew warriors marched once around the city and then went back to their camp. On the seventh day they circled the city seven times. Then the trumpets sounded and the walls fell down flat. Thousands of Hebrew soldiers scrambled over the tumbled stones to destroy everybody and everything in town.

The war went on for about seven years, but everywhere God gave his people victory. When they had taken as much land as they could use, they settled down to farming. For a long time they had peace and prosperity. Our lessons begin near the end of Joshua's life.

Lesson 4. More than a hundred years old, Joshua called the people together. They had a choice, he said. There were the gods their fathers had served centuries ago by the Euphrates; there were the pagan gods of the land they had taken; there was the Lord who had led them from Egypt and given them this land. Which God would they serve? Loudly the people declared they would serve the Lord.

UNIT TWO: THE RULE OF THE JUDGES

OCTOBER 2, 9

For a long time the Hebrews kept their promise to serve the Lord. But, one by one, the valiant warriors who had won the land were replaced by a softer generation, blessed by rain and sun and good harvests instead of mighty miracles and victory in battle. They were not so acutely aware of the Lord among them (Judges 2:10).

Lesson 5. Envy grew, and dishonesty, and violence, and murder. People even began to join in the feasts of pagan gods. God's punishment came in the form of invaders who stole livestock and harvest, killing anyone who stood in their way. Hungry and afraid, the people thought again of the Lord, stopped worshiping other gods, and began pleading for help. Mercifully, God provided a leader (judge) to rally them and defeat the invaders. But when peace and prosperity were restored, all too soon the people began to forget God again. This happened over and over through the three hundred years we call the period of the judges.

Lesson 6. Here is an example of that repeated process. Midianites from the desert occupied Israel. When the people turned to the Lord, he called Gideon to rescue them. Gideon raised an army of 32,000, but the Lord reduced it to 300. With that handful the Lord chased the innumerable host of invaders back to the desert. Convinced of the Lord's power, the people again were loyal to him—but not for long.

UNIT THREE: THE BEGINNING OF THE KINGDOM

OCTOBER 16, 23, 30

Samuel, the last of the judges, rallied the people to drive out the Philistines who had oppressed them. Then he led the nation in righteousness. But in his old age he made his sons judges, and they were greedy and crooked (1 Samuel 7:3—8:3).

Lesson 7. Leaders of the people asked Samuel to give them a king. Samuel and the Lord did not approve of that. The Lord was the proper king of Israel. The people had only to obey him to have peace and prosperity forever. But the leaders persisted in their request for a king, and the Lord said to let them have their way.

Lesson 8. The Lord chose Saul to be the first king of Israel, and the people gladly acclaimed him.

Lesson 9. Saul began his reign with a brilliant victory over Ammonites who threatened a city of Israel (1 Samuel 11). But soon he faced a greater test of his trust in the Lord. When Philistines invaded Israel, the Lord told Saul to hold his troops at Gilgal till Samuel would come to offer sacrifice and direct the campaign. After a week, Saul became impatient and went ahead with the sacrifice before Samuel came. For that he was told his family would not continue on the throne of Israel.

UNIT FOUR: THE KINGDOM UNDER DAVID AND SOLOMON

NOVEMBER

The Lord chose David to be the next king, but Saul continued to rule for many years while David was maturing and being prepared to rule. When Saul was killed in battle, David became king and established his capital at Jerusalem. He brought the ark of the covenant there and proposed to build a temple for the Lord. Nathan the prophet brought God's answer: David was not to build the temple, but God promised that people of David's line would continue to rule forever (2 Samuel 1:1—7:17).

Lesson 10. Humbly David accepted God's will and gave thanks for his promise. But even David was not immune to temptation. He committed adultery with a neighbor's wife, and then had the neighbor killed in battle (2 Samuel 11).

Lesson 11. God sent Nathan to denounce David's sin, and David humbly confessed his guilt.

Solomon was the next king. At his request, God gave him special wisdom. God also gave riches and honor that Solomon did not ask. The new king improved David's empire, and built the temple that David was not allowed to build. His reputation spread far and wide.

Lesson 12. The queen of Sheba was one of many who came to see if Solomon lived up to his reputation. She found that he did, and more.

Lesson 13. Having everything his own way, Solomon neglected to give enough attention to God's way. For political purposes he brought pagan princesses to Jerusalem as his wives. They brought their pagan religions, and Solomon built places of worship for their pagan gods. The Lord's rebuke was plain, and his punishment was severe. Solomon's glorious empire would be lost; his kingdom would be divided; his son would rule only one tribe of Israel's twelve.

This series of lessons proclaims the power of God and the weakness of men. Showered with God's blessings, people turn away from him. The people of Israel did it over and over in the time of the judges. Their kings did it too. Elevated by God's power and blessed by his favor, Saul and David and Solomon all disobeyed him. Their failure is the common failure of mankind. Who among us will not say with David, "I have sinned against the Lord"? (2 Samuel 12:13).

So all history unites in proclaiming this truth: People need a Savior. Praise the Lord, he has provided one—Jesus Christ his Son. By his gracious forgiveness we sinners can have "the righteousness that comes from God and is by faith" (Philippians 3:9). There is no other hope for mankind.

The Subject of Our Lives

by Gary E. Weedman

Political revolutions, changing national boundaries, and uprootings of ethnic peoples are not unique to the latter part of the twentieth century; they also make up much of the narrative of the book of Joshua. The political changes in central and eastern Europe and in the former Yugoslavia have monopolized our headlines in recent months without much understanding from western observers. Yet one of the clear messages of Scripture is that similar events described in the book of Joshua have meaning that we are able to know from the revelation of God himself.

There is some temptation to assume from the Israelite conquest of Canaan that God "blesses" the nation that honors him by enhancing their military might, their expansionist interests, or their national stature. Coming to the book of Joshua with this world view will cause one to misunderstand the events recorded in it as well as affect any meaning this book holds for our own times.

GOD, THE SUBJECT OF JOSHUA

Joshua is an intriguing character. He led the Israelites across the Jordan River with its waters "piled up in a heap," even though it was at flood stage (Joshua 3:16). Fearlessly he led the priests, the ark of the covenant, and the armed men around the city of Jericho. He asked God to stay the sun over Gibeon to give the Israelites the needed time for victory. Near the end of his life he stood before the Israelites and delivered one of the most famous addresses of all history—one that revealed a great faith and a single devotion.

Yet, Joshua is not the subject of the book that bears his name; God is. Note the following references: God told Joshua, "I will give you every place where you set your foot, as I promised Moses. . . . I will never leave you nor forsake you" (1: 3, 5). After Joshua sent two men on a spy mission and they were befriended by Rahab, they returned to Joshua with this report: "The Lord has surely given the whole land into our hands" (2:24). As the Israelites made preparations to cross the Jordan and claim the covenant made to Abraham, God told Joshua, "Today I will begin to exalt you in the eyes of all Israel, so they may know that I am with you as I was with Moses" (3:7).

Joshua knew who the subject of the narrative really was. After the people crossed the Jordan and set up the stones as a memorial at Gilgal, Joshua told them, "The Lord your God dried up the Jordan before you. . . . The Lord your God did to the Jordan just what he had done to the Red Sea" (4:23). At Jericho it was not clever strategy that provided a victory for the Israelites. Even before the battle, God said, "See, I have delivered Jericho into your hands, along with its king and its fighting men (6:2). Joshua's cry on the seventh day was, "The Lord has given you the city" (6:16). And so goes the narrative of Joshua. It is the narrative of God at work. God said, "For I have delivered into your hands the king of Ai" (8:1). In the campaign against the southern cities, "the Lord, the God of Israel, fought for Israel" (10:42). Neither the intelligence nor the courage nor the power nor the resourcefulness of Joshua or the Israelites are the subject of this book. They may have been wise and courageous and resourceful. The subject, however, is God himself.

WHAT ABOUT US?

When the narratives of our lives are written, who will be the subject? In our western, enlightened, and increasingly secular society, one does not expect God to be made the subject of life; it is common for humans, or events, or other things to occupy that position. It is tragic, however, to see this secularist tendency creeping into the lives of believers. The examples are many.

When a crisis occurs in the lives of others, we hear believers say, "You're in our thoughts," or "We're remembering you," or, "You have our sympathy." These well-intentioned responses reflect the impact of secular society. How hard it has become for many believers to say, "We'll pray to God for your difficulty"!

A local congregation finished a much-needed education wing for their building. During the celebration reception, many of the members were observing how many persons had worked, sacrificed, and given to the project. A local minister associated with another fellowship came through the reception line and noted, "It looks like the Spirit of God has been at work here!" God's Spirit had been at work in that congregation, and still is at work; why is it so difficult for those good people to say so?

In an Austrian village not far from Haus Edelweiss, the European headquarters of the mission agency TCM International, there is a small hotel named Die Auge des Gott ("The Eye of God"). When asked about this unusual name, the proprietors explained that they were so aware of the presence of God throughout their lives, they wanted to affirm that faith by such a name for their hotel; the name seemed natural to them. The very fact that I regarded this name as "strange" is evidence of the effect that this secularist trend can have on those of us living in the western world.

This attitude, a reluctance to make God "the subject of our narratives," has at least two causes. First, I suspect that many do not want to appear to be religious zealots in the same mold as the religious cults, who attribute the events of their own history, as extreme and bizarre as they are, to the acts of God. The world remembers the fanaticism of Jim Jones and David Koresh, persons who seemed obsessed by the idea of God in their lives.

Second, the scientific world view has influenced us all more than we may know. During the eighteenth century a movement known as "The Enlightenment" emerged. The leaders of this movement not only believed that one could understand the world from a purely secular perspective, they also believed that human effort could control the events of the world. Persons did not need God to understand the world or to control its events. Humans, they believed, had the capacity to solve their own problems, whether social, material, physical, or "spiritual" by the application of the same kind of inventiveness used in scientific advances. Joshua, however, had a different viewpoint.

A HEAVENLY PERSPECTIVE

The perspective from which one sees any object or event greatly affects the understanding of it. While living in England, my sons and I watched cricket matches as baseball-loving Americans. What we "saw" was very different from what cricket-loving Englishmen saw. It was only when we began to see the game as they saw it, to understand cricket separate from the perspective of baseball, that we had any real understanding of what was going on.

So it was with the man, Joshua. God is the subject of the book of Joshua because Joshua saw his world from the perspective of God himself.

Joshua saw God fulfilling his eternal purpose of keeping his covenant with Abraham, Isaac, and Jacob. He saw God giving the land of Canaan to the people of Israel, the descendants of those patriarchs (Genesis 12:1, 7; 15:7, 18). Joshua saw God making of them "a great nation" (Genesis 12:2). Joshua knew as surely as if it had already happened that in the Israelites, "all peoples on earth [would] be blessed" (Genesis 12:3). He saw God's hand in those events, a divine involvement elaborated upon by the apostle Paul nearly fifteen hundred years later when he wrote, "For I do not want you to be ignorant of the fact, brothers, that our forefathers were all under the cloud and that they all passed through the sea. They were all baptized into Moses in the cloud and in the sea. They all ate the same spiritual food and drank the same spiritual drink; for they drank from the spiritual rock that accompanied them, and that rock was Christ" (1 Corinthians 10:1-4).

God is working in the world today through Christ, bringing to fulfillment his great plan of redemption. May we all, like Joshua, be aware of God's eternal purpose and make him the center, the subject as it were, of our lives.

From the Conquest to the Kingdom
Unit 1. The Conquest of the Land
(Lessons 1-4)

Sep
4

SPYING OUT JERICHO
LESSON 1

WHY TEACH THIS LESSON?

Contemporary society is awash with "self-esteem" and "self-improvement" courses. Unfortunately, many people enroll in seminar after expensive seminar and have as little esteem as before. They lack confidence in themselves, their government, their society, and even their God.

It is to be expected, actually. A generation that has grown up being told they are here by chance (the product of evolution) and they have nowhere to go (no Heaven or Hell) is naturally pessimistic. In what or whom can they have confidence?

Ancient Israel had the advantage in this respect. They knew they were God's people. They knew where they had come from (most recently, Egypt) and where they were going (to be a "great nation"). They believed and had confidence in the God who had called them. When their confidence waned, he gave them reassurance.

We today can have the same confidence. God has called us and has promised us the victory. This lesson reminds us that the same God who led Israel into the promised land is leading us to our own "promised land"!

INTRODUCTION

"I will make you into a great nation." So said the Lord, and Abraham believed it. Even when he was seventy-five years old and had no child, he believed God's promise. Depending on that promise, he set out for a country unknown (Genesis 12:1-4; Hebrews 11:8).

Abraham was a hundred years old before he had a son to inherit the promise. When his son Isaac was sixty, he had two sons; but only one of them inherited the promise. So in the third generation the nation-to-be was only one man.

Then expansion began. Jacob had twelve sons, and all of them were heirs of the promise. Jacob was 130 years old when he led the family to Egypt, and it numbered about seventy people. In a few centuries it grew to perhaps three million. Jacob's other name, Israel, became the name of the nation.

A. THE BIRTH OF A NATION

Those years in Egypt may be called the prenatal period of Israel. There was growth in numbers, but not in independence. The growth alarmed Egypt's king. What if the people of Israel would join some outside enemy and overthrow him? He made slaves of them and tried to work them to death, but they thrived on hard work.

Then came the time for the infant nation to be delivered. The birth was difficult, but Israel was free—free, but feeble and fearful. For forty years God nurtured it in the desert, till it became mature enough to inherit the land he had for it—the land of Canaan at the east end of the Mediterranean Sea.

B. LESSON BACKGROUND

From the southern desert, God led his people northward east of the country of Moab that lay along the east shore of the Dead Sea. When they turned west toward the Jordan, the Amorites opposed them with deadly force; but Israel quickly van-

DEVOTIONAL READING:
JOSHUA 1:1-9
LESSON SCRIPTURE:
JOSHUA 1, 2
PRINTED TEXT:
JOSHUA 2:1, 8-14, 22-24

LESSON AIMS

After this lesson a student should be able to:

1. Retell the story of Israel's daring spies in Jericho.

2. Explain why the people of Israel were confident as they prepared to invade the promised land.

3. Confidently undertake some needed service for the Lord.

KEY VERSE:

"The Lord has surely given the whole land into our hands."
—Joshua 2:24

LESSON 1 NOTES

quished those opponents and took over their country. Moving north on the east bank of Jordan, they captured Bashan as well.

Israel camped in the eastern plain, looking across the flooded Jordan toward Jericho. Moses died, and Joshua became the nation's leader.

I. DANGEROUS MISSION (JOSHUA 2:1)

Winter was giving way to spring as the new leader prepared to take his people across the river and conquer the tribes in Canaan.

A. INFORMATION NEEDED (V. 1A)

1a. Then Joshua son of Nun secretly sent two spies from Shittim. "Go, look over the land," he said, "especially Jericho."

Israel's camp was in Shittim, an area of indefinite size a few miles east of the Jordan. Its name means acacias, so we suppose those trees grew abundantly there. Across to the west, Jericho lay in the narrow plain between the river and the mountains beyond. Obviously it would be the first place to be captured. Joshua sent two daring young men to see what they could learn about the place: the lay of the land, the strength of the walls, the number of people, the kind of weapons they had. No less important was the morale. Were the people of Jericho confident and resolute, or were they frightened?

B. BOLD BEGINNING (V. 1B)

1b. So they went and entered the house of a prostitute named Rahab and stayed there.

As the rainy season was just ending, the Jordan was deep and wide, overflowing its banks (Joshua 3:15). But the Israelites may have captured some boats along with the land of the Amorites. Crossing the river was not very difficult, even at night.

On the west bank, apparently the spies thought a bold approach would be best. Perhaps they hoped people would think they were ordinary travelers, not men from the camp of Israel. They simply walked into Jericho and found lodging in the house of a prostitute. It may seem strange that men of Israel would stop in such a place. Only a short time before, some had died for their sins with sexy women of Moab (Numbers 25:1-5). But perhaps all the hotels in Jericho were of the same kind. Some think the Hebrew word *zonah* means primarily a hostess or innkeeper, and that Rahab may not have been a prostitute. Gesenius, the famous lexicographer, rejects that thought; but others hold it strongly. It would not be surprising if every lodging house in town was a house of prostitution. The people of that land were corrupt beyond any hope of reformation. The Lord ordered them to be destroyed—men, women, and children (Deuteronomy 20:16-18).

If the spies hoped to find safety in their boldness, they were disappointed. Someone knew or guessed where they came from and why they were there. The king was told of it, and he sent his men demanding that the prostitute turn in her guests. Rahab put on an innocent face. "Why, yes, some men were here," she said, "but I had no idea where they came from. They left just before the gates were closed for the night. Hurry after them! Surely you can catch them."

If the officers were suspicious enough to search the house, they found no men of Israel. Rahab had hidden them under a pile of flax on the roof. So the king's men raced toward the Jordan, and the gate was locked behind them so the spies could not escape if they were hidden somewhere in the city (vv. 2-7)

II. MAKING A DEAL (JOSHUA 2:8-14)

Rahab was wise as well as wily. Protecting her guests was not just a matter of good business, hoping they would come again or recommend her place to

---

VISUALS FOR THESE LESSONS

The Adult Visuals/Learning Resources packet contains classroom-size visuals designed for use with the lessons in the Autumn Quarter. The packet is available from your supplier. Order No. ST 192.

WHAT DO YOU THINK?

It has been suggested that Joshua showed a lack of faith by sending the spies into Jericho. After all, God had promised them a victory; what need did they have to spy out the city?

Others say this is not a lack of faith, but just good sense. God does not always give us all the details of a plan, but expects us to use careful planning and sound judgment in combination with our faith.

What do you think? And how does that apply to your own exercise of faith in the Lord?

their friends. Neither was it mere kindness of heart that made her keep them safe. The woman had sized up the situation accurately, and she meant to save her own life by saving the spies.

A. FEAR (vv. 8-11)

8. Before the spies lay down for the night, she went up on the roof.

Before her guests bedded down for the night, Rahab came up to the roof to make a deal with them.

9. And said to them, "I know that the LORD has given this land to you and that a great fear of you has fallen on us, so that all who live in this country are melting in fear because of you.

If the spies wanted to learn about the morale of Jericho's defenders, they had come to the right place. Rahab's eyes and ears had been open. She was convinced that *the Lord,* the God of Israel, had given her country to his people, and they would surely take it. She knew that God by name, for *the Lord* here represents the personal name that has come into English as *Jehovah.* She knew her fellow citizens were terrified by the approach of the fearsome Israelites, and that all the inhabitants of the land were *melting in fear. To melt* is to lose strength of body and mind. We might say the people of Jericho "had no backbone" in the face of the Israelites.

10. We have heard how the LORD dried up the water of the Red Sea for you, when you came out of Egypt, and what you did to Sihon and Og, the two kings of the Amorites east of the Jordan, whom you completely destroyed.

Forty years had passed since the Lord had *dried up the water of the Red Sea* for Israel. Perhaps that great event happened before Rahab was born; but news of it had come across the years and the miles to Jericho, and it had not been forgotten.

Recent events were no less alarming. Just *east of the Jordan,* and in recent months, *the two kings of the Amorites* had opposed Israel; and Israel had *completely destroyed* them. Those were strong and warlike kings. Not long before, Sihon had taken some of the territory of Moab (Numbers 21:26). Probably they could muster more troops than Jericho could. What would happen when the destroyers of the Amorites came across the Jordan to Jericho?

11. When we heard of it, our hearts melted and everyone's courage failed because of you, for the LORD your God is God in heaven above and on the earth below.

Morale in Jericho was not just low; it was missing! There were no strong hearts there, no courage. There was no hope of victory, and therefore no will to fight. The people were convinced that the Lord ruled both Heaven and earth; and he was for Israel and against Jericho. The hearts of the spies must have soared at the news. This town would be a pushover!

RECOGNIZING GOD'S POWER

Sometimes it seems one can point to the time when a major shift in culture or history takes place. The year 1948 is an example. When the year began, there were nineteen television stations broadcasting in the United States, and Americans owned 186,000 TV sets. By year's end the number of stations had more than doubled and a million sets had been sold. We had entered the video age, and nothing could turn back the clock. Few people could have guessed the amazing changes—for both good and bad—that would take place in American culture because of television.

Rahab seems to have had an insight about the changes that would take place in her land when Israel invaded Canaan. She told Joshua's spies that the reputation of their God had preceded them. He was feared as the One who had miraculously delivered Israel from slavery and had led them in conquering the Amorites. Rahab could see that only those who were on the side of Israel's God had hope for survival.

WHAT DO YOU THINK?

Rahab lied about her knowledge of the two spies, and the Bible does not speak disapprovingly of her act. Thus, some have asserted, it is not always wrong to lie. In time of war, for example, the taking of lives is not called murder. Is the sacrifice of truth sometimes similarly not "lying"? If the two spies had been discovered and Rahab had used physical violence to defend them, would she not have been honored for it? Is she less a hero if her defense took a less violent form?

Others are quick to point out that the Bible's silence here is not an endorsement. The Bible does not speak disapprovingly of many recorded actions that are contrary to its laws. The checkered career of Samson is one example that comes to mind. In addition, Colossians 3:9 says, "Do not lie to each other, since you have taken off your old self with its practices." Further, Revelation 21:8 and 22:15 state that liars will be excluded from Heaven.

What do you think?

We naturally desire to be on the "winning" side in life's great battle. Just as important, however, is that we recognize that God has been at work in history and that we take part in the redemptive work he is doing through his people at this moment in time

—C. R. B.

B. DEAL (vv. 12-14)

12, 13. Now then, please swear to me by the Lord that you will show kindness to my family, because I have shown kindness to you. Give me a sure sign that you will spare the lives of my father and mother, my brothers and sisters, and all who belong to them, and that you will save us from death."

The deal was simple. Rahab had saved the lives of these two spies. She asked them to guarantee her safety and the safety of her whole family in the coming destruction of Jericho. And she meant the entire family with no exceptions: father and mother and brothers and sisters, and all who belong to them—all their wives and husbands and sons and daughters.

Rahab wanted the spies to agree to this deal and to give her a *sure sign*. Perhaps that means she wanted them to specify some sure sign by which she and other members of her family could be recognized and spared in the rightful confusion when the city was being destroyed.

14. "Our lives for your lives!" the men assured her. "If you don't tell what we are doing, we will treat you kindly and faithfully when the Lord gives us the land."

Promptly the spies agreed. Rahab had saved their lives and their mission, and now they saw how important that was. News of the terror in Jericho would give courage to the warriors of Israel. If the spies had failed to come back, that would have generated doubts and fears. So the men promised safety to their hostess, but only if she would continue to keep their movements secret.

UNLIKELY HEROES

Matewan, West Virginia, is a little mountain town with a checkered past and a difficult present. In 1878, the famous Hatfield-McCoy feud began there for reasons no one is sure about today. In the 1920s, Matewan's bloody "coal wars" occurred. That labor rebellion has been called by some America's largest armed insurrection since the Civil War. Since 1957, thirty-three floods have destroyed much of the town.

In light of this, Matewan's hope for the future is especially interesting. The leaders of the town have decided to revive their community by attracting tourists, capitalizing on the feud between the Hatfield and McCoy clans. If their plans succeed, people who share the blame for the town's infamy will become the unlikely "heroes" bringing a brighter future to Matewan!

God has used many unlikely heroes to accomplish his will throughout history. Rahab is just one example. A prostitute in Jericho who recognized the power of God, she protected the Israelite spies. The lesson for us is that none are so disreputable or so evil that they cannot further God's cause today if they will acknowledge his power and his rightful place in their lives.

—C. R. B.

III. MISSION ACCOMPLISHED (JOSHUA 2:22-24)

Verses 15-21 supply additional details. Rahab's house was on the city wall. From her window she lowered a rope outside the wall so the men could climb down in the darkness. The king's men were searching the plain, so she told her guests to hide in the hills for a few days. They could go back to their camp in safety after the search was over.

The red rope by which the spies escaped became the "sure sign" Rahab had requested (v. 12). She was to tie it in her window where it could be seen by Israel's warriors when they came. It would mark the only safe house in all Jericho. Rahab must see that all her relatives were in that house when the attack came. Any outside would die with the rest of the inhabitants.

A. RETURN (vv. 22, 23)
22. When they left, they went into the hills and stayed there three days, until the pursuers had searched all along the road and returned without finding them.

Following Rahab's advice, the spies went west *into the hills* instead of east to the river. They did not have far to go; rugged mountains rise steeply only a little way from Jericho. Rocky ravines provided good hiding places. The rainy season was near its end, but water could be found in little streams and pools. Perhaps Rahab had given the fugitives enough food for a few days. Meanwhile the king's men scoured the plain between the Jordan and Jericho. If the searchers found a boat the spies had used, that encouraged them to think the intruders had not escaped across the river. So they searched diligently, but within *three days* they concluded that the spies had got away.

23. Then the two men started back. They went down out of the hills, forded the river and came to Joshua son of Nun and told him everything that had happened to them.

Probably in the darkness of night the spies came down out of the hills, forded the river, and came to Joshua with their report.

B. REPORT (v. 24)
24. They said to Joshua, "The Lord has surely given the whole land into our hands; all the people are melting in fear because of us."

Of course the spies had not talked with *all the people* of Jericho, but they may have talked with a number of them before they stopped at Rahab's house for the night. Even Rahab was not in touch with all the people; but she entertained guests from various places. She said "all who live in this country" were terrified, and the spies believed her. She thought the Lord, the God of Heaven and earth, was giving the land to the Israelites; and the spies thought so, too.

CONCLUSION
Athletes and coaches are aware of two dangers: overconfidence and the lack of confidence. The overconfident competitor, sure of victory, may lose because he trains halfheartedly and competes carelessly. The one who lacks confidence may lose because he is too tense to do his best.

These dangers are not confined to the world of sports. The overconfident student may fail a test because he neglects his homework; the one lacking confidence may fail because anxiety paralyzes his mind. One businessman overextends himself and goes into bankruptcy; another fails because he is too timid to take advantage of his opportunities. One candidate loses the election because he does not campaign seriously; another loses because in his anxiety he resorts to wild exaggeration or outright lying.

A. JERICHO'S CONFIDENCE
To say the people of Jericho lacked confidence would be an understatement. Rahab said they were terrified—and not only the people of Jericho, but the people of the whole country.

Those people had good reason for their terror. It was not the people of Israel alone. It was the Lord, the God of Israel, the God of Heaven and earth. He had brought Israel through the Red Sea, showered them with manna from Heaven, refreshed them with water from the arid rock, and given them victory over the Amorites east of Jordan.

WHAT DO YOU THINK?

Joshua was a man of confidence and courage as he led the people of Israel. On this occasion, Israel followed his lead and acted with confidence. Years before, however, Israel had rejected the confident leadership of Joshua and Caleb. Given the opportunity to enter the land of Canaan within two years of the time they left Egypt, they refused. Fearful of the Canaanites, the people of Israel actually contemplated returning to Egypt (Numbers 13:25— 14:10).

What determines which way a people or an individual will respond to a challenge? More to the point, what makes the difference in your life so that you accept God's challenges courageously and not with fear?

OPTION

The reproducible activity on page 24, "Success in Our Lives," gives students an opportunity to apply the principle of confidence to a real life situation facing them.

THOUGHT TO REMEMBER

"So do not throw away your confidence; it will be richly rewarded" (Hebrews 10:35).

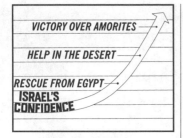

Visual 1 illustrates the point made in the "Conclusion."

PRAYER

Our Father in Heaven, you have given us some wonderful abilities, physical, mental, and spiritual, for which we are grateful. Even more we are grateful that your abilities are far more marvelous than ours, and you are with us as truly as you were with Joshua. May we have wisdom enough to know what you want us to do, and confidence enough to do it. In Jesus' name we pray. Amen.

DAILY BIBLE READINGS

Monday, Aug. 29—Praise for God's Leading (Psalm 105:37-45)

Tuesday, Aug. 30—Joshua's Commissioning to Lead the People (Deuteronomy 31:14-23)

Wednesday, Aug. 31—God Encourages Joshua to Be Courageous (Joshua 1:1-9)

Thursday, Sept. 1—Joshua Organizes to Cross the Jordan (Joshua 1:10-18)

Friday, Sept. 2—Joshua's Spies Are Hidden by Rahab (Joshua 2:1-7)

Saturday, Sept. 3—The Promise to Protect Rahab's Family (Joshua 2:8-14)

Sunday, Sept. 4—The Spies Report to Joshua (Joshua 2:15-24)

Now those people favored of the Lord were looking across the river at Jericho, and the sinners of Jericho were trembling behind their walls. Westward and northward and southward the rest of the people of Canaan were trembling too. It was not only the people of Israel that scared them; it was the God of Heaven and earth.

B. ISRAEL'S CONFIDENCE

Israel's confidence was built by the same events that shattered the confidence of Jericho. Israel walked through the sea on dry ground; Israel followed an unfailing pillar of cloud and fire; Israel lived on manna from Heaven and water from the rock. Israel defeated the Amorites with the sword, but not without the support of the Lord.

Now, poised to invade the main part of the promised land, Israel seemed confident. Moses was dead, but he and the Lord had appointed Joshua to take his place. We wonder if Joshua's own confidence wavered a little. After forty years in a subordinate position, he was suddenly thrust into the position of leadership at a critical time. It was an awesome responsibility. The first nine verses of Joshua record the Lord's repeated encouragement to him: "Be strong and courageous."

The Lord repeated also the reason for confidence: "As I was with Moses, so I will be with you; I will never leave you nor forsake you" (Joshua 1:5).

The promise of success also was repeated: "I will give you every place where you set your foot. ...No one will be able to stand up against you all the days of your life.... You will lead these people to inherit the land I swore to their forefathers to give them" (Joshua 1:3, 5, 6).

Such assurance provided all the support Joshua's confidence needed. He gave the order for the people to advance (Joshua 1:10, 11).

C. OUR CONFIDENCE

There may be Christians who are overconfident. Those brethren who take poisonous snakes to church to prove that God will keep the promise of Mark 16:18—perhaps they should remember that Jesus quoted, "Do not put the Lord your God to the test" (Matthew 4:7). The church that "steps out on faith" to construct a building bigger, more ornate, and more expensive than it needs or can pay for—perhaps it should recall what Jesus said about counting the cost (Luke 14:28-30). But lack of confidence handicaps more of us than overconfidence does.

Consider your own congregation and community. Have you been noticing something that they ought to do? Have you been saying sadly, "Oh, no, I couldn't do it"?

Maybe you can, if you approach it with confidence, with prayer, with thoughtful study and preparation, with training, with eagerness, with the help of friends and the help of God.

Can you be present, alert, attentive, and happy in all the meetings of the church?

Can you participate thoughtfully in those meetings where participation is invited?

Can you help with the cleaning and maintenance of the church building and property?

Can you teach a class or lead a group in discussion?

Can you contribute more than ten percent of your income to the Lord's work?

Can you talk to a neighbor about your faith as freely as you talk about baseball?

Or whatever you see that ought to be done—can you do that?

Maybe you can.

Discovery Learning

This page contains an alternate lesson plan emphasizing learning activities. Classes desiring such student involvement will find these suggestions helpful. The next page is a reproducible activity page to further enhance discovery learning.

LEARNING GOALS

As students participate in today's class session, they should:

1. List the risks that Joshua, Rahab, and the spies undertook for God.

2. Choose at least one risk they believe God wants them to take for him soon.

INTO THE LESSON

Before class, write each of the following words, scrambled, on your chalkboard for class members to see as they arrive:

IKRS (risk), TRVOCIY (victory), DEECEIBON (obedience), VRESCIE (service).

Distribute pencils and half sheets of paper, and ask your students to unscramble the words. To begin the class, let volunteers share their unscrambled words. Then ask class members to write sentences about the Christian life and use these words in the sentences. After about three minutes, let volunteers read the sentences they have written.

Discuss with the class, "Which word suggests to you the biggest challenge to your Christian life? Why?"

Mention that each of these words summarizes the theme of one of the four lessons in the first unit of this quarter's study, the conquest of Canaan. For those who chose *risk* as the most challenging word, today's lesson will be the most challenging, for "risk" is the theme of this lesson.

INTO THE WORD

Use the material in the "Introduction" section on page 17 to establish the background for this lesson. If you have time, do both of the following Bible-study activities. If you have time for only one, do the second one.

Before either activity, have a volunteer read Joshua 2:1, 8-14, 22-24 aloud. As he or she does so, have the students listen to decide why "risk" is the key word in this account.

And I Quote! Write the following quotes on index cards, one quote per card. Make enough of the "quote" cards so that half of your students can each have one. If you repeat quotes, that's OK. Give each of the other half of your students a card with one of the following names on it: *Joshua, Spies, Rahab.* Ask class members to stand. Each one with a quote card should find a student with a matching name card. When all have done this, they can be seated. Then check to see if the matches are correct. (Correct answers are indicated after each quote for the teacher's convenience.)

"Go, look over the land, especially Jericho." (Joshua)

"I don't know which way they went." (Rahab)

"The Lord dried up the water of the Red Sea when you came out of Egypt." (Rahab)

"Give me a sure sign that you will spare the lives of my family." (Rahab)

"Our lives for your lives!" (spies)

"The Lord surely has given the whole land into our hands." (spies)

After this activity, discuss the following questions: "What adjectives would you use to describe Rahab? What motivated her to act as she did? What did the spies learn about Jericho from their visit there? Why did they respond to Rahab as they did? What can we learn about God from this account?"

Take a Risk! Divide the class in half. The first half should form groups of three to five. Examining today's text, they should answer the following questions about Joshua and the spies:

What risks did Joshua and the spies take? Why did they take them? Were they foolish or wise to take these risks? Why? What was the outcome? How would the outcome have been different if they had been unwilling to take the risks?

The second half also should form groups of three to five and answer the same questions about Rahab.

INTO LIFE

Ask, "What does this passage seem to teach about risk-taking? Is risk-taking something God may approve? When and why?"

Ask the students to pair off, and have each pair think of three situations in which God may require Christians to take risks today. After three minutes, write their suggestions on the chalkboard. Ask, "When was the last time you took a risk for God? What happened? Did it make you more or less willing to risk for him again?"

Challenge class members to look at the list on the chalkboard and to decide whether it contains an area where God might want them to take a risk for him this week. Then conclude with a time of prayer.

Spies in Canaan

Some forty years before Joshua sent the two spies into Jericho, he himself had been part of a spy mission in Canaan (Numbers 13:17–14:45). Compare that mission with the one described in the lesson today.

	Mission 1	Mission 2
Number of Spies		
Purpose of the Investigation		
Scope of the Mission		
Result of the Mission		
Consequences of the Mission		

What do you think was the key to the success of the second mission after the first had failed?

_____

_____

_____

Success in Our Lives

Think of a challenge facing you personally, your family, or your church? Write it below:

_____

How can the spies' mission in Jericho encourage you to face this challenge with confidence? Write a plan of action that incorporates some of the principles at work in the spies' successful mission.

_____

_____

_____

From the Conquest to the Kingdom
Unit 1. The Conquest of the Land
(Lessons 1-4)

ACTING ON FAITH

LESSON 2

WHY TEACH THIS LESSON?

If you believe the media, faith and "real life" are mutually exclusive concepts. Faith is okay for the church building, but it dare not be expressed in the marketplace. If a politician should make a statement of faith, he or she is immediately branded an extremist out to upset the supposed barrier between church and state.

Real faith, however, is integral to real life. Biblical faith is based on truth, and truth is compatible with truth. Nowhere is this more dramatically illustrated than in the Israelites' crossing of the Jordan River. As the priests stepped into the flooded Jordan, the moment of truth had arrived. If their faith was based in truth, they would cross safely. If it were false, they would soon be swept away in the flooding torrent. This was real life!

This lesson will challenge your students to consider the practical ramifications of living by faith day by day.

INTRODUCTION

"Now faith is being sure of what we hope for and certain of what we do not see" (Hebrews 11:1).

A. EVERYDAY FAITH

We live by faith day by day, in the most practical affairs of life.

We set the alarm clock and go to sleep, "being sure" it will wake us at the set hour; and it does, usually.

We sit down at the table with calm faith in our breakfast cereal. Oh, yes; we know perverted people have slipped into stores and poisoned stock on the shelves, but we are "certain" that our cereal is wholesome and nourishing, having all the vitamins and minerals announced in small type on the box.

Fearlessly we drive to work, trusting the cross traffic to stop when our light is green.

Workplaces have burned down in a night, and employees have arrived to find themselves fired; but we are confident that both workplace and job will be there when we arrive.

In faith we work all week, expecting to be paid. On payday we take a check, confident that it will be good at the bank.

B. FAITH AND ACTION

James 2:26 says, "Faith without deeds is dead." That applies to everyday faith as well as to religious faith. What happens if we trust the alarm clock, but fail to set it? What if we have faith in our breakfast cereal, but do not eat it? How far can we go by faith in an automobile if we never get behind the wheel and drive? Can we live on faith in an employer if we never go to work? Will faith in a paycheck sustain us if we keep the check in our pocket?

C. LESSON BACKGROUND

The opening chapters of Joshua are not organized as modern writers are taught to arrange their material. Perhaps the inspired writer made notes at various times,

---

DEVOTIONAL READING:
HEBREWS 11:23-31

LESSON SCRIPTURE:
JOSHUA 3, 4.

PRINTED TEXT:
JOSHUA 3:7-17.

LESSON AIMS

After this lesson students should be able to:

1. Tell how the people of Israel crossed the Jordan River in time of flood.

2. Tell of some other events that helped the Israelites to believe in God's power and goodwill.

3. Mention some things that give strength to their own faith in God, Christ, and the Bible.

OPTION

The reproducible on page 32 contains an activity to help your students explore "everyday faith."

KEY VERSE:

"The priests who carried the ark of the covenant of the Lord stood firm on dry ground in the middle of the Jordan, while all Israel passed by until the whole nation had completed the crossing on dry ground."

—JOSHUA 3:17

and later put the notes together without caring that some things are mentioned more than once and that the chronology is not always clear. Here we suggest a possible order of events leading up to those recorded in our lesson text.

1. Having destroyed two kingdoms on the east bank of Jordan, Israel camped in the plains of Moab opposite Jericho and a few miles east of the river (Numbers 22:1).

2. Joshua was appointed to take Moses' place as the leader of Israel (Numbers 27:18-23).

3. Moses died in the land of Moab, and God buried him in a place unknown to man (Deuteronomy 34:5, 6).

4. Israel remained in camp for a month of mourning for Moses (Deuteronomy 34:8).

5. Joshua sent two spies to investigate Jericho and its vicinity. They must have been gone at least five days, perhaps several days longer (Joshua 2).

6. The people of Israel moved their camp close to the river (Joshua 3:1).

7. Three days were allotted for preparation to cross the river (Joshua 1:10, 11).

8. The people were alerted to follow the priests who would carry the ark of the covenant (Joshua 3:2, 3).

9. Joshua gave the signal, and the priests began the march (Joshua 3:6).

I. PROMISE TO JOSHUA (JOSHUA 3:7, 8)

God's promise and directions to Joshua are recorded more fully in Joshua 1:1-9. The promise was that God would be with him and that he would be successful in capturing the land west of the river. The directions were two-fold. First, Joshua must be strong and very courageous. Second, he must remember, teach, and obey all the law that had been given earlier. Now we see a summary of the promise.

A. PROMISE OF GREATNESS

7. And the LORD said to Joshua, "Today I will begin to exalt you in the eyes of all Israel, so that they may know that I am with you as I was with Moses.

The Lord was going to build Joshua's status and credibility in the sight of all Israel. That enlargement would begin that very day. Joshua would promise a safe passageway across the river, and it would appear. Joshua's reputation would continue to grow as every campaign he would direct would be successful. The purpose of this was not just to exalt the new leader; it was to let everyone know God was with Joshua as he had been with Moses.

HUMILITY AND EXALTATION

When Prime Minister Margaret Thatcher of England was reelected to her third term of office, she promised to continue her work of leadership with, in her words, a sense of "great humility." In her speech, she quoted from Rudyard Kipling's "Recessional":

> The tumult and the shouting dies;
> The Captains and the Kings depart:
> Still stands Thine ancient sacrifice,
> An humble and a contrite heart.

Kipling, writing when Britain ruled a worldwide empire, had an insight into the fleeting nature of earthly pomp and circumstance, and he emphasized the quality that every leader should possess.

Joshua was exalted by God to become Moses' successor in leading the nation of Israel and being God's spokesman to his people. Joshua did not—indeed, he could not—exalt himself to that position.

WHAT DO YOU THINK?

The Lord exalted Joshua in the sight of all Israel. Does this suggest that Christian leaders today are entitled to a certain level of exaltation and adulation from church members? If so, to what extent? And if not, why not?

What significance do you see in the fact that the Lord exalted Joshua and not himself? How can you tell when a person's prestige is God's doing and when it is a result of self-exaltation?

Do you ever find yourself attempting to exalt yourself rather than wait for the Lord's exaltation?

How do humility and leadership status work together?

Those who are great in God's eyes are the humble. Knowing themselves to be weak, they trust in the strength of the Lord, and find his strength becoming their own.   —C. R. B.

B. AN ORDER TO BE PASSED ON
8. "Tell the priests who carry the ark of the covenant: 'When you reach the edge of the Jordan's waters, go and stand in the river.'"

The *priests* were to lead the way to the river, but not all the way across. They were to *stand still in the river* while the people passed them and went on to the west bank. The people would see that even the priests obeyed Joshua as Aaron had obeyed Moses, and so the new leader would seem greater in their sight.

Here again it seems probable that the events are not recorded in the order in which they occurred. Perhaps God gave this command to Joshua and Joshua passed it on to the priests before they picked up the ark of the covenant and led the march (v. 6).

II. PROMISE OF A SIGN (JOSHUA 3:9-13)
Now we come to Joshua's promise to the people. It would begin to be kept that very day, and therefore Joshua would be greater in the eyes of his people.

A. CALL TO LISTEN
9. Joshua said to the Israelites, "Come here and listen to the words of the LORD your God.

Joshua had sent officers through the camp to tell the people to get ready (Joshua 1:10, 11). Now the people were ready and massing for the march. It seems that Joshua stood up and shouted to the entire three million. What a voice!

B. SIGN OF SUCCESS
10. "This is how you will know that the living God is among you and that he will certainly drive out before you the Canaanites, Hittites, Hivites, Perizzites, Girgashites, Amorites and Jebusites.

Israel was not moving into empty country west of the Jordan. Seven powerful tribes lived there. Forty years earlier, their tall men and strong city walls had intimidated ten of the twelve scouts Moses had sent to spy out the land (Numbers 13, 14). Tall men and strong walls were still there. If the men of Israel considered only their human resources, they might again decide the land could not be taken. But God was among the people of Israel. He had determined that those tribes were too evil to be tolerated any more. He was going to use Israel to wipe them out, and he would do it without fail. Joshua said God was about to give the people of Israel a sign by which they could know he was among them and was able to do whatever he determined to do.

11. "See, the ark of the covenant of the LORD of all the earth will go into the Jordan ahead of you.

The *ark of the covenant* was a symbol of God's presence among his people. When they were in camp, it rested in the Holy of Holies in the tabernacle. When they were on the march, it was carried by the priests. It was a wooden chest covered with gold and holding the stone tablets engraved with the Ten Commandments, the basic part of God's covenant (Deuteronomy 10:3-5). God was and is the *Lord of all the earth*; not only the people of Israel, but also those doomed tribes west of the Jordan were subject to him. That ark leading the way into Jordan meant that God was leading.

12. "Now then, choose twelve men from the tribes of Israel, one from each tribe.

HOW TO SAY IT

Amorites. AM-uh-rites.
Canaanites. KAY-nan-ites.
Girgashites. GUR-ga-shites (G as in get).
Hittites. HIT-ites or HIT-tites.
Hivites. HI-vites.
Jebusites. JEB-yuh-sites.
Perizzites. PAIR-iz-zites.

WHAT DO YOU THINK?

"This is how you will know," God promised the Israelites. And how we may wish for an equally conclusive sign of God's presence and guidance in our own lives.

How does one know whether or not he is following God's will? Does this account have anything to say to people today about that? What help do 1 Corinthians 10:11 or Hebrews 11:30, 31 offer in this regard?

What do you think?

These representatives of the twelve tribes were to take stones out of the Jordan for a memorial monument on the west bank. As future generations of the people of Israel would pass the monument, children would ask about that structure of twelve stones, and parents would tell again how God had helped his people across the river (Joshua 4:1-7).

13. "And as soon as the priests who carry the ark of the LORD—the LORD of all the earth—set foot in the Jordan, its waters flowing downstream will be cut off and stand up in a heap."

Carrying the *ark*, the symbol of God's presence, the priests would walk into the shallow water at the edge of the flooded stream. The water then would be *cut off* from its supply up the river. The water in front of Israel would run on down to the Dead Sea; the water up the river would be piled up *in a heap* instead of flowing past the waiting people. The bed of the river would be empty so the people could walk across. This control of the stream would demonstrate that God himself was there as truly as the symbol was, and the people would be assured of his help in all their battles (v. 10).

III. THE PROMISED SIGN (JOSHUA 3:14-17)

What did the people think of the promise Joshua gave them? Some of them had crossed the Red Sea as children forty years before. They had seen the water standing like a wall to the right and the left (Exodus 14:22). But after forty years, could they expect to see another such miracle? All the people under forty years of age, of course, had lived all their lives in the desert. They had never even seen such a flood of water as they were seeing now. But they had seen little streams after desert storms, and copious springs flowing from dry rock (Numbers 20:11). They knew water runs downhill, and now Joshua said it would rise up in a heap. Whatever doubts they may have had, they had faith enough to act. They loaded their donkeys, picked up their packs, and followed the priests toward the river.

A. FORWARD INTO THE FLOOD

14. So when the people broke camp to cross the Jordan, the priests carrying the ark of the covenant went ahead of them.

Carrying God's symbol on their shoulders, the priests marched toward the river. The people followed half a mile behind (Joshua 3:4), probably spread out in a wide front so all of them could see what would happen.

15. Now the Jordan is at flood stage all during the harvest. Yet as soon as the priests who carried the ark reached the Jordan and their feet touched the water's edge. . . .

The river was out of its banks and spreading over the plain, so it was shallow at the *edge*. Boldly the priests walked into the shallow water as if they were going to walk all the way across the river—as indeed they were, but not without stopping till all the people crossed it.

B. A HEAP OF WATER

16. The water from upstream stopped flowing. It piled up in a heap a great distance away, at a town called Adam in the vicinity of Zarethan, while the water flowing down to the Sea of Arabah (the Salt Sea) was completely cut off. So the people crossed over opposite Jericho.

As Joshua had promised, the water *stopped flowing* past. It just *piled up in a heap* somewhere up the river. The water in front of the people of Israel kept running down to the sea, leaving a stretch of empty riverbed many miles long. As to the place where the heap of water rose, the city of *Adam*, no one now can be sure

OPTION

Page 32 has some discussion on "Getting Your Feet Wet" that you may find useful to use here. The page is reproducible so you can photocopy it and give each member of your class a copy. Or just ask the questions and discuss it together that way.

where that city was or where *Zarethan* was. The Jordan in flood carries a lot of water, and the flow must have been stopped for hours. Even if they moved in a wide column, three million people with all their belongings would require quite some time to cross. The heap of water must have been a very big one.

C. THE CROSSING

17. The priests who carried the ark of the covenant of the LORD stood firm on dry ground in the middle of the Jordan, while all Israel passed by until the whole nation had completed the crossing on dry ground.

From verse 8 some students conclude that the priests stood at the spot near the east side where they first waded into the water, but verse 17 sounds as if they went on to the *middle* of the riverbed. In either case, God's symbol stood there like a barrier in the bed of the river, and God's will made the water stop far up the stream, allowing the people to cross safely to the west side.

The travelers laid down their burdens at a new campsite on the plain between the river and Jericho. The twelve selected men (v. 12) carried twelve stones out of the river to be built into a monument (Joshua 4:1-8). The crossing was complete. At God's command, Joshua called to the priests to bring the ark of the covenant to the bank beyond the reach of high water, the piled-up water was released, and the flooded river flowed by as before.

Some scholars imagine that a huge landslide blocked the whole channel of the Jordan at a narrow place some miles north of Jericho. This made a dam, they suggest, north of which the water spread out to form a lake till it was high enough to run over the top of the dam. Then the dam was swiftly eroded, and the river flowed on as before. But if the water was spread out in a lake, would it be called a heap? The record seems to indicate a *mound* of water. That would defy the law of gravitation as we know it, but every miracle shows that God knows some laws we do not know.

Even if we suppose a landslide stopped the water, we must recognize a marvelous miracle in the timing of the events. Joshua assigned three days for preparation (Joshua 1:10, 11), and the stoppage came promptly at the end of those days. Just at the moment when the priests with the ark marched into the edge of the stream, the water started to go down. The riverbed was empty just long enough for the people to cross; then promptly it was full again. This was no accident of nature, but a miracle of God. It was provided not only to get the people across the river, but to assure them that God was with them and would give them success (Joshua 3:10).

ACTING ON GOD'S WORD

In 1986 an iceberg—fifty miles wide and seventy miles long—broke off the Antarctic ice shelf. Moving northward, by early 1991 the iceberg was approaching the shipping lanes near the southern tip of South America.

As it drifted into warmer waters, it "calved" numerous smaller icebergs to litter the sea lanes with dangerous obstacles. Its cliffs towered two hundred feet above the ocean and created its own weather system around it. The fog that surrounded the giant iceberg made it difficult for navigators to locate it. It was a dangerous, forbidding obstruction.

Israel confronted an imposing deterrent to their goal of reaching the promised land: the Jordan River in flood stage. They had no trouble seeing the obstacle, however; their problem was finding a way through it. But the problem was not a problem. Joshua gave Israel the instructions God had provided, Israel followed God's commands, and God did the rest.

Life is like that. In situations concerning which God has spoken explicitly, we may expect him to help us with our problems if we follow the directions in his Word.

—C. R. B.

WHAT DO YOU THINK?

The lesson writer points out that some scholars attempt to find a natural explanation for the miraculous crossing of the Jordan —as they do for other miracles recorded in the Bible. How would you answer a friend who suggested the story in today's text was a fictionalized account of what must "really" have happened? Would you answer a Christian with such doubts differently from the way you would answer a non-Christian? If so, how?

Visual 2 illustrates the thoughts in the Conclusion of the lesson (p. 30).

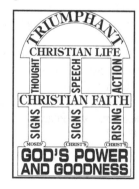

Prayer

Thank You, Father, for giving us solid reasons for our faith. We do believe in You; may we have grace and power to act on our faith. Amen.

Thought to Remember

How firm a foundation, ye saints of the Lord,
Is laid for your faith in His excellent Word!

Daily Bible Readings

Monday, Sept. 5—They Acted by Faith (Hebrews 11:23-31)

Tuesday, Sept. 6—Instructions to Follow the Ark (Joshua 3:1-6)

Wednesday, Sept. 7—The Jordan Will Stop Flowing (Joshua 3:7-13)

Thursday, Sept. 8—Israel Crosses Over the Jordan (Joshua 3:14—4:7)

Friday, Sept. 9—Twelve Stones Carried With Them (Joshua 4:8-14)

Saturday, Sept. 10—Stones for Remembering the Crossing (Joshua 4:15-24)

Sunday, Sept. 11—God Offers Restoration and Protection (Isaiah 43:1-7)

CONCLUSION

With awe the people of Israel stood looking back at a roaring torrent where they had walked a little while before. That torrent had stood aside to let them pass! They knew it was no accident. God had done the impossible, and he was with them! It is small wonder that they were ready to act on faith again. Resolutely they advanced to Jericho.

A. More Faith-Building Facts

This mighty miracle was one of many in Israel's memory. Older people could remember the night they left Egypt. The sound of wailing was around them, for in each Egyptian household was one dead; but there was no death in Israel that night. They could remember walking through the Red Sea and seeing the pursuing Egyptians dead on the seashore. Younger ones had lived all their lives with a pillar in the sky to guide them. Old and young alike could remember water gushing from the rock at the tap of Moses' rod; and even yet each morning brought new manna for their daily bread. It is no wonder that they moved with powerful faith; the marvel is that their faith could sometimes fail.

B. How Is Our Faith?

"These things happened to them as examples, and were written down as warnings for us" (1 Corinthians 10:11). The stopping of the Jordan built the faith of Israel; can it do any less for ours? The God who did impossible things is our God. How is our faith?

John the Baptist was in jail because he told the truth. Wondering, he sent a question to Jesus: "Are you the one who was to come, or should we expect someone else?" Jesus answered with facts, not philosophy: "Go back and report to John what you hear and see: The blind receive sight, the lame walk, those who have leprosy are cured, the deaf hear, the dead are raised, and the good news is preached to the poor" (Matthew 11:2-5). The facts were enough to establish John's faith; are they not enough to establish ours?

Paul summarized the good news he proclaimed in Corinth:

"that Christ died for our sins according to the Scriptures, that he was buried, that he was raised on the third day according to the Scriptures, and that he appeared to Peter, and then to the Twelve. After that, he appeared to more than five hundred of the brothers at the same time. . . . Then he appeared to James, then to all the apostles, and last of all he appeared to me also" (1 Corinthians 15:3-8).

On those facts the Christians in Corinth stood (1 Corinthians 15:1). Do we stand as firm as they?

C. Acting on Our Faith

"What should we do then?" listeners asked John the Baptist, and he told them to share with people in need. Read more in Luke 3:10-14.

"Brothers, what shall we do?" listeners asked the apostles, and Peter told them to repent and be baptized. Read more in Acts 2:36-42.

Without a specific question, Paul told Christians to be transformed so as to demonstrate what is God's will. Read some details in chapters 12 to 15 of Romans. Add those in 1 Corinthians 12, and see chapter 13 for what is even better. For more rich thoughts about acting on our faith, read the whole New Testament. But "do not merely listen to [or read] the word. . . . Do what it says" (James 1:22).

Otherwise you're only fooling yourself when you talk about your faith.

Discovery Learning

This page contains an alternate lesson plan emphasizing learning activities. Classes desiring such student involvement will find these suggestions helpful. The next page is a reproducible activity page to further enhance discovery learning.

LEARNING GOALS

As students participate in today's class session, they should:

1. Discover how little the Israelites needed to do in order to enter the promised land and how much, by contrast, God did to make the entrance possible.

2. Identify God's magnificent responses to our small steps of obedience.

3. Choose one significant step to take soon in obedience to God.

INTO THE LESSON

Write these two open-ended sentences on your chalkboard: "Obeying God is easy because—" and "Obeying God is difficult because—"

Divide the class in half. Have the students in each half pair off with a classmate sitting nearby. The pairs in the first half are to complete the first sentence; those in the second half are to complete the second sentence.

After three minutes, let volunteers share what they have decided. Tell your class, "The key word in today's lesson is obedience. We'll look at a Bible story that can help us decide how obedience is easy and how it is difficult.

INTO THE WORD

Connect this lesson with last week's by giving a brief lecture based on the material presented in the "Lesson Background" (pages 25, 26). Begin today's Bible study by having three volunteers read Joshua 3 to the class, following these verse divisions: 1-6, 7-13, and 14-17. Then ask class members to tell everything that Joshua and his people did as recorded in this chapter. Write them on the chalkboard.

Then, beside that list, write what God did in response to what Joshua and the people did.

Discuss with your class members, "Who did more in this incident, God or his people? Who did the more difficult thing, God or the people?"

There may be some difference of opinion on these questions; if so, don't press for the differences to be resolved yet. That can come later.

Ask your students to complete the following comparative Bible study. Distribute copies of the Bible-study chart shown at the top of the right column. The answers, which are given in italics, are for the teacher's convenience and should not be given to the students ahead of time.

Person and Scripture	How God Was Obeyed	What God Did in Response
Shadrach, Meshach, Abednego (Daniel 3)	*Refused to worship Nebuchadnez- zar's idol*	*Saved them from harm in the fiery furnace*
Elijah (1 Kings 18:20-40)	*Preached against Baal and challenged his prophets*	*Consumed Eli- jah's offering with fire*
Abraham (Genesis 22:1-19)	*Showed willing- ness to sacri- fice Isaac*	*Miraculously provided an offering*

Write these verse headings on the chalkboard: 1-6; 7, 8; 9-13; 14-17. For each paragraph from Joshua 3, students should jot a word, phrase, or sentence to describe what they think were Joshua's feelings at each time.

Allot five minutes for this. Then, for each paragraph, let volunteers share what they have written. Discuss, "What do you suppose Joshua learned from these events? What about the people? What can we learn from their experience?"

INTO LIFE

Write this sentence on your chalkboard: "If we will take the first step, God will do the rest." Discuss: "How true was this principle in the examples we have studied today? Can you think of other Bible stories that show the truth of this principle? (Possibilities: Noah, Joseph, Moses, the apostle Paul.)

Ask class members to think of this principle in relation to their own lives. Have there been times when God has provided magnificently in response to their obedience? Possible examples would be as a result of tithing, confessing a sin, or saying "no" to an unethical business practice or some other temptation.

Discuss this with the class: "Why are we sometimes so hesitant to take the first step?"

Ask, "Is there a step in obedience to God that you should take before the end of this year?"

If any students will share what they are thinking, make special mention of their goals in your closing prayer. Otherwise, lead them to pray silently about how they need to obey God.

Focus on Faith

Unbelievers frequently claim to live without "faith"; that is, they rely on proven commodities only. "Faith," they claim, is a "blind leap" into the unknown. Yet consider the following situations. How is it true that everyone, Christian and non-Christian alike, must approach each one "by faith"?

Air travel

Buying a house (or having one built)

Grocery shopping

Marriage

What happens when the object of one's faith turns out to be untrustworthy?

What convinced you that God is worthy of putting your faith in him? How can you share that confidence with someone else?

Getting Your Feet Wet

Sometimes faith demands action in the face of what appears to be an insurmountable obstacle. Only when the first step of faith has been taken does the way become clear. Crossing the Jordan is an example: not until the priests carrying the ark actually stepped into the river and the water was lapping at their ankles did the river stop and the way across open to Israel. How is that principle demonstrated in the following situations?

Beginning to tithe

Taking on a new ministry (e.g., teaching a class, leading a small group, etc.)

A church's deciding to call a new staff member or to launch a building program

Have you ever been in a similar situation, when you had to act before you had all the answers or could see the way? How did you handle it?

Is there some action you ought to take right now that you have been hesitating about because you can not see the way? What can you do today to "get your feet wet" and make the first step of faith?

From the Conquest to the Kingdom
Unit 1: The Conquest of the Land
(Lessons 1-4)

WINNING THE BATTLE

LESSON 3

WHY TEACH THIS LESSON?

The fall of Jericho has been dismissed by unbelievers as utterly impossible. Marching around the city blowing trumpets is no battle plan. Nor do walls simply collapse at the sound of human shouts. Improbable, illogical, impossible!

Yet that is precisely what the Bible says happened. And the Bible, inspired of the God who cannot lie, must be believed. The story of the fall of Jericho is true!

The Christian life is often seen by the world as illogical, impractical, impossible. But it is still the right way. This lesson can be a powerful reminder that doing things God's way, no matter how unusual or unlikely to succeed the world may say that is, is still the way to go.

INTRODUCTION

D day—do you remember it? Men and munitions and material had been massing for months in Britain. The world waited on tiptoe, and defenders in Europe waited in anxiety. Few people knew just when the great day would be; but when the word was given, the response was swift. Waves of boats and aircraft swept across the English channel; thousands stormed the beaches of France and plunged into conflict.

Israel's D day was that famous day when Jordan's water rose up in a heap and a nation of people walked dry-shod through the river. But unlike the invaders of Europe, the people of Israel did not plunge into instant combat. No troops were massed to meet them on the west bank. The defenders were scared. They had heard how these invaders had walked through the Red Sea forty years before, and how they had trodden down two nations on the east bank just recently (Joshua 2:10, 11). Now in addition they knew how the Jordan had stopped to let these people cross (Joshua 5:1). Obviously someone more than human had these invaders in his care. No one came to fight them. Anxious sentinels must have watched and worried on the wall of Jericho as the people of Israel made their camp in the nearby plain. No doubt scouts of tribes farther west were perched in the mountains above Jericho. But in that plain beside the Jordan no one was seen coming to meet the men of Israel.

A. PEACEFUL PASSOVER

The day Israel crossed the Jordan was the tenth day of the first month (Joshua 4:19). That was the very day when each family was to select a lamb to be eaten in its Passover feast four days later (Exodus 12:1-8). Just forty years after the first Passover in Egypt, Israel celebrated its first Passover in the land of promise (Joshua 5:10). The next day the Israelites ate some of the grain grown on the west bank, and manna came no more. The wanderers were in their homeland now, but they still had to vanquish the people who lived there.

B. LESSON BACKGROUND

Then one day a stranger came with sword in hand, and Joshua hurried to confront him. "Are you for us or for our enemies?"

DEVOTIONAL READING:
PSALM 149
LESSON SCRIPTURE:
JOSHUA 6
PRINTED TEXT:
JOSHUA 6:1-5, 15-20

LESSON AIMS

After this lesson a student should be able to:

1. Retell the story of the fall of Jericho.

2. List at least five attitudes and activities that are included in God's plan for His people today.

3. Find at least one way to follow God's plan better this week.

KEY VERSE

Joshua commanded the people, "Shout! For the Lord has given you the city!" —Joshua 6:16

LESSON 3 NOTES

WHAT DO YOU THINK?

What difference do you see between being "on the Lord's side" and having him "on our side"? How can you be sure you are on his side and not merely claiming him for yours?

WHAT DO YOU THINK?

What effect do reports of archeological discoveries like John Garstang's have on your faith? Why?

OPTION

There is a crossword puzzle on page 40 that you may copy and distribute to your students to use as an introduction to today's lesson text.

"Neither," he replied, "but as commander of the army of the Lord I have now come" (Joshua 5:13-15).

No doubt Joshua got the message. The Lord's army was in the field and ready, but it was on the Lord's side rather than any human side. It would fight against any who opposed the Lord; it would fight for any who obeyed him. This was both an encouragement and a warning. Joshua and Israel had better take care to be on the Lord's side, too.

I. PROMISE OF VICTORY (JOSHUA 6:1, 2)

Digging in the plain of Jordan from 1930 to 1936, John Garstang found what he believed to be the ruins of Joshua's Jericho. The small city was protected by a double wall about thirty feet high. The outer wall was six feet thick, the inner one, twelve feet. Both walls had tumbled down, and ashes showed that the town had been burned. Later diggers thought that that town was destroyed *before* Joshua's town, but they found much less evidence of a later one. Whether Joshua saw that particular town or not, we know he saw a town protected by a wall.

A. ANXIETY
1. Now Jericho was tightly shut up because of the Israelites. No one went out and no one came in.

With that horde of Israelites camping near by, the people of Jericho were taking no chances. They went inside the walls and barred the gates. Their cisterns were full of water (Passover came at the end of the rainy season). No doubt they had stored food enough to last for a long time. There were quantities of charred wheat and barley in the ashes of that city Garstang found. Well supplied with food and water, and seeing no battering ram in that huge camp of Israel, the anxious men of Jericho may have felt safe behind their well-built wall. But none can be safe when they are godless.

B. PROMISE
2. Then the Lord said to Joshua, "See, I have delivered Jericho into your hands, along with its king and its fighting men.

The Lord had his own army in the field (Joshua 5:14), and he would deliver the city to Joshua. Neither the *king* nor his soldiers would be able to keep it safe. That did not mean Joshua and his men would have no part in the capture; it meant that success was certain.

II. BATTLE PLAN (JOSHUA 6:3-5)

God himself gave Joshua the plan of battle; and that was well, for surely Joshua never would have thought of such a plan. And if he had devised it, it would not have worked without God's help. God both planned the work and worked the plan; and yet the fighting men of Israel had a part in it, and the plan would have failed if they had not done their part.

A. SIX CIRCUITS
3. "March around the city once with all the armed men. Do this for six days.

Imagine the puzzled surprise of the watchers on the city wall. Israel's entire fighting force came out and marched once around the city, then went back to camp. The next day they did it again, and every day for six days. Some of the marchers may have been puzzled, too. What could be the purpose of this daily hike? But at least the marchers had a sound reason for doing what they did. God told them to do it.

B. MARCHING MUSIC

4a. "Have seven priests carry trumpets of rams' horns in front of the ark.

More details of the procession are given in verses 6-14. Imagine yourself on the wall of Jericho watching the parade. A feature that catches your eye is the *ark* of the covenant, carefully shrouded from view (Numbers 4:5, 6), supported on long poles, and carried on the shoulders of priests. *Seven priests* go ahead of the ark, blowing on *trumpets* made *of rams' horns*. Are they playing a lively march, or a somber dirge for the doomed city? On that point we have no information. Part of the armed men march ahead of the trumpeters, and the rest follow behind the ark. The fighting men of Israel number six hundred thousand (Numbers 26:51). It has been estimated that they could march seventy-five abreast in a column long enough to surround the city completely while staying out of reach of an arrow shot from the wall. Quite an impressive sight to the defenders of a small city!

C. THE SEVENTH DAY

4b "On the seventh day, march around the city seven times, with the priests blowing the trumpets.

The *seventh day* was different. This time the procession was not to stop after one circuit. It was to march on around the city *seven times*.

5. "When you hear them sound a long blast on the trumpets, have all the people give a loud shout; then the wall of the city will collapse and the people will go up, every man straight in."

After the seventh circuit, the trumpeters would stop their marching music and give the signal with a *long blast*. At that signal, all the marching troops would shout with a *loud shout*. At the shout, the wall of the city would fall down flat. The procession of Israel's fighting men would be stretched out all around the city. With the wall out of the way, every man of the six hundred thousand would charge straight ahead up the slope and into the city.

Such was the plan God gave to Joshua. Verses 6-14 tell how it was carried out through the first six days of the marching.

III. VICTORY (JOSHUA 6:15-20)

Verses 4 and 5 describe the plan of action for the seventh day. Now we are to see how that plan was carried out.

A. SEVEN CIRCUITS

15. On the seventh day, they got up at daybreak and marched around the city seven times in the same manner, except that on that day they circled the city seven times.

The marchers *got up* early because they had much to do that day. First, they would walk around Jericho *seven times*. Of course, we do not know how far they walked or how long it took. For example, suppose their path around the city was three miles long, making a circle somewhat less than a mile in diameter around the city. Then seven circuits at an unhurried pace would take about seven hours. The time needed to destroy the city would be added to that, making a long day for Israel's warriors. If they made a smaller circle around the city, of course, the time would be less. The ruined city that Garstang described was small and compact, having only six or seven acres inside the wall.

16. The seventh time around, when the priests sounded the trumpet blast, Joshua commanded the people, "Shout! For the Lord has given you the city!

Again we see that the writer does not always record events in the order in which they happened. The seven trumpets could be heard all around the circle, even if it

WHAT DO YOU THINK?

At least some of the Israelite army must have wondered at the irrational battle plan that had been announced to them. Yet they all obeyed and the victory was won. Are there times in your life when obedience to God's Word seems irrational or impractical? When? What is the key to obedience even when it doesn't seem to make sense?

was a mile wide. That was the signal for the people to shout (v. 5), so we cannot suppose Joshua took time after the trumpet call to give the instructions in this verse and those that follow. And we need not suppose he shouted to the troops spread out in a mile-wide circle. He must have given these instructions (through verse 19) before the march began that morning. At that special long blast of the trumpets, the men were to "give a loud shout," trusting the Lord to break down the walls so they could take the city as his gift.

B. DEVOTED CITY

17. "The city and all that is in it are to be devoted to the Lord. Only Rahab the prostitute and all who are with her in the house shall be spared, because she hid the spies we sent.

Jericho was the first city to be taken in the campaign west of the Jordan. It must be given to the Lord, as were the firstfruits of the harvest (Deuteronomy 26:1-11). People of Israel might live in towns taken later, but all Jericho must be destroyed. Stores of food must be burned, along with clothing and household goods. Animals and people must be killed. *Only Rahab* and her family were to be spared, because she had saved the lives and the mission of Israel's spies. That was the subject of our lesson two weeks ago. Apparently one bit of the city wall would not collapse with the rest, for Rahab's house was on the wall (Joshua 2:15), and all her people were to gather there (v. 18). The spies whom Rahab had saved were appointed to see that she and her family were kept safe (Joshua 6:22-25). Probably the whole family was accepted in Israel along with her. Rahab has an honored place among the faithful (Hebrews 11:31).

THE MOST SIGNIFICANT REWARD

At dawn on April 15, 1865, two men on horseback came to the home of Dr. Samuel Mudd, asking him to set the broken leg of one of them. After doing so, he gave them food and a place to rest. Dr. Mudd might have lived his whole life in obscurity were it not that the man whose leg he treated was John Wilkes Booth, "on the run" after assassinating Abraham Lincoln.

Mudd was convicted of conspiracy in the assassination and sentenced to life imprisonment. (Some legal experts today feel the evidence presented was insufficient to prove Mudd's guilt.) While in prison, he saved the lives of fellow inmates and soldiers during a yellow fever epidemic. For this, President Andrew Johnson pardoned Mudd after only four years in prison.

Rahab, a prostitute, would have been forgotten long ago but for one thing: when Joshua's spies came into Jericho, she hid them and then helped them escape to freedom. For her act of kindness (and faith, as Hebrews 11 tells us), her life and the lives of all in her household were spared when the Israelites took the city.

Sometimes other people reward us in significant ways for the good we do; at other times they ignore it entirely. Nevertheless, God knows, and that is the most significant reward for the person who loves God. —C. R. B.

WHAT DO YOU THINK?

If anyone disobeyed the command to "keep away from the devoted things," he would "bring trouble" on the whole camp of Israel. Have you seen examples in which one person's disobedience brought trouble on a whole family or a whole church—a whole nation? Do you believe one person's obedience can similarly bless large numbers of people? Why or why not?

18. "But keep away from the devoted things, so that you will not bring about your own destruction by taking any of them. Otherwise you will make the camp of Israel liable to destruction and bring trouble on it.

A soldier might enrich himself with spoil from other cities, but not this one. Jericho was *devoted* to the Lord, a sacrifice, and therefore to be destroyed. Anyone who would steal from that sacred sacrifice must also be destroyed. Worse than that, such theft from the devoted city would make the whole camp of Israel a curse. Chapter 7 gives an example. One man did steal some of the spoil of Jericho, and all Israel was shamefully defeated until that man was detected and destroyed.

19. "All the silver and gold and the articles of bronze and iron are sacred to the LORD and must go into his treasury."

Metal things would not be destroyed but neither would they be taken for private property. They must be put in the *treasury* of the Lord.

THE WEALTH BELONGS TO GOD

George Walker filed an affidavit in Pretoria, South Africa, in July, 1886, staking his claim for gold, and then sold his claim for fifty dollars. Thus began one of the greatest gold rushes in history. Within three years, people bitten by the gold bug had swarmed into the shantytown of Johannesburg from all over the world. No one knows what happened to George Walker.

This story has parallels among the "forty-niners" of the California gold rush and among those who braved the frigid dangers of the Alaskan frontier in the rush of 1898. The prospect of fabulous wealth has lured many people to their destruction, either physical or moral.

God warned the Israelites against taking for themselves any of the wealth they might find in Jericho. He sought to protect them from the moral destruction that sometimes accompanies great wealth gained with too little expenditure of personal effort. But more than that, this city and everything in it was devoted to the Lord. Israel was to recognize that and see that all the precious things were put into his treasury. We today do well to remember that all our riches really belong to God.

—C. R. B.

C. TRIUMPH

20. When the trumpets sounded, the people shouted, and at the sound of the trumpet, when the people gave a loud shout, the wall collapsed; so every man charged straight in, and they took the city.

This was just what the Lord had promised (v. 5). The *trumpets sounded* their long blast, the *people shouted* with a *loud shout*, and the wall fell down flat. Many scholars have suggested that the united shout of six hundred thousand men might generate sound waves powerful enough to shake a wall apart; others doubt that any number of human voices could do that. We must remember that an unseen army of the Lord was there, too (Joshua 5:13-15). No doubt that army could demolish a wall with ultrasound, or by some method entirely unknown to us.

If this was the city described by Garstang, it was built on the top of a knoll. The outer wall tumbled down the slope; the inner one collapsed into the space between the walls. More than half a million fighting men of Israel were surrounding Jericho. With the wall out of the way, they went up the sides of the knoll, over the fallen bricks, and into the city from all sides. Imagine the surprise of the people in the town. Paralyzed by shock and fear, they made no effective resistance. The invaders slaughtered them all—men, women, and children (v. 21).

If such a massacre seems revolting, we need to remember that it was ordered by the Lord, not by the men who carried out the order. "The Lord is compassionate and gracious, slow to anger, abounding in love" (Psalm 103:8). But when he determines that people are too evil to live, he is not squeamish about killing them. Remember the destruction of Sodom (Genesis 19:24, 25) and the flood that destroyed most of mankind (Genesis 7:21, 22). Innocent children died, yes; and for them it was far better to die in innocence than to grow up and die in sin.

So the Lord's battle plan worked perfectly, for the Lord and his people worked it together. Israel took the city, but no one in Israel was richer because of the taking. Like the firstfruits of harvest, this first-captured city was a sacrifice, an offering to the Lord.

WHAT DO YOU THINK?

Some say the God of the Old Testament, ordering wholesale slaughter of men, women, and children, is not the same God of love portrayed in the New Testament. How do you reconcile the harsh judgment that fell on the inhabitants of Jericho with the grace of God revealed through Christ? Does the fact that many will spend eternity in Hell for their disobedience have any bearing? If so, what?

THOUGHT TO REMEMBER

Any life lived by God's plan is a successful life.

Visual 3 of the visuals packet relates to the thoughts included in the "Conclusion" section.

SUCCESS NEXT RIGHT

Learn and follow God's plan

PRAYER

Father, how wonderful it is that You have a faultless plan for us! How good it is to know that Your plan is revealed in Your Word! In gratitude we promise that we will try to know Your plan and follow it. In Jesus' name, amen.

DAILY BIBLE READINGS

Monday, Sept. 12—Joshua's Preparation for Battle (Joshua 5:10-15)

Tuesday, Sept. 13—The Lord Is Near (Psalm 145:14-20)

Wednesday, Sept. 14—God's Promise to Joshua (Joshua 6:1-5)

Thursday, Sept. 15—Beginning the March Around Jericho (Joshua 6:6-11)

Friday, Sept. 16—The Fall of Jericho (Joshua 6:12-21)

Saturday, Sept. 17—Rahab's Family Is Spared (Joshua 6:22-25)

Sunday, Sept. 18—God Gives Victory (Psalm 98:1-6)

OPTION

Use the activity, "Tearing Down the Walls," on page 40 to apply this lesson on obedience.

CONCLUSION

How can we win life's battles? By accepting God's plan and following it. We all know that. But that is not so simple as it sounds. We don't always find such clear instructions as God gave to Joshua. God gives us principles and leaves us to work out details in our own lives. Can we accept our responsibility and find joy in it?

A. KNOWING GOD'S PLAN

God's plan for us is in the Bible. But do we spend more time with the Bible than we do with TV, which often presents life-styles that are contrary to God's plan?

Bible study seems so indirect. We look for step-by-step instructions like those in a cookbook; God gives us life-guiding principles. If we really want to follow God's plan, we can figure out how to apply his principles.

Bible study seems so slow. We would like to have each guiding principle stated in ten words or less. But we learn about faith from the lives of Abraham and Rahab and Stephen. We learn about sacrifice from Abel and Jesus on the cross. We learn about prayer from Hannah and Elijah and Jesus in Gethsemane. We learn about fortitude from Joseph and Jeremiah and John the Baptist. Do we care enough about right principles to learn them in this way?

Bible study seems so impractical. We want to know how to make the mortgage payment, and God tells us how Joshua took Jericho. But Joshua took Jericho by following God's instructions, and we know we had better not make the mortgage payment by stealing or cheating.

Really, we know how to make that payment. We do it by getting along with one car instead of two or three, by preparing meals at home instead of dining out, by wearing old clothes longer. But we don't like self-denial, even if it is a sound principle. *Following* God's plan may be harder than *knowing* it.

B. FOLLOWING GOD'S PLAN

The Israelites didn't take Jericho the day after they crossed the river. The Passover was at hand, and they took time to celebrate it properly. Following God's plan involves taking time for reverence, time for worship, time to be holy. It takes time to absorb Bible principles from the lives of heroes and from the teaching of Jesus and the apostles. Do you have time for Sunday school and church, other group Bible studies, and your own daily study at home?

God's plan includes sincerity, honesty, and truth (Ephesians 4:25). Did you try to fool anyone last week?

God's plan includes self-control (Ephesians 4:26). Did you get through the week without blowing up?

God's plan includes clean talk (Ephesians 4:29). Did you lapse into any "unwholesome talk"?

God's plan includes wholesome thinking (Philippians 4:8). Are you ashamed of any of your thoughts?

God's plan includes kindness, consideration, compassion (Ephesians 4:32). How did you do with those?

God's plan includes helpfulness (1 Corinthians 10:24). Did you go out of your way to help someone last week?

God's plan includes humility (1 Peter 5:5). Are you happy when someone gets ahead of you?

God's plan includes sacrifice and self-denial (Hebrews 13:16). What did you do without last week for the sake of some good cause?

Don't stop now. List some other things that you know are included in God's plan for you.

Discovery Learning

This page contains an alternate lesson plan emphasizing learning activities. Classes desiring such student involvement will find these suggestions helpful. The next page is a reproducible activity page to further enhance discovery learning.

LEARNING GOALS

Students in today's class should:

1. Summarize the facts in the story of Israel's battle against Jericho.

2. List some principles for achieving spiritual victory today.

3. Choose one principle to put into practice more fully in their own lives.

INTO THE LESSON

Write the following words on your chalkboard: *risk, obedience, victory.* Class members may remember that the word *risk* summarized lesson one of our current unit, and *obedience,* lesson two. Today's lesson focuses on *victory.*

To begin today's session, ask the class members to work individually and to write a sentence or two in which all three of the words are used to express a truth concerning the Christian life. Here are some possibilities:

• Those who risk obedience to God will enjoy spiritual victory.

• Obedience to God brings victory, but it may require risk.

• One doesn't really risk anything when one knows that obedience to God ultimately brings victory.

Allow class members two minutes to write their sentences; then ask for volunteers to share what they have written. Tell the class, "Today's study lets us look at a victory Israel experienced under Joshua's leadership. We'll see how many of your statements seem true in light of our discussion of today's text."

INTO THE WORD

Divide your class into four sections and assign each section a different portion of Joshua 6 according to the verse divisions that follow. Within each section, class members should work in pairs or groups of three. Each small group should write a one-sentence summary of the group of verses assigned to its section. Allot five minutes for this.

1. Promise of victory (vv. 1, 2)

2. Battle plan (vv. 3-5)

3. Prelude to victory (vv. 6-14)

4. Victory (vv. 15-21)

As students are working, write the four headings on the chalkboard or an overhead projector transparency.

When time is up, ask for volunteers to share their summaries. Write at least one summary under each heading.

Ask class members, "What do you find interesting or surprising about this story? Why? What does it teach about victory? About risk-taking? About obedience?"
Option.

Some of your students could do a Bible study about the subject of victory. (If you wish, divide the class into five sections instead of four. Four of them could do the study described above, while the fifth does the study of victory as described in the following paragraph.

For each of the following Scriptures, students should jot down an answer to the question, "What does this verse teach about spiritual victory?" The verses are Psalm 44:5; John 16:33; Romans 8:35, 37; 1 John 5:4; Revelation 3:5.

INTO LIFE

Use the material in the "Conclusion" section of the first lesson plan (page 38) to apply this lesson to life today. Read aloud the first paragraph, which begins, "How can we win life's battles?" Discuss with your class, "Why hasn't God given us day-by-day, step-by-step instructions as he did Joshua in the event recorded in our lesson text? What role does Bible study have in helping us to find spiritual victory?"

Proceed to section A, entitled "Knowing God's Plan." Introduce it; then read aloud the topic sentences ("Bible study seems so indirect." "Bible study seems so slow." "Bible study seems so impractical.") You may even want to write these on the chalkboard. Ask students to decide how each of these sentences is true and in what sense they may be false.

Then ask, "How, then, can we hope to get God's guidance for our lives? How can we find victory?"

Read to the class section B, "Following God's Plan." Ask, "Which of the principles suggested here seem most challenging to you? Why?"

Write the word *victory* down the center of your chalkboard. Ask students to suggest principles for achieving spiritual victory in their lives; each principle should begin with a word that begins with a letter in *victory.* Write some of these on the chalkboard as students suggest them. Ask volunteers to share which of these principles could most effectively promote their spiritual growth.

End with sentence prayers for victory.

Victory Crossword

Use today's text to complete the following crossword puzzle.

DOWN

1. Musical instruments made from rams' horns.
2. What each man did, straight ahead of him, when the walls fell.
4. Number of circuits made around the city on the final day.
5. God promised the walls would do this.
6. God told Joshua that the city, its king, and its army had been ____ into Joshua's hand.
8. Joshua warned the people not to bring ____ on the camp by taking plunder from the city.
10. Time of day when the Israelites got up on the day of battle.
12. The commander of the Israelites.
15. Some of the metal objects were made of this precious metal.
16. Jericho's army was called its "____ men."
17. How Jericho was "shut up."
18. What kind of trumpet blast the Israelites would hear.
21. What they were to do when they heard the trumpet blast.

ACROSS

3. Only she and her family were spared.
4. The metal objects were "____ to the Lord."
7. The Israelites did this around the city once each day.
9. "Keep away from the ____ things!"
11. These men carried the ark of the covenant.
13. Failure to observe the ban on taking plunder could make Israel ____ to destruction.
14. Some of the metal objects were made of this alloy.
19. Number of days the Israelites made the circuit around the city one time.

20. The trumpet sound that was to be the signal to shout.
22. The first city to be taken west of the Jordan.
23. Stealing from the spoils of the city could bring ____ on both the thief and the whole camp of Israel.
24. Some of the metal objects were made of this.
25. All the metal objects were to be put into the Lord's ____.
26. Some of the metal objects were made of this precious metal.

Tearing Down the Walls

The land of Canaan belonged to the Israelites by God's promise. But Jericho with its imposing walls threatened to withhold that promise. Yet, when the Israelites obeyed God's command, the walls—strong though they must have seemed—came tumbling down.

What "walls" stand between you and the promises of God? _____

_____

By what acts of obedience could these walls be torn down? _____

From the Conquest to the Kingdom
Unit 1: The Conquest of the Land
(Lessons 1-4)

CHOOSING TO SERVE GOD

LESSON 4

WHY TEACH THIS LESSON?

Options. Choices. That's what people want today. The problem is, their choices are too often selfish. People choose a car for its comfort options even when it is not practical for the needs of the family. They choose a church for its programs and convenient starting times even if its doctrine is not sound. They choose independence from parental duties even if it means killing an unborn baby to get it.

Such choices are not what Joshua had in mind when he said, "Choose for yourselves. . . ." Usually, the right choice is not the easy choice. Choosing to serve God is not a choice of convenience. It will require sacrifice and self discipline. But it is a choice that must be made. Our lives depend on it.

INTRODUCTION

Looking eastward from their highland pasture, Abraham and Lot saw the valley of the Jordan. The "whole plain . . . was well watered, like the garden of the Lord." Lot thought it would be a fine place to live (Genesis 13:10, 11).

That valley must have looked even better to the people of Israel some centuries later when they came in from the desert and looked westward from the plains of Moab. Many of them had never seen a river; now they saw the Jordan overflowing with life-giving water. For most or all of their lives they had walked among pale gray desert shrubs; now they saw Jericho lying in a valley green with springtime, for spring comes early in that garden spot eight hundred feet below the level of the sea. Like Lot of old, the Hebrew people thought that verdant valley would be a good place to live—and God had said it would be their own. So they moved in.

A. MOVING IN

Lessons 1-3 have told us how the Hebrews moved into the valley. Lesson 1 told how the spies of Israel ventured into Jericho and escaped with the help of their hostess, Rahab. Lesson 2 told how the overflowing waters of the the Jordan were built into a mountain so the newcomers could walk across a dry riverbed. Lesson 3 told how the wall of Jericho fell down flat, and how half a million fighting men raced across the fallen bricks and wiped out the city.

From Jericho the fighting men went on to capture more of their promised land. They lost one battle when one man of Israel was guilty of outrageous sin; but the sinner was detected and destroyed, and then the others went back to fight and win (Joshua 7, 8). They were tricked into a treaty by crafty men of Gibeon (Joshua 9). With these exceptions, the men of Israel went from victory to victory, for the Lord was with them. He had decreed destruction for those depraved tribes of Canaan, and destroyed they were.

It was a war of infantry, slogging on slow feet from place to place. The Lord had said, "I will give you every place where you set your foot" (Joshua 1:3), and they did set their feet on all the land they conquered. So it was about seven years before they could stop fighting. They distributed among their tribes the land they had conquered. The division is recorded in chapters 13-22 of Joshua.

DEVOTIONAL READING:
PSALM 116:12-19
LESSON SCRIPTURE:
JOSHUA 24
PRINTED TEXT:
JOSHUA 24:1, 2, 11-16

Sep
25

LESSON AIMS

After this lesson a student should be able to:

1. List at least three great things the Lord did to help Israel.

2. Tell what the people of Israel promised to do in response to God's help.

3. State his or her choice to serve the Lord.

4. Consider God's will in every choice he or she makes.

KEY VERSE:

Choose for yourselves this day whom you will serve. . . . But as for me and my household, we will serve the LORD.

—JOSHUA 24:15

Display visual 4 of the visuals packet and let it remain before the class.

"*Prayer of* COMMITMENT

*The dearest idol
I have known,
Whate'er that idol be,
Help me to tear it
from Thy throne,
And worship only
Thee.*

WILLIAM COWPER

LESSON 4 NOTES

B. LESSON BACKGROUND

The goodness and power of God were evident in the help he gave to Israel in the invasion and conquest. The people of Israel were so deeply impressed that they were faithful in their worship and obedience. The pagans around them were impressed, too. None of them wanted to attack those fearsome newcomers who had wiped out so many tribes and peoples. So Israel lived in peace in the new land for a long time, while Joshua grew old (Joshua 23:1). But Joshua could not live forever, and he knew it. With more than a hundred years behind him, he wanted to impress his people once more with God's power and their duty. So he called a meeting.

OPTION

Use the reproducible activity, "Service, Please," on page 48 to introduce this lesson's emphasis on service.

I. GOD'S WORD (JOSHUA 24:1, 2, 11-13)

It is puzzling to see that chapters 23 and 24 of Joshua are so much alike. The explanation seems to be that chapter 23 records Joshua's meeting with leaders of the nation, while chapter 24 records a mass meeting of all the people. As the president of the United States consults leaders of Congress before he announces a policy publicly, Joshua made his presentation to leaders of the nation and gained their support before he talked to the whole nation. Our lesson goes straight to his talk to all the people.

A. THE MEETING (V. 1)

1. Then Joshua assembled all the tribes of Israel at Shechem. He summoned the elders, leaders, judges and officials of Israel, and they presented themselves before God.

Joshua gathered all the tribes, plus the leaders he had gathered before. *Shechem* was a central place located between two mountains. It was a good place to speak to a big crowd. Perhaps that was the reason it had been chosen for a reading of the law soon after Israel arrived in the promised land (Joshua 8:33-35). It was also the place where God had spoken to Abraham when that patriarch arrived in the promised land (Genesis 12:6, 7). Now Joshua called the millions of Abraham's descendants to hear God's message to them. They did not just meet with Joshua; *they presented themselves before God.*

B. THE SPEAKER (V. 2)

2. Joshua said to all the people, "This is what the LORD, the God of Israel, says:

It was Joshua's voice the people heard, but the words he spoke were the words of God. Speaking as a prophet, Joshua quoted the words God gave to him. In the verses that follow, *I* is not Joshua; it is God. The Lord began by recounting the history of his people from the time of Abraham. The Lord had brought Abraham from Mesopotamia to the land of promise, and later had brought Abraham's descendants from Egypt to that same land (vv. 2-10). The next part of our printed text takes up the story as these emigrants from Egypt crossed the Jordan.

HOW TO SAY IT

Amorites. AM-uh-rites.
Canaanites. KAY-nan-ites.
Euphrates. U-FRAY-teez.
Girgashites. GUR-ga-shites (G as in get)
Hittites. HIT-ites or HIT-tites.
Hivites. HI-vites.
Jebusites. JEB-yuh-sites.
Perizzites. PAIR-iz-zites.
Shechem. SHEE-kem or SHEK-em.
Sihon. SYE-hun.
Terah. TEE-ruh.

C. GOD'S HELP (VV. 11-13)

11. "'Then you crossed the Jordan and came to Jericho. The citizens of Jericho fought against you, as did also the Amorites, Perizzites, Canaanites, Hittites, Girgashites, Hivites and Jebusites, but I gave them into your hands.

The men of Jericho fought as well as they could; but their fighting was futile. God had first terrified them by his miraculous help to Israel, and then he demolished their wall and let the army of Israel take them by surprise. The other tribes mentioned in verse 11 were not in Jericho, but they all fought against Israel one or a few at a time through the next seven years. Their fighting was as futile as that of the men of Jericho. Israel won victory after victory, not because the men of Israel were such fierce fighters, but because God *gave* each enemy to them.

12. "'I sent the hornet ahead of you, which drove them out before you—also the two Amorite kings. You did not do it with your own sword and bow.

The Hebrew word for *hornet* appears only three times in the Old Testament. Each time it is used for an instrument God used to drive out the enemies of Israel. Some students think it is to be taken literally, that God sent such a plague of hornets that Israel's enemies were forced to leave the area. However, the historical record in the book of Joshua does not record such a plague. It indicates rather, as does verse 11 of our text, that each tribe fought the Hebrews, though feebly and futilely. Some students suggest that the hornet may be a figure of speech for the fear that tormented the pagans when the Hebrews came near, such as the fear Rahab described (Joshua 2:8-11). The Hebrew word for *hornet* comes from a verb that means to hit, strike, or smite. Possibly it means that the enemies were so terror-stricken that they could not fight effectively, or possibly it refers to an epidemic of disease that struck down the enemies. In any case, the point is that the defeat of Israel's enemies was due to the Lord more than to the sword and bow of Israel. This began even before Israel crossed the Jordan. The two kings of the Amorites, Sihon and Og, were routed on the east bank (Numbers 21:21-35).

13. "'So I gave you a land on which you did not toil and cities you did not build; and you live in them and eat from vineyards and olive groves that you did not plant.'

The victorious Israelites were not pioneers in a wild, rough land. They took over fields already cleared of brush and stones, plowed and planted without any work by those who now possessed them. The Israelites had lived in tents for forty years; now they took over whole cities of houses furnished and ready to be lived in. They took over fruit trees and grapevines mature and bearing fruit. All of these were gifts from God.

II. JOSHUA'S WORD (JOSHUA 24:14, 15)

In these verses, Joshua spoke in his own person. The *me* in this paragraph means Joshua, not God. But still Joshua was God's prophet, speaking as God directed him.

A. SERVE GOD ONLY (V. 14)

14. "Now fear the LORD and serve him with all faithfulness. Throw away the gods your forefathers worshiped beyond the River and in Egypt, and serve the LORD.

To *fear the Lord* is not to run away from him and try to hide, as guilty sinners sometimes do. It is to seek his presence and his will with reverence and awe; it is to be afraid to do wrong. To *serve him* is to worship and obey him. Joshua appealed to the people to do this in *all faithfulness*: not with formal ceremonies only, but willingly and gladly in all the acts of daily living. God's power is plain in verses 11-13, giving ample reason to regard him with reverence. His goodness to his people is no less plain in those verses, leading good people to obey him with gratitude and love.

The Lord is the only real God there is. Other so-called gods are not gods at all. Terah, Abraham's father, was among the *forefathers* who served other gods (Joshua 24:2). He lived in Ur, where the moon was worshiped along with many imaginary gods. The location of Ur is described as *beyond the River.* In the Bible the Euphrates is sometimes called simply "the River." The Hebrew term for *beyond* is used loosely.

WHAT DO YOU THINK?

Do you believe the "hornet" that went before Israel was a literal plague of stinging insects or something figurative, like the terror that many of the tribes experienced before attempting to fight against Israel? Why do you think so?

Have you ever experienced something similar? That is, have you seen God clear the way of obstacles for you or your church as you attempted some bold venture for him? If so, describe the event.

The meaning seems to be simply that Terah and other fathers lived "beside" the Euphrates. Now Joshua urged his people to have nothing to do with the non-gods that were worshiped long before in that faraway place. Furthermore, he urged them to renounce the non-gods the older ones had lived among in *Egypt*. Nowhere in the world or out of it is there any other real God; so *serve the Lord!*

B. CHOOSE (V. 15A)

15a. "But if serving the LORD seems undesirable to you, then choose for yourselves this day whom you will serve, whether the gods your forefathers served beyond the River, or the gods of the Amorites, in whose land you are living.

Joshua acknowledged that the people were free to choose. The Lord was the only real God, and these people were indebted to him for freedom from slavery in Egypt, guidance and provision through the desert, and victory in the promised land. Both good sense and gratitude would lead them to worship and serve the Lord "in all faithfulness." But the Lord demanded that his people obey his law, that they live upright and moral lives, that they be good and do good. If that seemed *undesirable* to anyone, he was free to choose another way. There was the moon worship of faraway Ur, and there was the Baal worship of the nearby Amorites. Neither of these put any restraint on greed and cheating, booze and promiscuous sex. Make up your mind!

C. JOSHUA'S CHOICE (V. 15B)

15b. "But as for me and my household, we will serve the LORD."

Joshua and his family had made their choice. They had chosen good sense and gratitude. They had chosen truth and right. They had chosen upright, moral living. They had chosen the Lord!

THE MARK OF GREATNESS

Dave Dravecky's life is one of the great heartbreak stories in modern major league baseball. Dravecky, who is a Christian, was pitching for the San Francisco Giants when his career was cut short by cancer. In October, 1988, he had surgery to remove a tumor from his pitching arm.

Amazingly, ten months later Dravecky pitched and won a game. In his next game, however, his arm broke as he made a pitch in the sixth inning. After his arm was broken accidentally two months later, his "miraculous" comeback had to be abandoned. Eventually, doctors would have to amputate his arm in order to save his life. When asked about his faith in the face of the cancer that destroyed his career, Dave Dravecky said, "My focus is not just on how I can become healed, but how I can serve God through all this."

Real greatness is seen in the decision stated by Joshua in our lesson today, and expressed in similar words by Dave Dravecky: "Regardless of what may happen to me, I will serve God."

We may be unable to control history, our health, or the actions of others, but each of us can decide to serve God regardless of circumstances or consequences. This is true greatness.   —C. R. B.

III. THE PEOPLE'S PLEDGE (JOSHUA 24:16, 22-25)

We are left to imagine how the whole huge assembly of Israel expressed its answer to Joshua. Perhaps some well-known leader took it on himself to speak for the nation, or perhaps a group of leaders conferred together and put forward one of them to say what all were thinking. When the spokesman made his statement, the people could express their assent by shouting, "Amen!" In some such way an answer came from the huge assembly, and it is recorded for us.

WHAT DO YOU THINK?

In a culture that values personal choice above virtually all else, Joshua may be thought presumptuous to speak for his family: "We will serve the Lord." How important do you think it is that the head of the family take the lead in spiritual matters? What dangers are present when he does not? What dangers are present when he takes the lead, but in the wrong direction?

A. PROMPT PLEDGE (V. 16)

16. Then the people answered, "Far be it from us to forsake the LORD to serve other gods!"

Forsake the Lord? Serve other gods? Such ideas were utterly abhorrent to these people. The Lord had set them free from Egypt; he had preserved them in the wilderness; he had secured the promised land for them (vv. 17, 18). These were the same reasons the Lord had given through Joshua (vv. 5-13).

Perhaps Joshua perceived that the answer was too quick and easy, that it was not thoughtful enough to represent a true commitment. Instead of accepting it with thanks and approval, he hurled back an unexpected challenge: "You are not able to serve the Lord" (v. 19).

Now certainly the people stopped to think. Joshua had been urging them to serve the Lord. They had promised to do it, and now he said they couldn't. What could he mean?

Joshua explained. These people could not serve the Lord because he is holy and he is jealous. He will not accept halfhearted service or worship shared with imaginary gods. He will not tolerate sin. If the people would violate their pledge and do wrong, he would hurt them instead of helping them (vv. 19, 20).

More thoughtfully now the people reaffirmed their promise: "No! We will serve the Lord" (v. 21).

B. WITNESSES (V. 22)

22. Then Joshua said, "You are witnesses against yourselves that you have chosen to serve the LORD."

"Yes, we are witnesses," they replied.

When an important contract is made, disinterested parties are called to witness the signing of it. In this case there were no disinterested parties present, so Joshua called the people themselves to be witnesses of their pledge. If they would break the pledge, they would be condemned by their own words. Solemnly the people accepted the responsibility. If the promise should be broken, they would testify against themselves.

C. REPEATED PLEDGE (VV. 23, 24)

23. "Now then," said Joshua, "throw away the foreign gods that are among you and yield your hearts to the LORD, the God of Israel."

It seems that the pledge was already being broken in some degree: some *foreign gods* were even then being possessed by some of the people. Joshua urged them to get rid of every false god among them, whether Mesopotamian, Egyptian, or Amorite (vv. 14, 15). The people of Israel should give their hearts completely to the Lord God of Israel.

24. And the people said to Joshua, "We will serve the LORD our God and obey him."

The people reaffirmed the pledge they had made twice before (vv. 16-18, 21). They said they would without fail be loyal to the Lord.

THE IMPORTANCE OF PILOTS

Air traffic controllers lost radio contact with a Royal Air Force jet fighter while it was flying five hundred miles an hour at an altitude of thirty-one thousand feet over Salisbury, England. An American pilot flying nearby in another plane was asked to make a visual inspection of the fighter. He discovered the fighter's cockpit canopy to be missing, as were the pilot's seat and the pilot. The plane was continuing on the last course set by the pilot, but on its own.

WHAT DO YOU THINK?

Joshua told the people they would not be able to serve the Lord, and he called them witnesses against themselves. Serving the Lord must be hard! But Jesus said, "Come to me, all you who are weary . . . and I will give you rest. . . . For my yoke is easy and my burden is light" (Matthew 11:28-30). How would you reconcile these two passages? When should we stress the difficulty of serving the Lord (as Joshua did) and when should we stress the rest (as Jesus did)?

PRAYER

Long ago we pledged our loyalty to you, our Heavenly Father; and now we promise anew to seek your will in every choice we make. In Jesus' name we pray. Amen.

THOUGHT TO REMEMBER

"We will serve the Lord."

WHAT DO YOU THINK?

The meeting at Shechem is one of several occasions in Scripture when some of God's people formally renewed their covenant to serve the Lord. How important do you think such formal, public rededications were for the Israelites? Should Christians have such rededications today? Why or why not? What format would you suggest for such a service?

OPTION

Use "Renewing the Covenant" on page 48.

DAILY BIBLE READINGS

Monday, Sept 19—Praise for God's Care (Psalm 116:12-19)

Tuesday, Sept 20—Joshua's Reminder of God's Protection (Joshua 23:1-8)

Wednesday, Sept. 21—Joshua's Charge to Remain Faithful (Joshua 23:9-11, 14-16)

Thursday, Sept 22—Joshua's Recall of Their Deliverance History (Joshua 24:1-10)

Friday, Sept 23—Joshua's Call for Commitment (Joshua 24:11-15)

Saturday, Sept 24—The Promise to Serve God (Joshua 24:16-23)

Sunday, Sept 25—The Stone of Witness (Joshua 24:24-31)

The American pilot flew his plane alongside the fighter for seven hundred miles until it finally ran out of fuel and crashed into the sea. The British pilot's body was later found near Salisbury, where radio contact had first been lost.

Some persons are like the pilotless plane, moving along through life apparently quite well, generally staying on course, but with no controlling spirit to guide them safely to their destination. As long as no obstacle gets in front of them or no unforeseen crisis develops, they seem to function normally. Ultimately, however, such persons will crash-land with disastrous results.

The people of Israel committed themselves to serve the Lord, and to obey his voice. Those today who seek God's guidance, and who thoughtfully decide to submit to his control, will be able to avoid "mid-air collisions" as well as the final "crash-landing."

—C. R. B.

D. FORMAL COVENANT (V. 25)

25. On that day Joshua made a covenant for the people, and there at Shechem he drew up for them decrees and laws.

We cannot be sure of the precise meaning of the words *decrees and laws*, but the main thought of the verse is clear. Joshua put the people's pledge into a formal *covenant*, an agreement or contract, and put it in writing (v. 26). The covenant reaffirmed the one made at Sinai by the fathers of these people (Exodus 19:8).

Joshua erected a monument as a permanent reminder of the covenant reaffirmed. The meeting adjourned, and the people went home, pledged anew to be faithful to the Lord (vv. 26-28).

CONCLUSION

The people kept their promise as long as Joshua lived, and longer. They were faithful to the Lord as long as they were guided by men who remembered the mighty miracles that brought them into the promised land (Judges 2:7).

In next week's lesson we shall see how later generations abandoned the sacred covenant.

OUR CHOICES

We who are Christians have made our choice to serve the Lord, but keeping our pledge to him brings us to smaller choices day by day.

Now that the children are away, you're getting rid of that second car. You can tell a buyer that it runs all right, which is true; or you can add that it uses an outrageous amount of oil, which also is true. What do you choose to say?

You hear a very ugly rumor about the woman next door, whom you don't like very well. You can say you don't believe it; you can say nothing; you can repeat the rumor to a few close friends. What do you choose?

Good friends invite you on a Sunday trip to see some beautiful autumn foliage. Will they stop for church along the way? No, no; they don't have time for that. What do you choose?

The PTA is planning some gambling games for its carnival. Such games are illegal in your state, but the authorities will look the other way. You can help with the planning; you can say nothing; you can protest against teaching children that it's okay to break the law if you can get away with it. What do you choose?

People are asking to have the Bible removed from the school library. They are influential people; probably your voice would have no effect. Besides, who ever reads the Bible in a school library? You can ignore the matter; or you can talk with the librarian, the principal, the school board. What do you choose?

Perhaps you will not face any of these choices this week, but you will face others. Choose thoughtfully.

Discovery Learning

This page contains an alternate lesson plan emphasizing learning activities. Classes desiring such student involvement will find these suggestions helpful. The next page is a reproducible activity page to further enhance discovery learning.

LEARNING GOALS

As students participate in today's session, they should:

1. List the spiritual choices that were presented to the Israelites, and some that Christians confront today.

2. Recommit themselves to their choice to serve God only.

INTO THE LESSON

Ask class members to mention areas of everyday life, regarding which many choices are open to us. (Examples may include markets for grocery shopping, malls where we can buy clothes, gas stations for the purchase of fuel, places for dining out, and the like.) Are all of these choices good for us? Have your students ever been in a situation where the choices open to them were bewildering or bad instead of good?

Tell your students that today's session explores the spiritual choices that the ancient Israelites faced, and those that God's people face today.

INTO THE WORD

Once again write this unit's summary words, one under the other, on your chalkboard: *Risk, Obedience, Victory, Service.*

Beside *Risk* write "Lesson One" and ask a volunteer to tell what that lesson taught about risk.

Write "Lesson Two" beside *Obedience* and ask someone else to summarize that lesson.

Write "Lesson Three" beside *Victory* and have a student summarize that lesson.

Then use material under the heading "A. Moving In" in the "Introduction" section (page 41) to connect Lesson Three with this one. Briefly mention the events recorded in the book of Joshua that occurred between the fall of Jericho and the event in today's lesson.

Tell the class that today's lesson emphasizes "service." (Write "Lesson Four" beside *Service.*) Have a student read Joshua 24:1-27, and instruct the others to listen for what this text teaches about serving God.

Next, distribute the questions listed below. You may want to discuss these with the whole class in the order shown. Or you may choose to divide the class into groups of five to seven and have each group discuss a different question. After about six or eight minutes, reconvene the class into one large group and hear answers to all the questions.

1. Why did Joshua remind the people of the great heroes from their past? What could be learned from remembering the stories of the patriarchs (vv. 2-4), Moses (vv. 5-7)? Their own possession of the promised land (vv. 8-13)?

2. What choices did Joshua present to the people (vv. 14, 15)? How did the people respond to this challenge (vv. 16-18)? Why?

3. Why did Joshua seem to reject their initial response (vv. 19, 20)? How would you summarize this challenge to the people?

4. As recorded in Joshua 24, how many times did Joshua prompt the people to proclaim their faithfulness to God? Why did he make them repeat their vows so often? By what physical signs did Joshua summarize their commitment? What was the value of these?

5. What clues about the people's faithfulness to God do you see in Joshua's comments (vv. 14, 20, 23)? Given the many ways God had worked among them and their forefathers, how could they still have a problem with making him Lord? What does this teach you about faithfulness? Peer pressure? Sin and temptation?

INTO LIFE

Discuss the following questions with the class:

1. Why do you suppose Joshua said, "Choose this day whom you will *serve*"? Why didn't he say, "Choose whom you will *believe*"? Or "Choose whom you will *worship*"? What is significant about the idea of service, both for Israel and for us today?

2. In a sense, it may be said that each of us is serving someone or something. What are some choices available to people in our culture as to whom or what they will serve?

Perhaps you should list on the chalkboard the answers to this second question. Keep prodding the class for responses until you have a couple dozen. Then, if you have time, ask class members to decide on the six or eight that are most chosen by people today. Put a star beside each of these items on the board.

Ask class members if they have been tempted to choose these starred items instead of God. How have they been able to choose God instead?

End with a time of sentence prayers, during which class members will reaffirm their commitment to serve God only.

Service, Please

Use each letter of the word *service* to suggest another word or a phrase that describes Christian service. One example has been done for you.

S _____

E _____

R _____

V Voluntary _____

I _____

C _____

E _____

Renewing the Covenant

The covenant at Shechem was nothing new to the Israelites. The call to serve God went back half a millennium, to Abraham's days in Ur of the Chaldees. But they had slipped in their faithfulness and needed to be challenged anew to serve the Lord.

In the box below, list some ways Christians today can renew their own covenant to serve God, either individually or as a congregation.

What can *you* do—right now or sometime this week—to recommit yourself to serving the Lord?

From the Conquest to the Kingdom
Unit 2. *The Rule of the Judges*
(Lessons 5, 6)

ISRAEL'S TRAGIC PATTERN OF LIFE

LESSON 5

WHY TEACH THIS LESSON?

In *The Autobiography of Benjamin Franklin,* the author describes his attempts to attain perfection by working on his sins, one at a time, until he had overcome them. The problem, Franklin said, was that his old sins, supposedly corrected, kept recurring when he took his attention off one to deal with another.

It is the same problem Israel had. God would get their attention by allowing invaders to plunder their land. But when the crisis was over, their attention was soon diverted and they returned to their sinful ways.

Christians today may struggle with the same sort of problems. When they try to break old habits by their own strength alone, they find themselves running through cycles of success and failure. This lesson serves as a warning against treating only the symptoms instead of strengthening our commitment to the Lord.

INTRODUCTION

Going downhill is easier, but going uphill is safer. On the climbing road we use more energy, but control is easy. On the downward slope we gain speed but lose control. The runner is more likely to stumble and fall; the wheeled vehicle may leave the road on a curve.

This is true in the moral realm as well. It takes effort to be upright and noble; but on the downhill side one coasts easily from small lies to big lies, from minor cheating to major fraud.

A. ISRAEL'S CLIMB

Israel's journey from Egypt to the promised land was uphill all the way. The generation that started the journey lacked the courage and stamina to complete it quickly. Fearful and faltering at the border of the promised land, the people of Israel were turned back and made to live the next forty years in the desert (Numbers 13, 14).

The Israelites who grew up in the desert were toughened by their rugged life. Better than that, they learned to depend on the Lord, who supplied manna from Heaven and water from the rock. Trusting in the Lord, they advanced boldly into the promised land and destroyed nations much greater and stronger than they were (Deuteronomy 9:1-3).

B. ISRAEL AT THE TOP

In about seven years the people of Israel captured as much of the promised land as they were ready to use. Heathen tribes still surrounded them, but they divided the land and settled down to farming (Joshua 13—19). The people worshiped God and obeyed him faithfully (Joshua 23:1). Peace and prosperity prevailed. Israel lived on the summit for possibly sixty years or more after the long climb ended and the land was theirs.

DEVOTIONAL READING:
PSALM 81:6-16

LESSON SCRIPTURE:
JUDGES 2:6–3:6

PRINTED TEXT
JUDGES 2:11-19

Oct
2

LESSON AIMS
After this lesson students should be able to:
1. Recall at least one improvement in their own Christian living during the past year.
2. Specify at least one improvement to be made in the coming year.

KEY VERSE:
Then the Israelites did evil in the eyes of the LORD and served the Baals. They forsook the LORD, the God of their fathers, who had brought them out of Egypt. They followed and worshiped various gods of the peoples around them. They provoked the LORD to anger.
—Judges 2:11, 12

LESSON 5 NOTES

WHAT DO YOU THINK?

Failure to complete the task of destroying the inhabitants of Canaan was one reason for Israel's downfall recorded in Judges. Sometimes Christians start tasks for the Lord and then fail to finish. Do you think that is a major problem for the church? Why or why not? Is it a bigger problem for the church who may have been counting on that person or on the person himself? Why?

Are you sometimes guilty of promising to do a job but failing to complete it? How can we encourage Christians to finish what they start?

C. PREPARING TO PLUNGE

Two things conspired to prepare Israel for a plunge from the happy summit of righteousness, prosperity, and peace.

First, the people failed to finish the job. They had been told to destroy or drive out all the pagans in their new land (Deuteronomy 7:1-5). But when Israel was firmly in control, it seemed unnecessary to kill the defeated people. Certainly it was more profitable to let them live and make them pay tribute. So many of the Israelites became accustomed to pagan neighbors and pagan ways (Judges 1:21—2:5).

Second, the passing of years brought the passing of all the people who remembered how God had helped them in the long climb from slavery to victory. A new generation grew up in the land, and they knew only peace and comfort and the support of tribute from pagan neighbors. Accustomed to easy living, these Israelites lacked their fathers' strength and steadfast trust in the Lord (Judges 2:10).

I. THE PLUNGE (JUDGES 2:11-13)

Humans seem designed to keep moving. Spiritually and morally, if we stop going forward, we begin to go backward; if we stop climbing, we start descending. After perhaps sixty years at the top, Israel began the downward plunge.

A. EVIL AND IDOLATRY (V. 11)

11. Then the Israelites did evil in the eyes of the LORD and served the Baals.

Baal is a name given to various idols and imaginary gods of the pagan of Canaan. Each tribe might have its own Baal. Ceremonies of worship might vary, but none of the Baals had any regard for the Lord's standards of honesty, decency, and morality. Those who served Baals also *did evil in the eyes of the Lord* in other ways as well.

How could Israel make such a drastic change? Of course, it was not so abrupt as it sounds here. There must have been a very gradual change of attitude. Perhaps it began with a few rebellious teenagers who kept on sowing wild oats after they grew up. The following scenario is purely imaginary, but it could have happened this way.

Waking at midnight, an eighteen-year-old Hebrew heard faint sounds of music and happy shouting from a distant pagan festival. The next week he took his flock to a water hole just as a pagan boy arrived with his sheep. Curious, the Hebrew asked about the festival.

The answer told of things the Hebrew boy has been taught to believe were acts of sin and depravity, not acts of worship. "You're kidding!" he charged.

The pagan boy shrugged. "Why don't you come and see?"

Perhaps not at the very next festival, but in time the Hebrew got one or two other daring young men to go with him. What they saw was more shocking than what he had heard. The beef was good, the wine was plentiful, the entertainment was X-rated, and the women were seductive. The boys left with their minds in a whirl, but they went back to another festival and took some other fellows along. Not wanting to be freeloaders, they took a calf from somebody's father's herd to be sacrificed. After several such festivals, they got drunk enough to join in the sex orgy.

In some such way, the downward slide began in various places around Israel. Worship of the Lord must have begun to seem dull and to make the boys feel guilty—so they dropped out. Those were the days when everyone did as he saw fit (Judges 17:6). No one disciplined the defectors, and the slide gained momentum.

B. PROVOKING THE LORD (V. 12)

12. They forsook the LORD, the God of their fathers, who had brought them out of Egypt. They followed and worshiped various gods of the peoples around them. They provoked the Lord to anger.

HOW TO SAY IT

Ashtoreth. ASH-toe-reth.
Canaanites. KAY-nan-ites.
Midianites. MID-e-un-ites.
Moabites. MO-ub-ites.
Othniel. OTH-ni-el.
Philistines. Fi-LISS-teens or FIL-iss-teens.

Those who joined in pagan rites were uncomfortable in meetings to worship the Lord, especially if God's law was taught and sin was rebuked. Increasingly they *forsook the Lord,* forgetting they were indebted to him for their freedom and prosperity. The first of the Ten Commandments proclaimed, "You shall have no other gods before me" (Exodus 20:3). By ignoring this basic rule, the Israelites *provoked the Lord to anger.* As Joshua had reminded his people, the Lord is holy, and he is jealous (Joshua 24:19).

C. MRS. BAAL (V. 13)
13. Because they forsook him and served Baal and the Ashtoreths.

The *Ashtoreths* were imaginary goddesses supposed to be associated with the Baals. As each pagan tribe had its own Baal, it had also its own Ashtoreth. Each tribe might represent her by a different idol; but all the pagan tribes regarded her as a very sexy deity.

TRYING TO LIVE IN TWO WORLDS

In tropical American waters lives a strange species of fish, the Anableps. It is known as the "four-eyed fish," due to the unusual construction of its eyes. Each of its two eyes has an upper and a lower part, each part functioning independently of the other. As the fish swims at the surface of the water, the upper part of its eyes project above the water. This enables the fish to search for food and watch for enemies. At the same time the lower part enables it to survey its underwater environment. In a sense, the Anableps lives in two worlds, something few of God's creatures are able to do.

Some persons try to live in two worlds, spiritually speaking. Wanting to enjoy all this world offers, they conduct their business and daily affairs as if God did not exist. By occasionally "looking up" and acknowledging God, however, they convince themselves that they are maintaining a vital relationship with him.

If, after the death of Joshua's generation, Israel practiced similar self-deception, in time they completely forsook the Lord to serve Baal. Let us not be deceived into thinking we can live safely in two worlds. "Set your minds on things above," Paul said, "not on earthly things" (Colossians 3:2). —C. R. B.

II. DISASTER (JUDGES 2:14, 15)
As God revealed himself to Moses, he is "compassionate and gracious . . . slow to anger, abounding in love and faithfulness, maintaining love to thousands, and forgiving wickedness, rebellion and sin" (Exodus 34:6, 7). We do not know how long he tolerated Israel's defection, or how complete that defection was. But with all his mercy, God will "not leave the guilty unpunished" (Exodus 34:7). Sooner or later, those who persist in guilt must face the anger they have provoked.

A. THE SPOILERS (V. 14)
14. In his anger against Israel the Lord handed them over to raiders who plundered them. He sold them to their enemies all around, whom they were no longer able to resist.

The Lord's method of punishment was simple. He had been supporting Israel against all enemies; now he simply switched his support to the other side.

Of course, this was due in part to natural causes. The Israelites of this generation were soft. They had lived all their lives in peace and comfort. They knew nothing of war. They had no military organization or leaders. When armed marauders swept into their land, what could they do but run for the hills, leaving their homes and fields to be spoiled? So the marauders drove off sheep and cattle, took away wheat and barley from threshing floors and granaries, helped themselves to ripened fruit. When they were gone, the people came back from the hills to find themselves destitute.

WHAT DO YOU THINK?

It is possible that the excitement of the pagan festivals made worship of the Lord seem dull by comparison, leading to Israel's departure from faith in the Lord. What activities tend to appeal to bored believers and entice them away from "sincere and pure devotion to Christ" (2 Corinthians 11:3)? What can you do to be sure you are not attracted to these things and led to compromise your devotion to the Lord?

Should the church make worship more exciting to appeal to the young and to outsiders? If so, how? If not, how can the church reach out to those not inclined to worship in the style practiced by your church?

WHAT DO YOU THINK?

The lesson writer suggests easy, comfortable living may have been part of the problem for the generation after Joshua. Is that a problem today? If so, in what ways? Is having things too difficult also a danger? If so how? Which is the greater problem? Why? (Consider Proverbs 30:8, 9.)

The statement that God *sold them to their enemies* does not mean the enemies made any payment to God. It says merely that God handed them over to the enemies as if they had been sold. The natural weakness of the Israelites may have been enough to accomplish this. If not, God used other methods as they were needed. It is not recorded, however, that he did for the pagans any such mighty miracles as he had done for the people of Israel.

B. A PROMISE KEPT (v. 15)

15. Whenever Israel went out to fight, the hand of the LORD was against them to defeat them, just as he had sworn to them. They were in great distress.

Not always did the people of Israel run for the hills when enemies approached. Sometimes they went out to battle. But as the *hand of the Lord* had been with them in the conquest of their land, now it was *against them*. As they had won before, now they lost. The Lord's hand is the decisive factor in any struggle in which he takes a part. The people should have known that God would be against them when they had turned against him. Defeat by enemies was one of many ways he had promised to punish their disobedience (Leviticus 26:14-25).

III. SUMMARY OF THREE CENTURIES (JUDGES 2:16-19)

These four verses summarize the history of Israel for almost three hundred years. It can be done thus briefly because basically the same events happened over and over, only with wide variations. Many different times Israel turned away from God and was troubled by "raiders" (v. 14). The raiders were different groups with different ways. Verse 14 seems to speak of raiding parties that came and went, taking spoil with them; but at one time the Canaanites dominated a part of Israel for twenty years (Judges 4:1-3). Seldom if ever did a raider gain control of the whole country. The Canaanites dominated the north part; the Philistines harassed the south; the Midianites came across the Jordan to strike at Israel's heartland. Periods of oppression and periods of peace are recorded separately as if one had followed another, but some of them may have overlapped. There may have been different oppressors in different parts of Israel at the same time; or there may have been different judges at the same time in different areas.

A. DELIVERANCE (v. 16)

16. Then the Lord raised up judges, who saved them out of the hands of these raiders.

When raiders brought them to poverty and misery, the people of Israel remembered who had helped them before. Again they appealed to the Lord, and he provided a leader to help them get rid of the raiders. These leaders are called *judges*, but they were very different in their personalities and their methods. Gideon was a distinguished military leader who turned down the invitation to rule Israel when victory was won. Deborah was more like what we call a judge. She held court under a palm tree (Judges 4:4, 5). Shamgar was an individual hero who brought relief by his single-handed conquests (Judges 3:31). There were many more judges in three hundred years, and no two of them were alike.

B. DOWNHILL AGAIN (v. 17)

17. Yet they would not listen to their judges but prostituted themselves to other gods and worshiped them. Unlike their fathers, they quickly turned from the way in which their fathers walked, the way of obedience to the LORD's the commands.

The people listened to their leaders till the spoilers were gone, and perhaps for some years longer. But all too soon they lapsed again into idol worship and wicked-

---

WHAT DO YOU THINK?

The Israelites' cycle of blessing, sin, suffering, repentance, deliverance, and restoration to blessing was repeated again and again through 300 years. The beginning seems each time to have been an attitude of taking God's blessings for granted. Do you see signs of the same thing happening in the lives of believers today? What is the evidence that a person is taking God's grace and blessings for granted? How can you prevent such an attitude from beginning in your life?

ness instead of going on in the godly way of *their fathers* who had lived in the time of Joshua. Then the Lord sent spoilers again. Israel's forsaking of the Lord to worship idols is compared to infidelity in a marriage.

C. THE LORD'S LOVING HELP (v. 18)

18. Whenever the LORD raised up a judge for them, he was with the judge and saved them out of the hands of their enemies as long as the judge lived; for the LORD had compassion on them as they groaned under those who oppressed and afflicted them.

"This hurts me worse than it does you." So said the old-fashioned father as he applied the paddle. The paddled child never believed it, of course—till he grew up and became a parent. Then he knew it was true. Likewise the Father in Heaven was grieved by the pain of his children on earth, though he himself sent the spoilers to inflict the pain. When the punished children in their groaning turned to the Lord, admitting their sin and pleading of relief, the Lord *raised up a judge.* He *was with the judge* to help defeat the enemies and to exert a godly influence on the people when the oppression was ended. Chapter 3 gives an example. Idolatrous Israel was punished by an invasion from Mesopotamia, and oppressed for eight years. When the suffering people cried to the Lord, he raised up Othniel not only to lead in defeating the invaders, but also to lead in loyalty to the Lord after the invaders were gone. So Israel was true to the Lord and at peace for forty years, till Othniel died (Judges 3:7-11).

D. ANOTHER PLUNGE (v. 19)

19. But when the judge died, the people returned to ways even more corrupt than those of their fathers, following other gods and serving and worshiping them. They refused to give up their evil practices and stubborn ways.

Look again at the example in chapter 3. After forty years of peace and prosperity with Othniel, the people of Israel lapsed into sin and idolatry again. This time the Moabites and some allies moved in. For eighteen years the Israelites had to give up produce and livestock in tribute to Moab (Judges 3:12-14).

Would the people of Israel never learn? No, not in three hundred years. When God blessed them with peace and plenty, in time they pursued pleasure rather than righteousness. Pursuing pleasure, they fell into immorality and idolatry. Then came the spoilers, bringing oppression and misery. Misery brought the sinners to grieve over their sin and turn away from it, appealing to the Lord for relief. So the gracious Lord provided a judge, a leader to rally the penitent people and defeat the raiders. Victory brought the people of Israel to another era of peace and plenty. Why couldn't they stay there?

AFTER OTHER GODS

Israel had a hard time learning that unfaithfulness to God brought them only pain and suffering. Time and again they turned from God to paganism, and each succeeding generation was more corrupt than the one before it.

The United States of America has traditionally been thought of as a "Christian" nation. Whether God considers this to be so is open to question, of course. Some of the founders of the nation were Deists, not Christians; nevertheless, they came to their conclusions about government and society within the context of a culture that was based on Christian principles.

So it is somewhat surprising to most of us to read about the advance of paganism in modern American culture. The evidences are many: In Los Angeles, a coffeehouse is billed as "a meeting place for pagans"; multitudes convene in the desert to be part of

OPTION

The reproducible activity, "The Judges of Israel," on page 56 will lead your students in a Bible study to compile a list of the judges who led Israel between the time of Joshua and of Samuel. It can be kept as a handy reference later.

Display and refer to Visual 5 as you comment on verse 19.

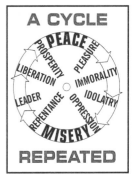

PRAYER

Father in Heaven, how wonderfully you care for us! With all our failings, your love will never fail. With praise and gratitude we pledge anew to continue in the upward way, bringing honor and glory to you and your Son. Amen.

WHAT DO YOU THINK?

If we are not growing, we are declining. What are some specific ways in which we can make sure to continue our growth in Jesus Christ? What things are you presently doing to make sure you grow? What activities could you add? What activities do you perhaps need to stop?

THOUGHT TO REMEMBER

Keep on climbing.

DAILY BIBLE READINGS

Monday, Sept. 26—God's Goodness Calls for Faithful Response (Psalm 81:6-16)

Tuesday, Sept. 27—After Joshua's Death, Israel Forsook God (Judges 2:6-12)

Wednesday, Sept. 28—God Sent Judges to Help Israel (Judges 2:13-19)

Thursday, Sept. 29—A Time of Testing (Judges 2:20—3:6)

Friday, Sept. 30—Another Cycle of Apostasy and Deliverance (Judges 3:7-15)

Saturday, Oct. 1—Again God Rescues a Wayward People (Judges 4:4-10)

Sunday, Oct. 2— Israel Known as "a Rebellious People" (Isaiah 30:8-14)

"harmonic convergences" of the "spiritual" powers of the universe; "New Age" believers, astrologers, psychics, and dabblers with crystals mix their paganism with small portions of Christian teaching; Eastern religions are building temples all across America.

As America moves from one spiritual aberration to the next, are we different from ancient Israel? It's a question we need to ask.   —C. R. B.

CONCLUSION

People of our time are moving, too. Are we climbing up or coasting down?

As young people we advance automatically. We grow taller and stronger. We get our permanent teeth. We advance in school. We go out and get jobs. As adults we tend to level off. Easily we get into a comfortable rut, and we start downhill before we know it.

A. WHICH WAY?

Which way are you going? Think of yourself as you were a year ago and as you are now.

• Are you taking better care of yourself physically? What improvement have you made in diet, exercise, habits of work, recreation, and rest? What improvement can you make now?

• Have you grown mentally? What important things have you learned? What do you need to learn now?

• Are you kinder, more sympathetic, more forgiving? Do you see some room for improvement?

• If you are married, are you more attentive to your mate? Do you see how you can do better?

• How about your job? Are you doing it better and more happily, and improving your relationship with fellow workers? Is there some improvement you need to be planning?

• Has your praying become more meaningful and more satisfying? Do you need to give it more time and more thought?

• Are you finding Bible study more helpful, and doing more of it? Could you get more out of it if you would put more in?

• Have you taken any new responsibility in the work of the church? Do you think of one you can take now?

• Have you increased your contribution to the Lord's work? You know church expenses are going up just as yours are.

You can think of other ways to compare you as you are with you as you were. Do you think you are climbing up, staying still, or coasting down? What will you be doing from now on?

B. THE GOAL AND THE WAY

Where are we going? What lies at the end of our upward way? Is it worth the climb?

We are moving toward "the whole measure of the fullness of Christ" (Ephesians 4:13-15). Our aim is to be like Jesus; and, yes, it is worth all the effort we can make. All the effort we can make is not enough, of course; our transformation depends on the grace of God. But at his bidding, we press on in the upward way. So "when he appears, we shall be like him, for we shall see him as he is" (1 John 3:2).

The way to the top is not to exalt ourselves. That is the way down (Luke 14:11). The way to take is the way Jesus took. He took "the very nature of a servant"; he "humbled himself and became obedient to death" (Philippians 2:5-11).

Discovery Learning

This page contains an alternate lesson plan emphasizing learning activities. Classes desiring such student involvement will find these suggestions helpful. The next page is a reproducible activity page to further enhance discovery learning.

LEARNING GOALS

As students participate in today's class session, they should:

1. Describe the cycle of sin, suffering, and deliverance that characterized the experience of the Israelites in the time of the judges.

2. Compare and contrast this cycle with the experience of Christians today.

3. Determine how to get out or stay out of this cycle of behavior.

INTO THE LESSON

Divide the class members into groups of from five to seven members each. One half of the groups should discuss the following statement to decide on reasons that prove it to be true:

When we disobey God, we put ourselves in peril. God always punishes disobedience.

The other half of the groups should discuss the following contrasting statement to prove it is true:

Although our sins grieve God, he never gives up on us. As a merciful God, he always provides his children with a way back to him.

Write the two sentences on your chalkboard or duplicate them onto sheets of paper for distribution to the groups. Allot five minutes for the groups to discuss their statements. When they have come up with their "proofs" (they may use common sense reasons as well as biblical examples), lead the whole class in a discussion along the following lines of thought: "The two sentences seem to contradict each other. Is one right while the other is wrong? Are they both wrong? Is there a sense in which each is correct?"

Tell the class that today's Scripture text shows both the wrath and the mercy of God in relation to his people when they sin against him.

INTO THE WORD

Use material from the "Introduction" section on page 49 as the basis for a brief lecture that connects the book of Joshua with the book of Judges, and last week's lesson with the lesson for today.

After you have given the lecture, ask students to summarize the sections of Judges 2 indicated by these verse divisions: verses 6-9; 10-13; 14 and 15; 16 and 17; 18; and 19. Let students choose one of the following four ways to summarize each verse or group of verses:

- a *color* to characterize the section
- a *word* to summarize the section
- a *song* to depict the meaning of the section
- a *weather report* to portray the mood of the section

Write the verse sections and the italicized words above on the chalkboard. Have the students work individually or in pairs to do a single summary. You may find it better, however, to have your students work in the same groups that were formed for the introductory activity. If so, ask each group to choose at least three of the four options for their summaries of the text. After about ten minutes, ask class members to share what they have written.

Then lead the class in discussing these questions: "What was the cycle of behavior that characterized the Israelites during this time of their history? Why do you suppose they behaved as they did?"

If you have time, ask class members to browse through the rest of the book of Judges to see illustrations of this pattern.

INTO LIFE

Discuss the following five questions with the whole class:

1. In what sense is it surprising to know that the Israelites repeated this cyclical pattern of behavior so many times? In what sense is it understandable?

2. What similar cycles of behavior have you seen in the lives of Christians you know?

3. Think of contemporary counterparts to each of the following elements in the Israelites' experience:
- gods other than the Lord God (vv. 11-13, 17)
- powerful enemies that win victories against God's people (v. 14)
- judges (vv. 16, 18, 19)

4. Why do God's people sometimes refuse to "give up their evil practices and stubborn ways"? (v. 19).

5. What can we learn from the experience of the Israelites in the time of the judges? How can we get ourselves out of their cycle of despair and keep ourselves out of it?

Close with sentence prayers from volunteers who will thank God for the lessons learned from the portion of his Word we have studied today.

Judges of Israel

Israel repeated a cycle of sin, oppression, repentance, and deliverance many times during the 300-year period from Joshua to Samuel. Each time a leader—or judge—was instrumental in leading the people in repentance and deliverance. Look up each of the following Scriptures and list the name of each judge identified. The name of the major oppressor is given in column 3 as a reference guide for you.

SCRIPTURE	JUDGE	OPPRESSOR
1. Judges 3:8-11	_____	Mesopotamia
2. Judges 3:12-30	_____	Moab
3. Judges 3:31	_____	Philistia
4. Judges 4:2–5:31	_____	Jabin of Canaan
5. Judges 6–8	_____	Midian
6. Judges 9	_____	(Period of Civil War)
7. Judges 10:1, 2	_____	Ammon
8. Judges 10:3-5	_____	Ammon
9. Judges 10:6–12:7	_____	Ammon
10. Judges 12:8-10	_____	Philistia
11. Judges 12:11, 12	_____	Philistia
12. Judges 12:13-15	_____	Philistia
13. Judges 13–16	_____	Philistia

The Value of Leadership

The repentance stage in each of Israel's cycles was led by a strong leader. Christian leadership always has the result—not merely of growing large congregations, though that may well be a by-product—but of stimulating spiritual growth and repentance among people. Who has been instrumental in your own life as a Christian leader? Write the name of a leader who has had a significant influence on your life, and a sentence or two about what his or her leadership has done for you.

_____

_____

In the space below, write one or two suggestions for how you might be a leader and influence someone else's life.

DELIVERANCE BY GOD'S HAND

LESSON 6

WHY TEACH THIS LESSON?

The name of Gideon has been appropriated by a group of businessmen who distribute Bibles in hospitals, hotels, the armed services, and schools. They have chosen his name because Gideon was not a professional prophet, statesman, or military leader when God called him to his great task. These businessmen—not professional "ministers" or "preachers"—identify with Gideon's "layman" status as they do what they believe God has called them to do.

But the lesson of Gideon speaks to all Christians, those in vocational ministry as well as those who are not. Even if Gideon had been a capable general, a strategist *par excellence,* he would not have been prepared for the task God called him and his 300 to do. The lesson of Gideon is a clear reminder that we, of ourselves, are incapable of accomplishing the victories God would win through us. The lesson of Gideon is total dependence on God, not upon one's training and skill. This is not to say training is unimportant, but it reminds us that our training is always the *second* step in our preparation. First comes dependence on God.

INTRODUCTION

Three hundred years is a long time in the life of a nation. The Roman Empire lasted longer than that, but the Babylonian Empire not nearly so long. The Constitution of the United States is only 207 years old. Three hundred years ago the British had taken New York from the Dutch, but were contesting with the French for Nova Scotia and debating the boundary of Florida with the Spanish. Three hundred two years ago, nineteen alleged witches were hanged in Massachusetts. Three hundred sixty-one years ago, the authorities compelled Galileo to retract his bold announcement that the earth moves.

In Israel, the time of the judges lasted about three hundred years. During this time there were great and momentous changes, but the most notable feature about this period was that the people of Israel repeated the same pattern over and over. At ease and affluent, the people cared more about getting rich and having fun than about doing right. Consequently they resorted to dishonesty and idolatry. Punishment came by means of invaders who took away their riches and their fun. In poverty and misery, the people turned to the Lord, and he provided a leader to rally them and defeat the enemies. Peace and prosperity returned.

This repeated cycle was the subject of our study last week. This week we are to study one example of it.

A. DOWN TO THE DEPTHS

In forty peaceful and prosperous years, the people of Israel more and more "did evil in the eyes of the Lord" (Judges 5:31—6:1). This time the invaders came across the Jordan from the east.

DEVOTIONAL READING:
PSALM 33:10-22

LESSON SCRIPTURE:
JUDGES 6:1–8:21

PRINTED TEXT:
JUDGES 7:2-7, 19-21

Oct
9

LESSON AIMS

After this lesson a student should be able to:

1. Tell how the Lord drove the Midianites out of Israel.

2. Mention one victory of the Lord that the student has participated in.

3. Mention a present or future struggle that the Lord can win with the student's help.

KEY VERSE:

Get up! The Lord has given the Midianite camp into your hands.   —Judges 7:15

The Midianites and other tribes were nomads. In the desert country east and south of Israel, they had to keep moving to find pasture for their sheep, cattle, and camels. Now they moved across the Jordan into Israel. The fields of growing wheat and barley were lush pasture for flocks and herds used to the sparse growth of the desert. The invaders fanned out over the country all the way to the Mediterranean coast and south to Gaza. The land was utterly devastated. Probably the nomads then went back to the desert, to come again the next year when the fields were green with a new crop. This went on for seven years.

Intimidated by the huge number of invaders, the Israelites fled to the hills and became cave dwellers. The record in Judges 6:1-6 sounds as if whole tribes of desert people moved in, bringing women and children as well as livestock; but the next chapter seems to describe a military camp. Perhaps the people and animals spread out over a wide area, while corps of tough fighting men camped together, ready to go swiftly to any place where there seemed to be a threat of attack.

Now the hungry people of Israel cried unto the Lord (Judges 6:6). His first response was to send a prophet to remind them of his former benefits, which they seemed to have forgotten (Judges 6:7-10). Then he summoned Gideon to raise an army and drive out the invaders (Judges 6:11-14).

B. LESSON BACKGROUND

Gideon undertook the task reluctantly, but moved energetically to get it done. Thirty-two thousand volunteers responded to his call. They camped on the north slope of Mount Gilboa with the widespread camp of the Midianites below them on the floor of the valley. Then came a surprise.

I. DISMISSING THE FEARFUL (JUDGES 7:2, 3)

The invaders were innumerable as a plague of grasshoppers (Judges 6:5), but an estimate of their number emerges later in the story. Fifteen thousand were left after a hundred twenty thousand were killed. There must have been at least a hundred thirty-five thousand in the camp that Gideon and his men saw before the fight began. It would be natural to think that thirty-two thousand were far too few to attack that multitude, but God said they were far too many.

A. TOO MANY (v. 2)

2. The LORD said to Gideon, "You have too many men for me to deliver Midian into their hands. In order that Israel may not boast against me that her own strength has saved her. . . .

Outnumbered though they were, the thirty-two thousand men of Israel still made an impressive army. If they would rout the Midianites, they might think they had done it by their own strength and heroism. The Lord wanted all of them to understand that the victory was due to him, not to them.

B. SWIFT REDUCTION (v. 3)

3. "Announce now to the people, 'Anyone who trembles with fear may turn back and leave Mount Gilead.'" So twenty-two thousand men left, while ten thousand remained.

"Anyone who is afraid may be excused." That was a sure-fire way to reduce the size of an army in sight of the enemy. More than two-thirds of the troops took Gideon at his word and dropped out. Only *ten thousand* were left. If Gideon himself began to be afraid, who can blame him? But the reduction was not yet complete.

It is surprising to see the name *Gilead* here, for that is best known as the name of an area east of the Jordan. Perhaps some spur or hump of Mount Gilboa also had

OPTION

The reproducible activity, "The Battle Is the Lord's," on page 64 will lead the students to discover several biblical examples where God won the victory for his people. It may be used to introduce this lesson.

WHAT DO YOU THINK?

God reduced the size of Gideon's army so the Israelites could not take the credit for the victory over Midian. What measures ought the church today take to be sure God is glorified instead of human effort in our ministries? Does this suggest our churches should deliberately stay small? But if so, then what about the large numbers reported in Acts 2:41; 4:4?

What about in your own life? Do you take conscious measures to give God the credit for your personal victories? If so, how do you do it?

that name. Some students think an ancient scribe copying the record may have made a mistake, writing Gilead for Gilboa. At this late date, there seems to be no way of proving either of these theories.

II. DISMISSING THE OVERCONFIDENT (JUDGES 7:4-7)

Ordinary human thinking would conclude that ten thousand men had no chance to defeat that horde of invaders in the valley. But ordinary human thinking does not include the Lord in the equation. A handful of men plus God would utterly overwhelm all the myriads of Midian. God had called these men to conflict, and he would give them victory; but God would not win the victory by himself. The men of Israel must do their part, and do it heroically; but they must not think their heroism could win without the Lord.

A. STILL TOO MANY (v. 4)

4. But the LORD said to Gideon, "There are still too many men. Take them down to the water, and I will sift them for you there. If I say, 'This one shall go with you,' he shall go; but if I say, 'This one shall not go with you,' he shall not go."

Wisely Gideon had assembled his men at a place where there was an adequate supply of drinking water. Their camp was beside the spring of Harod (v. 1), a large spring on the north side of Mount Gilboa. It supplied a little stream where Gideon could have his men get a drink of water before the battle. There the Lord would point out the men to be excused and those to stay with Gideon.

B. STRANGE TEST (v. 5)

5. So Gideon took the men down to the water. There the LORD told him, "Separate those who lap the water with their tongues like a dog from those who kneel down to drink."

One lapping with his tongue would not lap directly from the stream, but would cup a little water in his hands and drink from that (v. 6). One bowing on his knees would kneel at the edge of stream or pool, bend forward, and put his lips to the surface of the water to drink. People who have camped by unpolluted streams know what a satisfying way that is to drink one's fill. But soldiers and athletes and hard workers know it is unwise to drink one's fill just before vigorous action. Encamped in the valley below, the Midianites certainly saw the Hebrews assembled on the hillside. They might come out to battle at any time. Those who scooped up water with their hands would drink less and be more ready for combat. Each of them was to be set on one side; those who bowed on their knees on the other.

C. THE CHOSEN FEW (vv. 6, 7)

6. Three hundred men lapped with their hands to their mouths. All the rest got down on their knees to drink.

When the division was complete, only three hundred men stood on one side. All the rest of the ten thousand were on the other side.

7. The LORD said to Gideon, "With the three hundred men that lapped I will save you and give the Midianites into your hands. Let all the other men go, each to his own place."

Gideon may have been hoping to keep the larger group; but no, the Lord assigned the *three hundred* to him. Along with the little group, however, he gave a very big promise. He, the Lord, would use that little group to bring the whole huge horde of Midian under the power of Gideon. So the rest of the ten thousand were told to go home. Verse 8 seems to indicate that the departing men left enough supplies so each of the three hundred had plenty of food.

Gideon may have been getting nervous as his band was getting smaller. Verses 9-14 tell how one more bit of encouragement was given to him. After nightfall the Lord sent him and his servant down to the camp of Midian. In the darkness they sneaked close enough to hear two Midianites talking.

One Midianite was telling about a dream. He had seen a loaf of barley bread come tumbling into the camp to crush a tent. The Hebrew text says *the* tent, perhaps meaning the commander's tent, the army's headquarters.

The other Midianite was quick to interpret the dream. He said the barley loaf represented Gideon, who was about to tumble into camp with his troops to crush it.

Obviously the Midianite intelligence division had done its work well. The men not only knew about the nearby Hebrews, but they even knew the name of the commander. They must have seen the thirty-two thousand soldiers assemble on the hill. In spite of their numeric superiority, the Midianites were nervous and uneasy. God was preparing *them* for the battle as well!

III. ROUTING THE FOE (JUDGES 7:19-21)

Gideon and his servant went back up the hill to waken their men. Quietly they distributed equipment and gave instructions. Each man had a trumpet. Each one also had a torch, which he probably lighted at the campfire before he covered it with a clay jar to hide it till the proper moment. In three companies they moved out in the darkness and silently surrounded the Midianite camp (vv. 15-18).

A. READY? (v. 19A)
19a. Gideon and the hundred men with him reached the edge of the camp at the beginning of the middle watch, just after they had changed the guard.

Gideon and the men with him crept as close to the enemy camp as they could without alerting the sentries. They timed their arrival between ten and eleven o'clock, just after the changing of the guard. The new sentries, wakened from their early sleep, were nervous but still sleepy.

B. NOW! (v. 19B)
19b. They blew their trumpets and broke the jars that were in their hands.

Suddenly the sound of a hundred trumpets blasted the silence. Suddenly a hundred torches flared in the darkness. It was a startling signal.

C. RESPONSE (v. 20)
20. The three companies blew the trumpets and smashed the jars. Grasping the torches in their left hands and holding in their right hands the trumpets they were to blow, they shouted, "A sword for the LORD and for Gideon!"

Like twin echoes, a hundred trumpets blasted from this side, and a hundred more blasted from that. Two hundred more torches flared. Between trumpet blasts the battle cry rang out. The name of *Gideon* was alarming, for the Midianites knew he commanded those gathering Hebrews (v. 14). The name of *the Lord* was even more alarming, for the Midianites had heard from their grandparents what terrifying things the Lord had done in years gone by.

D. TERROR (v. 21)
21. While each man held his position around the camp, all the Midianites ran, crying out as they fled.

The Israelites did not rush the camp; they just let the trumpets and the torches do their work. The Midianites woke to the sound of trumpets and the sight of a ring of fire. Normally one bugler is enough for a battalion, or perhaps a regiment.

How many vengeful Hebrews were massed behind three hundred trumpets? Bewildered and befuddled, groping in darkness for shoes and swords, the Midianites fled in terror.

Panic and confusion must have been fatal to many of the Midianites, for "the Lord caused the men . . . to turn on each other with their swords" (v. 22). We can imagine the scene: stumbling out of his tent with sword in hand, a man saw a running figure bearing down on him and struck it down—but it was one of his comrades. Or perhaps the runner struck first, and the other died. There may have been hundreds or thousands of such deaths as comrades fought each other "throughout the camp" (v. 22).

THE POWER OF ONE

Several computer networks—one of them involving sixty thousand computers—were rendered useless in November 1988. A "virus" attack began to rapidly infect computers across the nation. As word of the epidemic spread, operators of thousands of computers not yet infected "quarantined" their systems by disconnecting them from the networks.

This relatively benign virus didn't destroy any files; it merely duplicated "garbage" so rapidly that the computers' memory banks were filled up so they could not operate. The crisis was caused by only one person, a graduate student in computer science, who thought his experiment would be harmless. Because the system his virus attacked was one used by the U. S. Defense Department, the FBI found the case very interesting!

Gideon and his select band of soldiers had their part in routing the huge Midianite army, but they, more than anyone else, would know that they could not take credit for the victory. It was God's victory alone—beginning with the winnowing down of Gideon's army from thirty-two thousand to the plan for surprising the Midianites. It is said that "one person and God make a majority." Actually, God is a majority without anyone else. Wisdom dictates that we align ourselves with him.   —C. R. B.

CONCLUSION

So with torches and trumpets and three hundred men, the Lord put an army to flight. The Midianites ran southeast toward the Jordan River and their homeland beyond it, but their troubles were far from over.

A. MOPPING UP

Thousands of Israelites started for home before the trumpet blast (vv. 2-8). Now runners caught up with them, inviting them to turn back and join the pursuit (v. 23).

Spread far and wide over Israel, Midianite families with flocks and herds soon learned what was happening. They too started for home, but they could not move swiftly with their livestock. Gideon called on the tribe of Ephraim to intercept them as they fled. The men of Ephraim captured and killed two princes of the enemy. There is no record of how many more they killed, or how many cattle and sheep were captured (vv. 24, 25).

Meanwhile the remnant of Midian's fighting men escaped beyond Jordan to a place where they felt secure. But Gideon and his three hundred followed, surprised them, and defeated them again. The two kings of the Midianites were captured, and later they were slain (Judges 8:10-12, 18-21).

Again loyal to the Lord, Israel was at peace for forty years (Judges 8:28).

B. THE LORD'S VICTORY

Thirty-two thousand men were too many, the Lord said. Even ten thousand were too many for the Lord's army. If the Lord would win the victory by so many,

WHAT DO YOU THINK?

Of course, Gideon's victory was a special case. How much do you think it should cause us to expect victory in our own lives? Consider 1 Corinthians 15:57: "But thanks be to God! He gives us the victory through our Lord Jesus Christ." Is that a blanket promise? Why or why not? How much should Christians anticipate victory in their own lives and in the life of the church? What if we encounter failure? How should we handle that?

Display visual 6 of the visuals packet, and you refer to it in reference to points B, C, and D of the Conclusion section.

PRAYER

"Now unto the King eternal, immortal, invisible, the only God, be honor and glory for ever and ever. Amen" (1 Timothy 1:17).

THOUGHT TO REMEMBER

The Lord can do wonders— through you.

OPTION

The reproducible activity, "The Battle Is Still the Lord's," on page 64 can be used to lead your students to apply the principles expressed here. Reproduce and distribute the activity or simply lead your class to discuss the material printed there.

DAILY BIBLE READINGS

Monday, Oct. 3—A Faithless People Cry for Help (Judges 6:1-10)

Tuesday, Oct. 4—Gideon's Call to Lead the Israelites (Judges 6:11-18)

Wednesday, Oct. 5—A Sign to Reassure Gideon (Judges 6:19-24)

Thursday, Oct. 6—Gideon Destroys the Altar of Baal (Judges 6:25-32)

Friday, Oct. 7—Two More Signs Affirm God's Call (Judges 6:33-40)

Saturday, Oct. 8—The Selection of Gideon's Army (Judges 7:2-14)

Sunday, Oct. 9—The Enemy Flees From Gideon's Army (Judges 7:15-21)

they might think they did it by themselves. So the Lord's army was cut down to a mere three hundred. No one could possibly think such a tiny handful would defeat that huge army in the valley.

Gideon saw the Lord's angel and heard the Lord's voice to give him courage, but the three hundred saw no angel and heard no voice but Gideon's. Still, in faith they moved out to surround and destroy an army four hundred fifty times as big as theirs. They trusted the Lord.

The Lord won the victory through men of faith, but he did it in such a way that faithless persons could still say—and they do—that the Lord had nothing to do with it. They suggest that the three hundred simply used a clever stratagem of their own to scare the enemies out of their wits. But people of faith know the Lord won the victory.

C. MORE OF THE LORD'S VICTORIES

Early in the fourth century special coins of the Roman Empire were struck to celebrate the extermination of Christianity; but only about a decade later, a Roman coin displayed Chi-Rho, a symbol of Christ. Let credit be given to hundreds of Christians who gave their lives to keep their faith, and let credit be given to the emperor who made Christianity legal; but the Lord won the victory.

Next month our Thanksgiving celebration will call to mind the Pilgrim fathers who survived a bitter winter on the stern New England coast, who toiled hard through the summer, and who paused in the autumn to give thanks. Let us honor their courage and fortitude and hard work; but they knew the Lord won the victory, and they gave him thanks.

In 1992 a Florida church building was demolished by a hurricane. Promptly the members set about rebuilding, though they had their own homes to rebuild, too. Give credit to their devotion and sacrifice, and give credit to Christians all over the land who sent funds to help; but the Lord won the victory.

Mr. Chumbley was ninety-three years old when he gave his life to Christ. For seventy years his wife had been telling him he ought to be a Christian. At least a dozen Christian ministers through the years had tried to teach him the way of the Lord. Christian friends at work had tried to win him, and later his associates in a Christian retirement home had made like efforts. Perhaps he never would have been won without such efforts, but still the victory belonged to the Lord.

In these instances and many more, no one saw the Lord or heard his voice; but he was there. No earth-shaking miracle proclaimed his presence, but he was at work. From the human point of view the odds against him seemed long, but he won.

Take a few minutes to think about your own life. In how many of God's victories have you had a part? What victory is he now about to win through you?

D. GOD IS CALLING

"Moses," called the Lord. "Moses."

"Here I am," said Moses, before he knew who was calling.

After Moses learned who was calling, the Lord said, "I am sending you to Pharaoh to bring my people the Israelites out of Egypt" (Exodus 3:10).

Then Moses said, "Who, me?"

But Moses took his life in his hands and went to Pharaoh, and through every difficulty and danger he "persevered because he saw him who is invisible" (Hebrews 11:27). Through Moses, God won a mighty victory.

You may not hear God's call with your ears, but you will hear it with your faith. Will you answer the call? God can win through you.

Discovery Learning

This page contains an alternate lesson plan emphasizing learning activities. Classes desiring such student involvement will find these suggestions helpful. The next page is a reproducible activity page to further enhance discovery learning.

LEARNING GOALS

As students participate in today's class session, they should:

1. List what God did and what Gideon did in Israel's victory over the Midianites.

2. Discover ways God's methods for bringing us victory may be surprising or unusual.

3. Decide one way to accept God's surprises for their own lives.

INTO THE LESSON

After all the class members have arrived, ask them to pair off. In their pairs, have each student tell a two-minute story about himself or herself relating to one of these topics:

"A time when victory was particularly sweet."

"A time when God surprised me."

"A time when I worried for nothing."

After four minutes (two minutes for each partner's story), ask for three volunteers to share their stories with the class, one for each heading. Then tell your class, "As we look at how God worked in Gideon's life, decide how your stories relate to the themes in today's study."

INTO THE WORD

Use the material in the "Introduction" on page 57 to remind class members of last week's study and to connect it with this week's. Then read all of Judges 7 aloud to the class.

A dramatic way to do this is to have a dialogical reading. One person reads all the words of God in this passage. Another reads everything that Gideon said. A third person reads the words of the first Midianite (v. 13), and another reads the second Midianite's words (v. 14). All of the remaining words are read by the narrator.

Divide the class in half and instruct one half to listen for "everything that God did." The other half is to listen for "everything that Gideon did." When the reading of the text is finished, ask the students in each half of the class to arrange themselves in groups of three and to list under their respective headings the actions they detected. Then ask volunteers to share with the class as you write the items under each heading on your chalkboard.

Optional activity. If you have time, divide your class into groups of from four to seven members each. One person from each group should volunteer to deliver a monologue before the whole class. The other class members in each group are to help the speaker prepare his or her monologue.

The monologues are to be no longer than two minutes in length and are to begin with one of the following statements:

"I am Gideon—"

"I am the Lord—"

"I am Purah, Gideon's servant—"

"I am a soldier in the Midianite army—"

"I am one of Gideon's three hundred warriors—"

If you have five or fewer small groups, make certain that each group selects a different topic. Students are to prepare their monologues by studying and discussing chapter 7 of Judges.

After either or both of these Bible-study activities, lead a class discussion based on the following questions: "Why did God command Gideon to limit his army as he did? What might Gideon and his forces have learned from this experience? What did it teach the rest of the Israelite nation? What can we learn from it?"

INTO LIFE

Ask the students to arrange themselves into groups of from four to seven members each (the same groups they were in for the Bible study above). As they do so, write this statement on your chalkboard: "God's ways are not man's ways." Each small group should list as many examples as they can think of that show that this statement is true.

After five minutes, ask volunteers to share some of the examples they have noted. Discuss with the class, "How have you been surprised by the way you have seen God work in your world? Has your response to God's actions matched Gideon's? Has God's work in your life matched what he did for Gideon? What happens when we ignore God's commands and insist on doing his work in our own way instead of his? How can we become more willing to follow his methods instead of insisting on our own?"

Ask class members to reflect privately for a moment on this question: "What is the situation in your life where you most need God to provide the victory?"

Perhaps volunteers will share what they are thinking. Then ask several to pray sentence prayers to close today's session.

The Battle Is the Lord's

The victory of Gideon's 300 is but one of many examples in the Bible where victory in a military campaign must be ascribed to God's intervention and not to human power or plans. Look up each Scripture passage cited on the chart below. Identify the enemy defeated and write a description of the victory that the Lord provided

SCRIPTURE	ENEMY	HOW THE LORD PROVIDED VICTORY
Exodus 14:21-31		
Joshua 6:12-25		
Joshua 10:1-5		
1 Samuel 7:3-14		
1 Samuel 14:6-23		
2 Samuel 5:17-25		
1 Kings 20:13-30		
2 Kings 6:8-23		

The Battle Is *Still* the Lord's

Over what enemies has the Lord given you victory in your own life that you could not have conquered on your own? List two or three, such as habits that you have put aside, relationships that have been mended, etc. Offer God praise for the victory he has won.

What enemies continue to confront Christians individually and/or the church as a whole today? List several below. Then, next to each one, note any progress you feel you have seen in the Lord's working victory in that situation. Pray daily for the Lord to bring about the victory over each enemy you listed.

From the Conquest to the Kingdom

Unit 3: The Beginning of the Kingdom
(Lessons 7-9)

ISRAEL DEMANDS A KING

LESSON 7

WHY TEACH THIS LESSON?

Spiritual nearsightedness is a common affliction. It dates back at least as far as the period of the judges, when the people of Israel did as they "saw fit," but they did not see very clearly. Even when they saw fit to follow the Lord, they saw only the external result and not the internal motivation.

The elders of Israel knew Samuel was a godly man and a good judge. They also knew his sons were not godly and would not be good leaders. They knew another solution needed to be found. That much was easy to see.

But the long view was not so clear. They knew Samuel's leadership had provided for security and prosperity, and they hoped to produce the same result by means of a monarchy such as the nations around them had. They equated the result with the cause. If they could provide a stable government, then they would have the Lord's blessing. They should have pursued the Lord's blessing directly, and the stable government would have followed.

And so Christians today often seek to have God's blessing by performing external acts of supposed righteousness. Inside, they remain unconverted. They are looking for a king like everyone else rather than allowing God to be king in their lives. This lesson challenges that notion.

INTRODUCTION

"Everyone did as he saw fit," or, as the King James Version puts it, "what was right in his own eyes." This is the repeated description of Israel's conduct in the time of the judges (Judges 17:6; 21:25). In deciding between right and wrong, one's own eyes are not a safe guide unless they are enlightened by God's Word.

Without that light, one's own eyes may mistake what is *pleasant* for what is *right*. So luxury and laziness may be perceived as right, along with overeating and overdrinking, idol worship and adultery. Or one's own eyes may foolishly conclude that what is *profitable* is right. Then one may approve of lying and cheating and stealing because they make him or her rich.

Such blunders were the bane of Israel in the time of the judges. When things went well, people ran wild in pursuit of pleasure and profit. Doing as they saw fit, they did what the Lord saw as evil. God's way of correcting their eyesight was to bring in a pagan tribe to steal their profits and end their pleasures. In poverty and misery the people could see their mistake. They began again to worship God and obey him; then he provided a leader to drive out the invaders. Obedient Israel found the way back to prosperity. This cycle rolled on and on for three hundred years.

A. THE LAST JUDGE

Samuel was the last of the judges. Dedicated to the Lord before he was born, and brought up by a godly priest, he became a godly man and a prophet. But in his youth the people of Israel again did as they saw fit and evil in the sight of the Lord.

This time God's punishment came through the Philistines, who lived in the coastal plain. They continued to dominate and oppress Israel for twenty years (1 Samuel 4:1—7:2)

DEVOTIONAL READING:
PSALM 47:1-9

LESSON SCRIPTURE:
1 SAMUEL 7:15–8:22; 12:19-25

PRINTED TEXT:
1 SAMUEL 8:4-9, 19; 12:19-25

Oct
16

LESSON AIMS

After this lesson students should be able to :

1. Explain how Israel got a king, and what was wrong with that.

2. Accept responsibility for what they do.

3. Specify one way they can follow God's leading more perfectly.

KEY VERSE:

Appoint a king to lead us, such as all the other nations have.
—1 Samuel 8:5

Then Samuel sounded a call to repentance, and the people responded. They got rid of their idols and gave their worship and obedience to the Lord. Samuel summoned them to a big prayer meeting in Mizpah (1 Samuel 7:3-6).

Seeing the nation gathering for prayer, the Philistines thought an army was assembling to rebel against their rule. Quickly mustering their own troops, they marched to put down the insurrection. This time the Lord fought for Israel. He upset the Philistines with a terrific thunderstorm, and the Israelites chased them back to their plain (1 Samuel 7:7-14).

With peace restored, Samuel moved to maintain righteousness. He became a circuit judge, going from place to place so people could more easily come to him with cases to be decided according to God's law (1 Samuel 7:15-17).

B. LESSON BACKGROUND

When Samuel was growing old, he sent his sons to be judges in the south part of Israel. That would have been an excellent move if the sons had been like their father. But those young men cared nothing for justice or God's law. They "accepted bribes and perverted justice" (1 Samuel 8:1-3).

I. CALL FOR A KING (1 SAMUEL 8:4-8)

The elders of Israel were disturbed, as they should have been. They could remember how they had suffered under Philistine rule, and how God had helped them with a thunderstorm at just the right moment. But in a few years these elders would die, and so would Samuel. The new generation would not have the same memories to warn them against evil; and if justice could not be found in the courts, soon it would not be found anywhere in Israel. How could the nation be saved from another slide into evil and idolatry and disaster?

A. TROUBLED ELDERS (V. 4)

4. So all the elders of Israel gathered together and came to Samuel at Ramah.

Something had to be done, and Samuel was the man to do it. He was the undisputed leader of the nation, the one who had guided them to freedom from the Philistines, the one who had blessed them with equal and exact justice in his court, the one they trusted. So the huge group of *elders* came to his home *at Ramah*.

B. PROBLEM AND SOLUTION (V. 5)

5. They said to him, "You are old, and your sons do not walk in your ways; now appoint a king to lead us, such as all the other nations have."

The elders stated the problem very simply. First, Samuel was *old*. He would not be there to dispense justice much longer. Second, his sons were not walking in his ways: there was no prospect that they would dispense true justice. Some kind of change was needed, and the elders suggested a change that looked good to them: *appoint a king to lead us, such as all the other nations have*. All the nations around Israel had kings. Monarchy seemed to work. It was simple and effective. The king was the head: everybody did what he said to do. If anyone was disposed to object, the king had a standing army to keep him in line. Not being under a king themselves, the elders did not see the many abuses that arise in that kind of government. Apparently they expected Samuel to find them a king like himself, godly and wise and incorruptible.

C. RELUCTANT PERMISSION (VV. 6-8)

6. But when they said, "Give us a king to lead us," this displeased Samuel; so he prayed to the LORD.

OPTION

The reproducible activity, "Kingly Plans," on page 72 may be used to lead your students to discover God's instructions for Israel's king given under Moses.

WHAT DO YOU THINK?

Samuel was a very godly man, but his sons were morally corrupt. It is the same pattern seen earlier with Eli (1 Samuel 2:12) and later, at least to some extent, with David. (Consider his sons Amnon, 2 Samuel 13, and Absalom, 2 Samuel 15:1–18:18.) Why does it seem so common that the children of godly leaders fail to live up to the same standards as their parents? What about Proverbs 22:6? What bearing does that verse have on rearing godly children?

Perhaps Samuel was *displeased* because he thought the request reflected dissatisfaction with him personally (v. 7). More than that, his wisdom and inspiration from the Lord must have led him to know the proposed solution would not work. Even if he appointed a man as capable and upright and unselfish as himself, who could guarantee that his sons would not be as bad as Samuel's sons were?

A lesser man might have denounced the elders' plan instantly and loudly, but Samuel was too wise for that. He took the matter to a higher judge: *he prayed to the Lord.*

7. And the LORD told him: "Listen to all that the people are saying to you; it is not you they have rejected, but they have rejected me as their king.

The Lord gave consent, but not approval. Samuel should listen to the elders and do what they asked. It would not solve their problem, but it would show them and their children that such a solution would not work.

God said Samuel should not feel hurt by the elders' request. They were not rejecting him; they were well pleased with his leadership. Their problem lay deeper than that. The Lord said, *They have rejected me as their king.*

God was the proper king of Israel. He made his will known in the law given through Moses. In the law itself he promised blessing and help to israel when israel obeyed his law; he promised disaster when the law was ignored. He did not provide a king on earth to make the people obey the King in Heaven; instead, he made all persons responsible for their own obedience and for teaching their children to obey. Whenever the people did not obey, they were rejecting the Lord.

It was not impossible for the people to keep God's law well enough to receive his blessing and help. They did it as long as Joshua led them, and for years after he died (Judges 2:7). They did it for forty years after God and Gideon rescued them from Midian (Judges 8:28). They did it for years after God and Samuel rescued them from the Philistines (1 Samuel 7:13-17).

Now the elders saw the beginning of another slide into disobedience and disaster. Why didn't they assume the responsibility of teaching obedience to their families and clans? Why didn't they resolve to establish the reign of God so fully that no one would ever feel a need to appeal to those rascally sons of Samuel?

In our own communities, do we take upon ourselves the responsibility of teaching God's Word and will so thoroughly that no one will ever disobey? No, we banish God and his Word from our classrooms, and we establish police and courts and jails to restrain the disobedience of the untaught. The elders of Israel wanted a king to do that for them.

8. "As they have done from the day I brought them up out of Egypt until this day, forsaking me and serving other gods, so they are doing to you.

The people of Israel had a long history of pledging their loyalty in words but rejecting God in fact. If they now were rejecting Samuel and his advice, it was just what they had been doing to the Lord for centuries.

II. WARNING IGNORED (1 SAMUEL 8:9, 19)

The Lord let his people in Israel have their own way, but he told Samuel to explain the perils of it.

A. SOLEMN WARNING (V. 9)

9. "Now listen to them; but warn them solemnly and let them know what the king who will reign over them will do."

Samuel was to let the people have their way; he was to help them get the best king that was to be had. But he was to let them know that being ruled by a king was no bed of roses. The king would draft their young people for military service,

Display visual 7 of the visuals packet as you refer to verse 7.

GOD GAVE
HIMSELF— *a faultless king*
HIS WORD— *a faultless guide*
AND THE RESPONSIBILITY *to know, obey, and teach*
HIS MESSAGE TO ALL.

WHAT DO YOU THINK?

If God was to be Israel's king, and it was a sin to ask for a human king, then why did God give instructions in Deuteronomy 17 about a human king for Israel?

Some say the sin of asking for a king was simply one of motive, to be like all the other nations. Had they wanted a king for a godly reason, God would have been pleased to have given them one. Others suggest the sin was one of running ahead of the Lord's plan, that God intended for David to be the first king over Israel. Others say God never intended for Israel to have a king at all. The instructions in Deuteronomy 17 show his foreknowledge, not his intention.

What do you think? What application can be drawn from each suggestion?

OPTION

The reproducible activity, "Just Like Everybody Else," on page 72 is designed to lead your students in a discussion of peer pressure. Copy and distribute the activity, or simply discuss the issues raised there.

WHAT DO YOU THINK?

God told Samuel the people's request for a king was a rejection of him. The monarchy they proposed was certainly not what God intended, but still he allowed it. Similarly, when the Pharisees asked Jesus why Moses had given commands regarding divorce, Jesus said God allowed divorce because of the hardness of human hearts. It was not God's intention for men and women, but he allowed it.

Why do you think God allows certain situations even though he does not approve? Are there other similar cases? What can we learn from this toleration of less-than-ideal relationships? How ought we to approach situations where God's ideals are not being upheld?

HOW TO SAY IT

Ammonites. AM-un-ites.

Philistines. Fi-LISS-teens *or* FIL-iss-teens.

Jabesh Gilead. JAY-besh GIL-e-ud.

and civilian service, too. He would requisition fields and vineyards, slaves and livestock, for his officials. He would levy a ten percent tax. The people would find all of this to be oppressive (vv. 10-18).

B. REPEATED REQUEST (V. 19)

19. But the people refused to listen to Samuel. "No!" they said. "We want a king over us."

Samuel's protest made small impression on the elders. They had been thinking about this matter, and their minds were made up. The injustice of Samuel's sons was a clear and present danger. They repeated their request for a king.

The following verse records the elders' three reasons for their insistence:

1. No one could tell them a monarchy wouldn't work. All the other nations had kings, and they seemed to be doing all right.

2. They needed a king to judge them as Samuel had been doing. He would settle their disputes, he would tell them what to do, he would enforce the law. The elders would be relieved of the responsibility of learning and teaching and enforcing that long and wordy law.

3. The king would be responsible for national defense. It would be his job to muster an army and repel any invasion of Israel, and to lead any necessary invasion of another country.

Again Samuel took the matter to the Lord, and again he was told to go ahead with plans for a king. So the meeting adjourned (vv. 21, 22).

III. REASSURANCE AND WARNING (1 SAMUEL 12:19-25)

The elders went home, and Samuel waited for the Lord's leading. First he was led to a man named Saul, whom he anointed privately to be the king of Israel (1 Samuel 9:1—10:1). Then he called a mass meeting for the purpose of choosing a king by lot. The lot fell on Saul, thus confirming the choice already made in private and letting all the people see that the choice was made by the Lord, not by Samuel. Saul was tall and handsome, a fine figure of a man. With a few exceptions, the people acclaimed him with enthusiasm (1 Samuel 10:17-27).

Soon came the first test of the new king. Ammonites from the east threatened Jabesh Gilead, a city on the east bank of Jordan. Saul quickly recruited an army and soundly defeated the Ammonites. Samuel led the people to Gilgal to celebrate the victory and confirm the establishment of the kingdom (1 Samuel 11).

To the crowd at Gilgal, Samuel reviewed the great help that God had given to Israel through the centuries. Plainly he told the people they had sinned by asking for a king instead of obeying the Lord as their king. It was wheat-harvest time, a time when it never rains in Israel. But Samuel asked God to confirm his statement by thunder and rain, and God responded. Thus convinced of their sin, the people were frightened.

A. PRAYER REQUEST (V. 19)

19. The people all said to Samuel, "Pray to the LORD your God for your servants so that we will not die, for we have added to all our other sins the evil of asking for a king."

Freely the people confessed not only former sins but also the sin of asking for a king instead of recognizing God as their king and obeying him. Now they begged Samuel to pray that they would not die for their sin.

B. REASSURANCE (VV. 2-23)

20. "Do not be afraid," Samuel replied. "You have done all this evil; yet do not turn away from the LORD, but serve the LORD with all your heart.

Samuel did not make light of the people's sin, nor did he withdraw his accusation. Rather, he repeated it with emphasis. Still he said, *"Do not be afraid."* The important thing was what they were going to do, not what they had done in the past. From now on, they had better not turn aside from the straight line of wholehearted service to the Lord.

21. "Do not turn away after useless idols. They can do you no good, nor can they rescue you, because they are useless.

If God's people would turn away from God, to what would they turn? To idols or imaginary gods. These things are *useless.* They cannot give their followers rain and sunshine and good crops as the Lord does. They cannot *rescue* their followers from enemies as the Lord does. They *can do* their followers *no good* at all.

ANTIDOTE TO FEAR

Pëtr Ilich Tchaikovsky was one of the world's greatest composers, but fear and depression clouded his life. When he was ten, his mother left him in a Saint Petersburg preparatory school. He so feared being left alone that he ran after her carriage, trying to grab its wheels to stop her departure. His mother died four years later, and he became obsessed with his misery.

Finally, in music he found some consolation. In time he taught harmony at the Conservatory of Moscow. During a brief, unhappy marriage he attempted suicide. Thereafter he suffered from frequent depressions. Toward the end of his life, he sank into extreme depression and thought he was going mad. During this period he wrote what many regard as his greatest composition, the "Symphonie Pathetique." He conducted its premiere, which was not well received, and a week later Tchaikovsky was dead.

Sometimes, like Tchaikovsky's, our troubles come from the way others have treated us or from a temperamental disposition to gloominess that seems beyond our control. More often, discouragement and fear are the natural consequences of bad choices we have made.

Samuel told the Israelites that their request for a king was wrong, but he urged them neither to fear nor turn away from serving the Lord. That would lead only to futility. Repentance of sin and wholehearted obedience to God were the keys to their spiritual health. It is so even today.   —C. R. B.

22. "For the sake of his great name the LORD will not reject his people, because the LORD was pleased to make you his own.

To many other sins the people of Israel had added the sin of demanding a king. They did not deserve the Lord's favor and help, but he was going to help them anyway *for the sake of his great name:* his reputation, his honor, his position as the one and only God who can do great things. Back in the time of Abraham he had chosen this particular family of people for a great purpose. Through them he was going to bring a blessing to all families of the earth (Genesis 12:3), for through them he would send his Son to redeem the lost and offer salvation and eternal life to all mankind.

23. "As for me, far be it from me that I should sin against the LORD by failing to pray for you. And I will teach you the way that is good and right.

The people had asked Samuel to pray for them (v. 19). That he would do; it would be a *sin against the Lord* to stop his praying. But he would also continue to denounce their sins and to teach them the good and the right way.

C. FINAL WARNING (VV. 24, 25)

24. "But be sure to fear the LORD and serve him faithfully with all your heart; consider what great things he has done for you.

WHAT DO YOU THINK?

God said the request for a king was evil, and the people finally agreed. So why not dissolve the monarchy and go back to the government they had followed before? Instead, Saul remained king. Why do you think repentance of the sin of asking for a king did not require revoking Saul's kingship?

WHAT DO YOU THINK?

Why would it have been a sin for Samuel not to pray for the people? Because they had asked him to? Because it was his "job" as a prophet? Why? When is it a sin for Christians today to fail to pray for others?

Is there someone for whom you need to pray right now?

WHAT DO YOU THINK?

Has the Lord done great things for you? Name some. What ought your response to them be?

PRAYER

How gracious you are, dear Heavenly Father! Out of your goodness you have provided both forgiveness of sin and a faultless guide to righteous living. In love and gratitude we pledge ourselves anew to do your will. In Jesus' name we pray. Amen.

THOUGHT TO REMEMBER

"The Lord will not reject his people" (1 Samuel 12:22).

DAILY BIBLE READINGS

The people had asked for a king, and now they had one. In spite of past sins, all would be well if they now would hold the Lord in reverence and give him wholehearted obedience. Samuel already had assured them of that (v. 14). Now he reminded them again that their well-being depended on their wholehearted obedience. God had done great things for them all through their history. They ought to remember all those things and serve God both out of gratitude and in the hope that he would continue to do great things for them in the future.

25. *"Yet if you persist in doing evil, both you and your king will be swept away."*

The people had thought a king would solve all their problems. Not so! Their problems could be solved only by doing right. If they would do wrong in the future, disaster would come to them and their king together.

CONCLUSION

"Righteousness exalts a nation: but sin is a disgrace to any people" (Proverbs 14:34). Israel was not alone. Doing right is beneficial everywhere, and doing wrong is disastrous.

A. DO IT YOURSELF

The righteousness that exalts a nation is a do-it-yourself project. You are responsible for what you do; I am responsible for what I do. Neither of us can escape responsibility by blaming parents or spouse or associates, government or society or the system.

In our society we need police and courts and jails to deal with people who do not accept their responsibility; but a frequent complaint about our justice system is that it does not make bad people good. Criminals who go into our jails are still criminals when they come out. They remain criminals till they themselves decide to change.

God can help us do right, of course; and we can help one another do right or wrong. But all who do wrong do it themselves, and none does right without doing it himself.

B. LOOKING AHEAD

One of the responsibilities of our generation is to teach God's way to the next generation. Our public schools give us no help in this; it is our own responsibility. We are not only to teach God's way when we are sitting at home; we are also to show how the teaching is applied in all our going and coming, all the activities of daily living (Deuteronomy 6:6, 7).

Our failure to teach the next generation does not excuse its failure to obey the Lord, but neither does its failure to heed our teaching excuse our failure to teach.

C. THE WAY THAT WORKS

We cannot become good unless we desire in our hearts to be good, but we cannot become good by our effort alone. It takes a greater power than ours.

"All have sinned" (Romans 3:23), and "the wages of sin is death" (Romans 6:23). If we do nothing but good from now on, that cannot atone for the sins of the past. The only way to escape from sin and death is to be justified by God's grace "through the redemption that came by Christ Jesus" (Romans 3:24). The only way to become good is to have our sins forgiven; and we have our sins forgiven when we give ourselves to Jesus: believing in him, trusting him, obeying him (Acts 16:30-33; 2:37-42; 22:16). Thus we become good with a righteousness not our own, "the righteousness that comes from God and is by faith" (Philippians 3:9).

Discovery Learning

This page contains an alternate lesson plan emphasizing learning activities. Classes desiring such student involvement will find these suggestions helpful. The next page is a reproducible activity page to further enhance discovery learning.

LEARNING GOALS

As students participate in today's class session, they should:

1. Decide why God did not want the nation of Israel to have a king, and why he allowed them to have one anyway.

2. List practical steps they can take to make their nation more pleasing to God.

INTO THE LESSON

Write the following sentences on your chalkboard for students to see as they arrive:

• *Our job is to make our nation a Christian nation.*

• *Our job is to live like Christians in our non-Christian nation.*

To begin, ask class members which sentence they agree with more. Ask for a show of hands and tell class members they must vote for one or the other of the two sentences.

Ask class members to form groups of two or three. Each group must have at least one person who chose the first sentence and one who chose the second. In their groups students should tell each other why they chose as they did. Allow five minutes for them to do this. Then lead a brief class discussion of the sentences.

INTO THE WORD

Connect this week's lesson with last week's lesson. The material under the "Introduction" heading (page 65) will provide the information that you need. Ask your students to open their Bibles and look at the chapter and section headings for the first eight chapters of 1 Samuel. As they read the headings to you, review the events in those chapters and the significance of each. Then ask a volunteer to read today's printed text aloud while the class listens for these three things:

1. What did the people want?

2. What did Samuel want?

3. What did God want?

You may want to divide the class in thirds and have each third listen for the answer to a different one of the questions as the Scripture is read. Then answer each question by leading the whole class in discussing them.

Next, give each class member a copy of the following Bible-study questions. If you have time, divide the class into groups of from five to seven students each, and ask the groups to answer the questions. After several minutes lead the whole class in discussing them.

1. Why did the elders of Israel want a king? (1 Samuel 8:5).

2. How did Samuel react to their request? Why? (v. 6). What does Samuel's response to the elders show about his character?

3. What was wrong with the elders' request for a king? Why did God allow what he did not approve?

4. What was God's assessment of the Israelites? (v. 8). Give some examples to substantiate God's assessment of his people.

5. What warnings did God tell Samuel to give the people regarding having a king rule them? (vv. 9-18).

6. Read verse 20 and list the three reasons the elders gave for wanting a king. Does their rationale seem reasonable? How may one account for their insistence upon wanting a king to reign over them?

7. According to 1 Samuel 12:19-25, how did Samuel respond when the people finally saw the error of their request? Would God bless them, even though their having a king was against his will? On what conditions? What did Samuel regard as a valid reason why Israel should obey the Lord wholeheartedly?

INTO LIFE

Ask a volunteer to read Proverbs 14:34 aloud to the class. Then read to the class only the first paragraph under the heading "A. Do It Yourself" in the "Conclusion" section on page 70. Lead the class in discussing the following questions: "Is our nation more or less righteous today than it was ten years ago? How about twenty years ago? What evidence can you give for your answer? Are Christians more or less visible today than a generation ago?"

To make personal application of this lesson, ask class members to consider this question: "What can you do to make our nation more righteous this week?" Distribute slips of paper and ask each student to write down at least one answer to the question. Collect the slips and read them back to the class. Then let several volunteers close with sentence prayers for the nation, for the class, and for the specific ideas noted on the slips of paper.

Kingly Plans

Although God was not pleased with the people's wish for a king, he had anticipated it and gave instructions regarding the king years before. Read Deuteronomy 17:14-20 and answer the following questions.

1. What qualifications must the king meet to be chosen? (v. 15)

2. What prohibitions must the king observe? (vs. 16, 17)

3. What commands must the king follow? (vs. 18-20)

Just Like Everybody Else

The people wanted a king to rule them so they would "be like all the other nations" around them (1 Samuel 8:20). Their motive, while not proper, was understandable. Peer pressure continues to convince people—even Christian people—to act in ways not necessarily consistent with scriptural teaching.

What examples have you observed of people's responding to peer pressure to an undesirable degree in the following areas?

Fashion

Car style/model

Entertainment

Moral standards

Adherence to biblical command or precedent

How have you resisted peer pressure to take a stand for what you felt was right according to the Bible? Cite one example. What was the result?

From the Conquest to the Kingdom
Unit 3: The Beginning of the Kingdom
(Lessons 7-9)

SAUL'S OPPORTUNITY AS KING

LESSON 8

WHY TEACH THIS LESSON?

People today need a word of grace. "To err is human," we say, and Scripture echoes, "All have sinned." Last week's lesson brought another example. The people of Israel added one more sin to their long list of sins by asking for a king.

Today's lesson supplies the word of grace. Though the people had sinned, God was still concerned about them. Their cry had reached his ears (1 Samuel 9:16). Though they had chosen a form of government other than what God had intended for them, as long as they would submit to him anew, God would use that government to provide peace and prosperity.

Sometimes we make mistakes that cannot be undone. Through wrong choices, we have created situations that cannot be reversed. Does God still love us? Is his grace still sufficient? Yes! *Our* cry reaches his ear, too. This lesson provides assurance of our own deliverance!

INTRODUCTION

Change was brewing in Israel. The people were going to have a king, and they were optimistic. Samuel had been their chief judge for a long time, and they had prospered. Samuel was old now; he would not be with them much longer. Furthermore, his sons were greedy and crooked. The people wanted a king to banish greed and crookedness, to manage the economy so everyone would prosper, and to vanquish all foreign foes.

Samuel warned the people that a king would bring new problems instead of solving the old ones. With or without a king, doing right brings prosperity and doing wrong brings disaster. But the people were not listening. All the other nations had kings, didn't they? Obviously that was the kind of government that worked.

God agreed to give them a king without giving his approval to their request. God himself chose the king, but neither the prophet nor the people knew who he was.

LESSON BACKGROUND

Kish was a prosperous man of the tribe of Benjamin. Somehow a few of his donkeys got out and wandered away. So Kish told his son Saul to take one of the servants and go out to find the strays.

Saul was not a mere boy on the farm. He was a man in the prime of life. His son Jonathan was an adult; not much later he commanded a thousand fighting men (1 Samuel 13:2).

Saul and the servant tramped over a lot of territory in the next three days, but found no donkeys. They were about to give up and go home when they thought of Samuel. They happened to be near the town were he was. Samuel was God's prophet, and he often gave God's messages to the people. Surely God knew where the donkeys were. If he would tell his prophet, the prophet could tell the searchers (1 Samuel 9:1-13).

DEVOTIONAL READING:
PSALM *106:40-48*

LESSON SCRIPTURE:
1 SAMUEL 9:15–10:1A, 20-24

PRINTED TEXT:
1 SAMUEL 9:15-17, 10:1A, 20-24

KEY VERSE:

Then Samuel took a flask of oil and poured it on Saul's head and kissed him, saying, "Has not the Lord anointed you leader over his inheritance? —1 Samuel 10:1

Oct
23

LESSON AIMS

After this lesson a student should be able to:

1. Tell how God's choice of a king was made known to God's prophet and God's people.

2. Outline the qualifications of a king of Israel, and compare the qualifications of a citizen of God's kingdom today.

3. Find a way to improve his or her understanding of and obedience to God's will.

LESSON 8 NOTES

I. INFORMING THE PROPHET (1 SAMUEL 9:15-17; 10:1A)

Saul and the servant hurried to the town where Samuel was. At the gate they met the prophet himself, who was going out to give his blessing to a sacrifice and feast at a nearby high place (1 Samuel 9:14).

A. ANNOUNCEMENT IN ADVANCE (vv. 15, 16)

15. Now the day before Saul came, the LORD had revealed this to Samuel:

The Lord not only knew where the donkeys were; he also knew where Saul and the servant were and just when they would come to see Samuel. So a *day before Saul came,* the Lord foretold his coming.

16. "About this time tomorrow I will send you a man from the land of Benjamin. Anoint him leader over my people Israel; he will deliver my people from the hand of the Philistines. I have looked upon my people, for their cry has reached me."

Years earlier, the Philistines had oppressed Israel for a long time. Samuel had rallied the Israelites to drive them out with the help of a thunderstorm from the Lord, so at that time they "did not invade Israelite territory again" (1 Samuel 7:3-14). But the Philistines were watchful and persistent. They meant to come back. Through the years they probably saw signs of weakness in Israel. Now they were beginning to step up their pressure, and had established at least one outpost in Israelite territory (1 Samuel 10:5). Israel, however, had not turned so far away from God that he was willing to let the Philistines subdue them. This time he wanted the new king to take the lead in defeating those enemies, and Saul was to be the new king. Samuel was to designate him as king by anointing him.

B. IDENTIFICATION ON ARRIVAL (v. 17)

17. When Samuel caught sight of Saul, the LORD said to him, "This is the man I spoke to you about; he will govern my people."

When Samuel caught sight of Saul, the Lord plainly told his prophet that this was the one to be king. Samuel took Saul to the feast and seated him in the place of honor, then gave him lodging for the night. The record centers on Saul, but no doubt the servant remained with him. As the two were leaving in the morning, Samuel went a little way with them. He asked Saul to tell the servant to go on ahead so the prophet could speak privately with Saul (vv. 18-27).

C. ANOINTING THE KING (10:1A)

1a. Then Samuel took a flask of oil and poured it on Saul's head.

From time immemorial there has been a custom of anointing a king to induct him into office or to indicate his dedication to that office. David, for example, was anointed three times: once long before he actually became king, once when he became king of Judah, and once when he became king of all Israel (1 Samuel 16:1-13; 2 Samuel 2:4; 5:1-3). In Israel, priests were anointed for their office long before there was a king (Exodus 28:40, 41). There is one mention of the anointing of a prophet (1 Kings 19:16). Some students think that among God's people the anointing oil signified a special gift of God's Spirit (1 Samuel 16:13). But, of course, God's Spirit comes as he will, with or without anointing (Judges 3:10; 6:34; Acts 8:14-17; 10:44).

Anointing was used to dedicate things as well as people to sacred uses. Jacob anointed a stone, making it a monument in memory of God's appearing to him (Genesis 28:18). The tabernacle in the wilderness was anointed, along with the things in it (Exodus 30:22-29).

So the first king of Israel was chosen by the Lord and anointed by the Lord's prophet, but no one knew it except the Lord, the prophet, and the king.

WHAT DO YOU THINK?

God told Samuel that Saul would be the leader of God's people and would deliver them from Philistine oppression, noting that the people's cry had reached him. Yet the request for a king had been condemned as sin—as we saw in last week's lesson. What a marvelous example of God's grace, then, this becomes. In spite of their sin in asking for a king, God promises deliverance from their enemy. And the instrument of deliverance is the king himself!

Have you observed other examples of such grace—where God has used someone who might represent a sinful situation to bring about his own purposes in spite of the sin? Perhaps a person who has divorced without scriptural grounds in time has become a model spouse and parent. Perhaps a divisive person has caused a church split, but later is now an advocate of peace and unity in the church. What examples have you seen?

OPTION

The reproducible activity, "First King?" on page 80 is designed to lead your students in a Bible study of today's text by comparing Saul's coronation with an earlier incident.

Certainly Saul was not seeking or expecting any such honor and responsibility. In his own view, he was a member of the most unimportant family in the most unimportant tribe of Israel (1 Samuel 9:21). After he left Samuel, do you suppose he might begin to wonder if it was really true? Could it be possible that he was to be the king? To quiet any such doubts, Samuel told Saul exactly what was going to happen to him as he was going on his way, and each thing happened just as Samuel had foretold. So each event became added evidence that Samuel was a true prophet (1 Samuel 10:2-12).

II. INFORMING THE PEOPLE (1 SAMUEL 10:20-24)

Now that the king was chosen, the next step was to let all the people know about the choice. For that purpose Samuel called a national meeting and told the people to present themselves before the Lord (1 Samuel 10:17-19). The Lord was going to select a king from among them, and apparently some way of casting lots was to be used to show the choice to the people.

When we flip a coin to decide a matter, we expect the result to be entirely by chance. But when the Hebrews cast lots to decide a matter of national importance, they confidently expected God to decide the outcome, and he did.

The Scripture does not give a description of how lots were cast. We do know that part of the high priest's equipment was the mysterious Urim and Thummim by which questions were decided (see Exodus 28:30; Numbers 27:21). Some scholars speculate that these were two pebbles of the same size and shape, but of different colors. To answer a question, the priest would reach into his pouch without looking and take out a pebble. The white one meant yes and the black one meant no.

In this way or some other, the people expected God to let them know whom he had chosen to be king. So they began to present themselves before the Lord, first by tribes and then by thousands, the smaller family groups within a tribe (1 Samuel 10:19).

A. SELECTING THE KING (VV. 20, 21)

20. When Samuel brought all the tribes of Israel near, the tribe of Benjamin was chosen.

For a tribe to come near before the Lord, it was not necessary for the whole tribe to step forward. One man could simply mention the name of the tribe, and wait for an answer. To each tribe the answer was no, till *the tribe of Benjamin* was mentioned. Then the answer was yes. The king was a man of that tribe.

21. Then he brought forward the tribe of Benjamin, clan by clan, and Matri's clan was chosen. Finally Saul son of Kish was chosen. But when they looked for him, he was not to be found.

After the tribe of Benjamin was chosen, the next step was to name the clans within that tribe. These were presented one by one, and the Lord said yes to *Matri's clan.* Possibly there was another step, not specifically mentioned, by which the family of Kish was chosen from among those of his brothers in Matri's clan. But at last the members of a family were presented one by one, and *Saul the son of Kish was chosen.* And now we see that it was not necessary for a man even to be present to be presented before the Lord. Someone merely put forward Saul's name, and the Lord said yes. Now all the people knew who was their king, but he could not be found.

B. FINDING THE KING (VV. 22, 23)

22. So they inquired further of the LORD, "Has the man come here yet?" And the LORD said, "Yes, he has hidden himself among the baggage."

If the Lord was giving yes or no answers, then a series of questions must have been needed as they inquired of the Lord further:

Is this man Saul going to arrive later?

No.

Is he already here in camp?

Yes.

Is he in his tent?

No.

Is he taking care of the animals?

No.

Is he in the baggage area?

Yes.

So some of the people raced to the place where baggage was stored, and found Saul hidden there.

A RELUCTANT HERO

Victor Frisbie was for many years one of the most quoted persons in Los Angeles, although he was never seen in public! His opinions on numerous matters were often seen in the *Los Angeles Examiner*. His obituary appeared in the January 6, 1962, issue of the *Examiner*. "Victor Frisbie, well-known sportsman and traveler, died today."

The cause of death for Victor Frisbie was that the *Examiner* "died" that day also. Frisbie was the fictitious creation of bored copy writers on the newspaper's staff, who used Frisbie's "quotes" to enliven articles concerning recurring events such as the New Year's Day Rose Parade. Apparently, the editors never caught on to the ruse, but when the paper stopped publication, Frisbie died with it.

Saul really did exist, but when the time came for him to be presented as God's choice for Israel's first king, he was nowhere to be seen. Saul preferred anonymity to public acclaim.

Was it humility or lack of self-confidence that caused Saul to hide? We may never know. But for one to have a bit of reticence when faced with a task of great importance is far better than to be filled with braggadocio. An assignment of great responsibility calls for humble reliance on God, not boastful posturing. —C. R. B.

23. They ran and brought him out, and as he stood among the people he was a head taller than any of the others.

Reluctant Saul was brought to the meeting, and he was *a head taller* than the crowd. He was good-looking, too (1 Samuel 9:2). Of course, the Lord did not choose him for that reason, for "the Lord looks at the heart" (1 Samuel 16:7). But the outward appearance made a fine impression on the people.

Saul, with all his height and good looks, was not arrogant or aggressive at this time. He was modest, even bashful. He described himself as the most insignificant man in Israel (1 Samuel 9:21). When he heard that he was to be king, he told no one (1 Samuel 10:15, 16). And when he knew the secret was about to come out, he hid instead of stepping forward to claim his place. But when it was time for action, he proved to be bold and capable (chapter 11).

No doubt, both Saul's noble appearance and his modesty helped to make him acceptable to the people. Added to these was the fact that the Lord chose him.

C. ACCEPTING THE KING (v. 24)

24. Samuel said to all the people, "Do you see the man the LORD has chosen? There is no one like him among all the people." Then the people shouted, "Long live the king!"

OPTION

The reproducible activity, "Godly Leadership," on page 80 may be used to help your students compare their own leadership qualities with those of Saul.

WHAT DO YOU THINK?

Leadership can bring out the best in a person or it can bring out the worst. Saul appears to have been quite modest when he was chosen to be king. Later, however, he became an egotistical tyrant. What do you think went wrong in Saul's life? Why did leadership bring out the worst in him? What do you do, or what can you do, to keep the same thing from happening to you when you are in leadership positions?

The new king looked more kingly than anyone else in the crowd, and he was the Lord's choice. Samuel was quick to point out both these facts, and the people responded with a great shout of acclamation: *"Long live the king!"*

THE MEASURE OF A PERSON'S WORTH

In 1931, the 1,250-foot Empire State Building in New York City became the world's tallest building. In 1972, New York's World Trade Center grabbed the honors at 1,350 feet. Then, in 1973, the Sears Tower in Chicago became the world's tallest building at 1,454 feet.

Another member of the "world's tallest" club is "Bullwinkle," a 1,615-foot offshore oil drilling rig in the Gulf of Mexico. One would never guess it to be that tall, since only 262 feet of it is above water!

We are fascinated with things and people of gargantuan proportions. From basketball players to national leaders, tall people seem to have an advantage. So it was that Saul's height was something for everyone to remark about as he was designated king of Israel.

However, Saul's later behavior demonstrated that there is more to the measure of a person than height. Like the oil-drilling rig, "Bullwinkle," what is beneath the surface may be far more significant than what can be seen at first glance. What is in one's heart—moral character and spiritual sensitivity—is far more vital than how tall a person is or any of the other physical standards the world uses to measure a person's worth. —C. R. B.

CONCLUSION

Let's conclude our study with 1 Samuel 10:25, the verse that follows our lesson text: "Then Samuel explained to the people the regulations of the kingship. He wrote them down in a scroll and deposited it before the Lord."

A. THE REGULATIONS OF THE KINGSHIP

The Lord was the proper king of Israel. When he gave his law, about four hundred years before Saul's time, he neither commanded nor encouraged the people to have any other king. Still he foresaw the time when Israel would have a human king, and he set down regulations for the king and the kingdom (Deuteronomy 17:14-20). No doubt these were the regulations Samuel told the people about. Let's consider them.

1. The king must be one chosen by the Lord.

2. He must be an Israelite, not a foreigner.

3. He must not have many horses. Horses were not used for plowing; they were used for war. Israel was to be a peaceful nation.

4. The king was not to have many wives.

5. He was not to have much silver and gold.

6. The king must make a copy of God's law, keep it with him, and read from it every day. Thus he would learn to fear the Lord and obey his law.

Notice how Saul fitted the legal description of a king:

1. He was chosen by the Lord. The Scriptures make that very plain.

2. He was an Israelite.

3. Probably he had no horses at all. Donkeys matched his style of life.

4. Second Samuel 12:8 seems to indicate that Saul had more than one wife, and that David took Saul's wives along with his kingdom. Apparently monogamy was not recognized as ideal in those days.

5. As to silver and gold, it seems that Saul's family was moderately wealthy; but certainly it was not among the idle rich. Saul was put on foot in search of lost donkeys.

KEEP IT HANDY
STUDY IT DAILY

Holy Bible

LEARN IT THOROUGHLY
OBEY IT FULLY

Refer to visual 8 of the visuals packet as you discuss the thoughts in the "Conclusion" of this lesson.

OPTION

The reproducible activity, "Kingly Plans," on page 72 (from lesson 7) may be used to lead your students in a Bible study of the "regulations for the kingship." If you did not use it in the previous session, you may use it to introduce the ideas in part "A" of the "Conclusion."

WHAT DO YOU THINK?

Even though Saul was king, and others after him would be king, the law of God was still the supreme law of the land. Even the king was to submit to it. How does the place of God's law in the kingdom illustrate the place it should hold in our lives and in the church today? What can you do to be sure it holds that position?

PRAYER

Our Father and our King, with the psalmist we pray, "Open my eyes, that I may see wonderful things in your law" (Psalm 119:18). Among other things, may we see a wonderful vision of what we ought to be doing in the work of your kingdom, and by your grace may we be doing it with joy and determination. In Jesus name, Amen.

THOUGHT TO REMEMBER

"The Lord your God was your king" (1 Samuel 12:12).

DAILY BIBLE READINGS

Monday, Oct. 17— Saul Seeks Help From a Seer (1 Samuel 9:1-10)

Tuesday, Oct. 18—Saul Comes to Samuel (1 Samuel 9:11-21)

Wednesday, Oct. 19—Samuel Anoints Saul to Be King (1 Samuel 9:22—10:1)

Thursday, Oct. 20—Signs to Confirm Saul's Appointment (1 Samuel 10:2-8)

Friday, Oct. 21—Saul's Heart Is Changed (1 Samuel 10:9-16)

Saturday, Oct. 22—Saul's Kingship Affirmed by Israel (1 Samuel 10:17-26)

Sunday, Oct. 23—Saul's Victory Over Israel's Enemy (1 Samuel 11)

6. Without having any definite information, we may suppose Saul took home a copy of the law. Humble as he was at this time, perhaps he read it diligently and learned much. Next week we shall see that his obedience faltered at a critical time. Before we condemn him, let's consider our own Bible study, assess our own learning, and check our own obedience.

As God designed it, Israel was to be an absolute monarchy with God as its king and with every citizen obedient to his law. Still there were to be judges and officers in every community to lead the way, to teach all the people to know the law and obey it, and to rebuke and punish when it was necessary (Deuteronomy 16:18).

On the other hand, Saul's kingdom was a limited monarchy. The king himself must obey God's law as strictly as the lowliest citizen did. The king must not issue any decree contrary to God's law. The Lord was still supreme.

Samuel put these regulations in writing so they would be available for reference at any time. He laid them up before the Lord so they would be preserved for posterity.

B. GOD'S KINGDOM TODAY

The kingdom of God as we know it is not the kingdom of Israel. It is not limited to the descendants of Israel, or Jacob, as he is more often called. It is open to anyone who chooses to be ruled by God. Nevertheless the kingdom of God is similar to Israel in several ways.

One came into the kingdom of Israel by being born to parents who were Israelites. One comes into the kingdom of God by being born again, born of water and the Spirit (John 3:3-5).

Like the old kingdom of Israel, God's kingdom is designed to be an absolute monarchy with God as its king. If we say Christ is its king, that also is true, for God and Christ are one (John 10:30).

Like those in Israel, each person in God's kingdom is responsible for his own obedience to God. Many people, especially beginners, need help with this responsibility. Israel had judges and officers to keep the people in line; God's kingdom has elders to help and guide those who need their help. All of us in the kingdom should respect and follow those leaders (Hebrews 13:17), but only as long as they lead in God's way. No one has a right to overrule the Lord God Almighty.

Since there is no human king and each person is responsible for his own conduct, the regulations set down for the king of Israel may well be applied to each person in God's kingdom.

1. The king of Israel must be chosen by the Lord, and all those in God's kingdom also are chosen by him (1 Peter 2:9, 10).

2. The king of Israel must be an Israelite, and each person in God's kingdom must be reborn as a child of God (1 John 1:12, 13).

3. The king of Israel must not have many war horses, and the citizen of God's kingdom must keep the peace if he can (Romans 12:18).

4. The king of Israel must not have many wives. An overseer in the church must be a one-woman man (1 Timothy 3:2). Is that not the standard for those he oversees as well?

5. The king of Israel must not have much silver and gold, and people of God's kingdom are urged to lay up treasure in Heaven, not on earth (Matthew 6:19-21).

6. The king of Israel must have a copy of God's law and read from it daily, reading carefully and learning to fear God and obey him. Every citizen of God's kingdom needs to be a diligent Bible student with the steadfast purpose of knowing God's will and doing it. How much time have you spent with God's Word in the past week? What have you learned about his will for you? How will you do God's will better this week?

Discovery Learning

This page contains an alternate lesson plan emphasizing learning activities. Classes desiring such student involvement will find these suggestions helpful. The next page is a reproducible activity page to further enhance discovery learning.

LEARNING GOALS

This lesson should help students:

1. List Saul's qualities and potential for success as a leader.

2. Decide how God may be calling them to leadership today.

INTO THE LESSON

Ask students to complete one of the following sentences and to share their completion with a friend:

I most want a leader to be—

When I'm asked to lead, I usually—

My example of a good leader is—

Tell class members that today's lesson is about leadership. The lesson text focuses on the choice of Saul as Israel's first king, and you will want them to consider Saul's leadership potential.

INTO THE WORD

Before class write the following phrases on slips of paper, one phrase per slip. Make enough slips so each class member may have one:

How God chose the leader

How Samuel felt about the new king

How Saul felt about being king

How the people felt about the new king

To begin today's Bible study, explain the background of today's text. Then put all the slips face down in a basket so the students cannot see what is written on them. Ask them to take a slip from the basket as it is passed to them.

Next, read today's printed text aloud to the class. As you do so, each student is to listen for information about the topic on the slip he or she has drawn.

After the Scripture has been read, have your class members stand and ask each other what is written on their slips. Each is to find a partner whose slip matches his or her own. Once everyone is paired, give students five minutes to discuss their topics. Then lead the whole class in a discussion of the four topics.

Option.

Make enough copies of the following instructions for each class member to have one:

Pick your activity. Decide which of the following Bible-learning activities you would like to complete. Then find at least one other person who will work with you on that activity. Your group will have six minutes to complete the activity. Then the teacher will ask several volunteers to share what they have prepared. Pencils, paper, and drawing materials are on a table in the front of the room.

Choice one: Suppose you are Saul talking to your son Jonathan about the events of the day preceding your coronation, and the coronation day itself. What do you say to him? Be ready to have this conversation in front of the whole class. One person will need to be Saul, and the other Jonathan.

Choice two: Suppose you are a member of the nation of Israel writing a diary entry on the events of the days mentioned in our lesson text. How do you feel about the new king? Write down your impressions.

Choice three: Suppose you are an artist who wants to depict the historical events described in today's lesson text. How would you picture them? Draw one picture, or perhaps a series of pictures, to tell the story.

Encourage students to work together to complete these projects. Not everyone needs to do the actual acting, writing, or drawing. But members of the groups can give ideas to the ones actually completing the "creative" part of the project. If you choose the "Pick-your-activity" option for the Bible-study activity, try to see that all three choices are selected by different groups.

INTO LIFE

Lead the whole class in discussing the following questions.

1. How might the events of 1 Samuel 10 have been designed to equip Saul for leadership? Consider each following verse or group of verses individually in this regard: verse 1, verses 2-8, verses 9-13, verses 20-24, and verse 27.

2. How do you think Saul felt about being chosen to be king of Israel? Consider especially 1 Samuel 9:21; 10:14-16; and 10:22, 23.

Perhaps one or more students will share their responses to these questions: Have you ever been tapped for some service in the church that you didn't feel qualified to perform? How did you react? How did you decide whether or not God wanted you to do it?

As you ask the following questions, have the students reflect on them privately: Are you more of a leader or a follower? Are you sure? If God were going to use you as a leader in some situation today, what would it be?

First King?

Saul is regarded as the first king of Israel. While he was the first legitimate king, about a century before Saul's time another leader usurped the title and called himself "king." Read Judges 8:29–9:57 and compare the two men below.

	USURPER	TRUE KING
Name		Saul
Father	Gideon	
Tribe (see Judges 6:15)		
Length of Reign (see 1 Samuel 13:1)		
How he became king		
Religious devotion		
How he treated those who did not want him as king (see 1 Samuel 10:27; 11:12, 13)		

Godly Leadership

Those familiar with Saul's career must wonder at how he changed from a humble and gracious appointee to the throne to become the jealous and vindictive pursuer of David, God's choice to replace Saul. What qualities, evident at his coronation, made Saul a potentially good leader?

Do you share those qualities? What can you do to develop and preserve such qualities in your life?

From the Conquest to the Kingdom

Unit 3: The Beginning of the Kingdom
(Lessons 7-9)

KING SAUL DISOBEYS GOD

LESSON 9

WHY TEACH THIS LESSON?

How close is "close enough"? So often we are tempted to settle for just a little less than what God's Word demands. Complete obedience is too difficult. Besides, isn't it legalistic to demand strict adherence to the Word?

Saul thought he had come close enough. Samuel told him to wait seven days for the prophet to come and offer the sacrifice before Saul and the army went into battle. He waited the seven days, but he didn't wait for Samuel to come. But he did not go to battle without having the sacrifice offered. He just had it done without waiting for Samuel.

But Samuel said it was not close enough. In fact, it betrayed a presumptuous attitude that disqualified the king from having his line continue on the throne.

This lesson stands in stark opposition to the notion that we can set our own standards or that we can presume upon God's grace. It is not legalistic to follow God's Word precisely. To the contrary, if Jesus is Lord, then nothing less than complete submission to his will is proper.

INTRODUCTION

What is a king supposed to do? Saul must have wondered about that. He was snatched suddenly from the farm to the throne, with no training or experience in politics. There was no former king to set an example, no government organization. The law said the king should study it and obey it; but specifically it said more about what the king should not do than about what he should do. Samuel was still the chief judge. As God's spokesman, he gave instructions to the nation. So what was a king to do?

What Saul did was to go back home to the farm (1 Samuel 10:26; 11:5). There he received news from the east, and suddenly he knew what the king ought to do.

A. A JOB FOR THE KING

A strong force of Ammonites from the desert besieged Jabesh, a town on the east bank of Jordan. Hopelessly outnumbered, the men of Jabesh offered to surrender and pay tribute; but the arrogant Ammonite king wanted to humiliate them further by gouging out the right eye of every man. At that, the besieged people of Jabesh sent messengers throughout Israel to beg for help.

Saul's response was fully worthy of a king. He sent out an urgent demand for volunteers, and 330,000 men responded. With superb generalship, Saul led them to surround the Ammonite force and cut it to bits (1 Samuel 11:1-11).

B. CONFIRMING THE KINGDOM

Samuel then called the people to meet in Gilgal to celebrate the victory, confirm the kingdom, and give thanks to the Lord. Though Saul had been a magnificent leader, Samuel at last convinced the people that they had done wrong in asking for a king. Nevertheless, Samuel assured them that peace and prosperity could be had exactly as before. With or without a king, they must simply obey the law of God (1 Samuel 11:14—12:25).

DEVOTIONAL READING:
1 SAMUEL 15:22-26

LESSON SCRIPTURE:
1 SAMUEL 13

PRINTED TEXT:
1 SAMUEL 13:5-14

LESSON AIMS

After this lesson a student should be able to:

1. Tell how King Saul disobeyed the Lord's command, and what sentence was pronounced by the Lord's prophet.

2. Explain how the Lord's commands come to us.

3. Give more attention and better obedience to God's Word.

Oct
30

KEY VERSE:

But now your kingdom will not endure; the Lord has sought out a man after his own heart and appointed him leader of his people, because you have not kept the Lord's command.
—1 Samuel 13:14

The places mentioned in this lesson are included on the map identified as visual 9 of the visuals packet.

C. LESSON BACKGROUND

Saul then dismissed most of his army, keeping only three thousand men. He deployed two thousand of them in the high country at Micmash and Bethel. Saul's son Jonathan took command of the other thousand and led them to Gibeah, his hometown. The Philistine outpost at Geba was between these detachments of Israelites.

It was Jonathan who began the hostilities. With his thousand men he "attacked the Philistine outpost at Geba." Whether any Philistines escaped alive or not, the news soon reached the Philistine homeland down on the coast by the Mediterranean Sea.

It seemed certain that the Philistines would be out in force to avenge the crushing of their outpost in Israel. Saul sent a call to all the land, and the men he had recently dismissed began to assemble again at Gilgal, down in the Jordan Valley (1 Samuel 13:1-4).

I. DANGER IN ISRAEL (1 SAMUEL 13:5-7)

The Philistines had a number of city-states, but they had remarkable success in stifling rivalries among them and acting together. Now some of them remembered a former defeat in Israel (1 Samuel 7:10, 11). Intending to be successful this time, they put together all the armed forces they could muster.

A. FEARSOME INVADERS (v. 5)

5. The Philistines assembled to fight Israel, with three thousand chariots, six thousand charioteers, and soldiers as numerous as the sand on the seashore. They went up and camped at Micmash, east of Beth Aven.

There is some question about the number of chariots that were actually involved here. Some of the ancient manuscripts say *thirty thousand* instead of *three thousand*. Thus, the King James Version records that higher number. However, the charioteers ("horsemen" in the King James) in an army are usually many more than the chariots (2 Samuel 10:18; 1 Kings 10:26; 2 Chronicles 12:3). It is hard to believe that the Philistines had thirty thousand chariots and only *six thousand charioteers*. Besides, students find no other record of as many as thirty thousand chariots. Therefore, without doubting the truth of the Bible, many students think the inflated number came about when some uninspired scribe in ancient times made a mistake in copying the number from the inspired original. Some students think it is more likely that the original number was *one thousand*.

In any case, it was a fearsome army that swept their way into Israel. Besides the chariots and charioteers, there were foot soldiers so numerous that the reporter did not even venture to estimate their number. It is probable that the Israelites had no chariots at all. If they could recall the 330,000 men who had gone to Jabesh (1 Samuel 11:8), we can only guess how that number compared with the uncounted horde of Philistines now camped at Micmash. Saul and his two thousand men had been at Micmash not long before (v. 2), but they had withdrawn to Gilgal in the Jordan Valley to wait for the rest of their army (v. 4).

B. FEARFUL ISRAELITES (v. 6)

6. When the men of Israel saw that their situation was critical and that their army was hard pressed, they hid in caves and thickets, among the rocks, and in pits and cisterns.

The sheer size of the Philistine army was frightening. Israelites living near the invasion route hid in the hills, leaving their homes and farms to be pillaged by invaders in search of grain, meal, and animals for food.

FIGHTING FEAR WITH FAITH

A phobia is an exaggerated and often disabling fear. There are names for literally dozens of phobias. For example, there is hydrophobia (fear of water), claustrophobia (fear of closed-in places) and its opposite, agoraphobia (fear of open spaces).

A phobia recently come to light is shared by tens of thousands of persons who formerly drove automobiles. They now have an uncontrollable fear of getting behind the wheel of a car. It seems that long bridges trigger the phobia. A police dispatcher in the area around the Chesapeake Bay Bridge in Maryland says that on some days there are as many as ten drivers who cannot make it across the bridge. These drivers "freeze up" on the bridge and come to a halt, making it necessary for someone to come out and drive their cars the rest of the way across the bridge.

When the Philistine forces invaded the land, the Israelites were overcome with fear, and they hid themselves in caves, in thickets, or anywhere else they could seclude themselves from what seemed like sure disaster. At times our fear of what lies in the future threatens to undo us. Sometimes those fears are unreasonable, exaggerating the danger we face. But whether our fear is reasonable or not, like Israel we need to find our refuge in God, who holds both us and the future in his hands. —C. R. B.

C. FLIGHT AND FEAR (V. 7)

7. Some Hebrews even crossed the Jordan to the land of Gad and Gilead. Saul remained at Gilgal, and all the troops with him were quaking with fear.

Instead of hiding near their homes, *some Hebrews* looked for safety farther away. Hoping the war would be confined to the west side of the Jordan, they crossed to the other side of the river.

Saul stayed *in Gilgal* on the west side of the river, but all the people who joined him there were *quaking with fear.*

II. DISOBEDIENT SACRIFICE (1 SAMUEL 13:8, 9)

Waiting may be harder than fighting, especially if the waiting people are scared. So it was with Saul and his soldiers at Gilgal. We can readily imagine they were too nervous to sleep well, their appetite failed, and fear grew bigger day by day.

A. SCARY WAITING (V. 8)

8. He waited seven days, the time set by Samuel; but Samuel did not come to Gilgal, and Saul's men began to scatter.

This looks back to the day when Samuel anointed Saul to be king. At that time Samuel had told what was going to happen in the near future, and it had happened just as he had predicted (1 Samuel 10:2-6). Samuel also had said that Saul then should do what he would see occasion to do (1 Samuel 10:7). Saul had seen occasion to rescue Jabesh, and he had done that (1 Samuel 11:1-11). He had seen occasion to smash a Philistine outpost, and Jonathan had done that with a detachment of the army (1 Samuel 13:2-4). We do not know how much time it took to do all that; but afterward the time came to obey the last part of the instruction Samuel had given on that anointing day. (See 1 Samuel 10:8.)

While Saul was at Micmash, Samuel may have reminded him of those instructions. With or without such a reminder, Saul remembered. He went down to Gilgal (1 Samuel 13:4). Hard as it was to wait there idly, *he waited seven days, the time set by Samuel.* He knew Samuel was a prophet who relayed God's commands, and he needed the prophet to tell him what to do next (1 Samuel 10:8.)

But the seventh day came, and Samuel did not. It must have seemed to Saul that the waiting was becoming unendurable. His situation grew worse day by day, as his soldiers *began to scatter,* that is, desert. Each morning the army was smaller, and in seven days the loss seemed ominous. Saul felt that he could wait no longer.

WHAT DO YOU THINK?

For all their talk of needing a king to lead them in battle, the people of Israel had precious little faith that their new king could do so when the Philistines began to assemble their troops. Their fear led, at least in part, to Saul's disobedience. Do you think the failure of Christians to support their leaders similarly tempts those leaders to compromise their obedience to God's Word? Why or why not? Cite examples if you can. Has lack of support from others ever caused you to consider compromising your obedience? What can you do to support your leaders and encourage obedience to God's Word?

B. FRIGHTENED SACRIFICE (V. 9)

9. So he said, "Bring me the burnt offering and the fellowship offerings." And Saul offered up the burnt offering.

We need not suppose Saul usurped the place of a priest and made the sacrifice with his own hands. There were priests in his camp, enough of them to carry the ark of the covenant (1 Samuel 14:3, 18). Probably they conducted the sacrifice with the proper ceremony (Leviticus 1). But the king had been told to wait till Samuel arrived (1 Samuel 10:8). That was the Lord's command given through his prophet, and Saul had disobeyed it.

III. EXCUSES (1 SAMUEL 13:10-12)

Like most of us who disobey a command of the Lord, Saul had reasons that he thought were compelling. But were they?

A. CAUGHT IN THE ACT (V. 10)

10. Just as he finished making the offering, Samuel arrived, and Saul went out to greet him.

How often we disobedient ones are embarrassed by being caught in the act! We ought to be embarrassed whether anyone sees us or not, for we know the Lord sees every disobedience.

Some students think it is unfair to condemn Saul for his act. They say he waited seven days according to his instructions. They say Samuel broke his promise by failing to come in seven days, and therefore Saul was no longer bound to obey the command. Other students think Saul did not wait till the seven days were *ended*, but only till the seventh day *began*. They think Saul made his offering on the seventh day, and Samuel came on that day as he had promised.

We can leave that difference of opinion unsettled. The command to Saul was not only to wait seven days, but also to wait till Samuel came. That he failed to do.

B. FRIGHTENING SITUATION (V. 11)

11. "What have you done?" asked Samuel. Saul replied, "When I saw that the men were scattering, and that you did not come at the set time, and that the Philistines were assembling at Micmash. . . .

What Saul had done was plain enough. The fire was still blazing on the altar. Saul had violated God's command by offering the burnt offering instead of waiting for Samuel to arrive. So Saul did not answer the question by telling what he had done. Like a guilty child caught in the act, the king began to tell why he had done it. He gave three excuses:

1. His troops were deserting. Every day made his army less capable of conflict.
2. Samuel did not come *at the set time*.
3. The Philistines at Micmash were poised to strike. They might strike any day.

If Saul had put more trust in God and less in human resources, he could easily have seen the fallacy in his reasoning.

1. It would be better to lose his whole army than to lose the Lord's help by disobeying him.
2. Samuel's delay called for more trust in God, not for disobedience.
3. The gathering of Philistines provided a perfect opportunity for the Lord to defeat them.

C. DESPERATE NEED (V. 12)

12. "I thought, 'Now the Philistines will come down against me at Gilgal, and I have not sought the LORD's favor.' So I felt compelled to offer the burnt offering."

WHAT DO YOU THINK?

Saul "felt compelled to offer the burnt offering" (1 Samuel 13:12). In his mind, apparently, he had a choice between having no sacrifices made or having them made the wrong way (without Samuel). He must have felt he was choosing "the lesser of two evils." But Samuel showed him that choosing the lesser evil was still choosing evil!

How many of us have not found ourselves in similar situations? Do you think Samuel's response to Saul's choice is relevant to such choices today? If so how? What insights do James 1:14 and 1 Corinthians 10:13 offer when we feel compelled to choose evil?

OPTION

The reproducible activity, "Difficult Obedience," on page 88 may be used to lead your students in a Bible study of occasions when obedience to God's commands was especially difficult. The second activity, "It Doesn't Get Any Easier," will help students make application. Use the two together or wait until near the end of the lesson to do the second activity.

"I had no choice." How often we hear that excuse, or make it ourselves! So Saul said, "I didn't want to do it, but I just had to." The imminent danger demanded immediate action. The Philistines might swoop down at any time, and it was unthinkable to go into battle without asking for the Lord's help.

Here Saul displayed a mixture of good thinking and bad. It is wise to seek God's help in any crisis, yes; but it is foolish to think his help can be gained by disobeying him.

IV. SENTENCE (1 SAMUEL 13:13, 14)

We may feel inclined to sympathize with Saul. The man was in a critical situation, and it was getting worse. After all, he did wait a week, and then all he did was to seek the Lord's help. What's wrong with that? But Samuel pronounced the sentence of the Lord, and his word is more reliable than our feeling.

A. FOOLISH DISOBEDIENCE (V. 13)

13. "You acted foolishly," Samuel said. "You have not kept the command the LORD your God gave you; if you had, he would have established your kingdom over Israel for all time.

It is foolish to disobey *the command* God had given him. No matter how critical the situation, no matter how urgent the need, no matter how plausible the excuses, it is foolish to disobey the Lord. If Saul had been as wise as he was valiant, he would have been obedient. Then the Lord would have established his kingdom *for ever.* His descendants would have been rulers in Israel through all the generations. But now there was no chance of that, for Saul had *acted foolishly.*

B. SEVERE PENALTY (V. 14)

14. "But now your kingdom will not endure; the LORD has sought out a man after his own heart and appointed him leader of his people, because you have not kept the LORD's command."

Your kingdom will not endure. This does not mean Saul was finished ruling Israel as of that moment. It means his kingdom was not to continue through the generations of his descendants, as it would have done if Saul had been wise and obedient (v. 13). To head that lasting line of kings the Lord now had chosen someone else, *a man after his own heart.* We know that man was David, but perhaps only God then knew who he was. Even Samuel may have learned at a later time, and certainly David himself did not yet suspect that such a destiny awaited him.

As for Saul, God did not cast him off after that one disobedience. The Lord used him and his daring son Jonathan to win a tremendous victory over those fearsome Philistines at Micmash (1 Samuel 14:1-23). He used them to defeat other enemies as well (1 Samuel 14:47, 48). Later disobedience brought rejection of Saul (1 Samuel 15), but even then he continued to rule for years. Meanwhile, through danger and hardship and valor, David was being prepared to become king. Chapters 16—30 of 1 Samuel tell about it.

CONCLUSION

You acted foolishly. When all our explanations are made and all our excuses are offered, the word of God's prophet still rings through the centuries at every misdeed of ours: "You acted foolishly." That same word comes to all mankind: to Adam and Eve in the garden, to the many who drowned in the great flood, to those burned up in Sodom, to the disobedient ones who died in the destruction of Jerusalem in A.D. 70, to you and me and every sinner of today, for "all have sinned and fall short of the glory of God" (Romans 3:23). It's foolish.

WHAT DO YOU THINK?

Samuel said Saul had disobeyed God's command. Yet the command to wait came to Saul from Samuel, not from God. Why, then, did Samuel say Saul had disobeyed God?

Some say the answer is seen in Samuel's office. As an inspired prophet, he spoke for God. Thus, his words were God's words. (See 2 Peter 1:20, 21.) Others say this is evidence that Saul himself offered the sacrifice, taking over the role of a priest and, thus, violating the Lord's command.

What do you think—how did Saul disobey the Lord? Why do you think so? What difference does it make in the application of the principle at issue here?

WHAT DO YOU THINK?

Samuel accused Saul of acting "foolishly." In the Bible, foolishness is often more serious than mere ignorance or even stupidity. It is a term that suggests a lack of moral discernment. See Psalm 53:1; Proverbs 10:23; 14:16; Luke 12:20. What do you think, was Samuel merely criticizing Saul's mental judgment, or was he making a statement about Saul's morality? Why do you think so?

PRAYER

How good you are, our Father: how precious, how kind, how loving! Not only have you given us your faultless Word to guide us in your way; you also have given your faultless Son to atone for the foolish failures in which we have turned away from your Word. We thank you, Father; and in gratitude we pledge ourselves anew to read your Word and follow it. In Jesus' name, amen.

THOUGHT TO REMEMBER

"Fear God, and keep his commandments."

DAILY BIBLE READINGS

Monday, Oct. 24—Saul Battles the Philistines (1 Samuel 13:1-7a)

Tuesday, Oct. 25—Samuel Condemns Saul's Offering and Leadership (1 Samuel 13:7b-14)

Wednesday, Oct 26—Saul's Army Lacks Weapons (1 Samuel 13:15-22)

Thursday, Oct. 27—Saul Disobeys God's Command (1 Samuel 14:52—15:9)

Friday, Oct. 28—Samuel Confronts Saul's Excuses (1 Samuel 15:10-19)

Saturday, Oct. 29—God Has Rejected Saul as King (1 Samuel 15:20-28)

Sunday, Oct. 30—Samuel's Commission to Anoint Another King (1 Samuel 15:34—16:3)

WHAT DO YOU THINK?

Some people say all this talk of obedience was okay for the Old Testament, with its system of law, but it is irrelevant under the New Testament, the covenant of grace. Yet consider such passages as 2 Corinthians 9:13; 2 Thessalonians 1:8; Hebrews 5:9; 2 John 6. Is not obedience still important?

What do you think? Does Ecclesiastes 12:13 still describe "the whole duty of man"? Why or why not?

OPTION

Use "It Doesn't Get Any Easier" on page 88 to further apply the lesson of obedience from this text.

A. GOD IS UNSEEN

Saul's failure was a failure of faith, and so is ours. He could see the threat of the Philistines, but the Lord was hidden from his sight. So he yielded to the visible threat and disobeyed the invisible Lord. That was foolish. In like manner we yield to the pressure of circumstances and tell a lie, or join in malicious gossip, or turn away from a brother in need. It's foolish.

God has chosen to be invisible so we may walk by faith (2 Corinthians 5:7). Yet the invisible God is not without a visible witness. Rain and sun and harvest speak of his power and his love (Acts 14:17). The heavens declare his glory (Psalm 19:1), and the whole earth is full of it, too (Isaiah 6:3). The testimony of earth and sky is so conclusive that there is no excuse for any who fail to believe in God and obey him (Romans 1:20-22).

B. GOD IS UNHEARD

Saul heard Samuel speak; but when Samuel was not present, Saul did not hear the voice of God. Still, Saul had good reason to be sure the voice of Samuel spoke the message of God. Samuel told him what was going to happen, and it did happen. Saul should have kept the word of the prophet in mind.

God has chosen to be unheard by most of us, but he has not left us without his Word. He spoke to his prophets and gave them his message for us. "For prophecy never had its origin in the will of man, but men spoke from God as they were carried along by the Holy Spirit" (2 Peter 1:21).

God spoke to a few prophets. Each prophet spoke to a few people, or a few hundred, or a few thousand. But some of the prophets also wrote their messages, and some of their writings have been collected in a book, the Bible. The book speaks to the whole world. Specifically, it speaks to you. It speaks to me. This is the Word of God that we need to carry in our minds so we will not disobey it. "I have hidden your word in my heart that I might not sin against you" (Psalm 119:11).

To hide God's Word in your heart is not to conceal it or to keep it away from anyone. It is to treasure it, to love it, to know it—and above all to obey it. Of course, the one who thus treasures God's Word will be more than eager to share it with others.

The king of Israel was charged to have his own personal copy of God's law in a time when copies were few. He was not only to have it, but also to read from it every day. And he was not only to read from it, but also to learn to fear God and obey him (Deuteronomy 17:18, 19).

When Israel decided to have a human king, this was God's law for him. Now we have decided to have no human king. The kingdom of God is nearer to its original plan. God is the only king, and each one of us is personally responsible to him. Then each one of us had better have his own copy of God's Word, and read it, and learn to fear God and obey him.

C. CONCLUDING THE CONCLUSION

"Here is the conclusion of the whole matter; Fear God and keep his commandments, for this is the whole duty of man." So wrote Solomon, one of God's prophets—at least, that is how it is translated in English (Ecclesiastes 12:13, *New International Version*). However, the word *duty* is not in the original writing. The Hebrew reads simply, "This is the whole of man." This is not just what man does; it is who man is. This is the essence of humanity; this is what God designed each person to do; this is the way to be truly human: "Fear God, and keep his commandments."

Discovery Learning

This page contains an alternate lesson plan emphasizing learning activities. Classes desiring such student involvement will find these suggestions helpful. The next page is a reproducible activity page to further enhance discovery learning.

LEARNING GOALS

Today's session will help students:

1. Understand Saul's situation while he waited for Samuel to come and offer the prescribed sacrifice.

2. Compare Saul's situation with that of Christians today who are waiting for God to answer a prayer or provide direction in their lives.

3. Name one situation in their lives in which they will continue to wait on God.

INTO THE LESSON

Make a copy of the multiple-choice statements printed here and in the next section, "Into the Word," for each student, or read the statements to the class as you conduct your discussion.

To open today's session, ask your students to complete the following three multiple-choice statements (more than one completion may be chosen).

1. When I think my prayers are unanswered, I
   a. quit praying
   b. pray harder
   c. change my prayer
   d. ask a Christian friend for advice

2. When I wonder what I should do in a specific situation, I usually
   a. pray
   b. read the Bible
   c. go to church
   d. do what seems best at the moment

3. When I realize I've done something wrong, my first reaction is usually to
   a. make excuses
   b. ask forgiveness
   c. get down on myself
   d. ask if it was really so wrong after all

Tell your class that in the event recorded in today's text, King Saul faced situations similar to those listed above. As you study today's Scripture, your students should decide how their responses compare with Saul's.

INTO THE WORD

Use the material in the "Lesson Background" section to connect last week's lesson with this lesson. Then have a student read today's text aloud to the class. The multiple-choice statements below may then be used as an outline for your discussion of today's text.

1. The Israelites were afraid because
   a. the Philistines were strong
   b. they didn't trust God
   c. they didn't trust Saul
   d. anyone would have been under the circumstances

2. Saul offered the burnt offering himself because
   a. he was afraid he would lose the battle
   b. his army was deserting him
   c. he didn't trust Samuel
   d. he was obeying the spirit of the law, if not the letter of it

3. Samuel asked Saul, "What have you done?" because
   a. he didn't know what Saul had done
   b. he couldn't believe what Saul had done
   c. he wanted Saul to admit what he had done
   d. he was hoping to hear a good reason for what Saul had done

4. Saul's response to Samuel showed that
   a. Saul ignored what God had commanded
   b. Saul tried to make himself look good
   c. Saul trusted God
   d. Saul trusted himself

5. Samuel's response to Saul proved that
   a. Samuel was displeased with Saul
   b. God was displeased with Saul
   c. Saul would no longer be king
   d. God had another king in mind for Israel

INTO LIFE

Distribute copies of the following five incomplete statements. For numbers 1, 2, and 3, have students write down their answers, share their answers with a neighbor, or discuss them with the whole class.

1. When I think about "waiting on God," I remember the time when—

2. The hardest thing about waiting on God to act or direct is—

3. It's always a good idea to keep waiting on God, because—

Ask volunteers to read these Scriptures at this time: Psalm 27:14; 37:7; Proverbs 20:22; Isaiah 40:31; Lamentations 3:25.

Then ask students to respond privately to these two open-ended sentences:

4. I am presently waiting on God to—

5. I will continue to wait on God because—

Difficult Obedience

Saul saw his situation deteriorating. He waited seven days, as Samuel had told him to do, and saw more of his men desert each day. While the Philistines prepared for war, Saul decided he could wait no longer; he had to act. But Samuel had never said obedience would be easy; he just said it was necessary.

Saul was not the only one who found obedience difficult. Look up the following Scriptures. In the appropriate columns record who had to obey, in what situations, and how successful they were.

Scripture	Person	Situation	Result
Genesis 6:9-22			
Genesis 12:1-5			
Genesis 19:15-26			
Exodus 3:4–4:18			
Numbers 13:1-3, 17–14:45			
Joshua 3:7-17			
Judges 4:4-24			
Judges 11:29-40			
Daniel 3:8-30			
Matthew 1:18-25			
Matthew 26:36-46			
Acts 4:1-20			
Acts 9:10-19			

It Doesn't Get Any Easier

What situations have you faced when obedience to the Lord seemed especially difficult? What made it so difficult? How did you do (or how could you have done) the right thing in spite of the difficulty? How can you now help others facing similar dilemmas?

DAVID CLAIMS GOD'S PROMISE

LESSON 10

WHY TEACH THIS LESSON?

It is said that familiarity breeds contempt, and often that seems to be so. Even the most wonderful of God's blessings can be treated as commonplace if we fail to contemplate them anew but instead take them for granted.

We who have known Christ for many years can easily begin to take for granted the grace of God. Worse yet, we may sometimes act as if we believe we somehow *deserve* his favor.

David's prayer of gratitude for God's promise ought to challenge our complacency. It is by God's grace that we have hope of eternal life, not by personal merit. Let David's prayer become your prayer, and the prayer of your students, as you claim the very great and precious promises that God has made to us.

INTRODUCTION

Saul couldn't wait. The job facing him was dangerous as well as difficult—he had to drive out a big army of well-armed Philistines. He wanted to get on with it, but the Lord had said to wait till Samuel came with instructions. So Saul waited, but not quite long enough. Disobedience was still disobedience, even after seven days of obedience. Last week's lesson told about that.

A later disobedience was even worse. Off to the south was a tribe of people who had attacked Israel repeatedly. The Lord judged that tribe to be too wicked to live. He told Saul to take his army and destroy the tribe of Amalek, every man, woman, and child. This was an expedition for punishment, not plunder. Sheep and cattle and other property were to be destroyed along with the people.

Again Saul obeyed, but not quite enough. He took his army and destroyed most of the tribe, but he caught the king and brought him back alive. He also saved some of the best of the cattle and sheep—for a sacrifice to the Lord, he said. You can read about this in 1 Samuel 15.

Saul was rejected. He continued as king until his death, and his doings are recorded in the first book of Samuel; but now David took center stage.

A. DAVID THE SHEPHERD-MUSICIAN

God sent Samuel to Bethlehem to anoint David as the next king. Not many people were allowed to know about that, however. Saul, once modest and unselfish, had become an arrogant and egotistical tyrant. He would kill both Samuel and David if he knew about this anointing (1 Samuel 16:1-13).

David was a shepherd. He also was such a fine musician that his fame had spread far from Bethlehem. When King Saul was troubled by an evil spirit, his advisers thought he might be calmed by music. David was recommended and brought to the king (1 Samuel 16:14-23). His music worked so well that David became a frequent traveler between the pastures of Bethlehem and the palace of the king. He was a shepherd at home till he was called to play for the king (1 Samuel 17:15).

DEVOTIONAL READING:
PSALM 86:1-12
LESSON SCRIPTURE:
2 SAMUEL 7
PRINTED TEXT:
2 SAMUEL 7:18-29

LESSON AIMS

After this lesson a student should be able to:

1. Recall the main thoughts of David's prayer that is recorded in our text.

2. Mention two or three of God's promises that are precious to the student.

3. Identify one way of doing God's will more perfectly this week.

Nov
6

KEY VERSE:

And now, LORD God, keep forever the promise you have made concerning your servant and his house. Do as you promised..
—*2 Samuel 7:25*

Lesson 10 Notes

B. David the Hero

The Philistines invaded again. As their army faced Saul's army across a valley, one of the Philistines stepped out with a challenge. Why should whole armies fight? he asked. Let the Hebrews send a man to fight him in single combat. Whoever lost, his side would concede the victory to the other.

This Philistine was over nine feet tall. No man of Israel volunteered to meet him, till David came to the camp. When he saw the situation, he promptly volunteered to fight the giant. He said the Lord would deliver the big man into his hand, and that was what happened (1 Samuel 17:1-54).

With that victory to his credit, David came into the army. Soon he was its commander. His troops were so successful that David was the hero of the victory celebration. But Saul was furious. He could not stand to see the general more celebrated than the king (1 Samuel 18:5-9).

C. David the Fugitive

The jealous king decided to assassinate his popular general, but David escaped to the desert. There he was joined by members of his family and others who were out of favor with the king (1 Samuel 18:10—22:2).

Instead of resorting to robbery, this outlaw band protected people of Judah against raiding Philistines. They moved about in the desert, while Saul and his army tried to catch them. For a while they tried to find refuge with the Philistines, but that did not work out very well. So David and his band went on living in the desert, defeating Saul's enemies and dodging Saul's army. This went on till Saul died in a battle with the Philistines (1 Samuel 22:3—31:13).

D. From Fugitive to King

David belonged to the tribe of Judah, and he had won the gratitude of his tribe by defending its people against the Philistines and other raiders. So when Saul was dead, the men of Judah soon made David their king (2 Samuel 2:1-4).

Ishbosheth became king of the other tribes. He seems to have had no ability as a leader, but he was Saul's son and was backed by Abner, capable commander of Saul's army (2 Samuel 2:8-11). There was spasmodic war between David's troops and Abner's, and the advantage was with David (2 Samuel 2:12—3:1).

When both Ishbosheth and Abner were dead, their tribes had no strong national leader. Eventually, tribal leaders went to David and anointed him as king of all Israel (2 Samuel 5:1-5).

Display visual 10 of the visuals packet. Refer to it during the "Lesson Background" and the "Conclusion" sections.

E. David the King

Now united under an able king, Israel prospered. Soon David captured Jerusalem. The tribe of Judah had taken that town centuries before (Judges 1:8), but the Jebusites had reoccupied it and had lived there for a long time. Now David made it his capital (2 Samuel 5:6-10) and wanted to bring the ark of the covenant there. The ark had been kept in a private house in Kiriath Jearim since before Saul was king (1 Samuel 4:1—7:2). From there David moved the ark to Jerusalem, where a special tent became its new home (2 Samuel 6:1-19).

F. Lesson Background

The immediate background of this lesson is seen in 2 Samuel 7:1-17. King David relaxed in a fine house built by artisans from Tyre, and the ark of the covenant rested in a tent. That ark represented the presence of God among his people. David thought the ark should have a finer house than the king had, and he proposed to build such a house.

Nathan the prophet promptly approved, but he did it without waiting to hear from the Lord. When God spoke, Nathan had to retract his approval. With all good intentions, David was running ahead of the Lord's plan. God would have his house, but David would not build it. The reason is not given at this point in the record, but the Lord explained it to David at this time or later. It was because David was a warrior, a man of blood (1 Chronicles 22:7-10). This does not mean David's wars were wrong. God expressly directed many of his battles. But the battles were fought to make peace. God's kingdom is properly a peaceful kingdom, and it was more fitting for God's house to be built by a man of peace, David's son.

David must have been disappointed that he was not allowed to build a house for the Lord, but the message in 2 Samuel 7:5-16 softened the disappointment in several ways:

1. The house was David's idea, not the Lord's. The Lord had never had a house, he had never asked for one, and he was not asking for one now (vv. 5-7).

2. The Lord's favor to David was clear in the shepherd's rise from farm to palace (vv. 8, 9). Being so blessed and favored, David should accept God's will concerning the house.

3. God was going to provide a permanent place for his people Israel (vv. 10, 11). That was reassuring to David, who had been fighting to secure such a place.

4. God's house would be built, though David would not build it (vv. 12-15).

5. Though David would not build a house for the Lord, the Lord would build a house for David (vv.11, 16). God would not build a house of stone and wood, but a household, a family, that would continue to rule forever. We do not know how fully David understood that promise; but with inspiration of the Holy Spirit he was able to sing of the king eternal, the Christ, whose kingdom has no end (Psalm 16:8-11; Acts 2:25-36).

I. GOD AND DAVID (2 SAMUEL 7:18-20)

Surely the message from the Lord brought disappointment to David; but it brought also such reminders of past favors and such assurance of future favor that disappointment was lost in humble gratitude and praise and hope. Out of an overflowing heart David uttered the prayer that we read in our text.

A. WHO IS DAVID? (v. 18)

18. Then King David went in and sat before the LORD, and he said: "Who am I, O Sovereign LORD, and what is my family, that you have brought me this far?

David found a private place for his prayer. Some students think he went into the tent where the ark of the covenant was kept (2 Samuel 6:17). Perhaps, but it was not necessarily so. He could go into a private room of his own palace and sit *before the Lord,* for he understood that God was with him everywhere. It was David who sang the beautiful assurance of Psalm 139:8-10: "If I go up to the heavens, you are there; if I make my bed in the depths, you are there. If I rise on the wings of the dawn, if I settle on the far side of the sea, even there your hand will guide me, your right hand will hold me fast." David could sit before the Lord in any private place, and so can we.

Who am I? David was a shepherd boy, the youngest of eight sons. That boy had not elevated himself to the throne of Israel; the Lord had lifted him (2 Samuel 7:8, 9). Humbly David admitted that the Lord did not owe any such favor either to him personally or to his house, his *family.* God's own will and God's own power had made the shepherd boy a king. All this is true, but David's modesty does not conceal from us the fact that God lifted this particular boy because he looked at David's heart and saw that it was like God's own (1 Samuel 16:7; 13:13, 14).

What Do You Think?

Several times in his prayer David addressed God as "Sovereign Lord." The sovereignty of God is his authority to rule absolutely and without question. Apparently David was struck by the fact that the almighty God, who could do whatever he pleased in any place, at any time, and with anyone, had chosen him for special honor. In what ways does the sovereignty of God impress you? What praise can you offer as a result?

What Do You Think?

Several times in his prayer David addressed God as "Sovereign Lord." The sovereignty of God is his authority to rule absolutely and without question. Apparently David was struck by the fact that the almighty God, who could do whatever he pleased in any place, at any time, and with anyone, had chosen him for special honor. In what ways does the sovereignty of God impress you? What praise can you offer as a result?

B. Divine Promise (v. 19)

19. "And as if this were not enough in your sight, O Sovereign Lord, you have also spoken about the future of the house of your servant. Is this your usual way of dealing with man, O Sovereign Lord?

To be lifted from sheepfold to throne was no small thing in David's sight, and it is no small thing in ours. But the Lord went on with something else beyond the power of human wisdom: He foretold the *future* of David's house, his family. Members of that family would continue to rule forever (vv. 12-16). Such prediction for eternity is not ordinary. David recognized the unique nature of the promise. Yet, because it was God who promised, he could be sure the divine promise would be kept. So can we. Jesus, the son of David, is the king eternal.

C. Divine Knowledge (v. 20)

20. "What more can David say to you? For you know your servant, O Sovereign Lord.

David was feeling very humble, unworthy of the great help God had given him and of the great promise given for the future. He had expressed his feeling in the words we read in verse 18. Now he saw no need to say any more about it, for he was sure God understood his heart. In the opening lines of the psalm quoted above, David wrote: "O Lord, you have searched me and you know me. You know when I sit and when I rise; you perceive my thoughts from afar."

It is good to realize that we too are helpless without God, and unworthy of his help. But dwelling too much on these thoughts may keep us from doing what we really can do with God's help. We need to remember that he does help his people even if they are not worthy.

II. GOD AND HIS PEOPLE (2 SAMUEL 7:21-24)

From thoughts of himself, small and weak, David turned to thoughts of God, who is great and powerful. Our thinking may well follow the same pattern. We are unable to do much, but God is able to do wonderful things through us.

A. The Greatness of God (vv. 21, 22)

21. "For the sake of your word and according to your will, you have done this great thing and made it known to your servant.

It was not for David's sake alone that God made him king; it was for the sake of God's *word*. God had promised a man after his own heart (1 Samuel 13:14), and David was that man. It was not according to the wish of David's heart that he was made ruler of Israel; it was according to the wish of God's own heart. By the great things he had done, God made his *servant* David not only to know those great things, but also to know the great God who did them. David then could be sure God would do the great things he promised for the future.

22. "How great you are, O Sovereign Lord! There is no one like you, and there is no God but you, as we have heard with our own ears.

Wherefore, because of the great things God had done, David could say with assurance, *"How great you are!"* God not only is great; he is the greatest: *"There is no one like you,"* and not only is there no other God like the Lord; there is no other God at all. That was proved by all that David had seen in his lifetime, and also by all that he had *heard*. The stories handed down through generations confirmed the conclusion drawn from David's own experience. The Lord had rescued his people from Egypt; he had kept them in the desert for forty years; he had brought them into the promised land in spite of the opposition of bigger and stronger nations. There was no one else in all the universe who could do such things.

How to Say It

Amalek. AM-uh-lek.
Ishbosheth. Ish-BO-sheth.
Jebusites. JEB-yuh-sites.
Kiriath Jearim. KEER-i-ath JAIR-um.
Philistines. Fi-LISS-teens or FIL-iss-teens.

ALONE IN THE UNIVERSE?

On October 12, 1992, the five hundredth anniversary of Columbus's discovery of the New World, NASA scientists turned on an extremely powerful computer to begin an intensive "Search of Extraterrestrial Intelligence." The computer is connected to huge radio telescopes in the Mojave Desert and Puerto Rico. It will listen for radio signals that might indicate the existence of other civilizations.

There are those who are fervent proponents of the idea that numerous intelligent civilizations exist throughout the star systems of the cosmos. Many people believe "UFOs" represent some of these civilizations trying to contact (or at least, observe) us. Among scientists, opinions vary. A Vatican representative visited the NASA experiment, and after studying the project he made this telling observation: "They are looking for God." It is likely that he was right.

Whether we are unique in the universe is probably irrelevant. What is important is that our (and Israel's) God is unique. David said there is none like him, and there is no God other than our God. All who worship him can be assured that they have a place in the will of the God who alone rules the universe.   —C. R. B.

B. THE GREATNESS OF GOD'S PEOPLE (VV. 23, 24)

23. "And who is like your people Israel—the one nation on earth that God went out to redeem as a people for himself, and to make a name for himself, and to perform great and awesome wonders by driving out nations and their gods from before your people, whom you redeemed from Egypt?

In all the world there was no nation like Israel. However, Israel's unique greatness was not due to the goodness or strength of the people. It was due to the Lord. In his relationship with Israel he set out to do three things:

1. He set out *to redeem . . . a people for himself,* to rescue Israel from every peril and make it his own nation. He did save Israel from Egypt, and then from the nations and their gods in the promised land.

2. The Lord set out *to make a name for himself,* to create a reputation for himself, to let many nations know there is no god to compare with him. The kind of reputation he built is seen in Joshua 2:9-11. The people of Canaan were convinced that the Lord was God of Heaven and earth.

3. The Lord set out *to perform great and awesome wonders* for his people and for his land. With great miracles he rescued his people from Egypt, led them and fed them in the desert, and gave them victory in the land of promise.

24. "You have established your people Israel as your very own forever, and you, O LORD, have become their God.

Established means set in place. Not by any merit of Israel, but by the Lord's own will and power he set up Israel as his own nation and placed himself as Israel's God. That was what made Israel unique.

III. GOD AND HIS WORD (2 SAMUEL 7:25-29)

David proposed to build a house for God; but that was not what God wanted, so David gave up his wish. The Lord proposed to build a house for David; and that prospect was so magnificent that David now prayed that God would do according to his own will and keep his promise.

A. PRAYER FOR DAVID'S HOUSE (V. 25)

25. "And now, LORD God, keep forever the promise you have made concerning your servant and his house. Do as you promised.

God had said David's house, his household, his family, would continue to rule forever. Now David merely said amen—so let it be.

PRAYER

Eternal Father, we rejoice in the long record of your promises that have been kept, and we rejoice in the many precious promises you have given us. We trust you, Lord; and we promise you our faithful service.

THOUGHT TO REMEMBER

"Your will be done."

WHAT DO YOU THINK?

In his prayer recorded in our lesson text, David reminded God of the promise he had made regarding David's household, and asked that it be fulfilled. Do you ever mention specific promises in your prayers, and ask that God fulfill them? Why or why not?

WHAT DO YOU THINK?

David said he would not have found the courage to offer his prayer except that God had promised it before he asked. Does that suggest we should only pray for things God has specifically promised already? Why or why not? If not, then how do you find the courage to ask the Sovereign Lord for special blessings not already promised? (Consider Matthew 7:7-11; 18:19, 20; John 14:13, 14; 16:26; Romans 8:26, 27; Hebrews 4:16.)

DAILY BIBLE READINGS

OPTION

Page 96 contains two activities to help your students recall many of the "precious promises" of God and to praise him for them. Photocopy the page and distribute the copies to your students. They may work individually or in small groups to complete the activities.

B. PRAYER FOR GOD'S NAME (V. 26)

26. "So that your name will be great forever. Then men will say, 'The LORD Almighty is God over Israel!' And the house of your servant David will be established before you.

One thing God set out to do was to make a name for himself (v. 23). Now David prayed that God's name would be magnified forever by people acclaiming him as God over Israel. His name would be the more famous as he would keep his promise about the house of David.

C. PRAYER BASED ON PROMISE (VV. 27-29)

27. "O LORD Almighty, God of Israel, you have revealed this to your servant, saying, 'I will build a house for you.' So your servant has found courage to offer you this prayer.

David would hardly dare to ask such a future for his family if God had not promised it. But God did promise it, and with all confidence David prayed that God would do as he said he would.

28. "O Sovereign LORD, you are God! Your words are trustworthy, and you have promised these good things to your servant.

David was sure that God's words were *trustworthy,* so he did not hesitate to ask for what the Lord had promised.

29. "Now be pleased to bless the house of your servant, that it may continue forever in your sight; for you, O Sovereign LORD, have spoken, and with your blessing the house of your servant will be blessed forever."

Once again David prayed that the Lord would do just what he wanted to do, what he had said he would do. So good was his promise that David could ask nothing better.

CONCLUSION

The house David wanted to build was built by his son, Solomon. It was a magnificent temple of stone and cedar lined with gold, but it has been gone for two thousand years.

The house God built for David is standing today, and it will continue to stand for eternity.

A. PRAYER OF GOD'S PEOPLE

Disappointed in his wish to build a temple, great David prayed that what God proposed would be done. Facing death on the cross, great David's greater son prayed, "Not my will, but yours be done" (Luke 22:42).

How many followers of the Master have echoed that same prayer! In disappointment or loss, in grief or in pain, this is the prayer of God's people: "Your will be done."

B. PRECIOUS PROMISES

Not only to David and to Israel, but also to you and me God has given "very great and precious promises" (2 Peter 1:4). "Whoever believes and is baptized will be saved" (Mark 16:16). "If we confess our sins, he is faithful and just and will forgive us" (1 John 1:9). "The dead in Christ will rise first. After that, we who are still alive and are left will be caught up together with them in the clouds to meet the Lord in the air. And so we will be with the Lord forever" (1 Thessalonians 4:16, 17).

What other precious promises are you cherishing today? They will be kept. Praise the Lord!

Discovery Learning

This page contains an alternate lesson plan emphasizing learning activities. Classes desiring such student involvement will find these suggestions helpful. The next page is a reproducible activity page to further enhance discovery learning.

LEARNING GOALS

As a result of this lesson, your students should be able to do the following:

1. Consider the fact that great men of God have sometimes failed to obey him.

2. List the attitudes of David, the deeds of God, and the requests of David as seen in David's prayer recorded in 2 Samuel 7.

3. Thank God for keeping all his promises.

INTO THE LESSON

Read the following agree/disagree statements to your students. After each statement is read, those who agree should raise their hands. If there is significant difference of opinion concerning any statement, pause to let the students explain why they responded to the sentence as they did. Then go to the next sentence.

1. A spiritually mature person is less likely to displease God than an immature Christian.

2. The longer one lives for God, the easier it is to please God in one's life.

3. The longer one lives for God, the more difficult it is to please God in one's life.

4. When God has a special task for a special leader, he provides that leader with special protection against sin.

5. God may forgive any sin, but the consequences of that sin cannot be removed.

Discuss these ideas as much as your class time will allow. Just make sure that you don't take time that you need for Bible study and life application later.

Tell class members that today's lesson begins the last unit in this quarter's lessons, and in this unit you will be studying the lives of David and Solomon.

Ask class members if they can discern what these agree/disagree statements have to do with David and Solomon. After brief discussion remind them that both David and Solomon were great men of God, and that both fell to great sins against God. In this unit we will look at both the promise and the failure of each of these men. And we will try to see how we can avoid the same failures in our lives.

INTO THE WORD

Begin the Bible study by reminding class members of the latter days of Saul's reign, of how David became king, and how he prospered as king early in his reign. You can find this information in the "Introduction" section on pages 89 and 90. You may want to give this material to a class member during the week before class so that he or she can present this review for your class.

However you conduct your review, make sure it also includes the summary of 2 Samuel 7:1-17 from the "Lesson Background" section of this Introduction. That will prepare your class for the inductive Bible study suggested below.

Write on the chalkboard the three column headings indicated by the bold lettering below. Then ask your class members to examine today's printed text and to make lists under each heading. Have them work in groups of from five to seven students. Provide pencil and paper for each group.

Allow ten minutes for the groups to do their work. As you discuss the results of their study, record their answers under the headings on the chalkboard. (The answers given in each paragraph below are for the teacher's convenience.)

Attitudes of David: humility, gratitude, awe (vv. 18, 19, 22, 23); faith (vv. 25, 26, 28, 29); courage (v. 27); submission (vv. 28, 29).

What God Did: raised David from humble beginnings to the throne of Israel (v. 18); made great promises to David (vv. 19, 21): redeemed Israel as a people for himself (v. 23); redeemed Israel from Egypt (v. 23); performed great and mighty wonders to establish and protect Israel (v. 23); established Israel as his own nation forever (v. 24).

David's Requests to God: Keep your promise concerning the future of David's "house" (vv. 25, 26); bless the house of your servant so that it may continue forever (v. 29).

INTO LIFE

Ask half of your students to decide, "What does this lesson teach us about David?" and the other half, "What does this lesson teach us about God?" Have class members pair off to discuss their assigned question for three minutes. Then discuss with the whole class.

End the class session with sentence prayers of thanks and praise to God for (1) his plan to establish a people unto himself, for (2) including Christians among them, and for (3) his faithfulness to keep this and all his promises from generation to generation.

Precious Promises

David was filled with praise and thanksgiving because God had made some amazing promises to him. God's promises to us are even more amazing. Look up the following Scriptures and record the promise given in each one.

Matthew 10:38, 39

Matthew 18:19, 20

Mark 16:16

Luke 11:9, 10

Luke 12:31

John 3:16

John 11:25, 26

John 13:17

John 14:2, 3

John 16:12, 13

Acts 2:38, 39

Galatians 3:29

Hebrews 4:1, 2

Hebrews 9:15

James 1:12

Revelation 2:10

Precious Praise

David's response to God's promise to him was praise. Use the space below to write a prayer of praise for one of God's promises to you. Include praise for what God has already done for you, a statement of the promise of what he will do, a commitment to meet any stated conditions attached to the promise (e.g., "who perseveres under trial," James 1:12; "if you do them," John 13:17), and the request for God to "keep forever the promise you have made" (2 Samuel 7:25).

DAVID SINS AGAINST GOD

LESSON 11

WHY TEACH THIS LESSON?

The story of David and Bathsheba is well known—too well known, in some respects. Glamorized by Hollywood and legitimized by those who no longer hold to biblical standards of morality, the story becomes an excuse for many who would rationalize their own sin. If David could "get away with it," then why can't I?

This lesson focuses not on the event but on the result. Those who seek to find an excuse for their own sin in David's behavior would do well to take this lesson to heart. There was no easy forgiveness here. Though he did find grace, bitter and long-lasting consequences accompanied it. This lesson serves as a reminder that while wounds may heal, they often leave scars.

INTRODUCTION

Last week we saw how humbly David gave up his wish to build a house for God and accepted the will of God. Now we shall see how tragically he, on one occasion, ignored God's will.

A. BUILDING AN EMPIRE

When David was fully established as king of all Israel, he soon moved to subdue the pagan nations that had troubled his country. King Hiram of Tyre gladly became a friend, sending men and materials to build David's palace (2 Samuel 5:11). King Toi of Hamath gratefully sent rich presents to thank David for defeating Toi's chief enemy (2 Samuel 8:9, 10). The other nations around Israel were defeated and forced to pay tribute. Thus David's empire came to include most of the land promised to Israel much earlier (Joshua 1:4).

While extending his rule abroad, David also attended to domestic affairs. He organized the government for effective control, and established justice in the land (2 Samuel 8:15-18). It seemed that the king was doing just what the elders had hoped he would do (1 Samuel 8:19, 20).

B. THE BIG WAR

David's wars came to their climax when the Ammonites and Syrians joined forces against him. After some hard fighting the Syrians gave up and agreed to pay tribute, but the Ammonites were harder to subdue. Apparently winter brought a temporary end to the campaign against them. In the spring, Joab took the army to besiege a chief city of the Ammonites, while David stayed in Jerusalem to manage the domestic affairs of the kingdom (2 Samuel 10:1—11:1).

C. LESSON BACKGROUND

From the roof of his palace in Jerusalem, David saw a woman taking a bath—a beautiful woman. On inquiry he learned that her name was Bathsheba and that her husband Uriah was away with the army. So David brought her to his palace and to his bed. Then he sent her back home (2 Samuel 11:2-4).

How did the woman feel about this? Was she a virtuous wife, dragged to the king against her will? Or was she a lonely woman, pleased and flattered by the royal

DEVOTIONAL READING:
1 JOHN 1:5-10
LESSON SCRIPTURE:
2 SAMUEL 11:1–12:19
PRINTED TEXT:
2 SAMUEL 12:1-10, 13

LESSON AIMS

After this lesson a student should be able to:

1. Tell the story of David's sin, Nathan's parable, and David's response to the parable.

2. From his or her own observation, recall at least one of sin's consequences that forgiveness did not remove.

3. Be alert to avoid sin.

Nov
13

KEY VERSE:

David said to Nathan, "I have sinned against the LORD."
—*2 Samuel 12:13*

LESSON 11 NOTES

HOW TO SAY IT

Absalom. AB-suh-lum.
Adonijah. Ad-o-NYE-juh.
Bathsheba. Bath-SHE-buh.
Hamath. HAY-muth.
Sheba. SHE-buh.
Toi. TOW-eye.
Uriah. Yu-RYE-uh.

WHAT DO YOU THINK?

Nathan used a story to help David see his sin before he saw himself in it. Perhaps it's a good model for us to follow as we attempt to fulfill the admonition of Galatians 6:1, "Brothers, if someone is caught in a sin, you who are spiritual should restore him gently." What elements from Nathan's approach do you see as especially helpful? What others might you add?

invitation? Or did she deliberately entice the king by exposing herself in his sight? These questions are not answered. The lady was indiscreet, at least, but we have no clear indication of her moral character.

In any case, the king was responsible. We cannot excuse him with a plea that he was starved for love. The record indicates that he had a number of wives. Though David was a man after God's own heart, he certainly was far from the Creator's ideals of love and marriage. He must have known that adultery was forbidden by law and punishable by death (Leviticus 20:10).

In due time David learned that Bathsheba was pregnant (2 Samuel 11:5). That would be embarrassing to the king as well as to her. Could Uriah and the neighbors be led to think her husband was the father of her child?

David called Uriah to Jerusalem to report on the siege, then told him to go home for the night. But Uriah was a dedicated soldier. He thought it would not be fair to enjoy a night with his wife while his comrades had to stay in the field. He spent two nights with the king's servants and then went back to the battle (2 Samuel 11:6-13).

David's next plan was more sinister. He ordered Joab to see that Uriah died in battle, and Joab did. The widow mourned for the customary time, then became the wife of David (2 Samuel 11:14-27).

I. PARABLE (2 SAMUEL 12:1-6)

David himself was a prophet (Acts 2:29-31), but sometimes God spoke to him through another prophet. We saw an example in the background of last week's lesson (2 Samuel 7:1-17), and now we see another.

A. RICH MAN, POOR MAN (vv. 1-3)

1. The LORD sent Nathan to David. When he came to him, he said, "There were two men in a certain town, one rich and the other poor.

The Lord sent Nathan. In chapter 7 we saw that Nathan gave his own opinion and then had to correct it after he heard from the Lord. Now the record makes it clear that Nathan came as the Lord's messenger.

The prophet began as if he were presenting a case for the king to judge.

2. "The rich man had a very large number of sheep and cattle.

The rich man may have had stores of gold and silver, too, but the story focuses on livestock.

3. "But the poor man had nothing except one little ewe lamb he had bought. He raised it, and it grew up with him and his children. It shared his food, drank from his cup and even slept in his arms. It was like a daughter to him.

The poor man had no livestock for market. He had only one *lamb*. Poor as he was, he had *bought* it for a family pet. Quite literally, the lamb was like one of the family.

B. ROBBERY (v. 4)

4. "Now a traveler came to the rich man, but the rich man refrained from taking one of his own sheep or cattle to prepare a meal for the traveler who had come to him. Instead, he took the ewe lamb that belonged to the poor man and prepared it for the one who had come to him."

The duty of hospitality was taken seriously in that time and place. It would be unthinkable not to have a good dinner for a traveling friend who stopped at one's house. But even a rich man had no freezer in his house. The only way to keep fresh meat was to keep it alive. An unexpected guest had to wait for his dinner till an animal was slaughtered and cooked.

Rich as he was, this host was too stingy to use one of his own lambs. He stole the poor man's pet and *prepared it* for his guest.

C. PUNISHMENT (VV. 5, 6)

5. David burned with anger against the man and said to Nathan, "As surely as the LORD lives, the man who did this deserves to die!

That rich man might well be called "the meanest thief." With plenty of lambs in his own flock, he stole a beloved pet and left a family bereaved. David's *anger* flared at that. He said, literally, that the man was a "son of death." That means he "ought to die," but it is not necessarily a death sentence.

6. "He must pay for that lamb four times over, because he did such a thing and had no pity."

The four-fold restoration David demanded was the legal penalty for stealing a sheep (Exodus 22:1). With strict justice, David pronounced the sentence the law required, though special circumstances in this case made the theft so heinous that the thief deserved the death penalty.

II. REALITY (2 SAMUEL 12:7-10)

Months had passed since David's sin. Bathsheba was now his wife, and the child of their adultery had been born (2 Samuel 11:26, 27). Through all those months David had been tormented by conscience, as he reveals in Psalm 32:3, 4. Still he did not suspect that Nathan's story had anything to do with his own sin. The prophet's next words must have come as a total surprise.

A. GUILT (V. 7A)

7a. Then Nathan said to David, "You are the man!

"Who, me?" David must have thought. "Me? That heartless wretch who stole a poor man's pet?" Perhaps he was shocked and insulted by Nathan's charge, but he must have been puzzled even more. Before explaining the charge, the prophet paused to recall what wonderful things the Lord had done for David.

B. FAVOR (VV. 7B, 8)

7b. "This is what the LORD, the God of Israel, says: 'I anointed you king over Israel, and I delivered you from the hand of Saul.

Very clearly David must have remembered that day when he had been called from the pasture to be anointed as king (1 Samuel 16:1-13). No less clearly he recalled the years when Saul's army had combed the desert to catch him and kill him, but still he had been safe. David well knew he had been highly favored by the Lord.

8. "'I gave your master's house to you, and your master's wives into your arms. I gave you the house of Israel and Judah. And if all this had been too little, I would have given you even more.

It seems that it was customary for a new king to take over the former king's *wives* along with his palace. The record names one wife of Saul (1 Samuel 14:50), but this verse suggests that there were more—probably the choicest ladies in the land. The Lord had given David everything that belonged to Saul, including the kingship of Israel and Judah. The Lord was willing to give even more, but what else could David want?

C. INGRATITUDE (V. 9)

9. "'Why did you despise the word of the LORD by doing what is evil in his eyes? You struck down Uriah the Hittite with the sword and took his wife to be your own. You killed him with the sword of the Ammonites.

WHAT DO YOU THINK?

Some people find David's response to the acts of the rich man in Nathan's story surprising in light of his own terrible sins. Others suggest it is quite natural, reminiscent of Paul's admonition in Romans 2:1, when he noted that "at whatever point you judge the other, you are condemning yourself, because you who pass judgment do the same things."

What do you think? Does a persistent sin in one's life make him more or less critical of others guilty of the same sin? Do you think being critical suggests the person's conscience is troubling him? Why or why not?

WHAT DO YOU THINK?

David's sins were shown to be particularly bad in view of all the good things God had done for him. Perhaps this suggests a different standard of judging which sins are "worse" than others: the sins themselves have no varying degree of intensity (sin is sin), but their comparison with the blessing received by sinner does.

What do you think? Does the amount of blessing we receive from God make it all the worse when we fail him and commit sin? What blessing has God given you that you can reflect on to resist sin?

It was wrong for anyone to break God's commandment; but it was doubly wicked for David to disobey after the Lord had done so much for him. He was guilty of the sin of ingratitude along with his other sins.

The Lord had said, "You shall not murder," and, "You shall not commit adultery" (Exodus 20:13, 14). Moreover, the Lord had said that either of these crimes should be punished with death (Exodus 21:12; Leviticus 20:10). Surely stealing the one wife of a loyal soldier was worse than stealing the pet lamb of a poor man, a crime for which David had said the thief deserved to die. But to the theft of a wife David had added the murder of a husband. He had earned the death penalty twice!

TO SEE OURSELVES

O wad some power the giftie gie us
To see oursels as others see us!
It wad frae monie a blunder free us,
An' foolish notion.

The eighteenth-century Scottish dialect of Robert Burns's poem, "To a Louse," sounds a bit strange to our ears, but we can understand its message: If we could just see our lives through the eyes of other people, we might be saved from entertaining many foolish ideas and from the sinful actions that result from them!

Perhaps most of us have been tempted to do something foolish or worse, thinking, "No one will ever know; surely, I can get away with it! It would be so enjoyable, and besides, what could it possibly hurt?" In those moments, we are blessed if we have a friend who knows what we are contemplating and says, "Don't be foolish!"

Unfortunately, King David did not have such a friend to prevent him from the arrogant use of his royal power. As a result, he committed adultery with Bathsheba. Then, compounding his sin, David arranged to have her husband murdered in battle so David himself could marry her.

God, however, would not be mocked. By means of a simple parable, his prophet Nathan confronted David with the enormity of his sin. Finally, David saw himself as God saw him, and (as the saying goes) it was not a pretty picture!   —C. R. B.

D. PUNISHMENT (v. 10)

10. "'Now, therefore, the sword will never depart from your house, because you despised me and took the wife of Uriah the Hittite to be your own.'"

The Lord announced punishment to fit the crime. Read the first part of verse 10 with the last part of verse 9: "You killed him with the sword of the Ammonites. Now, therefore, the sword will never depart from your house." David had murdered Uriah with violence; through the rest of his life David would be grieved by violent deaths in his family. Then read the last part of verse 10 with the first part of verse 11: "'You . . . took the wife of Uriah the Hittite to be your own.' This is what the Lord says, . . . 'I will take your wives and give them to one who is close to you.'" Later chapters reveal that the one who took David's wives was his own rebellious son, Absalom.

Conscious of his own adultery and murder, David failed to deal sternly with his sons when they committed similar crimes. Partly because he failed to deal sternly, such crimes multiplied.

David's son Amnon raped his half sister, Tamar. David was angry, but apparently did not punish Amnon. Two years later, David's son Absalom, full brother of Tamar, had Amnon killed. Absalom then fled the country, but after a while he was allowed to return. Perhaps encouraged by David's leniency, Absalom gathered followers and staged a revolt to take his father's throne for himself. David had to flee from Jerusalem, and Absalom made a show of taking his father's wives as his own. David

OPTION

Allow the students to discover for themselves how the "sword" plagued David and his family after this event by using the reproducible activity, "The Sword Will Not Depart," on page 104.

soon gathered his forces and put down the revolt, but Absalom was killed along with many others in the civil war. (See 2 Samuel 13—18.)

In David's last years, his son Adonijah also plotted to take the throne. This time the plot was nipped in the bud; but soon after David died, Adonijah was executed for his continuing ambition to be king (1 Kings 1, 2). So to the end of David's life and beyond, the sword did not depart from his house.

III. PARDON (2 SAMUEL 12:13)

Throughout the Bible David is honored as a hero and a prophet, the sweet singer of Israel, and a man after God's own heart. Yet no effort is made to hide his sin. His wicked acts are exposed in all their horror.

This emphasizes the goodness of God. He is "compassionate and gracious, . . . slow to anger, abounding in love and faithfulness" (Exodus 34:6). Such a sinner as David was not beyond the reach of his grace, and neither are we.

A. CONFESSION (V. 13A)

13a. Then David said to Nathan, "I have sinned against the LORD."

David offered no excuses. He did not say that the woman tempted him, or that the one he killed was a Hittite and not a man of Israel, or that the death of a soldier is a small matter, or that a king has rights that others do not have. He was not angry with Nathan for denouncing him. In the plainest language he declared the awful truth: I have sinned against the Lord.

The thought was not new to David. It had burdened his secret mind for a long time. In his penitential song he wrote, "My sin is always before me" (Psalm 51:3). It had been to him like the searing heat of a dry summer (Psalm 32:3, 4). Now at last he made open and honest confession, not only to Nathan, but also to the Lord. This is the way to pardon (Psalm 32:5). So it is for us: "If we confess our sins, he is faithful and just and will forgive us our sins and purify us from all unrighteousness" (1 John 1:9).

BIG ENOUGH TO ADMIT IT

Rudy Ruiz came home from work and discovered his wife sick in bed. His two teenage sons had not done their chores. Rudy told the boys how important their mother was to him after helping him recover from two heart attacks. His unfortunate "parting shot" was, "I love you boys, too, but I don't need you—not the way I need your mother." His fourteen-year-old son, John David, was especially stung by the remark.

Several weeks later Rudy, John David, and a friend were fishing on a rain-swollen river when the current sucked their rubber raft into a culvert beneath a concrete bridge that was under a foot of water. John David was thrown onto the bridge, but Rudy could only grab the edge of it. His foot was caught in a rope on the boat, and he was being pulled under. John David grabbed his dad, and he and their friend held on desperately until help came. Through his son's courage and strength, Rudy survived. After his rescue, Rudy said to his son, "I'll never say 'I don't need you' to anyone again."

When confronted with his sin, David showed how "big" a person he was by facing the truth and admitting his guilt. To be able to admit, "I was wrong," may be the best evidence there is of the maturity of spirit that leads to repentance and restoration.　　　　　　　　　　　—C. R. B.

B. FORGIVENESS (V. 13B)

13b. Nathan replied, "The LORD has taken away your sin. You are not going to die."

Display visual 11 of the visuals packet as you discuss verse 13 and the "Conclusion" of the lesson.

WHAT DO YOU THINK?

When confronted with his sin, David humbly confessed and yielded to the prophet's announcement of God's will. The Pharisees, by contrast, chafed at Jesus' condemnation of their sin and plotted to kill him. What makes the difference in how a person responds to accusations of sin? What makes a person open to receiving it graciously and confessing repentantly? How do you usually respond when confronted with your sin?

WHAT DO YOU THINK?

David's experience raises a question about the extent of God's forgiveness: if God is willing to forgive our sins, why do you think he does not also take away the consequences of our sins?

OPTION

Use the reproducible activity, "Sin and Consequences," on page 104 to pursue this discussion further and to make application to life today.

PRAYER

O Lord, we are overwhelmed by your goodness. Like David we confess that we have sinned against you, and like David we rejoice in your forgiveness. Today and tomorrow and all the days of our lives, so lead us that we will not need to be forgiven so often. This we pray in the name of Jesus our Redeemer. Amen.

THOUGHT TO REMEMBER

*As we hope to go to Heaven
And our Lord's "well done" to win,
It is good to be forgiven,
But it's better not to sin.*

DAILY BIBLE READINGS

Monday, Nov. 7—David's Sin (2 Samuel 11:1-13)

Tuesday, Nov. 8—David Causes Uriah's Death (2 Samuel 11:14-25)

Wednesday, Nov. 9—Nathan Rebukes David (2 Samuel 11:26—12:9)

Thursday, Nov. 10—God's Judgment and Forgiveness (2 Samuel 12:10-15a)

Friday, Nov. 11—A Prayer of Repentance (Psalm 51:1-14)

Saturday, Nov. 12—Thanksgiving for Forgiveness (Psalm 32:1-7)

Sunday, Nov. 13—Death of the Child (2 Samuel 12:15b-23)

So David was forgiven. Like the rich man of the parable he deserved to die, but he did not die. He lived for many years to build up the empire of Israel. Exultantly he sang, "Blessed is he whose transgressions are forgiven, whose sins are covered. Blessed is the man whose sin the Lord does not count against him" (Psalm 32:1, 2).

Yet how often the joy of forgiveness was marred! Forgiveness takes away sin, but it does not take away all the consequences of sin. David was forgiven, but he prayed in vain for the life of the child born of his sin. The child died (2 Samuel 12:14-23). David was forgiven, but the dire prophecies spoken by Nathan were not withdrawn. David seethed with anger when his daughter was raped (13:21); but with his own adultery in mind, how could he chasten the rapist? Though forgiven, David grieved when one son killed another and fled to a foreign country (v. 37). David had to flee from Jerusalem (15:14-17) while his rebel son stole his wives (16:20-22). David agonized in grief at the death of that rebel son (18:33). He had to put down another rebel, a scoundrel named Sheba (chapter 20). Feeble with age, he had to rouse himself and act vigorously to thwart the plotting of his son Adonijah (1 Kings 1). Truly, through all his life, the sword never departed from his house.

CONCLUSION

If God's forgiveness is sure, why should we worry about our sin? Why not trust him to forgive us, and sin whenever it seems convenient or pleasant? Strongly Paul warns against that silly notion: "We died to sin; how can we live in it any longer?" (Romans 6:1-4).

A. CONSEQUENCES

A city councilman was detected in adultery. He said he was sorry, and loyal constituents forgave him and elected him to another term. But when he ran for a higher office, he suffered a humiliating defeat. Many voters thought a man who would cheat on his wife might cheat the taxpayers as well.

After an angry quarrel at work, Joe was driving furiously when he was maimed in a wreck. He may be forgiven, but he is still maimed. And an innocent motorist killed in the accident is still dead.

Angered by a snub, Mabel told a vicious lie about the woman who snubbed her. When her anger cooled, Mabel apologized. The other woman forgave her, and probably the Lord did, too. But the falsehood is still being whispered all over town.

A usually decent man got drunk and beat his wife severely. When he became sober, he repented with tears and was forgiven, but the wife is still scarred.

Tempted by hard times, Frank stole some money he was taking to the bank. He said he had been robbed, and robberies were so frequent that he was not suspected. But his conscience tormented him till he told the truth. His employer is a good-hearted man, so Frank is forgiven—but he is no longer trusted.

B. RUN AWAY

How many times David must have regretted that day when he watched a woman at her bath! Joseph had a better idea. When a woman tried to seduce him, he took to his heels (Genesis 39:7-12).

"Flee from sexual immorality" (1 Corinthians 6:18). Get away from it. Turn off the TV programs that encourage it or make light of it. Avoid the pornography that flourishes everywhere. Pray, "Lead us not into temptation"; and don't go where the Lord doesn't lead.

"Finally, brothers, whatever is true, whatever is noble, whatever is right, whatever is pure, whatever is lovely, whatever is admirable—if anything is excellent and praiseworthy, think about such things" (Philippians 4:8).

Discovery Learning

This page contains an alternate lesson plan emphasizing learning activities. Classes desiring such student involvement will find these suggestions helpful. The next page is a reproducible activity page to further enhance discovery learning.

LEARNING GOALS

As students participate in today's class session, they should:

1. Review the story of David's adultery with Bathsheba and his plotting to cover his sin.

2. Paraphrase the parable of Nathan.

3. Understand that sin may produce unpleasant consequences in this life, even though the sin is forgiven.

INTO THE LESSON

Write the following scrambled sentence on the chalkboard:

sure will out your find be sin you.

Ask class members to unscramble the sentence ("be sure your sin will find you out"). Ask them to think of examples from their own lives, or from history, or from current events to prove the truth of this divine pronouncement found in Numbers 32:23.

Ask how the sentence applies to the lives of David and Solomon, the two great kings we are studying in this unit of lessons. Some students may refer to the Bible story that is the text of this lesson. Tell the class that today we will look at this story in depth to see what we can learn about how God feels about our sin.

INTO THE WORD

Before class, write the following ten headings and Scripture references on note cards:

David's Sin (2 Samuel 11:1-5)
David's Ploy (2 Samuel 11:6-13)
David's Plot (2 Samuel 11:14-17)
The Messenger's Report (2 Samuel 11:18-24)
David's Response (2 Samuel 11:25-27)
Nathan's Parable (2 Samuel 12:1-4)
David's Reaction (2 Samuel 12:5, 6)
Nathan's Rebuke (2 Samuel 12:7-12)
David's Punishment (2 Samuel 12:13-15)

Distribute the cards to different class members. They are to look up the references and read the assigned Scripture verses aloud to the class in the order given here. Ask your class members to listen for ideas under the following four headings as the Scriptures are read (write these on the chalkboard):

1. What surprises you about David.

2. What you learn about Nathan.

3. What surprises you about God.

4. A question you would like to ask about this story.

Have each volunteer read aloud the heading on his or her card before reading the assigned text to the class.

After all the Scriptures are read, discuss with the class their ideas under the four headings suggested above.

Following this discussion divide your class members into groups of four to six students. Ask each group to write a modern-day paraphrase of Nathan's parable in 2 Samuel 12:1-4. Each paraphrase should be in a contemporary setting, with twentieth-century counterparts to each element in the story.

After ten minutes, let volunteers read their paraphrases. Comment on their insights. Then ask class members to list the punishments that God said would follow David's sin (vv. 10-12, 14). Discuss: "Why was the Lord so angry at David's sin? (vv. 7-9, 14).

INTO LIFE

Continue your discussion with the following questions:

1. Why do you think God insisted on punishing David, even after David had repented and God had forgiven him?

2. Does repentance and forgiveness blot out the need for punishment of an infraction?

Ask class members if they can remember the consequences that David suffered because of his great sin involving Bathsheba and Uriah. Ask them to share specific examples. Then, referring to the list under "B. Forgiveness" beginning on page 101, remind them of incidents they omitted. Discuss, "Do such dire consequences always follow our sin?"

Then ask class members to share examples, hypothetical or real, of how consequences often follow a sin, even after it has been forgiven. Possibilities are suggested under "A. Consequences" in the "Conclusion" section on page 102.

Discuss: "What should we learn from the story of David?" Possible answers:

"God forgives the one who repents sincerely, but the consequences of one's sin remain."

"It is a blessing to be forgiven, but it is better not to sin in the first place."

"One should think twice before sinning; sin never delivers what it promises."

The Sword Will Not Depart

David's later life provides dramatic proof that the prophet's warning had been true. As a consequence of David's sin, The sword did not depart from his house. Fill in the blanks in the chart below to see for yourself how violence plagued David's family.

Scripture	Incident Family Involved	Members of David's	Result
2 Samuel 13:1-22			
2 Samuel 13:23-39			
2 Samuel 15:1-16; 16:20-22; 18:1-18			
2 Samuel 20:1-22			
1 Kings 1: 5-10, 32-53			
1 Kings 2:13-25			

Sin and Consequences

Though David and Bathsheba were forgiven, bitter consequences followed their sin for many years. Cite some examples where you have seen that forgiven sin still has consequences.

Sometimes God allows things to happen to us to discipline us (Hebrews 12:7-13). Do you think this may explain why the consequences of sin are not removed, or does discipline come to rebuke the unrepentant and to lead him to repentance? Why do you think so? What, then, should be our response to difficulty in our lives?

From the Conquest to the Kingdom

SOLOMON'S GLORIOUS REIGN

LESSON 12

WHY TEACH THIS LESSON?

Many people, for obvious reasons, will find it difficult to identify with Solomon. They are not wealthy, nor do they see themselves as especially wise. But in one key respect, every Christian should identify with and learn from Solomon. The queen of Sheba "heard about the fame of Solomon and his relation to the name of the Lord" (1 Kings 10:1). Every Christian—*Christ*-ian—wears the name of the Lord. Those who know us should also know of our "relation to the name of the Lord." Use this lesson to challenge your students to that high standard.

INTRODUCTION

Old King David turned over the kingdom to young King Solomon, and gave two bits of advice along with it. "Be strong," and, "Observe what the Lord your God requires" (1 Kings 2:1-3). Young Solomon took both bits of advice seriously.

A. STRONG KING

Solomon's half brother Adonijah had tried to steal the throne for himself; but David had learned of it, and the plotting had been interrupted by the sound of trumpets announcing that Solomon was king. Adonijah's plotters had swiftly deserted him then (1 Kings 1:5-49).

Solomon tried to be lenient with Adonijah. He said, "If he shows himself to be a worthy man, not a hair of his head will fall to the ground" (1 Kings 1:50-53). But Adonijah did not show himself worthy. At the first sign that he was still plotting, Solomon showed himself strong. He executed both Adonijah and the tough old army general who had supported him (1 Kings 2:13-35).

B. GODLY KING

Following his father's second bit of advice, "Solomon showed his love for the Lord by walking according to the statutes of his father David" (1 Kings 3:3). He went to Gibeon, the nation's chief place of worship, and offered a thousand burnt offerings. There the Lord appeared to him in a dream. The Lord said, "Ask for whatever you want me to give you." Solomon asked for wisdom and understanding to rule the nation well. Pleased with that request, the Lord not only granted what was asked, but promised riches and honor as well. And if Solomon would continue to obey the Lord, he would have a long life, too (1 Kings 3:4-14).

C. WIDE EMPIRE

Following his father's advice to be strong, Solomon built a formidable military force (1 Kings 4:26). This secured his hold over the wide empire David had built, reaching from "the River," the upper Euphrates, in the north to the border of Egypt in the south. The kings of that area paid tribute, and Israel lived in peace and safety (1 Kings 4:21, 24, 25).

DEVOTIONAL READING:
PROVERBS 3:5-15

LESSON SCRIPTURE:
1 KINGS 9:1-9; 10:1-24

PRINTED TEXT:
1 KINGS 9:1-3; 10:1-7, 23, 24

LESSON AIMS
After this lesson a student should be able to:

1. Tell why the queen of Sheba visited Jerusalem and what she learned about Solomon and his kingdom.

2. Explain why Solomon was wiser and richer than other kings of the world.

3. Resolve to seek God's kingdom and his righteousness.

Nov
20

KEY VERSE
King Solomon was greater in riches and wisdom than all the other kings of the earth.
—1 Kings 10:23

Lesson 12 Notes

What Do You Think?

Solomon wrote, "Wisdom is supreme; therefore get wisdom. Though it cost all you have, get understanding" (Proverbs 4:7). How do we "get wisdom"? How do we know whether the wisdom we have is from God or from the world? James says we should pray for wisdom (James 1:5). Is that all there is to it? If not, what else is involved? If it's so simple, why did Solomon suggest it might "cost all you have"?

What if two people have prayed for God's wisdom to decide an issue, and then they disagree? How can we determine which of them, if either, has the answer that corresponds to God's wisdom?

How to Say It

Adonijah. Ad-o-NYE-juh.
Ethiopia. E-thee-O-pee-uh (th as in thin).
Euphrates. U-FRAY-teez.
Gibeon. GIB-e-un.
Mesopotamia. Mes-uh-puh-TAY-me-uh.
Sheba. SHEE-buh.
Yemen. YEM-un.

D. Great Buildings

Mindful of David's wish for a temple for the Lord, Solomon set about building it. He enlisted the king of Tyre to procure timber from the famous cedars of Lebanon (1 Kings 5). From Tyre came also a master craftsman to supervise the construction. His name was the same as the king's name, Hiram (1 Kings 7:13, 14). Actual building of the temple began in the fourth year of Solomon's reign, and was finished seven years later (1 Kings 6:37, 38).

It took another thirteen years to build Solomon's own house (1 Kings 7:1). This was a magnificent palace for the nation's headquarters as well as for Solomon's home. Second Chronicles 8:1-6 tells briefly of other building projects that Solomon undertook "throughout all the territory he ruled."

Tyre was noted for seamen and traders as well as builders. King Hiram and his people helped Solomon build a fleet of ships on the Red Sea, and Israel became a power in world commerce (1 Kings 9:26-28).

Voyages of the trading ships helped to spread Solomon's reputation for wealth and power, and above all for wisdom. The king of Israel was world famous as the outstanding authority in many fields, and "men of all nations came to listen to Solomon's wisdom" (1 Kings 4:29-34). The second part of our lesson text tells of one who came, but the first part records the Lord's own response to Solomon.

I. THE LORD'S APPROVAL (1 KINGS 9:1-3)

At this time in his career, Solomon loved the Lord and obeyed him (1 Kings 3:3). The Lord's approval was more important to him than all the tributes of kings and all the accolades of scholars, and the Lord took occasion to express his approval.

A. Occasion (v. 1)

1. When Solomon had finished building the temple of the Lord and the royal palace, and had achieved all he had desired to do. . . .

Two phases of Solomon's activity were completed: the temple and the royal palace. Probably all Solomon "had desired to do" means all he wanted to do on those buildings, not all he wanted to do throughout the whole land. Temple and palace together took twenty years to build (1 Kings 6:38; 7:1; 9:10). When they were done, the Lord took that occasion to give additional revelation to the king.

B. Appearing (v. 2)

2. The Lord appeared to him a second time, as he had appeared to him at Gibeon.

The earlier appearing at Gibeon has been mentioned in section B of the Introduction above. The Lord had appeared in a dream and had promised wisdom, riches, and honor. Now he appeared again.

C. Approval (v. 3)

3. The Lord said to him: "I have heard the prayer and plea you have made before me; I have consecrated this temple, which you have built, by putting my Name there forever. My eyes and my heart will always be there."

Chapter 8 of 1 Kings records the dedication of the temple, including Solomon's prayer on that occasion (8:22-53). What we read in this verse is God's answer to that prayer. God said he had *heard the prayer,* that he had *consecrated* the temple to put his *Name* there forever, and that his *eyes* and his *heart* would be on it perpetually.

While the prayer was offered when God's house was completed—thirteen years before the events of this chapter—one should not be concerned that God delayed in answering Solomon's prayer. Solomon had prayed that God would accept the temple as his dwelling place. God responded then, making his acceptance plain by filling the house with a visible cloud of his glory (8:10, 11). When the king's house was finished thirteen years later, there were some signs that Solomon was becoming more worldly and less godly. Therefore the Lord took that occasion to remind Solomon of his prayer. He had asked God to accept the house, and God had done so. Now, thirteen years later, God reminded Solomon of that prayer and added a warning that his acceptance was conditional. If king and people would continue to obey the Lord, the temple would continue to be honored as God's house (9:4, 5). But if they would turn away from the Lord, he would reject both them and the temple they had built (9:6-9).

CONSECRATING THE TEMPLE

Eighty-three years after President Theodore Roosevelt laid its cornerstone in 1907, the Washington National Cathedral was formally dedicated (although it will take another thirty years before it is completed). It is built in the classic manner of many European cathedrals: Gothic in style and intricately decorated with the work of craftsmen skilled in wood and stone.

The National Cathedral is like some others in that it is taking several generations to complete. The most extreme example may be the Protestant Cathedral in Ulm, Germany, which was begun in 1377 and not completed until 1890!

When Solomon had completed the most exquisite house of worship ever built for God, the Lord announced that he had consecrated it to himself "for ever." There is a sense, however, in which the dedication of any house of God is not a once-for-all matter. Some buildings that were dedicated to God in years past became cultural relics, or museums devoted to secular purposes, or unused shells that were finally torn down. Indeed, the temple Solomon built was in time destroyed. Regardless of its beauty or cost of construction, a house of worship remains consecrated to God only by the faithfulness of God's people who worship him there.   —C. R. B.

II. A QUEEN'S HOMAGE (1 KINGS 10:1-7)

The location of ancient Sheba has long been disputed. Many students have thought it was Ethiopia, on the east coast of Africa; but now the prevailing opinion seems to be that it was Yemen and some surrounding territory in southwestern Arabia. Ethiopia and Yemen face each other across the Red Sea. Both were in easy reach of Solomon's merchant ships (1 Kings 9:26-28).

A. ARRIVAL (VV. 1, 2A)

1. When the queen of Sheba heard about the fame of Solomon and his relation to the name of the LORD, she came to test him with hard questions.

Solomon was famous both for wisdom and for wealth (1 Kings 4:22-34). It is to his credit that his fame was connected with the name of the Lord. Apparently he let it be known that his wisdom and wealth were God's gifts (1 Kings 3:3-14).

The *queen of Sheba* was not one to believe everything she heard. She may have doubted both that Solomon was wiser than her scholars and that the Lord was greater than her gods. She meant to find out for herself instead of trusting the tales told by sailors and travelers.

We are not told what *hard questions* the queen brought. Some students think they were riddles. Indeed, the Hebrew word is the one used of the riddle that Samson invented to challenge the guests at his wedding (Judges 14). But apparently our translators thought the lady brought more serious problems. She may have collected hard questions in science, philosophy, religion, commerce, government, and other fields.

2a. Arriving at Jerusalem with a very great caravan—with camels carrying spices, large quantities of gold, and precious stones—

WHAT DO YOU THINK?

Solomon took nearly twice as long to build his own house than he did to build the house of the Lord. It was at that point that the Lord appeared to him to remind him of his commitment to the Lord and warning him of the consequences should that commitment fail. Do you think there is evidence in the time spent on each house that suggests a reminder and a warning were necessary? If so, what warning might God give you or your church based on the time you and others in the church spend on secular activities compared to the time you commit to ministry purposes?

WHAT DO YOU THINK?

People knew that Solomon's fame was associated with the name of the Lord God of Israel. Do people associate what they know of you with God? How can we make sure that whatever fame we achieve is connected with the name of the Lord?

Of course, there is a danger connected with this. Once the connection is made between your reputation and the Lord, then whatever you do—good or bad—reflects on him. How can you be sure to present a consistently positive portrayal of the Lord you serve?

The queen had learned what things were valued in Jerusalem—*spices, large quantities of gold, and precious stones*—and she brought them in abundance. She had no fleet of ships at sea to match Solomon's, but perhaps she had more camels than he had. We are not told how many of them were in her *very great caravan*, but surely there were enough to make an impressive entrance into *Jerusalem*, capital city of the famous Solomon.

B. CONFERENCE (VV. 2B, 3)

2b. She came to Solomon and talked with him about all that she had on her mind.

Solomon gave the queen a royal welcome and spent as much time in conference as she wanted to spend. *All that she had on her mind* seems to indicate that she brought real problems rather than clever riddles, or perhaps in addition to clever riddles.

3. Solomon answered all her questions; nothing was too hard for the king to explain to her.

Here is clear evidence that Solomon was specially gifted with wisdom from above. An ordinary man is not able even to answer *all* the questions of an ordinary person, much less the difficult questions of a head of state burdened with all the affairs of a nation.

C. OBSERVATION (VV. 4, 5)

4. When the queen of Sheba saw all the wisdom of Solomon and the palace he had built. . . .

As we have mentioned, Solomon was famous for two things: his wisdom and his wealth. Great *wisdom* was plain in his answers; great wealth was plain in the size and splendor and masterly craftsmanship of *the palace he had built*.

5. The food on his table, the seating of his officials, the attending servants in their robes, his cupbearers, and the burnt offerings he made at the temple of the LORD, she was overwhelmed.

In that magnificent palace, Solomon's *table* required a lot of fine food for his family and *officials* and guests, plus even more food, not quite so fine, for a multitude of servants. See 1 Kings 4:22, 23 for his daily grocery list: more than five hundred bushels of flour and meal, thirty beef cattle, a hundred sheep, plus wild game and poultry. No wonder the queen was *overwhelmed*.

We have no such clear picture of the other things that won the queen's admiration. Evidently two classes of attendants are called *officials* and *servants*. No doubt the queen was impressed by the huge number of them as well as by their fine apparel. The *cupbearers*, waiters at the table, may have been impressive, too; but some students think the Hebrew word here refers to the drinks that were served rather than to the waiters.

The King James Version mentions also his "ascent by which he went up to the house of the Lord," meaning an elaborately decorated path or ramp or stair by which he went to the temple. The NIV gives a different meaning to the Hebrew words: *the burnt offerings he made at the temple of the Lord*.

It is not necessary to know exactly what all these details were. Together they made a profound impression on the visiting queen. She had come in a high-spirited way; hoping her long camel train loaded with precious things would make an impression on Solomon. But she found her glory completely eclipsed.

D. HOMAGE (VV. 6, 7)

6. She said to the king, "The report I heard in my own country about your achievements and your wisdom is true.

WHAT DO YOU THINK?

Solomon was able to answer the queen of Sheba's hard questions. Today's world faces some hard questions that Christians need to answer: Who we are? Where did we came from? Where are we going? What must I do to be saved?

Without appearing falsely pious or acting as if you think you know everything, what can you do to encourage people to ask you such questions and to trust you to have a good answer? What can you do to be prepared to answer them?

The queen was convinced. The reports she had heard back in Sheba were not myths, not exaggerations, not the bragging of sailors far from home. They were sober truth.

7. "But I did not believe these things until I came and saw with my own eyes. Indeed, not even half was told me; in wisdom and wealth you have far exceeded the report I heard."

Seeing was believing. Far from exaggerations, the reports heard in Sheba had understated the truth. Solomon's wisdom and prosperity far surpassed them. His *wisdom* was proved by his ready answers to all questions (v. 3). Verses 14-22 tell something of his *wealth*. For example, in one year Solomon received 666 talents—twenty-five tons—of gold!

Read the rest of the queen's tribute in verses 8-10. Notice that she gave homage to the Lord as well as to Solomon. She even gave the Lord credit for Solomon's high position. No doubt Solomon himself had assured her that God had made him what he was.

TELLING THE OTHER HALF

While Communism still held sway throughout Eastern Europe and much of Asia, it was common for the Communist press to present current events with a propagandized slant in opposition to the Western world. History books were rewritten to remove from the historical record whatever was embarrassing to the Communist leaders.

Then Mikhail Gorbachev gained power in the Soviet Union. As a part of his widely hailed *glasnost* (openness) policy, censors no longer peered over the shoulders of historians. A new high school history book was published in 1989, telling much of the truth that had been falsified for decades. But even its authors admitted that so much new information about past lies was coming to light that they had to begin immediately to write another, still more accurate, version of history. Perhaps more than half the truth about Soviet history was yet to be told!

When the queen of Sheba visited Solomon, the "half that had not been told her" was not covered over by lies. On the contrary, the truth of how God had blessed Solomon far exceeded even the truth about him that the queen previously had heard.

It has been said that truth is stranger than fiction. God's blessings are not fiction. The truth about how he blesses those who are faithful to him would be hard to exaggerate.

—C. R. B.

III. THE WORLD'S HOMAGE (1 KINGS 10:23, 24)

The queen of Sheba was one of many who came to Jerusalem to see whether the reports they heard were true, to admire Solomon's splendor, and to learn from his wisdom.

A. COMPARISON (v. 23)

23. King Solomon was greater in riches and wisdom than all the other kings of the earth.

In other times, when the Lord was not properly honored, little Israel was overshadowed by great empires in Egypt and Mesopotamia. Pagan kings exceeded faithless kings of Israel in riches and wisdom. But in Solomon's time both Egypt and Mesopotamia were weaker. Israel was the dominant nation, and Solomon was famous far and wide for *riches* and for *wisdom*. Note again the indications of wealth in this chapter, verses 14-22 and 26-29. Review the praise of his wisdom in 1 Kings 4:29-34. And remember that both wisdom and wealth were the Lord's special gifts to a king who honored him (1 Kings 3:3-14).

WHAT DO YOU THINK?

The queen of Sheba was overwhelmed by Solomon's wisdom and the splendor of his kingdom. Is it legitimate for a church to aim to make visitors to its services feel "overwhelmed" by what they observe? If we seek such a worship experience, how can we be sure it is the majesty of God that overwhelms them and not the mere trappings of wealth and splendor, the extravagant display of human talent?

In regard to a church's fellowship, we might recall the famous exclamation of an observer of the early church: "Behold how these Christians love one another!" Would a visitor to your church be led to make such an observation? Would she say it of you? Why or why not?

THOUGHT TO REMEMBER

"But seek first his kingdom and his righteousness" (Matthew 6:33).

Visual 12 illustrates the "Conclusion" of this lesson.

PRAYER

Father in Heaven, we are thankful for your Word, which teaches us to know what is right. We are thankful also for the Savior, through whom we are forgiven and we have the righteousness that is from you by faith. As we seek your kingdom and your righteousness, may we have wisdom to understand the Word and grace to follow the Savior. In his name we pray. Amen.

DAILY BIBLE READINGS

B. HOMAGE (V. 24)

24. The whole world sought audience with Solomon to hear the wisdom God had put in his heart.

The whole world, of course, means that part of the earth that heard about Solomon: Mesopotamia and the countries bordering on the Mediterranean Sea and the Red Sea. From all of these, the wisest seekers of truth came to learn from Solomon; and again the historian pauses to give credit to God, who gave Solomon his wisdom.

CONCLUSION

Solomon's wealth and wisdom are extolled again and again, but let it never be forgotten that his devotion to the Lord preceded them and accompanied them. The king began his reign by following the parting advice of David: "Observe what the Lord your God requires: Walk in his ways, and keep his decrees and commands, his laws and requirements, as written in the law of Moses, so that you may prosper in all you do" (1 Kings 2:3). Solomon did keep God's law, and he did prosper in everything. His was no lip service or conforming to tradition; he loved the Lord.

A. THE KING'S DEVOTION

The king's devotion is seen in the thousand offerings he made early in his reign (1 Kings 3:4) and in his humble prayer for wisdom to rule the people of God (1 Kings 3:9). It is seen in the magnificent temple he built for the Lord, and in the prayer he offered when the temple was completed (1 Kings 8:22-53). "Three times in a year" Solomon continued his sacrifices, probably celebrating the three annual feasts established by the law (1 Kings 9:25; Exodus 23:14-17).

Solomon made no secret of his devotion and his indebtedness to the Lord. Plainly the record says his wisdom and wealth were special gifts (1 Kings 3:12, 13). The queen of Sheba acknowledged it (1 Kings 10:9), and so did the king of Tyre (1 Kings 5:7). It seems that all who came to hear Solomon's wisdom heard also that God had put it in his heart (1 Kings 10:23, 24).

The Lord himself acknowledged Solomon's devotion by appearing to him twice with great promises (1 Kings 3:5; 9:2), by granting him wisdom and riches and fame (1 Kings 3:12, 13), and by accepting the completed temple and filling it with glory (1 Kings 8: 10, 11).

B. RIGHTEOUSNESS EXALTS

"Righteousness exalts a nation" (Proverbs 14:34). Never was Solomon's proverb illustrated more clearly than in Solomon's Israel. A country smaller than half of New Jersey ruled an empire eight times as big, and received honor from all the world.

More remarkable still, it seems that "the whole world" responded as the queen of Sheba did, with respect and admiration rather than envy and enmity. Apparently Solomon in all his glory was so modest about his accomplishments and so persistent in giving God the glory that he made friends instead of foes. In his wisdom he illustrated what David's greater descendant was to say centuries later: "Do not worry, saying, 'What shall we eat?' or 'What shall we drink?' or 'What shall we wear?' For the pagans run after all these things, and your heavenly Father knows that you need them. But seek first his kingdom and his righteousness, and all these things will be given to you as well" (Matthew 6:31-33). Solomon sought God's righteousness. He asked for wisdom to lead God's people in God's way, and riches and honor were given to him along with what he asked.

Discovery Learning

This page contains an alternate lesson plan emphasizing learning activities. Classes desiring such student involvement will find these suggestions helpful. The next page is a reproducible activity page to further enhance discovery learning.

LEARNING GOALS

As students participate in today's class session, they should:

1. Discover that God's blessing was the foundation for Solomon's wisdom and wealth.

2. Decide how to make their nation wealthier, wiser, or more righteous so as to please God.

INTO THE LESSON

Before class write the words *wisdom* and *wealth* on your chalkboard. To begin today's session, distribute slips of paper and ask class members to write a sentence that includes the two words. Collect the slips and read the sentences back to the class.

As you read each sentence, or after you have read them all, analyze them with the class. Do class members agree with all of them? Why or why not? Are the ideas of wisdom and wealth mutually exclusive? Is it possible for the same person to enjoy both wisdom and wealth?

Tell class members that this lesson is the first of two about Solomon, perhaps the wisest man who ever lived, and one of the wealthiest. Like his father, David, Solomon brought great glory to God and also failed before him. Today's lesson looks at the glory, and next week's study examines the failure.

INTO THE WORD

Ask class members to share what they know about Solomon. Write on your chalkboard the headings in the introduction section on pages 105 and 106 (Strong King, Godly King, Wide Empire, Great Buildings). Use these headings as an outline for a brief lecture to explain how Solomon became king and what he had accomplished already before the events recorded in today's text. As much as possible, relate the ideas about Solomon shared earlier to this outline.

Ask two volunteers to read the following Scriptures aloud to the class: 1 Kings 3:4-15 and 1 Kings 9:1-9. Then divide the class into groups of about six or eight to compare and contrast the two passages. What is different about the two visions from God? What is the same about them?

Discuss with the class: What is present in the second vision that was not in the first? Why do you suppose God added warnings that he had not mentioned when he first spoke with Solomon?

Ask another volunteer to read 1 Kings 10:1-7, 23, 24 aloud. Then ask your class members to work in the same small groups to examine all of chapter 10 for (a) Evidences of Solomon's Wisdom and (b) Evidences of Solomon's Wealth. (The first activity on the reproducible page, 112, provides room under these two headings to complete this study. Make a copy for each student or for each group to complete.) Allow about ten minutes for the groups to study; then put the headings on your chalkboard and let class members suggest what to list under each one.

Ask class members, "Why was Solomon so prosperous?" Have one member look up and read aloud 1 Kings 3:9, 12, 13 and another 1 Kings 10:9, 23, 24; then discuss the question fully. Help class members to see that God was the source of Solomon's success, and that Solomon and the surrounding nations readily acknowledged God's blessing in Solomon's kingdom.

INTO LIFE

Ask a class member to read aloud Proverbs 14:34 for Solomon's own analysis of how God responds when a nation acknowledges him.

Once again write the word *wisdom* on your chalkboard. Beneath it write *wealth;* then write *righteousness* beneath both words. Next, put the following series of numbers beside each word: -3 -2 -1 0 +1 +2 +3.

Ask your class members to decide whether their nation has more or less wisdom, wealth, and righteousness than it had ten years ago. They should use the above numbering system to quantify their answers. For example, if they feel their nation has much less wisdom now than it did a decade ago, they should put a -3 beside *wisdom*. If they feel the country is about as righteous now as it was a decade ago, they should put a 0 beside *righteousness*.

Ask students to write the words and their number/vote on slips of paper. Then poll the class for each word. If you have time, you may want to write a cumulative number score on the board beside each word.

Which of the three elements did your class decide their country needs most? How would the presence of the other two help the third one to increase? Lead the class in discussing how individual Christians can make a country more righteous, wiser, or wealthier. What steps could they as individuals or your class as a whole take this week or this month to improve the character of their country?

Wisdom and Wealth

Read 1 Kings 10 and then list below all the evidences of Solomon's wisdom you find there and all the evidences of his wealth.

EVIDENCES OF SOLOMON'S WISDOM	EVIDENCES OF SOLOMON'S WEALTH

A Good Name

Solomon had quite a reputation, drawing the elite of many nations to see him to find out whether the reports of him they had heard were true. Yet, it was clear that his fame was from "his relation to the name of the Lord." Consider the following professions. How would it affect one in that profession to be known for his or her "relation to the name of the Lord"? How should each one approach his or her duties to maintain that relationship?

Public School Teacher

Government Official

University Biology Professor

Corporate Mid-level Manager

Your Profession

SOLOMON TURNS FROM GOD

LESSON 13

WHY TEACH THIS LESSON?

"Do not think of yourself more highly than you ought, but rather think of your-self with sober judgment, in accordance with the measure of faith God has given you" (Romans 12:3). "So if you think you are standing firm, be careful that you don't fall!" (1 Corinthians 10:12). The Bible repeats the warning several times, but it never seems enough. It is said that a picture is worth a thousand words. Maybe that is the reason the Bible gives us the picture of Solomon we find in this lesson. Wiser than all the kings who came before or after him, still he stumbled and fell. This lesson reminds us that we are not so wise we can dabble with sin and escape its consequences. Better to flee and be safe!

INTRODUCTION

Solomon was the wisest man in the world. The Lord said, "I will give you a wise and discerning heart, so that there will never have been anyone like you, nor will there ever be" (1 Kings 3:12).

Solomon was the richest man in the world. The record says he "was greater in riches and wisdom than all the other kings of the earth" (1 Kings 10:23). Gold abounded in the temple (6:20-22), and scarcely less in the palace (10:14-21). Sil-ver was plentiful as stones in Jerusalem (10:27).

Solomon was the most powerful man on earth. His military machine was fear-some (1 Kings 4:26). He stationed strong forces in fortified cities "in all the land of his dominion" (9:17-19). So "during Solomon's lifetime Judah and Israel . . . lived in safety" (4:25).

A. POWER CORRUPTS

Power corrupts. That saying has been illustrated so many times that few will doubt its truth. In recent lessons we have seen that Saul was humble and modest in his youth, but as king he became a tyrant without conscience. He disobeyed God (1 Samuel 15), and he tried diligently to kill his best supporter (19:1). David was a man after God's own heart (13:14), but with the power of a king he became an adulterer and a murderer (2 Samuel 11, 12).

Solomon was the most powerful man on earth. Could he escape the corruption of power?

B. WEALTH CORRUPTS

How many small businessmen, honest and industrious, have become big busi-nessmen and then crooks! Some wealthy entrepreneurs of Wall Street multiply their riches by illegal "insider trading." Millionaire bankers and financiers find it easy to defraud customers and investors. Sadly Jesus commented, "It is easier for a camel to go through the eye of a needle than for a rich man to enter the kingdom of God" (Mark 10:25).

DEVOTIONAL READING:
PROVERBS 16:1-7

LESSON SCRIPTURE:
1 KINGS 11

PRINTED TEXT:
1 KINGS 11:1-13

LESSON AIMS

After this lesson a student should be able to:

1. Tell about Solomon's folly and explain how it could have been avoided.

2. Tell how we can keep our-selves from similar folly.

3. Find more time for Bible study.

KEY VERSE:

Solomon did evil in the eyes of the Lord; he did not follow the Lord completely. —1 Kings 11:6

Display visual 13 of the visuals packet and let it remain before the class throughout this session.

GOD'S GIFT OF WISDOM

Nov 27

LESSON 13 NOTES

WHAT DO YOU THINK?

Solomon was among the many rulers in history who fell prey to the corrupting effects of power. Kings and presidents still fall prey to this corruption. Do you think this is a problem for civil leaders only, or does the same thing happen in businesses and school boards and churches? How can those who lead today avoid this corrupting influence? How can you, in whatever leadership position you may hold, avoid this influence?

WHAT DO YOU THINK?

God forbade the Israelites to intermarry with people of pagan nations. The same principle is surely true for "spiritual Israel," the church. "Do not be unequally yoked together with unbelievers," Paul warned the Corinthian Christians (2 Corinthians 6:14). Clearly marriage is included in the application of this principle.

Why, then, do we see so many examples of young men and young women from the church marrying non-Christians and often drifting away from the church afterward? How can the church provide solid teaching to its young people regarding courtship and marriage? How can Solomon's example be used to counsel young people in this important regard?

Solomon was the richest man on earth. Could he escape the corruption of riches?

C. DOES WISDOM CORRUPT?

The Lord approved Solomon's wish for wisdom, and Solomon's proverbs praise wisdom over and over. But Paul reminds us that not many who are "wise by human standards" are called to God's kingdom (1 Corinthians 1:26).

Isaiah notes that "the wisdom of the wise will perish" (Isaiah 29:14). Is it possible that wisdom can corrupt the wise as power can corrupt the powerful and wealth can corrupt the wealthy? If so, could Solomon escape the corruption of wisdom?

Whether we can blame power or wealth or wisdom, Solomon's glory was terribly corrupted in his later years. The Lord's favor depended on Solomon's obedience. The Lord made that plain more than once (1 Kings 3:14; 6:11-13; 9:4, 5). A man as wise as Solomon should have remembered. But the time came when Solomon trusted his wisdom more than he trusted God's law.

I. FORBIDDEN WIVES (1 KINGS 11:1-3A)

Solomon wrote, "He who finds a wife finds what is good" (Proverbs 18:22). His other writings seem to approve lifelong faithfulness to one wife (Proverbs 5:18, 19; Ecclesiastes 9:9), but it seems that he himself found one as often as possible.

A. MANY WIVES (v. 1)

1. King Solomon, however, loved many foreign women besides Pharaoh's daughter—Moabites, Ammonites, Edomites, Sidonians and Hittites.

Early in his reign, Solomon made a peace treaty with Egypt and strengthened the alliance by marrying the daughter of Pharaoh (1 Kings 3:1). Then Solomon proceeded to strengthen ties with other nations in the same way. The nations named were subject to Solomon. After the custom of the time, he left them free to manage their own affairs as long as they paid tribute to him regularly. Women of these royal families could serve as hostages as well as wives. When a princess of Moab, for example, was in Jerusalem, the king of Moab would hesitate to offend Solomon. That might mean his daughter in Jerusalem would lose favor with the king, and then who knew how she might be mistreated?

Long before Israel had a king, the Lord made specific laws for the king who would come in the future (Deuteronomy 17:14-20). Among other things, the law said the king should not "take many wives" (Deuteronomy 17:17). David ignored that law, and Solomon ignored it even more outrageously. It seemed wise to take all those wives for political reasons, and Solomon chose to follow political wisdom rather than divine law. The wisest man in the world acted foolishly when he chose to follow his own wisdom rather than God's own word.

B. PAGAN WIVES (v. 2)

2. They were from nations about which the LORD had told the Israelites, "You must not intermarry with them, because they will surely turn your hearts after their gods." Nevertheless, Solomon held fast to them in love.

According to the law, no one in Israel was allowed to marry a pagan from one of the other nations (Deuteronomy 7:3, 4). A pagan wife or husband would turn the Israelite's heart away from the real God. So Solomon's marriages violated the law in two ways: his wives were many, and they were pagan.

C. THE NUMBER OF WIVES (v. 3A)

3a. He had seven hundred wives of royal birth and three hundred concubines.

Special mention is made of the princess of Egypt (1 Kings 3:1; 7:8), but some nations must have contributed groups of princesses to Solomon's harem. We cannot count seven hundred different nations near Israel. Perhaps Solomon thought he needed a princess from each of the influential families or clans within a nation.

Concubines were second-class wives, not so important as the princesses. Still they may have been the most attractive ladies in the harem, chosen for beauty and charm rather than for political reasons; and so they may have enjoyed more of the king's attention. Even the wisest man on earth could hardly find time to give much personal attention to each of a thousand wives. Some humorist has computed that if Solomon spent a one-month honeymoon with each of the thousand, that was eighty-three years of honeymoons—and he reigned only forty years (1 Kings 11:42).

II. IMPORTED SINS (1 KINGS 11:3B-8)

The law forbade marriage with pagans, "because they will surely turn your hearts after their gods" (v. 2). Solomon may have smiled at that: "Not me! Nobody is going to turn away my heart." But who is wise enough to know his own heart and his own weakness? Have you ever caught yourself doing something you had thought you would never, never do?

A. IMPERFECT HEART (VV. 3B-5)
3b. And his wives led him astray.

How could that be? Wasn't Solomon wise? Yes, he was wise, and he was strong. But the wise man acted foolishly when he ignored God's Word and took those pagan wives, and the strong man acted weakly when lovely ladies begged to be allowed to worship their own gods.

4. As Solomon grew old, his wives turned his heart after other gods, and his heart was not fully devoted to the LORD his God, as the heart of David his father had been.

Solomon did not deny the Lord. The Lord still had his heart, or maybe ninety-nine percent of it. He just made a bit of room for phony gods. A man can make a few concessions to get along with his wives, can't he?

So Solomon's *heart was not fully devoted to the Lord his God.* Perhaps only a small percent of it was given to phony gods to please seven hundred wives. But God's demand is firm, uncompromising, intolerant: "No other gods" (Exodus 20:3).

5. He followed Ashtoreth the goddess of the Sidonians, and Molech the detestable god of the Ammonites.

Ashtoreth was the love goddess worshiped in Sidon north of Israel. *Molech* was the brutal king-god of the Ammonites east of Israel.

How much did Solomon have to do with the worship of these imaginary gods? Scholars debate that question. Some think *followed* means he himself joined his wives in worshiping. Others think he only permitted it and provided places for it. In either case, Solomon was at fault. If his heart had been fully devoted to the Lord, he would not have tolerated the worship of any other god.

B. EVIL DOINGS (VV. 6-8)
6. So Solomon did evil in the eyes of the LORD; he did not follow the LORD completely, as David his father had done.

When one's heart is not fully devoted to the Lord (v. 4), soon his actions reflect it. "For from within, out of men's hearts, come evil thoughts, sexual immorality, theft, murder, adultery, greed, malice, deceit, lewdness, envy, slander, arrogance and folly" (Mark 7:21, 22). Solomon's heart did not lead him into all of these, but it did at least lead him into some foolishness. He should have followed his own advice: "Above all else, guard your heart, for it is the wellspring of life" (Proverbs 4:23).

7. On a hill east of Jerusalem, Solomon built a high place for Chemosh the detestable god of Moab, and for Molech the detestable god of the Ammonites.

A *high place* is a place of worship. The *hill east of Jerusalem* is the Mount of Olives. Not in Jerusalem itself, but just across a narrow ravine to the east, Solomon built a place of worship for Chemosh. *Moab* and *Ammon* were kindred nations descended from two sons of Lot (Genesis 19:36-38). Their imaginary gods, *Chemosh* and *Molech*, were supposed to be similar in nature. Possibly both could be worshiped in the same place. If not, Solomon built two high places for them.

8. He did the same for all his foreign wives, who burned incense and offered sacrifices to their gods.

Of course the Moabites and Ammonites could not be favored above the rest of the seven hundred wives. Each of them had to have a place to worship her phony god. Some students have supposed that every hill near Jerusalem was crowded with places of pagan worship. It seems probable, however, that dozens of the wives worshiped the same god, so huge numbers of high places were not needed.

III. SEVERE PENALTY (1 KINGS 11:9-13)

Part of Israel's mission in the promised land was to destroy all the idols and altars and places of pagan worship (Exodus 34:13; Deuteronomy 7:5; 12:2, 3). When Solomon built what he ought to destroy, the Lord's response was severe.

A. ANGER OF GOD (vv. 9, 10)

9. The LORD became angry with Solomon because his heart had turned away from the LORD, the God of Israel, who had appeared to him twice.

It was wrong for anyone to turn away from the Lord, but it was worse for Solomon to turn away after the Lord had *appeared to him twice* with special favor and promises. Though Solomon did not turn away very far, *the Lord became angry.*

10. Although he had forbidden Solomon to follow other gods, Solomon did not keep the LORD's command.

Besides the commands given to all Israel and written in the law, Solomon had God's word given to him personally. Plainly the Lord had warned him that turning away would have terrible results (1 Kings 9:6-9). In spite of that, *Solomon did not keep the LORD's command.*

B. LOSS OF KINGDOM (v. 11)

11. So the LORD said to Solomon, "Since this is your attitude and you have not kept my covenant and my decrees, which I commanded you, I will most certainly tear the kingdom away from you and give it to one of your subordinates.

Solomon had been ignoring God's commands more and more. In violation of the law he took pagan wives, and he took many wives. He also acquired many horses contrary to the law, and he got them from Egypt (Deuteronomy 17:16; 1 Kings 10:26-29). But when he gave some recognition to phony gods, that was the last straw. God had given him a glorious empire, and God was going to take it away from him.

C. MODIFIED PENALTY (vv. 12, 13)

12. "Nevertheless, for the sake of David your father, I will not do it during your lifetime. I will tear it out of the hand of your son.

The punishment was modified, not for the sake of Solomon, but for the sake of David. This was not done as a personal favor to David, who had died years before; it was done so God's promise to David would be kept. Concerning Solomon, the Lord had said to David, "My love will never be taken away from him, as I took it

---

WHAT DO YOU THINK?

It is alarming to imagine the Lord's being angry with us. But he was angry with Solomon when he turned away from the Lord. Do you think the Lord might similarly be angry with us at times? Why or why not? If so, what should be our response? How might recognizing God's anger be related to the idea of fearing God (Matthew 10:28; 1 Peter 1:17; 2:17)?

away from Saul" (2 Samuel 7:15). Deprived of God's mercy, Saul had died in bloody defeat (1 Samuel 31:1-6). But by God's mercy, Solomon's glorious empire would remain intact till Solomon would die of natural causes. Then the kingdom would be taken swiftly from his son.

13. "Yet I will not tear the whole kingdom from him, but will give him one tribe for the sake of David my servant and for the sake of Jerusalem, which I have chosen."

The punishment was modified in a second way. One of the twelve tribes would be left for Solomon's son to rule. This would not be done for the sake of Solomon or his son, but for the sake of David and Jerusalem. This, too, must be understood in the light of God's promises and purposes. God had chosen David's family to continue on the throne forever (2 Samuel 7:12, 13, 16), and God had chosen Jerusalem as the special place of his presence (1 Kings 9:3). Neither of these choices would be nullified by Solomon's misdeeds, but Solomon's glorious empire would end. Only David's own tribe, the tribe of Judah, would still be ruled by men of David's family.

FAR-REACHING CONSEQUENCES

Galena, Illinois, was once the commercial and cultural center of the Midwest. In the middle of the nineteenth century, it was a progressive city on the American frontier. Its setting on the Galena River was just a short distance from the Mississippi.

The produce of the surrounding region and the ore from local mines could be traded for goods brought upstream from the South and other parts of the country on the great inland waterway formed by the Mississippi and Ohio Rivers. The "city fathers" were so sure of their future as a riverboat town that when the railroad wanted to build a terminal there, they said they didn't want it.

In those days, Chicago was just a small town that also had access to water transportation. But Chicago's leaders said yes to the railroads, and the rest is history. Galena's mines gave out, the population dwindled, and the town declined. A decision on the part of a few had far-reaching consequences for many.

Solomon had his rationalizations for marrying foreign women: we know it was considered good international politics; he may also have thought it made Jerusalem a more cosmopolitan city. But Solomon's unwise decision was in direct opposition to God's specific command. The price to be paid was the decline and destruction of a whole nation. Sin still has its price today.   —C. R. B.

CONCLUSION

How could such a wise man be so foolish? It wasn't hard at all. Solomon began to trust his wisdom too much, and he failed to check it by God's Word. While we mourn over his folly, let's give a bit of thought to our own. Our wisdom is less than Solomon's, but do we always live by the wisdom we have? How many times have you said, "I should have known better," or "Why did I do that?" or "How could I be so stupid?" With the good sense we have now, all of us can do better than we have been doing. Can't we? At the same time, all of us can be growing wiser.

A. GETTING WISDOM

Solomon's wisdom was a gift from God (1 Kings 3:12), and so is ours. "If any of you lacks wisdom, he should ask God, who gives generously to all without finding fault, and it will be given to him" (James 1:5). But that does not mean we receive his gift without any effort on our part.

God gives our daily bread, but we work for it, too. With the muscles and minds God gives us, we work with the materials he gives, and so we get the food he gives. With the same minds God gives, we study the Scriptures he gives, and thus we get the wisdom he gives.

HOW TO SAY IT

Ammonites. AM-un-ites.
Ashtoreth. ASH-toe-reth.
Chemosh. KEE-mosh.
Edomites. EE-dum-ites.
Hittites. HIT-ites or HIT-tites.
Moabites. MO-ub-ites.
Molech. MO-lek.
Pharaoh. FAIR-o or FAY-ro.
Sidonians. Sye-DOE-nee-uns.

WHAT DO YOU THINK?

We speak of a person's being "worldly wise." Sometimes this type of wisdom is legitimate, but sometimes it can lead one astray. What are some means by which we can test it?

Consider Romans 14:19; 1 Corinthians 10:31; and Galatians 5:13.

PRAYER

Dear Father in Heaven, thank you for sharing your wisdom and truth with us. Confessing that we have neither learned nor followed your Word as well as possible, we beg you to forgive our neglect and help us to do better. In Jesus' name we pray. Amen.

THOUGHT TO REMEMBER
Read the Bible!

DAILY BIBLE READINGS

Monday, Nov. 21—Solomon's Achievements (Ecclesiastes 2:4-9)

Tuesday, Nov. 22—God Sees Into the Heart (Proverbs 16:1-9)

Wednesday, Nov. 23—Solomon Disobeys God's Command (1 Kings 11:1-8)

Thursday, Nov. 24—Solomon's Kingdom Will End (1 Kings 11:9-13)

Friday, Nov. 25—Edomite Foes Organize Against Solomon (1 Kings 11:14-22)

Saturday, Nov. 26—Other Adversaries Take Action (1 Kings 11:23-27)

Sunday, Nov. 27—Ahijah's Prophecy About Jeroboam's Reign (1 Kings 11:28-40)

Do you suppose Solomon neglected his homework? The law said he should have a copy of God's Word and read from it every day (Deuteronomy 17:18-20). But Solomon had a nation to rule, a big commercial enterprise to manage, and seven hundred wives to keep happy. Do you suppose daily Bible reading was crowded out of his busy schedule? The Book said he shouldn't multiply horses (Deuteronomy 17:16). But what if he hadn't seen that part of the Book for ten years? Could that explain why he ignored it?

Are there some parts of the Bible that you haven't read for ten years? Maybe you do not have as much wisdom as God wants to give you.

B. TESTING WISDOM

The devil is no fool. He tries to deceive us with wisdom that is as phony as the gods of Moab and Sidon.

Eve thought it would be wise to eat from the forbidden tree. If she became wiser, she became sadder, too. She lost her home in Eden (Genesis 3).

Solomon thought it would be wise to take hundreds of pagan wives. The strategy seemed to work: he had little trouble with their fathers. But his kingdom was split in two when he died (1 Kings 12:1-20).

King Herod thought it was wise to kill anyone who might possibly take his throne, including a baby who was called King of the Jews (Matthew 2). But Herod died, his kingdom was split four ways, and Jesus still is King.

Soviet dictators thought it was wise to destroy all dissenters and ultimately to take charge of the whole world. But they made their downfall sure when they decreed that God did not exist. Their country is split more ways than Herod's.

Eve could have had a very simple way to test her thinking. She knew what God said: "Don't eat from that tree." That settled it.

Solomon could have checked his thought just as simply if he had kept up his homework. God's law said, "Not many wives; no pagan wives; no other gods."

Herod knew how to find out where the Christ was to be born. He called the Bible students, and they gave him the information from Scripture (Matthew 2:4-6; Micah 5:2). If Herod had pursued the matter further in the same way, he could have learned that Christ's kingdom cannot be destroyed (Daniel 2:44).

Russian Communists may have been misled by corrupt church officials who misrepresented God, but they could have bypassed the officials and read God's Word for themselves. It gives no support either to church corruption or communist tyranny.

How do you think you and I can test our thinking to see whether it is wise or not?

C. TOO BUSY?

If anyone could claim to be too busy for Bible study, Solomon could. Some of us make that claim while our responsibilities are far less than his. But an empire was lost because Solomon did not live by Bible teaching. Can we afford to risk whatever empires we have?

Some of us assign ourselves a certain number of chapters a day, and neglect whatever we have to neglect in order to read those chapters. But some chapters take longer than others, so some of us reserve a certain time each day. Many of us plan to read the entire Bible each year, and some eager ones read it two or three times in a year. Many of us could read it four times a year simply by giving up the worse half of the television programs we watch. If anyone is too busy for Bible study, that person is too busy.

Are you wise enough to find time to become wiser?

Discovery Learning

*This page contains an alternate lesson plan emphasizing learning activities. Classes
desiring such student involvement will find these suggestions helpful. The next page
is a reproducible activity page to further enhance discovery learning.*

LEARNING GOALS

As students participate in today's class session, they
should:

1. List the factors that contributed to Solomon's downfall.

2. Discuss six principles related to God and how
Solomon's downfall illustrates the importance of each
one.

3. Choose one of the principles to remember and
apply in the following week.

INTO THE LESSON

Write the following scrambled sentences (with the
punctuation and capitalization shown here) on note
cards, one sentence per card. (Each scrambled sentence is
in italics. What follows is the solution, given for the convenience of the teacher.)

To begin this session, divide your class into pairs or
groups of three or four and give a card to each group. Ask
each group to unscramble its sentence to reveal an important truth.

*1. conventional we God. become wisdom wisdom, we
world's may blindly blind to When accept the the from*

When we blindly accept the world's conventional wisdom, we may become blind to the wisdom from God.

*2. blessing wisdom, When wisdom. comes habit of God's
lose lose the the that may from living studying by we we God's*

When we lose the habit of studying God's wisdom, we
may lose the blessing that comes from living by God's
wisdom.

*3. often disobedience. with failure minimal Monumental
starts*

Monumental failure often starts with minimal disobedience.

*4. governed with God. God; with be by rules from otherwise,
Relationships relationships relationship others others can with
interfere must with our*

Relationships with others must be governed by rules
from God; otherwise, relationships with others can interfere with our relationship with God.

*5. first straw the hearts last Our for is another god God. in
our making*

Our making another god first in our hearts is the last
straw for God.

*6. depending Those by God God. are blessed most suscepti-
ble on their most blessings failing to to and follow*

Those most blessed by God are most susceptible to depending on their blessings and failing to follow God.

When the groups have finished their work, ask them
to share the results with the class. (You may want to prepare a poster before class with the correct sentences on it.
If so, display it after the groups report so all may see the
unscrambled sentences.) Ask class members to comment
briefly on them. Which sentence most "strikes a chord"
with them? Which do they have the most trouble understanding? Is there a sentence with which they disagree? Is
there a sentence that explains a principle that class members can illustrate with examples from their own lives?

After several minutes of discussion, tell the class that
each of these sentences contains a truth that is illustrated
by the story told in today's Scripture text.

INTO THE WORD

Remind the class of last week's study of Solomon, the
world's wealthiest and wisest man. Tell them that today's
text describes the sad decline of Solomon. Ask a volunteer
to read the Scripture text aloud while class members listen and decide why Solomon failed.

If students worked in pairs or groups for the first activity, ask them to return to the same groupings. Distribute
paper and instruct the groups to examine today's text and
list what it indicates Solomon did that was wrong. After
about five or six minutes, ask volunteers to share as you
make a list on the chalkboard. Ask, "What was so wrong
with these things?"

Then have the class decide how the example of
Solomon illustrates each of the principles stated in the unscrambled sentences. You may want to assign a different
sentence to each group, or let each group choose a sentence.

INTO LIFE

Ask students to decide which of these principles is the
greatest challenge to them. Invite each student to choose
one of the sentences and to write it on a note card as a reminder of today's discussion.

Ask volunteers to share which sentence they chose,
and why. Close the class session with sentence prayers,
mentioning especially the concerns that your students
have shared.

Royal Mistakes

The law was very clear on several points about how the king of Israel should or should not behave. Solomon, wise as he was, failed on several of them. In addition, he failed to live up to the standards God set for all his people, including kings. Read the following Scriptures and complete the chart below to see how Solomon failed to live up to the standard God set for the king and the people.

THE LAW SAID . . .	BUT SOLOMON . . .
Do not make an _____ or _____ of any kind Deuteronomy 4:15-20	Followed _____ and _____ 1 Kings 11:5
Destroy all the _____ ;"Do not worship the Lord your God in _____ way." Deuteronomy 12:2-7	Built _____ _____ for Chemosh and other pagan gods. 1 Kings 11:7, 8
Make _____ in one place only Deuteronomy 12:13, 14	Offered sacrifices on the _____ _____ 1 Kings 3:3, 4
Not many _____ Deuteronomy 17:16	Had 12,000 _____ 1 Kings 4:26
Don't get horses from _____ Deuteronomy 17:16	Imported horses from _____ and Hue 1 Kings 10:28
Not many _____ Deuteronomy 17:17	Had 700 _____ and 300 _____ 1 Kings 11:3
No large amounts of _____ or _____ Deuteronomy 17:16	Received 666 talents of _____ yearly; made silver as common in Jerusalem as _____ 1 Kings 10:14, 27

Personal Mistakes

Little by little, Solomon's devotion to the Lord eroded. God did not immediately punish him for violating his laws. But the effect was cumulative. Finally, the time of judgment had arrived. Is there some habit or weakness in your life that threatens to compromise your relationship with the Lord. Maybe it seems small now, but it can grow. Write below the habit or weakness you need most to deal with. How will you handle it?

Winter Quarter, 1994-95

Theme: Jesus the Fulfillment (Matthew)

Special Features

Lessons

Unit 1. Jesus and John: Setting the Scene

Unit 2. Immanuel: God With Us

Unit 3. Jesus: The Son of David

Unit 4. Jesus Christ: Victor Over Sin and Death

About these lessons

The focus of this quarter's study is on Jesus Christ as the fulfillment of the Old Testament promises. This emphasis is begun with two lessons on John the Baptist's ministry of preparation, prophesied by Isaiah. The theme is carried out in succeeding lessons on Jesus' birth, ministry, death, and resurrection.

Dec 4
Dec 11
Dec 18
Dec 25
Jan 1
Jan 8
Jan 15
Jan 22
Jan 29
Feb 5
Feb 12
Feb 19
Feb 26

Jesus, the Promised One

by Carl Bridges

This quarter's lessons focus on Jesus as portrayed by Matthew. Even though the writers of all four Gospel accounts agreed on who Jesus was, what he did, and what he means to everyone, still each of them emphasized certain aspects of his character. Matthew, more than any other writer, highlighted Jesus' role as fulfiller of prophecy. He called attention to an Old Testament prophecy by means of an introductory statement such as this one in chapter 1, verse 22: "All this took place to fulfill what the Lord had said through the prophet." Other similar statements are found in 2:15, 2:17, 2:23, 4:14, 8:17, 12:17, 13:35, 21:4, 27:9. These "formula quotations," as some scholars call them, serve as only the most noticeable mark of Matthew's concern with prophecy. All through his Gospel account we see him present Jesus as the promised One, the son of David, the divine Savior to whom all the prophets pointed.

A secondary theme of this quarter's lessons comes to the surface as we see how different people responded to Jesus. John the Baptist, the Magi, King Herod, and Jesus' own disciples, among others, could accept him or reject him, but they couldn't ignore him. We see in their varied responses to God's Son a pattern repeated in our day as people accept Jesus, turn him away, or try to ignore him.

In all four Gospels we find the *kerygma*, the proclamation, of Jesus as Messiah, Son of God, and Savior. As people have often said, the Gospels do not function simply as biographies of Jesus. In addition to telling us facts about his life, they provide a God-inspired interpretation of who he is. When Peter preached to the Pentecost crowd (Acts 2), when Philip talked to the Ethiopian (Acts 8), when Paul spoke in the synagogue at Antioch in Pisidia (Acts 13), or when any early proclaimer of Jesus told anyone else about him, they gave the same message. The facts of Jesus' ministry, his teaching, his death and resurrection, together with the promise of his coming again to judge the world, provided the "pegs" on which the apostolic preachers hung what they had to say. These basic facts about Jesus, his nature and work, we find highlighted in all the Gospels, including the one we study this quarter. Matthew's Gospel, like the other three, serves not just as fact but also as interpretation, not only as biography but as proclamation as well.

DECEMBER 4, 11

JESUS AND JOHN: SETTING THE SCENE (UNIT 1)

The lessons in this study don't go in strict chronological order. The first unit has to do with John the Baptist, who served as Jesus' forerunner, and Jesus' reaction to John. In lesson 1 we hear John's stern message of repentance to the Israelites of his time, as he called them to turn away from evil and turn to the God of Abraham in order to get ready for the judgment to come. We also hear his promise of the coming Messiah, and we see that promise begin to find fulfillment in Jesus' baptism and the descent of the Holy Spirit upon him.

The Scripture text for lesson 2 comes from later in Jesus' ministry, when John the Baptist sent a message from prison to ask Jesus if he really was the promised One. After telling John's messengers to go back to John with a report of the messianic signs they saw Jesus performing, Jesus addressed the crowds, evaluating John's character and ministry. John was not a weakling, Jesus said, nor did he desire a life of luxury. Instead this rugged man, who lived an austere life in the desert, was strong and immovable. He was a dedicated servant of God, who had been privileged to announce the coming kingdom.

IMMANUEL: GOD WITH US (UNIT 2)

The second unit of the Winter quarter focuses on Jesus as Immanuel, "God with us." In lesson 3 we consider Mary's miraculous pregnancy and the reaction to it of her fiancé, Joseph. We learn of the angel's appearance to Joseph, the divine name the new child was to bear, and a seven-hundred-year-old prophecy, which promised that he would be born of a virgin. This lesson reveals Jesus' birth to be both a historical event, something that happened to real people in a real time and place, and as a cosmic event, something that affects all people of all times and places.

In lesson 4 we meet some of the most mysterious characters in the Bible, the "Magi from the east" (2:1). Profound students of nature, they came to greet the infant King after seeing a special star rise when he was born. In this lesson we also meet Herod the Great, the king who sat uneasy on his throne and saw the baby Jesus as a dangerous rival.

JESUS: THE SON OF DAVID (UNIT 3)

In the third unit, we see how Matthew presented Jesus as the son of David, the royal descendant of the ideal king, the one who would sit on his ancestor's throne and rule God's people with justice. In the Scripture passages contained in this unit, we find the record of some of Jesus' marvelous deeds, the messianic signs that proved who he was.

Lesson 5 deals with two notable miracles, the healing of two demon-possessed men in the region of Gadara, and the restoration of a paralyzed man whom some friends carried to Jesus for help. In these miracles we see Jesus' power over the forces of disease and evil that darken people's minds and twist their bodies.

As time went by, Jesus' enemies began to press him, and in lesson 6 we see how he dealt with them. Jesus entered a synagogue, where he met a man with a withered hand. Jesus' antagonists, less concerned with the man's wholeness than with the question of whether Jesus would "break" the Sabbath by healing him, made the man's situation a test case. After Jesus healed many more persons among the crowds who followed him, the amazed people wondered aloud, "Can this be the Son of David?" (12:23).

Lesson 7 tells of Jesus meeting a Canaanite woman, a Gentile, and how he dealt with one who was not a member of God's chosen people. It shouldn't surprise us to find him meeting her deep need by healing her daughter. From this incident in Jesus' life, we learn one of the truths Matthew points to again and again: God loves people of all kinds and doesn't play favorites.

Lesson 8 deals with the dramatic event in Jesus' ministry known as his transfiguration. While on a mountain with three of his disciples, Jesus was visibly changed before them and then joined by Moses and Elijah. Thus those disciples were given a glimpse of Jesus' true nature. At the same time, God the Father spoke out of Heaven with words of approbation similar to those spoken at Jesus' baptism.

Lesson 9 covers Jesus' triumphal entry into the city of Jerusalem. At this time many people, including children, proclaimed him as the son of David, the messianic king. By riding on a donkey in fulfillment of prophecy, Jesus deliberately declared himself as the promised deliverer of Israel.

JESUS CHRIST: VICTOR OVER SIN AND DEATH (UNIT 4)

The fourth and final unit of this quarter's study deals with Jesus' death and resurrection, and events associated with them. Lesson 10 tells of the Passover meal Jesus ate with his disciples shortly before his arrest. During the meal he designated the bread as a memorial of his body, about to be broken on the cross, and the cup as a memorial of his blood, about to be shed to atone for the sins of the world.

Lesson 11 presents us with one of the ugliest events recorded in Scripture, the trial of Jesus. Confronted with faked evidence and facing a hostile court, Jesus maintained his integrity as the Son of Man and bore without flinching the rage of his enemies. We can hardly fail to be moved by such a graphic picture of what our Lord went through for the people he loved so much.

Jesus' crucifixion serves as the subject of lesson 12. Although we may be shocked by the brutality and injustice of what people did to him, we cannot help being grateful for his suffering on our behalf. When the soldiers mockingly said, "Hail, king of the Jews!" (27:29), they spoke more truth than they knew.

Lesson 13 presents Matthew's account of the resurrection, the event that showed Jesus to be the Son of God and Savior of mankind. Some women who followed Jesus came intending "to look at the tomb" (28:1), but found instead an angel who told them that their Friend and Master was not there, that he had been raised from the dead. Leaving the tomb "afraid yet filled with joy" (28:8), they hurried to tell Jesus' disciples. By Jesus' appointment, these men met Jesus again on a mountain in their native Galilee and received a commission from him that is still in force today, the command to "go and make disciples of all nations, baptizing them in the name of the Father and of the Son and of the Holy Spirit, and teaching them to obey everything I have commanded you" (28:19, 20). They also received from Jesus a promise that his followers claim even today: "And surely I am with you always, to the very end of the age" (28:20).

At the end of John's Gospel we find these words: "Jesus did many other things as well. If every one of them were written down, I suppose that even the whole world would not have room for the books that would be written" (John 21:25). We, too, are aware of the abundance of material from which to draw in considering the life of Christ, since the study we are now beginning can deal with only a few passages taken from Matthew's long Gospel. Still, the record of Jesus' sayings and doings is precious, and we gain much even if we study but a limited part of it. The good news of Jesus, if we will let it, will change our lives forever.

God's Royal Son

by Dennis C. Gaertner

Justin Simon remembers a "brush with history" few of us would be able to keep to ourselves. In the summer of 1949 he sat in a Chicago airport with forty-six students ready to fly to war-damaged Europe as youthful ambassadors of goodwill. Discovering in Alaska Airlines a fare that would allow each student to fly at a cost of only two hundred dollars, Justin rounded up his group and waited for departure time.

A few hours before departure, Justin discovered that a snag had developed. The Alaska Airline flight did not have permission from the Civil Aeronautics Authority to land. Justin frantically began phoning every official he could think of in order to get help, but to no avail.

When he ran out of names, he decided to act on a truly desperate idea. He called person-to-person to the White House in Washington, D. C. It was 4:30 in the morning, but on the third ring he heard a man answer with "a slow, deliberate voice that twanged with a Midwestern accent." It was President Harry Truman. Justin apologized profusely for bothering the president at that hour. Truman responded by saying, "Well, I don't much mind that you've called me. I was up anyway." After Justin explained the situation with the college students, the president gave him instructions—a name and a phone number to contact—and the problem was on its way to solution.

Few Americans expect this kind of access to their president. In the ancient world the distance between the king and his subjects was even more pronounced. Ordinary people had no expectation of gaining access to the king. This fact of life provides the element of surprise in Jesus' parable about the king who ordered his servants to "go to the street corners and invite to the banquet anyone you find" (Matthew 22:9).

JESUS AS ROYALTY

Passages in the Old Testament speak of One who was to come at some time in the future and rule in the Spirit and power of Jehovah. His rule would be characterized by righteousness and faithfulness. His coming is pictured as one for which the Jews should prepare. "In the desert prepare the way for the Lord; make straight in the wilderness a highway for our God," says Isaiah (40:3). His arrival would inspire celebration and hope because "the Sovereign Lord comes with power, and his arm rules for him" (Isaiah 40:10).

This coming ruler is portrayed as one who would be established in the line of David, the royal line of Israel. Isaiah calls him "the Root of Jesse" and describes his influence as reaching far beyond Israel (11:10). As the kings of ancient Israel were consecrated to their office by being anointed with oil (see 1 Samuel 10:1; 16:13; 1 Kings 1:39), this ruler would be anointed to his office. He was known as the "Messiah," a Hebrew term that means "anointed one." The Greek equivalent is "Christ." In the case of the Messiah, the anointing would come from God.

By the time of the birth of Jesus, expectations about the Messiah, the coming King, were being heard from several sources within Judaism. Today scholars can read Jewish literary works such as the Apocalypse of Ezra, the Apocalypse of Baruch, 4 Ezra, and the Dead Sea Scrolls to see what the Jews thought the Messiah would be like.

When the Magi came from the east inquiring about the one who was born king of the Jews, the chief priests and scribes furnished the information that the king would be born in Bethlehem (Matthew 2:5, 6). The New Testament describes Simeon's waiting in Jerusalem "for the consolation of Israel" (Luke 2:25). When he saw the baby Jesus he recognized the One designated as "the Lord's Christ" (vv. 26-32). Samaritans also were anticipating the coming of the Messiah (John 4:25, 29).

EVIDENCE OF JESUS' ROYALTY

Much of what Jesus did during his ministry raised in his audience the anticipation of his position as king. His miracle of feeding the multitudes caused some of the Jews to plan to force Jesus to be their king (John 6:15). Jesus' miracles were proof to them that he was the Prophet who was "to come into the world" (v. 14). However, these nationalistic Jews misunderstood the nature of the divine rule spoken of by the prophets. When Jesus declared its spiritual nature, many of these people lost interest in him (vv. 25-66).

By riding on a donkey into Jerusalem at his triumphal entry, Jesus was declaring that he was the king of David's line spoken of by the prophets (Zechariah 9:9). Those who lined the way into the city understood this and shouted, "Hosanna to the Son of David! Blessed is he who comes in the name of the Lord!" (Matthew 21:9).

Nevertheless, Jesus made clear that his reign was to be spiritual, not political. The tension between these concepts surfaced on several occasions during Jesus' final hours. At Jesus' hearing before Pontius Pilate, the accusers of Jesus charged him with claiming "to be Christ, a king" (Luke 23:2). Their accusations were built on the notion of a reign in which taxes would be raised and armies formed for the defeat of Rome. Though Jesus freely admitted that he was "king of the Jews" (Matthew 27:11), he was not the worldly, political king his accusers were trying to make him out to be (see John 19:12). To Pilate he said, "My kingdom is not of this world. If it were, my servants would fight to prevent my arrest by the Jews. But now my kingdom is from another place" (John 18:36).

The misunderstanding of this point explains some of the treatment of Jesus during the hours of the crucifixion. The soldiers placed on him a scarlet robe, a crown of thorns, and then put a staff in his hand and mockingly bowed before him as if showing respect to a monarch (Matthew 27:27-30). At the cross some ridiculed him by jeering, "Let this Christ, this King of Israel, come down now from the cross, that we may see and believe" (Mark 15:32). Meanwhile the inscription over his head announced: "JESUS OF NAZARETH, THE KING OF THE JEWS" (John 19:19).

JESUS' SPIRITUAL REIGN

Soon after the resurrection of Jesus, the apostles understood the spiritual nature of Jesus' reign. On the Day of Pentecost the residents of Jerusalem heard Peter proclaim that God had raised Jesus from the dead. For this reason Peter could confidently announce that "God has made this Jesus, whom you crucified, both Lord and Christ" (Acts 2:36). At God's right hand Jesus could exercise authority to grant forgiveness of sins, and Peter insisted that the audience must, therefore, turn to Jesus through repentance and baptism in his name in order to receive salvation from sin (v. 38).

Whenever a repentant sinner responds to the gospel invitation, the reign of Jesus is advanced. Whenever we confess that we believe that Jesus is the Christ, the Son of the living God, we pledge our loyalty to the spiritual king of our lives.

Beginning at the Day of Pentecost the apostles consistently declared Jesus to be the Son of God with power. Paul affirms that Jesus descended from the royal line of David (Romans 1:3). John wrote his Gospel account in order that readers might believe "that Jesus is the Christ" (20:31). Descriptive terms such as "Lord," "Christ," and "Son of David" demonstrate how exalted is Jesus' status in God's eyes. Paul further states that "God exalted him to the highest place and gave him the name that is above every name." Honor is to be given him, for "at the name of Jesus every knee should bow, in heaven and on earth and under the earth, and every tongue confess that Jesus Christ is Lord, to the glory of God the Father" (Philippians 2:9-11).

The decision we make about whom we acknowledge as king and ruler of our lives brings eternal consequences. The New Testament assures us that we are making no mistake by extending our worship to Jesus as king. John records the scene in Heaven, in which the four living creatures give "glory, honor and thanks" to God, who sits on the throne, and the twenty-four elders fall down before him and worship him (Revelation 4:1-11). In the next chapter (5:11-14) John records another scene. He heard multiplied thousands of angels praising the Lamb who had been slain, singing that he is worthy of "honor and glory and praise." As if in echo, "every creature in heaven and on earth and under the earth and on the sea, and all that is in them," could be heard singing, "To him who sits on the throne and to the Lamb be praise and honor and glory and power, for ever and ever!" To that the four living creatures said, "Amen," and "the elders fell down and worshiped." As the royal Son of God, Jesus deserves our worship.

JOHN HERALDS JESUS' COMING

WHY TEACH THIS LESSON?

It is considered neither wise nor polite to call someone a "snake" these days, but that is exactly the term John the Baptist used of many of the religious leaders of his day. "Poisonous snakes," to be precise. It was not their position that bothered John, but their attitude. He preached repentance, and they refused. They believed they were too righteous, too sophisticated, too dignified to need repentance.

This lesson will not have been successful unless your students are led to see that they, too, need to repent. Even if they have served Christ faithfully for many years, they, as all of us, still have areas in which further growth is needed. Repentance clears the way for growth.

INTRODUCTION

A. I'LL PREACH UNTIL YOU REPENT!"

A preacher preached on repentance every Sunday until his congregation got tired of it. It wasn't always the same sermon—he would use different texts, different illustrations, and different words—but it was always about repentance.

Finally a delegation of the church's leaders went to the preacher and asked him to change his theme. "Why do you always talk about repentance?" they asked. "Don't you have anything else to say?"

The preacher replied, "I'll stop preaching about repentance when you repent. Then I'll go on to something else."

John the Baptist was a preacher whose theme was repentance. He urged Israel to turn from sin and get ready for the Messiah, God's chosen Deliverer, who was soon to make his appearance. Today's text contains a sample of John's preaching and the record of Jesus' coming to John for baptism in order to comply with God's will.

B. LESSON BACKGROUND

The lesson text tells of John the Baptist's great work of announcing the coming of the Messiah. Luke indicates that the word of God came to John in the fifteenth year of the Roman Emperor Tiberius, that is, A.D. 26 or 27 (Luke 3:1). John then began his ministry of calling God's people to prepare to receive the Christ.

In chapter 1 of his Gospel account, Matthew tells of Jesus' human family line and his virgin birth. Chapter 2 contains the record of the visit of the Magi and Joseph and Mary's flight to Egypt with the young child Jesus to escape King Herod's attempt to kill him. Nearly thirty years of Jesus' life are passed over in silence from the end of chapter 2 and the beginning of chapter 3. There Matthew records John the Baptist's entrance upon the scene and his startling announcement.

I. JOHN'S MINISTRY (MATTHEW 3:1-6)

A. FORCEFUL PREACHING (VV. 1, 2)

1. In those days John the Baptist came, preaching in the Desert of Judea.

DEVOTIONAL READING:
ISAIAH 40:3-11
LESSON SCRIPTURE:
MATTHEW 3
PRINTED TEXT:
MATTHEW 3:1-15

LESSON AIMS

At the completion of this lesson the students should:

1. Be able to describe briefly the message of John the Baptist.

2. Be able to define repentance.

3. Believe that Jesus is the Christ prophesied in Scripture and make him Lord of their lives.

VISUALS FOR THESE LESSONS

The Adult Visuals/Learning Resources *packet contains classroom-size visuals designed for use with the lessons in the Winter quarter. The packet is available from your supplier. Order no. 292.*

KEY VERSE:

I baptize you with water for repentance. But after me will come one who is more powerful than I, whose sandals I am not fit to carry. He will baptize you with the Holy Spirit and with fire.
—Matthew 3:11

OPTION

The first activity on the reproducible page 134 provides a creative way for your students to study today's text. It may be used as an introduction to your study.

Visual 1 of the visuals packet summarizes the lessons for this quarter in chronological order. Visual 14 illustrates the theme of the quarter. It will be helpful if both visuals are displayed for several weeks.

WHAT DO YOU THINK?

John's life-style was different from that of most people, to say the least. He lived in the wilderness, he wore a camel's pelt for a garment, and he ate wild honey and locusts.

Do you think this strange lifestyle increased the effectiveness of his call for repentance, or would it have made it easier for "sensible" people to dismiss him and his message? Why do you think so?

How would you respond to a preacher who was more than a little unorthodox in his methods? Why?

What can the church do to attract the kind of attention John attracted in order to deliver the message of the gospel? What can you do?

In those days. This evidently points back to the last verse of chapter 2, and refers to the days when Jesus was still living in Nazareth. *John the Baptist.* In the Synoptic Gospels—Matthew, Mark and Luke—John is identified as the "baptizer" or the "baptist." This description refers to John's most noticeable activity, the practice of immersing people in water as a sign of their change of heart toward God and his moral requirements.

The Desert of Judea was the desert area by the Dead Sea. Verse 6 tells us that John was baptizing in the Jordan, so we conclude that he was preaching by the Jordan where it flows through the wilderness just before entering the Dead Sea.

2. And saying, "Repent, for the kingdom of heaven is near."

John called for people to turn from sin and to dedicate themselves to obeying God; that's what repentance is. They needed to repent because God was about to do something marvelous in their time. That which had been predicted both in the law and by the prophets—the coming of the Messiah and the establishment of his heavenly rule—would soon occur. If they were indifferent regarding obedience to the law that they had already been given, they would not be prepared to receive the revelation the King would bring.

The kingdom of heaven is near. The idea is that the kingdom was poised on the edge of the stage of history, "waiting in the wings" to appear. With the beginning of Jesus' ministry, the kingdom would break in upon God's creation in all its majestic power.

Today, as well as in John's time, people need to repent to get ready for God's kingdom. Only when our hearts and minds are turned toward God and we are ready to do wholeheartedly what he wants us to can Jesus enter our hearts to rule our lives.

B. FULFILLMENT OF PROPHECY (V. 3)

3. This is he who was spoken of through the prophet Isaiah: "A voice of one calling in the desert, 'Prepare the way for the Lord, make straight paths for him.'"

Matthew refers to the prophecy in Isaiah 40:3. There the prophet called on God's people to prepare the way for God to come and rescue them from captivity in Babylon. Just as God delivered Israel from physical captivity in the sixth century B.C., he would now rescue from the power of sin and death all who would accept the Deliverer he was sending.

John the Baptist's mission was to get people ready for the Messiah. He called on them to *prepare the way* and to *make straight paths for him.* By preaching repentance and administering a preparatory baptism, John prepared people to hear and receive Jesus, God's own Son. We have a similar task today as believers in Jesus; part of our job is to prepare the way for people to come to faith in him, a process one writer has called "pre-evangelism." By pointing people to God's moral requirements and gently helping them to see their need for a Savior, we can get them ready to meet Jesus and put their lives in his hands.

C. PERSONAL CHARACTERISTICS (V. 4)

4. John's clothes were made of camel's hair, and he had a leather belt around his waist. His food was locusts and wild honey.

John's clothing was a coarse fabric woven from *camel's hair,* held around him by a *belt* of animal hide. This unusual clothing, similar to the "prophet's garment" of Zechariah 13:4, marked John as a prophet. *Locusts,* declared edible by the law (Leviticus 11:22), were easily captured; and *honey,* stored in caves by wild bees, was available for John's eating. His total life-style was characterized by austere self-denial—most appropriate for one who was calling a nation to repentance.

John's dress and diet marked him as different from the people of his time and place. Most of us who are followers of Christ today don't stand out from our contemporaries in the same manner as John did. But people should be able to tell that we are different from those who are controlled by the world's system of values. Can others tell by our attitudes and actions and speech that we have committed our lives to Christ?

D. THE PEOPLE'S RESPONSE (VV. 5, 6)

5. People went out to him from Jerusalem and all Judea and the whole region of the Jordan.

A road that was much traveled forded the Jordan River near Jericho. Perhaps it was here where John began his preaching. His first hearers were so impressed that they told others. Soon people were coming in multitudes from the whole surrounding area to hear John.

6. Confessing their sins, they were baptized by him in the Jordan River.

Perhaps curiosity for this unusual-appearing preacher drew the people to him in the wilderness region by the Jordan, but something more kept them there. Verse 2 indicates that the theme of John's preaching was repentance, and it is obvious from the people's response that his preaching carried great conviction. The people were confronted with their sins, they admitted their guilt, and were baptized by John in the river. Thus they committed themselves anew to God in preparation for the coming of his kingdom.

CREDIBILITY

On October 28, 1992, the announcement appeared in at least one newspaper in Oregon and one prestigious newspaper on the East coast. The head of a world mission church based in Korea had proclaimed that the world would end on October 31 of that year. There appeared to be very few believers. Perhaps the fact that the head of the mission had been accused of fraud by the government of Korea and had purchased long-term bonds that would mature after the advertised date of the end of the world undermined his credibility!

John the Baptist came preaching that people should repent because the kingdom of Heaven was at hand. Multitudes went out to hear him, and they believed and obeyed his message. His announcement was based in the prophecy of Isaiah, which his hearers knew and believed. Furthermore, John's life-style was consistent with his message. Everything about John spoke of self-denial and surrender to God. Nothing in his manner or message gave even the least hint of a desire for personal gain.

Few will believe an announcement if they doubt the credibility of the proclaimer. Let's be sure that our motives, our methods, and our manner of life are in line with the gospel we preach and teach.   —W. P.

II. JOHN'S MESSAGE (MATTHEW 3:7-12)

A. CHALLENGE TO LEADERS (VV. 7-10)

7. But when he saw many of the Pharisees and Sadducees coming to where he was baptizing, he said to them: "You brood of vipers! Who warned you to flee from the coming wrath?

Among the great crowds who came to hear John's preaching were leaders of the two principal religious sects in Israel—*the Pharisees and Sadducees.* The name *Pharisees* came from a Hebrew word that meant *separated.* Members of this party were very careful to keep themselves separated from anything and anyone regarded as legally "unclean." They had elevated the traditions of the elders to such an extent that they were regarded as being equal in authority to the written law of God. The

---

HOW TO SAY IT

Isaiah. Eye-ZAY-uh.
Pharisees. FAIR-ih-seez.
Sadducees. SAD-you-seez.
Tiberius. Tie-BEER-ee-us.
Zechariah. Zek-uh-RYE-uh.

WHAT DO YOU THINK?

Popular thinking often confuses sorrow for sin with repentance. Judas felt remorse for his betrayal of Jesus, but he did not repent (Matthew 27:3). Sorrow for sin leads to repentance (2 Corinthians 7:9, 10); it is not to be equated with repentance. The Greek word in the New Testament literally means "to have another mind." So repentance is "a change of mind that reveals itself in a changed life." Thus, John called for "fruit in keeping with repentance."

Do you think people take repentance seriously today? Why or why not? Should the church demand "fruit in keeping with repentance" before accepting one's confession of Christ? After? Why or why not?

Pharisees made a great show of keeping the outward forms of the law, but they had little regard for the spirit of it. Late in his ministry Jesus exposed this group for the hypocrites that they were (see Matthew 23:1-36).

The Sadducees held views that were directly opposite of those held by the Pharisees. The Sadducees openly cooperated with the pagan Romans who ruled Palestine at this time. They rejected the authority of oral tradition, and instead of making a great show of piety they lived in a luxurious manner. Whereas the Pharisees believed in the resurrection of the dead and the existence of angels and spirits, the Sadducees denied both (Acts 23:8).

John was aware of the true character of these leaders, so he knew that they had not come with good motives. Rather than coming in humble penitence, it seems that they came to reject and ridicule his baptizing.

8. "Produce fruit in keeping with repentance.

Here John represents human beings as fruit trees. He called on all persons, even these religious leaders, to repent of their sins and to produce *fruit*, that is, to live in a manner that would indicate their change of heart. Pretense of piety would not obtain God's mercy; only genuine repentance followed by godly living is acceptable to him.

9. "And do not think you can say to yourselves, 'We have Abraham as our father.' I tell you that out of these stones God can raise up children for Abraham.

Many of John's hearers, and certainly the Pharisees and Sadducees, were intensely proud of their Jewish heritage. The mere fact that they were Abraham's descendants, the chosen people of God, led them to believe that they had nothing to fear from the wrath of God. It was a general feeling among those in John's audience that when the Messiah came and established his kingdom, all the Jews would be a part of it. In contrast to this way of thinking, John made it plain that no one is born into God's favor, that behavior counts more than birthright in his sight. We can easily picture John pointing to the *stones* on the ground to illustrate that God could take any material he desired and by his power make *children for Abraham* if that generation despised him and refused to live as he required.

We, too, need to be careful that we don't depend on others to put us in good standing with God. The faith of one's parents, spouse, or children cannot, by itself, bring one into God's favor. Each individual must establish and maintain a relationship with God through sincere faith and the wholehearted commitment of his or her life to the Lord.

10. "The ax is already at the root of the trees, and every tree that does not produce good fruit will be cut down and thrown into the fire.

Here John returned to the metaphor of fruit trees introduced in verse 8. He compared his hearers to trees in an orchard. Each tree, of course, occupied valuable space in the orchard and was expected to bear fruit for its owner. If it did not, the tree would be *cut down and thrown into the fire.*

John was announcing the coming of the Messiah, who would establish his kingdom and bring salvation to mankind. But the Messiah was to be Judge as well as Savior. Those among his chosen people who were corrupt, who refused to produce the *good fruit* of righteousness in their lives, would be removed, just like a fruitless tree in an orchard. The *fire* is a reference to Hell.

This passage shouldn't terrify us, but it should remind us that God put us on earth for a reason. He expects our lives to count for something, to "bear fruit" in the biblical sense. The fruit we bear should include the "fruit of the Spirit" that the apostle Paul identifies in Galatians 5:22, 23. It should also include acts of service to God and to other people. It is appropriate to ask ourselves from time to time what our lives have counted for in the past, and what they count for now. Is the way of

OPTION

Explore this issue further with "Fruit in Keeping With Repentance," a reproducible activity on page 134.

WHAT DO YOU THINK?

John warned of impending judgment. The Pharisees and Sadducees dismissed his message, however, instead of responding. Today, it is easy for church members to dismiss warnings of judgment. It is true that God's message of judgment is for those who do not obey the gospel of Jesus Christ. However, let it be remembered that judgment begins with the church! Peter writes "For it is time for judgment to begin with the family of God" (1 Peter 4:17). What do you think the church should do to prepare for this "judgment"? What should you do?

someone in need being made easier by what we do? Is someone who is outside of Christ being drawn closer to him by the attitudes we manifest, by our speech, and by our conduct?

B. COMING OF THE MESSIAH (VV. 11, 12)

11. "I baptize you with water for repentance. But after me will come one who is more powerful than I, whose sandals I am not fit to carry. He will baptize you with the Holy Spirit and with fire.

Here John drew a contrast between his baptism and that of the mighty One who would come after him. John's baptism was *with water,* which may also be translated "in water." Water was the substance in which the person was plunged, the physical medium by which the baptism was accomplished. More than that, John's baptism was *for repentance.* It publicly marked a person's turning away from sin and toward God and his ways.

Speaking of the One who was coming, John said, *he will baptize you with the Holy Spirit and with fire.* When Jesus was about to ascend into Heaven, he repeated the first part of the promise to his chosen apostles: "In a few days you will be baptized with the Holy Spirit" (Acts 1:5). This was fulfilled about ten days later on Pentecost (Acts 2:1-4). Some suggest that the baptism with the Holy Ghost and fire were the same event, noting that "what seemed to be tongues of fire" sat on those who received the Holy Spirit on Pentecost (Acts 2:3). Jesus, however, made no mention of a baptism with fire in his statement in Acts 1:5. John's statement recorded here by Matthew is set in a context of fiery destruction, first of fruitless trees (v. 10) and then of useless chaff (v. 12). It seems more likely, therefore, that John was speaking of two different events: the baptism of the Holy Spirit on Pentecost and the baptism of fire for the wicked at the last day (Matthew 25:41; Revelation 21:8).

The One who was coming after John was the Messiah, and John confessed to being unworthy even to carry his shoes. At this point the other Gospels quote John as saying that he was not worthy to untie the straps of his sandals (Mark 1:7; Luke 3:16, John 1:27). Either way John meant that the Messiah was so much greater than he that John felt himself unworthy even of the most menial service to this great figure.

12. "His winnowing fork is in his hand, and he will clear his threshing floor, gathering his wheat into the barn and burning up the chaff with unquenchable fire."

Once again John referred to the separation of the wicked and the pretenders from God's people. In this verse he presents another picture of the separation of the useless from the valuable.

The *winnowing fork* was used to toss the grain into the air after it had been trampled to separate the kernels of grain from the husks and stalks. The wind blew away the useless chaff, while the heavy grain fell to the threshing floor. The grain was stored for use, but the chaff was burned up. Thus, the winnowing fork in the Messiah's hands would serve as an instrument of judgment, like the axe of verse 10.

WHOM SHALL WE FEAR?

Jim and John walked slowly home from school, deep in conversation about what had happened on the school grounds that day. They had seen and heard it all. One of their classmates had been beaten up by the gang of toughs who dominated the students. Jim was in favor of telling their father about it and asking him what to do. John felt differently. He said, "Dad will make us tell the principal, and then we'll be the next ones in trouble with the gang."

WHAT DO YOU THINK?

Christians are sometimes reluctant to speak out for their faith for at least four reasons: (1) They fear they will lose popularity. What others think about them dominates their decisions and behavior. (2) They fear that the unpopular stand may cost them financially. One who is in business may lose customers. (3) They wish to minimize pain. Normal people don't want to suffer. If one is in the minority, one could become a martyr. (4) They fear that they will not be able to answer adequately the challenges of unbelievers.

John the Baptist seemed to have none of these fears. Are you more like John or the fearful Christians described above? Why? How can Christians today develop the same kind of boldness John had?

THOUGHT TO REMEMBER

May we show by the way we live that Christ rules our lives.

WHAT DO YOU THINK?

When Jesus presented himself to John for baptism in the Jordan, John protested. Jesus insisted on being baptized, however, to "do all that God requires" (Matthew 3:15, TEV). Christian baptism is different from John's baptism, as seen in Acts 19. Still, Jesus did give the command, "Therefore go and make disciples of all nations, baptizing them. . . ." (Matthew 28:19). In the practice of Christian baptism, how instructive is Jesus' example when he was baptized by John? Why do you think so?

PRAYER

Lord, deliver us from a shallow "repentance" that fails to touch our hearts or our behavior. May we turn from the ways of evil and walk wholeheartedly in the paths of righteousness through the strength that Christ provides. In his name, amen.

DAILY BIBLE READINGS

Monday, Nov. 28—The Lord's Messenger (Malachi 3:1-7)

Tuesday, Nov. 29—John the Baptist Preaches Repentance (Matthew 3:1-6)

Wednesday, Nov. 30—One Greater Than John Is Coming (Matthew 3:7-12)

Thursday, Dec. 1—Jesus Convinces John to Baptize Him (Matthew 3:13—4:1)

Friday, Dec. 2—Jesus Preaches Repentance (Matthew 4:12-17)

Saturday, Dec. 3—Jesus Calls Disciples and Begins Ministering (Matthew 4:18-25)

Sunday, Dec. 4—God's Promise Fulfilled in Jesus (Acts 13:16-26)

As it turned out, the boys did tell their father, and he went with them to bolster their courage in telling what they had witnessed.

John the Baptist spoke of the Messiah's blessing and judgment. Pride, prejudice, worldly desires—perhaps these or other motives kept many of the religious leaders from responding to John's prophetic message. Others heard and obeyed John's call to reformation of life. They chose to do right rather than keep silent and find favor with those who rejected God's call for change.

Don't let fear of any person determine your response to Jesus. Wiser is it to fear him who "can destroy both soul and body in hell" (Matthew 10:28).   —W. P.

III. JOHN'S MASTER (MATTHEW 3:13-15)

A. OBJECTION TO JESUS' REQUEST (VV. 13, 14)

13. Then Jesus came from Galilee to the Jordan to be baptized by John.

Jesus grew up in Nazareth and then, when ready to begin his ministry, came south to where John was baptizing. He came for the particular purpose of receiving baptism at John's hands.

14. But John tried to deter him, saying, "I need to be baptized by you, and do you come to me?"

At this point, John had not received the divinely promised sign that would identify the Messiah. That came *after* Jesus was baptized (John 1:33, 34). Yet John now recognized Jesus' greatness and, in proper humility, confessed that it was more appropriate for Jesus to baptize him. Since the mothers of John and Jesus were related (Luke 1:36), the families quite possibly were together often in Jerusalem for the annual feasts. Surely John knew of Jesus' miraculous birth and his superior sanctity. It may be that when Jesus came to him, John was virtually certain of Jesus' true nature; but he would not know positively until the Holy Spirit descended upon Jesus after his baptism.

B. ACQUIESCENCE TO JESUS (v. 15)

15. Jesus replied, "Let it be so now; it is proper for us to do this to fulfill all righteousness." Then John consented.

The *Good News Bible* has this translation: "Let it be so for now. For in this way we shall do all that God requires."

John then baptized Jesus, and, as the following verses state, God's Holy Spirit descended like a dove and lit on Jesus. God's voice echoed from Heaven to confirm the sign and to declare his approval of this act of obedience performed by his Son.

CONCLUSION

Repentance is more than sorrow for sin; it is more than the decision to stop following the devil and to begin following God. Repentance is complete when one actually stops pursuing the ways of the world and begins to do the will of God.

John called the people of his time to repentance, to reject sin and to turn toward God in their hearts and minds and to express that change in the way they lived. The exciting reason for John's demand was that "the kingdom of heaven is at hand." The Messiah was in their midst and would soon make himself known. Only by turning their hearts and lives back to God would they be prepared to receive the long-awaited Redeemer.

For nearly two thousand years now the message has rung out: "The Messiah has come, and he has made a way of escape from our sins!" Turn to God through him and receive forgiveness and eternal life.

Discovery Learning

This page contains an alternate lesson plan emphasizing learning activities. Classes desiring such student involvement will find these suggestions helpful. The next page is a reproducible activity page to further enhance discovery learning.

LEARNING GOALS

After this session, the class members will be able to:

1. Describe the person and ministry of John the Baptist.

2. Define repentance.

3. Demonstrate repentance by changed action (living in a way that indicates a change of heart).

INTO THE LESSON

Before the class session begins, write the following questions on the chalkboard or overhead transparency:

What is the most unusual food you have ever tasted?

What is the most unusual type of clothing you have ever seen? Would you wear such clothes?

As your students arrive, encourage them to think about the questions and to be prepared to give their answers in a few minutes.

Begin the session by asking for your students' responses to the questions. List on the chalkboard the unusual foods and clothing styles mentioned. Allow four to five minutes for this opening discussion.

Point out that John the Baptist was known for his unusual diet and dress. Even more significant, however, was the powerful message he preached. It's a message we still find relevant today.

INTO THE WORD

Begin the Bible study by sharing the information from "Lesson Background," page 127. Then have a class member read the text aloud (Matthew 3:1-15). Malachi 4:5, 6 may also prove helpful to the class as you teach about John's role in fulfilling prophecy and preparing people for the beginning of Jesus' ministry.

By means of the following questions, encourage the students to examine and discuss the Scripture text:

1. What does this passage say about the life-style of John the Baptist? Why do you think he chose such an unusual life-style? Do you think he was different *on purpose?* Why? (*The text describes his appearance, wearing a camel's hair garment and a leather belt, and his diet: locusts and wild honey.*)

2. What one word best describes John's message? (Divide the students into groups of two or three to discuss this and compile a list. Have them consider also Luke 3:1-18 for a more detailed account. Allow four or five minutes for discussion, and then let the groups share their conclusions. *John was stern and bold in his preaching. Luke empha-*

sizes that he was also very practical in teaching about changes the people needed to make in their lives.*)

3. Do you think John *chose* his life-style, or was he *called* to it? What makes you think so? Do you think his message would have been as powerful if he had looked more normal? Would his life-style and message draw you to him or push you away? Why? (*Luke records that the angel dictated to John's father certain aspects of his life-style—Luke 1:13-17. Still, his message was filled with power from the Holy Spirit—Luke 1:15—not merely from his external appearance.*)

4. People came with different motives to hear John. What were some of those motives? (*Some came out of curiosity and some out of a sincere desire to hear a message from God. The Pharisees and Sadducees came to hear John, perhaps out of curiosity, or fear of his success, or the desire to catch him in error to discredit him.*)

5. Why was the message of John to the Pharisees and Sadducees so negative? (*See comments under verse 7.*)

6. The core of John's message was repentance. In the biblical sense, what does it mean to repent? (*It means to turn one's heart and mind from sin and to dedicate oneself to obeying God in all of life.*)

7. John encouraged the people, "Produce fruit in keeping with repentance" (verse 8). What does this mean? (*It means that our conduct will give evidence of our changed heart and mind. For specifics, see Galatians 5:22, 23.*)

8. On what basis did John at first refuse to baptize Jesus? (*John's baptism was a baptism of repentance. He refused on the basis of Jesus' holiness and his own sinfulness.*) What thoughts do you think were going through John's mind?

INTO LIFE

Ask, "What are some specific ways each of us can be a 'John the Baptist' to prepare someone to receive Jesus?"

Note that John preached repentance. Discuss, "What sins might there have been in that society from which the people needed to repent? How different are the sins in our society?"

Remind the class of the unusual foods and clothing you discussed at the beginning of your class time. Ask each student to examine his or her own life. Ask the class to consider this: Would it be easier to repent and change your behavior than it would be to eat such food or wear such clothes? Immediately close with prayer.

Picture This!

Read Matthew 3:1-15. Draw a picture (or write a word or brief phrase) in each box below to represent items in the verse indicated. Then mark the message of the verse positive (+), negative (-), or neutral (0).

verse 4 + - 0	verse 7 + - 0	verse 10 + - 0
verse 11 + - 0	verse 12 + - 0	verse 15 + - 0

Fruit in Keeping With Repentance

Answer these questions as you think John the Baptist would have answered them.
What would happen to those who did not repent?

What would those who decided to repent do next?

How would others know that someone had repented?

When we accept Jesus, we receive his perfect righteousness and we have the Holy Spirit to help us please God. We demonstrate the fruit of the Spirit listed in Galatians 5:22, 23.

"The fruit of the Spirit is love, joy, peace, patience, kindness, goodness, faithfulness, gentleness and self-control."

Galatians 5:22, 23

Jesus the Fulfillment
Unit 1: Jesus and John: Setting the Scene
(Lessons 1, 2)

JESUS AFFIRMS JOHN'S MESSAGE

Dec 11

LESSON 2

WHY TEACH THIS LESSON?

Bible heroes sometimes become larger than life to us. Thrilled with the record of the great acts of faith they performed, we sometimes forget they were, after all, human and subject to the same emotions as we. Including doubt.

John the Baptist's question of Jesus, "Are you the one?" is the question we all face from time to time. Even long-time Christians, especially in a period of stress or fatigue, may question their faith. John's situation provides relief, for Jesus' answer to John is his answer to us. Look at the evidence and renew your faith!

This lesson will provide this reassurance to your students.

INTRODUCTION

A. THE ANATOMY OF DOUBT

There are two kinds of faith. The first is the acceptance of facts as being true. We might call this *intellectual* belief. The other kind of faith involves confidence in a person. It is the assurance we feel regarding a person that he or she is reliable and will not let us down. This is a matter of trust, which we might call *interpersonal* belief.

For example, a woman who meets a man and dates him for a while may have faith in the first sense but not in the second regarding him. She may be convinced that every fact he has told her about himself is true, that he has the job he says he has, that his family background is what he claims, and so on. But she may not trust him enough as a person to marry him. Even so, we may believe the facts of the Christian faith—that God exists, that he sent his Son to die on the cross, and that he raised him from the dead— and yet be unwilling to trust God personally, unwilling to put our lives in his hands.

The faith that leads to salvation is both intellectual and interpersonal. It is, first of all, acceptance of the facts of the good news of Jesus. But more than that, it is complete trust in Jesus, a trust that leads us to base our whole lives on him. We need to believe *that* certain things are true regarding Jesus, and we also need to believe *in* Jesus Christ as one who is a trustworthy person.

Our Christian faith can come under attack at either of these points, the intellectual or the interpersonal. The devil may try to persuade us that what we have believed simply isn't true, that we have been factually deceived. If this strategy doesn't work, he may try to lead us to mistrust God, to refuse to put our lives in his hands. Most people who doubt God don't doubt the facts of who he is or what he has done so much as they doubt his ability or willingness to take care of them; they are unwilling to trust him with their lives. Either kind of doubt, the intellectual or the interpersonal, can be fatal to our faith if it becomes a way of life.

B. LESSON BACKGROUND

Our quarter's study began last week with the introduction of John the Baptist. He preached of One who was coming to establish "the kingdom of heaven." Boldly

DEVOTIONAL READING:
JOHN 1:1-14
LESSON SCRIPTURE:
MATTHEW 11:2-15
PRINTED TEXT:
MATTHEW 11:2-15

LESSON AIMS

After participation in this lesson a student should:

1. Know the circumstances of John's arrest and imprisonment.

2. Understand why John began to have doubts about Jesus.

3. Recognize the signs that proved Jesus to be God's Messiah.

4. Know how to resolve doubts.

WHAT DO YOU THINK?

The lesson writer makes the point that faith that leads to salvation is more than belief of facts but is also belief in a person. James concurs, noting that "even the demons believe . . . and shudder" (James 2:19). What do you think leads a person to move beyond intellectual belief, accepting the facts, to interpersonal belief, trusting the Lord with one's life? What can you do to help a friend, relative, or neighbor to take that step?

KEY VERSE:

I will send my messenger ahead of you, who will prepare your way before you.
—Matthew 11:10

WHAT DO YOU THINK?

The lesson writer observes that doubt "can be fatal to our faith if it becomes a way of life." Does that suggest that brief periods of doubt, like John's, that do not become "a way of life" are not harmful? Why or why not?

Can good come from doubt? If so, how?

WHAT DO YOU THINK?

John the Baptist experienced "the dark night of the soul" while he was in prison. Questions (some would say doubt) arose in his mind as to whether Jesus was the Messiah. Regardless, he did the right thing: he sent trusted followers to Jesus to get straight, reliable answers to his questions.

What if Jesus had rebuked John for his doubt? Do you think John would have been brought back to faith? Would others have felt brave enough to raise questions later?

How should Christian leaders respond to doubts and questions raised by young people and new Christians in such a way that they both provide reliable answers and keep the door open to help with future doubts and questions? How can you tell the difference between an honest question and a skeptic's taunt? How should you respond to either?

OPTION

Thomas faced a similar "dark night" after the death of Jesus. Your students might enjoy and learn from a comparison of John and Thomas. Use the reproducible activity on page 142.

he called for all persons, even the arrogant and self-righteous religious leaders, to repent and to prepare to receive the Lord. In response to his forceful preaching, many of his hearers confessed their sins and were baptized. Jesus also came and was baptized by John.

Immediately Jesus was led into the wilderness, where he faced a period of temptation by the devil. Afterward Jesus embarked on his ministry.

The event recorded in our lesson text occurred more than a year later. John had continued preaching, but his ministry declined as Jesus' popularity grew, and John accepted that fact without jealousy (John 3:25-30). At some point, John was arrested and imprisoned for reproving Herod the tetrarch for the evils he had done, notably for taking the wife of his brother Philip (Luke 3:19, 20). This Herod, known as Herod Antipas, ruled the territories of Galilee and Perea, the areas where the ministries of both Jesus and John were, for the most part, conducted.

While Jesus was in the midst of his Galilean ministry, messengers came to him from John with an important question.

I. JOHN'S DOUBTS (MATTHEW 11:2-6)

A. HE QUESTIONED JESUS (VV. 2, 3)

2. When John heard in prison what Christ was doing, he sent his disciples.

The Jewish historian Josephus tells us that John was imprisoned in the fortress of Machaerus, near the eastern shore of the Dead Sea. Herod had a winter palace there. Even though John was in prison, he was not isolated from the outside world. Apparently he was allowed visitors, from whom he heard about Christ's ministry. He was permitted also to send messages by them, as we see in this verse.

3. . . . to ask him, "Are you the one who was to come, or should we expect someone else?"

John had previously seemed certain of who Jesus was. When Jesus came to John for baptism, John didn't want to baptize him because he knew Jesus was so much greater than he (Matthew 3:14). Furthermore, John had publicly identified Jesus (John 1:29). Why, then, did John seem to be expressing doubt concerning Jesus now?

The Bible doesn't give us a direct answer to this question, but several thoughts come to mind. First, John was a rugged person who had spent his entire life in the outdoors. For months, some say for six months or more, he had been cooped up in prison. His confinement and enforced inactivity may have had a debilitating effect on his spirit. Contributing to this, perhaps, was the fact that Jesus had made no move to free him. Second, it seems certain that John did not understand the program that would be developed by the Messiah. He knew that the Messiah was going to establish a kingdom of godly rule. He may have wondered, therefore, why Jesus had not announced himself as the Messiah and begun to seize the government from the hands of godless rulers. From the reports John had received, Jesus was conducting a simple ministry of preaching and healing. John's resulting disappointment and perplexity, therefore, may have prompted his question.

B. HE RECEIVED AN ANSWER (VV. 4-6)

4. Jesus replied, "Go back and report to John what you hear and see:

The best cure for doubt is fact. Jesus didn't rebuke John, nor did he ask, "Why don't you trust me?" Instead, he gently urged John to weigh again the facts that he already knew. He had heard of Jesus' miracles, and now Jesus instructed John's disciples to report to their teacher about the miracles they themselves were witnessing (see Luke 7:20-22). These were supernatural works and provided undeniable evidence that he whom John had announced was indeed "the Son of God" (John 1:34).

5. "The blind receive sight, the lame walk, those who have leprosy are cured, the deaf hear, the dead are raised, and the good news is preached to the poor.

The prophet Isaiah spoke of a time when God would open blind people's eyes and unstop deaf ears, when a lame person would "leap like a deer, and the mute tongue shout for joy" (Isaiah 35:5, 6).

In another place Isaiah spoke of the Messiah, who would be "anointed . . . to preach good news to the poor. . . . to bind up the brokenhearted, to proclaim freedom for the captives and release from darkness for the prisoners" (Isaiah 61:1, 2). Through his preaching and miraculous healing, Jesus was doing what Isaiah said the Messiah would do. If John would simply believe the evidence his representatives brought back to him, he would have no doubt at all that Jesus really was "the one who was to come."

6. "Blessed is the man who does not fall away on account of me."

Here Jesus came as close as he ever did to correcting John, but notice the Master's gentleness and the positive nature of his words. Instead of scolding, he pronounced a blessing on John or anyone else who would not *fall away* because of him.

One might fall away if Jesus did not conduct his plan of redemption as he or she saw fit. Some fell away because Jesus saw through their hypocrisy and condemned their sins. Others, who desired a worldly Messiah, fell away because Jesus did not raise an army to overthrow the Gentile oppressors. The Messianic kingdom was spiritual in nature, and Jesus' ministry was being conducted according to the will of his heavenly Father. Blessing would come to all who trusted Jesus, even through what they regarded as delay and disappointment. The same promise of blessing comes to all today who hold on to faith in Jesus and follow him rather than to follow their own concept of the kingdom.

GOING TO THE SOURCE

The Sacramento River irrigates the Central Valley of California. Beginning just below Mount Shasta in northern California, it winds its way 382 miles to the delta, where it joins with the San Joaquin River, and both then flow into the north arm of San Francisco Bay. Along the way it supplies water to the tremendous farm lands that produce food for millions of people all across America.

One of the river's amazing features is the huge, flowing spring from which it arises. Almost immediately the river is born, and animal and bird life are instant users of its life-sustaining water. Until a person goes and sees that spring, it is hard to believe that a river could begin so suddenly and in just a few feet start to fulfill the function of feeding and blessing so many.

So it is with Jesus. John wondered whether he was truly the source of life come into the world. When John sent his disciples to ask, Jesus made no claims; he simply told them to tell John of his works of healing and of his preaching of the "good news."

Here is the test of reality. One may doubt, but the results of blessing and truth reveal the power of the source. Jesus, who is the water of life, had God's power from the moment he began his ministry. He was able to do the works of God because he was God in human form. He was the Source. —W. P.

II. JOHN'S CHARACTER (MATTHEW 11:7-11)

A. HE WAS STRONG (VV. 7, 8)

7. As John's disciples were leaving, Jesus began to speak to the crowd about John: "What did you go out into the desert to see? A reed swayed by the wind?

Visual 2 of the visuals packet draws attention to John the Baptist, "My Messenger" of Matthew 11:7-10.

WHAT DO YOU THINK?

Jesus affirmed that John had faithfully fulfilled his mission of preparing the people to receive him. He paid John the highest compliment possible: "Among those born of women there has not risen anyone greater than John the Baptist" (Matthew 11:11). Of significance to Christians today is this "tag line" Jesus added to the compliment of John: "yet he who is least in the kingdom of heaven is greater than he."

What do you think he meant, that the least in the kingdom of heaven is greater than John? Is that automatic, or does one have to maintain a certain standard to be so great? If so, what? Is the blessing of verse 6—"Blessed is the man who does not fall away on account of me"—related? If so, how?

As the disciples of John left Jesus to return to their imprisoned teacher, Jesus began to speak to the crowds surrounding him. Among his hearers were some who had been disciples of John the Baptist. Perhaps they were inclined to think the less of John because of the question John sent.

By means of three questions directed to these in the crowd, Jesus issued a stirring tribute to John. First, when they went out to hear John speak, did they expect to see a weakling, like a *reed swayed by the wind?* Of course not! John was a strong, bold proclaimer of God's word. Then let them not interpret any doubt in John's question as an indication of weakness.

8. "If not, what did you go out to see? A man dressed in fine clothes? No, those who wear fine clothes are in kings' palaces.

More than that, John did not seek luxury or comfort. Nor did he wear *fine clothes,* such as was worn by royalty. He lived in the outdoors, and the rough clothing he wore indicated it. He was a plain-speaking man of God, whose only concern was to tell people what God wanted them to know, regardless of his own comfort or even his own safety.

B. HE WAS A PROPHET (V. 9)

9. "Then what did you go out to see? A prophet? Yes, I tell you, and more than a prophet.

Having heard of John's bold preaching by the Jordan River, the people had thronged to see and hear him. Was it because they suspected he was a prophet? Whatever their expectations that drew the people to him, all came to conclude that he was indeed a prophet (see Matthew 21:26). With this opinion Jesus concurred, but added that John was even more.

C. HE WAS A MESSENGER (V. 10)

10. "This is the one about whom it is written:
"'I will send my messenger ahead of you,
who will prepare your way before you.'

This explains what Jesus meant by "more than a prophet." He referred to Malachi 3:1, and identified John as the one foretold there, the special *messenger* who would prepare the way for God's chosen One. John did this by calling the nation to repentance and urging all to make the Messiah's paths straight so he could enter their hearts and lives.

MY MESSENGER

In one of her poems, Amy Carson Phillips describes God working in creation with the names "Hack" and "Hew." Hack carved out the mountains, scooped out the seas, and dug the great valleys. These were the frames for the creative artistry of Hew. Hew gave song to the birds and the colors to dawn and sunset. He caused the rose to bloom, and made all creation beautiful. The poet called Hack and Hew the "Sons of God." By them God made the world ready for the creation of man.

In the Gospels, John the Baptist was God's messenger to prepare the way for Messiah's coming. John was "Hack," the rugged instrument of God who made the road straight and the call for repentance clear. Our Lord honored John for his tough message and his faithfulness as the preparer for Jesus' own ministry that brought healing to those needing his touch of love and grace.

The world today still needs to hear the clarion call of those who will turn people's hearts to the Lord, for he alone can restore the wholeness that all were created to have. God used John to begin the restoration that Christ would complete. He can use us also to bring people to the cross, where they can find forgiveness and eternal life.

—W. P.

D. HE WAS GREAT (V. 11)

11. "I tell you the truth: Among those born of women there has not risen anyone greater than John the Baptist; yet he who is least in the kingdom of heaven is greater than he.

Because of John's courage and faithfulness in fulfilling his mission, Jesus gave high praise to him. Up to this time, Jesus said, no human being, no one *among them that are born of women,* was greater than John. This tribute gave reassurance to any who might be inclined to think ill of John for his doubt. From there, Jesus moved on to an important truth regarding the *kingdom of heaven* that John could only announce, and that is that the lowliest citizen of that kingdom has higher standing than John. By saying this, Jesus wasn't putting John down. Instead, Jesus emphasized as strongly as he could what wonderful blessings would be bestowed on those in God's kingdom that was being established.

III. JOHN'S MISSION (MATTHEW 11:12-15)

A. HE PROCLAIMED THE KINGDOM (V. 12)

12. "From the days of John the Baptist until now, the kingdom of heaven has been forcefully advancing, and forceful men lay hold of it.

Bible translators and commentators have proposed differing views of the meaning of this verse. The reading here leads us to understand Jesus to be saying that God's kingdom is a powerful, world-changing force, whose coming shakes things up. More than an academic philosophy or a gentle appeal to people to live better, the gospel causes drastic changes in the way people think, talk, and behave. Furthermore, halfhearted, fainthearted people aren't quickly drawn to it. Only the brave, the ones who seek God with their whole hearts, will have the courage to embrace the kingdom message. It takes "forceful" people to follow Jesus. But where our version says that *the kingdom of heaven has been forcefully advancing,* the King James has, "the kingdom of heaven suffereth violence." In place of *forceful men lay hold of it,* that version has "the violent take it by force." If this translation is correct, Jesus meant that as soon as John the Baptist appeared with his dramatic announcement concerning the coming kingdom, and right on up to the time Jesus spoke, people attacked what God was trying to do in the world. Examples may be seen in Herod's seizure and imprisonment of John, the opposition of the Jewish religious establishment to Jesus, and the attempts of the Zealots, who advocated the violent overthrow of Rome, to turn Jesus' power and popularity to the accomplishment of their purposes (see John 6:15).

Would these violent people succeed? Can anyone take God's kingdom by brute force? Of course not. *"The violent take it by force"* doesn't necessarily mean that anyone can seize God's kingdom. Perhaps the *Good News Bible* has captured the meaning in its translation, "violent men *try to seize it."* The idea is that people who try to pervert God's plan, to hammer God's kingdom into a movement that will serve their own ends, will not succeed.

It is difficult to choose between these two ways of understanding the verse, because both of them have merit.

B. HE BEGAN A NEW ERA (V. 13)

13. "For all the Prophets and the Law prophesied until John.

All the Prophets and the Law prophesied. The whole Old Testament, even the parts that we call law or history or poetry, as well as the portion that we identify as prophecy, looked forward to the coming of God's glorious kingdom.

WHAT DO YOU THINK?

Of the two interpretations given for verse 12, which do you think is more in keeping with what Jesus was trying to say? Why do you think so? What specific application would you draw from your understanding of this verse?

WHAT DO YOU THINK?

Jesus and John both preached repentance—change. But many find change difficult. Pride may be a barrier; they cannot admit they have a need to change. Fear of the unknown and the comfort of the known can also erect barriers. We have our "comfort zones," and most persons prefer to stay in them. The effort (and pain) that may be involved may also be a barrier to change.

How can the church provide help in removing these barriers from persons, within and without the church, to make appropriate changes in their lives? What can you do to overcome such barriers? To help someone else overcome them?

PRAYER

Father in Heaven, we confess that we haven't always trusted you as we should. Grant us assurance of your love and concern for us, and enable us to trust you enough to base our whole lives on your promises. We want to be people of faith, not doubters. Through Christ our Lord we pray, Amen.

THOUGHT TO REMEMBER

Jesus' words and works verify that he is the Christ.

DAILY BIBLE READINGS

Until John. John the Baptist's ministry marked a turning point in God's plan for the world. As the forerunner of Christ and the one who announced that "the kingdom of heaven is near" (Matthew 3:2), John marked the change from the old agreement between God and his people, the covenant with Israel, to the new agreement sealed with Jesus' blood (Matthew 26:28). John's ministry was the hinge point upon which the new era turned.

C. HE FULFILLED PROPHECY (vv. 14, 15)

14. "And if you are willing to accept it, he is the Elijah who was to come.

More than four hundred years earlier, the prophet Malachi promised that God would send the prophet Elijah "before the coming of the great and dreadful day of the Lord" (Malachi 4:5). This is not to say that God would reincarnate Elijah. The meaning is clarified by the words of the angel Gabriel spoken to Zechariah, the father of John the Baptist, when the angel told Zechariah that he and his barren wife would have a son. The son to be born would go before the Lord "in the spirit and power of Elijah" (Luke 1:17). Here Jesus corroborates the angel's message, while affirming that the prophecy of Malachi was fulfilled in John the Baptist. If Jesus' hearers would *accept it,* that is, if they had spiritual eyes to see what God was doing at this point, they would realize that John fulfilled Malachi's prophecy.

15. "He who has ears, let him hear."

John's question led Jesus into a discussion concerning this great man and his place in God's overall plan. John's mission, prophesied centuries earlier, was to announce the coming of the One who would bring redemption to the world. Jesus pronounced that John had done his job well, thus indicating that he, Jesus, was the one of whom John spoke. With the statement in this verse Jesus implied that God had given all the ability to understand these things, and that the wise would act on their understanding.

CONCLUSION

A. LEARNING FROM JOHN

We have seen in this lesson that John the Baptist, great man though he was, came to a period in his life when questions were raised in his mind concerning Jesus. And from John we learn a valuable lesson; namely, when questions or doubts trouble us, we must work at resolving them. If one begins to doubt God, it is too easy not to do anything to settle those doubts, simply to go along in an indifferent manner until doubt solidifies into a permanent viewpoint. Equally, if not more important, is what we do to resolve our questions. Notice: John had questions about Jesus, so he went directly to Jesus for answers. So must we. If we have questions about the Christian life or about God's care for his people, let us go to him in prayer and study his Word anew. It may be that our doubts are the result of faulty understanding of God's promises.

Another valuable lesson we learn from John's experience is that we who belong to God's kingdom rate highly with him. Even though we stand in awe before a man like John, when we hear Jesus' words, "He who is least in the kingdom of heaven is greater than he" (v. 11), we can't help but be overwhelmed by the magnitude of what God has done for us through his Son.

B. LESSONS FOR LIFE

Where does John's story leave us, then? It should move us to gratitude toward God for what he has done for us. It should also help us with the doubts that may come to us from time to time, making us determined to resolve them before they poison our relationship with Christ.

Discovery Learning

*This page contains an alternate lesson plan emphasizing learning activities. Classes
desiring such student involvement will find these suggestions helpful. The next page
is a reproducible activity page to further enhance discovery learning.*

LEARNING GOALS

After this session, class members will be able to:

1. Describe how Jesus responded to John the Baptist's question about his Messiahship.

2. Identify circumstances that may influence people to doubt their belief in Jesus as Savior.

3. List actions to take when faith is challenged by doubt.

INTO THE LESSON

As the class time begins, ask class members to assemble themselves in groups of four or five. To half of the groups assign the first activity below; assign the second activity to the rest of the groups. For the first activity, bring several newspapers for the students' use.

1. Those doing this activity are to scan the newspapers to find articles about situations in which people showed trust or faith. A member from each group should prepare to share one or two of the best illustrations of trust, and the role trust played in the situation.

2. Have groups work to compile a list of everyday actions or events that require trust or faith. You may need to help get their thinking started by sharing one or two examples (such as, when driving a car, we trust that the car will work and that the other drivers will stay on their side of the road).

Give the groups five to seven minutes to work, and then ask for a report from each group.

Make the transition to Bible study by sharing insight from the lesson introduction ("The Anatomy of Doubt," page 135). Point out that today's lesson focuses on John the Baptist. We will consider the question he raised about Jesus, and how Jesus reassured John and affirmed John's message and role as the forerunner of Christ.

INTO THE WORD

Begin the Bible study by having a class member read the Scripture text aloud to the class. Then use the following questions to develop class discussion:

1. Verse 2 indicates that John the Baptist was in prison. Why was he there? (See the lesson background; see also Mark 6:17-20.)

2. At Jesus' baptism, John was certain that Jesus was the Messiah (John 1:29-34). Why, then, did John ask the question recorded in verse 3? (See lesson notes on verse 3. John had been in prison for months, and Jesus had not

made any attempt to rescue him. Perhaps this had something to do with John's question. Also, John, like many others, may have been expecting the Messiah to be the strong leader of a political kingdom, not a meek, mild, servant king.)

3. Have class members read aloud the following passages: Isaiah 29:18-21; 35:4-6; 61:1-3. Based on these prophecies, what might have been some of John's expectations of Jesus as the Messiah? What expectations was he meeting? What expectations was he not meeting?

4. What six proofs of his messiahship did Jesus give John's disciples? (See verses 4-6. Luke 7:20, 21 indicates that Jesus performed these miracles *after* John's disciples had posed the question to him; therefore, they would have witnessed these miracles of Jesus.) Why do you think Jesus answered John's question with evidence, rather than specifically with a "yes"?

5. While Jesus affirmed that John was indeed a great man, he said that the "least" in the kingdom of Heaven is greater than John. How are we "greater" than John?

6. What are some examples of how Jesus' kingdom has been "forcefully advancing"? (See the comments for verse 12.) Encourage your students to think about times they have had to be bold for the sake of the kingdom.

OPTION

Have your students complete the reproducible activity, "Thomas and John the Doubters" on the next page. You may photocopy the page for each student to have a copy.

INTO LIFE

Have your class members return to the small groups in which they worked at the beginning of the class. Give each group a copy of the following assignments. Plan your lesson to allow about ten minutes for discussion.

1. The Scripture text does not indicate that Jesus criticized John for asking his question. What circumstances in life may cause a person today to question God?

2. In those times of questioning, how can a person find renewal of faith and hope?

3. The event we have studied shows us that even leaders need encouragement. List ways you can be of encouragement to the church leaders.

Challenge each class member to select one way he or she can encourage a church leader and then offer that encouragement in the next week.

Thomas and John the Doubters

Answer the following questions by reading the Scriptures and filling in the chart.
1. How did the person view his relationship with Jesus?
2. For what proof did he ask?
3. What did Jesus tell him to do?
4. How did Jesus comfort him?
5. How did he express faith in Jesus?

JOHN THE BAPTIST	THOMAS THE DISCIPLE
1. Matthew 3:13, 14	John 11:7, 8, 16
2. Matthew 11:2, 3	John 20:24, 25
3. Matthew 11:4-6	John 20:26, 27
4. Matthew 11:7-11	John 20:29
5. John 1:29	John 20:28

I'll Be an Encourager

Think of someone who could use some encouragement. Could you minister to this person?

Who? _____

When? _____

How? _____

Look up the following Scriptures. Circle one that could help you encourage the person's whose name you wrote.

John 20:29   Matthew 21:21, 22   Romans 8   Ephesians 2:1-10

JESUS IS BORN

LESSON 3

WHY TEACH THIS LESSON?

Every year the stores begin selling Christmas a little earlier. In the midst of this secularized and commercialized event, many become depressed. Perhaps they are alone and lonely. Perhaps they are sensitive to the plight of the poor, the homeless, the victims of war and famine. How can anyone have parties when such suffering goes on.

This lesson reminds us that the reason for our joy is that there is Someone who sees the suffering. That's what Christmas is all about. Immanuel! God with us! With the homeless, with the lonely, with the victims. This lesson reminds us of the true message of Christmas—a message we must share as well as celebrate!

INTRODUCTION

A. THE MIRACLE OF LIFE

"I believe in miracles," Barry said. "Every time I see a sunset, or hear a newborn baby cry, every time I look into the night sky and see the stars, I realize that all of life is a miracle." Do you agree that we see miracles all around us in nature and in human life? Or is a miracle something else?

Of course, in one sense we have to agree with Barry. All the things God has created are wonders, things that cause us to marvel. One of the Hebrew words translated "miracle" in the Old Testament emphasizes this thought. But the miracles of the Bible are to be understood in a more restricted sense. It is obvious that they are God's special actions that lie outside the normal course of events.

C. S. Lewis, the well-known Christian writer of this century, describes a miracle in this narrower meaning of the word. He defines it as a new event that God puts into the normal chain of cause and effect that makes up our world. Regular patterns of events, involving both the inanimate and animate, may be observed in our world: the sun rises and sets daily, the seasons change in an unvarying manner, the crops go through their appointed growing cycle, and all living creatures go through their life cycles, too. One event causes another, which causes the next, which causes the next, and so on. It is only right for us to see God's hand in these events and to thank him for the beauties and bounties of nature, as well as the joys of human life, because all these flow out of God's original creative act. Because he set these events in motion, they display his glory. But now and again, for a special purpose at a special time, God has "slipped in" an event that we can't account for by the natural laws of cause and effect: a sea that parted, someone who walked on water, someone who rose from the dead. These events are signs, evidence, of a power that is able to control, indeed override, the forces we observe in nature. These meanings also are found in words translated "miracle" in the Bible.

What do you think of Barry's statement? Is he wrong, then, to call all of life a miracle? Of course not, because everything God has provided produces wonder in our hearts. But in a more technical sense, only certain events properly may be called miracles because they supersede the normal course of events as a result of God's direct intervention in his world.

DEVOTIONAL READING:
ISAIAH 9:2-7
LESSON SCRIPTURE:
MATTHEW 1
PRINTED TEXT:
MATTHEW 1:18-25

Dec
18

LESSON AIMS

After participation in this lesson a student should:

1. Be able to tell why belief in the virgin birth of Christ is vital to the Christian faith.

2. Recognize the importance of predictive prophecy.

3. Believe that Jesus is the Son of God and our Savior.

4. Commit his or her life to Jesus as Lord.

KEY VERSE:

The virgin will be with child and will give birth to a son, and will call him Immanuel.
—Isaiah 7:14

LESSON 3 NOTES

HOW TO SAY IT

Almah (Hebrew). *Al-MAH.*
Babylonian. Bab-uh-LOW-nee-un.
Jehoshua. Je-HOSH-u-a.
Jeshua. JESH-yoo-uh.
Parthenos (Greek). *Par-THEN-ahss (th as in thin).*
Septuagint. Sep-TOO-uh-jint.

WHAT DO YOU THINK?

Because unfaithfulness carried a severe social stigma, Joseph certainly would have felt humiliated by Mary's apparent misconduct. At first he probably would have felt resentment and anger—he knew he was not the father of the child to be born. Surely he would have been disappointed with Mary. Yet, even with these feelings, he did not feel vindictive or vengeful. He cared for her and cared about what would happen to her. Still, her "sin" could not be ignored.

How does a person develop such a sensitivity? How can one take a stand against sin without being vindictive against the people involved? In what areas do you think this balance is most needed today? Why?

Could you be as gracious to a person guilty of gross sin, as Mary appeared to be, especially when you yourself had been wronged in the process? Why or why not?

This lesson deals with Jesus' birth. The Bible plainly states that Jesus was born of a virgin, an event that qualifies as a miracle by any standard. Though one may call the birth of a baby in 1994 a miracle in the larger sense, Jesus' birth was a miracle in a special sense, because God's own Son came into the world without the involvement of a human father.

The virgin birth of Jesus plays an essential role in our understanding of who he is. It marks him as a human being, yet one who is more than human; it identifies him as God's own Son, one who is qualified to be our Savior.

B. LESSON BACKGROUND

In beginning his account of the life of Jesus, Matthew traces Jesus' human ancestry starting with Abraham, from whom sprang the Jewish race. The first seventeen verses of chapter 1 deal with this genealogy.

Matthew presents Jesus' ancestors in three groups, corresponding to three periods of Israel's history. The first group includes those from Abraham to David, the second group those from David to the Babylonian captivity, and the third group those from the captivity to Jesus. Those named in the first group were patriarchs, those of the second were kings, and those of the third were citizens. By identifying Jesus as a descendant of Abraham, Matthew shows that Jesus was a member of God's covenant people. As a descendant of David, Jesus was in the royal line and was qualified to rule over God's people. Mention of the Babylonian captivity calls to mind the fact that Jesus' purpose in coming was to release his people—all people who would accept him—from eternal captivity to sin.

Without further introduction, Matthew begins to relate the miraculous birth of Jesus, the one whose coming would change the whole world forever.

I. THE SITUATION (MATTHEW 1:18, 19)

A. MARY'S PREGNANCY (v. 18)

18. This is how the birth of Jesus Christ came about: His mother Mary was pledged to be married to Joseph, but before they came together, she was found to be with child through the Holy Spirit.

Matthew begins the account of Jesus' birth without any preliminary remarks. We learn that Jesus' mother, Mary, was *pledged to be married* to a man named Joseph. Such a pledge in that day meant more than an engagement means today. It was a publicly recognized commitment to marry, a solemn contract that could be set aside only by an explicit, written statement such as was used in the divorce of a married person. This explains why Matthew refers to Joseph and Mary as husband and wife as he relates this narrative (see verses 19 and 20). *Before they came together.* Although this couple could be called husband and wife, Matthew is very clear in stating that they were not living together; they had not yet experienced the intimacies reserved for those who are living in matrimony. It was while Joseph and Mary were pledged to one another that Mary was *found to be with child through the Holy Spirit.* Writing many years after this event, Matthew could give the identification given here. But, at the time, Joseph knew only that his betrothed was carrying a child that was not his. Luke 1:26-38 records the angel's announcement of this miraculous conception.

B. JOSEPH'S RESPONSE (v. 19)

19. Because Joseph her husband was a righteous man and did not want to expose her to public disgrace, he had in mind to divorce her quietly.

Did Mary tell Joseph of the angel's visit and announcement? If so, how did he react to it? We are not told. Judging from the verse before us, Joseph believed what was most natural to believe: that Mary had been unfaithful to him and was about to bear a child by another man.

Joseph was *a righteous man,* that is, one who obeyed the law of Moses. If it could be proved that Mary had willingly engaged in fornication, punishment called for by the law might be administered. This would require a court trial and would involve an investigation into Mary's conduct. Joseph, however, did not want *to expose her to public disgrace.* These, then, were the options before Joseph. He could be vindictive and push for the law to take its course, or he could let the matter drop as quietly as possible and simply dissolve the marriage before it even began. Joseph *had a mind to divorce her quietly.* Being a righteous man, Joseph wanted to do what was right; but his justice was not the type that considers only the letter of the law. It was tempered with mercy and compassion. He loved Mary, and he could not expose her to shame and punishment. But neither could he proceed with the marriage. He decided, therefore, to terminate their relationship quietly.

II. THE VISION (MATTHEW 1:20, 21)

A. GOD'S INTERVENTION (v. 20)

20. But after he had considered this, an angel of the Lord appeared to him in a dream and said, "Joseph son of David, do not be afraid to take Mary home as your wife, because what is conceived in her is from the Holy Spirit.

After he had considered this. How many heartbreaking, sleepless nights of reflection both Joseph and Mary experienced is not indicated. Finally Joseph came to the decision mentioned in verse 19, and even now he must have dreaded the thought of informing his beloved of it. Perhaps he was in the throes of deciding how to do that when God brought an end to his anguish. *An angel of the Lord.* It was the angel Gabriel who had come to Mary some months before with the announcement that she would give birth to a son, but the angel who spoke to Joseph is not named.

Son of David. Though an obscure carpenter in a Galilean town, Joseph was a descendant of David, a member of the royal line. Predictions in the Old Testament were clear that the Christ would be of the seed of David. Did the angel's form of address cause Joseph to think that his wife's son could possibly be the Christ? If not, what the angel said next certainly could have. Joseph was not to be afraid of marrying his betrothed wife. She had done nothing wrong. The power of God had overshadowed her (Luke 1:35), so that that which was conceived in her was of the Holy Spirit. Mary's pregnancy did not come about in the normal manner. The conception was miraculous.

B. GOD'S PROMISE (v. 21)

21. "She will give birth to a son, and you are to give him the name Jesus, because he will save his people from their sins."

As the legal father, Joseph would name Mary's Son; but he would not be free to choose the name. The angel told him that he was to name the child *Jesus.* This name is the Greek equivalent of the Hebrew name *Joshua,* which also appears in the Bible as *Jehoshua* or *Jeshua.* This name contains the Hebrew name for the God of Israel, and the whole name means "Jehovah is salvation."

Mary's child would bear a name that described his role as Savior: *he shall save his people from their sins.* In the full light of New Testament revelation, it is clear that God didn't intend to restrict this promise to any one people. *His people* are all the people of the world who will accept Jesus. Whosoever comes to him will be saved from the eternal consequences of the wrongs they have done.

Visual 3 of the visuals packet illustrates Joseph's dream (Matthew 1:20, 21). It also previews events to be studied in future lessons in this quarter.

WHAT DO YOU THINK?

The name Jesus is the Greek equivalent of the Hebrew Joshua, which means "Jehovah is salvation," and Jesus would "save his people from their sins." The child would also be called Immanuel, meaning "God with us."

Do you think names are still important to people today? Why or why not? Do you think giving a child a name with special meaning, and them reminding the child throughout childhood of that special meaning, will motivate the child to "live up to" the name, or would it put undue pressure on the child? Why?

OPTION

The reproducible activity on page 150, "What's in a Name?" will enable your students to explore the significance of names in Scripture.

Answers for reproducible chart, page 150:
1. father of many nations
2. Christ/Messiah
3. Christians
4. God with us
5. Jesus

WHAT DO YOU THINK?

Matthew frequently calls attention to the prophecies regarding Jesus. How important is predictive prophecy to you? How much does it strengthen your faith to know that hundreds—even thousands—of years in advance, God already knew what would happen and directed events to ensure that they occurred just as he said they would? How might you use prophecy to convince a friend in the truth of Scripture and the fact that Jesus is truly God's Son?

WHAT DO YOU THINK?

There are those who claim Mary was not a virgin, but had had relations with Joseph or some other man (and suggestions of who vary widely) to become pregnant with Jesus. The Hebrew word used in Isaiah 7:14 is cited as evidence, for it may be a virgin or it may be just a "young woman." But Matthew and Luke are very clear about her virginity. (Why so much is made of one word in the Old Testament and the overwhelming evidence of the New is dismissed as faulty is never explained!)

How would you explain the truth and the significance of the virgin birth to a skeptical neighbor?

III. THE PROPHECY (MATTHEW 1:22, 23)

A. MATTHEW'S COMMENT (V. 22)

22. All this took place to fulfill what the Lord had said through the prophet:

Jesus' divine conception wasn't a last-minute decision on God's part. He had planned it long ago and had revealed it through one of his ancient spokesmen, *the prophet* Isaiah.

This is the first of ten times in his Gospel that Matthew called attention to the fact that an event he was reporting was the fulfillment of prophecy. (The other places are 2:15, 17, 23; 4:14; 8:17; 12:17; 13:35; 21:4, and 27:9). In each of these ten instances he said, "Now all this happened in order that the word of the prophet might be fulfilled," or words to that effect. This suggests that the people to whom this Gospel account was written were Jewish Christians, who would have been very familiar with the Old Testament and the prophecies it contained.

Several values of predictive prophecy may be noted. First, such prophesies underscore the importance of the events that came to pass in time, showing that those events were part of a plan; second, they enabled God's people to be prepared for those events when they occurred; and third, they give assurance that the events predicted were of God, for the passing of many centuries between prophecy and fulfillment rules out the possibility of human origin for them.

B. ISAIAH'S PREDICTION (V. 23)

23. "The virgin will be with child and will give birth to a son, and they will call him Immanuel"—which means, "God with us."

This statement quoted by Matthew was part of a prediction spoken by the prophet Isaiah in the eighth century B. C., at a time when the land of Judah was in danger of invasion by Israel and Syria. The prophecy was fulfilled within a few years, except the part that Matthew quotes.

The virgin will be with child. There is no doubt that Matthew, here, and Luke in his Gospel, make it very clear that Mary was a virgin before and after Jesus was conceived. He was the result of God's visitation of Mary through the Holy Spirit.

The passage in Isaiah, in the original Hebrew, contains the word *almah,* which, according to many capable scholars, may be translated "young woman." Thus it does not necessarily mean "virgin," but may properly be so used, depending upon the circumstances. However, the Greek translation of the Old Testament, known as the Septuagint, was the "Bible" most in use in the time before Jesus' birth, and in this translation the word *almah* is translated as *parthenos,* which means "virgin." Thus, from at least as early as the middle of the third century B. C., the date generally accepted for the translation of the Septuagint, the prophecy had been understood to say that a *virgin* would conceive. Matthew, who wrote under the inspiration of the Holy Spirit, also uses the term *parthenos* where the prophecy in Isaiah has *almah.* Thus we are led to understand the meaning of Isaiah's prophecy of this miraculous event centuries earlier. The Bible must be allowed to interpret itself. The same Holy Spirit who moved Isaiah to speak also spoke through Matthew, and the message was the same: this special child was conceived of a virgin.

They will call him Immanuel. This does not seem to have been literally applied to Jesus as a name by which he is called in the Gospels. However, the whole emphasis of the New Testament is focused on the fact that God did become man and came to be "with us" in Jesus. In his teaching and ministry Jesus would reveal his true nature. It would be very clear that in him God was indeed with mankind.

CHILD OF PROMISE

Look through a Bible dictionary and you will see that the names given to persons mentioned in the Bible had significance. They were not just letters put together to form a word (name) that was pleasant-sounding. The names were a word, or a combination of words, that had a meaning. Some of the name choices are explained for us in the biblical text. For example, Abram's name was changed to *Abraham* ("father of a multitude") because of God's promise that he would have great progeny. One Joses was given the name *Barnabas* ("son of consolation") because of encouragement he gave the church in Jerusalem.

The angel who told Joseph in a dream that the child conceived in Mary was of the Holy Spirit also instructed him what to name the child. *Immanuel* means "God with us," and *Jesus* means "Savior." This holy child's person and work were indicated by his names. He was the promised Messiah sent from God. His names revealed his mission among us.

We might do well to give our children names indicating value and virtue, in hopes that they might try to live up to them. Regardless, in Jesus, all believers wear the name *Christian.* Are you living up to the meaning of that name?   —W. P.

Jesus is identified in Scripture as the Son of God and the Son of man, titles that he alone deserves. The fact that he was born without a human father shows him to be Son of God in a unique sense. The fact that he was born of a woman shows him to be Son of man, a human being like the rest of us. It is difficult for us to understand how one person could be fully God and fully human. But this was a miracle, and we are not called upon to understand it, only to believe. Only thus can we receive the eternal blessing Immanuel came to bestow.

IV. THE BIRTH (MATTHEW 1:24, 25)

A. JOSEPH'S OBEDIENCE (V. 24)

24. When Joseph woke up, he did what the angel of the Lord had commanded him and took Mary home as his wife.

We can only imagine Joseph's thoughts when he awoke: to know that Mary's character was vindicated. Though we are not told what he thought, we know what he did—he obeyed the angel's order and brought Mary into his home. Thus he gave Mary the protection and social standing that was necessary for God's Son to be brought into the world. Joseph's quiet obedience serves as a model for many of us, whose roles in the church and in the world may not be very noticeable but are still important to the accomplishing of God's purposes.

B. JESUS' BIRTH (V. 25)

25. But he had no union with her until she gave birth to a son. And he gave him the name Jesus.

He had no union with her. Here Matthew indicates that Mary remained a virgin *until* she gave birth to Jesus. The natural understanding of this expression is that *after* the birth of Jesus, the relationship of Joseph and Mary was that of a normal married couple.

In Luke 1:31 we read that Mary was to call her Son's name "Jesus." In the verse before us we are told that Joseph did as the angel commanded (v. 21) and bestowed that name on her Son. So they acted in harmony in giving the child the specified name, which indicated that in him the salvation of Jehovah would be brought to mankind.

FOLLOWING ORDERS

The mountain gorge looked deep and foreboding, the rushing stream, far below, frightening. All the exhilaration of climbing the mountain trail evaporated as the

WHAT DO YOU THINK?

Mary and Joseph obeyed the Lord to the letter and without hesitation. In this they become an example worthy of our imitation today. Of course, each of them was visited by an angel to reassure them they were on the right track!

How can we today act with the same conviction and unswerving devotion? How do you maintain your own commitment to the Lord in spite of difficulty and opposition?

PRAYER

O Lord our God, for your faithfulness in fulfilling your promise of old to come and dwell among us, we praise you. For Christ Jesus, who relinquished his heavenly glory and became one with us that he might bring us to you, we are truly grateful. May our gratitude be seen in our obedience to all he has commanded us. Amen.

THOUGHT TO REMEMBER

"You are to give him the name Jesus, because he will save his people from their sins" (Matthew 1:21).

DAILY BIBLE READINGS

Monday, Dec. 12—The Darkness Becomes Light (Isaiah 9:2-7)

Tuesday, Dec. 13—The Salvation of God Is Coming (Isaiah 52:1-10)

Wednesday, Dec. 14—The Angels' Message About Jesus (Matthew 1:18-25)

Thursday, Dec. 15—The Birth of Jesus (Luke 2:1-7)

Friday, Dec. 16—Praise From Angels and Shepherds (Luke 2:8-20)

Saturday, Dec. 17—Jesus' Presentation in the Temple (Luke 2:21-35)

Sunday, Dec. 18—Anna Gives Thanks for Jesus (Luke 2:36-40)

group of boys came to the narrow path that hugged the mountainside above the roaring river.

Clifton, the trail leader, walked slowly ahead in the sight of the boys until he reached a wider, safer part of the path. Then he invited the boys to do as he had done, one by one. Soon all but Gene had made it across. Gene couldn't move—he hugged the cliff wall and, in fright, stared down at the stream. Clifton walked carefully back to him, took his hand, and said, "Gene, I'll hold on to you. Don't look down at the river. We'll move just one step at a time. Hang on! Do exactly what I tell you to do."

The fearful boy inched along the path, leaning into the cliff wall, and, with Clifton's help, safely negotiated the dangerous part of the trail.

Clifton let go of his hand, patted his shoulder, and said, "I knew you could do it!"

Gene's reply was, "I couldn't do it alone, but I knew you wouldn't ask me to do it if you thought I would fall."

Joseph faced a problem he did not know how to solve. The victory came when he abandoned his fears and did exactly what he was told to do. The Lord will guide us through life by his Word if we will let him.

—W. P.

CONCLUSION

A. HE WILL SAVE HIS PEOPLE

We sometimes sing a song that goes like this: "Jesus, Jesus, Jesus—there's just something about that name." There certainly is "something about that name." It means "Savior," and it means he has come to rescue us from the penalty of the wrongs we have done and the power of those wrongs to corrupt our lives.

"You are to give him the name Jesus," the angel instructed Joseph, "because he will save his people from their sins." We who have put our trust in Jesus, who obey him with our whole hearts and look for nothing better in life than to be like him, know that this is true. We have experienced in our own lives God's saving power through Jesus Christ his Son. Did the angel say, "He will save his people"? We can say, "He *has* saved his people, and *we* are those people!"

This is a message worth proclaiming. The message of Jesus isn't primarily one of judgment, though judgment has a part in it. First and foremost it is the good news that God has come to the aid of the people he made, that he hasn't left them to suffer the consequences of the evil in their lives. He offers them full and free pardon and life eternal with him. Can we believe these truths and not find our lives changed? Can we know these things and not tell others who need to hear them?

B. GOD IS WITH US

Years ago a preacher preached an unforgettable sermon on Jesus as "Immanuel, God With Us." In the development of his message, the preacher gave the word *with* several different meanings. "God is 'with' us in Jesus," he said, "in the sense that he became one of us and lived right here among us. More than that, God is 'with' us in Jesus in that he is on our side, standing shoulder to shoulder beside us in the troubles of life."

Many people throughout history have believed in gods who are far removed from them and care little about them. The essence of the Christian faith, and the heart of the Christmas message, is that the high and holy God, who "lives in unapproachable light" (1 Timothy 6:16), has come to earth to be one of us and will take us to Heaven to be with him. Our God is not remote, nor is he unconcerned about our needs. To the contrary, he cared so much for us that he became one of us, so we might eventually become like him. That's something to celebrate—at Christmastime or anytime!

Discovery Learning

This page contains an alternate lesson plan emphasizing learning activities. Classes desiring such student involvement will find these suggestions helpful. The next page is a reproducible activity page to further enhance discovery learning.

LEARNING GOALS

After this lesson, class members will be able to:

1. Describe God's intervention in the lives of Mary and Joseph, her husband-to-be.

2. Explain the need for God's intervention in human form.

3. List evidence of God's intervention in our lives today.

INTO THE LESSON

Begin the session by saying, "The genealogies recorded in the Bible are often overlooked. In addition to studying Matthew's record of the events leading up to the miraculous birth of Jesus, we will examine Jesus' family history to consider its importance."

INTO THE WORD

Divide the class into groups of five or six students each. Assign to the groups different sections of the genealogy for study according to these verse divisions: verses 2-6a: 6b-11; and 12-16. Give each group a copy of the following questions and allow ten minutes for discussion.

• *What names do you recognize in this genealogy?*

• *What facts can you remember about these persons?*

• *Which persons in the list are most significant in establishing who Jesus is?*

• *What word would you use to summarize the generations in this section of the genealogy?*

Ask for a brief summary from each group. Then ask, "How does this genealogy show God's intervention in human events?" (These and other concepts should come from this discussion: he intervenes *deliberately*, having planned for the Messiah for centuries. He intervenes with *grace*. Tamar and Rahab were prostitutes, but still he could use them. He intervenes *personally*. The names of these people were important. He intervenes *miraculously*. The climax of the genealogy is the virgin birth!)

Pursue the concept of God's intervention by exploring his intervention in the lives of Mary and Joseph. Have someone read Matthew 1:18-25 aloud. Ask the groups you formed earlier to list ways God intervened directly in the lives of Mary and Joseph. Suggest they look at Luke 1:30-38, also.

Guide the class in discussing these questions:

Matthew uses two titles for Jesus (vv. 1, 16). What are they? (Son of David and Christ, or Messiah.) What significance would each of these names have to Matthew's readers? What significance do they have to us?

What reason does Scripture give for the choice of Mary to be the mother of Jesus? What commendable qualities are revealed about her character?

What was Joseph's initial reaction to Mary's news? How did his plans change following his dream? What does this tell you about Joseph?

Read aloud Isaiah 7:14. Share with the class a summary of the lesson notes on verses 21-23, and emphasize the significance of Jesus' virgin birth. Apart from fulfilling prophecy, why do you think it was necessary for Jesus to be born of a virgin?

INTO LIFE

Much is made of the gossip Mary and Joseph must have endured as a result of Mary's pregnancy—except in Scripture. Though we can learn much from their commitment to face the jokes and snide remarks and ignore the false perception many must have had of them, Scripture offers not a word.

Instead, the Bible simply tells the true story: God stepped into the course of human events and worked a miracle. A virgin became pregnant, and her fiancé was assured that she was a virgin still.

Suggest to the class that this provides an example for us. Rather than focus on the potential problems of serving the Lord, perhaps we should focus on his presence. Ask class members to suggest evidence of his intervention in our lives today. Answered prayer, healing of the sick, deliverance from bad habits, and comfort in a time of grief are just a few of the types of examples that may be offered. Try to get the class to be specific—what prayer was answered, and how?

After about ten minutes, make application by discussing these questions:

What does this lesson teach us about submission to God? Obedience to God? Commitment to others?

How does the fact of God's intervention in our lives motivate us to get involved in other peoples' lives to bring the grace of God to them?

Close with sentence prayers of submission and commitment offered by volunteers.

What's in a Name?

Use your Bible to fill in the sections of the chart left blank.

NAME	RELATED NAME	REFERENCE	MEANING
1. Abraham	Abram	Genesis 17:5	
2.		John 1:41	anointed one
3.	Christ	Acts 11:26	disciples first called this at Antioch
4. Immanuel	Emmanuel	Matthew 1:23	
5.	Joshua	Matthew 1:21	Jehovah saves

What's in My Name?

Fill in your name writing one letter in the vertical squares. Build an acrostic. (An example, using the name *Jesus,* is shown below, with an explanation at each step of the instructions.)

1. Including the first letter of your name, write a word that will remind you of a promise of God. (In the case of the example, the word is *justification.* God promises to justify us, to declare us "not guilty," in Christ.)

2. Including the last letter of your name, write a word that will remind you to share God's love and forgiveness with others. (Like Jesus, our mission is to seek and to save the *lost.* Note your words do not have to *start* with the letters in your name; they just have to *include* them.)

3. Including another letter, write a word that will remind you how God's presence has made a difference in your life. (Hebrews tells us Jesus is sympathetic to our weaknesses. This encourages us to take our burdens to him and to find grace to help us.)

Explain why you chose those words.

[J] ustification
[E]
[S] ympathy
[U]
Lo [S] t

Jesus the Fulfillment

Unit 2: Immanuel: God With Us

(Lessons 3, 4)

THE WISE MEN WORSHIP JESUS

LESSON 4

WHY TEACH THIS LESSON?

Why, indeed? Haven't we heard this story enough? Can we not all repeat it by heart? What can we possibly learn from such a well rehearsed story?

Sometimes the purpose of a lesson is not to provide new information so much as it is to provide motivation. Even if we know the story, we don't seem to practice the same zeal and dedication as the wise men. Their commitment to obey God's Word, their willingness to go to extremes to worship the King, and their joy through it all demonstrate we still can learn a thing or two from even this most familiar story!

INTRODUCTION

A. WRITTEN IN THE STARS

It's hard to tell if we are seeing a trend or not, but it seems that every year more and more people advertise themselves as palm readers, psychics, or astrologers. For a modest fee they will tell us what the future holds for us—whether we will get the job we want, find a loving mate, or enjoy good health, etc.

The astrologers make especially interesting claims, believing as they do that the stars, planets, and other heavenly bodies control or, at least influence, human life. The more we know about how the stars influence us, they say, the more we will know how to handle our lives, avoid disaster, and reach our personal goals.

Scripture teaches differently, however. There we learn that we have life as a gift of God and that to a large extent the things that happen to us in life are the result of the deliberate choices we make. The heavens don't determine our fate. Rather, as David affirmed in Psalm 19:1, "The heavens declare the glory of God." The stars don't map out the path that lies ahead of us. To the contrary, we choose the direction our lives will take. Each individual's personal choice of good or evil, and one's personal responsibility for the choices he or she makes, are clear teachings running through all of Scripture. (See Joshua 24:15.) For the safest and happiest future, let us not look to the stars, but to him who created the heavens and the earth.

B. LESSON BACKGROUND

In today's lesson we meet some men who might be called astrologers, who came to honor the child Jesus after they saw a star that signaled his birth. The fact that these men are spoken of in a favorable manner in Matthew's Gospel might surprise us, in view of the fact that the Bible speaks against astrology and similar arts. (See Isaiah 47:8-15, especially verses 13 and 14.) Daniel in his day overcame all the "magicians, and the astrologers, and the sorcerers" (Daniel 2:2) who competed with him as they served King Nebuchadnezzar of Babylon.

Perhaps it is not fully accurate to describe these men as astrologers. They were Magi, learned men, instructed in the wisdom of the East. From history we form a picture of them as the ancient equivalents of scientists, philosophers, and advisers,

DEVOTIONAL READING:
ISAIAH 11:1-9
LESSON SCRIPTURE:
MATTHEW 2
PRINTED TEXT:
MATTHEW 2:1-12

Dec
25

LESSON AIMS

This lesson should lead students to:

1. Understand that the revelation granted to the wise men and their coming to worship the King indicated that the salvation Jesus brought was for all people.

2. Join the wise men in their adoration of the King.

3. Select one way they will express their love and devotion to Christ.

KEY VERSE:

On coming to the house, they saw the child with his mother Mary, and they bowed down and worshiped him. Then they opened their treasures and presented him with gifts of gold and of incense and of myrrh. —Matthew 2:11

LESSON 4 NOTES

WHAT DO YOU THINK?

Consider the expense of money, time, and effort required of the Magi to get them to the presence of the Christ child. Do you think Christians today display the same devotion and commitment in their worship of Christ? Why or why not?

What changes would you suggest for the worship of Christ in your church that might draw out the same kind of devotion to Christ as displayed by the Magi?

OPTION

Use the reproducible activity on page 158, "Follow the Star," to enable the students to investigate some of the obstacles the Magi overcame in visiting the Christ child, and to see how they can overcome obstacles to service.

ANSWERS TO REPRODUCIBLE ACTIVITY:

1. The star was sometimes hidden from view.

2. Travel was expensive.

3. The trip took a long time.

4. The gifts were costly.

5. Herod tried to use them for evil purposes.

all rolled into one. Of particular interest to them was the study of astronomy. When the Son of God came into the world, he "made his mark" on the natural order of things, and his star arose. In some way the wise men recognized this mark when they saw it, and they came to honor him. How much they understood of Jesus' divine nature, either at first or later on, the Scripture does not state, but at least they honored him as no ordinary person.

In the first two lessons of this quarter's study we considered John the Baptist, whose divinely appointed task was to prepare God's people to receive the Messiah when he began his public ministry. Last week's lesson took us back thirty years before that time, to the occasion when God's angel announced to Joseph that his promised wife, Mary, who was a virgin, would give birth to a child conceived in her of the Holy Spirit. The first chapter of Matthew ended with a matter-of-fact reference to the birth of her child, whom Joseph named *Jesus* according to the angel's instruction (1:21). The event recorded in this lesson took place some time after Jesus was born.

I. THE NEW KING'S STAR (MATTHEW 2:1, 2)

A. JOURNEY OF THE WISE MEN (v. 1)

1. After Jesus was born in Bethlehem in Judea, during the time of King Herod, Magi from the east came to Jerusalem.

Jesus was born. Matthew gives us but a brief account of the birth of Jesus, as noted above. We turn to the Gospel of Luke for the information that all this took place in Nazareth of Galilee. It is Luke who explains why Joseph and Mary were *in* Bethlehem when Jesus was born. Luke also tells of the crowded conditions there, the stable, the song of the angels, and the visit of the shepherds.

During the time of King Herod. This was Herod the Great, who ruled Judea under the Romans as a client king. In 40 B.C. the Roman senate appointed Herod king over the Judean territory, but it took him three years to conquer it and come into full power as its ruler.

Herod was a man of great natural abilities, physical strength, and intellectual powers. He was a shrewd military leader and a great builder. He rebuilt the old city of Samaria, built Caesarea as a port city, and started construction on the Jerusalem temple that was standing during Jesus' earthly ministry. Known for his ruthlessness, Herod would do nearly anything to keep his subjects under his control and thus retain the favor of the Romans. In the waning years of his life, Herod became insanely jealous of his power. Becoming suspicious of his favorite wife, Mariamne, and his two sons by her, Herod had the three of them executed. Another son met the same fate shortly before Herod's own death.

From the Jewish historian Josephus, other historians, and archaeological data, we know that Herod the Great died in 4 B.C. The mistake in our calendar was made by a monk in the sixth century. By the time the mistake came to light, the calendar was too familiar to change. Allowing a year or two for the events of Jesus' early life before Herod died, and remembering that Jesus was about thirty in the fifteenth year of Tiberius Caesar, that is in A.D. 26 or 27 (Luke 3:1), we conclude that Jesus was born in 5 B.C., give or take about a year.

Magi from the east. Where exactly in the East these Magi, often called wise men, came from we are not told. The usual guess is Persia. The plural indicates that there were more than one. The fact that they brought three types of gifts has led to the speculation that there were three of them.

To Jerusalem. The wise men were looking for one who was born "King of the Jews," as we see in verse 2. It was natural, therefore, that in their search they should come to the capital city of the Jews.

B. QUEST OF THE WISE MEN (V. 2)

2. . . . and asked, "Where is the one who has been born king of the Jews? We saw his star in the east and have come to worship him."

Where is the one who has been born king of the Jews? Arriving in Jerusalem, the wise men must have immediately asked this question in the city streets. Wouldn't everyone know of such a great event and be able to give them the information they sought? We can see these men going from person to person, repeating their inquiry, but gaining no information.

We saw his star in the east. These men studied the heavens, and when a special star made its appearance, it did not escape their notice. Attempts have been made to explain this star on the basis of natural occurrences, but these explanations are unsatisfactory. The biblical account leads us to conclude that the appearance of this star was miraculous. How, then, did these men know what this star signified? The most satisfactory explanation is that they received a direct revelation from God concerning it. The history of the events surrounding the birth of Jesus suggests this conclusion. The shepherds were informed of the birth in this way, as were Simeon and Anna. And by God's direct communication with them, the wise men were instructed not to return to Herod with word of the child's whereabouts, but to go home by another route.

The Greek word translated *to worship* means "to bow down to do homage." We do not know how much the wise men understood of the divine nature of the King who was born. Surely, however, they knew that he was more than the heir to the throne of a tiny kingdom enslaved by Rome. Why else would they come from so far away with expensive gifts to do homage to him?

A SIGN FROM ABOVE

On a clear night in Chile the stars in the southern hemisphere are bright and glistening. The wonder of God's creative power is fully displayed in the innumerable luminaries hung across the limitless reaches of space.

On such a starry night a few years ago, during the week of Christmas, several missionaries were having a retreat near the ocean. At a break time we all watched as two luminaries moving in opposite directions crossed overhead and disappeared in the horizon. Were they a sign from Heaven? Were they two comets speeding through the velvet black sky? No, they were two space satellites, one American and the other Russian, racing in their orbits around the earth. Eerie, beautiful, mysterious, silent in their journey, they held us entranced as we watched their passage.

Imagine the wonder and the excitement of the wise men when they observed in the Eastern sky the star of the King of the Jews. This sign in the heavens brought them westward to Judea to worship. By contrast, that same sign greatly troubled King Herod.

It is Christmas once more. God's signs given through his Word still beckon us to come to Jesus and to worship him as the King. How do you respond to God's call?

—W. P.

II. THE OLD KING'S PLOT (MATTHEW 2:3-8)

A. DEMAND OF THE KING (VV. 3, 4)

3. When King Herod heard this he was disturbed, and all Jerusalem with him.

Word of the wise men's inquiry soon was brought to the attention of *Herod the king.* The aged monarch knew nothing of the birth of One who was held to be a claimant to his throne. Learning of it, the king *was disturbed.* Even though Herod was nearing the end of his own reign, he was consumed with jealousy and fear for his position. *All Jerusalem* was troubled as well, for the people knew the crimes an enraged Herod was capable of committing against anyone he imagined was a threat to him.

4. When he had called together all the people's chief priests and teachers of the law, he asked them where the Christ was to be born.

Whatever the wise men understood concerning this One who was born "King of the Jews," Herod understood him to be *Christ*, the Messiah, God's anointed one. Herod knew that the Scriptures of the Jews predicted the coming of the Messiah and that the people were looking for him, so he assembled those persons who would be able to answer his question. *The chief priests* were the men in charge of the temple worship; *the teachers of the law* were the experts in the law of Moses. *He asked them.* We might have expected him to "demand" or "order"—but Herod could be courteous when it served his purposes.

B. REPORT OF THE PRIESTS AND TEACHERS OF THE LAW (vv. 5, 6)

5. "In Bethlehem in Judea," they replied, "for this is what the prophet has written:

The chief priests and teachers of the law answered immediately that the Messiah was to be born in *Bethlehem*, King David's hometown, just five miles south of Jerusalem. God had said this through his *prophet* long ago.

The main role of the prophets of Old Testament times was to give God's message to his stubborn people and to call them to turn from their sins and come back to God. Although predicting future events wasn't the prophets' main task, they often did make predictions, and the predictions always came true.

6. "'But you, Bethlehem, in the land of Judah, are by no means least among the rulers of Judah; for out of you will come a ruler who will be the shepherd of my people Israel.'"

The prophecy came from the writings of the prophet Micah (Micah 5:2), who lived more than seven hundred years earlier. In poetic utterance, Micah addressed Bethlehem, a small village in the *land of Judah*. Though insignificant when compared with the splendid capital of Jerusalem, Bethlehem would gain fame in all the world and for all time. From this village would come *a ruler*, the great King of Israel.

C. INSTRUCTIONS FOR THE WISE MEN (vv. 7, 8)

7. Then Herod called the Magi secretly and found out from them the exact time the star had appeared.

Having received the information he needed from the chief priests and scribes, Herod dismissed them. Then he summoned the wise men *secretly* for a private conference. He now knew where the child was born, but he needed to know *the exact time* the birth had taken place. Apparently Herod felt that the child had been born at the very time the star had appeared. We learn from verse 16 that Herod ordered the killing of all the male children in and near Bethlehem who were two years old and under. This suggests that the star appeared perhaps as much as a year earlier. Herod probably would have increased or even doubled the time mentioned by the wise men in order to make sure he included the child he feared when the killings at Bethlehem took place.

8. He sent them to Bethlehem and said, "Go and make a careful search for the child. As soon as you find him, report to me, so that I too may go and worship him."

In his private interview with these men, Herod not only was successful in obtaining the information he sought, but he also was able to assess their character. It seems that he judged them to be honest men, for he sent them unaccompanied to Bethlehem and piously requested that they bring him word when they found the young child so that he might *go and worship him.* Of course, Herod had no intention of paying any kind of homage to the child. His intention was to kill the child, and deceitfully he would use these innocent men to accomplish his malicious purpose.

III. THE WISE MEN'S SUCCESS (MATTHEW 2:9-12)

A. APPEARANCE OF THE STAR (VV. 9, 10)

9. After they had heard the king, they went on their way, and the star they had seen in the east went ahead of them until it stopped over the place where the child was.

With the knowledge that the child whom they sought was in Bethlehem, the wise men departed the king's presence and started for the village, even though night was falling. *The star they had seen in the east.* Some think this implies that they had seen the star when they were in the East, and that they had not seen it since then. *Went ahead of them.* Because the star led them directly to where Jesus was, others conclude that the star had given them similar guidance throughout their journey.

10. When they saw the star, they were overjoyed.

Seeing the miraculous star again, they rejoiced greatly. The divine guidance given by the star clearly confirmed the prophecy of the Old Testament. The travelers knew that they were nearing the end of their search.

LOCATING THE KING

In the story, *The Prince and the Pauper,* the exchange of roles between the future king and another young man who looked like him was rather easily accomplished because of the fixed ideas surrounding royalty. Princes are found in castles; paupers in humble abodes. Princes wear royal garments; paupers wear peasant garb. Princes act with assurance of position; paupers go quietly about their everyday tasks.

To locate a child who is to become king, one would look in the king's palace. So the wise men came to Jerusalem, expecting to find him who was born King of the Jews. Herod, however, knew nothing of the birth. But he learned that God's prophet had said the King would come out of Bethlehem of Judea, so he sent them there.

The star they had seen earlier led them from the palace in Jerusalem to the place where the young child was. Without God's direction by Scripture and star, they could not have found the King whom they sought. If they had not trusted the revelation given to them, they would have continued to inquire in the wrong place.

God says we must come to the manger, the cross, and the empty tomb to find the One who alone qualifies to be the King of our lives. The world says royalty is found elsewhere. To whom will you listen?   —W. P.

B. GIFTS FOR THE CHILD (V. 11)

11. On coming to the house, they saw the child with his mother Mary, and they bowed down and worshiped him. Then they opened their treasures and presented him with gifts of gold and of incense and of myrrh.

We notice that Matthew refers to Jesus as a young *child,* and that the family was living in a *house,* not a stable. This indicates that some time had passed from the time of Jesus' birth until the arrival of the wise men in Bethlehem.

When they entered the house and saw Jesus, they *bowed down* before him and *worshiped* him. They knew from the events in Jerusalem that this child was the Christ. How much beyond that they knew of his nature we do not know. The valuable gifts they brought included *gold,* a fitting present for a king, *incense,* of a kind such as a priest might burn before God (see Exodus 30), and *myrrh,* a spice used in

WHAT DO YOU THINK?

The wise men presented gifts of gold, incense, and myrrh to the Christ child. Some Bible students see in the three gifts symbols of Christ's identity and mission. Gold was the gift fit for a king. Incense was a gift for deity, appropriate for a priestly offering before God. Myrrh, used in the preparation of bodies for burial, suggested the fact that he was "born to die." Thus they see these as gifts for One who would serve as king, priest, and sacrifice! Others have suggested that Joseph and Mary were of limited financial means, and that the price these gifts brought assisted them in their stay in Egypt, which followed immediately upon the departure of the wise men.

Still others point out that Scripture is silent regarding the gifts, other than stating that valuable gifts were given. They feel, then, that the value is the greatest significance regarding them, suggesting that token gifts have no place in the genuine worship of Christ.

What do you think? What is the significance of the gifts? Could all of these suggestions hold an element of truth for us? Why or why not?

Visual 4 of the visual packet pictures the magi presenting their gifts to the Christ child.

WHAT DO YOU THINK?

What a marvelous example of God's providence is this story. Murderous King Herod thought his plan to eliminate this new "King" was working perfectly. These honest wise men would lead him right to the cradle. And if not, then "Plan B" would surely take care of him, along with hundreds of other innocent babes. But God had things in control. Warning first the wise men and then Joseph, his Son escaped the wiles of Herod.

Even without talking to us in our dreams, God can control the events surrounding us so that we can do his will. What examples of God's providence have you seen at work in your own life?

PRAYER

Father, we thank you for the marvelous gift of your Son. May we show our heartfelt gratitude by giving him the best gift we can, the gift of ourselves. Amen.

DAILY BIBLE READINGS

Monday, Dec. 19—The Rule of the Messiah (Isaiah 11:1-9)

Tuesday, Dec. 20—The Day of Deliverance (Zechariah 9:9-13)

Wednesday, Dec. 21—The Deliverer to Come From Bethlehem (Micah 5:1-5a)

Thursday, Dec. 22—Wise Men Directed to Bethlehem (Matthew 2:1-6)

Friday, Dec. 23—The Wise Men Worship Jesus (Matthew 2:7-12)

Saturday, Dec. 24—The Escape to Egypt (Matthew 2:13-18)

Sunday, Dec. 25—Return From Egypt (Matthew 2:19-23)

burial (see John 19:39). Taken together, these offerings were most suitable for One who would serve as king, priest, and sacrifice.

C. DEPARTURE OF THE WISE MEN (V. 12)

12. And having been warned in a dream not to go back to Herod, they returned to their country by another route.

Herod had duped the Magi, but God intervened so that they would not unwittingly give Herod the information he sought. Just as God spoke to Joseph in a dream (Matthew 1:20) and would do so twice again (2:13, 19) to protect the Christ, he warned these visitors from the East not to return to Herod in Jerusalem. In obedience to God's word, they went to their homeland by a different route, and stepped off the stage of the gospel story.

CONCLUSION

A. GIFTS FIT FOR A KING

"The Little Drummer Boy" has been a popular Christmas song in America for many years. Of course, the song is fictional. Even so, it carries truth worthy of consideration. You probably remember how the song goes. A boy with a drum goes along with the shepherds to visit the infant Jesus. Troubled because he doesn't have a gift fit for a king, the boy finally plays on his drum to please the baby. "I'll play my drum for him," the boy says. "I'll play my best for him."

From the drummer boy's statements two thoughts emerge. The first is this: If we do not have possessions of great value to offer to Christ, let us recognize the value of what we do possess and of it make an offering to him. The wise men presented to the Christ child gifts of gold, frankincense, and myrrh. These were wonderful gifts, and they enabled Joseph and Mary to flee to Egypt with Jesus and to provide for him there. But one wonders if the lowly shepherds on the day following Jesus' birth did not return to the stable with warm, wholesome food and other necessities—simple gifts that they had in their power to bring.

Some persons today can and do give to the Lord plots of land, buildings, and large sums of money. These are wonderful gifts and they advance the Lord's cause. Most persons, however, do not possess resources of such magnitude. But what we do have can be offered to Christ, and he will not reject it. When we give what we have, our Lord is pleased.

The second thought is that we should give our best for Christ. No half-hearted effort would express the reverence the drummer boy felt in his heart for the Christ child at his birth. How, then, can we, who know not only of his wondrous birth but also of his life and sacrificial death in our behalf, give him anything less than our best? We begin by giving him ourselves without reservation. Once we have done that, can we ever entertain the thought of giving to him of our resources only after we have satisfied our own selfish desires? God gave his Son, the most precious gift mankind has ever received. The wise men made great sacrifice of time and effort to present to Jesus gifts fit for a king. Let us do no less today.

B. FOR ALL PEOPLE

Today's Scripture passage indicates that God's plan of salvation is intended for the whole world. God's Son came to earth as a child born of the Jewish nation, in keeping with God's plan announced as far back as the time of Abraham (Genesis 12:1-3). But God's promise revealed his intention to bless all nations through Abraham. By sharing the announcement of Jesus' birth with the wise men, who were Gentiles, God showed that this good news was meant for all persons—Jew and Gentile alike.

Discovery Learning

*This page contains an alternate lesson plan emphasizing learning activities. Classes
desiring such student involvement will find these suggestions helpful. The next page
is a reproducible activity page to further enhance discovery learning.*

LEARNING GOALS

After this lesson, class members will be able to:

1. State in proper sequence the events included in the visit of the wise men to Jesus.

2. List problems the wise men overcame to find and worship Jesus.

3. Name something they need to overcome, or that they have overcome, to honor God.

INTO THE LESSON

As you begin, take some time to allow class members to share some of their childhood memories about Christmas Day.

After several members have shared, make transition to the lesson time. Though the visit of the wise men is often associated with the events of the night of Jesus' birth, we will see today that it actually occurred some time later.

INTO THE WORD

Prior to class time, write the following events from today's lesson text on sheets of paper, one event per sheet. (Write the words large enough so that your students will be able to read them from where they are seated.) The events in their proper order are as follows: Jesus is born; Wise men see the star; Wise men come to Jerusalem; Wise men talk with Herod; Herod consults Jewish priests and teachers; Herod secretly talks to wise men; Wise men are led by the star; Wise men go to Bethlehem; Wise men present gifts to Jesus; Wise men return home.

Ask for ten volunteers to come to the front of the room. Scramble the sheets and give each of the ten students a sheet. Ask them to hold up the sheets so all in the class may see the events written on them. Then have the class, without referring to the Scripture text, move the students around so as to arrange the events in order.

When the class is certain they have the events in the proper order, ask a volunteer to read aloud the lesson text, Matthew 2:1-12. Then, using the following questions, plus insights from the lesson commentary, lead the class in a discussion of the lesson.

Where was Bethlehem? What Old Testament events and persons were associated with this town?

(It was about five miles south of Jerusalem. Rachel was buried there {Genesis 35:19}; the story of Ruth and Boaz took place there; Bethlehem was David's home.)

What was the significance of Jesus' being born in Bethlehem? (Micah prophesied that the Christ would come out of Bethlehem. See Micah 5:2.)

Who were the wise men who came searching for the King of the Jews?

What was King Herod's reaction to the news of the birth of a King? Why did he react in this manner? (See comments under verse 1.)

Why were the citizens of Jerusalem troubled? (See verse 3.)

When Herod spoke with the wise men, what specific information did he seek from them? (See verse 7.) What was his motive for wanting to know this? (See also Matthew 2:16.)

It has been estimated that the journey of these men from their home in the East to Jerusalem occupied a number of weeks, if not months. Why do you suppose they were willing to leave everything and make such a long trek after seeing that special star in the sky?

(For a different approach to exploring the difficulties endured by the wise men, make copies of the first reproducible activity on the next page, "Follow the Star.")

What are some of the "stars" people today are willing to follow? (Focus your discussion on false gods people follow today. Some examples are money, job status, power over others, pleasure.) Where are these "stars" leading them?

(The second reproducible activity on the next page, "Stars in Our Eyes," provides another way to explore some of the stars people follow today. Use of the reproducible sheets is encouraged to increase student involvement.)

INTO LIFE

What was the response of these men when they finally found Jesus (v. 11)? How was their response similar to the response of an unbeliever who finds Jesus for the first time?

Take some time to have volunteers from your class share the story of their own search for Jesus. Limit each testimony to one or two minutes. If you know of class members whose testimonies are especially dramatic or moving, plan for them to share last. Otherwise, some might feel that their testimony is "boring" or of no value, and thus might be unwilling to share.

Close the class with prayer, thanking God for the incomparable gift of his Son Jesus.

Follow the Star

The wise men followed God's star. They certainly faced many obstacles as they traveled. Decode these statements, replacing the stars with letters. (Answers are on page 152 of *The NIV Standard Lesson Commentary*.)

1. ✪h✪ ✪✪✪r w✪✪ ✪om✪✪✪m✪✪ h✪dd✪n fr✪m v✪✪w.

2. ✪r✪v✪l w✪✪ ✪xp✪ns✪v✪.

3. ✪h✪ ✪r✪p ✪ook ✪ long ✪✪m✪.

4. ✪h✪ g✪f✪s w✪✪✪ co✪✪ly.

5. H✪✪od ✪✪✪✪d ✪o u✪✪ ✪h✪m fo✪ ✪v✪l pu✪p✪✪✪.

The Magi overcame obstacles to bring gifts of great worth to Jesus. What obstacle must you overcome to worship Jesus with your life? Some ideas are listed below. Add as many others as you can think of; then rate them, with 1 being the most troublesome for you, 2, the next most troublesome, and so on.

RATING	OBSTACLE	RATING	OBSTACLE
_____	ambition	_____	pride
_____	avoid conflict	_____	laziness
_____	too little time	_____	too little money
_____	selfishness		

What happens when people are hindered by these obstacles? What evidence demonstrates that they are being influenced by these obstacles?

Stars in Our Eyes

Think of the expression, "They had stars in their eyes." Then think of some words that identify things that were important to you as a child. What put stars in *your* eyes? Write some of them on the stars below.

Are you still following these stars? Why or why not? What better stars have you found to follow?

Jesus the Fulfillment

Unit 3: Jesus: The Son of David

(Lessons 5-9)

DELIVERANCE AND FORGIVENESS

LESSON 5

WHY TEACH THIS LESSON?

Why do so many people still reject the Lord? Is it because they feel so overwhelmed by sin they are beyond hope? Is it because they have been so paralyzed by fear or guilt they cannot act. Do they doubt the power of God to deliver them through Jesus?

This lesson addresses all these needs. The cleansing of the Gadarene demoniacs—completely overwhelmed by the power of Satan's demons—proves no one is beyond Jesus' power to redeem. And the episode with the paralytic proves his power to forgive as well as his power to heal. Whatever is troubling your students in resisting evil, this lesson assures them "the one who is in you is greater than the one who is in the world" (1 John 4:4).

INTRODUCTION

A. EVERYONE NEEDS DELIVERANCE

Everyone needs deliverance. We need deliverance from the snares of Satan, from the evil that holds us captive and helpless in its power. We need deliverance from our guilt. We need deliverance from the burdens, the disappointments, the problems of life. We must have deliverance, because we cannot deliver ourselves.

The ancient Israelites needed deliverance from the Philistines and other enemy nations, and God raised up David to lead in their deliverance. God sent Jesus to be our Deliverer. Jesus deals with us as individuals, not just as a mass. In the lesson for today we will see three persons whom Jesus delivered. Two he freed from the shackles of Satan, and one he freed from guilt and disease.

B. LESSON BACKGROUND

In the lessons of Units 1 and 2 of this quarter's study, we have seen that Old Testament prophecies were fulfilled in the ministry of John the Baptist, who heralded Jesus' coming, and in the events surrounding our Savior's birth. Unit 3 further emphasizes Jesus' connection with persons and prophecies of the Old Testament.

As we begin our study of Unit 3 it is important to remember that this is a topical, rather than a chronological, study of the life of Christ. The title of this unit is, "Jesus: The Son of David." The lessons in this unit focus on events that illustrate how Jesus fulfilled the title, "Son of David."

David was the most heroic and beloved of Israel's kings. Under his leadership the nation prevailed over her neighboring enemies and was free and prosperous. David was a good king, not a tyrant. He was concerned for the welfare of his people. His great sin notwithstanding, David was a religious leader who led the people to remain faithful to the Lord. The Lord promised David that in time to come he would set one of his descendants on the throne of an everlasting kingdom. (See 2 Samuel 7:12-16.) This promised descendant came to be known as "the Son of

DEVOTIONAL READING:
LUKE 4:16-21

LESSON SCRIPTURE:
MATTHEW 8:1–9:8

PRINTED TEXT:
MATTHEW 8:28–9:8

Jan
1

LESSON AIMS

As a result of studying this lesson the students should understand that Jesus, the Son of David:

1. Has power to overcome all the evil forces that seek to destroy people.

2. Has power and authority to forgive and heal the effects of sin in man's heart, life, and body.

3. Is concerned and willing to help each person who comes to him.

KEY VERSE:

When Jesus saw their faith, he said to the paralytic, "Take heart, son; your sins are forgiven."
—Matthew 9:2

David." The Jews looked for him to be a second David, one who was like David but was even greater than the ancient king.

This lesson shows that Jesus was a deliverer just as David was. Jesus, however, performed the greater work of delivering the people from spiritual enemies and bondage. Furthermore, his work was not limited to the people of the nation of Israel. Jesus brought deliverance for all of mankind.

The first event recorded in our lesson text, the healing of the two demoniacs, took place as Jesus and his disciples reached the eastern shore of the Sea of Galilee after Jesus calmed the storm. The second event, the forgiveness and healing of the paralytic, though it immediately follows in the text, probably took place some time earlier. Both Mark and Luke record it as taking place earlier in Jesus' ministry. This is not a contradiction between the accounts, because Matthew evidently wrote a topical account of Jesus' life rather than a strictly chronological one.

I. DELIVERANCE FROM THE FORCES OF EVIL (MATTHEW 8:28—9:1)

A. CONFRONTATION WITH EVIL (vv. 28-31)

28. When he arrived at the other side in the region of the Gadarenes, two demon-possessed men coming from the tombs met him. They were so violent that no one could pass that way.

Jesus and the disciples landed on the eastern shore of Galilee in the region of the *Gadarenes*. A town named Gergesa, or Gerasa, was located near the lake shore. Gadara, a larger town, was located a few miles to the southeast. The people of the area were known by each of these names (see Mark 5:1; Luke 8:26).

Two demon-possessed men. Mark and Luke also record this event, but they mention only one man. Probably one was much more prominent in the scene, and so they focused on him. Mark 5:9 indicates that many demons were living in one man, making him exceedingly strong at times. The demons who possessed these men reduced them to a pitiful existence. The men were without rational control. Violent and raving, they wore no clothes and lived in caves that were used as tombs.

The demons actually took over the minds and bodies of these men, producing the extreme effects noted. The same effects to a lesser degree are seen in all who are under the influence of Satan. Such persons often are violent and behave irrationally. The more evil takes over their lives, the more they are cut off from others.

29. "What do you want with us, Son of God?" they shouted. "Have you come here to torture us before the appointed time?"

As spirit beings, the demons recognized Jesus to be the Son of God, and they feared him. It was they who cried out, using the men's voices. They knew that eternal torment was their ultimate destiny and that Jesus had the power to bring that about. They were afraid their torment might begin immediately.

30, 31. Some distance from them a large herd of pigs was feeding. The demons begged Jesus, "If you drive us out, send us into the herd of pigs."

Many Gentiles lived in this area, so it seems most likely that the hogs were raised by some of them. The request of the demons leads us to conclude that evil spirits will go to extremes to keep from being disembodied. Living in a hog doesn't seem like much of an existence, even for demons, but apparently they considered the alternative to be worse.

B. DELIVERANCE (v. 32)

32. He said to them, "Go!" So they came out and went into the pigs, and the whole herd rushed down the steep bank into the lake and died in the water.

WHAT DO YOU THINK?

Some people believe demon possession no longer takes place— that Satan and his demons were allowed much more power when the greater power of the Son of God was present and that such power is no longer granted to the forces of evil. Others believe it takes place yet. They tell chilling stories of people involved in the occult and voo-doo rituals performing superhuman feats.

What do you think? Do demons still possess people? If so, what defense does the Christian have? If not, to what extent do you think Satan and his demons are allowed to influence our world?

HOW TO SAY IT

Capernaum. Kuh-PER-nay-um.
Gadara. GAD-uh-ruh.
Gadarenes. GAD-uh-reenz.
Gerasa. GAIR-uh-sah.
Gergesa. GUR-guh-sah.
Pharisees. FAIR-ih-seez.
Philistines. FIL-iss-teens or Fi-LISS-teens.

Mark 5:13 tells us that about two thousand pigs were in the herd. Apparently the demons couldn't control the pigs as they could the two men, for in their terror and madness the hogs stampeded down the hill. In the locale where this event took place, the hill slopes steeply down to within about forty feet of the shore. The herd rushed on, plunged into the lake, and were drowned.

Jesus, who knows all things, surely knew that this would happen, and this raises the question of why he allowed the destruction of this property. It seems likely that he permitted it in order to provide a very dramatic demonstration of the forces that were at work. These events showed Jesus to be a deliverer and the demons to be destroyers. The deliverance of the demoniacs drew attention, but the destruction of the herd strengthened the impact on the people of the area. Intended or not, this was the evident result, because, as verse 34 mentions, everyone from the city came out to see what had happened.

It has become common in modern times to discount the existence of demons as superstition. And many Christians believe that demons existed on earth in Jesus' day only. It is true that in the New Testament period there was a concentration of demon possession. It is evident that when God was bringing to fulfillment his plan of redemption through his Son, Satan did all in his power to oppose him. However, there is no indication in Scripture that all demon activity has ended. Our knowledge of the spirit world is extremely limited. From Hebrews 1:14 we learn that God's angels are "ministering spirits, sent to serve those who will inherit salvation." Since this is so, is it too much to believe that demonic spirits exist to achieve Satan's purposes? Exactly what form this spiritual activity takes is difficult to say.

The apostle Peter warns that "the devil prowls around like a roaring lion looking for someone to devour" (1 Peter 5:8). We are urged to resist him by "standing firm in the faith" (v. 9). Those who disregard the Bible's warnings of danger from Satan and engage in witchcraft, spiritualism, and the like are seeking a communion with a spiritual power that can only lead to the most horrible kind of enslavement.

Most persons, however, are not possessed by demons in the way the two men in our text were. But this does not mean that people today are not bound by Satan's power. All people sin and come under the curse of death. And all sinners are bound by the chains of sin, being unable to resist it and unable to escape its grim curse. Jesus came to deliver all from this bondage, to rescue us from Satan's dark kingdom and power and bring us into his glorious kingdom of light (Colossians 1:13). Jesus is willing and able to be deliverer for all who call upon him today.

C. REJECTION (VV. 33—9:1)

33, 34. Those tending the pigs ran off, went into the town and reported all this, including what had happened to the demon-possessed men. Then the whole town went out to meet Jesus. And when they saw him, they pleaded with him to leave their region.

Those tending the pigs, filled with consternation, fear, and amazement, quickly carried the news to the nearby city. Almost everyone in town hurried out to the scene, and when they saw Jesus, they asked him to *leave.*

Why did these people react this way? Were they afraid that Jesus would cause further economic losses? Were they angry? Perhaps they realized that they were in the presence of deity and they feared him. It is impossible to say what their reasons were, but we can say with certainty that they were very foolish in asking Jesus to leave.

Jesus had performed a wonderful, miraculous work of deliverance on the two demoniacs. Surely many sick people and perhaps even other demoniacs lived in the region. These townspeople would have been wise to beg Jesus to stay and

WHAT DO YOU THINK?

Why the Gadarenes begged Jesus to leave their territory after he had cast the demons out of two persons who were demon-possessed is a mystery. One would have thought they would have begged him to stay and to heal others.

Bible students have offered two suggestions for their rejection. The first is that the residents may have feared additional economic loss. The loss of two thousand hogs must have cost the owners of the hogs plenty. Perhaps the citizens of the area were more concerned about protecting their possessions than they were about the relief of human suffering that Jesus could bring.

Others suggest that the people feared Jesus' supernatural power. The people may have feared that the power that freed the demon-possessed and commanded demons might be turned on them for their sins.

What do you think? What are some reasons people reject him today? To what extent are these reasons mirrored in the reaction of the Gadarenes?

WHAT DO YOU THINK?

We are amazed and dismayed by the response of the Gadarenes. We call them foolish, or selfish, or both. They asked Jesus to leave.

But another man said, "Go away from me, Lord; I am a sinful man!" (Luke 5:8). Why do you think we regard the Gadarenes as foolish but honor Peter, who made such a similar remark? What is different about their situations? What response ought we to make?

Display visual 5 of the visuals packet throughout the class session. Based on the account of the paralytic, it illustrates the concept of forgiveness.

Option

The activity, "Harmonize Your Answers," on the reproducible page 166 may be used to lead your students in a Bible study of this passage and the two other Synoptic accounts (Mark and Luke) to get a complete picture of this event.

What Do You Think?

If you had come to Jesus for physical healing and he said, "Your sins are forgiven," would you have been disappointed or encouraged? Could you have gone home content at that point even if Jesus had not also cured your paralysis? Why or why not?

Of course, Jesus ministered to both the physical and spiritual needs of the man. Do you think the church continues to address both types of needs? Why or why not? What can you do to keep your own response to both kinds of needs in balance? What can your church do?

heal others. He did as much elsewhere. The miracle established that Jesus was sent from God; and so they would have been wise to ask him to stay and teach them God's will. He did elsewhere. If Jesus had stayed, he would have enriched people's lives many times more than the cost of the dead hogs. As it was, only the two men, and perhaps their families, profited from Jesus' visit on this occasion.

The continuing tragedy is that many people today refuse to allow Jesus to come into their lives. They reject the deliverance, freedom, and healing that he can give and wants to give. They forfeit so much by making the same foolish decision that these people made.

Could it be that all of us keep Jesus out of some areas of our lives? Are there sins that we won't let him help us overcome? Are there hurts that we won't let him heal?

9:1. Jesus stepped into a boat, crossed over and came to his own town.

Jesus did as the people requested and returned to Capernaum on the western side of the lake.

II. DELIVERANCE FROM THE EFFECTS OF EVIL (MATTHEW 9:2-8)

In chapter 8 Matthew has given a collection of Jesus' miracles, showing the different kinds of miracles Jesus performed in this early period of his Galilean ministry. To this list he now adds the healing of the paralytic in Capernaum, although this miracle probably occurred at an earlier time in that city.

A. Forgiveness (v. 2)

2. Some men brought to him a paralytic, lying on a mat. When Jesus saw their faith, he said to the paralytic, "Take heart, son; your sins are forgiven."

From the parallel accounts of this event (Mark 2 and Luke 5), we learn that Jesus was teaching in a house that was filled to overflowing. Scribes and Pharisees from many cities of Galilee and Judea, and even from Jerusalem, were among the great crowd that filled the house in Capernaum. They *brought to him a paralytic.* Mark 2:3 says there were four men carrying the stricken man. The cause and extent of the man's paralysis is not stated, but evidently he was unable to move about on his own.

The *faith* of all five of these men was demonstrated in the unusual steps taken to get the paralytic into Jesus' presence. Unable to enter the crowded room, the four carried their friend up to the roof of the house, broke loose some of the tiling, and lowered him to the feet of Jesus. Matthew does not include this fact, but it is recorded in both Mark (2:4) and Luke (5:19).

Your sins are forgiven. The Jews commonly believed that disease was the direct result of some personal sin (compare John 9:2). Perhaps this man felt a great burden of guilt and condemned himself for his pitiable condition. Perhaps he feared that Jesus would not heal him because of his sins. If that was the case, then Jesus' words certainly were reason for him to *take heart.* Jesus' statement was not a prayer that the man be forgiven; it was a statement of fact, a direct pardon. The paralytic had come to Jesus seeking healing, but he received much more.

True Wholeness

Wholeness is the longed-for vision of man. We want to be free from disease, injury, disability—any and all infirmities of the body. Andy Cole wanted wholeness, too. However, his dissolute life, including addiction to alcohol and drugs, prevented him from coming even close to it. Dissipation had disturbed his emotional stability and diminished his work skills. In his thirties, he was already an old man, shunned by most and an alien to his own family. Those who had tried to help Andy had long before given up in their attempts.

Then Andy heard the gospel—the message of God's love and forgiveness—and he let Jesus come into his life. What nothing else could do, Andy's genuine conversion to Christ accomplished. The scars of abuse remained, but Andy, new in spirit and forgiven of sin, found freedom from its chains by believing and following Jesus. He became a man of integrity and a Christian example to all. Andy Cole's changed life was little short of miraculous.

We make a mistake if we treat symptoms only and neglect their cause. Jesus knew that sin is the cause of all of our problems, and he provided its cure. Only in him can we be made truly whole.   —W. P.

B. THE QUESTION OF AUTHORITY (vv. 3-6)

3. At this, some of the teachers of the law said to themselves, "This fellow is blaspheming!"

The *teachers of the law* immediately seized on Jesus' words. Their reasoning went like this; No one can forgive sin except God, and any man who claims the prerogatives of God is guilty of blasphemy. (So far, they were correct.) But their conclusion that Jesus was only a man, hence guilty of blasphemy, was false.

4. Knowing their thoughts, Jesus said, "Why do you entertain evil thoughts in your hearts?

Hearts are an open book to Jesus, and he knew *their thoughts*. These teachers probably were rather startled when Jesus looked them in the eyes and revealed their evil, accusing thoughts for all to hear.

5. "Which is easier: to say, 'Your sins are forgiven,' or to say, 'Get up and walk'?

Both of these statements are easy *to say*, but both require God's power to perform. In effect, Jesus asked which was easier to demonstrate. Anyone could claim to forgive sins, because it would be impossible to know whether the sins were actually forgiven. But if someone said, *Get up and walk*, immediate, visible, miraculous results would be required to show that the speaker possessed supernatural power.

6. "But so that you may know that the Son of Man has authority on earth to forgive sins. . . ." Then he said to the paralytic, "Get up, take your mat and go home."

Jesus proposed to demonstrate his invisible power and authority *to forgive sins* by visibly demonstrating his power to heal. If Jesus could heal the man, which could be done only by God's power, then it would prove that he also could forgive sins. This is based on the premise that God would not give anyone the miraculous power to heal the most hopeless physical ailments if that person were at the same time blaspheming. If Jesus could heal the man, then he could not be blaspheming.

Without hesitation Jesus ordered the paralyzed man to get up, pick up his mat, and walk home. The truth would soon be known.

C. HEALING (vv. 7, 8)

7. And the man got up and went home.

Instantaneously the man was healed and able to do what Jesus commanded. (See Mark 2:12.) One can imagine that he raced home in order to be the first to tell the joyous news to his family.

PROVING HIS WORD

Millie Phillips, the wife of a Canadian preacher, is an excellent fisher. One day, however, she made a claim that seemed too bold. Her husband and his brother just returned from a morning of fishing on Buffalo Lake in Alberta, each with his limit of

OPTION

Pursue further the idea of balancing the spiritual and the physical with the second activity on the reproducible page 166.

WHAT DO YOU THINK?

There are those who say Jesus never claimed to be divine. He was just a man who went around teaching love and doing great things. "Deity" was something later disciples read into his words and actions.

How does this event demonstrate Jesus' deity? What evidence does it present that Jesus himself acknowledged his deity and expected others to accept it as fact?

PRAYER

Lord of all, thank you for sending our deliverer. He has overcome your enemy and ours, Satan. Through him you have freed us from the bonds of evil so that we might serve you in righteousness. We are proud yet humbled, overjoyed even overwhelmed, to acknowledge him as the Son of David, our eternal King. Help us, Lord, to be faithful to him. Amen.

WHAT DO YOU THINK?

The two crowds in today's lesson reacted very differently to Jesus. One said, "Go away!" The other said, "Praise God!"

What do people say in response to the witness of Christ presented by your church? To your own witness of him? If they reject him, is it because the witness is faulty or, as in the case of the Gadarenes, that the response is unjustified? How can you be sure it is not the former?

THOUGHT TO REMEMBER

David was a great deliverer, but a greater deliverer has come—Jesus Christ, the Son of God.

DAILY BIBLE READINGS

Monday, Dec. 26—Teaching on the Mountain (Matthew 5: 1-13)

Tuesday, Dec. 27—Do Not Judge Others (Matthew 7:1-5)

Wednesday, Dec. 28—Hearers and Doers of Jesus' Words (Matthew 7:24-29)

Thursday, Dec. 29—Healing a Leper and a Centurion's Servant (Matthew 8:1-13)

Friday, Dec. 30—Healing and Fulfillment of Prophecy (Matthew 8:14-22)

Saturday, Dec. 31—Restoring Two Demoniacs (Matthew 8:23-34)

Sunday, Jan. 1—Forgiving and Healing a Paralytic (Matthew 9:1-8)

ten pike. Millie said, "Let me fish for just one hour, with Jim running the boat and taking off the hook the fish I catch, and I'll catch as many as you did. And mine will be bigger!" Jim agreed, and in a few minutes they were out on the lake.

In one hour they were back at the shore. Millie had her limit of ten fish, and they were as big as, and perhaps bigger than, the fish the men had taken all morning to catch. It really was no contest. Millie had proved her word.

To make a claim is one thing; to prove one's words is another. Jesus proved his claim to possess divine authority to forgive sins when he demonstrated divine power to heal the paralytic. The proof that Jesus could offer such a gift silenced his accusers.

In Christ we have the promise of the forgiveness of our sins. Must we wait to see proof that he can do all he has promised, or will we walk by faith in his Word?

—W. P.

8. When the crowd saw this, they were filled with awe; and they praised God, who had given such authority to men.

Jesus was vindicated. His power and authority were demonstrated beyond reasonable refutation. The crowd, seeing what happened, was filled with awe They were astounded. They knew of Jesus' power and believed he could heal, else they would not have come to him in the first place. Beyond this, Jesus had challenged them to think more deeply about the source and extent of his power. He claimed power that God did not delegate—the power to forgive. The discerning among the people must have realized the implications, Jesus claimed to be equal with God, and he had given sufficient proof to establish his claim.

The reaction of the teachers of the law is not mentioned. While they may have marveled, it is unlikely that they praised God. Sadly, most of the Pharisees and teachers chose to remain blind to the truth and to oppose Jesus throughout his ministry.

Jesus has furnished sufficient evidence for belief in him today. He does not ignore the educated and sophisticated and appeal only to the masses. Sadly, however, the more worldly wisdom one has, the harder it seems for that person to see the simple, obvious truth that Jesus is indeed the Son of God.

Again, the Son of David was greater than his noble ancestor. David could not deliver his people from guilt; nor could he heal. But he who descended from him could do both.

CONCLUSION

Today's lesson shows that Jesus can deliver us in two important ways.

First, he is able to deliver us from the power of Satan. Many, on their own, have tried to break sin's dreadful hold on their lives, only to fail. Jesus delivers today just as surely as he delivered the two possessed of demons. He takes the liar, the drunkard, the thief, the adulterer, the abuser, the addict, and delivers them from the bondage of their sins. He has changed countless lives. He can change the lives of the people in your class, of their families, of their friends and neighbors.

Second, Jesus delivers us from the dreadful effects of sin, namely guilt and death. We all need forgiveness, and he extends it. We all need fresh starts, and he gives them. And those he forgives he also heals. It is true that we still suffer disease and death, but Jesus has conquered death so that he might deliver us from it once and for all when he returns to gather his own.

David was a great deliverer, but a greater deliverer has come. Jesus delivers people of all nations from the worst of enemies. May all claim his deliverance, and not make the foolish error of those who asked Jesus to depart from their midst. To reject Jesus is to reject the only possible hope of deliverance.

Discovery Learning

This page contains an alternate lesson plan emphasizing learning activities. Classes desiring such student involvement will find these suggestions helpful. The next page is a reproducible activity page to further enhance discovery learning.

LEARNING GOALS

As a result of participating in today's lesson, a student will be able to:

1. Describe Jesus' power over sin in each example of healing.

2. Explain how evil is displayed in many different forms.

3. Choose a relationship with Jesus and sharing in his ministry over personal preferences and convenience.

INTO THE LESSON

Before class, write the following statement on the chalkboard or on a poster visible to the entire class:

The spiritual forces of evil exhibit their power in many forms.

Allow a brief time for the students to discuss the statement and to suggest a variety of expressions of the power of evil (evil behavior in people, sickness and death, demon possession?). List in a single column on the chalkboard or poster all the ideas that are suggested.

Explain that today's lesson deals with the spiritual warfare that is recorded in Matthew 8:28—9:8. Jesus handled a variety of expressions of Satan's power, and offered deliverance in each case.

INTO THE WORD

Divide the class into two groups. Assign one group the first narrative (Matthew 8:28—9:1) and the second group the other narrative (9:2-8). Ask each group to develop a five-minute TV newscast of the event assigned to it, with one or two reporters and others playing the various roles (the first group has demoniacs, tenders of the pigs, and townspeople; the second group has a paralytic, those who carried him, the teachers of the law, and the observing crowd). The students are to work together within their groups to create the dialogue for interviews concerning what events happened, how they happened, what the results were, why the persons thought the events happened, and how they felt about them. For example, questions might be: *How long had you been demon-possessed? Why did you want Jesus to leave? What did you think when Jesus said you were forgiven? Why were you scribes so upset when Jesus said the man was forgiven?*

Encourage creativity within the facts presented in the Scripture. The point is to probe the realities of the spiritual warfare that took place and the reactions of the various people in both of these incidents.

After each group has had adequate time to prepare, each is to present its newscast. Lead directly into a discussion with this question: *When people realized that Jesus had the power and authority to overcome evil and forgive sin, why were their reactions to him so different?* Wrap up the discussion with conclusions regarding how evil appears in different ways in these events (the demoniacs, the paralytic, and the scribes) and how the reactions of the Gadarene townspeople and the Capernaum crowd were so different. The important thing is for each of us to respond in faith to Jesus' deliverance and forgiveness.

INTO LIFE

Refer back to the list you made at the beginning of class. Now ask how evil can show up in *our* lives, and list the responses in a second column next to the first. Possible responses include: angry outbursts, materialism, gossip, pursuit of pleasure.

Have the class divide into groups of four or five persons each to discuss in what ways they could relate to each of the persons who were involved in the events of today's text.

1. The two demoniacs (out of control, straining relationships).

2. The Gadarene townspeople (concerned with possessions, uneasy about power encounters, unsure about Jesus' impact on life-style).

3. The paralytic (weak, a victim, needing forgiveness).

4. The teachers of the law (self-righteous, critical, overly skeptical).

5. The Capernaum crowd (filled with awe because of Jesus' power, praising God).

Let those who are willing share their responses with the class.

Compare the two crowd responses in the text. The Gadarene townspeople sent him away; the people of Capernaum praised God. The Gadarenes, apparently were too preoccupied with their business (hogs) or their comfortable life-style (which Jesus might challenge) to appreciate the deliverance he had to offer. Challenge the class members to be sure they are putting their relationship with the Lord ahead of personal preferences or convenience.

Then have the class separate into pairs. Ask each person to share a response to these two questions and then pray for one another: How do I need Jesus' deliverance and forgiveness right now? How will I respond?

Harmonize Your Answers

Some events are told in more than one Gospel. By harmonizing all the accounts of an event, we get a more complete picture. Read the Scriptures cited below to get all the facts about the healing of a paralyzed man.

	MATTHEW 9:1-8	MARK 2:1-12	LUKE 5:17-26
1. Where was Jesus teaching?			
2. Who was listening to Jesus teach?			
3. How was the man brought to Jesus?			
4. What did Jesus say to the man before healing him?			
5. What silent accusation was made against Jesus?			
6. How did Jesus know he was being accused?			
7. What contrasting statements do Jesus offer as comparison?			
8. What should the teachers of law have learned from the healing?			
9. What did the man do after he was healed?			
10. What did the crowd do and say?			

Careful Balance

Jesus addressed both the physical needs of the paralytic (healing) and the spiritual needs (forgiveness). The church today needs to maintain the same balance. Write below one or two physical needs you and your church can address in your community. Next to each idea, suggest how that may be used to open the door to perform some spiritual ministry.

PHYSICAL NEED   SPIRITUAL NEED

What cautions must one exercise so that the ministering to the physical needs is not misinterpreted as exploiting people in order to proselytize them?

JESUS, THE SON OF DAVID

LESSON 6

WHY TEACH THIS LESSON?

"Tradition! Tradition!" sang Tevye in *Fiddler on the Roof*. For him and his Jewish contemporaries, tradition was a source of comfort. It gave them a sense of identity and solidarity in a strange land.

Tradition makes a wonderful servant, but it is an onerous master. When traditions serve people's needs, like drawing them together and teaching them the lessons of their history, it fills a needed role in society. But when tradition begins to rule, it riders rough shod over human need and squeezes out mercy.

It was this second role of tradition Jesus confronted and condemned in the religious leaders of his day. It is that same role he would confront in your church and in your students' lives (and in your own). This lesson offers the reminder that mercy is to be valued above tradition.

INTRODUCTION

A. EYES THAT WILL NOT SEE

No one is so blind as the one who closes his or her eyes to the truth and refuses to see. To some extent, we all close our eyes to things we don't want to see. We refuse to see a loved one's failing health. We refuse to see problems in relationships. We refuse to see the need to make hard choices and hard changes. We refuse to see our own faults.

Hatred also causes deliberate blindness. Hatred can be so strong that it causes one to see truth or fairness or innocence. The Pharisees had such hatred for Jesus. They refused to hear the truth of his words. They refused to acknowledge the power of his miracles. They were blind to the obvious.

Others, however, looked at Jesus with open eyes. They saw his miraculous deeds and understood that these words verified his message. They accepted what he said, and Jesus was able to show them many things.

We must ask ourselves whether or not we have open eyes.

B. LESSON BACKGROUND

The Pharisees, who were offended by Jesus, continually sought ways to criticize and attack him. One charge they pursued vigorously was that Jesus and his disciples violated the Sabbath. The first part of Matthew 12 introduces this controversy, as the Pharisees criticized the disciples for supposedly violating the Sabbath by plucking heads of grain and eating them. Jesus said they were innocent (see verse 7) and appealed to Hosea 6:6, to prove his point. He also appealed to the case of David, who on one occasion ate the bread of the tabernacle, which was intended for the priests only. This is interesting in the context of this lesson, which proclaims Jesus as the Son of David. The Son appealed to the example of the father (Matthew 12:1-7).

Jesus concluded that confrontation by stating, "For the Son of Man is Lord of the Sabbath" (v. 8). As the lawgiver himself, Jesus had the authority to interpret the

---

DEVOTIONAL READING:
ISAIAH 42:1-9
LESSON SCRIPTURE:
MATTHEW 12
PRINTED TEXT:
MATTHEW 12:9-23

Jan
8

LESSON AIMS
After this lesson the students should:
1. Be convinced that doing God's will is more important than keeping man-made traditions.
2. Be able to state at least two facets of Jesus' servanthood.
3. See clearly that Jesus is the true Son of David.

KEY VERSE:
It is lawful to do good on the Sabbath. —Matthew 12:12

LESSON 6 NOTES

law of the Sabbath and pronounce whether or not it had been violated. The Pharisees caught the implications of this statement, and at the earliest opportunity sought to trap him regarding appropriate conduct on the Sabbath.

I. LORD OF THE SABBATH (MATTHEW 12:9-14)
A. A DOUBLE-EDGED QUESTION (VV. 9, 10)
9. Going on from that place, he went into their synagogue.

Matthew's transitional statement, *Going on from that place,* is intended only to convey that he is moving from one event to another. Luke makes it clear that this confrontation in the synagogue took place on another Sabbath than the one just mentioned, perhaps the next one. However, it did occur in *their synagogue.* Therefore, the same Pharisees who questioned Jesus about the grain now put another question before him.

10. . . . and a man with a shriveled hand was there. Looking for a reason to accuse Jesus, they asked him, "Is it lawful to heal on the Sabbath?"

Whether by accident or by prearrangement, *a man with a shriveled hand* was in the synagogue on this day. The Pharisees asked Jesus, *Is it lawful to heal on the Sabbath?* According to their tradition, certain treatments might be given on the Sabbath to keep a patient from becoming worse; but efforts to bring healing were not to be made until the following day. It seems clear that these legalists expected Jesus to heal this impaired man, for they posed this question so that they would have a *reason to accuse* him, that is, that they might publicly declare him to be a Sabbath breaker.

This incident reveals the perversity of the hearts of these men. They had seen Jesus heal many who were diseased, disabled, and demon-possessed, and they knew that his healings were genuine miracles. Going on the logical presumption that only God can work miracles, (and take note that all of Jesus' miracles brought only healing, and not hurt, to mankind), they should have realized that Jesus was from God. As Nicodemus said, "No one could perform the miraculous signs you are doing if God were not with him" (John 3:2). At the very least they should have regarded him as a prophet. In fact, Jesus worked so many miracles and such great miracles that he eclipsed any of the Old Testament prophets. And if Jesus was a prophet, then they should have come to him humbly seeking God's message and God's will. But they were not seekers of truth. Closing their eyes to it, they approached Jesus with the intention of overcoming him and obscuring the truth.

B. DO GOOD ON THE SABBATH! (VV. 11-13)
11. He said to them, "If any of you has a sheep and it falls into a pit on the Sabbath, will you not take hold of it and lift it out?

As he did on many occasions, Jesus answered his questioners with questions of his own. In so doing he exposed their hypocrisy and wickedness. So here he posed a situation that would have been familiar to all. He asked what one of them would do if one of his sheep fell *into a pit on the Sabbath.* Would he say, "Hold on little sheep; I'll rescue you tomorrow"? Everyone in the synagogue knew the answer to this. Anyone would naturally rescue the sheep immediately, even on the Sabbath, and no one would accuse him of breaking the Sabbath for doing so.

12. "How much more valuable is a man than a sheep! Therefore it is lawful to do good on the Sabbath."

If it is permissible to help a sheep on the Sabbath, then obviously *it is lawful to do good* to one's fellowman *on the Sabbath.* This conclusion is so clear and powerful that it exposes the foolishness of the original question. Why would anyone even ask if healing on the Sabbath is right? On the face of it, it is always right to heal and help.

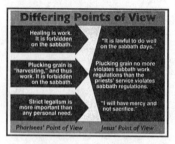

One might even ask how it would be possible to heal on the Sabbath if God did not approve of it. Who could heal but by God's power? If a miracle of healing were done on the Sabbath, it must be done with God's permission and cooperation.

God's Commandment regarding the Sabbath was, "Six days you shall labor and do all your work, but the seventh day is a Sabbath to the Lord your God. On it you shall not do any work" (Exodus 20:9, 10). *Labor* means all the work involved in earning a living and running a household, be it plowing, building fences, making pots, cooking, cleaning, or any such thing. God allotted six days for these activities, but prohibited them on the seventh. The idea was for the people to have rest from their daily toils. These were the kinds of activities that were prohibited. The Jewish scholars' interpretations of this Commandment over the course of time became hardened into traditions, which transformed the Sabbath law into something that God never intended it to be.

13. Then he said to the man, "Stretch out your hand." So he stretched it out and it was completely restored, just as sound as the other.

Jesus did not do any visible work. He simply told the man to *stretch out* his hand. Jesus did not even say he intended to heal it. Yet when the man stretched out his hand it *was completely restored*. That which had been useless to the man became strong and functional. It was obvious to all that Jesus used his power to heal the man's hand, but what work did he do? He did not prepare an ointment or massage the hand or even touch it. How could the Pharisees object to this? Yet they did.

C. MINDLESS TRADITION KILLS TRUTH (V. 14)

14. But the Pharisees went out and plotted how they might kill Jesus.

The Pharisees left the synagogue in such a rage that they immediately began to make plans to *kill him*. Their actions make obvious that they really had no interest in learning whether healing on the Sabbath was legal. They wanted one thing only: to discredit and eliminate Jesus. How twisted and perverted and hardened their consciences were! They could not approve an act of mercy on the Sabbath, but they saw nothing wrong with plotting murder on the sacred day.

We see from this that the Pharisees' mindless devotion to their traditions blinded them to the truth revealed by Jesus. He gave sufficient proof that he spoke with God's authority, but the Pharisees rejected this proof and Jesus along with it.

Let us take care not to harden our hearts against Jesus, as the Pharisees did. Rather, whatever Jesus has said in explaining God's will, let us accept, no matter how it may contradict what we have believed or done, or want to do or don't want to do. May our attitude be that we will do whatever Jesus has said we must do in order to be pleasing and acceptable to God, even if it means changing our lives, our beliefs, or our traditions.

CONFLICTING VALUES

Hundreds of thousands of people died of starvation in 1992. The news of the drought and the desperate need for food to sustain life touched the world. From many nations, and especially from the United States, millions of tons of wheat and other food staples, along with medical supplies, poured into ships and transport planes to relieve the hunger and to fight illness and disease.

Volunteer workers from many relief organizations came to Somalia to see that the food was properly distributed and that medical aid was offered. These volunteers were committed to relieving the suffering of the Somali people; but factional warlords, bent on gaining control of the land, hindered them from their humanitarian efforts. The warlords' greed for power was more important in their eyes than the lives of their suffering countrymen.

WHAT DO YOU THINK?

The Pharisees based their prohibition of healing on the Sabbath on Scripture. The law said no work was to be done on the Sabbath, and healing, they said, was work.

Do you think similar situations arise in the church, when a decision, based on Scripture, is the cause of problems because it is, even so, still an opinion? How can such problems be avoided? Can even good decisions be the source of problems if they are actually opinions based on Scripture and not clear scriptural commands? Why or why not?

WHAT DO YOU THINK?

A tradition is a handed-down pattern of thought or action. Families and communities may have traditions of various kinds, and these provide continuity from generation to generation. Churches may have traditions, too. Some people find great comfort in the traditions of the church.

To others, however, the very thought of tradition causes a negative reaction. It is equated with something extra- or anti-scriptural. Jesus' opposition of the Pharisees' devotion to tradition is cited for support.

Yet Paul calls for Christians to hold to the traditions taught by the apostles (2 Thessalonians 2:15). How does one know whether a tradition is good or bad? How can you be sure traditions are kept in their proper place and not elevated to the status of Scripture?

As one relief worker put it, "The old and young get the least aid, but I have not seen an unfed soldier on either side." Such always seems to be the result when self-interest and concern for the needy meet head-on.

When Jesus healed the sick and infirm, there should have been universal rejoicing among all of his countrymen. Instead, the Pharisees plotted Jesus' destruction. They rejected Heaven's values and replaced them with their own. Let us not be guilty of the same.   —W. P.

II. GOD'S SERVANT (MATTHEW 12:15-21)

A. MANY ARE HEALED (vv. 15, 16)

15. Aware of this, Jesus withdrew from that place. Many followed him, and he healed all their sick.

Aware of the Pharisees' intention to kill him, Jesus *withdrew* from the area. He would not use force or miraculous power to resist his enemies. Instead, he fulfilled his own injunction to his apostles: "When you are persecuted in one place, flee to another" (Matthew 10:23).

Many followed him. The leaders may have been angered by Jesus' action, but not the common people. Many persons afflicted with all sorts of diseases and disabilities thronged after him, hoping that he would heal them. Mark indicates that the crowds came from Galilee, Judea, Jerusalem, and from areas inhabited by Gentiles (Mark 3:7, 8). This throws light on the reference to "the nations" below. Jesus may have been angered by the hardhearted, hypocritical leaders, but he had unbounded compassion for those who suffered, and *he healed all their sick.*

16. . . . warning them not to tell who he was.

It is easy to see how the people's excitement resulting from Jesus' miracles could have got out of control. Among his hearers were many militaristic Zealots, who desired to throw off forcibly the rule of Rome. If the knowledge of Jesus' miraculous power spread, the people might be encouraged to rebel, expecting him to use his power to overcome the enemy. But such a program had no part in Jesus' ministry. He came to reveal God's will to man, and the miracles were signs to show that the revelation came from God. Overemphasis on the miracles could cause the people to ignore the revelation.

B. THE CHOSEN SERVANT (vv. 17-21)

17, 18. This was to fulfill what was spoken through the prophet Isaiah: "Here is my servant whom I have chosen, the one I love, in whom I delight; I will put my Spirit on him, and he will proclaim justice to the nations.

Verses 18-21 are a quotation from Isaiah 42:1-4. Isaiah spoke of the Christ as God's servant, who was loved by God and who pleased God by doing his will. It is obvious that Jesus was he. God's Spirit came to Jesus when he was baptized, and remained with him (Matthew 3:16; John 1:32, 33). Jesus' miracles gave further demonstration that God was pleased with him.

He will proclaim justice to the nations. That is, he would rule justly. The prophecy stated that Christ's kingdom was for all nations. As noted above, Gentiles were among the many who followed Jesus, even at this time. Before returning to his Father in Heaven, Jesus commanded that the gospel message be proclaimed to all nations so that the Gentiles as well as the Jews might be included in God's kingdom (Matthew 28:19).

19. "He will not quarrel or cry out; no one will hear his voice in the streets.

This verse and the next give a general description of the manner in which Jesus conducted his ministry. This verse does not mean that the Christ would not teach in public. To the contrary, he preached and taught continually. And repeatedly he

WHAT DO YOU THINK?

Jesus' healing ministry gained him wide popularity. Rather than exploit that popularity, Jesus often instructed those he healed not to tell others (as in verse 16). He was not interested in gaining fame or in wielding political power. Spreading the word of his miracles of healing at this point would have taken the emphasis of his ministry from the spiritual and placed it on the physical.

How can popular Christian leaders today resist the temptation to exploit their popularity for personal, political, or material profit?

was engaged in controversy with the religious leaders, but he always moved to keep such controversies from becoming more intense. In his teaching he usually did not raise his voice in strife; instead, he spoke quietly and logically. A rabble-rouser might take to *the streets* to stir up a mob and create an uprising against the authorities, and this is exactly what many wanted Jesus to do. Stirring up a violent mob, however, was just what he was trying to avoid.

20. "A bruised reed he will not break, and a smoldering wick he will not snuff out, till he leads justice to victory.

A bruised reed is hardly strong enough to stand erect, or perhaps it is bent with its head toward the earth. In this weakened condition it is easily broken off entirely. A *smoldering wick* is one that has been left untended; it will soon die out. That God's chosen servant would not break the weak reed or extinguish the flickering wick was an emphatic way of declaring that his mission was to heal and restore, not to destroy. His manner would be to show tenderness and compassion, not harshness.

This is exactly the kind of ministry that Jesus conducted. When he walked among his people during his earthly ministry, there were brought to him those who were diseased, disabled, and possessed of demons, and he healed them. Tenderly he cared for those who were hurt, not only physically but spiritually also, those under stress, caught up in sin, oppressed, depressed, and downtrodden. These too he restored to wholeness. Jesus' compassion extends to us today. To those who respond to him and accept him, he shows himself to be tender and loving. Christ knows the weakness of his people and will not lean on them too much or give them a load heavy enough to break them. See 1 Corinthians 10:13. His people are the light of the world (Matthew 5:14). Often their light is smoky and dim, but Christ preserves them instead of putting them out. How long will he continue to do this? *Till he leads justice to victory.* Though in his ministry Jesus showed tenderness and compassion, he will be the conqueror of all. In the end the gospel will prevail; Christ will bring his just and righteous kingdom to complete victory.

21. "In his name the nations will put their hope."

Isaiah's prophecy indicated that Christ's kingdom would be opened to the Gentiles (v. 18). In this verse that thought is completed; the Gentiles would respond to the invitation and receive the gospel. They would *put their hope* in Jesus Christ and trust him to be their Savior and king.

Verse 21 of our text is different from our version of Isaiah, but it follows the Greek version that was used in Matthew's time.

III. THE SON OF DAVID (MATTHEW 12:22, 23)

A. SIGHT AND SPEECH (V. 22)

22. Then they brought him a demon-possessed man who was blind and mute, and Jesus healed him, so that he could both talk and see.

Demons evidently had differing effects on those whom they possessed. The man afflicted here was made *blind* and *mute*. Jesus cast the demon out of the man and *healed him*, so that he could both see and speak.

This miraculous healing gave sight to the man who had been possessed by a demon, and it also caused the people who witnessed it to take a close look at Jesus, perhaps really seeing him for the first time. They saw one who was much more than an ordinary man.

B. SEEING JESUS CLEARLY (V. 23)

23. All the people were astonished and said, "Could this be the Son of David?"

From our perspective, some two thousand years removed, we may be inclined to become casual when reading about another healing; but on the day it occurred,

Gracious Lord, help us see clearly the service that you would have us render for you. Keep us from becoming so attached to familiar practices that we become blind to your commands. Give us hearts full of gratitude for the healing you have brought to our lives. May all that we do bring glory to your holy name. Amen.

THOUGHT TO REMEMBER

None is so blind as a person who will not see.

DAILY BIBLE READINGS

Monday, Jan. 2—The Lord's Servant Will Establish Justice (Isaiah 42:1-9)

Tuesday, Jan. 3—Lord of the Sabbath (Matthew 12:1-8)

Wednesday, Jan. 4—Healing on the Sabbath (Matthew 12: 9-14)

Thursday, Jan. 5—The Mission of God's Chosen Servant (Matthew 12:15-21)

Friday, Jan. 6—Jesus' Power Comes From God (Matthew 12:22-37)

Saturday, Jan. 7—Request for a Sign (Matthew 12:38-42)

Sunday, Jan. 8—Jesus' True Family (Matthew 12:46-50)

all the people were astonished. They were so impressed that they asked each other whether Jesus could be *the Son of David.* This was equivalent to wondering whether he was the Messiah. How this reaction contrasts to that of the Pharisees! Those leaders of the people were blinded by their jealousy, hatred, and traditions. These common people, however, had the honesty to consider Jesus and his works objectively. Doing so led them to ask the right question.

Matthew included this question not only as a record of the thoughts of the people on that day long ago, but as a question for all of his readers to consider and answer for themselves. Indeed, the purpose of his book is to record enough of Jesus' deeds and words to convince people from that day forward that Jesus is in fact the Son of David, the Messiah.

WHY?

"We prayed for both newborn twins. We believe God hears our prayers. One baby lived, and the other died. Why did God make a choice? Why weren't both healed?" The young parents' inquiry to their minister came from faith, not from doubt. The loss of their child brought them seeking an answer to a great mystery. When we pray, why do some become well and others die? Why, under the skilled hands of a gifted surgeon, does one heart patient survive to live a full life and another perish during the procedure?

Perhaps we view healing from the wrong perspective. Death will come to us all. Even Lazarus, who was raised from the grave by Jesus, died again. The main purpose of Jesus' miracles of healing must be kept in mind. First and foremost they attested to his deity. The crowds who saw Jesus heal the demon-possessed man who was blind and mute asked the right question. They did not challenge the miracle. They had seen it occur. They knew the Messiah was to come, and their question was not, "Why this healing and not another?" Their question was, "Could this be the Son of David," the promised one?

Healing does occur. It is a mystery in its distribution, but an evidence of God's power in our Lord Jesus Christ. Accept the gift and honor the Giver, no matter who is the recipient. Perhaps at a later time the mystery will be explained.   —W. P.

CONCLUSION

People often give what they want to give rather than what the recipient needs or wants. Parents may give their children money or things rather than the time and attention they crave and need. Friends sometimes give advice rather than a listening ear.

God's people sometimes do the same thing with him. The ancient Jews developed a great number of traditions regarding their religious life. They were very zealous in observing these traditions, and in doing so they felt that they were serving God. But their traditions often became more important to them than God's revealed law. In fact, Jesus charged the scribes and Pharisees with setting aside God's laws in order to keep their traditions. See Matthew 15:1-9. They gave God what they wanted to give instead of what he asked for.

One who loves Christ and is devoted to him will give to him what he requires. Basically, he requires us to follow his example in attitude, in holiness of life, and in serving others. He calls us to be peaceful and meek, to tenderly heal broken hearts and lives and bodies. He asks us to carry the message of salvation to all peoples of the world. As members of Christ's church, it is appropriate for us to be concerned about maintaining attractive and functional church buildings, providing programming that we feel is appealing and uplifting, and the like. These are good, but let us not allow them to become substitutes for giving to Jesus what he has asked of us— lives that proclaim his glory and saving power.

Discovery Learning

This page contains an alternate lesson plan emphasizing learning activities. Classes desiring such student involvement will find these suggestions helpful. The next page is a reproducible activity page to further enhance discovery learning.

LEARNING GOALS

As a result of participating in today's lesson, a student will be able to:

1. Contrast God's purpose for the Sabbath with man's Sabbath traditions.

2. Name traditions that keep us from helping others.

3. Choose a way to show mercy by putting ministry ahead of tradition.

INTO THE LESSON

Ask the class to define the following: *tradition* and *status quo.* Allow individuals to make a brief clarification of the meaning of each term. If no one brings it up, point out the following:

(a) *Tradition* is a man-made belief or custom that achieves a high degree of importance.

(b) *Status quo,* which comes from Latin, means "the existing condition."

Next, probe why so many people insist on maintaining traditions and the *status quo.* Expect to receive answers such as the following: (1) That's all some people have ever known. (2) They provide security and safety. (3) Some don't like risks at all. (4) Some confuse them with God's will.

Make the transition to the study of today's Bible text by saying that Jesus was confronted by the Pharisees more than once regarding his apparent disregard for their traditions.

INTO THE WORD

Divide the class into three groups for study. Give each group one of the following assignments:

1. Research these Old Testament passages to discover what God intended when he instituted the Sabbath: Exodus 20:8-11; 31:14-17; 35:2, 3; Leviticus 23:3; and Deuteronomy 5:12-15.

2. Summarize Jesus' teachings in Matthew 12:1-8.

3. Analyze Matthew 12:15-21 and clarify how Jesus fulfilled each point in Isaiah 42:1-4. For assistance, see the comments under these verses in this manual.

Allot approximately ten minutes for the groups to complete their study. When the groups have finished, ask a spokesperson from each group to present their conclusions in the same order as the above assignments.

Summarize and explain that the issue in Matthew 12:9-23 is tradition *versus* a ministry of love and kindness.

The Pharisees were blinded by their allegiance to their traditions and battled to maintain the *status quo.* In doing that, they were missing what the crowds were beginning to see—that Jesus was fulfilling his messianic role as the Son of David by acts of compassion and power.

If we are to be faithful to him, then we must avoid the attitude of the Pharisees and place above all else God's will for us to evangelize and to minister to others.

INTO LIFE

Make and distribute copies of the six statements below, leaving a blank for each italicized word. Mention that these are statements that are sometimes used by people who want to keep things the way they are. Allow some time for each one to complete the sentences by filling in the blanks. Approach this as a light-hearted and fun activity.

1. We've never *done it* that *way before.*

2. This is not the *time.*

3. We *tried* it before and it didn't *work.*

4. That's not our *responsibility.*

5. It *costs* too much.

6. We are doing *okay* without it.

Ask the class to suggest some traditions or customs in your church that, while not really scripturally based, are highly valued and would cause quite a stir if changed. These might include the order of worship, who can give a Communion meditation, and what is considered proper Sunday attire.

Discuss how holding onto a tradition could possibly keep the church from ministering with love and compassion. For example, "To be welcome in our church, a person must wear a coat and tie, not jeans and a sweatshirt."

Ask if anyone is aware of a tradition in *this* church that has hindered the church's ability to minister effectively to members or to the unchurched community. Keep the discussion focused on the need for us to follow Jesus' priorities, emphasizing ministry over man-made traditions.

Conclude by asking the class to work in pairs to share answers to these questions:

1. What can we as a church do to make sure that we do not allow man-made traditions to take precedence over doing Christ's will?

2. How can I minister to others with compassion and kindness?

They Missed the Point!

In order to enforce the law, the Pharisees added their traditions. The law said no one could work on the Sabbath; the tradition defined what was "work." Writing two letters of the alphabet was work—unless one or both were written in the dirt or were otherwise not permanent. Walking too far (based on the distance of the farthest encampment from the tabernacle during the wilderness wanderings) was work. If a man threw an object more than six feet, it was work—unless a dog or another person intercepted it before it traveled six feet!

One can appreciate the intent of the Pharisees' interpretations, but in practice they completely missed the point. Striving for literal obedience, they failed to allow the law to minister to their hearts and produce loving, merciful attitudes. How much better to have literal obedience with love and mercy! Explore the possibilities with the following questions:

I understand that God planned the Sabbath for these reasons—

It sounds as if the Pharisees wrongly interpreted the Sabbath in these ways—

How could limiting travel on the Sabbath fit within God's plan for the Sabbath?

How could limiting travel on the Sabbath be used to contradict God's plan for the Sabbath?

Have We Missed the Point?

"For I desire mercy, not sacrifice, and acknowledgment of God rather than burnt offerings," Hosea 6:6. How could an appreciation of this verse have prevented many of the Pharisaic abuses in Jesus' day? How could it prevent some of the problems that arise in your church today?

A FOREIGNER'S FAITH

LESSON 7

WHY TEACH THIS LESSON?

"Something there is that doesn't love a wall, that wants it down." So wrote Robert Frost in "Mending Wall." But something there is that does love a wall and wants it up, too! "Good fences make good neighbors," or so we have convinced ourselves. Perhaps we like the fact that behind the wall we cannot see their need. If we saw it, we would be obliged to do something to help. But, behind the wall, we can dwell in ignorant bliss.

In this lesson, we will see how Jesus tore down the walls that separated him from people. A Gentile woman, and then a number of other Gentiles after that, found in Jesus a good neighbor instead of a wall.

Use this lesson to challenge your students to look behind the walls, to see the needs, and to share the grace of God.

INTRODUCTION

A. BOUNDARIES

Who can forget the day the television cameras brought into our homes images of people dancing with glee atop the Berlin Wall? Half the population of Berlin, it seemed, chipped away at this monument to the Cold War. Once this wall had been patrolled by border guards armed with machine guns. And from time to time the guards used their lethal power to stop those who sought to flee. But suddenly this broken and disappearing wall symbolized freedom. Friends and relatives shut off from one another for so long were free to visit again. And, after a time, a city and a nation were reunited. A repressive regime had crumbled. The hated wall had become irrelevant, something to be carted away in slabs to museums or to be broken into bits by souvenir hunters. Soon little chunks of the wall began showing up on desks and coffee tables.

Walls, whether literal or figurative, play important parts in our lives. Some walls are indeed hated. But in other instances walls or boundaries are, in fact, appropriate and helpful. The owners of a vacation home in the mountains of North Carolina have named their cabin simply, "Four Stone Walls." Walls can help to provide a place of comfort, a place protected from the elements. Walls also provide protection from various threats to the welfare of a family. When we are responsible for the care of children, for example, we spend a considerable amount of our time calling attention to "walls," or boundaries. Responsible parents of young children must often draw distinctions between those things that are good for them and those things that are not. And so they tell their children, "Do this, but don't do that." The point is that safety is to be found in certain circumstances, within certain parameters, and threats lurk beyond.

The problem, of course, is that some boundaries have been drawn improperly. The surveyor was in a hurry. The person who drew the map was careless. And sometimes the parent was filled with animosities, was unreasonably fearful, or was poorly informed.

Sometimes the boundaries that have been drawn improperly have been in place for longer than anyone can remember. And if tradition prescribes inappropriate

DEVOTIONAL READING:
ISAIAH 35:5-10
LESSON SCRIPTURE:
MATTHEW 15:1-31
PRINTED TEXT:
MATTHEW 15:21-31

Jan
15

LESSON AIMS

This lesson should help students:

1. Recall with gratitude that Jesus broke through barriers to reach people.

2. Identify boundaries that need to be crossed today so that all people may have an opportunity to respond to God's reconciling love.

3. Examine their actions, attitudes, and prejudices in light of the example of Jesus.

KEY VERSE:
Woman, you have great faith!
—Matthew 15:28

LESSON 7 NOTES

HOW TO SAY IT

Caesarea Philippi. Sess-uh-REE-uh Fih-LIP-pie or FIL-ih-pie.
Canaanite. KAY-nan-ite.
Decapolis. Dee-KAP-uh-lis.
Pharisees. FAIR-ih-seez.
Phoenicia. Fih-NISH-uh.

OPTION

Use the reproducible map on page 182 to introduce this lesson and give your students an appreciation of the geography. You might also use this map for other lessons in the quarter to further your students' understanding.

Four factors essential to faithful living, which are drawn from the Canaanite woman's faith and action, are highlighted on visual 7 of the visuals packet.

lines, it can be extraordinarily difficult for the heirs of that tradition to sense that anything is wrong, much less to feel free to cross the boundary.

Jesus often encountered people who were stubbornly committed to maintaining improperly drawn boundaries, inappropriate barriers, walls that divided people from people, walls that kept people from doing the will of God, walls that had "always" been there. Jesus frequently encountered people who were confused about such questions as the lines between pleasing and displeasing God, between respectable and disrespectable people, between righteousness and sin, and between what was possible and impossible. We often find Jesus confronting people whose world was topsy-turvy. Not only were lines improperly drawn, but the wrong labels were used. "Up" was "down"; "down" was "up."

In the first century, as in every century since then, what Jesus had to say was not what many people wanted to hear. It was not, and is not, easy to listen to the Master. Discipleship is rewarding, but it is also costly. As followers of Jesus, we are often called upon to struggle against opposition, against barriers to faithfulness. Even though Christians draw strength from the grace and mercy of God and have the support of fellow believers, the struggles are real. Through the centuries, listening to Jesus has sometimes cost believers their lives. At the very least, listening to him will often inconvenience us and sometimes set us at odds with family and friends. Squaring our lives with our faith is the work of a lifetime. Listening to the Master requires us as honestly as possible to examine our actions, our attitudes, and, yes, our prejudices. What is more frustrating than to recognize that a wall that has provided us with a certain sense of security is not God's wall? What is more frustrating than to recognize that we have sometimes been on the wrong side of a wall?

B. LESSON BACKGROUND

The fifteenth chapter of Matthew begins with Jesus in Galilee responding to Pharisees and teachers of the law who had come all the way from Jerusalem. They were concerned. They had come a long way to ask why the disciples of Jesus were "crossing over the line." Why were they violating tradition? The disciples, after all, did not wash their hands before they ate a meal. How offensive!

Of course, we are inclined to think that people ought to learn to wash their hands before they eat. It is traditional for us, too. Besides, we know something about bacteria and personal hygiene. But for a group of grown men to undertake an arduous journey to tell another adult that he and his disciples should wash their hands in the prescribed fashion—and as a matter of religious obligation—is a bit much! As is often the case as we consider the questions put to Jesus by the religious leaders of the day, we wonder if there is not more than meets the eye here. Is there a hidden agenda?

Jesus then turned the tables on his critics. Why did they nullify the clear command of God? Why did they use the tradition of the elders as a means of evading their responsibilities to their mothers and fathers? These defenders of orthodoxy, these "border guards" from Jerusalem, were, in a word, hypocrites! They never neglected to wash their hands, but thought nothing of neglecting the needs of their parents. Ignoring weighty matters, these men from Jerusalem specialized in the trivial (vv. 1-9).

Jesus went on to explain that cleanness and uncleanness were ultimately matters of the heart. From an unclean heart came such sinful behavior as evil thinking, murder, adultery, other sexual immorality, stealing, lying, and slander. His critics would do well to give more attention to real uncleanness. Sinful actions issuing from the heart mattered infinitely more than eating with unwashed hands. Real defilement mattered infinitely more than ritual defilement. In comparison to obeying God out of a sense of gratitude, merely going through a routine prescribed by the tradition of the Pharisees mattered not at all (vv. 10-20).

Then Jesus and his inner circle crossed a geographical, ethnic, and religious border. They left Galilee for a time. They made their way toward the coastal region of Phoenicia, where Galileans were outsiders.

I. JESUS RESPONDS TO A WOMAN OF FAITH (MATTHEW 15:21-28)

A. LEAVING GALILEE (V. 21)

21. Leaving that place, Jesus withdrew to the region of Tyre and Sidon.

As was often the case, Jesus went from one place to another, not just for a change of scenery, but also hoping for a change of activity. Jesus often sought solitude, especially after attending to the needs of the multitudes. We recall, for example, Jesus' crossing the Sea of Galilee searching for solitude, a time for prayer and rest, but finding a crowd that grew to more than five thousand. After healing the sick who were among them, and then miraculously feeding that vast throng, he sent the multitudes home for the night. Then he walked alone up the mountainside to pray (Matthew 14:13-23).

Jesus rarely ventured into Gentile areas. (We read of his going to Samaria, to Caesarea Philippi, and to the Decapolis, the region southeast of the Sea of Galilee.) Another occasion is described in this text, when he and his disciples made their way into Phoenicia, and particularly to the area around *Tyre and Sidon*, the principal cities of the *region*.

We cannot be certain how long this visit lasted or how many miles it covered. It is about thirty-five miles from the northern edge of the Sea of Galilee to the ancient port of Tyre. The coastal city of Sidon was more than twenty miles north of Tyre, but the record does not say they went into these cities, just that they were in the area. Thus Jesus and his disciples did not necessarily undertake a trip of more than a hundred miles, but any of us would consider their journey to be a very ambitious walk.

This region offered Jesus and the disciples the prospect of a retreat, the prospect of relief from the stress of the crowds and the controversies with Israel's religious leaders. Here thousands would not be seeking his healing touch. Here, in fact, Jesus and his disciples might be more or less anonymous.

B. AN URGENT PLEA (V. 22)

22. A Canaanite woman from that vicinity came to him, crying out, "Lord, Son of David, have mercy on me! My daughter is suffering terribly from demon-possession."

Even in the region of Tyre and Sidon, however, Jesus' coming was known by at least one person. A certain Gentile woman (called here *a Canaanite woman*) learned somehow that Jesus had come into the area, and she came out to meet him. Furthermore, she doubtless knew that Jesus had cast out demons from many persons in Galilee. This woman was not timid. She was determined to get help for her daughter. With her insistent cries for mercy for herself and for her daughter, this devoted mother disturbed whatever peace and quiet Jesus and his party may have been enjoying. Convinced that Jesus had it within his power to end the suffering of her demon-possessed daughter, the distressed woman cried out, explaining her plight and begging Jesus to help. We cannot know how much this woman knew about Jesus or precisely what the words she used to address him meant to her. *Lord* was used commonly in that day as a term of respect. It was often used in a way equivalent to our word *sir*. *Son of David* is recognized by Christians as a Messianic title, but we cannot know that she used it in this manner. At the very least, however, she honored Jesus greatly and had the highest confidence in him. And she clearly believed that he had the power to work miracles.

C. THE DISCIPLES' RESPONSE (V. 23)

23. Jesus did not answer a word. So his disciples came to him and urged him, "Send her away, for she keeps crying out after us."

Usually Jesus helped all who came to him. In this instance, however, he *did not answer a word*. The silence of Jesus constituted a barrier for the woman. But she kept crying out. The disciples appear to have been annoyed with the woman, and they urged Jesus to send her on her way. They may have meant that he should grant her request promptly so that peace and quiet could be restored. Or they may have been urging him to send her away without granting her request. We can't be sure which. As on other occasions, so here, they were quick to give Jesus advice. And they seem quite self-centered in this instance. They were insistent: "Do something!" they said in effect. "We've heard enough from this noisy Gentile woman!"

D. PERSISTENT PLEADING (VV. 24-27)

24. He answered, "I was sent only to the lost sheep of Israel."

First, the woman encountered the barrier of silence, and then came these discouraging words that served as yet another barrier. He was sent *only to the lost sheep of Israel*, and this woman was not a part of that flock. Jesus' words remind us that his mission during his earthly ministry was not to right every wrong throughout the world all at once. His mission was limited by the restrictions related to his humanity. He had only so much energy. He could travel only so far. But his mission was also limited by an intentional design. While Jesus made rare exceptions to this general rule of devoting his attention to the house of Israel, later he would commission his disciples to take his gospel throughout the world.

25. The woman came and knelt before him. "Lord, help me!" she said.

The woman may have heard Jesus' response to the urging of his disciples. But, regardless, she had no intention of slipping away in defeat. Instead, she continued to seek Jesus' mercy relentlessly. Kneeling before him, she continued to beg for his help.

26. He replied, "It is not right to take the children's bread and toss it to their dogs."

Now another barrier is noted, and words that are expressed constituted a further test of the woman's faith. On the face of it, Jesus' statement appears to be an insensitive response to the heartbroken woman's cries. *It is not right*, Jesus observed, as he used what was perhaps a common saying about the inappropriateness of giving the food intended for children to dogs. The contempt of the Jews for Gentiles was deeply rooted. *Dogs* was a term used among Jews of that day to express their contempt for Gentiles. The epithet called to mind undesirable, unclean animals, not cuddly household pets. Jesus was indicating that he was sent to the Jews, and that the woman was a Gentile. By employing a term that was in common use, he meant merely that it was not in keeping with the design of his personal ministry to grant to Gentiles the benefits that were intended for the Jews. In our day of heightened sensitivity to language that is "politically correct," this remark likely will strike many as awkward. It is evident, in light of his teaching in general as well as his ultimate response to this woman, that Jesus did not regard her as an inferior person. Nor

WHAT DO YOU THINK?

These disciples frequently surprise us. In essence, they were saying to Jesus, "Get rid of this woman! She's bothering us." If nothing else, they were presuming to tell their Master what to do—hardly appropriate behavior for a disciple. Even more, they give every appearance of being self-centered. There is no evidence of their having any sensitivity to this woman's desperate need, no compassion such as Jesus showed. It may well be that because of their inappropriate response, Jesus engaged in the "repartee" with the woman for his disciples' benefit as well as for hers!

Why is it so easy for good people, like the disciples, to get so caught up with their own situation that they become insensitive to people in need? What can you do to be sure you are not guilty of the same?

WHAT DO YOU THINK?

Commentators have made much of Jesus' statement about giving the children's food to dogs. For some, it has caused no little concern that Jesus would call someone a dog!

Think about our own expression, "You can't teach an old dog new tricks." Are we calling someone a dog whenever we cite this old adage? Do you think Jesus' expression might have been understood as a mere comparison—that some things are appropriate and some things are not—rather than as a personal epithet? Why or why not?

was he giving his approval to the abusive term. Once again, the statement may have been as strong as it was because it was intended as another test of the woman's spirit. It was a recognition of the barrier that existed between the two peoples. Would she allow that barrier to keep her from receiving a favor from a Jew?

27. "Yes, Lord," she said, "but even the dogs eat the crumbs that fall from their masters' table."

Regardless of precisely how Jesus delivered his words, the essential point was that at this time his mission had limits. But the humble, persistent woman protested. Granting that the main course was for Israel, did the Gentiles not have a right to the scraps? She was convinced that all would be well if Jesus would grant her just a little attention. She had encountered several barriers, but she would not give up her hope that Jesus would help.

E. REQUEST GRANTED (V. 28)

28. Then Jesus answered, "Woman, you have great faith! Your request is granted." And her daughter was healed from that very hour.

Jesus paid the woman a high compliment. Her faith was great! Perhaps the Canaanite woman did not fully comprehend what she was saying. Perhaps she could not have presented a carefully reasoned discourse on God's boundless love for the whole world. But the persistent cries that the disciples found so bothersome were an eloquent testimony to her faith as far as Jesus was concerned. He paid this Gentile woman a compliment that any of his Jewish disciples would have been grateful to receive. Great was her faith! Her faith was tough. Her faith struggled against obstacles. (We are reminded of the account in Mark 2:1-12 of the faith and the struggle of those who tore a hole in the roof so that they could lower their paralytic friend into the house where Jesus was. See lesson 5.) Thus Jesus granted her request.

It may be of interest to note similarities between this passage and Matthew 8:5-13. When Jesus paid tribute to the Roman centurion who successfully pleaded with Jesus to heal his servant, he declared that this Gentile had faith greater than he had found in Israel. And in response to the urgent requests of both the centurion and the Canaanite woman, Jesus worked the miracles at a distance.

TENACIOUS FAITH

Roy Gault's light plane ride had turned into a tragic nightmare. Just a few minutes out of the airport near Anchorage, Alaska, the pilot had run into trouble. The plane was too close to the mountain. As the pilot tried to turn to avoid a crash, Roy knew they were not going to make it. The plane plowed into the mountainside, and both pilot and passenger were thrown clear. They were too injured to call, signal, or do anything to attract attention.

Night fell, and Roy awoke to hear the sound of animals nearby. "How horrible," he thought, "to live through the crash only to be mauled or eaten by bears!" Morning light showed the animals to be goats, but no rescue plane cheered their hopeless situation. Finally, however, the two were found.

Roy had broken bones throughout his body. The doctors said he would live but never walk again. In time he was dismissed from the hospital, but he was in a special bed and unable to care for himself. His mother and father took care of him, and they refused to give up hope. Slowly the impossible began to happen. Bathed in his parents' faith and prayers, Roy was nursed back to health. Their faith would not be deterred from seeking wholeness for their son. Roy now captains a large fishing vessel in Alaskan waters.

Jesus healed the Canaanite woman's daughter for the same great, overcoming faith. Listen to his words: "O woman, your faith is great; be it done for you as you

WHAT DO YOU THINK?

The account of the Canaanite woman can teach us some valuable lessons about prayer. We learn that Jesus is approachable by anyone. Even though this woman was a Gentile, Jesus heard her request. He would help her with her need. We also learn that Jesus works in his own time. He did not immediately answer her request. By delaying, he challenged her faith in him and taught the disciples (and us) an important lesson about persistence and patience when approaching God with our requests. We also learn that we can approach the Lord openly, honestly, and without fear of rejection.

Which of these lessons—or some other you see here—is most significant to you in your prayer life? Why? Which is most reassuring? Which do you think most needs to be talked about in the church? Why?

PRAYER

You were in Christ reconciling us, O God. You loved us while we were content to live in sin, while we were separated from you by our own waywardness. You saw the barriers and broke through them. You came seeking us. You came in Jesus Christ, who refused to observe artificial boundaries of man's making. You came in Jesus Christ, crucified, risen, victorious! Because we are grateful, help us to seek others for you with the same compassion and persistence. Help us to break through the walls that separate us from those you are seeking today. Amen.

THOUGHT TO REMEMBER

Jesus said to the Canaanite woman, "You have great faith!" How do we respond to the challenges and barriers we confront as believers? What would Jesus say of our faith?

DAILY BIBLE READINGS

Monday, Jan. 9—Help Promised for God's People (Isaiah 35:3-7)

Tuesday, Jan. 10—Gentiles Are God's People (1 Peter 2:4-10)

Wednesday, Jan. 11— Traditions: Good or Bad? (Matthew 15:1-9)

Thursday, Jan. 12—Living From the Heart (Matthew 15: 10-20)

Friday, Jan. 13—Jesus Responds to a Gentile's Faith (Matthew 15:21-28)

Saturday, Jan. 14—A Man's Hearing and Speech Restored (Mark 7:31-37)

Sunday, Jan. 15—We Are One in Christ (Galatians 3:23-29)

wish" (New American Standard Bible). Christ will reward those who refuse to relinquish their faith in him.

—W. P.

II. JESUS PERFORMS MANY MIRACLES (MATTHEW 15:29-31)

A. RETURN TO THE SEA OF GALILEE (v. 29)

29. Jesus left there and went along the Sea of Galilee. Then he went up on a mountainside and sat down.

After his visit to the region of Tyre and Sidon, Jesus returned to the vicinity of the Sea of Galilee. Perhaps wishing to avoid the excitable multitudes and the hostile Pharisees, Jesus did not return to Galilee itself. Instead, he went to the region of the Decapolis southeast of the Sea of Galilee (Mark 7:31).

B. RETURN OF THE CROWDS (v. 30)

30. Great crowds came to him, bringing the lame, the blind, the crippled, the mute and many others, and laid them at his feet; and he healed them.

Earlier, Jesus had cast the demons out of two men in this area, and the citizens had asked Jesus to leave (see lesson 5). Now great multitudes came to him gladly. People from Decapolis had followed Jesus on his first tour through Galilee (Matthew 4:25). It would seem that their testimony and that of the healed demoniac (see Mark 5:18-20) brought about the people's marked change of attitude toward Jesus.

In great numbers they came seeking healing. They brought with them those who were lame, the blind, the crippled, the mute and many others. And Jesus healed them.

C. AMAZEMENT AND PRAISE (v. 31)

31. The people were amazed when they saw the mute speaking, the crippled made well, the lame walking and the blind seeing. And they praised the God of Israel.

Jesus broke through the barriers of what could ordinarily be expected. Those who saw him heal the sick were amazed, for most of them probably had never seen such mighty acts performed before. The phrase the God of Israel strongly suggests that the crowd was drawn largely from the Gentile population in the Decapolis area. One wonders if any of these were led to a faith as invincible as that of the Canaanite woman of Phoenicia.

CONCLUSION

In the eyes of some, the Canaanite woman was not worthy of attention for many reasons. She was "from the wrong side of the tracks." She was a Gentile. She did not worship in Jerusalem.

Like those who thronged around Jesus when he was on the shore of the Sea of Galilee, she sought him eagerly, expectantly.

But Jesus singled out this woman for praise. Great was her faith! There were all sorts of boundaries that could have deterred her. She could have given up, retreating in sullen silence. But she was as relentless as an army with a battering ram at the gate to a besieged city. For her persistence, for her great faith, Jesus praised her. And even though we don't know her name, we remember her. We, like Jesus, pay tribute to her for her persistent faith.

If all we do is admire this woman, however, our response to these verses in Matthew is incomplete. What boundaries do we need to cross for the sake of our relationship to Jesus Christ? What prejudices limit our effectiveness as his servants? Just how great is our faith?

Discovery Learning

This page contains an alternate lesson plan emphasizing learning activities. Classes desiring such student involvement will find these suggestions helpful. The next page is a reproducible activity page to further enhance discovery learning.

LEARNING GOALS

At the conclusion of this examination of Matthew 15:21-31, the students will be able to:

1. Explain how Jesus used this event to break through barriers to reach people.

2. Name people who are outsiders to class members.

3. Identify the boundaries that must be crossed if they are to reach those "outsiders" with the gospel.

INTO THE LESSON

As class members arrive, have them form groups of three or four students each. Ask each group to brainstorm to see what images come to their minds when they think of the word *wall*. Allot three to five minutes for this. Have a person from each group write their responses on the chalkboard or newsprint. Then lead a brief discussion as the groups share their responses.

Make the transition into the Bible study section by stating that today's passage of Scripture looks at invisible walls that sometimes divide people, and that Jesus will show us how to deal with those barriers.

INTO THE WORD

Use the material from the "Lesson Background" section (pages 176, 177) to establish the context of the event in today's Scripture text. Then have a class member read Matthew 15:21-31 aloud as class members follow along.

Assign the class members to work in pairs to find the answers to the following questions from the text:

1. What specific barriers are present in this passage that could have prevented the woman from asking Jesus for what she needed? (The woman was not a Jew; her daughter was possessed by a demon; what she asked defied natural law.)

2. After the woman pleaded for mercy, why did Jesus state that he was sent only to "the lost sheep of Israel"? (v. 24). (Perhaps he wanted to test the extent of her faith.)

3. Jesus responded to the woman's second plea by saying, "It is not right to take the children's bread and toss it to their dogs" (v. 26). His answer seems abrupt and uncaring. How would you explain this? (This saying pointed up the barrier that separated Jew from Gentile. It seems that Jesus was probing to see if the woman's faith would overcome that barrier. See the comments and "What Do You Think?" questions in the commentary section, pages 178, 179.)

4. What do you conclude about the woman by her response recorded in verse 27? (She was humble and persistent. She was convinced Jesus could help her daughter.)

5. Why do you think Jesus eventually granted the woman's request? (v. 28). (It was surely because of the depth of her faith.)

6. What was the response of the multitudes who witnessed Jesus' miracles? (They praised the God of Israel.)

Allot ten to twelve minutes for the pairs to work together to find the answers. Then at the designated time, call the groups together and proceed with a discussion of the text, using the students' answers as the basis for the discussion. Be sure to fill in any details that were missed by the groups. Summarize the teaching of this passage.

INTO LIFE

To apply this lesson, quote the lesson writer's statement in the Conclusion: "If all we do is admire this woman, however, our response to these verses in Matthew is incomplete." Use his questions to guide a discussion:

1. What barriers exist today that inhibit the proclamation of Jesus Christ to those who need to hear? (The answers may include ethnic and cultural barriers; concern for health and personal welfare, such as when working with AIDS victims; indifference to the needs of those who are different from us.)

2. What boundaries do we in this congregation need to cross for the sake of our relationship to Jesus Christ? (Keep probing until specific barriers are mentioned.)

3. What prejudices limit our effectiveness as his servants? (Seek specific answers.)

Distribute paper and pencils or pens to your students. Lead them to make personal application by asking them to write the names of three or four people that would be considered as "outsiders" to them. Next to each name, the student should write one or two barriers that cause them to be outsiders. (These may be some of the barriers discussed above or other ones.)

Conclude by asking, "How great is your faith? Could you overcome barriers to take Christ to another? How persistent are you?" Ask each student to complete this sentence at the bottom of the papers they have been writing on: "I want to overcome barriers that keep me from sharing my faith by. . . ." If time allows, let them share their answers with two others. Then close with prayer.

Map It Out

Read the Matthew 15:21-31. Circle on this map the locations referred to. Draw lines to indicate Jesus' travel.

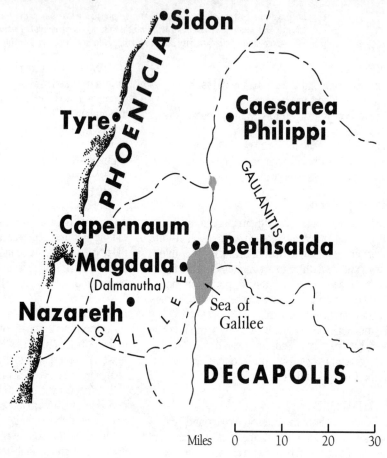

Don't Fence Me Out!

Imagine you have just arrived in your church auditorium and discovered a section of seating "Reserved for Super Saints." You do not know how these people qualify for "super saint" status, but since you have not been notified that you are included, you sit elsewhere. Then you notice that some of the people in the special section are very much like yourself. In time given to church activities, faithful attendance, and Christian witness in society, you can see no reason to elevate their "sainthood" over your own. Still, they are in and you are out.

How do you feel about the separation?

How is that similar to the separation non-Christians may sometimes feel as they look at the church as a whole?

What can you do to be sure your church walls are not a barrier keeping the world out and away from the "super saints"?

Jesus the Fulfillment

Unit 3. Jesus: The Son of David
(Lessons 5-9)

JESUS IS TRANSFIGURED

LESSON 8

WHY TEACH THIS LESSON?

If you listen to television sports announcers, you know no team ever simply wins or loses anymore. The Cats *maul* the Raiders and the Vikings *storm* their opponents' turf; the Bengals are *annihilated* and the Braves are *scalped*. Even when the margin of victory is slim, it seems the verb has to be more dramatic than *won* or *lost*.

Overstatement may be the way of sportscasting, but there are still some things that cannot be overstated. One of them is the majesty of Christ. God himself put on a display greater than any created by modern pyrotechnic experts. And when that did not adequately impress the disciples, who still wanted to elevate Moses and Elijah to his stature, God's own voice echoed on the mountain.

We are prone to ingratitude. We easily take for granted what is common. God's grace in Jesus is so abundant, we can easily fall into the trap of taking it, and him, for granted. This lesson should challenge your students to see Jesus as the unique and awesome one he is. While it may be too much to hope your students will fall with their faces to the ground, as the three disciples did, such a response would not be an overstatement.

INTRODUCTION

A. CHRIST, OUR FOCAL POINT

Being the father of two teenagers who love amusement parks, I have learned how to survive roller coaster rides. My method is simple: I find something inside the coaster to focus my eyes on while the ride is in progress. That object becomes my focal point: my eyes never deviate from it. By being able to do this I have found that the heights and depths of the rides no longer frighten me.

The disciples were in their third year of close association with Jesus. During this time they had heard his marvelous teaching, had seen him confound the religious leaders and the teachers of the law in debate, and had been eyewitnesses of his tremendous miracles of healing wherever he went. Varied and exciting were the many high points they shared in ministry with their Master.

At the time of the event recorded in our lesson text, however, the bottom had dropped out of everything for the disciples—grief and dismay had overtaken them. Jesus knew the cause of their spiritual "low," and he had a remedy for it. They needed a positive, spiritual focal point. Our lesson shows how Jesus provided for the disciples' need.

B. LESSON BACKGROUND

Last week's lesson ended with Jesus in the region known as the Decapolis, southeast of the Sea of Galilee. He spent three days there healing those who were lame, blind, mute, and those suffering from various other physical disorders. At the end of that time he miraculously fed the multitude, which numbered four thousand. After dismissing the multitude, he entered a boat with the disciples and crossed over to the western shore of the Sea of Galilee to the town of Magdala (Matthew 15:32-39).

DEVOTIONAL READING:
2 PETER 1:16-21

LESSON SCRIPTURE:
MATTHEW 17:1-23

PRINTED TEXT:
MATTHEW 17:1-13

LESSON AIMS

The study of this lesson is designed to help the student:

1. Understand the significance of the transfiguration to Jesus, to the disciples, and to us.

2. Appreciate who Jesus is and what he did for us on the cross.

3. Seek to be a witness to God's grace and Christ's glory.

Jan
22

KEY VERSE:

This is my Son, whom I love; with him I am well pleased. Listen to him! —Matthew 17:5

LESSON 8 NOTES

In Magdala Pharisees and Sadducees demanded that he show them a sign from Heaven. Exposing their hypocrisy, Jesus rebuffed them briskly and departed. Returning by boat with the disciples to the eastern shore of the lake, Jesus warned them to beware of the leaven (the teachings) of these corrupt leaders (Matthew 16:1-12).

Next the little band moved northward to the vicinity of Caesarea Philippi. There Peter answered Jesus' inquiry with words that are among the most sublime in all of Matthew's Gospel. Speaking for himself and all of the disciples, he declared their conviction that Jesus was the Christ, the Son of the living God. In response, Jesus spoke a blessing upon Peter.

Soon, however, the mood changed. Jesus' ministry was turning toward its climax, and the disciples needed to know it. And so he revealed to them clearly for the first time that he must go to Jerusalem and suffer at the hands of the nation's religious leaders and be killed. Peter expressed the horror of the whole group at this suggestion, but he was silenced by the stern rebuke of Jesus. The Lord continued speaking to them on the theme of taking up one's cross and following him. This turn of events left the disciples in the darkness of despair (vv. 13-28).

I. THE SON CHANGED (MATTHEW 17:1-4)

A. A PLACE APART (V. 1)

1. After six days Jesus took with him Peter, James and John the brother of James, and led them up a high mountain by themselves.

After six days. Nearly a week had passed since Jesus announced to the disciples that he was to suffer and die. They must have found this week the heaviest of their lives. Surely much earnest discussion had taken place among them, and they probably had got little sleep. They needed help in dealing with their despair. Understanding this, Jesus took the three leaders of the group into a *high mountain by themselves,* where they could be given private instruction and encouragement to help them conquer their doubt and dismay. The spiritual uplift these three were to receive would soon be radiated to the rest of the disciples. Peter had made the good confession in the vicinity of Caesarea Philippi, and it seems that Jesus and the disciples were still in this same general area. The *high mountain* Jesus and the three disciples ascended was probably Mount Hermon, the highest in the region. Less likely is Mount Tabor, twelve miles southwest of the Sea of Galilee. From as early as A.D. 326 it has been suggested as the site, but it is not in the same area as Caesarea Philippi (though it could easily have been reached in *six days*) and it is not nearly as high.

B. A CHANGE IN CHRIST'S APPEARANCE (V. 2)

2. There he was transfigured before them. His face shone like the sun, and his clothes became as white as the light.

The word *transfigured* means "transformed" or "changed." From Luke's account, we learn that Jesus' appearance changed while he was praying (Luke 9:29). His *face* and his *clothes* began to shine brilliantly. The disciples were given a glimpse of Jesus' majesty; his glory was shown before their very eyes. The darkness of sadness, confusion, and despair that had filled their hearts regarding their beloved Master was dispelled by the radiance that issued forth from him. Years later Peter wrote of this scene and its message: "We were eyewitnesses of his majesty. For he received honor and glory from God the Father . . . when we were with him on the sacred mountain" (2 Peter 1:16-18).

C. A COMFORTING CONVERSATION (V. 3)

3. Just then there appeared before them Moses and Elijah, talking with Jesus.

WHAT DO YOU THINK?

Jesus took only three of the disciples with him up on the mountain, and only those three were privileged to witness his transfiguration. The same three were often granted privileges the other nine were not. Some might consider this unfair. Others say Jesus was training these three for special leadership roles. Still others say everyone needs an "inner circle" of friends who are closer than other friends.

What do you think? Why did only these three get invited to the mountain top? What does this suggest about interpersonal roles in the church today? Does it suggest a style of leadership training, for example? To what extent ought we to imitate Jesus' example here?

"This is my beloved Son . . .

hear ye him."

Visual 8 is a photograph of Mount Tabor, which some think was the site of Jesus' transfiguration.

Apparently the three disciples were asleep when the transfiguration occurred and Moses and Elijah appeared and began talking with Jesus. Awaking from their slumber, the disciples saw the three and overheard their conversation: they were talking about Jesus' death, which was to occur in Jerusalem (Luke 9:30-32). Moses and Elijah may be considered key representatives of the law and the prophets. Did the disciples at this time understand the significance of Moses and Elijah's appearing with Jesus and discussing his death? If not, they would in time come to realize that Jesus' death was completely in harmony with God's will as revealed in the Old Testament (see Luke 24:44).

D. A CHALLENGING RESPONSE (v. 4)

4. Peter said to Jesus, "Lord, it is good for us to be here. If you wish, I will put up three shelters—one for you, one for Moses and one for Elijah."

Luke indicates that Peter uttered these words as Moses and Elijah started to leave (Luke 9:33). Not knowing what to say, Peter suggested that they make *three shelters*, one for each of these great teachers (see Mark 9:6). The word here probably means shelters made from tree branches, such as the Jews dwelt in during the Feast of Tabernacles (Leviticus 23:39-43). Perhaps Peter thought that by providing shelter for the three they would stay awhile longer so the disciples could hear them all. Did he also think that by having them all stay on the mountain Jesus' death could be forestalled?

In the Christian life there are occasions we call "mountaintop experiences." These may be quiet times of retreat from the world's influences, when we can reflect privately on things spiritual. Or they may be times when we gather with other Christians to share our hope and joy in the Lord and thus encourage one another. Peter wanted his mountaintop experience to continue. We can understand that. But we also know that in order for God's will to be fully accomplished, one must come down from the mountaintop and, with Jesus, walk in the paths of service, even the way of the cross.

II. THE SON CONFIRMED (MATTHEW 17:5)

A. THE FATHER'S TESTIMONY (v. 5A, B)

5a. While he was still speaking, a bright cloud enveloped them, and a voice from the cloud said, "This is my Son, whom I love; with him I am well pleased.

God interrupted Peter. A brilliant cloud appeared, and a voice came out of the cloud—both indications of the presence of God. Only days before, Peter had proclaimed that Jesus was God's Son. Now God confirmed what Peter had spoken. Jesus was indeed the Son of God. And because Jesus had chosen to follow the path to Calvary, fulfilling God's purpose, the Father expressed his pleasure in the Son.

We note the similarities between Jesus' baptism and his transfiguration. By means of his baptism, Jesus publicly affirmed his purpose to shed his blood for a world lost in sin. At that time God spoke from Heaven, indicating his approval of his Son. Only a week before the transfiguration, Jesus rejected Satan's attempt to get him to avoid the cross (Matthew 16:23); and, while on the mount, Jesus calmly spoke with Moses and Elijah about his coming death in Jerusalem. Both incidents were reaffirmations of Jesus' desire and determination to fulfill God's will, to make possible the redemption of a lost world, by sacrificing himself. And, as at Jesus' baptism, God clearly identified Jesus as his Son and spoke his approval of him.

B. THE DISCIPLES' RESPONSIBILITY (v. 5C)

5b. "Listen to him!"

WHAT DO YOU THINK?

Peter was guilty of elevating human leaders to the status of Christ by suggesting to honor each of the three equally. Do you think human leaders today are sometimes elevated to the position Christ alone should hold? If so, how? How can you appreciate the contributions of Christian leaders but still listen to Christ in the sense God ordered the disciples to "listen to him" on the mountain?

WHAT DO YOU THINK?

While the transfiguration was a unique event that declared the deity of Christ, there is a sense in which all Christians are to be transfigured—or transformed, as it is usually expressed. What do the following Scriptures suggest about the transformation of Christians?

Romans 12:1, 2; Philippians 2:5-8; 2 Corinthians 3:18; 1 Corinthians 15:52; 1 John 3:2

What should declare that such a transformation has taken place in a Christian's life? What evidence declares it of you?

HOW TO SAY IT

Decapolis. Dee-KAP-uh-lis.
Magdala. MAG-duh-luh.
Pharisees. FAIR-ih-seez.
Sadducees. SAD-you-seez.

WHAT DO YOU THINK?

The disciples' response to God's voice was to fall on the ground. Then Jesus tenderly touched them and reassured them. When we truly understand who Jesus is, should we not respond to him with awe in a similar fashion? How can we express the awe we should feel at recognizing Jesus' nature, and at the same time be comforted by his presence? Which aspect of his nature should we emphasize to others, his awesomeness or his tenderness? Why?

To Peter and the other two disciples, God said, "Listen to my Son. Because of who he is, accept his teachings. Accept his words that he is to suffer and die."

Do you remember "Follow the leader," the game you played as a child? No matter what the leader did, you imitated him. So the Christian life, from beginning to end, is a life of following our leader—Jesus. We are to understand who Jesus is and what his life was all about. It was about service to others, about self-denial, about bearing the cross. We are to listen to him and follow in his steps.

LISTEN TO HIM!

The Mall, stretching westward from the U. S. Capitol in Washington D. C., is lined with important buildings. Among them are the White House, the Smithsonian Institute, and the National Art Gallery. Millions of people have come to the nation's capitol to visit these structures and to view their historic contents.

The Washington Monument, the Lincoln Memorial, and the Jefferson Memorial occupy places of prominence here, also. These are not tombs. The men whose names they bear are buried in other places. These structures are memorials to these great presidents who led in the founding and the preserving of the United States of America. These memorials help us remember that this country was established on the principles of liberty and justice for all.

Peter may have felt the need to build monuments at the site of the transfiguration of Jesus. Here Jesus talked with Moses, the great leader and legislator of Israel, and with Elijah, one of the nation's great prophets. They were men to remember!

Peter's suggestion was made in haste. God used the proposal as a means of elevating Jesus as his beloved Son, whom everyone should hear and honor. He would create a new people out of all who would come to him. The church, the body of Christ, is his living memorial. We remember and honor him best as we live by his teachings and share him with all the world.

—W. P.

III. THE SON COMFORTS AND COMMANDS (MATTHEW 17:6-13)

A. COMFORT FOR CHRIST'S DISCIPLES (VV. 6, 7)

6. When the disciples heard this, they fell facedown to the ground, terrified.

When they first saw Jesus transfigured before them, the three disciples were frightened. Now, having seen this brilliant cloud and having heard God speak, Peter, James, and John were *terrified* and fell down with their faces to the ground. Indeed, they made the only appropriate response that weak and sinful man could make in the presence of the Almighty.

7. But Jesus came and touched them. "Get up," he said. "Don't be afraid."

With tenderness and compassion Jesus came to the terrified disciples to banish their fear. What can be more comforting to one who is frightened than the reassuring voice and touch of a trusted loved one? Even so, nothing could have stilled the minds and hearts of these three disciples more than the touch and the voice of the Master they knew so well.

B. FOCAL POINT FOR THE DISCIPLES (V. 8)

8. When they looked up, they saw no one except Jesus.

In the Greek text the word *only* appears at the end of this sentence for emphasis. Moses the lawgiver and Elijah the prophet were gone; only Jesus remained. Thus was signified that the Old Covenant had done its work and must make way for the new dispensation. God's purpose centered on Jesus, and on him alone, and he was soon to complete the great work he had come to earth to do.

As disciples we must focus on Jesus alone. He will prove sufficient for our needs. When all else leaves or fails, Jesus remains to comfort and to guide.

WHO IS LEFT?

When men began to climb Mount Everest, in attempts to reach the pinnacle of earth's highest mountain, expedition after expedition ended in failure. Avalanches, crevasses, and extreme steepness combined with strong winds and thin air to keep most climbers from even getting close to the mountain's summit.

Finally, in 1953, the news flashed around the globe that Edmund Hillary of New Zealand and Tenzing Norway, a Nepalese Sherpa tribesman, had scaled the mountain, stood at the highest point on earth, and safely returned to their advance camp. Their feat was acclaimed by the whole world. Since then others have made the rugged climb to Everest's peak, but none have had the instant fame that Hillary and Norway attained by their historic climb.

Perhaps Peter, James, and John felt that what they had witnessed on the mount of transfiguration was the highest spiritual experience one could have. They had seen and heard Moses and Elijah, giants in the Old Testament galaxy of heroes, talking with Jesus. But God wanted them to climb higher, to the mountaintop of all spiritual reality. They must understand that Jesus stands alone as the pinnacle of man's return to God. Men would come to know in him life on its highest plane. Don't settle for anything or anyone as a substitute for Jesus.   —W. P.

C. COMMAND FOR THE DISCIPLES (v. 9)

9. As they were coming down the mountain, Jesus instructed them, "Don't tell anyone what you have seen, until the Son of Man has been raised from the dead."

As recently as a week before the transfiguration, Jesus had instructed the disciples not to tell the people at large that he was the Christ (see Matthew 16:20). The disciples themselves didn't understand what was involved in his messiahship, namely that he must die for the sins of the people and be raised again. If the disciples didn't understand that, the crowds certainly did not. The people were bent on having an earthly messiah, one who would be their political savior. To announce publicly Jesus' deity and messiahship would only stir up national excitement and lead to reckless actions by the zealous militarists.

As Jesus and the three disciples came down from the mount of transfiguration, he cautioned them not to tell anyone at that time of the vision they had been given on the mountain. To do so would only increase the excitement of the multitudes and cause them to interfere with the course his ministry must take. The time would come when they would be able to speak of the vision, and that would be after he was raised from the dead. Then the disciples themselves would better understand the nature of his kingdom, and the people would be better prepared to receive their teaching concerning it.

The months that lay ahead in Jesus' ministry were going to be difficult ones for the disciples, and the vision of the transfigured, glorified Christ would sustain them during that time. Knowing that death could not hold Jesus should sustain every disciple today through the hard times of life.

D. QUESTION AND ANSWER (vv. 10-12)

10. The disciples asked him, "Why then do the teachers of the law say that Elijah must come first?"

The word *then* indicates that the disciples' question related to something in the immediate past, and that seems to have been Elijah's appearance with Jesus when Jesus was transfigured. Explaining the prophecy in Malachi 4:5, 6, the scribes taught that Elijah would come and fulfill the work assigned to him before the Messiah arrived. The disciples acknowledged Jesus as the Messiah, but Elijah had only now shown himself. Furthermore, Elijah appeared to the three of them only, and

WHAT DO YOU THINK?

Jesus said the prophecy that Elijah would come had already been fulfilled. He referred not to a literal appearance of Elijah, however, but to John the Baptist. What does this suggest about the fulfillment of prophecy? How do we know when a literal fulfillment is required, and how can we tell when a figurative fulfillment will suffice? How should we respond to someone who understands a prophecy literally that we believe has a figurative fulfillment? Or who views figuratively what we believe to have a literal fulfillment?

PRAYER

O God, who reveal the glory of your only Son upon the mountain, grant to us a vision of his coming glory so that we may be strengthened to obey your command to carry the cross and carry the gospel to the people around us, and throughout the entire world. Until we are changed into his likeness from glory to glory, may we live for and pray in Jesus' name, Amen.

THOUGHT TO REMEMBER

Let us keep our eyes focused on Jesus and our ears attuned to his words.

DAILY BIBLE READINGS

Monday, Jan. 16—Elijah to Appear Before the Messiah (Malachi 4:1-5)

Tuesday, Jan. 17—Witnesses to Christ's Glory (2 Peter 1: 16-21)

Wednesday, Jan. 18—Peter Says Jesus Is the Messiah (Matthew 16:13-20)

Thursday, Jan. 19— Conditions of Discipleship (Matthew 16:21-28)

Friday, Jan. 20—The Transfiguration of Jesus (Matthew 17:1-8)

Saturday, Jan. 21—Jesus Will Suffer (Matthew 17:9-13)

Sunday, Jan. 22—Jesus Heals an Afflicted Child (Matthew 17:14-23)

they couldn't see how, in his brief appearance, he could accomplish the work spoken of by the prophet. The disciples were confused.

11. Jesus replied, "To be sure, Elijah comes and will restore all things.

In his reply, Jesus harked back to the prophecy in Malachi, which explains his use of the future tense, "will restore." Jesus confirmed that the scribes were correct in their teaching in this instance. Elijah was to come before the Messiah and *restore all things*. Some have interpreted Malachi's prophecy to mean that Elijah will appear in person before the second coming of Jesus and effect some great work of restoration. The following verses, however, indicate that the restoration spoken of was the repentance preached by John the Baptist to prepare for Jesus' ministry.

12. "But I tell you, Elijah has already come, and they did not recognize him, but have done to him everything they wished. In the same way the Son of Man is going to suffer at their hands."

Jesus said that Malachi's prophecy had been fulfilled: Elijah had already come. Jesus made it clear that he was not referring to Elijah's appearance on the mountain, but to John the Baptist (v. 13; see also Luke 1:17). The ruling powers in Palestine had not acknowledged John as a messenger of God. Instead, they did to him *everything they wished*. John worked to restore people to God, but he was rejected and killed. Even so would Jesus suffer at the hands of the rulers and be slain.

We are reminded that we must be sensitive to God's work and God's will. We must not be like the religious leaders of Jesus' day who resisted God's actions and desires because he was not acting the way they thought he should.

E. UNDERSTANDING (v. 13)

13. Then the disciples understood that he was talking to them about John the Baptist.

As the disciples came to this understanding, did they begin to understand also what the cost of their discipleship might be? Jesus had begun to speak of his death at the hands of the nation's rulers, a fate already suffered by John. Surely they would recall Jesus' teaching just six days before: "If anyone would come after me, he must deny himself and take up his cross and follow me. For whoever wants to save his life will lose it, but whoever loses his life for me will find it" (Matthew 16:24, 25). Though the cost of discipleship is great, the reward is infinitely greater. These disciples remained faithful to Christ—may we do likewise.

CONCLUSION

The transfiguration of Jesus was an event filled with reassurance not only for him, but for the disciples. It had been more than two years since Jesus' baptism, and the beginning of his ministry. He had been received by the common people, but vehemently opposed by the leaders of the nation. When for a brief time Christ's essential glory shined through the body of Jesus, and he heard the Father's words of approval, surely God's chosen Servant was encouraged in the way he was going and was strengthened to continue in it to the end.

The disciples had been facing despair over Jesus' announcement of his death. But seeing the glory of God shining in and through Jesus gave them reassurance that their Master would ultimately be victorious. There was much they did not understand, but certainly they descended the mount with an understanding and a hope that they did not have before.

We too are blessed by this event. The testimony of these eyewitnesses strengthens our faith in Jesus (see John 1:14; 2 Peter 1:16-18). Further, we are assured that one day we will be like him (1 John 3:2). O glorious day! Until then, may we heed the Father's words spoken of his Son and "listen to him."

Discovery Learning

This page contains an alternate lesson plan emphasizing learning activities. Classes desiring such student involvement will find these suggestions helpful. The next page is a reproducible activity page to further enhance discovery learning.

LEARNING GOALS

This lesson should enable the students to:

1. Describe the transfiguration of Jesus.

2. Tell how the transfiguration could have encouraged the disciples.

3. Acknowledge a desire to "listen to" Jesus and obey his teachings.

INTO THE LESSON

As the class members arrive, have them form groups of four to six. Give each group a copy of the following situation:

You are among a privileged few who have been permitted to catch a glimpse of Heaven. You take the trip and discover that Heaven is as it is described in Revelation 21. It is a beautiful place, perfectly formed with all kinds of precious jewels. A river runs through the middle of the city. On each side of the river are fruit-bearing trees. No lamp is needed there, for God and his Son Jesus are in the very middle of the city. You receive one message from Jesus while you are there: "Behold, I am coming soon! Blessed is he who keeps the words of the prophecy in this book" (Revelation 22:7). When you and your group return, what will you tell those waiting to hear your report?

Let the groups work together for five to seven minutes to determine the message they would give. Then let the groups share their responses. Try to draw from the group more than a description, but also a challenge: what kind of motivation would such an experience provide?

After the group sharing, make the transition to the study of today's Scripture text. Point out that in a special moment, three of Jesus' disciples were given a brief glimpse of his essential glory as it shone through the human form that he wore. At that time they were given a most important word from God. This event is known as the transfiguration.

INTO THE WORD

Present the thoughts in the "Lesson Background" section to connect last week's lesson to the event we are studying in this lesson. Then read the Scripture text aloud in its entirety. After that is completed, lead the class in a Bible discussion, using the questions below as a guide. (Option: Use the reproducible activity on the next page for Bible study.)

1. Who went with Jesus to the mount of transfiguration? (v. 1). (Peter, James, and John—the three disciples who were closest to Jesus.)

2. What did Peter, James, and John see during the transfiguration? (vv. 2, 3). (Jesus' face shone like the sun, and his clothes were white as the light. Moses and Elijah were speaking with him.)

3. What proposal did Peter make? (v. 4). That they build three shelters there—for Jesus, Moses, and Elijah.)

4. Why were Peter's plans not acted on? (vv. 5, 6). (A brilliant cloud appeared; God spoke from the cloud, announcing that Jesus was his Son and that he was to be listened to.)

5. Why would Jesus ask the disciples not to tell anyone what they had seen until after his resurrection? (v. 9). (Not long before this, the crowds had thoughts of forcing Jesus to be their political leader {John 6:15}. Word of his transfiguration would only intensify these misguided efforts. After his resurrection the true nature of his kingdom would be understood.)

6. What prompted the disciples' question recorded in verse 10? (See the lesson comments on this verse.)

7. What was the gist of Jesus' answer to the disciples' question? (vv. 11, 12). (The prophet Malachi spoke figuratively when he said Elijah would precede Messiah's coming. The prophecy was fulfilled in John the Baptist.)

8. How would this event have encouraged Jesus' disciples? (They were given convincing evidence that Jesus truly was the Son of God, and that he alone was worthy of their praise and obedience. They were also given divine testimony to help them understand that Jesus' impending death in Jerusalem was in accordance with God's will.)

INTO LIFE

We have considered Jesus' transfiguration from the disciples' viewpoint, but what does it mean to us? Have a student read 2 Peter 1:16-18 aloud to the class at this time; then lead a discussion of this passage. Consider the blessing that it gives us (the certainty that the disciples were not duped regarding Jesus, the fact that they were eyewitnesses of his divine majesty, the solid basis we have for our faith in Jesus).

Ask, "What do we learn from Jesus' transfiguration that we are to do?" (Let the students express the need to listen to Jesus, obey him, and proclaim him to all.) Close with prayer.

A Sensory Experience

Read Matthew 7:1-13. Also read the parallel passages in Mark 9:2-13 and Luke 9:28-36. Fill in the chart with facts found in the Scripture.

Next, use your five senses to imagine what Peter, James, and John must have seen, heard, smelled, touched, or tasted.

SEE	HEAR	SMELL	TOUCH	TASTE

On the Mountain Top

Peter, James, and John were literally on a mountain top when they saw Jesus transfigured. We use the same terminology for climactic emotional or spiritual events today, and this event qualifies as a mountain-top experience for the disciples in that sense as well.

Recall a mountain-top experience you have had that caused you to appreciate Christ a little more than before.

What was the event?

Why was it so uplifting?

What did it motivate you to do?

How can the inspiration of mountain-top experiences be sustained even after you leave the mountain?

Jesus the Fulfillment
Unit 3. Jesus: The Son of David
(Lessons 5-9)

THE PEOPLE PROCLAIM JESUS THE SON OF DAVID

LESSON 9

WHY TEACH THIS LESSON?

"Who is this?" the people of Jerusalem asked of Jesus, and they still ask today. The "prophet from Nazareth" may be sufficient answer for some, but it is incomplete. The praise of God's people today should echo the true answer, "He is 'the Christ, the Son of the Living God.'" Today's lesson is intended both to demonstrate that fact and to challenge your students to praise him as such.

INTRODUCTION

A. SPEAKING A DIFFERENT LANGUAGE

Many years ago, a man from Greece committed a minor crime while visiting in an American city. The police were unable to communicate with the man in his native language, so they placed him in a mental hospital, intending to deal with his case in a short time.

Unfortunately, the records of this incident were misplaced, and this Greek-speaking gentleman was left for years in the mental hospital. There he learned to speak English, but he learned it from English-speaking mental patients. As a result, he learned only the dysfunctional language of the mental patients. This led his doctors, who spoke with him only in English, to diagnose him as mentally ill. In fact, the man could have demonstrated himself healthy if he had been given the opportunity to communicate with his doctors in his own language. Before the mistake was corrected, the man had spent half his life in a mental hospital.

Jesus Christ was God's Son who came to earth as God's Messiah. He came speaking the language of the kingdom of God, but many people were unprepared to understand that language.

In Jesus' miracles the people saw the power of God; in his teaching they recognized an authority greater than man's. Together, these created in the people's hearts the hope that Jesus would become their deliverer. The hopes and expectations they had placed in Jesus were given full expression in his triumphal entry, when they acclaimed him as the king who came in the name of the Lord. The events of the week that followed, however, revealed that they really didn't understand the deliverance he brought, nor the nature of the kingdom he came to establish.

B. LESSON BACKGROUND

Jesus' disciples were slowly learning the nature of his divine purpose on earth. At Caesarea Philippi, Peter had demonstrated his growing awareness of the identity and mission of Jesus when he testified, "You are the Christ, the Son of the living God" (Matthew 16:16). On the mount of transfiguration, Peter, James, and John had heard the voice of God proclaim, "This is my Son, whom I love; with him I am well pleased" (Matthew 17:5).

Jesus spent the next six months preparing his disciples for his coming death. In his third passion prediction (Matthew 20:17-19), Jesus warned his disciples that

---

DEVOTIONAL READING:
MATTHEW 20:17-28
LESSON SCRIPTURE:
MATTHEW 20:17–21:17
PRINTED TEXT:
MATTHEW 21:1-11, 14-16

LESSON AIMS

This lesson is designed to help the students:

1. Affirm that Jesus is the Messiah, who came as the fulfillment of biblical prophecy.

2. Recognize that Jesus is the King of kings, whose kingdom is not of this world.

3. To allow Jesus to reign in their lives, governing their attitudes and actions.

Jan 29

KEY VERSE:

Hosanna to the Son of David! Blessed is he who comes in the name of the Lord!
—Matthew 21:9

HOW TO SAY IT

Bartimeus. BAR-tih-MAY-us.
Bethphage. BETH-fage.
Caesarea Philippi. Sess-uh-REE-uh Fih-LIP-pie or FIL-ih-pie.
Decapolis. Dee-KAP-uh-lis.
Jehu.. JAY-hoo.
Zaccheus. Zak-KEE-us.
Zechariah. Zek-uh-RYE-uh.

Visual 9 of the visuals packet summarizes the multitudes' acclamation of Jesus at the triumphal entry.

catastrophic events were on the horizon: (1) The chief priests and scribes would deliver him to the Gentiles to be mocked and scourged; (2) he would be condemned to death by crucifixion; (3) he would rise again from the dead.

In today's lesson, the time of the fulfillment of the ancient prophecies is at hand. Jesus and his disciples are going to Jerusalem. Thousands of Jews from Galilee, Perea, and the Decapolis were also journeying there to celebrate the Passover.

On their way, Jesus and his disciples passed through Jericho, where Jesus bestowed sight on two blind men, one of whom was named Bartimeus (Matthew 20:29-34; Mark 10:46-52). In this city Jesus also visited in the home of Zaccheus (Luke 19:1-10). From Jericho, the Lord and his disciples traveled to Bethany, a small village on the southeastern slope of the Mount of Olives, and spent the Sabbath in the home of Mary, Martha, and Lazarus (John 12:1-8). On the next morning, Jesus made his descent from the Mount of Olives into Jerusalem, the event known as "the triumphal entry."

I. PREPARATIONS FOR THE KING (MATTHEW 21:1-7)

A. ARRIVAL AT THE MOUNT OF OLIVES (v. 1)

1. As they approached Jerusalem and came to Bethphage on the Mount of Olives, Jesus sent two disciples,

On the day following the Sabbath, Jesus and his disciples left Bethany and came to the small village of *Bethphage,* located on the eastern slope of *the Mount of Olives,* between Bethany and Jerusalem. The Mount of Olives, just east of Jerusalem, was separated from the city by the Kidron Valley. The summit of the mount, about a mile east of the city, rose about three hundred feet above the temple hill and provided a panoramic view of the city. In Jesus' day, this mount must have been thickly wooded with olive groves, palm trees, and other vegetation.

B. INSTRUCTIONS FROM JESUS (vv. 2, 3)

2, 3. . . . saying to them, "Go to the village ahead of you, and at once you will find a donkey tied there, with her colt by her. Untie them and bring them to me. If anyone says anything to you, tell him that the Lord needs them, and he will send them right away."

The two disciples, who are not named, were sent to Bethphage to secure a donkey and her colt. It is unclear as to whether Jesus had made arrangements for these animals to be available, or if he foreknew supernaturally that they would be there and that the owner would gladly let the disciples bring them to him.

The Lord needs them would imply that the owner of the animals was a disciple of Jesus. The same is indicated by the fact that, when the disciples gave explanation, the man would immediately comply with the request.

Only Matthew says there were two animals; Mark mentions only one (Mark 11:2) and describes it as a colt, that is, a young donkey. Mark also tells us that the animal was unbroken—it had never been ridden. Having the colt's mother alongside would perhaps make the animal easier to handle. In any case, the unbroken animal remained calm under the hands of Jesus.

C. FULFILLMENT OF PROPHECY (vv. 4, 5)

4. This took place to fulfill what was spoken through the prophet:

While Jesus was deliberately fulfilling messianic prophecies, there was no attempt on his part at manipulation. That is to say, he did not look into the Old Testament to find out what the Messiah would do, and then set out to fulfill those prophecies. Rather, God had directed the prophet to make this prediction, and Jesus, being the Messiah spoken of, now fulfilled those prophecies. This was for him an act of self-disclosure. In the past, Jesus maintained a cloak of limited secrecy over his messianic intentions; that cloak was now lifted.

5. "Say to the Daughter of Zion, 'See, your king comes to you, gentle and riding on a donkey, on a colt, the foal of a donkey.'"

Say to the Daughter of Zion. These opening words are quoted from Isaiah 62:11. *The Daughter of Zion* is a reference to Jerusalem herself. Zion was the principal hill on which the city was built. Of course, the inhabitants of the city were included in this term.

See, your king comes to you. These and the remaining words of this verse are quoted from the prophecy in Zechariah 9:9. The context in Zechariah shows that this was spoken concerning the Messiah. The nature of the Messiah's reign was indicated also by the prophet. He would be *gentle,* a fact that would be emphasized by his riding into Jerusalem on *the foal of a donkey.*

In Western societies the donkey is often a despised animal. This was not necessarily true in Eastern lands. In Israel of old, judges and chieftains often came riding them. To do so was a sign that these dignitaries came in peace (Judges 5:10; 10:4). The horse, on the other hand, was a mount of war.

In the manner of Jesus' coming to Jerusalem, therefore, Matthew indicates that Jesus fulfilled all that Zechariah had prophesied. He came in meekness as the Prince of peace, the ruler of a spiritual, not a material, kingdom.

Jesus came to Jerusalem as Israel's king, yet he was not the kind of king they were prepared to receive. They did not want a king who was meek, but one who was warlike, one who would reflect the power of Israel's past kings and reaffirm Israel's splendor among the nations.

D. OBEDIENT DISCIPLES (VV. 6, 7)

6. The disciples went and did as Jesus had instructed them.

These disciples were, no doubt, filled with confusion, curiosity, and apprehension about coming events. Only a few months earlier in Jerusalem, during the Feast of Dedication, the religious authorities had attempted to kill Jesus (see John 10:31, 39). The disciples were certain that danger still awaited their Master in the capital city (compare John 11:14-16). Yet, there was no hesitation or questioning when Jesus gave them instructions.

We have to be impressed at this point with the unquestioning obedience of the disciples. And what of us, Jesus' disciples today? In the New Testament, we have his commands for his followers in every generation. Do we obey without hesitation, or do we find reasons for not doing as he wishes us to do?

7. They brought the donkey and the colt, placed their cloaks on them, and Jesus sat on them.

The disciples brought the animals to Jesus, realizing that he was going to ride on one of them. Since they did not know which animal he planned to ride, they spread *their cloaks,* their heavy outer garments, on both animals. To surrender one's garment in such a manner was to extend great homage to Jesus.

Notice that (1) Jesus rode with no saddle, though he was seated on borrowed garments; (2) No one had ever ridden on this animal before. Only animals that had never been used were considered fit for sacred use. According to the law, the red heifer that was used for the ceremonial cleansing of sin must be an animal "that has never been under a yoke" (Numbers 19:2-9).

In God's design, Jesus was born to a woman who had never known a man (Luke 1:34; Matthew 1:20, 23). After his death on the cross, Jesus was buried in a tomb that had never been used (Matthew 27:60). It is appropriate that, at his triumphal entry, Jesus rode an animal that had never before been ridden.

On all previous occasions, Jesus had walked into Jerusalem; now he came like David or one of the judges—riding a donkey.

II. PRESENTATION OF THE KING (MATTHEW 21:8-11)
A. The Triumphal Entry (v. 8)
8. A very large crowd spread their cloaks on the road, while others cut branches from the trees and spread them on the road.

Many worshipers were coming to Jerusalem to observe the Passover, and as they came nearer to the capital city they merged into *a very large crowd*. Many of these people were from Galilee, and no doubt had either witnessed Jesus' ministry and miracles firsthand or knew others who had. Many believed him to be a prophet, or even the Messiah. As the people came to the realization that Jesus was in their midst, excitement began to rise. And when they saw him mount the animal, their enthusiasm increased. Would he at this time reveal his plan and use his great power to establish his kingdom?

Seeing the disciples remove their cloaks and put them on the animals for Jesus to sit on, some of the people in the crowd began to remove and *spread their cloaks on the road* for Jesus to ride on. Others in the crowd *cut branches from the trees* for the same purpose. John, in his Gospel account, mentions specifically that the branches of palm trees were used (John 12:13). However, olive and other trees grew there, so branches and leaves of those trees also may have been cut or plucked to lay in Jesus' path.

We read in the Old Testament that after Jehu was anointed king of the northern kingdom, "they hurried and took their cloaks and spread them under him on the bare steps. Then they blew the trumpet and shouted, Jehu is king!" (2 Kings 9:13). So, by spreading their garments and small branches in the way over which Jesus rode, the people were expressing their feeling that Jesus was royalty.

B. The King Acclaimed (v. 9)
9. The crowds that went ahead of him and those that followed shouted, "Hosanna to the Son of David!" "Blessed is he who comes in the name of the Lord!" "Hosanna in the highest!"

The crowds that went ahead of him and those that followed. This indicates two different groups. Some of the pilgrims to the Passover feast were already in Jerusalem. John mentions that when they heard Jesus was coming, many took palm branches and went out to meet and honor him (John 12:12, 13). At some point on the Mount of Olives this crowd met the one in the midst of which Jesus was riding. The former then turned back toward the city, so that they then were going before him.

The title *Son of David* must be understood against the backdrop of Jewish history. King David was among the most esteemed of Israel's rulers. During his reign, the united kingdom of Israel was a powerful, sovereign nation, one to be reckoned with. Israel's days as an international power were short-lived, however, and in time they lost their independence. For centuries they were ruled by other nations, a condition that continued in the days of Jesus by the domination of the Romans. Historically, Jewish hopes were centered on a future king who would come from the line of David—a son of David. This leader would be the Anointed One, or Messiah, who they believed would lead Israel back to her position of splendor and power. Jesus clearly left the impression that he was this king.

Hosanna means literally, "save now." Originally a prayer of supplication, this term had come to be an expression of joy and congratulation.

Blessed . . . in the name of the Lord. The crowds invoked God's blessing on him who had come "as the Lord's representative, God's Messiah."

Hosanna in the highest is somewhat equivalent to "Glory to God in the highest" (Luke 2:14). The people were thanking God in the highest heavens for sending the Messiah.

Whereas earlier in his ministry Jesus discouraged his disciples from spreading the word that he was the Christ, now he openly asserted his claims to that title. He accepted the homage of the multitudes, making no attempt to quiet them. His acquiescence encouraged the people to increase their shouts of acclamation, with the result that the excitement of throngs intensified as Jesus made his way down the Mount of Olives to the gate of the city.

Although the people were rightfully acclaiming Jesus as the Messiah, their concept of the Messiah was decidedly incorrect. They believed God's Anointed would lead a political-military movement that would deliver them from the yoke of bondage to Rome. Jesus, however, came in meekness, for his was a mission of peace and salvation.

C. CURIOUS CROWDS (V. 10)
10. When Jesus entered Jerusalem, the whole city was stirred and asked, "Who is this?"

As Jesus and the great crowd descended the Mount of Olives, they were in full view of the throngs of people assembled in the city of Jerusalem for the Passover. Matthew tells us that the vast crowds were *stirred* at this unusual procession as it made its way into the city. No doubt among the general populace many entertained hope that the moment of victory over Roman oppression had come. The religious authorities, on the other hand, were aroused to greater envy and hatred (see John 12:19).

Among the crowds in the city were Jews from all parts of the world who had come to celebrate the Passover. Perhaps they were the ones who asked, *Who is this?*

D. RESERVED REPLY (V. 11)
11. The crowds answered, "This is Jesus, the prophet from Nazareth in Galilee."

The crowds, that is, the people who were in the procession, kept repeating to the inquiries, *This is Jesus, the prophet from Nazareth in Galilee.* It was a modest reply, one that could not be denied. Nor would it stir up controversy. Had the crowds continued calling Jesus their "king" (Luke 19:38; John 12:13), the Roman authorities might have taken swift and strong measures to break up the procession.

III. PRAISE FOR THE KING (MATTHEW 21:14-16)
A. HEALING IN THE TEMPLE (V. 14)
14. The blind and the lame came to him at the temple, and he healed them.

Early in his ministry, Jesus cleansed the temple, driving out the money changers and those who sold animals there (John 2:13-15). He cleansed the temple once again following his triumphal entry. Mark, giving careful notations of time in his account, indicates that this cleansing took place on the day following the triumphal entry (Mark 11:11-15). The healings recorded in this verse in our text took place after this cleansing of the temple.

The authority Jesus assumed in cleansing the temple was supported by his miracles of healing. Both actions were steps in his revealing himself to be the Messiah.

B. CONTRASTING REACTIONS TO JESUS (V. 15)
15. But when the chief priests and the teachers of the law saw the wonderful things he did and the children shouting in the temple area, "Hosanna to the Son of David," they were indignant.

WHAT DO YOU THINK?

It is Luke who includes the notation that as Jesus neared Jerusalem, he wept over the city (Luke 19:41). What response do you think Jesus would make in observing our cities today? How would he respond to our churches? To this church?

If Jesus rode into your work place tomorrow, would he weep or rejoice? Why? What kind of response would he get from your coworkers? Why?

WHAT DO YOU THINK?

The people of Jerusalem were stirred to ask, "Who is this?" as Jesus entered the city. Do you think if we could pique the interest of people around us so that they, too, asked, "Who is this?" we could be more effective in our efforts of evangelism? Why or why not? What can the church or individual Christians do to make people ask "Who is this?" about Jesus today?

OPTION

The reproducible page 198 contains a summary of the various ways people in his day viewed Jesus. Distribute copies of this page to discuss those views and the way people view him today.

WHAT DO YOU THINK?

Verse 15 says children picked up the chants of praise that had resounded during the triumphal entry and repeated them. What does this suggest about teaching children to praise the Lord? At what age do you think children should be taught to praise him? Why?

PRAYER

Father, this day we declare with the angels in heaven: "To him who sits on the throne and to the Lamb be praise and honor and glory and power, for ever and ever!" (Revelation 5:13).

THOUGHT TO REMEMBER

Today and forever, Jesus is King!

DAILY BIBLE READINGS

Monday, Jan. 23—Thanksgiving for God's Salvation (Psalm 118:19-29)

Tuesday, Jan. 24—Followers of Jesus Must Serve Others (Matthew 20:17-28)

Wednesday, Jan. 25—Jesus Heals Two Blind Men (Matthew 20:29-34)

Thursday, Jan. 26—Jesus Approaches Jerusalem (Matthew 21:1-5)

Friday, Jan. 27—The Crowds Welcome Jesus (Matthew 21:6-11)

Saturday, Jan. 28—Jesus Cleanses the Temple and Heals (Matthew 21:12-17)

Sunday, Jan. 29—Jesus' Authority Questioned (Matthew 21:23-32)

The crowds were overjoyed as they saw miracle after miracle of healing, and the children took up the chant of the multitudes the day before (v. 9). Already furious because Jesus had expelled their crooked market from the temple, the religious leaders were filled with envy at the honor and acclaim being given Jesus.

C. SCRIPTURAL DEFENSE (V. 16)

16. "Do you hear what these children are saying?" they asked him.

"Yes," replied Jesus, "have you never read, "'From the lips of children and infants you have ordained praise'?"

The praises implied high homage. Professing to be zealous for God's honor, the chief priests and Pharisees appealed to Jesus to put a stop to this behavior. In essence, they said, "Jesus, why are you allowing the people to treat you like God? Stop immediately these blasphemous words from being spoken!"

In response, Jesus stated that the children's praise fulfilled the word of Psalm 8:2, a psalm acknowledged as messianic. Jesus affirmed that he was indeed God's Messiah and, therefore, worthy of the praise being given him.

It is noteworthy that little children hailed Jesus as the Messiah, whereas sophisticated religious leaders rejected him. Even today, the humble often perceive spiritual truth more readily than the sophisticated (1 Corinthians 1:26-28).

UNASHAMED PRAISE

Jamaican believers love to sing praises to Jesus. Across the hills and valleys of that lovely land one can hear the people singing hymns and choruses on Sunday and at street corners during the week. Their natural desire to praise Jesus causes them to share their faith in song.

Our family served as missionaries in Jamaica in the 1950s. Our four children began singing from early childhood, and they felt at ease singing hymns and choruses in the car while we were in that land. While we were on furlough in the United States, the children entertained themselves by singing as we traveled the highways from appointment to appointment. Even Mom and Dad would join in.

As we passed through a town or city with the car windows open, the singing would continue, and "Jesus Loves Me" would resound from the car for all to hear. Dad got nervous, and on one such occasion he made an unfortunate remark to Mother. "Couldn't you just quiet them down? I might not hear an ambulance or police car!" Mother's reply was, "You don't mind their singing the gospel when there is no one around to hear. Sing with them. I don't think we'll be arrested for praising the Lord with such joy!" Dad was properly rebuked.

The religious leaders in Jerusalem didn't want to hear the praise of Jesus either. Our Lord replied to their objection to the children's expressions of praise, "Have you never read, 'From the lips of children and infants you have ordained praise'?" Children have no fear in singing what they believe. Do you?   —W. P.

CONCLUSION

Jesus rode into Jerusalem amid the plaudits of crowds who hailed him as the One who came in the name of the Lord. His divine mission and authority had been revealed throughout his ministry among the people in the obscure towns and desert places of Galilee and elsewhere. That revelation continued right in the nation's capital following his triumphal entry, as he cleansed the temple and performed miracles of healing.

The religious authorities rejected him. It seems that even those who hailed him as king at his triumphal entry turned from him by week's end.

Is Jesus our King? Do we allow him to rule our hearts?

Discovery Learning

This page contains an alternate lesson plan emphasizing learning activities. Classes desiring such student involvement will find these suggestions helpful. The next page is a reproducible activity page to further enhance discovery learning.

LEARNING GOALS

After this lesson the students will be able to:

1. Relate what happened when Jesus entered Jerusalem on a donkey.

2. Describe the various responses to Jesus' ministry.

3. Identify ways to maintain personal enthusiasm in worshiping Jesus.

INTO THE LESSON

On a sheet of paper write, "Hosanna to the Son of David! Blessed is he who comes in the name of the Lord! Hosanna in the highest!" Cut the words apart, scramble them, and put them in an envelope. During the week before class, prepare one envelope for every three or four students you expect to have in class.

As the class members arrive, play a tape of songs that emphasize the majesty of Christ. Divide class members into groups of three or four. Give each group an envelope containing a set of the words, and ask them to put the words in the correct order. If they have difficulty doing this, tell them they can refer to Matthew 21:9 for help. Allot five to seven minutes for this; then have the class members read aloud the verse they unscrambled.

Make the transition into the Bible study by stating that this verse is central to today's lesson.

INTO THE WORD

The "Lesson Background" section mentions some of the events that occurred between Jesus' transfiguration (last week's lesson) and the triumphal entry, which we will examine today. Present these thoughts now to establish the background for today's study.

Ask several class members ahead of time to read the Scripture text. Have one be the narrator, who reads all of the connecting materials; another to read the words spoken by Jesus; a third to read the words of the prophet; and a fourth to read the words of the crowd. Have them read the text to the class at this time.

Now divide the class into five groups. Ask each group to read Matthew 21:1-11, 14-16 and to describe these events from one of the following points of view:

Group 1. Jesus' disciples.

Group 2. A person in the crowd who praised Jesus as he rode into Jerusalem.

Group 3. A resident of Jerusalem who witnessed the triumphal entry, but who was not a participant.

Group 4. The enemies of Jesus.

Group 5. Jesus.

Allow the groups six to eight minutes to complete their work. Then ask the groups to report their conclusions in the numerical order shown above. Take a few moments to add additional explanation of today's Bible text that did not surface in the reports.

INTO LIFE

Develop a discussion to apply the lesson to life. Use the following questions as a guide.

1. How does this event support the claim that Jesus is the Messiah? (Fulfillment of Old Testament prophecy; Jesus accepted their praise without rebuke; the Jewish leaders recognized the Messianic tone and were angered by it.)

2. The triumphal entry was a spontaneous event, in which the multitudes began praising Jesus. What reasons do we have to praise Jesus? What would have to happen for us to break out in public praise as these people did? (Let the pupils brainstorm reasons for praising Jesus. Be sure the list includes his redemptive work for us.).

3. The Jewish leaders did not accept the people's praise of Jesus. How should we respond when people reject our claims of the lordship of Jesus and that he is worthy of praise? (Encourage the students to suggest several ideas; be sure that a life-style consistent with our words is included.)

4. The title "Son of David" was especially significant to the Jewish worshipers in Jerusalem. What facts about Jesus are especially significant in our testimony of him today? (Let the class give suggestions. Try to move beyond the bare facts, most notably the death, burial, and resurrection of Jesus, to discuss terminology and the danger of using jargon not understood by people outside the church.)

5. The crowd was extremely enthusiastic in their praise of Jesus. What would it take for our praise to be as enthusiastic in our worship services? In our family devotions? In our lives? (Allow the class to share ways they praise the Lord.)

Conclude the session with these activities:

1. Ask class members to reconsider their personal commitment to Jesus Christ. Are their lives filled with praise, in word and action?

2. Ask them to share their responses to Jesus, and then pray together.

A Variety of Perspectives

The people of Israel in Jesus' day held differing views regarding him. Some of them are listed below.

(1) **Prophet.** Matthew 21:11 records that the multitude acclaimed him as "the prophet from Nazareth in Galilee." Many in the crowd regarded Jesus as a prophet who had come to foretell the reign of God.

(2) **Liberator.** The most nationalistic among the people felt that Jesus would be, or should be, a military leader. They looked for him to use his great power to lead them in throwing off the yoke of Roman tyranny.

(3) **Earthly king.** Many in the triumphal entry crowds expected Jesus to establish his kingdom and rule in the tradition of David.

(4) **Impostor.** The religious leaders in Israel knew that Jesus claimed to be equal with God, and for this they regarded him as a blasphemer and an impostor—one who was worthy of death.

(5) **Troublemaker.** The greedy and the powerful saw him as their enemy, for he exposed their selfish motives and was a threat to their influential position among the people.

(6) **The Son of God.** Those who were closest to Jesus, who received his teachings and observed his miracles with an open mind, came to this conviction.

Which of these views continue to be held today? Which have you seen or heard expressed by people around you?

What can Christians do to show people Jesus is the Son of God and not merely a prophet, and certainly not an impostor?

What can you do this week to praise Jesus as God's Son so that a friend or neighbor will be given reason to believe in him?

JESUS INSTITUTES THE LORD'S SUPPER

LESSON 10

WHY TEACH THIS LESSON?

No ceremony regularly observed by the church is more full of meaning than the Lord's Supper. Born of the symbolic Passover meal, the Lord's Supper is at the same time a memorial of a past event, a communion with a living Lord and with others of his people, and an anticipation of an eternal fellowship with him yet to commence. This lesson is intended to help your students renew their appreciation for this important activity.

INTRODUCTION

A. MEALS AND MEMORY

Many of the most memorable moments in my life have one thing in common—they were associated with meals. Perhaps the same is true for many others as well.

The disciples of Jesus shared a memorable meal with him after his resurrection (see John 21). The first Christians experienced happiness and unity in meals taken together (Acts 2:46). And the consummation of the ages will take place at the marriage supper of the Lamb (Revelation 19:6-9). We are not surprised, therefore, that Jesus chose the occasion of the Passover meal to impart to his disciples the significance of his death, and to establish a memorial to it.

No doubt Jesus and his disciples had celebrated the Passover meal together on other occasions. But this celebration would be different. A new and deeper meaning would be given to this ancient memorial, a significance that would have implications for eternity.

B. LESSON BACKGROUND

For centuries Jews had commemorated the Passover. The Passover meal was a memorial to Israel's exodus from Egypt.

Beginning on Passover and continuing for one week, the Jews ate their bread without leaven. This recalled that their forefathers left Egypt in such haste that they had no time to leaven the dough (Exodus 12:30-34, 37-39; 13:3-7). Also on the night preceding the exodus, at God's instruction, the Israelites daubed the blood of the Passover lamb on the lintel and door posts of their homes. Thus Israel was spared when the Lord brought death to all the firstborn of Egypt (Exodus 12:21-28). In this lesson we will see the new significance Jesus gave to the unleavened bread, and the eternal rescue that would be gained by the shedding of his blood.

The last supper occurred on Thursday evening of the "last week" of Jesus' earthly ministry. He entered the city to great acclaim on Sunday. On Monday he indicated the spiritual nature of his mission by cleansing the temple. Back in the temple on Tuesday, he engaged in discussion and debate for the final time with the religious leaders. It seems that he rested with friends in Bethany on Wednesday. Then on Thursday he instructed his disciples to prepare for the Passover meal.

DEVOTIONAL READING:
JOHN 6:30-40
LESSON SCRIPTURE:
MATTHEW 26:17-35
PRINTED TEXT:
MATTHEW 26:20-30

LESSON AIMS

This lesson should enable students to:

1. Understand the significance of the Lord's Supper.

2. Have a deeper love for Jesus, who gave his life for our redemption.

3. Participate in the Lord's Supper with renewed meaning.

Feb
5

KEY VERSE:

This is my blood of the covenant, which is poured out for many for the forgiveness of sins.
—Matthew 26:28

WHAT DO YOU THINK?

The primary focus of a shared meal is not on receiving nourishment. In a shared meal the focus belongs on feeding the relationship of those eating together, rather than simply feeding physical bodies. Eating together fosters bonding; it builds relationships.

How does eating the Lord's Supper build one's relationship with the Lord? With other Christians? (See 1 Corinthians 10:16, 17; 11:17-34.)

WHAT DO YOU THINK?

Matthew and Mark record the prediction of the betrayer before telling of the institution of the Lord's Supper. Luke reverses the order, citing the Lord's Supper first. John, who does not mention the Lord's Supper, tells that Judas left immediately after the prediction of the betrayer. That would suggest, if Matthew and Mark's accounts are chronological, that Judas was not present during the Lord's Supper. If Luke's is the chronological account, however, then Judas was present.

What do you think? Was Judas present as Jesus passed out the emblems of his sacrificial death? If so, what significance may we attach to that regarding the openness of the Lord's Table today? What does it suggest about our own "worthiness" to share in this memorial?

(See Matthew 26:20-29; Mark 14:17-25; Luke 22:14-23; John 13:18-27.)

I. THE MEAL BEGINS (MATTHEW 26:20)

20. When evening came, Jesus was reclining at the table with the Twelve.

In the upper room on the evening before his death, Jesus would deal with the disciples' desire for greatness, wash the feet of his disciples, command them to love one another as he had loved them, and reassure them of the presence of God's Spirit. Now he must turn to the matter at hand—his ensuing death.

The Twelve were Jesus' closest followers and comprised his family for the Passover celebration. They were more, however; they were his best hope for comprehending and carrying on his work.

II. THE BETRAYAL ANNOUNCED (MATTHEW 26:21-25)

A. SELF-EXAMINATION (VV. 21, 22)

21. And while they were eating, he said, "I tell you the truth, one of you will betray me."

The Passover meal was well under way when Jesus interjected a sobering thought—he would be betrayed by one of the disciples seated at the table! We should not become so quickly absorbed in the shocked reaction of the disciples that we fail to gauge Jesus' own feelings of sadness. Imagine the sense of betrayal he felt. One of those whom he had chosen and taught and loved was rejecting him, his teachings, and his care. An enemy might oppose, but only a friend can betray.

We who follow Jesus may also be betrayed by someone we love. If a family member or a fellow Christian lets us down, we have the assurance that Jesus understands our feelings. He experienced a similar hurt.

22. They were very sad and began to say to him one after the other, "Surely not I, Lord?"

Jesus' shocking words brought deep sadness to the disciples. Each of them except Judas knew he had no intention of betraying Jesus, but each feared the possibility that he might be the agent of betrayal. At different times some of the disciples had displayed attitudes and actions that were in conflict with him whom they called their Lord. James and John had suggested destroying a Samaritan village with fire from Heaven (Luke 9:54), and Peter had had the audacity to rebuke Jesus and try to keep him from going to Jerusalem. (Matthew 16:22). As it turned out, each one of them ran and hid at the moment of their Master's greatest need, and Peter even denied he knew him. Not only did each disciple recognize at this moment his potential for betrayal, but each acted it out in one way or another before this night had ended. It is to their credit, therefore, that each of them began to search his own heart instead of trying to determine which of the others was guilty.

We who are Jesus' disciples must realize that whenever our selfish agendas override our loyalty to Jesus, we are at risk of betraying him.

B. IT IS HE! (VV. 23, 24)

23. Jesus replied, "The one who has dipped his hand into the bowl with me will betray me.

During the Passover meal herbs, bread, and meat were dipped into a vessel of sauce, which was served to the participants in common. Thus Jesus would dip with all of the disciples, in a sense, since all at one time or other would dip his food into the common bowl. Some, however, feel that the expression *dipped his hand into the bowl with me* suggests that the traitor was seated near Jesus. From the Gospel of John we conclude that John, the beloved disciple, was reclining to the right of Jesus (see John 13:23-25), but we are not told who was on the left. Some believe it was Judas. If this is correct, then the exchange that took place between Jesus and Judas (see verse 25) may have been in an undertone that the others did not catch.

The seats on either side of Jesus were places of honor. Had Jesus invited his own betrayer to this position of intimacy and honor? Had he done so as one last appeal to Judas to alter his intentions?

24. "The Son of Man will go just as it is written about him. But woe to that man who betrays the Son of Man! It would be better for him if he had not been born."

Avoiding titles of power such as "Messiah" and "Son of God," Jesus usually called himself the *Son of Man,* a phrase rich in personal meaning and prophetic significance. The phrase sometimes served as a simple substitute for the pronoun *I.* It also would have reminded Jews of its use in Ezekiel, where it described the faithful prophet of God. Daniel used the phrase to prophesy the coming of one who would receive an everlasting kingdom, which would never pass away nor be destroyed (Daniel 7:13, 14). In other words, this title suggested appropriately enough Jesus' humanity, his humility, his suffering, his prophetic role, and his victorious rule.

The prophecy referred to here—*the Son of Man goes*—refers to the whole cluster of events surrounding his death. Psalm 22 and Isaiah 53 are two of the Old Testament passages that clearly foreshadow those events and indicate that Jesus died *as it is written about him.*

Jesus turned from the prophesied fact of his death to the personal facilitator of it—Judas. Some people think Judas was personally predestined by God to betray Jesus. Indeed, the book of Acts implies that the need to replace one of the twelve had been prophesied (Acts 1:20; Psalms 69:25; 109:8). However, because God knew in advance what would happen and inspired his prophets to write of it hundreds of years earlier does not mean that he caused it to happen. Speaking of Judas's betrayal of Jesus, the fourth-century church father Chrysostom said, "The prescience of God is not the cause of men's wickedness, nor does it involve any necessity of it; Judas was not a traitor because God foresaw it, but he foresaw it because Judas would be so." Jesus' words in this verse strongly suggest that the responsibility for the decision lay with Judas himself.

C. IS IT I? (v. 25)

25. Then Judas, the one who would betray him, said, "Surely not I, Rabbi?" Jesus answered, "Yes, it is you."

Like the others, Judas asked the same question. But why? Was it to hide his intentions from Jesus? Surely he knew of Jesus' ability to discern the heart (Matthew 9:4). Was it to conceal his plans from his fellow disciples? Perhaps. Or was it a desperate act of self-delusion, denying to himself the deed he had decided to do?

Perhaps the most enlightening facet of Judas's question is the title he used to address Jesus. The other disciples had called Jesus "Lord," even as they contemplated their own potential for betrayal. But Judas called Jesus *Rabbi* (Master), not "Lord." That title, meaning "honored Teacher," may indicate the deficiency in Judas's loyalty that led to the betrayal. To the rest, Jesus had become their Lord; but Judas's understanding of Jesus may have progressed little since the early days in Galilee.

Jesus responded to Judas with the same words he would use when Caiaphas would ask him if he were the Christ (Matthew 26:64). The NIV translation here, *"Yes, it is you,"* is accurate only in that the words convey an affirmative answer. At verse 64 it is better: "Yes, it is as you say." The Greek, *su eipas* (the same in both verses), is literally rendered, "You have said it." Judas's own words condemned him as the betrayer.

An important question for us remains: Is Jesus our Rabbi or our Lord? For many people, Jesus is little more than a great moral teacher whose insights can be followed on the path to a good life. But Jesus is Lord. He calls for absolute loyalty, and that loyalty is the path to eternal life.

HOW TO SAY IT

Caiaphas. KAY-uh-fus or KYE-uh-fus.
Chrysostom. Krih-SOS-tum or KRIS-us-tum.
Su eipas (Greek). Soo EYE-pahs.

WHAT DO YOU THINK?

Luke tells of a dispute that arose among the disciples about who was greatest (Luke 22:24-29). He records it after his account of the Lord's Supper, but the account may not be chronological. Many believe this dispute came early in the evening, perhaps as the disciples were being seated and were vying for seats of honor. It may well have been what prompted Jesus to wash the disciples' feet (John 13:1-17). In contrast to the "I-am-better-than-you" attitude that led to the dispute, each of the disciples displayed humble self examination as they asked, "Is it I?" when the Lord predicted one of them would betray him.

Which attitude do you think is more prevalent in the church today? Why? How does the Lord's Supper challenge the "I-am-better-than-you" attitude? How is the self-examination attitude important to the proper observance of the Lord's Supper? (See 1 Corinthians 11:17-22, 27-34.)

WHAT DO YOU THINK?

At least four crucial purposes may be noted for our observing the Lord's Supper. First, the Lord's Supper is a memorial to Jesus' death, so as we partake we remember his sacrifice for us. Second, by Jesus' death he established a new covenant between God and man. We who are Christians have entered this covenant, and each time we partake of the Lord's Supper we renew our commitment to that covenant. The third purpose is communion. We affirm our oneness with the Lord and his body, the church. The fourth purpose is one of anticipation. We "proclaim the Lord's death until he comes" (1 Corinthians 11:26). We look forward to the second coming of Christ.

How completely do you think Christians understand the breadth of meaning in the Lord's Supper? What difference do you think it would make in their daily behavior if Christians better understood what the Lord's Supper signifies? What can the church do to be sure it is better appreciated?

Visual 10 of the visual packet is a comparison of the new covenant with the old covenant based on Matthew 26:28.

III. THE MEAL WITHIN THE MEAL (MATTHEW 26:26-29)

A. THE BREAD AND THE BODY (v. 26)

26. While they were eating, Jesus took bread, gave thanks and broke it, and gave it to his disciples, saying, "Take and eat; this is my body."

Jesus took bread. This was the unleavened bread of the Passover feast. The practice of taking the flat loaf of bread, giving thanks to God, tearing it into pieces, and distributing it was part of the ceremonies observed at the Passover. Jesus had given the disciples instructions regarding preparations for the meal (see Luke 22:7-13), and he presided over it as the father of any Jewish family would do.

The words Jesus spoke at this point in the Passover meal, however, were a departure from every Passover the disciples had ever observed. Distributing the bread, Jesus said, This is my body. These new and shocking words shifted the focus from the past to the present, from history to him. Eating this bread is the means for disciples to maintain a spiritual communion with Jesus, whose body is given for them (Luke 22:19).

Every time we lift the loaf at the Communion table, we are participating in the history of God's deliverance then and now. But we are also participating in the mystery of "Christ in you, the hope of glory" (Colossians 1:27).

SYMBOL OF LIFE

The vast wheat fields of Kansas, stretching across the high plains, are green in winter until snow covers them. The warming sun of spring and summer mature the crop until the fields are a beautiful light tan, ready for harvest. Food for the hungry world can be seen in those fields of waving wheat. Marjorie was a city girl reading a book as the car sped eastward across Kansas. After a while she put the book down and looked up, eyed the acres of wheat, and remarked, "Isn't that the most desolate sight you have ever seen?"

Her husband was offended and speechless. That bountiful harvest would provide bread for multitudes of people and income for the farmers who planted and reaped their crops. How could anyone use the word desolate to describe the graceful undulation of ripe wheat gently swaying in the Kansas wind? His wife's statement seemed incomprehensible. He knew wheat and its worth; his wife did not.

Jesus is the bread of life. In the Lord's Supper, he offers himself in bread, the symbol for his body given as a sacrifice acceptable to God for our sins. Many do not know this truth. If one comes to the Lord's Supper unaware of its meaning, its spiritual value will be neither recognized nor received. Let us first remember our Lord's death, and give thanks for the life it makes possible.

—W. P.

B. THE CUP AND THE COVENANT (vv. 27-29)

27. Then he took the cup, gave thanks and offered it to them, saying, "Drink from it, all of you.

In recording the institution of the Lord's Supper, some translations say Jesus blessed the loaf (verse 26) and gave thanks for the cup (verse 27). Understanding the two terms to describe different actions, and assuming that both were done for both elements—that is, that Jesus both blessed and gave thanks for the loaf and the cup— many have come to the notion that Jesus did something to the loaf and to the cup, effecting a transformation of the bread and wine into his actual body and blood. The two terms, however, are virtually identical and are used synonymously. In thanking God for the loaf and the cup, Jesus was asking the Father to consecrate them for their intended purpose. Thus, in partaking of these elements, we remember Jesus' sacrifice of his life to effect our salvation and at the same time we give thanks for it. When we hear the "blessing of the loaf and cup," we should direct our thoughts in thanksgiving to the source of salvation, to God himself.

After taking a cup, giving thanks, and giving it to the disciples, Jesus gave a special invitation: *"Drink from it, all of you."* It is difficult to tell exactly at what point Judas left the upper room. (See "What Do You Think?" on page 200.) If he was still there at this time, the word *all* takes on added poignancy in view of the traitorous act he was contemplating.

The invitation in this verse is still a timely one. *Drink from it, all of you.* I have known Christians who have deliberately declined to partake of Communion, usually because on that day they felt especially unworthy of God's saving grace and were repentant for a week of thoughts and actions that disregarded God. But there is no better time to partake of Communion than when we feel overwhelmed by our sin. The Lord's Supper is spread for none other than sinners. No one is ever worthy of God's grace. This cup is for all of us, all of us who in some way have betrayed, denied, doubted, or disobeyed our Lord. This cup is always for us all.

28. "This is my blood of the covenant, which is poured out for many for the forgiveness of sins.

At this point Jesus gave new significance to the cup, even as he had to the bread. The cup stood for his *blood of the covenant.*

The word *covenant* is a word that was rich in meaning for the Jewish people. God had made a personal covenant with Abraham and had formalized it with his descendants by the law of Moses.

Blood was an important feature of that covenant. When Israel was encamped at Mount Sinai, they entered into the covenant with God, promising to do all he commanded. That covenant was ratified by blood, as Moses sprinkled the blood of the sacrificed animals on God's altar and on the people themselves (Exodus 24:6-8). According to the law, burnt offerings were offered daily in which the blood of the sacrificed animal was sprinkled on the altar. And once each year, on the Day of Atonement, the high priest sprinkled the blood of animals on the mercy seat of the ark of the covenant to make atonement for the priesthood and the people.

Jesus declared that a new covenant between God and man was being established, and it was based on the sacrifice of himself on the cross. *Forgiveness of sins* would come through the shedding of his blood, and the cup he now offered to the disciples was emblematic of it.

We see, therefore, that Communion is more than a ritual, or a remembrance. It is the renewal of a covenant initiated by the grace of God and entered into by all those who accept Jesus Christ as Savior and Lord. In partaking of the loaf and the cup of the Lord's Supper, we remember him who died to save us from our sins, and we recommit ourselves to him as his loyal servants.

Cup of Sacrifice

It was Memorial Day, 1988. At the Golden Gate National Cemetery, lying in the hills just south of San Francisco, the flags of all fifty states were displayed with the United States flag, which was at half-mast to commemorate the sacrifice of the men buried there. Rows of uniform white grave markers stood out against the green grass on the hills.

A gentle breeze ruffled the flags. Relatives of those who were buried there brought flowers to remember and to honor their dead. After some time, here and there a group would turn away after one final touching of a grave marker bearing the name of one dear to them.

There were no Memorial Day parades here—this was not the right location. This is a resting place to honor those who gave their life's blood to keep America free, and to thank others, now buried here, who survived their years of honorable service to be carried to this place and laid to rest with comrades lost in battle.

What Do You Think?

The Lord's Supper is an emotional event. We approach this time in a serious, thoughtful manner. After all, we are remembering the death of the Lord Jesus. Quiet, solemn feelings naturally accompany the time of Communion.

We also experience the feeling of gratitude. As we contemplate the great sacrifice Jesus made for us at Calvary, we are overwhelmed with this emotion. Upon reflection, we must acknowledge that without him we are sinners, lost, and without hope.

Another appropriate feeling is joy. We commune with a living Lord and a living body. We celebrate these relationships. We celebrate life.

Does one of these emotions dominate the Lord's Supper? If so, which one? Why? Should it? Why or why not? How can we communicate joy without appearing to take the sacrifice of Jesus lightly? How can we communicate all of these emotions in a healthy, balanced manner?

PRAYER

Our Father, we thank you for the Lord's Supper, which reminds us of Jesus' great love for us. As we partake, may we remember his sacrifice and find strength to rid our lives of sin. In Jesus' name we pray, amen

THOUGHT TO REMEMBER

The Lord's Supper is our link to the past—Jesus' saving death; to the present—his spiritual presence; and to the future—his victorious return.

DAILY BIBLE READINGS

Monday, Jan. 30—Jesus Is the Bread of Life (John 6:30-40)

Tuesday, Jan. 31—The Great Commandment (Matthew 22: 34-40)

Wednesday, Feb. 1—A Woman Anoints Jesus (Matthew 26:6-13)

Thursday, Feb. 2—Judas Will Betray Jesus (Matthew 26:14-25)

Friday, Feb. 3—Jesus' Last Supper With His Disciples (Matthew 26:26-30)

Saturday, Feb. 4—The Disciples Promise to Remain Loyal (Matthew 26:31-35)

Sunday, Feb. 5—In Remembrance of Jesus (1 Corinthians 11:23-29)

There is no place where the body of Jesus Christ lies buried. But there is a memorial to his blood, which was shed at Calvary in mortal conflict with sin. Come quietly, reverently; keep the memorial he gave us. It is not a tomb, but a cup. "Drink from it, all of you," he said. "For this is my blood of the new covenant, which is poured out for many for the forgiveness of sins" (Matthew 26:27, 28). Jesus won the battle; let us remember the sacrifice.   —W. P.

29. "I tell you, I will not drink of this fruit of the vine from now on until that day when I drink it anew with you in my Father's kingdom."

This was the last supper: Jesus would not again drink with his disciples before he shed his blood for them. Some believe *drink it anew with you in my Father's kingdom* refers to Jesus' fellowship with his disciples in the kingdom that was ushered in by his glorious resurrection a few days later. At that time Jesus did have meals with his disciples, as he communed with them, confirmed the reality of his resurrection to them, and commissioned them to preach the good news of salvation (Luke 24:30; Acts 10:41). Others think Jesus meant his fellowship with his people in the Lord's Supper in the church. Still others think this refers to Christ's fellowship with his people in the world to come at the marriage supper of the Lamb (Revelation 19:6-9).

In any case, we live with the assurance that when we partake of the Lord's Supper we share in the ever-present victory won by Christ's death and resurrection, and we share a foretaste of eternity with God.

IV. THE MEAL CONCLUDES (MATTHEW 26:30)

30. When they had sung a hymn, they went out to the Mount of Olives.

Jews customarily closed their Passover celebration by singing from Psalms 115-118. If custom was followed, Jesus and the disciples concluded this somber meal by singing songs of trust and love and praise and thanks to God. In them, however, were expressions such as the "sorrows of death" and the "cup of salvation" and the "sacrifice of thanksgiving" (116:3, 13, 17)—words suggestive not only of the meaning of the Passover, but also of the saving sacrificial death of Jesus.

The Mount of Olives, just east of the city of Jerusalem, was the place where the events that Jesus had just symbolized and prophesied would be set in motion. There, in an olive grove, he would pray that some other way might be found to fulfill God's plan—some way other than his death. But it was there also that Jesus would choose to conform his human will with the Father's will. This night he would be met by his betrayer and the temple police, and he would be arrested for claiming to be the Messiah.

CONCLUSION

The last supper was one of the most serious moments in the life of Jesus. It was a matter of life and death, and as such was a paradox. On the one hand it demonstrated the certainty of Jesus' death and of the sad complicity of one of Jesus' own disciples in it. On the other hand it intimated that there was something beyond that death, something to be remembered. The last supper was a matter of death and life.

The Lord's Supper, Communion, is one of the most serious moments of our lives. It, too, is a paradox because in partaking of it we clearly are involved in a matter of life and death. On the one hand it reminds us of our sin, which demanded Jesus' death, and of our potential for betrayal, which dishonors his death. On the other hand it celebrates his death, which made the hope of eternal life a reality for all who accept him as Savior and Lord. The Lord's Supper is a matter of death and life.

Discovery Learning

This page contains an alternate lesson plan emphasizing learning activities. Classes desiring such student involvement will find these suggestions helpful. The next page is a reproducible activity page to further enhance discovery learning.

LEARNING GOALS

After today's lesson, each student will be able to:

1. Identify the origin of the Lord's Supper.

2. Contrast the commitment implied by sharing in the Lord's Supper with the betrayal unintentionally effected by some of our actions.

3. Suggest some action an appreciation for the Lord's Supper motivates him or her to do.

INTO THE LESSON

Before the class enters the room, write the following dates on the board:

March 6, 1836   February 15, 1898   December 7, 1941

Begin the class period by asking the class if these dates remind them of an event. Most will associate the last with the Japanese attack on Pearl Harbor. Perhaps a few will recognize the first as the date of the fall of the Alamo, and the second as the date of the sinking of the U. S. battleship *Maine* in Havana Harbor. Point out that after each of these events, the nation was galvanized into action by a call to remembrance: "Remember the Alamo!" "Remember the *Maine*!" "Remember Pearl Harbor!"

Ask the class whether anyone knows of what event the Passover was intended to remind the Jews? If no one can answer, ask someone to read Exodus 12:12-17. Point out that it recalled their deliverance from Egypt when the Lord "passed over" their homes but struck the firstborn in every other home to secure their release.

Then note that it was out of that celebration Jesus instituted the Lord's Supper. Have someone read 1 Corinthians 11:23-25. Ask the class what Jesus intended the purpose of his Supper to be, based on his words here. ("In remembrance of me.") The Lord's Supper is a call to "Remember the cross!"

INTO THE WORD

Prepare a script from the text of Matthew, to be used by class members acting out the story of the last supper. Include dialogue from Luke's account (Luke 22:14-23) and from Paul's discussion in 1 Corinthians 11:24, 25. It may be helpful to use a contemporary translation of the text. Speaking parts include Jesus, Judas, and other disciples (see Matthew 26:22).

When the skit has concluded, point out that there are really two stories here: the prediction of the betrayal and the institution of the Lord's Supper. Divide the class into two groups. One will discuss the betrayal prediction, the other the Lord's Supper.

Give the first group the following questions:

1. What does *betray* mean?

2. How did Judas betray Jesus?

3. What is the significance of the fact that the eleven disciples addressed Jesus by using the word *Lord* whereas Judas addressed him as *Master* or *Rabbi* (v. 25)? Does it show a defect in Judas's understanding of who Jesus was?

Give the second group these questions:

1. What is a covenant?

2. Jesus said the cup represented his blood of the "new" covenant. What was the "old" covenant?

3. A covenant requires faithfulness to the terms. To what covenant do we pledge continued faithfulness when we share in the Lord's Supper?

After ten minutes, ask each group to report. During the first group's report, ask the class members to think of a time when they betrayed (that is, failed) Jesus by their action or lack of action. Let them have a minute or two to identify the incident and to decide what they should have done differently.

During the second report, note the discussion in the commentary section of this lesson for assistance. Note also the "What Do You Think" question about the purpose of the Lord's Supper, page 202.)

Ask, "How might our actions during the week sometimes unintentionally betray the Lord and violate the commitment we pledge in the Lord's Supper? How can we avoid such a conflict?"

INTO LIFE

Divide the class into three groups. Assign each a different one of these passages: Matthew 26:20-25; Matthew 26:26-29; 1 Corinthians 11:28, 29.

Ask the members of each group to take a few minutes to reflect on the passage assigned to them and to suggest several ideas that could be used in a Communion meditation. Have each group choose one or two of the ideas and compose a brief meditation. Ask them to include in their meditation some challenge to appropriate behavior that goes beyond the Communion service to daily life.

To conclude the class session, have a volunteer from each group present the group's meditation as though for a Communion service.

The Passover

"Jesus sent Peter and John, saying, 'Go and make preparations for us to eat the Passover'" (Luke 22:8).

After the Passover meal is eaten, the *matzah* is brought out, broken, and distributed among the meal participants. The matzah is unleavened—it is striped, and it is pierced. It was this matzah that Jesus pointed to as he said, "Take and eat; this is my body" (Matthew 26:26).

How is the matzah a suitable symbol for Christ?

Unleavened

Striped

Pierced

After the Passover meal is eaten, a third cup of the fruit of the vine is filled and raised. This cup represents God's promise that he would redeem his people from slavery. It is this cup after supper in the upper room that Jesus raised and stated, "Drink from it, all of you. This is my blood of the covenant, which is poured out for many for the forgiveness of sins" (Matthew 26:27, 28).

How is this cup a suitable symbol for Christ?

"Poured Out"

Redemption

Covenant

Keep It Fresh

No doubt, Jesus and his disciples had shared in the ritual of the Passover many times together. This night was different, however. How the disciples must have been startled when Jesus changed the wording to apply the elements to himself.

One need not be startled to avoid treating an activity as commonplace, however. What would you suggest to prevent the Lord's Supper from becoming commonplace in the worship service. Write your suggestions below. Then share them with the person who plans your worship services.

Unit 4. Jesus Christ: Victor Over Sin and Death
(Lessons 10-13)

JESUS IS REJECTED

LESSON 11

WHY TEACH THIS LESSON?

The nighttime trial of Jesus in the palace of the high priest is a study in contrast. On the one hand is Jesus, "the way, and the *truth*, and the life." On the other are the false witnesses, bribed to offer some shred of so-called evidence in order to convict Jesus. We see Jesus, calm and unshaken. Then we see the raving high priest and the brutal ones who struck and spit on Jesus. We see Jesus boldly answering the high priest. In the shadows, we see Peter cowering at the questioning of a maid.

And if we look closely, we see ourselves. We, too, are seated on the witness stand. What is our testimony? Will we answer brave and true, or will we hedge and dodge? Will we maintain our composure when falsely and hysterically accused (abused?), or will we answer in kind?

This lesson will challenge your students to stand with Jesus and to give the testimony of faith.

INTRODUCTION

A. PLEADING THE FIFTH

"I refuse to answer on the grounds that it may tend to incriminate me." Some of us may remember hearing these words in a radio broadcast of a real-life Senate hearing. Others have heard them only in a fictional television courtroom drama. We call it "pleading the Fifth Amendment." Under our system of justice, people are not required to give testimony that would indicate their own guilt.

At his trial before the Jewish authorities, Jesus was asked a question, which, if answered truthfully, would incriminate him in the thinking of his accusers. The question was, "Are you the Christ, the Son of God?" Jesus did not "plead the Fifth." Without hesitation he openly admitted that he was. To the religious leaders that confession was blasphemy. In fact, however, it is the truth, the whole truth, and nothing but the truth—the foundation of our faith and the basis of our hope of life in the world to come.

B. LESSON BACKGROUND

Last week's lesson ended with Jesus and his disciples going to the Mount of Olives following their observance of the Passover meal, during which Jesus instituted his memorial feast, the Lord's Supper. On the slopes of the mount, in a garden called Gethsemane, Jesus agonized over his impending death. Throughout the intense struggle, however, his prayer was, "Father . . . not as I will, but as you will." With the struggle came unfazed resolve: he was ready to fulfill his purpose in coming to earth. (See Matthew 26:36-46.)

Suddenly Judas came, leading a great crowd of armed persons from the chief priests and elders of the people. With a kiss Judas betrayed his Master, and at that signal the guards stepped forward and arrested Jesus (vv. 26:47-56).

After his late-night betrayal and arrest, Jesus endured a series of exhausting trials. First, he was taken before Annas, the former high priest who had been removed from that position by the Roman authorities but who was still highly respected among the Jews. Eventually Annas's son-in-law, Caiaphas, the current high priest,

---

DEVOTIONAL READING:
ISAIAH 53:1-12

LESSON SCRIPTURE:
MATTHEW 26:36-68

PRINTED TEXT:
MATTHEW 26:57-68

LESSON AIMS

As a result of this study, students should:

1. Know some key facts about the arrest and trials of Jesus.

2. Share the sense of rejection that Jesus experienced.

3. Resolve to respond to physical and verbal abuse without violence.

Feb
12

KEY VERSE:

Then the high priest tore his clothes and said, "He has spoken blasphemy! Why do we need any more witnesses? Look, now you have heard the blasphemy. What do you think?"

"He is worthy of death," they answered. —Matthew 26:65, 66

HOW TO SAY IT

Annas. ANN-us.
Caiaphas. KAY-uh-fus or KYE-
uh-fus.
Gethsemane. Geth-SEM-uh-nee
(G as in get).
Pontius Pilate. PON-chus PIE-lut.
Sanhedrin. SAN-huh-drun or
San-HEED-run.

WHAT DO YOU THINK?

The Sanhedrin was the most powerful religious and political body of the Hebrew people. Often called the "Council," it was made up of seventy-one of Israel's religious leaders. In a way, this Council was the Jewish supreme court. The Sanhedrin was allowed by Rome to make many of the local decisions affecting daily life. However, a death sentence had to be approved by the Romans. The Sanhedrin might try Jesus and decide that he deserved to die, but only Pilate, the Roman governor, could sentence him to be crucified.

The Sanhedrin operated in an illegal manner in its handling of Jesus, but Jesus did not protest. Do you think that suggests something of the way Christians respond when the political "system" is manipulated by unbelievers in such a way as to persecute Christians? Why or why not?

What about when church leaders misuse their authority? Does Jesus' response to the religious authorities of his day suggest a response for us? Why or why not?

convened a representative group of the Council to try Jesus. This is the hearing mentioned in our printed text.

The Council, or Sanhedrin, was the supreme judicial authority of the Jewish people. Headed by the high priest, it operated under the authority of Rome and by its own rules of conduct. One of those rules stated that court proceedings were to be conducted only in daylight. Because the trial recorded in today's lesson was held in the pre-dawn darkness, another hearing (see Matthew 27:1; Luke 22:66-71) had to be convened to make the guilty verdict official. Only then was Jesus escorted to the Roman governor Pontius Pilate, then to Herod, then back to Pilate for the final disposition of his case. But it was this trial before Caiaphas, which we study in our lesson today, that gave the Sanhedrin the grounds they sought for insisting on Jesus' crucifixion.

I. THE ARREST (MATTHEW 26:57, 58)

57. Those who had arrested Jesus took him to Caiaphas, the high priest, where the teachers of the law and the elders had assembled.

The soldiers who seized Jesus were not Roman soldiers but the temple police, a Jewish militia under the authority of the priests who controlled the temple. Jesus' cleansing of the temple and his recent authoritative teachings there had angered and threatened these priests, who now took the initiative to eliminate him.

Caiaphas was not especially religious, but he was wealthy and powerful. It was he who determined that it was expedient for one man to die for the sake of the people; that is, that Jesus must be killed (see John 11:49, 50).

Caiaphas's motives appear to have been purely political: Jesus had become a threat to priestly authority. Along with the priests were gathered teachers of the law and elders, spiritual leaders from around Judea.

It is a sobering thought that those who opposed Jesus so intensely were the very persons who should have recognized and welcomed his coming. Those who lead the church today must remain vigilant against allowing a desire for authority to undermine their loyalty to Jesus.

58. But Peter followed him at a distance, right up to the courtyard of the high priest. He entered and sat down with the guards to see the outcome.

The disciples of Jesus ran for their lives when Jesus was arrested (Matthew 26:56). Peter, however, and another disciple, probably John (see John 18:15) circled back to the city. Staying back and out of sight, Peter followed the crowd as Jesus was taken to the high priest's palatial mansion, where the Council had been hastily summoned.

Peter showed both boldness and cowardice. He brashly entered the courtyard of the palace where Jesus was being examined, but later he refused the opportunity to speak in Jesus' defense. Notice the hopelessness of Peter. He followed his Master, but only *to see the outcome*. In spite of Jesus' repeated predictions of his death and subsequent resurrection, the disciples appear not to have expected either.

We who follow Jesus today must have the courage to stand up and speak up for the Savior.

TO SEE THE OUTCOME

Queen Mary I of England, daughter of Henry VIII and Catherine of Aragon, attempted to revoke the Protestant Reformation achieved in England under the reign of her half brother, Edward VI. A sizable segment of the English clergy refused to accept the return to the Roman Church theology, which Mary demanded. Most Protestant clergy fled to the Continent to escape the persecution Mary instituted, but three hundred ministers in England were martyred for their faith. The best known of these men were Latimer, Ridley, and Cranmer.

Imprisoned by the authorities, Cranmer was forced to watch when Latimer and Ridley were burned at the stake. It was Latimer who, while in the flames, encouraged Ridley with the words, ". . . we shall this day light such a candle, by God's grace, in England as I trust shall never be put out." In his weakened condition Cranmer recanted the position he had taken favoring the Protestant Reform movement. In spite of that, his political enemies condemned him to be burned at the stake also.

Latimer's courage, which he had witnessed earlier, helped Cranmer retract his recantation. When he was burned, he put his right hand, with which he had signed away his religious conviction, in the flames so that it burned before his body was destroyed. Cranmer's courage was reborn by the example of Latimer.

Peter followed to see the outcome of the proceedings against Jesus. The courageous example of Jesus eventually brought Peter out of his denial and into a dynamic faith and witness.

How would we act under such harrowing testings? (Pray that your faith would overcome your fears.) Cranmer, as Peter, learned that "faith is the victory that overcomes the world."
—W. P.

II. THE TRIAL (MATTHEW 26:59-62)

A. THE COURT CONVENED (V. 59)

59. The chief priests and the whole Sanhedrin were looking for false evidence against Jesus so that they could put him to death.

It is clear that from the outset the religious authorities had only one thing in mind, and that was to kill Jesus. Having no interest in truth or justice where Jesus was concerned, they *were looking for false evidence* against him. The word for "false evidence" refers not to physical evidence, but to testimony. They were hoping to find someone to give testimony plausible enough to justify Jesus' execution. Not only were these authorities acting illegally in conducting this hearing at night, but they also hypocritically ignored their laws regarding fair testimony, most of which were meant to protect the rights of the accused.

B. THE PROSECUTION IN DISARRAY (V. 60)

60a. But they did not find any, though many false witnesses came forward.

The authorities bribed or pressured people to fabricate charges against Jesus. Because the hearing had been called so hastily, however, there was no time to coach these *false witnesses* in the giving of their testimony. As might be expected of those who deal in lies, their reports were inconsistent. Not one of the charges brought against Jesus met the Sanhedrin's own requirements for valid testimony—charges substantiated by two or three witnesses. The testimony of these false witnesses was so contradictory (Mark 14:56) that it was of no value.

C. THE CHARGE THAT MIGHT STICK (VV. 61, 62)

60b, 61. Finally two came forward and declared, "This fellow said, 'I am able to destroy the temple of God and rebuild it in three days.'"

Finally two false witnesses brought a charge in which they appeared to be in agreement enough to satisfy the Sanhedrin's requirements that a charge be confirmed by at least two witnesses. Three years earlier, Jesus had cleansed the temple in Jerusalem by driving out the money changers and those who sold animals. The testimony of these two false witnesses was a twisted report of what Jesus had said on that occasion. (See John 2:18-22.) They not only misinterpreted Jesus' words, they misquoted him. Jesus had said, "[You, not I] destroy this temple, and I will raise it again in three days" (John 2:19). Second, he was referring to his own body, prophesying his death and resurrection, and was not speaking of the temple building in Jerusalem (v. 21). The false witnesses twisted Jesus' words to make it look as

WHAT DO YOU THINK?

Peter followed Jesus to see how it all would end. He wanted to know what was going to happen to Jesus. Peter followed at a distance, however, because he did not want to suffer with Jesus. He did not want to assume any risk at this point in time. Thus, when he was accused of being a follower of Jesus, he vehemently denied any relationship to his Lord.

What do you think Peter should have done? Should he have walked alongside Jesus and possibly died with him? Should he not have followed at all and avoided the temptation to deny Jesus? Should he have stormed the Council chamber and denounced their illegal handling of Jesus? What do you think, and why?

What lesson do you think Christians should learn from Peter's behavior?

WHAT DO YOU THINK?

The two false witnesses misquoted and misrepresented Jesus by taking his words out of context. Have you seen examples where well-meaning individuals have misrepresented the Lord because they misquoted the Lord or the Bible, or they took the words out of context? What kind of harm was done?

How can we be sure our testimony of Jesus does not also misrepresent Jesus?

WHAT DO YOU THINK?

Jesus' response to the Council's threats and abuse is amazing. What calm in the face of extreme abuse! To what extent do you think we ought to respond in the same way? After all, it may be that Jesus' response was at least partly calculated to allow their plans for his crucifixion to succeed so that he could die for our sins and become our Savior. Since our response will not effect another atonement (Jesus died "once for all"), to what extent is his example one for us to follow, and in what ways, if any, ought our response to differ? Does Romans 12:14-21 offer any help?

Visual 11 of the visuals packet summarizes the rejection of Jesus and holds a challenge for us.

though he threatened destruction of the sacred temple, a charge of sufficient severity to warrant the death sentence. It is interesting to note that even these two witnesses had disagreement in their accusation (see Mark 14:57-59).

It ought to be clear that we who are friends of Jesus must be careful to present his statements accurately when we teach and share his message. Consideration must be given to the context of his words, as well as to whether he is speaking literally or figuratively in each instance, so as not to misrepresent him.

TRUE OR FALSE?

Jeremy became a youthful "truthful deceiver." His dad paid him five dollars a week to mow their lawn with their riding mower. At first Jeremy enjoyed the task, but after a while his enthusiasm for mowing waned.

Having recently read Mark Twain's tales of Tom Sawyer, Jeremy made a quick application of one of the stories. He always cut the lawn on Saturday, when his dad played golf and his mother visited the beauty shop. Many of his young friends wanted to run the riding mower. At twenty-five cents for fifteen minutes he let them do his work. Eight working rides in two hours added two dollars to the five he was paid by his dad. His scheme went well for several weeks, and his dad always complimented him on his faithfulness in mowing the yard.

Jeremy's enterprise came to a halt one Saturday when his dad came home early from his golf game. His words were stern. "Jeremy, it's your job. I warned you never to let anyone else ride the mower. An injury to a friend would be a disaster for us." Jeremy protested. "But, Dad, I did mow the lawn!" In his eyes the completed job was more important than his dad's rules.

Truth can be twisted, but it cannot be destroyed. Do we deceive ourselves and others by interpreting truth to suit our own ends? The false witnesses at Jesus' trial attempted that, but failed. Ultimately, truth will triumph. —W. P.

62. Then the high priest stood up and said to Jesus, "Are you not going to answer? What is this testimony that these men are bringing against you?"

With a pretense of fairness, the high priest gave Jesus the opportunity to respond to the charge brought by the two men. It was obvious that their twisted testimony was a deliberate attempt to discredit him before all the Jews who respected the temple as the place where God was worshiped. In all likelihood the high priest hoped Jesus would say something that could be used against him.

Self-defense was not a high priority for Jesus. On the other hand, when Jesus was asked a legitimate question, even when it was asked with an accusatory purpose, he answered openly.

How should the people of God respond to false charges? First, let us be certain to live our lives so as to ensure that such charges are in fact false. Second, we must learn not to retaliate when slandered, so that we may avoid adding a real offense to the false one. When we are attacked, silence may be the best defense. When we are questioned as to our allegiance to Christ, we must speak the truth in love.

III. THE SURPRISE WITNESS (MATTHEW 26:63-65)

A. DIRECT QUESTION (v. 63)

63. But Jesus remained silent. The high priest said to him, "I charge you under oath by the living God: Tell us if you are the Christ, the Son of God."

Jesus refused to dignify the false and malicious charges with even a reply. In response to Jesus' silence, Caiaphas made a strategic move. The false and fumbling testimony of the witnesses having failed, the high priest called the defendant to testify against himself, on an even more incriminating charge. He demanded that Jesus state under solemn oath whether or not he was *the Christ, the Son of God.*

For a person to claim to be *the Son of God* was to claim to be a divine person, one who was equal with God. (See John 5:18.) Jesus had said before that God was his Father (see John 8:13-20). Caiaphas hoped to force Jesus into a confession that would settle the matter once and for all. If Jesus said no, he would be discredited as an impostor; but if he said yes, he would be denounced as a blasphemer.

B. DIRECT ANSWER (v. 64)

64. "Yes, it is as you say," Jesus replied. "But I say to all of you: In the future you will see the Son of Man sitting at the right hand of the Mighty One and coming on the clouds of heaven."

When Jesus responded to the interrogation with the words, *It is as you say,* he acknowledged his true nature. But Jesus forced the actual testimony to come from the high priest's own lips—"It is as *you* say!" (See the comments under Matthew 26:25 in Lesson 10.) Jesus' answer turned the condemnatory question of Caiaphas into a proclamation of his person—the Christ, the Son of the living God—from Caiaphas's own lips.

Jesus proceeded to announce his glorious exaltation to God's *right hand.* These judges, who now were sitting in judgment of him and plotting to kill him, would one day stand before him to be judged. The imagery of *coming on the clouds of heaven* comes from Daniel 7:13, 14. There the prophet described the glorification of the Son of Man and announced the eternal kingdom that would be his. This was a forthright declaration by Jesus of his nature and power, one that would not be misunderstood by the men before whom he stood and which, he knew, would seal his condemnation.

C. DESIRED RESULT (v. 65)

65. Then the high priest tore his clothes and said, "He has spoken blasphemy! Why do we need any more witnesses? Look, now you have heard the blasphemy."

The tearing of one's clothes was done by slitting the garment at the throat and then tearing it downward for several inches. Among the Jews, this act indicated a deep grief, horror, or dismay. In the case of Caiaphas, the tearing of his garments was a hypocritical display. This illegal nighttime hearing was conducted for the sole purpose of fabricating a charge against Jesus so these authorities could put Jesus to death (v. 59). For all his histrionics, for all his feigned horror, Caiaphas was quite satisfied at the turn of events.

He has spoken blasphemy. The false witnesses that the Council had either bribed or blackmailed into testifying against Jesus had failed to produce credible testimony against him. Now, however, the high priest was convinced that Jesus had incriminated himself. Blasphemy is the act of showing contempt or lack of reverence for God. Caiaphas declared Jesus guilty of this for elevating himself, a mere man (in Caiaphas's view), to the position of God. Leviticus 24:16 makes the seriousness of the offense very clear: "Anyone who blasphemes the name of the Lord must be put to death. The entire assembly must stone him." In the Jewish religio-judicial system, blasphemy against God was the ultimate offense a person could commit. Caiaphas knew well that Jesus' self-incrimination was enough for a conviction by the Sanhedrin.

Why do we need any more witnesses? One can well imagine how relieved Caiaphas must have been not to have to seek any more witnesses and induce them to commit perjury in order to obtain the judgment he sought against Jesus.

You have heard the blasphemy. Everyone in the room had heard what Jesus said. Caiaphas pressed his advantage and declared that Jesus had convicted himself in their presence.

WHAT DO YOU THINK?

The apostle Paul states that "everyone who wants to live a godly life in Christ Jesus will be persecuted" (2 Timothy 3:12). If we are not facing any persecution for our faith, does that mean there is something wrong with our Christianity? If so, what? If not, why not? What, then, does this verse mean?

Should we, then, invite persecution? What do you think we should do if we are not being persecuted for our faith?

WHAT DO YOU THINK?

Do you think the boldness displayed by Jesus is typical of his followers today? Why or why not? What can we do to develop a boldness similar to that displayed by Jesus?

PRAYER

Forgive us, O God, when any of our actions bring disgrace upon your Son and our Savior. Help us to follow him all the way to his cross, and ours. In his name we pray. Amen.

THOUGHT TO REMEMBER

The confession that led to Jesus' death is the very confession of faith that leads us to life.

DAILY BIBLE READINGS

Monday, Feb. 6—Rejection of the Lord's Servant (Isaiah 53:1-5)

Tuesday, Feb. 7—Jesus' Prayer in Gethsemane (Matthew 26:36-41)

Wednesday, Feb. 8—Jesus Accepts God's Will (Matthew 26:42-46)

Thursday, Feb. 9—Refuge in God (Psalm 118:5-9)

Friday, Feb. 10—Judas Betrays Jesus (Matthew 26:47-56)

Saturday, Feb. 11—Jesus Before Caiaphas (Matthew 26:57-68)

Sunday, Feb. 12—Peter's Denial of Jesus (Matthew 26:69-75)

IV. THE VERDICT (MATTHEW 26:66-68)

A. VOICE VOTE (v. 66)

66. "What do you think?"
"He is worthy of death," they answered.

Caiaphas asked not for formal deliberation concerning Christ's guilt. He sought an immediate vote by acclamation, and he received it. All declared Christ *worthy of death*.

By conducting this hearing the way they did, these religious authorities violated almost every rule they had created to assure justice for the individual. They had met in the dark, although their rules specified that hearings were to be held only in daylight. They had gathered at the high priest's house instead of the appointed chamber where trials were to take place. And they knowingly had received the testimony of false witnesses, which, of course, was forbidden. Because this was not a regular session of the Sanhedrin, a meeting of the full body had to be convened in the morning to consider how this informal sentence should be carried out (Matthew 27:1). Capital punishment was in the hands of Rome. All that remained was to convince the Romans that Jesus was worthy of death.

There is a great irony in the death sentence that the priests (the leaders of worship), the teachers of the law, and the elders (the spiritual guides of the people) handed down upon Jesus. He died because of the guilt of the very ones who declared him guilty, and worthy of death.

B. VIOLENT REACTION (vv. 67, 68)

67. Then they spit in his face and struck him with their fists. Others slapped him.

With the pronouncement of the guilty verdict, all semblance of order in the room disappeared, and Jesus was subjected to brutal cruelty and mockery. Was it the rough temple guards, the servants, or the sophisticated priests and elders themselves who did the despicable things mentioned in this verse and the following verse? The text allows for the horrible possibility that the religious leaders, who condemned the Son of God by means of this miscarriage of justice, stooped even lower to the vicious, demeaning treatment described. If they did not actually spit with their own mouths—an indignity that all people of all times have regarded as extraordinarily vicious—and strike with their own hands, it is obvious that they permitted the others present to do it.

68. . . . and said, "Prophesy to us, Christ. Who hit you?"

Luke 22:64 says that at some point after the physical abuse began, Jesus was blindfolded. Then one after another they hit him in the face, challenging him to tell them which person had hit him. But through it all—the verbal and physical abuse and the blasphemies spoken against him (see Luke 22:65)—Jesus refused to retaliate. What an example he has given us of self-restraint in the face of persecution by our enemies!

CONCLUSION

The world has known judges and juries who have convicted innocent persons. But never was there a greater miscarriage of justice than when the Sanhedrin declared Jesus Christ, the Son of God, guilty of blasphemy and worthy of death.

Ironically, he whom these judges condemned would ultimately be their judge. His resurrection from the dead vindicated the quiet claim they had condemned as blasphemous, and his exaltation to the right hand of God confirmed his claim to divine power and authority. Ultimately, all of us must stand before him in judgment.

Discovery Learning

This page contains an alternate lesson plan emphasizing learning activities. Classes desiring such student involvement will find these suggestions helpful. The next page is a reproducible activity page to further enhance discovery learning.

LEARNING GOALS

After this lesson the students will be able to:
1. Relate the details of Jesus' trial before the Sanhedrin.
2. Describe Jesus' experience of being rejected.
3. Resolve to stand up for Jesus, whatever the cost.

INTO THE LESSON

Prior to class time, write the word *rejection* on the chalkboard or on a poster so everyone who comes into the classroom can see it. To begin, ask the students, "Have you ever had an experience of rejection? Maybe you had a crush on a girl in high school, but when you asked her out, she refused. Perhaps you applied for as job, or for a promotion, but you didn't get it. What experiences have you had that you wouldn't mind sharing?"

Allow several to share their experiences. Be sensitive; if the events related are recent, the people involved may still be smarting a little. Ask, "How does rejection make you feel? Why?" Note that rejection attacks a person's self-esteem. It is very easy, even though it is wrong, to feel the rejection is a valid statement of one's worth. It is actually only someone else's *opinion* of you or your qualifications for a particular task.

Still, we are almost always hurt by rejection. Today we are considering the rejection of Jesus.

INTO THE WORD

Begin this part of the lesson by having a class member read Matthew 26:57-75 aloud from a contemporary translation. Use the text as the springboard for a discussion of the various persons or groups present at Jesus' trial. Display the following phrases on the chalkboard or with an overhead projector:

Why there?
Desired result?
Outcome?

Divide the class into four groups and assign each group one of the characters below. Ask each group to answer the three questions above for their character. Encourage speculation, but be sure that what is actually in the text is included. Write the responses under the appropriate headings. Some possible answers are included here in case some of your groups need a little help getting started.

1. Peter. *Why was he there?* The text says he was there "to see the outcome" (v. 58), indicating curiosity. Perhaps he also wanted to be there in case Jesus needed him to ef-fect an escape. *What was Peter's desired result?* No doubt he was hoping for Jesus' release, so things could get back to normal for Jesus and his disciples. *What was the outcome?* Jesus was condemned (v. 66), and Peter decided it would be safer for him to disavow any knowledge of him (vv. 69-75).

2. The witnesses. *Why were they there?* Were they subpoenaed? Bribed? Blackmailed? *What was the witnesses' desired result?* Was it to please the rulers? To make money? To bring about Jesus' death? *What was the outcome?* Their testimony was discredited (v. 60). They distorted the truth (compare verse 61 with John 2:19). They became accomplices to the greatest crime in history.

3. Caiaphas. *Why was he there?* As high priest, he was head of the Sanhedrin. Besides, he lived there! *What was the desired result?* He had determined earlier that it was expedient for Jesus to die (John 11:49-53). He was guarding his political power. *What was the outcome?* He asked Jesus point blank whether he was the Christ, the Son of God, and Jesus affirmed it. This gave Caiaphas all he needed to get a guilty verdict.

4. The Sanhedrin. *Why were they there?* They were summoned, probably by Caiaphas. Some may have been simply "going along with the crowd." Most had such animosity for Jesus that they willingly resorted to lies to convict him. Some, like Nicodemus, may have been absent, deliberately excluded when the summons was issued. *What was their desired result?* Again, they wanted to kill him, no matter what it meant to their integrity. *What was the outcome?* They succeeded in having Jesus executed, but in rejecting him they brought upon themselves their own rejection by God (see Luke 20:9-19).

INTO LIFE

Give each group an additional five minutes to identify ways that people today imitate their assigned characters in rejecting Jesus. Then bring the class together and have the groups report the results of their discussions.

Have each student think about the times he or she has rejected Jesus, whether by silence or embarrassment (like Peter), or by putting material success ahead of integrity (like the witnesses). Then form a prayer circle and have them pray silently, asking God for strength to stand up for Jesus.

As a conclusion to the prayer, lead the class in singing the first stanza of "Have Thine Own Way, Lord!"

Rejected

Probably everyone has faced rejection at one time or another. How does it make you feel? How do you respond? Write below several words that express feelings, actions, or thoughts associated with being rejected. Use the letters of the word *reject* to begin each one. (One example has been done to get you started.)

R efused _____

E _____

J _____

E _____

C _____

T _____

In His Steps

Peter says we are called to follow in the steps of our suffering Savior (1 Peter 2:21). In fact, he spends almost the entire letter of 1 Peter suggesting how we ought to respond to rejection and persecution, based on Jesus' example. Look up the following passages and summarize the response it suggests for the times when we are called to suffer as Jesus did.

1 Peter 1:3-9

1 Peter 1:13-16

1 Peter 2:11, 12

1 Peter 2:21-23

1 Peter 3:8, 9

1 Peter 3:13-17

1 Peter 4:1

1 Peter 4:12-16

1 Peter 4:19

1 Peter 5:6-11

Peter, who failed to stand up for Jesus at his trial, is the one who wrote these things about suffering with Christ! What encouragement in the face of your own failures does it give you to see how the Lord used Peter even after his failure?

JESUS IS MOCKED AND CRUCIFIED

LESSON 12

WHY TEACH THIS LESSON?

"Must Jesus bear the cross alone, and all the world go free?" Yes! That is the essence of grace. We could not carry a cross like that of Jesus. He alone could die for our sin. This lesson should be used as a reminder of that great fact.

But while we could not and can not bear *the cross,* Jesus did say his disciples must each bear *a cross.* We will be opposed for our faith in the Lord. We will be challenged for our beliefs. The example of Jesus on his cross is our guide as we bear our own crosses. Let this lesson provide motivation to bear the cross graciously and with courage.

INTRODUCTION

A. FACES IN THE CROWD

Have you ever turned your gaze from the center of attention at a gathering of people—the basketball game, the parade, the bride and groom—and looked at the onlookers? In their faces you can see anguish and elation, excitement and disappointment, the twinge of loss and the joy of gain. In fact, you can almost follow the action just by watching the faces in the crowd.

The Gospel accounts record the details of Jesus' crucifixion. But they also focus on those who observed it. By looking at the onlookers—disciples, soldiers, religious leaders, bystanders, thieves—we see their varied reactions to Jesus' suffering and death. As we do, we experience the feeling of being there, of witnessing the crucifixion itself.

The crucifixion of Jesus occupies a central place in God's plan of redemption, thus, in all of Scripture. It is an event that is ever before us, confronting us with its horror and its power. It is filled with horror, because the sins of mankind, our sins, made the death of the innocent One necessary. In that same death, however, is "the power of God" that brings salvation to man (1 Corinthians 1:18). When we view the cross, what can be seen in our faces?

B. LESSON BACKGROUND

As we saw in last week's lesson, in a nighttime trial the Jewish authorities condemned Jesus to death for what they considered his blasphemous claim to be the Christ, the Son of God. They could not carry out the death sentence, however; only the Roman authorities could do that. Therefore, they had to convince the Roman governor, Pontius Pilate, that Jesus should be put to death.

Early in the morning, following the official meeting of the Sanhedrin in which Jesus was formally declared to be worthy of death, the authorities took him to Pilate (Matthew 27:1, 2; Mark 15:1; Luke 22:66—23:1). The Jewish leaders had difficulty convincing Pilate that Jesus was a rival king and thus a threat to Caesar's authority. But when they suggested that to release Jesus would be interpreted as a sign of disloyalty to Caesar, Pilate ordered the execution (see John 19:12-16).

DEVOTIONAL READING:
JOHN 3:14-21

LESSON SCRIPTURE:
MATTHEW 27:1-61

PRINTED TEXT:
MATTHEW 27:27-44

LESSON AIMS

The study of this lesson is meant to help students to:

1. Feel the sense of rejection that Jesus experienced when he was mocked and crucified.

2. Resolve to face scorn and mockery as Jesus did.

KEY VERSE:

Those who passed by hurled insults at him, shaking their heads and saying, "You who are going to destroy the temple and build it in three days, save yourself! Come down from the cross, if you are the Son of God!"

—Matthew 27:39, 40

Feb
19

LESSON 12 NOTES

YOU THINK?

While it might seem that only unbelievers, the enemies of Jesus, would be guilty of mocking Jesus, too often the most damaging mockery today comes from Christians who do not live what they profess. They mock him in their life-styles.

The soldiers pretended Jesus was king, but they had no real intention of serving or obeying him. How is that like the person who accepts Christ but makes no attempt to obey the Lord in life? How about the person who obeys the Lord in some matters, but not in all? Is there a difference? If so, what?

How does living a life focused on, or obsessed with, the material, mock the Lord? How does "living for the moment," without regard for eternity, mock him?

HOW TO SAY IT

Antonia. An-TONE-yuh.

Cyrene. Sye-REE-nee or Sye-REEN.

Gethsemane. Geth-SEM-uh-nee (g as in get).

Golgotha. GAHL-guh-thuh.

Pontius Pilate. PON-chus PIE-lut.

Praetorium. Pray-TOR-ee-um.

Sanhedrin. SAN-heh-drun or San-HEED-run

The Romans were not the inventors of crucifixion as a means of capital punishment, but by the first century A.D. it had become their favorite method of execution. The Jews were no strangers to crucifixion, for thousands of their countrymen had been crucified since Rome took control of Palestine. In Jesus' day it may not have been an uncommon sight to see the body of a rebellious Jew hanging on a Roman cross alongside a road in Palestine. For the Romans, and in a sense for the Jews, Jesus' death was business as usual.

By the time of the event in the opening verses of today's text, Jesus had been without sleep for at least twenty-four hours. During that time he had spent the evening instructing his disciples. Afterward, in the garden of Gethsemane, he experienced a period of intense, anguished prayer. Following his arrest he endured the night trial, which ended with the abuse and physical beating administered by those who were in attendance. Then came the morning trials before Pilate, then Herod, then last before Pilate once again.

Attempting to gain the crowd's assent that Jesus should be released, Pilate ordered Jesus to be scourged. This failed to satisfy them, however; they wanted Jesus put to death. Pilate then gave Jesus up to be crucified.

I. JESUS MOCKED (MATTHEW 27:27-31)

A. THE PRAETORIUM (V. 27)

27. Then the governor's soldiers took Jesus into the Praetorium and gathered the whole company of soldiers around him.

The Roman soldiers led Jesus from Pilate's judgment seat into *the Praetorium*, the quarters of the Roman governor. Here he would be held while preparations were made for the crucifixion. The *soldiers* were a special contingent of imperial troops numbering in the hundreds, whose duty was to guard and carry out tasks for the governor. The governor may have been occupying the Tower of Antonia, a fortress built just north of and overlooking the temple. From here the Romans could keep an eye on the Jews in the temple, where revolts were likely to start.

Some think the governor may have been residing in Herod's palace in the northwestern part of Jerusalem. In either case, the guard assigned to Jesus summoned their bored comrades for some entertainment at the expense of their prisoner.

B. PERVERSE PLEASURE (VV. 28-30)

28. They stripped him and put a scarlet robe on him.

This probably does not mean *stripped* naked. The soldiers removed Jesus' long outer robe, the one commonly worn by Jewish men, and draped around his shoulders the bright red or purple cloak of a Roman officer. Some think that the *robe* was a cast-off garment from the wardrobe of Herod, which the soldiers found. In either case, they deemed the garment a fitting costume for this Jewish peasant who had been sentenced as a pretender to royalty.

29. . . . and then twisted together a crown of thorns and set it on his head. They put a staff in his right hand and knelt in front of him and mocked him. "Hail, king of the Jews!" they said.

To continue the royal motif and the ridicule, the Roman soldiers took branches from a thorn-bush and fashioned them into a "victor's crown," similar in design to the laurels given to conquering generals or athletes. This one, however, had sharp *thorns*. Thorn bushes grew throughout Palestine, and their only practical use was as firewood or for the making of fences to contain grazing animals.

The soldiers' mockery continued as they placed a *staff* in Jesus' hand for a scepter, a token of his "royal" authority. This must have been a rather thick and solid cane for the soldiers to use it as described in verse 30.

Once Jesus looked the part, the callous soldiers knelt before him, doing mock obeisance to him as king. The irony, of course, is that the soldiers pretended that Jesus was what he in truth is, and they did in derision what they and all other persons one day shall do in all earnestness (see Philippians 2:9-11).

In that hall, hundreds of soldiers passed before Jesus, each kneeling and hailing him as *king of the Jews*. Eventually, however, they tired of the charade, and mockery gave way to violence.

30. They spit on him, and took the staff and struck him on the head again and again.

Contemptuously they *spit on him*, and each in turn took the *staff* from his trembling hands and hit him on the head with it, doubtless driving the thorns deeper into his flesh.

As we consider the horror of this scene, let us remember two things. First, we can add to Jesus' indignities by betraying him with our thoughts, denying him with our words, or rejecting him by our actions. Will we? Second, Jesus kept his dignity by refusing to retaliate against those who abused him. When we are treated with contempt, can we react as he did?

Apparently at this point Pilate had Jesus brought out before the people, and made one more futile attempt to save him from death (see John 19:4-16).

The truth that Jesus alone paid the price for our forgiveness is forcefully conveyed by visual 12.

C. ENOUGH (v. 31)

31. After they had mocked him, they took off the robe and put his own clothes on him. Then they led him away to crucify him.

The mockery finally ended. The scarlet robe they had put on Jesus (v. 28) was removed, and his own garment returned to him. All preparations having been made for the execution, the soldiers *led him away to crucify him.*

THE ROAD TO CALVARY

The pilgrims come year by year. They are the modern counterpart of those who have come throughout the centuries to remember the suffering Savior. They are believers who, in the week each year when Jesus' sufferings and death are commemorated, want to walk the road to Calvary. It is called *Via Dolorosa*, the Way of Sorrow.

Every follower of Jesus needs to walk with him to Calvary. We cannot, like Simon of Cyrene, carry Jesus' cross; but we can, at Jesus' invitation, take up our cross and follow him. We can look around us and see the pain, suffering, shame, and hopelessness of those without Jesus and begin to share the burden of their anguish. In so doing, we can be the bearers of the message of God's love, forgiveness, and reconciliation that came together at Calvary. We are not without modern examples. In Calcutta's morass of sin, idolatry, poverty, and death, Mother Teresa carries her cross. It is the caring ministry of love that comforts the dying and consoles the bereaved.

We cannot die to offer salvation to anyone. However, we can live as Jesus lived among us. We can feed the hungry, heal the wounded, encourage the stumbling, and thus reduce Satan's power and hold on mankind. We can carry our cross by fulfilling Jesus' ministry in the world, wherever we are. We can proclaim life, eternal life, by walking with humility and gratitude the road to Calvary and witnessing to the spiritual wholeness we were given there.   —W. P.

II. JESUS CRUCIFIED (MATTHEW 27:32-38)

A. THE APPROACH (v. 32)

32. As they were going out, they met a man from Cyrene, named Simon, and they forced him to carry the cross.

John 19:17 indicates that Jesus began the journey to the crucifixion site carrying his cross. No doubt weakened by the ordeal he had undergone, it must have been

WHAT DO YOU THINK?

Jesus said to his disciples, "If anyone would come after me, he must deny himself and take up his cross and follow me" (Matthew 16:24). Some people suggest that the responsibility of caring for an infirm parent or handicapped child is the cross of which Jesus spoke—or being stricken with a debilitating illness. But those experiences come to persons whether or not they are followers of Christ. One's "cross" is what one suffers and bears because, and only because, of his or her allegiance to Jesus Christ.

What are some experiences that might be considered "bearing the cross"? How does Jesus' experience with a cross motivate you in taking up your cross?

OPTION

In Psalm 22 there are several specific statements that relate to the crucifixion of Jesus. The reproducible activity on page 222 will help your students to explore these statements and relate them to the event of Jesus' crucifixion.

---

literally impossible for Jesus to bear the weight of the cross and walk along as fast as the soldiers wanted to go.

A man from Cyrene happened to be passing by. The soldiers seized him and compelled him to carry the heavy cross the rest of the way. *Cyrene* was a city of Libya on the north coast of Africa. *Simon* was probably a Jew who had come to Jerusalem for the Passover celebration. We have no idea if this Simon became a follower of Jesus, but his children were well known to many when Mark wrote his Gospel account (see Mark 15:21).

As we consider the fact that one was compelled to carry Jesus' cross, the real question is not who was Simon, but where were the disciples? Those whom Jesus had challenged to take up their cross and follow him had not followed him to help bear his. The disciples, who promised to follow Jesus to Jerusalem even if it meant dying with him (John 11:16), were not with him now because they were afraid they might really have to die.

And what of us? Will we abandon him when he needs us most?

B. THE PLACE (v. 33)

33. They came to a place called Golgotha (which means The Place of the Skull).

The place of crucifixion was called *Golgotha*, a Hebrew word meaning "skull." The Latin word *Calvary* has the same meaning. The location of this place is unknown. Why the place was given its name is unknown also. Some feel that the present Church of the Holy Sepulcher stands on the site. Others feel that "Gordon's Golgotha," a hill located north of the present city, is the actual site. Of greatest importance is not the location of Golgotha, but the death of God's Son that occurred there. The Person, and not the place, is to be revered.

C. THE PREPARATION (v. 34)

34. There they offered Jesus wine to drink, mixed with gall; but after tasting it, he refused to drink it.

Preparations for the crucifixion began. The drink the soldiers offered Jesus before they affixed him to the cross was a mild painkiller, a drop of kindness in the flood of contempt. When Jesus tasted it, however, *he refused to drink it*. He chose to endure all of the agony of the cross, and to do so with a clear mind. Some months earlier he had set his face to go to Jerusalem. Several times he had told his disciples of the violent death that awaited him there. He had wrestled in the garden with the agony of his impending death. He had faced the fear; he could face the fact. Jesus was no victim; his was a voluntary death.

D. THE CRUCIFIXION (v. 35)

35. When they had crucified him, they divided up his clothes by casting lots.

To be *crucified* is to be put to death by having one's hands and feet nailed or bound to a cross. When Jesus was crucified, large nails were driven through his hands and feet to hold him to the cross. It has well been said that one who was crucified "died a thousand deaths."

It was customary for the soldiers assigned to execution duty to divide the victim's clothing among themselves. *Casting lots* refers to some method whereby a chance decision could be reached, whether by throwing dice, flipping a coin, drawing straws, or some other way. When the soldiers did this, the prophecy of Psalm 22:18 was fulfilled.

E. THE WAIT (vv. 36-38)

36. And sitting down, they kept watch over him there.

The soldiers were responsible to see that no one came near, so they sat down to keep watch. Death on a cross could take days. Even when victims were nailed to the cross, death usually came by exhaustion or exposure, not from loss of blood.

37. Above his head they placed the written charge against him: THIS IS JESUS, THE KING OF THE JEWS.

In the case of prominent prisoners, a sign was affixed to the cross, indicating the crime for which the person was being crucified. It was to be a warning to passersby not to contemplate such criminal behavior. John 19:20 tells us that the message was written in three languages: Hebrew (probably meaning Aramaic, the language of the Jews), Latin (the official language of the Roman government), and Greek (the world language of commerce and culture). Ironically, the sign above Jesus' head proclaimed not a heinous crime but a wondrous truth about him.

38. Two robbers were crucified with him, one on his right and one on his left.

The *robbers* who were crucified with Jesus probably were not petty thieves. The word describing them means someone who stole with force and violence. The priests would not have been unhappy with this arrangement, because it suggested that Jesus was a common criminal like these robbers. Thus was the prophecy of Isaiah 53:12 fulfilled (see Mark 15:28).

III. JESUS REVILED (MATTHEW 27:39-44)

A. THE PASSERSBY (VV. 39, 40)

39. Those who passed by hurled insults at him, shaking their heads.

The crucifixion occurred out in the open for all to see. Some of those who passed by were the enemies of Jesus, and they *hurled insults* him as he hung on the cross. The word for *hurled insults* actually means "blasphemed." They were guilty of doing to the Son of God, however ignorantly, what he had been accused of doing to God.

40. . . . and saying, "You who are going to destroy the temple and build it in three days, save yourself! Come down from the cross, if you are the Son of God!"

They threw back in Jesus' face a completely twisted version of the statement he had made three years earlier. He had actually said, "[You] destroy this temple, and in three days I will raise it up" (John 2:19). He was speaking, of course, of his crucifixion and resurrection. Even though these enemies may not have understood what Jesus meant by his cryptic statement, it clearly implied that he possessed miraculous power. Coupling that with his own claim when he stood before Caiaphas (Matthew 26:64), these revilers challenged Jesus to give proof of his deity and *come down from the cross.*

B. THE AUTHORITIES (VV. 41-43)

41. In the same way the chief priests, the teachers of the law and the elders mocked him.

Some of the members of the Sanhedrin that had convicted Jesus were present. The *priests,* who had pressed the prosecution, seem to have taken the initiative once more. The *teachers of the law* and *elders* also lowered themselves to the level of the crude populace by joining in the mockery.

42. "He saved others," they said, "but he can't save himself! He's the King of Israel! Let him come down now from the cross, and we will believe in him.

The rulers could hardly deny that Jesus had healed people of grievous diseases and had raised people from the dead. Now, however, they seized their opportunity to undermine Jesus' credibility by pointing out his inability to rescue himself from suffering and death. Before Pilate he had asserted that he was the King of the Jews. The rulers now sneered that if that were true, he should now display his power and authority by freeing himself from the cross.

WHAT DO YOU THINK?

Modern research shows that most people respond with fear to the idea of dying. Their fear focuses on these questions: How will I respond to pain, particularly if it continues for a long period of time? Will I lose control? What will it be like if I am terminally ill for an extended time? If the terminal experience leaves me debilitated, how will I feel being completely dependent upon others? Will my loved ones be able to handle my dying—how will it impact them emotionally and psychologically?

Does the death of Jesus offer any assurance to us as we contemplate our own death? Why or why not?

WHAT DO YOU THINK?

What can we learn from Jesus' example that may help us when we must face criticism, insults, and even physical violence?

Why is it so difficult not to fight back, but to "turn the other cheek"? Do you think that is always the proper response? Why or why not?

THOUGHT TO REMEMBER

The scoffers said they would have believed in Jesus if he had come down from the cross. We believe precisely because he did not.

DAILY BIBLE READINGS

A great irony appears here. The religious leaders of Jesus' day claimed that they would believe in him if he came down from the cross; we believe in him precisely because he did not. The fact that he stayed on the cross is not a sign to us that he was a deceiver, but, rather, proof that his claims were authentic. We take it not as a sign of his weakness, but as the surest token of his strength of will to carry out the plan of God.

Sometimes we may forget just how strange it must be to the world when we Christians claim to believe that One who was executed as a criminal was the powerful Son of God. There was so much about Jesus—in his life and in his death— that the world counts for weakness. But the glory of the Son of God was in his suffering, his power was in his sacrifice, and his strength was in the voluntary nature of his death.

43. "He trusts in God. Let God rescue him now if he wants him, for he said, 'I am the Son of God.'"

The gist of the rulers' argument was that Jesus had lied in claiming to be *the Son of God*. If Jesus really was the Son of God, they implied, God would save his Son from death. These rulers took the death of Jesus as proof that Jesus was not the Son of God; we know that it was the clearest evidence that he was. The Jews took the death of Jesus as a sign that God had rejected him; we know that by his death Jesus was accomplishing the will of God.

C. THE CRIMINALS (v. 44)

44. In the same way the robbers who were crucified with him also heaped insults on him.

The robbers who were crucified with Jesus would have liked nothing better than for Jesus to demonstrate divine power and show that he was the king of Israel. The overthrow of the Roman government might mean rescue for them, also. Jesus' kingdom, however, was not a political/military one, and his victory was not of this type. When the robbers realized that there would be no miracle or display of divine power, they joined in the jeers. Luke 23:39-43 records that one of the two robbers repented, sought Jesus' favor, and was promised a place in paradise.

CONCLUSION

The death of Jesus is a mirror in which we see our own reflections. How do we respond to the death of Jesus? With whose voice do we speak?

Are we like the soldiers, oblivious to the spiritual revolution occurring around us, focused only on mockery, on the moment, on the material? Some who profess to follow Jesus mock him by their life-styles; they devalue eternal life, which he has won for them, by living only for the moment; and they reject the spiritual salvation he offers by living lives focused on the material.

Are we like the passersby, unwilling to consider seriously who Jesus is? As believers, do we just go through the motions, refusing to examine the implications of the death of Jesus lest we be challenged to change our priorities or our life principles?

Are we like the religious leaders, who sought to protect their own power by rejecting his? Do we also fail to see that the salvation God offers is founded not on spectacular display but on self-sacrifice?

Or are we like the thieves, who would minimize the fact of their sin and the extent of their guilt?

With our hearts and voices let us confess our sins before God and thank the Lord Jesus for his sacrifice that makes forgiveness of sin possible. Then by our lives let us honor him who suffered the greatest dishonor and shame that we might live eternally.

Discovery Learning

This page contains an alternate lesson plan emphasizing learning activities. Classes desiring such student involvement will find these suggestions helpful. The next page is a reproducible activity page to further enhance discovery learning.

LEARNING GOALS

After this session, the learners will be able to:

1. Contrast the horror and the glory of Jesus' crucifixion.

2. Offer praise and thanks to God for the victory Jesus won on the cross.

3. Commit themselves to follow Jesus in taking up their crosses.

INTO THE LESSON

Demonstrate the horror of crucifixion by comparing it with other methods of capital punishment. Prepare six large strips of paper and write one of the following methods on each:

Gas Chamber
Lethal Injection
Hanging
Firing Squad
Electric Chair
Crucifixion

Display these strips across the front of the room. (Or write them on the board, if you prefer.) Lead the class in a brief discussion of these forms of execution one at a time. Consider such questions as, "What physical suffering is involved?" "What humiliation is involved?"

Discuss *crucifixion* last. Point out the excruciating pain of having spikes driven through hands and feet (or wrists and ankles); the labor and agony of each breath, as a result of hanging in an unnatural position; the humiliation of hanging nearly naked (if not completely naked) before a crowd; the incredible thirst brought on by the dehydration of blood loss and hanging in the hot sun.

Note: the point of this introduction is to show the horrible death our Lord died, *not* to debate the pros and cons of capital punishment. The discussion here is physical, not ethical.

INTO THE WORD

Write on slips of paper the text of the following verses of today's passage, one verse per slip: 27, 28, 29, 30, 35, 37, 38, 39, 40, 41, 42, 43, 44. Pass these out to thirteen class members. Have the verses read one at a time in the order given. As each verse is read, ask the class to define the insult or mockery contained in it. (For instance, in verse 27 the humiliation is that of a large number of soldiers gathering around to ridicule Jesus.)

Also, have the class note the irony in such statements as verse 29 (their mocking statement was true!); verse 37 (again, Pilate's ridicule was absolutely true, see John 19:19-22); verse 42 (again, the insult was true: had he saved himself, all of us would be lost). Announce to the class, in your best Paul Harvey impersonation, "You know the news. Now, you're going to hear—the rest of the story!"

Point out that the other Gospel writers give additional details regarding the crucifixion, and that, most important, the story of Jesus does not end at the cross, either for himself or for the robbers.

1. *The robbers.* Have someone read Matthew 27:38, 44. Ask the class what they would assume the final destination of these men would be if we had only Matthew's Gospel. Then have someone read Luke 23:39-43. The "rest of the story" for one of the robbers is given here. What *two* promises made to him by Jesus are recorded in verse 43? (In addition to the promise of paradise, Jesus told him that he would be there *today;* he would not have to hang on the cross for several days, as was often the case.)

2. *Jesus.* Have someone read Matthew 27:50. What were the results of Jesus' death? (See, for example, Romans 4:25; Hebrews 2:14, 15.) Point out, however, that Jesus would have been just a statistic in a Roman archive if not for the "rest of the story," seen in Matthew 28:5-7; 1 Corinthians 15:3-8.

INTO LIFE

Have four students read to the class the stanzas of John Bowring's hymn, "In the Cross of Christ." As each student reads, have the class discuss briefly the reason given in that stanza for glorying in the cross.

Next, have someone read aloud Matthew 16:24, 25. Ask the class what it means to take up one's cross. Remind the class that a cross was a means of execution, and that verse 24 is explained by verse 25. Lead the class to see that taking up our cross is to endure reproach or dishonor in the eyes of the world, even the loss of life, in serving Christ. (Note the "What Do You Think?" question at the top of the left-hand margin on page 218.)

Urge the class members to commit themselves anew to a life of cross-bearing, putting their lives on the line for Jesus. Then close with a prayer of praise and thanks for Jesus' sacrifice on the cross.

Psalm 22

Psalm 22 is an important psalm, for it contains predictions of specific details relating to Jesus' crucifixion. Read all of Psalm 22; then go back and look at each verse cited below. Draw a line from the Psalm 22 reference to the New Testament reference in the right-hand column that describes its fulfillment.

Psalm 22:1 •   • Matthew 27:43

Psalm 22:7 •   • Hebrews 2:10-12

Psalm 22:8 •   • John 19:28

Psalm 22:15 •   • Matthew 27:39

Psalm 22:16 •   • Matthew 27:46

Psalm 22:18 •   • Matthew 27:35

Psalm 22:22 •   • John 20:25

Why Was Jesus Crucified?

Read the following Scriptures. How does each one help answer the question, "Why was Jesus crucified?"

Romans 5:6-11

Colossians 1:13, 19-23

Hebrews 9:11-17, 24-28

How do these verses make you feel about Jesus?

Jesus the Fulfillment

Unit 4. Jesus Christ: Victor Over Sin and Death
(Lessons 10-13)

THE RISEN CHRIST COMMISSIONS DISCIPLES

LESSON 13

WHY TEACH THIS LESSON?

So what? Someone has said that no sermon or lesson is complete until you ask, "So what?" What is the hearer supposed to do with this information? What is the significance of the details of the story.

In this lesson we have both the "what" and the "so what?" The "what" is the resurrection, central fact in the Christian faith. Evidence is cited to establish it as truth. At the end of our lesson text is the "so what?" Commonly called the "Great Commission," Jesus words at the conclusion of Matthew's Gospel tell us plainly what we are to do about the fact of the resurrection.

Challenge your students to see the Great Commission not as Jesus last words to eleven men of long ago, but his continual word to his disciples today.

INTRODUCTION

A. AFTERMATH OF THE RESURRECTION

In the appearances of the risen Christ, there was at first the urgent necessity to make sure that Jesus was actually risen from the dead. This surety was given.

The women who were on their way to tell his disciples of the empty tomb and angel's message met Jesus on the way. Coming to him, they fell down before him and clasped his nail-pierced feet (Matthew 28:9). They knew it was Jesus.

When Jesus appeared to ten of the apostles and those who were with them later in the day of the resurrection, he showed them his hands and his feet and urged them to touch him so they would know he was not an apparition. Then he ate food before them (Luke 24:36-43). They were convinced.

A week later Thomas, who was not present at the earlier meeting and who protested that he would not believe unless he saw the scarred body of his Lord, was given the same evidence, and he, too, confessed his belief in the risen Christ (John 20:26-29).

Once these witnesses were certain that Jesus was risen from the dead, they faced these questions: "What are we to do about this? May we tell others? When? How shall we proceed?" So, the great commission was the natural outcome of the resurrection.

We today still face the question as to what we will do about the resurrected Christ. It is not enough for us to strengthen our personal faith and to treasure our redemption in Christ. We must share it with others.

B. LESSON BACKGROUND

Although Jesus had been on the cross for only six miserably long, mercifully short hours, the Roman soldiers confirmed that Jesus was dead. To remove any possibility of doubt of this fact, one of the soldiers thrust his spear through the side of Jesus' body, causing blood and water to issue from it. Jesus' death occurred at 3:00 P.M. (Luke 23:44-46), so there was just enough time for his followers hurriedly

DEVOTIONAL READING:
ACTS 10:34-48
LESSON SCRIPTURE:
MATTHEW 27:62–28:20
PRINTED TEXT:
MATTHEW 28:1-10, 16-20

LESSON AIMS

As a result of studying this week's lesson, the students should:

1. Have a greater knowledge of the facts regarding Jesus' resurrection.

2. Rejoice in Jesus' victory over death.

3. Resolve to tell at least one person this week of what Jesus' resurrection means to mankind.

KEY VERSE:

Therefore go and make disciples of all nations, baptizing them in the name of the Father and of the Son and of the Holy Spirit, and teaching them to obey everything I have commanded you. And surely I am with you always, to the very end of the age.
—Matthew 28:19, 20

Feb
26

Lesson 13 Notes

to place his body in a borrowed tomb before the Sabbath began at sunset on that Friday evening. Attention to the corpse would have to wait until after the Sabbath, when the darkness of Saturday night gave way to Sunday morning's dawn. Only then could Jesus' faithful followers come to the tomb to complete the burial customs.

It is important to remember that the women who came to the tomb as the first day of the week was dawning came to minister to a dead Master, not a risen Lord. They could have expected his resurrection, perhaps they even should have. On three separate occasions Jesus had foretold that he would be handed over to the authorities, put to death, and raised on the third day (Matthew 16:21; 17:22, 23; 20:17-19). These women were among those disciples who had heard Jesus' dire predictions (see Luke 24:6-8), but they must have dismissed them as being incredible, just as Peter had done (Matthew 16:22).

Sadly, therefore, they came to Jesus' tomb that morning to attend to his permanent burial. What caused the transformation in their lives—and the lives of the eleven disciples—from defeat and disappointment to firm faith and courageous testimony? The resurrection of Jesus.

I. THE EMPTY TOMB (MATTHEW 28:1-8)

A. THE WOMEN APPROACH (v. 1)

1. After the Sabbath, at dawn on the first day of the week, Mary Magdalene and the other Mary went to look at the tomb.

These two women had been followers of Jesus since the days of his ministry in Galilee. They had traveled with him, ministering to him and giving financial support to his ministry (Matthew 27:55, 56; Luke 8:1-3). These two followed when Jesus' body was taken down from the cross and watched when it was placed in the tomb (Matthew 27:61; Mark 15:47).

The Sabbath had ended at sundown on what we call Saturday evening, but Sunday morning was the women's first opportunity to attend to Jesus. Elsewhere we learn that they came to the tomb bringing their prepared spices to complete the preparations for the burial of their dead Master, and that other women were in their company (Luke 23:55—24:1, 10; Mark 16:1). John tells us that the dark of the night had not yet completely disappeared when they arrived.

B. THE ANGEL APPEARS (vv. 2-4)

2. There was a violent earthquake, for an angel of the Lord came down from heaven and, going to the tomb, rolled back the stone and sat on it.

No mortal eye observed as Jesus came forth from the closed tomb, so we do not know the precise time when the resurrection occurred. It is implied, however, that the descent of the angel, the earthquake, and resurrection were nearly simultaneous in occurrence and that this all happened while the women were making their journey to the tomb. (Compare Luke 24:1, 2.) Clearly, it was not necessary for the angel to roll back the stone from the door to permit Jesus to come forth from the tomb. The angel's appearance struck terror in the hearts of the guards, and his opening of the tomb permitted the women and others to enter it.

3. His appearance was like lightning, and his clothes were white as snow.

The angel's appearance confirmed his identity as a being who had come from the presence of God. Jesus had revealed his divine identity to his disciples by a similar glorious appearance at the transfiguration.

4. The guards were so afraid of him that they shook and became like dead men.

The guards were Roman soldiers assigned by Pontius Pilate at the request of the Jewish religious leaders to keep watch over the sealed tomb. The angel seemingly

WHAT DO YOU THINK?

Jesus had given at least three clear predictions that he would be killed and would rise again (Matthew 16:21; 17:22, 23; 20:17-19). The chief priests and Pharisees had heard and understood him (Matthew 27:62-64). Why, then, do you think none of Jesus' followers seemed to have expected a resurrection?

How does the fact that the women and the disciples did not expect a resurrection assure us today it was true, and not just wishful thinking?

What is the basis for our believing that Jesus rose from the dead?

Is the failure of the disciples to understand Jesus' predictions of a resurrection similar to modern disciples' failure to understand some clear teachings in the Scripture? Why or why not?

If the disciples could spend so much time with Jesus and still not understand what he said about dying and rising again, how should we respond to believers who disagree with or understanding of his second coming? Can we be absolutely sure we are right and they are wrong? Why or why not?

had a countenance that was severe and fearsome, for as the guards looked at him they began to shake uncontrollably and fainted dead away. Although the soldiers did not see Jesus as he came forth from the tomb, when they regained consciousness and went into Jerusalem they were able to testify to the presence and power of this divine being and to the empty tomb.

C. THE ANGEL ANNOUNCES (VV. 5, 6)

5. The angel said to the women, "Do not be afraid, for I know that you are looking for Jesus, who was crucified.

When the women arrived at the tomb and saw that the stone was rolled away from it, they entered and discovered that the body of Jesus was missing (Mark 16:4-6; Luke 24:2-5). It was after this that the angel spoke to them.

The women naturally were afraid at the sight of a being who obviously was divine. Theirs was an appropriate fear, a fitting response in the presence of one who has come from the presence of God.

The angel knew, however, that their fear also centered about their thoughts of Jesus who had been crucified. He acknowledged this before leading them on to the undreamed-of truth of the resurrection.

Fear—reverential awe—is a proper response to almighty God as we realize that we live in his presence daily. But that fear does not terrorize us. By all he has done, especially in the death and resurrection of his Son, he has shown his love for us. The fear we have for God leads us to greater faith, and greater love for him.

6. "He is not here; he has risen, just as he said. Come and see the place where he lay.

He is not here. The first part of the angel's statement spoke only of absence and might have provoked further confusion and consternation in the women's minds. But the second part spoke of life, of resurrection. This is the great good news! Jesus is not held in the grip of the grave. He is freed from death and is able to free from death all those whose sins he bore. *Just as he said.* To give force to his assertion, the angel reminded the women that Jesus had promised to rise (see Luke 24:6, 7).

The women hesitated, still fearful, so the angel invited them to come close and examine the place where Jesus' body had lain. This at least confirmed his absence and for the time being suggested his resurrection. Before long, Peter and John would study that empty tomb and its contents—the linen bandages that had been wound around Jesus' body, limb by limb, and the neatly folded head scarf. The empty tomb, however, was not the ultimate basis for their faith, any more than it was the ultimate proof of the resurrection. The risen Lord himself would be the evidence and object of their faith.

Come and see is an invitation that is extended to every person in every age. We cannot with certainty examine the empty tomb of Jesus, but we can carefully consider all the evidence that shows that Jesus rose from the dead. The resurrection invites personal involvement as the basis for personal testimony.

D. THE ANGEL INSTRUCTS (VV. 7, 8)

7. "Then go quickly and tell his disciples: 'He has risen from the dead and is going ahead of you into Galilee. There you will see him.' Now I have told you."

The women were not allowed to linger at the empty tomb for long. They were commissioned to *go quickly and tell* the greatest good news the world has ever heard—Jesus *has risen from the dead!* The gospel has had many messengers, and these women were the first. Mary Magdalene apparently was the first of the women to reach the tomb. Without waiting to see or hear more than that the tomb was empty, she had run to tell Peter and John (see John 20:1, 2). The other women,

Visual 13 of the visuals illustrates the relevance of Jesus' resurrection and the Great Commission for every generation.

WHAT DO YOU THINK?

Jesus said he would rise from the dead, and he did! We can be confident, therefore, that he will do as he promises. One of his most precious promises to us is this: "I am the resurrection and the life. He who believes in me will live, even though he dies; and whoever lives and believes in me will never die" (John 11:25, 26).

What other promises especially encourage you? What would give you such courage if you could not believe in the resurrection?

WHAT DO YOU THINK?

There are some religious scholars who claim Jesus' resurrection was not a literal event, but the "resurrection" of his influence or the raising of his popularity. The Scriptures, however, tell of his being seen and heard and touched. He even ate with the disciples—more than once. This was a real, lasting resurrection. The living Lord is ruler of God's eternal kingdom.

What do you think? How does the fact that Jesus literally and bodily rose from the dead give you greater assurance than would a figurative resurrection? Why is it better to serve a living Lord than to follow a dead hero?

WHAT DO YOU THINK?

The women were afraid and joyful at the same time. Their fear, at least by the time they left the tomb, may have been the reverential awe that the presence of God or of his heavenly messengers always inspires.

What emotions does the resurrection evoke from you? Why? How can you share these feelings with others?

who had remained at the tomb were now commissioned by the angel to carry to the disciples the news of Jesus' resurrection.

He is going ahead of you into Galilee. The band of disciples had been shaken by the events of the past several days, and it had been temporarily disintegrated. This group, upon whom so much depended, needed to be formed again, and the peace, seclusion, and safety of Galilee was well suited for this. Many of these men were from Galilee, and it was there that they were called to be his followers. Now it would be the site of their recommissioning to an even greater ministry, service in the light of the resurrection. The foundation of their recommissioning would be their reunion with their living Lord himself.

Our lives, our ministries, must also be based on the person of Jesus Christ. Though we do not see him in the flesh, we meet him and come to know him as we read his Word. Thus "seeing" him, we too are led to serve him.

HE'S ALIVE!

"Missing in Action" has been an emotional, political, and personal tragedy for Americans ever since Vietnam. The pain of not knowing if one you love is dead or alive is devastating. The records of MIAs in Vietnam are still incomplete.

The long, black marble Memorial Wall in Washington D. C. testifies to the sacrifice of America's known dead in the war in Vietnam, and it honors their memory. MIAs are those whose bodies were not recovered or those who may have died as prisoners of war and their deaths not reported by North Vietnamese officials. Some speculate that there may be a few still alive somewhere in southeast Asia. It is a festering wound in the heart of our nation.

Jesus died on the cross and was buried in the tomb; but when the women came with their burial spices, he was not there. The greatest mystery and tragedy of all earth's history would have been the empty tomb with no certainty of where Jesus' body had been taken. Thank God, Jesus' death on the cross was true—it was an acknowledged and verified fact. He was buried, and the tomb's location was known. And the tomb was well guarded by Roman soldiers.

The angel did not say, "Jesus' body is missing." The angel's message from Heaven was an announcement that makes the gospel message the hope of mankind: "He is not here. . . . He has risen from the dead and is going ahead of you into Galilee. There you will see him" (Matthew 28:6, 7). No MIA. No mystery. History certifies that he is alive!   —W. P.

8. So the women hurried away from the tomb, afraid yet filled with joy, and ran to tell his disciples.

The women did as they were instructed by the angel, and they ran from the tomb *afraid yet filled with joy.* It may seem strange that these two emotions burned within the hearts of the women as they hurried to the disciples, but we can surely understand it. They had seen a heavenly visitor in blinding appearance who had spoken to them. They had been in the presence of the supernatural. Any response other than fear would have been most unnatural. No sooner than thinking of this divine visitation, however, their minds turned to the message that was given them—Jesus is risen! and they were filled with joy.

Convinced of the truth of Jesus' resurrection and all its meaning for a lost world, we too should hasten to *go* and *tell* those who have not heard.

II. THE RISEN LORD (MATTHEW 28:9, 10)
A. MEETING ALONG THE WAY (v. 9)
9. Suddenly Jesus met them. "Greetings," he said. They came to him, clasped his feet and worshiped him.

Even before the women reached the disciples to share their wonderful news, they were confronted with an even more wonderful reality. Jesus himself met them. He spoke the simple, quiet words of salutation common in their day: *"Greetings."* Thus their testimony would not just be word of an empty tomb, but the good news of, "We have seen the Lord."

Their reactions were wholly fitting: they knelt before Jesus in awe *and worshiped him.* As they did so they *clasped his feet* in their great desire to be fully assured that his presence was real. This passage shows that the sense of touch also attested to the resurrection.

B. MESSAGE REPEATED (v. 10)

10. Then Jesus said to them, "Do not be afraid. Go and tell my brothers to go to Galilee; there they will see me."

Once again the women received the instruction to let awe give way to action. An important message was to be given to the disciples. Neither in the angel's instructions to the women nor in Jesus' words here was mention made that the disciples would see Jesus that very day. The faith of the disciples, already sorely tested, would be tested further by the events of this day.

III. THE GREAT COMMISSION (MATTHEW 28:16-20)

A. THE AUTHORITY OF THE LORD (vv. 16-18)

16. Then the eleven disciples went to Galilee, to the mountain where Jesus had told them to go.

Matthew does not mention the exact time or location of this meeting with Jesus. More than a week had passed since the resurrection, however. Jesus appeared to the group on the evening of resurrection day when Thomas was absent, and again eight days later when Thomas was with the rest of the group (John 20:19-29).

On the eve of his crucifixion Jesus had spoken to the eleven disciples of this meeting (Matthew 26:32). The angel at the tomb gave the women instructions for the disciples regarding this meeting (28:7), as did Jesus when he met them in the way (28:10).

So *the eleven disciples* (Judas having hanged himself) went to a mountain in Galilee as Jesus had instructed them, doubtless in one of his earlier appearances to them. Galilee was the place where they were called to service, trained for service, and sent out in service. They surely knew that being summoned to Galilee meant that they were being summoned to service. The reality of the resurrection and our believing response to it are not ends in themselves. They anticipate a call to service. We too must move from our Jerusalems, our weekly worship services celebrating the resurrection, into our Galilees, to our own mountains of opportunity for witness and service to which we have been called.

17. When they saw him, they worshiped him; but some doubted.

The worship of God is the highest duty of human beings. Besides the Father himself none is worthy of worship other than the One who was God and had fully and finally manifested God to the human race. And there could be no greater moment to worship than in the presence of the risen Lord, who had nullified the unnatural domination of sin and death and had begun the process of restoring us to our natural relationship with God through the resurrection of the dead.

Matthew mentions that at the appearance of Jesus *some doubted.* This certainly cannot refer to any of the eleven disciples, for they had seen him more than once at Jerusalem and had been given indubitable proofs that he had risen from the dead. Perhaps this was the occasion when Jesus was seen by more than five hundred persons at once (1 Corinthians 15:6). The eleven were slow to believe that Jesus had

---

THOUGHT TO REMEMBER

Our risen Lord commissions us to go and tell others he is risen. Let's not fail him.

WHAT DO YOU THINK?

The command to "disciple the nations" continues to challenge us today. The nations, literally translated from the Greek text, means "people (or ethnic) groups." There are hundreds upon hundreds of "people groups." How might an emphasis on ethnic groups in the Commission challenge your church's fulfillment of this Commission? How does it challenge your own?

How many people of various ethnic groups live near you? Do they know of the resurrection? Have you told them?

OPTION

Use the reproducible activities on page 230 to help your students explore the significance of the resurrection and the imperative of the Great Commission in their own lives.

Obviously, the Great Commission puts great emphasis on Christian missions, so that all persons everywhere may learn of Jesus. But Jesus' Commission was for all his followers, not just for a relatively small group of workers willing to travel to far-off places. One can "Go" across the street as well as across the sea to fulfill the Great Commission.

Why, then, are not more Christians involved in evangelism? What can you do to be more involved in fulfilling the Great Commission?

PRAYER

O God of life, we thank you for the witness you provided to your Son's resurrection, and for the hope of eternal life that is ours in his victory over death. In the name of the risen Lord we pray. Amen.

DAILY BIBLE READINGS

Monday, Feb. 20—Witness to Jesus' Resurrection (Acts 10:34-43)

Tuesday, Feb. 21—A Guarded Tomb (Matthew 27:62-66)

Wednesday, Feb. 22—The Empty Tomb (Matthew 28:1-7)

Thursday, Feb. 23—Jesus' Resurrection Discounted (Matthew 28:8-15)

Friday, Feb. 24—He Has Risen! (Mark 16:1-8)

Saturday, Feb. 25—Jesus Appears to Mary and His Disciples (John 20:1, 11-23)

Sunday, Feb. 26—Jesus' Commission to His Disciples (Matthew 28:16-20)

risen (Mark 16:9-14), and Thomas's hesitance is well known (John 20:24-29). It is not surprising, therefore, that other followers of Jesus were hesitant to believe the resurrection reports. But consider this: if those who doubted had accepted the wonder of the resurrection too readily, too thoughtlessly, they would not be credible witnesses. Those on whose testimony our faith is based were not gullible. And their testimony was not based on wishful thinking or secondhand reports or mass hallucinations, but on what they themselves witnessed. We can be grateful for the faith of these first followers. But we can also be grateful for the doubt that assured that their eventual faith was founded in fact.

18. Then Jesus came to them and said, "All authority in heaven and on earth has been given to me.

Neither the church today nor anyone in the church possesses inherent *authority.* That belongs to the Lord alone. But like the apostles, we do the Master's bidding in the confidence that we are carrying out the Commission of the One to whom all authority is given and in whom all authority resides, our risen Lord.

B. THE COMMISSION TO THE DISCIPLES (VV. 19, 20A)

19. "Therefore go and make disciples of all nations, baptizing them in the name of the Father and of the Son and of the Holy Spirit,

All Christians of every age are bound by this command of our Lord. *Make disciples of all nations.* This is more than passing on information about Jesus. It is calling others to commitment to Jesus, to be his *disciples.* There are no national or ethnic or racial prerequisites to becoming a disciple, only wholehearted commitment to Christ. Baptism is not only the way in which our Lord commanded us to express our commitment to him, but it is an eminently appropriate way. Thus we are incorporated into Christ by a symbolic but real identification of ourselves with his saving death on the cross and his victorious resurrection.

20a. "and teaching them to obey everything I have commanded you.

Just as newborn infants must be fed to sustain life and promote growth, so those born again in Christ must receive *teaching* so they can mature in Christian thought, speech, and conduct.

C. THE PROMISE OF HIS PRESENCE (V. 20B)

20b. And surely I am with you always, to the very end of the age."

When God commissioned Moses, he said he would be with him. When God called Joshua, he gave the same promise. Here Jesus gives the promise of his presence to his disciples. It is the greatest promise we have—that he will continue to be with us until we are able to be with him.

CONCLUSION

As wonderful as the discovery of the empty tomb was, it was not enough. It was necessary for the women and the disciples to see and communicate with the risen Lord. And we have their testimony, the testimony of eyewitnesses, many eyewitnesses, who saw what they never expected to see, whose fear became faith, whose lives and attitudes were transformed, and who gave their lives—in more ways than one—for the One whom they had seen after he was risen from the dead.

The resurrection of Jesus cannot be explained, but their testimony to the reality of the resurrection cannot be explained away. Their testimony is the evidence of things we cannot see, and on that we base our faith. There will come a time when we will see Jesus face to face. Until then let us continue to tell the good news to all—he is risen from the dead!

Discovery Learning

This page contains an alternate lesson plan emphasizing learning activities. Classes desiring such student involvement will find these suggestions helpful. The next page is a reproducible activity page to further enhance discovery learning.

LEARNING GOALS

After participating in this lesson, the students will:

1. Experience the joy of the resurrection.
2. Understand the message of the Great Commission.
3. Resolve to be involved in the work of making disciples.

INTO THE LESSON

Give each class member a copy of the following three questions. Provide a pen or pencil for each person who needs one. Ask the questions aloud and give your class members two or three minutes to write an answer to each one.

1. What is the most joyful memory from your childhood (before you were eighteen years old)?

2. What factors made this a particularly joyful event?

3. What do you have that reminds you of the event? (For example, photographs, letters, home movies, etc.)

Have your class members divide into pairs (married students pairing off with those who are not their spouses) and ask them to share their answers to the questions. Allow about two minutes for each question.

Now, ask the class, "What do you think is the most joyful event in all of human history?" The answer you are looking for, of course, is the resurrection of Jesus. If other answers are given, acknowledge them as good answers!

Second, ask what it is about the resurrection that makes it particularly joyful.

Finally, ask the class what we have to remind us of Jesus' resurrection. Possible answers may include the Bible, the Holy Spirit, or Easter. But it is the Lord's Day, the first day of the week, that the church has set apart from earliest days as a time to celebrate the resurrection of the Son of God on the first day of the week nearly two thousand years ago.

INTO THE WORD

Have four students read aloud to the class the Scriptures in parentheses at the end of this paragraph. Before the readings, ask the class to be listening to discover something the verses have in common. (Luke 1:13; Luke 1:30; Luke 2:10; Matthew 28:5)

(The common element is the angel's command not to be afraid.) The women in our text obviously were terrified. Have the class examine the text to see what other emotion the women felt. (Joy, verse 8.)

Now lead into a discussion as follows: State, "We are convinced of the resurrection of Jesus by the testimony in the Word. We have identified with his death and resurrection through baptism, and we have the promise of his unfailing presence in our lives." Then ask, "Do we experience a great sense of joy as the women at the tomb did in thinking of his resurrection? If not, what can we do to rekindle the spark of sheer amazement and joy?"

Give two good readers the following short script, and have them read it now.

Doctor (*excitedly*): I've done it! I've just discovered the cure for cancer! It's been right under our noses all the time!

Assistant: That's great news, Doctor! Shall I call the media, the Centers for Disease Control, the president?

Doctor (*more subdued*): No, I don't really want all the publicity. I'm just a quiet kind of guy. Let's just forget about this and get back to the cure for the common cold we've been working on.

Assistant: OK. You're the boss.

Ask, "What is wrong here?" After a brief discussion, point out that we often are just like the doctor. We have the greatest news in history—Jesus is risen!—and we remain quiet about it!

Write on the board or overhead the words, "*Great Commission.*" Have someone read Matthew 28:18-20. Now write on the board or overhead these questions one at a time, or have a transparency prepared that will allow you to uncover them one at a time. Write each answer beside the question as the class gives it.

Whose authority? (Jesus')

When? (From now on, until the very end of the age)

What? (Make disciples)

How? (1. Baptizing them, 2. teaching them)

INTO LIFE

Ask each class member to think of one person they know who does not know the Lord. Just *one!* Then have them pray for the person, and for an opportunity to share Jesus with that person.

OPTION

Use the activity, "Go and Tell" on the next page to allow students to think of people with whom they can share the good news, and how. The page is reproducible so you can make as many copies as you need.

He Is Not Here. He Is Risen!

Read the following Scriptures to find more about this well-known phrase, "He is not here; He is risen." How do these facts make you feel? What do they cause you to want to do?

Romans 6:5, 9-11

1 Corinthians 15:42, 49, 57

Ephesians 1:20-22

Ephesians 2:4-7

Colossians 3:1-4

1 Peter 3:21b, 22

Go and Tell!

This news is really good news. Whom will you tell? How will you tell them?
Complete the following chart to make plans to tell the good news of Jesus. Then choose at least one person from the chart and act on your plans.

SOMEONE YOU KNOW WHO IS NOT A CHRISTIAN	NAME	OCCASIONS WHEN YOU ARE OFTEN TOGETHER	WAYS YOU COULD SHARE THE GOSPEL
A neighbor			
A coworker			
A relative			
Someone who shares the same hobby as you			
Someone else you see frequently			

Spring Quarter, 1995

Theme: Christians Living in Community (1 and 2 Corinthians)

Special Features

Lessons

Unit 1. Responding to Challenges of Life in Community

Unit 2. Nurturing the Life of the Community

Unit 3. Ministering as a Christian Community

About these lessons

The lessons of the Spring Quarter are based on the apostle Paul's letters of 1 and 2 Corinthians. In them Paul addressed a variety of problems and issues involving the first-century Christians in Corinth. The principles he enunciated provide guidance for Christians today as well. This study emphasizes that the church is a community, and that all Christians are to promote the health and growth of that community.

Mar 5

Mar 12

Mar 19

Mar 26

Apr 2

Apr 9

Apr 16

Apr 23

Apr 30

May 7

May 14

May 21

May 28

The Church as a Community

by Johnny Pressley

There is nothing quite like sitting in the grandstand and watching a baseball game. Of course, watching a game on TV has its advantages. The television camera allows you to witness a crucial play up close, and from a variety of angles, and even in slow motion replay. You are not affected by adverse weather or an inconsiderate crowd. You have the convenience of having your refreshments only a few steps away in the kitchen. And best of all, you get to watch the game in the comfort of your favorite chair.

What more could you want from a baseball game? Well, how about the feel of the crowd as their reactions to the game echo throughout the stadium? How about the sense of being there, of being able to say, "I was there when it happened"? For all the comfort and convenience of watching a game at home, it cannot match the excitement of actually being at the game.

The same can be said about our participation in the activities of the church. Many people prefer to watch from a distance. Some get their fill from religious programming on TV. Others attend worship services, but draw back from other activities of the church, such as Sunday school, Bible studies, and fellowship gatherings.

We cannot say these people are not receiving any spiritual benefits. Religious programs on TV can be edifying, and even a restricted diet of church worship provides some spiritual nourishment.

But interaction with people also is an integral part of the nature of the church.

From the beginning, the church has been associated with the Greek word *koinonia* (Acts 2:42). Our English Bibles translate *koinonia* with such words as *fellowship, sharing, participation,* and *communion.* All of these terms indicate that the members of the church are interacting with one another, providing mutual support, guidance, and encouragement. Those who worship from a distance never fully appreciate the idea that the church is a community.

The theme for this quarter's lessons is "Christians Living in Community." Each lesson spotlights some aspect participation in the church as an active member. No other New Testament epistles provide as much information regarding church life as the Scripture texts chosen for this quarter—Paul's letters to the church in Corinth.

Paul knew the church at Corinth in a very personal way. On one of his missionary journeys, he stayed and preached in Corinth for eighteen months (Acts 18:11). When he moved on to minister in other places, he continued to hear about activities in Corinth from friends in the church (1 Corinthians 1:11), and from fellow workers such as Titus (2 Corinthians 7:6, 7). With full knowledge Paul wrote about matters related to the community life of the church.

MARCH | *A PLACE FOR CHALLENGES (UNIT 1)*

Much of 1 and 2 Corinthians addresses difficulties in the church at Corinth. Thus, our studies for March focus on some of the problems that can arise in a church community today. This is not to bemoan the fact that churches often have problems, which would create a negative attitude regarding the church, but to view difficult situations as challenges that can be dealt with in positive and effective ways, resulting in the further growth of the church.

Lesson 1, March 5. To respond effectively to a difficulty in a church, one must present his resolution of the matter with clear reasoning that is grounded in the Word of God. Paul shunned the use of fancy words and fancy ideas, which are often a cover for worldly counsel (1 Corinthians 2:1-5). As Lesson 1 explains, Paul exemplifies a better approach to resolving issues: "Speaking the Truth Plainly."

Lesson 2, March 12. In a lesson entitled "Being Faithful Under Stress," we gain insights into how a Christian should deal with stressful situations. In 1 Corinthians 4, Paul describes the type of difficulties he and the other apostles had to confront as they ministered to the churches. Paul's advice is that his readers imitate him, and so this lesson concentrates on Paul's approach to dealing with tough situations.

Lesson 3, March 19. First Corinthians 10 draws upon Old Testament history to teach a lesson to New Testament Christians. The Israelites who left Egypt and wandered in the wilderness for forty years were often punished because they continued to find occasion for sin and rebellion against God. Their story shows the folly of repeatedly giving in to temptation. As Paul declares, "God is faithful; he will not let you be tempted beyond what you can bear. But when you are tempted, he will also provide a way out so that you can stand up under it" (v. 13). Lesson 3 gives practical guidance for "Resisting Temptation."

Lesson 4, March 26. This study reminds us that some difficulties in the church can escalate till firm disciplinary measures must be applied in order to resolve a situation and maintain the integrity of the church. In 2 Corinthians 13 Paul gives us some ideas for our disciplinary actions when we are "Dealing With Conflict."

A PLACE FOR GROWTH (UNIT 2)

One of the benefits of dealing responsibly with challenges is that we learn lessons that aid us in the future. But this is only one way that participation in the church fellowship helps us to grow in spiritual maturity and wisdom. In the Corinthian epistles Paul expresses a concern that individual Christians take advantage of the opportunities for growth afforded by the church. This will be evident in the five lessons for April. This group of studies is entitled "Nurturing the Life of the Community."

Lesson 5, April 2. This lesson is entitled "Building Up the Body." Attention is given to 1 Corinthians 12 and the matter of spiritual gifts. We may consider whether or not the Holy Spirit is still distributing miraculous gifts such as speaking in tongues, but the emphasis of the lesson will be the same as Paul's in chapter 12. Whatever gifts and abilities an individual has should be put to use for the growth and enrichment of the church.

Lesson 6, April 9. The study entitled "Growing Through Worship" focuses on 1 Corinthians 14, where Paul discusses tongues-speaking and prophesying in a worship service. For that large segment of the present-day church that does not practice the first-century miraculous gifts, it may seem that a study of this chapter would have little relevance. However, Paul's guidelines for the proper manner of participation in a worship service will speak to us as clearly today as they originally did to the church in Corinth.

Lesson 7, April 16. On Easter Sunday it is appropriate that the lesson centers on the resurrection of Christ. The account of the resurrection day is retold through a study of Luke 24, and the lesson also examines the way Paul links Christ's resurrection to our present life and future hope. The emphasis upon growing in the church will be evident in this lesson's suggestions for "Being a Resurrection People."

Lesson 8, April 23. Some of the difficulties that arise within a church community are related to the fact that the individual members are at different levels of spiritual growth. Often there is tension when we have to work with fellow believers who do things we think are inappropriate for Christians, and when our own practices are challenged by others. The study of 1 Corinthians 8 in Lesson 8 shows the challenge we each face in "Exercising Liberty Wisely."

Lesson 9, April 30. One of the sure signs of growth is that Christians begin to direct their attention away from their own needs and desires and give more thought to "Caring for One Another." Lesson 9 develops Paul's theme in 2 Corinthians 1: those who work through times of trial and tribulation without faltering in their faith prepare themselves to be a source of comfort for others when they must suffer.

MAY

A PLACE FOR SERVICE (UNIT 3)

Christians who actively participate in the various activities of the church experience spiritual growth as they interact with other members (April lessons), and as they deal with difficulties and conflicts in a biblical manner (March lessons). But the church also offers another means for Christian growth that is equally important: "Ministering as a Christian Community." Our lessons for May deal with this.

Lesson 10, May 7. "Living in Christian Freedom" is the title of a lesson that focuses on the ways in which Paul was willing to give up his rights as an apostle in order to serve the needs of the Corinthians and facilitate their growth (1 Corinthians 9). Since our present age is marked by the pursuit of individual rights by all kinds of special interest groups, this lesson should provide some much-needed balance between personal rights and ministry to others.

Lesson 11, May 14. Paul's desire to serve the needs of others reached its finest expression in his devotion to the ministry of preaching the gospel of Jesus Christ. In Lesson 11, "Working for Reconciliation," the text of 2 Corinthians 5 is used to remind us of our top priority as servants of Christ: to share the message of Calvary with those in need of reconciliation to God.

Lesson 12, May 21. An obvious way of carrying out this month's theme of serving others is by contributions of money and supplies to fellow Christians who are in need. The study of 2 Corinthians 9 in Lesson 12 will present the rationale and benefits of "Sharing Blessings With Others."

Lesson 13, May 28. There could be no grander conclusion to a study of the Corinthian epistles than to focus on 1 Corinthians 13, the famous "Love Chapter." Lesson 13 encourages us to be active in "Expressing Love to All," the key ingredient to make the church more than just a gathering of people, but a community.

Help One Another

by James B. North

When Thomas Campbell began the movement that grew into the Restoration Movement, one of his primary emphases was for the unity of the church. "The Church of Christ upon earth is essentially, intentionally, and constitutionally one," he wrote in the *Declaration and Address.* The unity of God's people on earth remained a firm commitment for him through his entire life.

Campbell could easily have taken much of his cue for this emphasis from Paul's letters to the Corinthians. Throughout these letters, Paul also emphasized the unity of God's people. Alternately cajoling and upbraiding, he urged the Corinthians to demonstrate that unity.

One of the applications of that theme is that the unified Corinthians were to help one another. This helping has both negative and positive aspects.

AVOID DIVISION

One of the negative applications of Paul's concern was to warn the Corinthians against division (1 Corinthians 3). Some Corinthians had formed a Petrine party;

others were Paulites, Apollosites, and even Christites. Such sectarian splits created stress in the body and worked against the healthy, wholesome attitudes necessary for mutual cooperation within the church.

Division is a corrosive factor wherever it is found. Division pits members of the same body against each other. This is counterproductive. The health of the body depends upon its wholeness, and that means the healthy acceptance of each member by all the other members. One of the major emphases of the Restoration Movement has been to work for the unity of Christ's body on earth. This is to be done not through creedal consensus, but by agreement of our common commitment to Christ. Whether we are thinking of a local congregation, or relationships between congregations, or even developments between different fellowships of believers, the commonness of Christians is found in their mutual commitment to Christ. If this is not present, there is no unity, and mutual help is strictly limited.

Paul was certainly aware of the frailties of human nature. He said we have the treasure of the gospel in jars of clay (2 Corinthians 4:7). Because we are weak clay we need to make every effort to avoid problems within the body.

YIELD TO A BROTHER

Another negative application came out in Paul's discussion of meat offered to idols (1 Corinthians 8 and 10). We are to refrain from any activity that might offend another member of the body. The principles of this passage lead us to sacrifice our rights so we can serve each other's needs.

One of the marks of a mature Christian is the willingness to yield to a weaker member of the body over issues that are not essential to salvation. In essential matters there can be no yielding. But in matters of discretionary activity, the mature Christian yields to keep from offending a weaker member.

The original context of this concern was in the matter of meat offered to idols. Paul said the meat itself was not the problem. The real problem lay with the implications and value judgments brought in by people who had just recently come out of paganism.

As Paul explains in 1 Corinthians 10:23-33, many things that are permissible may not be expedient. Christians help one another by foregoing what is allowed in order to do what is advisable. We can do all things to the glory of God, but we must do them in ways that keep others from stumbling. This is self-sacrifice for the good of the larger body.

There are numerous applications of these principles in the present. Christians today can demand the right to wear certain clothes, watch certain movies, have a certain hairstyle, purchase certain products, read certain books, patronize certain stores, listen to certain music. The list could go on and on. The real question, however, is not their right, but the effect it may have on someone else who is offended by such activities. Christians today can help one another by giving up their right to certain activities out of sensitivity to the conscience of others.

This yielding is not a matter of weakness, but of strength. It is done not out of cowardice or fear, but out of love and concern for one another. This is maturity in conscientious, discretionary behavior.

THE BODY IS A UNIT

We have mentioned some negative applications of Paul's teaching on unity. One of the positive aspects is his illustration of Christians as members of the same body (1 Corinthians 12).

Paul mentions that some members of the body are ears while some are eyes; some are hands while others are feet. It is not that these members are in competition with each other. It is simply that they have different abilities. All these abilities are used for the common good. By serving the common good, the members help each other. When the eye sends messages to the brain so the body does not walk into a wall, the eye helps itself at the same time it is helping all other members of the body. When the hand puts food in the mouth, the hand ultimately gets the nourishment; but, of course, the rest of the body does, too. Think what a mess it would be if the hand tried to get the nourishment directly without sharing it with the rest of the body. Members of the body help each other because they are a body. The whole idea of being a member means that each unit is part of a larger whole. A member of the body has life, usefulness, and purpose only if it is attached to the rest of the body. Various members best serve themselves when they help one another.

In Ephesians 4:16 Paul describes the whole body joined together, with each part doing its work. Some parts of the body are bone; others are muscle; others are the ligaments that tie the whole thing together. A body that is all bone without muscle is dead. A body that is all muscle without bone has no structure and can do nothing but flop around. Some Christians are like bones—hard, sometimes brittle. Some Christians are like muscle—they are active without a purpose. Bone-Christians provide the direction for the church, but muscle-Christians provide the action. Ligament-Christians are the ones who succeed in tying the whole thing together. Each fulfills its role, but it takes all together to get the job accomplished.

CONTRIBUTIONS

Paul also taught the Corinthians to help one another by sharing their financial resources (1 Corinthians 16; 2 Corinthians 8). Members of the church in Corinth could help members of the church in Jerusalem. Both the Galatian and the Macedonian churches were involved in this. The imagery is much the same as in the previous idea. The hand shares resources for the common good. The digestive tract and cardiovascular system share these same resources for the common good. Even so Christians in the body of Christ share their resources for the common good.

When a member of the body is wounded, white corpuscles rush to that spot to bring healing. Other members of the body do not respond by saying, "Serves him right. That's his misfortune; I'm only glad it didn't happen to me!" The body would soon die if its members acted in this way.

SHARING CONCERNS

A further positive application of Paul's emphasis on unity is seen in 2 Corinthians 1:7. Paul says the Corinthians have shared his sufferings as well as his comfort. When Paul wrote to the Galatians he said, "Carry each other's burdens" (6:2). The same idea is here.

When a physical body carries a burden, the entire body becomes involved. Muscles in the shoulders, the arms, the back, the abdomen, and the legs all strain under the load. Whatever the body undertakes, the entire body supports. Christians can help one another by doing likewise. We can share grief as well as joy, suffering as well as enjoyment, frustration as well as excitement.

The body is fitted together for the good of the whole. Members help one another as naturally as breathing. The body does not concentrate on breathing—it happens automatically. If the body had to think about breathing to get the job done, life could be very tenuous. Breathing happens almost all by itself, yet the entire body benefits. In the same way, members of the church help one another automatically. It does not take a good deal of concentration or thoughtful contemplation. It just happens. That is the body at work. Helping one another.

SPEAKING THE TRUTH PLAINLY

LESSON 1

WHY TEACH THIS LESSON?

We live in an age of consumerism. It puts some unique strains on the church. Somehow its timeless message of grace and redemption from sin must be packaged in the wrappings of the contemporary. The "consumers" must be enticed to come and see what the church has to offer. Contemporary music, lounge furniture in the foyer, coffee in the classrooms, gymnasiums, special programs, and many other features have been added to encourage people to participate in our programs and services. If it stops there, however, it stops short.

Use this lesson to remind your students that the heart of the gospel is not in the style, but in the Spirit. Its power is not in the calendar, but in the cross.

INTRODUCTION

A. "DEEPER WISDOM FROM BEFORE THE DAWN OF TIME"

In C. S. Lewis's story of *The Lion, the Witch, and the Wardrobe*, four children of one family find themselves in a magical country where a wicked white witch claims to be queen and wants to keep humans out of her territory.

Tension develops between Edmund and the other children, and Edmund plots to help the witch capture the others. In time he sees his error, and attempts to be reconciled with his family. But then the witch appears, demanding that Edmund be turned over to her to be killed. According to "deep magic from the dawn of time," she says, she is entitled to the blood of traitors.

Aslan the lion, however, knows a deeper magic from *before* the dawn of time. By that magic Aslan is able to redeem Edmund from the witch with his own blood. The witch is defeated and Edmund is reconciled to his family.

Here fiction touches reality. There was tension in the Christian community in Corinth, and Paul sought to overcome it by talking plainly about the foundation and center of the Christian faith, a deeper wisdom from before the dawn of time.

B. LESSON BACKGROUND

This lesson is taken from Paul's first epistle to the 1 Corinthians. About A.D. 55, perhaps 56 or 57, Paul wrote it from Ephesus to the church he had established in Corinth about five years earlier. Corinth was famous as the capital of the province of Achaia (Greece) and the most important commercial city of the region, but it was also infamous for its gross immorality.

Most of the Christians in Corinth were converted Gentiles. They were still struggling to overcome their former pagan life-style (1 Corinthians 6:9-11; 8:7). They had even sent Paul a letter with some questions. Paul would answer them in the letter we are studying (1 Corinthians 7:1, 2). But first he had to deal with a very urgent matter. He had heard that the Christians were dividing into cliques, each promoting its favorite teacher (1 Corinthians 1:10-12). In doing this, they were losing sight of God's deeper wisdom and the very center of their faith.

DEVOTIONAL READING:
1 CORINTHIANS 1:18-25
LESSON SCRIPTURE:
1 CORINTHIANS 1:18-2:16
PRINTED TEXT:
1 CORINTHIANS 2:1-13

LESSON AIMS
After this lesson, each student should:
1. Evaluate claims to Christian maturity according to the norm of a wise and holy life-style.
2. Defeat the world's attempts to undermine his or her confidence in the Word of God.

VISUALS FOR THESE LESSONS
The Adult Visuals/Learning Resources *packet contains classroom-size visuals designed for use with the lessons in the Spring quarter. The packet is available from your supplier. Order no. 392.*

KEY VERSE:
For I resolved to know nothing while I was with you except Jesus Christ and him crucified.
—1 Corinthians 2:2

LESSON 1 NOTES

OPTION

Use the reproducible activity, "Conventional Wisdom," on page 244 to help your students explore the difference between God's wisdom and the world's wisdom.

WHAT DO YOU THINK?

Paul's example has often been cited as a warning against using complex theological terms or scholarly discussions in communicating the gospel. We do not want to give the impression that the gospel is only for those who are highly educated or intellectually superior. At the same time, the more common accusation against Christians today is that they are "ignorant, uneducated, and easily led."

What do you think? Have we gone too far in the opposite extreme, not being eloquent enough with the gospel? Why or why not? Why do you think the secular world makes this charge? How do Paul's words here help us in communicating with the scientific and intellectual secularists of today?

WHAT DO YOU THINK?

Do you think your church puts enough emphasis on "Jesus Christ, and him crucified"? Why or why not?

Consider the following aspects of our worship. What suggestions would you offer to be sure that proper emphasis on Jesus Christ and him crucified is maintained in each? What dangers need to be avoided in each?

- The Lord's Supper.
- Hymns and gospel songs.
- Preaching.

I. CHRIST CRUCIFIED IS THE CENTRAL TRUTH (1 CORINTHIANS 2:1, 2)

A. FOCUSING ON LEADERS IS WRONG (v. 1)

1. When I came to you, brothers, I did not come with eloquence or superior wisdom as I proclaimed to you the testimony about God.

Before coming to Corinth, Paul was in Athens. There he preached to the most intelligent and the best educated people of that day (Acts 17:15-34). He saw the limitations of even the best of human *eloquence* and *superior wisdom*. So Paul came to Corinth determined to bring glory to Christ, not to the human messenger.

The focus of his ministry was on *the testimony about God:* he preached the word of the cross (literal translation of 1 Corinthians 1:18); he told what God had done in Christ. He would not let the cross be emptied of its power by emphasis on the wisdom of merely human words (1 Corinthians 1:17).

After those founding days, Paul had left Corinth and Apollos had arrived and ministered in the Corinthian church. He was an educated, eloquent man, having great boldness, vigor, and knowledge of the Scriptures (Acts 18:24-28). The apostle Paul valued Apollos greatly as a fellow Christian leader (1 Corinthians 3:4-9; 16:12).

Unfortunately, some of the Corinthians became enamored with Apollos's rhetorical abilities. Comparing the two leaders, they perceived that Paul was less eloquent, less polished in speech. Worse than that, they went on to conclude that his message was inferior. Perhaps they complained that he gave only elementary teaching, feeding them with milk rather than meat (1 Corinthians 3:2).

As a result, the church in Corinth was plagued by strife and tension (1 Corinthians 1:10-13; 3:3, 4; 11:18; 2 Corinthians 12:20). Underlying these were their perceptions of their leaders! How much tension and strife can be avoided in our churches today if people will think of their leaders as no more than servants and stewards! (See 1 Corinthians 3:5; 4:1.)

B. THE CROSS IS THE CENTRAL TRUTH (v. 2)

2. For I resolved to know nothing while I was with you except Jesus Christ and him crucified.

Paul regarded the Christians in the Corinthian church as brothers (1 Corinthians 1:10, 26; 2:1; 3:1). There should be no divisions among Christian brothers. All serve one Master, our Lord Jesus Christ (1 Corinthians 1:2, 10), and all experience one baptism in one name (1 Corinthians 1:13-15). All Christians stand on common and level ground before the cross! Wherever there is arguing and bickering in the church, almost certainly Christians have forgotten what life in sin was like before Calvary.

> Mercy there was great, and grace was free;
> Pardon there was multiplied to me;
> There my burdened soul found liberty,
> At Calvary!
>
> —William R. Newell

II. GOD'S POWER KEEPS FAITH STRONG (1 CORINTHIANS 2:3-5)

A. ARROGANCE IN LEADERS IS WRONG (vv. 3, 4)

3, 4. I came to you in weakness and fear, and with much trembling. My message and my preaching were not with wise and persuasive words, but with a demonstration of the Spirit's power.

Paul would not detract from God's glory in the gospel message or the church's life. When he first came to Corinth, he did not seek to impress the hearers with his powerful personality, but with his suffering Lord.

The power of the gospel lies in God (Romans 1:16), but the Corinthian Christians were boasting as if the faith were an achievement of human thought or wisdom (1 Corinthians 1:29, 31; 3:21; 4:6, 7). Paul would not boast of anything but his own *weakness* and what God's might had done through his weakness (2 Corinthians 11:30; 12:5-9), *a demonstration of the Spirit's power.*

What is this *demonstration of the Spirit's power*? It may be that Paul is referring to the special miraculous signs and wonders that he worked in Corinth as evidence of his authority as an apostle of Jesus Christ (2 Corinthians 12:12). But we can see from the rest of the letter that Paul thinks the Corinthians are already putting too much emphasis on the sensational and ecstatic signs of the Spirit (1 Corinthians 12—14). It may be, then, that he is referring to the moral change in the Corinthians' converted lives. This was very strong proof that the Spirit of God was at work in the message Paul preached.

There is no room for arrogant boasting and self-reliance among Christians. The cross must be kept central. At the foot of the cross, even leaders in the church can only acknowledge their unending and humble dependence on God. Many of the hymns that we sing today speak of giving God alone the glory for the cross: "My richest gain I count but loss, and pour contempt on all my pride." "Forbid it, Lord, that I should boast, save in the death of Christ, my God." "There to my heart was the blood applied; glory to his name." "King of my life I crown thee now; thine shall the glory be." "In the cross of Christ I glory." "In the cross, in the cross, be my glory ever"! Do our preaching and our living match our singing?

B. HUMILITY KEEPS ON DEPENDING ON GOD (V. 5)

5. . . . so that your faith might not rest on men's wisdom, but on God's power.

There was a very good reason Paul did not want the human presentation of the gospel to distract from the divine content of the gospel: he wanted the Christians' *faith* to depend on the supernatural reality of God, not on the persuasive power of human salesmanship.

Paul wanted the Corinthians to realize that once the power of God is lost in a Christian's life, that Christian's faith has lost the only foundation that can keep it plausible and credible in a naturalistic world (1 Corinthians 3:10-13).

This verse then cautions us to examine how we today present the gospel to outsiders. For instance, some professors in Bible colleges are concerned about how much we use sports and entertainment to recruit students. The reason for concern is expressed in the principle, "What you win them with is what you win them to." Do we want students whose focus is sports and entertainment or students who have a burden to win the lost and want to prepare themselves for that task?

The church must ask similar questions. Are we confronting prospective converts with the demands of the gospel for repentance and holiness, or are we winning them by telling of our convenient location, winsome preacher's family, and wonderful programs? "What you win them with is what you win them to."

THE SMOOTH DIVINE

Above is the title of a section in a long poem called *The Triumph of Infidelity.* It was written by Timothy Dwight and printed in 1788. This section is an attack on those who seek to preach or teach "with enticing words of man's wisdom" instead of stressing "Jesus Christ, and him crucified." Dwight says of this clergyman:

WHAT DO YOU THINK?

If your church were looking for a new minister, would you likely vote to hire a preacher who could be described as coming "in weakness and fear, and with much trembling," whose "message and …preaching were not with wise and persuasive words"? Why or why not?

How can this verse sometimes be used to excuse lack of careful preparation and research for preaching (i.e., refusing "human wisdom")? How is preaching filled with God's power instead of human wisdom different from preaching that has neither?

Does the same principle apply to a Christian's personal witness as well as to public preaching? Why or why not?

Visual 1 of the visuals packet illustrates the superiority of following God's Word instead of man's wisdom.

No terrors on his gentle tongue attend;
No grating truths the nicest ear offend.

. . . .

Plato's fine tales he clumsily retold,
Trite, fireside, moral seesaws, dull as old;
His Christ and Bible placed at good remove,
Guilt hell-deserving, and forgiving love.

We who speak about Christian truth, if we are faithful to our commission, do not aim to flatter our hearers, or to impress them with our eloquence, or to make them more civilized or "socialized." We aim to bring them to the cross of Jesus, where they can find a suffering Savior and forgiven sin.

—J. G. V. B.

III. GOD'S WISDOM REWARDS TRUE MATURITY (1 CORINTHIANS 2:6-9)

A. TRUE VERSUS FALSE MATURITY (VV. 6-8)

6, 7. We do, however, speak a message of wisdom among the mature, but not the wisdom of this age or of the rulers of this age, who are coming to nothing. No, we speak of God's secret wisdom, a wisdom that has been hidden and that God destined for our glory before time began.

Sometimes Christians fail to discern between what the world counts as *wisdom* and what God says is *wisdom*. Then they often act foolishly and inconsistently (1 Corinthians 3:1-8). That was happening in the Corinthian church with its immorality, boasting, and envying. When a Christian community has these kinds of activity, it looks foolish not only to God but also to the unbelievers around it.

Surely it is clear today that what the world counts as "grown-up" and "adult" is often more adolescent and childish than mature and responsible (1 Corinthians 3:1). Paul is appealing to every Christian who is truly adult and *mature* to take careful note of how shallow the world's wisdom really is in comparison to God's wisdom.

8. None of the rulers of this age understood it, for if they had, they would not have crucified the Lord of glory.

Worldly knowledge is great, and modern science and technology astound us with what human reason can know about our universe—but it cannot know God (1 Corinthians 1:21; 2:14; 3:19; 8:2, 3). Paul speaks the truth plainly on this matter: the cross of the crucified Messiah is the irrefutable historical proof of the inability of human wisdom to find God and to make peace with him. In fact, in their relentless pursuit of something to "glory" in (1 Corinthians 1:29, 31), the world and its leaders, both political and religious, wound up crucifying *the Lord of glory!* (Acts 4:23-30).

Unless God reveals his will to mankind, and unless humans accept his revelation, humanity's wisdom, power, and vaunted nobility will prove ultimately to be foolish, weak, and worthless. But once God's revelation of himself in the crucified Christ is accepted, God's alleged foolishness and weakness prove to be very wise, most powerful, and filled with the promise of glory! (2 Corinthians 4:16-18).

CRUCIFIED, YET CONQUEROR

Julian was a Roman leader in the fourth century A.D. He had been educated by Christians and had been a Christian teacher for a time, but then he abandoned Christianity. Known as "Julian the Apostate," he restored the pagan temples and showed extreme hostility to Christians. He was killed in a battle with Persian forces after reign-

HOW TO SAY IT.

Achaia. Uh-KAY-yuh.
Apollos. Uh-PAW-lus.
Corinth. COR-inth.
Ephesus. EF-eh-sus.

WHAT DO YOU THINK?

What comes to your mind when you think of "what God has prepared for those who love him" (v. 9)? Do you think only of eternity—what about the ministry he has prepared for you to fulfill in the meanwhile? Do you think only of the tasks at hand—what about the glory to be revealed? How can focusing on both be helpful in maintaining faithfulness? In sharing your faith with others?

ing as a Caesar only two years. While he was not actually fighting Christians at the time of his death, it is reported that his dying words were "Galilean, thou hast conquered."

"The rulers of this age" not only were responsible for Jesus' death on the cross, but through centuries they have often opposed his way and his people. A vivid modern example of this has been the oppression of Christians and the obvious attempt to eliminate the Christian religion from the atheistic, Marxist Union of Soviet Socialist Republics.

Just as Julian failed in his attack on the reality of Jesus and the church, so the Russian experiment came to naught. The "rulers of this age" in education, philosophy, science, art, and entertainment may be willing to ignore, demean, or destroy him, but they falter and are defeated. The "wisdom" of Paul's world scorned and scoffed at the crucified "Lord" of Christians, but he was ultimately victor. He will conquer the wisdom and power of our scornful world. "For it is written, 'I will destroy the wisdom of the wise; the intelligence of the intelligent I will frustrate'" (1 Corinthians 1:19; Isaiah 29:14)   —J. G. V. B.

B. TRUE WISDOM AND MATURITY REWARDED (v. 9)
9. However, as it is written:
"No eye has seen,
no ear has heard,
no mind has conceived
what God has prepared for those who love him"—

Truly wise and truly mature people are people who *love* God. Paul cited Isaiah 64:4 to show that God has *prepared* wonderful things to reward those who show their love by living in accordance with his revealed divine wisdom. Already in this life these people are receiving many blessings: they are chosen by God (1 Corinthians 1:27, 28), called by God (1:2, 9, 24, 26), and being saved by God (1:18).

But the blessings of God's grace and providence in this life, with all the love, peace, and joy they bring, are not all there is. More than the human *mind* can even think or imagine lies in store in the future for those who choose to live by divine wisdom. And all these present blessings and all our hope for future bliss are stored in Jesus Christ our risen Lord! (1 Corinthians 1:30; Ephesians 1:3).

THINGS PREPARED
I had learned to read and loved to do so, but as a child I was allowed to draw books from only the juvenile section of our city's public library. I've never forgotten the thrill of presenting proof of my admittance into high school and of being allowed to utilize the books of the adult department. Here were thousands and thousands of books, arranged, shelved, and made available. Things prepared!

I was thrilled again with the first art gallery I was able to visit. What gorgeous paintings, what colors, what portraits, what beautiful scenes! They all had been painted, purchased, and were now exhibited. Things prepared!

So it is with laboratories available for the use of microscopes, chemicals, Bunsen burners—all the equipment one can use to unlock physical conundrums and to explore our created world. So it is with autos to drive, planes to fly, and buildings to utilize. Things prepared.

Spiritually we learn of things we never could have conceived of by our human wisdom and observation. We are told in the Spirit-revealed Word about a city of God gleaming with eternal light, about a spiritual body that will be powerful, glorious, and incorruptible. We are informed about an everlasting fellowship of rejoicing, purified beings similar to the happy fellowship of a wedding feast. Things prepared!
                                                        —J. G. V. B.

WHAT DO YOU THINK?
As we attempt to speak "in words taught by the Spirit, expressing spiritual truths in spiritual words" (v. 12), how is the principle of using "Bible names for Bible things" helpful? How can we be sure this does not become "jargon" that alienates those outside the church?

WHAT DO YOU THINK?
Paul says "we have the mind of Christ" (v. 16). Some believe that means Bible study is unnecessary. Who needs to spend hours studying the Bible when we already have the "mind of Christ"? Others say this refers to God's revelation—thus, to the Bible. To make use of the "mind of Christ," we must study the Bible diligently.

What do you think? What does Paul mean? Who exactly is the "we"—all Christians, or Paul and other inspired teachers? How do you know?

How can we make full use of the "mind of Christ" in our lives today?

PRAYER

Dear Lord and Father of mankind,
   Forgive our foolish ways!
Reclothe us in our rightful mind;
   In purer lives Thy service find,
In deeper rev'rence, praise.
        —John G. Whittier

THOUGHT TO REMEMBER

Bind us together, Lord; bind us together with cords that cannot be broken. Bind us together with love.

OPTION

Use the reproducible activity, "Determining What Is Most Important," on page 244 to help your students apply the principle of this lesson in their own lives.

DAILY BIBLE READINGS

Monday, Feb. 27—The Power of Christ's Cross (1 Corinthians 1:18-25)

Tuesday, Feb. 28—God's Wisdom Revealed in Christ (1 Corinthians 1:26-31)

Wednesday, Mar. 1—God's Power Is Faith's Foundation (1 Corinthians 2:1-9)

Thursday, Mar. 2—God's Spirit Gives Understanding (1 Corinthians 2:10-16)

Friday, Mar. 3—Honor Christ as Lord (1 Peter 3:8-18)

Saturday, Mar. 4—Live as Children of God (Romans 8: 12-25)

Sunday, Mar. 5—Firm Counsel for Christian Living (Colossians 3: 1-7)

IV. GOD'S REVELATION GIVES CONFIDENCE (1 CORINTHIANS 2:10-13)

A. GUARANTEE OF TRUTH (VV. 10, 11)

10, 11. But God has revealed it to us by his Spirit. The Spirit searches all things, even the deep things of God. For who among men knows the thoughts of a man except the man's spirit within him? In the same way no one knows the thoughts of God except the Spirit of God.

Some Corinthian may have been wondering, as a Christian today may wonder: how do we know that what we teach is really God's wisdom and not just another form of human wisdom? How can we be sure that the Scriptures really express God's will for our lives? After all, other religions also claim to have revelations and sacred scriptures.

From the Garden of Eden on, Satan has always tried to use the world and the flesh (our human nature) to tempt us to distrust the Word of God. In today's world, entertainment, the media, education, and advertisement all seem united in attacking Christian beliefs and values.

Paul used a helpful analogy to bolster the Corinthians' confidence in the truth of God's Word. In each human being is a *spirit* that examines each thought, feeling, decision, and action of that person; God also—in whose image we are made—has a *Spirit* who knows *even the deep things of God*. This is the Spirit whom Jesus sent to guide Bible writers into all truth (John 16:13).

B. SPEAKING THE TRUTH (VV. 12, 13)

12, 13. We have not received the spirit of the world but the Spirit who is from God, that we may understand what God has freely given us. This is what we speak, not in words taught us by human wisdom but in words taught by the Spirit, expressing spiritual truths in spiritual words.

How this strengthens our confidence in the authority of the Scriptures! Paul and other apostles were guided by God's all-knowing Spirit. They passed on his revelation, not in the language of human wisdom, but *in words taught by the Spirit, expressing spiritual truths in spiritual words.*

This does not mean that we may use only the very words that we find in the Scriptures. To do this, we would have to speak in Greek and Hebrew. But it is important for all of us to express as closely as we possibly can those meanings intended by the original authors of the Scriptures.

This verse calls for a responsible and intentional mode of Christian thinking and speaking that is in harmony with the original revelation of God's wisdom as given to us by the Spirit.

Two important benefits result if Christians speak of spiritual matters in appropriate spiritual ways. First, the Christian community remains "perfectly united in mind and thought" (1 Corinthians 1:10). Second, the church maintains its confidence that the Scriptures reflect the mind of God.

CONCLUSION

On whose mind, then, should a community of believers unite? That of the preacher? Of a leading elder? Of a knowledgeable church member of long standing? Of Paul? Of Peter? Of Apollos?

The apostle Paul says our rallying point should be the mind of Jesus Christ (1 Corinthians 2:16). And we can know his mind from the Scriptures as we carefully study and reflect, and as the Holy Spirit conforms our minds more and more to that of Christ (Galatians 5:22, 23). Therefore, "do not conform any longer to the pattern of this world: but be transformed by the renewing of your mind" (Romans 12:2).

Discovery Learning

This page contains an alternate lesson plan emphasizing learning activities. Classes desiring such student involvement will find these suggestions helpful. The next page is a reproducible activity page to further enhance discovery learning.

LEARNING GOALS

Each pupil will be able to:

1. Contrast the preaching of Paul with the wisdom of the world.

2. Understand that the way of receiving spiritual wisdom differs radically from the ways in which people gain the world's wisdom.

3. Prepare a personal testimony.

INTO THE LESSON

Distribute paper and pencil and ask each student to write as many wise sayings as he can remember—not biblical sayings, but things the secular world deems wise. For example, "A penny saved is a penny earned." "Look out for number one." After about three to five minutes, ask people to share their sayings. Award a token prize, like a candy sucker, to the person who has the most.

Option: Use the reproducible activity, "Conventional Wisdom," on the next page.

Make the transition into the Bible study by stating that catchy maxims often have more appeal to people than do the deeper teachings of the Bible. The apostle Paul found his preaching being judged to be not as powerful as that of some other preachers. Consequently he defended his kind of preaching and contrasted it with the wisdom of the world. (Share insights from the "Lesson Background" as they apply.)

INTO THE WORD

Stimulate some practical insights by asking the class, "What are some qualities that a powerful, convincing speaker has?" Make two columns on the chalkboard. List the responses about a powerful speaker in the left column. Then ask students to read 1 Corinthians 2:1-13 and find out what kind of a communicator the apostle Paul was. Put their description of Paul's style in the other column. Lead the class to contrast the two columns. Point out that while Paul may have lacked some of the qualities that contemporary society applauds, he had one essential ingredient that made his communication powerful—content.

Let students find answers to the following questions by pairing off and searching the Scriptures. Write these questions on the board before the class arrives, or have them on handouts.

1. What one central truth had Paul tried to proclaim, according to 1 Corinthians 2:2? How was this different from what others had done?

2. What was the source of the wisdom Paul sought to share with the believers in the church at Corinth, as seen in 1 Corinthians 2:4, 10-13? How does this source differ from the world's source of wisdom?

3. How could the unity of the church at Corinth be disrupted because of the differing sources of wisdom?

4. What is meant by the phrase "rulers of this age" in 1 Corinthians 2:6, 8?

5. Why can't the wisdom of God be understood by the princes of this world?

6. What historical incident proves that people having only secular wisdom do not understand God's secret wisdom? (1 Corinthians 2:8). In your opinion, what is the primary content of God's secret wisdom?

After the pairs have worked on these questions for a few minutes, allow them to share their answers as you use them to develop the lesson for the class. Elaborate upon each question as you teach.

INTO LIFE

Help your students apply the lesson by teaching them to write their personal testimony about Jesus. Type and photocopy the following directives.

1. Choose a theme. Write about one area of your life that Christ has changed: for example, victory over a bad habit, peace of mind, etc.

2. Divide your testimony into three parts: (a) your life before meeting Christ (tell about a specific lack or problem);(b) how you came to believe and commit your life to Christ, and (c) how your life has changed since becoming a Christian. (Be specific.)

3. Helpful Insights: (a) don't use religious jargon or clichés. (b) Accentuate interesting aspects, but avoid boring details.

If time allows, or if someone is prepared in advance, have a personal testimony shared by a member of the class.

Close the session by reminding the class of Paul's example of a simple, straightforward witness to the person of Jesus Christ. Point out that personal testimonies should focus upon the Savior. If time allows, discuss some obstacles that must be overcome in sharing one's personal testimony.

Conventional Wisdom

List below as many contemporary maxims and "words to live by" as you can think of in five minutes. Don't worry about whether they are true or false, biblical or secular at first. Just write as many as you can.

Once you have a list developed, go back and analyze each item.
- Put a star (★) by each one you believe to be biblical. (Cite the reference if you know it.)
- Put a plus sign (+) by each one you believe to be consistent with the Bible's teachings even if not mentioned specifically.
- Put a minus sign (-) by each one you believe to be inconsistent with the Bible's teachings.
- Put a check (✔) by each one you believe to be commonly held by society today.

How many items have both a ✔ and a ★ or +? How many have a ✔ and a -? What does that say about the world's wisdom versus God's wisdom?

Determining What is Most Important

Paul was emphasizing the most important—God's wisdom—over the less important—everything else. What about you? When your day runs short, what gets cut? The diagram will help you sort through what is important and what is merely urgent. Complete the chart and keep it close by as a reminder of what is most important. The two quadrants under "Important" are where you should spend most of your time. In addition to the items you place in the chart, include the following: Bible reading, prayer, witnessing, and worship.

	IMPORTANT	NOT IMPORTANT
NOT URGENT		
URGENT		

Christians Living in Community

BEING FAITHFUL UNDER STRESS

LESSON 2

Mar 12

WHY TEACH THIS LESSON?

Adults are leaders. Not every adult leads in the same way or in the same set of circumstances, but virtually all adults lead in some way. Some of the adults in your class are church leaders, others are managers at their places of employment. Some may be active in community service projects or local government. Many are parents. Probably a few are teachers. Some wear a title of leadership—president, foreman, elder, director, principal. Others lead without a title; they simply "get the job done."

Whatever their sphere of leadership, your students need to hear Paul's words in today's text. Leadership is a sacred trust. It should display our submission to the Leader of us all. Challenge your students to follow Paul's example as he followed Christ.

INTRODUCTION

A. "YOUR OBEDIENT SERVANT, A. LINCOLN"

Near Springfield, Illinois, lies a little place called New Salem. Here Abraham Lincoln lived for a few years in the early 1830s. The little village has been carefully restored to look as it did in those days long ago.

Every year a play is performed on the grounds, dramatizing the events of Lincoln's life. For years the most famous play has been one entitled "Your Obedient Servant, A. Lincoln."

This title is taken from one of Lincoln's distinctive ways of signing his letters. It tells us much about the man as well as about his concept of leadership. Though mocked by the press, ridiculed by opponents, and often treated disrespectfully by people working closely with him, Lincoln shepherded the nation through very painful years on the strength of his character as a leader. He understood that leadership demands faithfulness and service.

This is what Paul wanted the Corinthian church to understand, as we see in our lesson.

B. LESSON BACKGROUND

In the first two chapters of 1 Corinthians, Paul has spoken the truth plainly about what should be central to all Christian thinking and preaching: the cross of Jesus Christ. In chapters 3 and 4 he shifts his focus away from the message to the relationship between the messengers and the recipients of the message.

There were some people in the Corinthian church who were beginning to view the church as just another human organization in which the leaders exist primarily to meet the felt needs of the followers, and in which the followers derive their self-worth primarily from their leaders' power and importance. Paul saw how very lethal this wrong perspective could be to the spiritual life of a church, and therefore he spoke of it with great urgency and also great love.

DEVOTIONAL READING:
ROMANS 12:1-10
LESSON SCRIPTURE:
1 CORINTHIANS 4
PRINTED TEXT:
1 CORINTHIANS 4:1,2,6-16

LESSON AIMS

After the completion of lesson, each student should:

1. Understand that servanthood is an essential part of being a Christian leader.

2. Know the value of faithful leadership in the church.

3. Imitate the faithfulness of good leaders.

OPTION

Use the reproducible activity, "Discover Your Leadership Style," on page 252 to introduce the idea of leadership.

KEY VERSE:

Now it is required that those who have been given a trust must prove faithful.
—1 Corinthians 4:2

LESSON 2 NOTES

HOW TO SAY IT:
Apollos. Uh-PAW-lus.
Cephas. SEE-fus.
Corinth. COR-inth.

Visual 2 of the visuals packet highlights the ministry of the apostles as described by Paul in the Scripture text.

WHAT DO YOU THINK?

What is the significance of Paul's view of leadership as a "trust" from God, that the leader is a servant or steward? Do you think most political leaders seem to have this concept? Why or why not? Do you think most industrial leaders seem to have this concept? Why or why not? Do you think most nationally known religious leaders seem to have this concept? Why or why not?

What about locally—do you see this concept displayed in your local church leaders? In yourself? Why or why not?

I. A PROPER PERSPECTIVE ON LEADERSHIP (1 CORINTHIANS 4:1, 2)

A. LEADERS ARE SERVANTS OF CHRIST (v. 1)

1. So then, men ought to regard us as servants of Christ and as those entrusted with the secret things of God.

Paul wanted the Corinthian Christians to see more clearly what it means to be leaders and followers in Christ's church. They would not need to boast so much about their leaders if they would fully realize how important they themselves were to God.

It seems quite clear that some of the Christians in Corinth were trying to bolster their feeling of self-worth by belonging to some important human leader and the group that called itself by his name (1 Corinthians 1:12; 3:4-9). Paul wanted them to understand that first they belonged to the most important leader of all: the Lord Jesus Christ. Because they belonged to Christ, all things that belonged to Christ also belonged to them, including Apollos, Cephas, and Paul himself (1 Corinthians 3:21-23).

If the Corinthian Christians would understand this, there would be no reason for one Christian to become "take pride in one man over against another" (1 Corinthians 4:6). Why not? Because all leaders would then be seen for what they really were: "servants, through whom you came to believe" (1 Corinthians 3:5). The Greek word translated *servants* in that verse is different from the one in the first verse of our text. This Greek word emphasizes the inferior and subservient position of the servant in relationship to his master. This is the proper view for Christian followers to have of their spiritual leaders. Every Christian leader is under Christ.

In our day of megachurches and multimillion-dollar television "ministries," Paul's words serve as an urgently needed reminder to both preachers and their supporters: leaders serve their followers because above all they are serving and following Christ (2 Corinthians 4:5).

In pagan Corinth, various heathen religious groups had "secrets" or "mysteries" that an outsider could not know until someone in the group revealed them to him. *The secret things of God* comprise that which was previously hidden but has now in the gospel been revealed: he wants Jews and Gentiles together to be saved as one new people in Jesus Christ (1 Corinthians 2:7; Ephesians 3:3-10). Christian servants are entrusted with the gospel to make that fact known!

B. LEADERS ARE STEWARDS OF GOD (v. 2)

2. Now it is required that those who have been given a trust must prove faithful.

Verse 1 says Paul and other Christian leaders are humble servants of Christ and stewards of God's mysteries. As stewards, they are accountable to God; they must be *faithful* in delivering the gospel entrusted to them, and faithful in managing their lives as directed by Christ the Lord.

Obviously Paul cared about what the Christians thought of him. But he was much more concerned about how God would judge him (1 Corinthians 4:3-5). Why is that? Because the apostles, and all leaders in the church, are accountable first and foremost to their Master, the Lord Jesus Christ.

In another place Paul asks, "Who are you to judge someone else's servant? To his own master he stands or falls. And he will stand, for the Lord is able to make him stand" (Romans 14:4).

God does sustain his faithful stewards; but we can be sure that neither God nor Paul would approve of a preacher today who lives immorally while warning potential critics not to speak against God's man.

Paul refused to let his followers be his ultimate judge, but that was not to lower the standards for his faithfulness. It was to raise them even higher! God was his judge.

BEING TRUSTWORTHY

Verse 2 in our lesson text speaks of "those who have been given a trust." We are familiar with situations in which some person is trusted to take care of something that belongs to others. We have grounds keepers on golf courses, baseball, football, and soccer fields. We have those who are responsible for the upkeep of swimming pools, and some who are gardeners on large estates or in public parks. Dietitians are responsible for supervising the food eaten by large numbers of people. There are administrators of hospitals, schools, and retirement homes. All of these people that are mentioned and large numbers of other people have responsibilities that are similar to what Paul is talking about here.

It is required that such stewards "be found faithful." They must honestly and carefully manage the property or oversee the group or agency of which they have charge. Such trustworthiness is essential. Stewards are praised and rewarded if efficient, and penalized or criticized if they are careless or negligent.

The apostle Paul tells us he and his co-workers had been entrusted with "the secret things of God." To them had been given the revelation that Jesus is Savior and Lord, and that the church is his body, purchased with his blood on the cross of Calvary. They must conserve and proclaim that revelation.

Is it not so with us? As Christians we are in responsible positions for God today. It is required of us that we be found faithful. If we do not love Jesus, seek to bring others to him, and make his church a living power in our world —who will?—J. G. V. B.

II. A PROPER PERSPECTIVE ON FOLLOWING (1 CORINTHIANS 4:6-8)

A. FOLLOWERS SHOULD NOT MISPLACE LOYALTY (v. 6)

6. Now, brothers, I have applied these things to myself and Apollos for your benefit, so that you may learn from us the meaning of the saying, "Do not go beyond what is written." Then you will not take pride in one man over against another.

Respect for worthy spiritual leaders in the churches is taught throughout the New Testament. But in the Corinthian church, the devotion of some to their leaders was threatening to become the kind of loyalty that is due to the Lord only. Paul wondered whether they were forgetting who had been crucified for them and in whose name they had been baptized (1 Corinthians 1:13).

In this letter Paul has been using Apollos and himself as examples to show how Christian leaders ought to relate to the Lord, to each other, and to their followers. Paul and Apollos were among the foolish, weak, and base things that God had chosen to use to reveal to the world his wisdom, power, and righteousness (1 Corinthians 1:26-31). They were fellow laborers in God's field, fellow builders in God's building (1 Corinthians 3:5-11), and fellow stewards accountable to the Lord (1 Corinthians 4:1, 2). It was wrong to champion one faithful preacher or teacher against another.

The phrase *beyond what is written* is puzzling. Paul does not say what writings he has in mind, nor does he cite the origin of the *saying* he quotes. But it is clear that Christians should not *take pride in one man over against another.* There was no quarrel between Paul and Apollos; there should be none between their followers.

B. FOLLOWERS SHOULD NOT FORGET THEIR ORIGINS (v. 7)

7. For who makes you different from anyone else? What do you have that you did not receive? And if you did receive it, why do you boast as though you did not?

WHAT DO YOU THINK?

Paul wrote, "Do not go beyond what is written." Several ideas have been suggested as to what writing he was talking about, such as the Old Testament or some rabbinical sayings, but we have no way of knowing for sure.

What application, then, can we draw from this? Do you think the principle may be applied to the Bible, even though the entire New Testament had not yet been written when Paul wrote this? Why or why not?

How does the slogan "Where the Bible speaks, we speak; where the Bible is silent, we are silent" suggest a similar concept to Paul's here? How strictly should this slogan be applied today?

WHAT DO YOU THINK?

When Paul says, "Who makes you different from anyone else?" two possible answers come to mind. One may say, "No one. There is no difference." Or one might recognize the difference of gifts and maturity among Christians and say, "God does."

In what sense is it true that there is no difference among Christians? What should we learn and do as a result?

In another sense, of course, it is not true, for there are differences. (See 1 Corinthians 12.) How does recognizing God as the source of those differences eliminate division that may arise as a result of such differences?

How can you keep the proper balance between seeing no difference among Christians and seeing the differences as God's gift? Are there some differences that should not be tolerated? Why or why not?

WHAT DO YOU THINK?

Those who take the Bible as literal truth and take seriously the Bible's call to an obedient and holy life may well find themselves labeled "fools" by many of their contemporaries. When they oppose what is "politically correct" because it is "biblically incorrect," there is little doubt that certain "enlightened" individuals in politics, in the media, in the entertainment industry, and elsewhere view them as fools.

Ironically, however, the label in Paul's letter seems to have come from within the church! Paul contrasts himself with the Corinthian Christians. Apparently the "wise" Corinthians had labeled Paul a "fool."

Why is it harder to remain faithful to the Lord when fellow Christians oppose our efforts than when outsiders oppose us? What is the proper response under such circumstances?

WHAT DO YOU THINK?

Paul said, "I am not writing this to shame you, but . . ." (v. 14). Who has not heard some busybody say, "It's none of my business, but. . ."? Or another say, "I don't want to hurt your feelings, but. . ."? How is such a line often used to justify treating another person wrongly?

How was Paul's use of this line different from the many today who use it as license to hurt people? After all, Paul did shame some of the people to whom he wrote! What cautions would you suggest to avoid using Paul's approach as a license to hurt others?

By use of three painfully honest questions Paul gets to the core of the mistake he is seeking to correct. Some people seemed to think they were worth more in God's eyes because they were won and taught by a superior leader, or because they had notable spiritual gifts (1 Corinthians 12). A Christian has much that is good and valuable; but it is nothing for him to brag about, because he has not received it by any merit or power or goodness of his own, but as a gracious gift from God.

It appears that some of the Corinthians had been Christians long enough to forget what life was like before God's grace in Jesus Christ called them, forgave them, and empowered them through the Holy Spirit to live new lives (1 Corinthians 6:9-11). Losing sight of their origins in grace, they began to idolize their favorite leaders, and to boast as if they had already reached perfection.

C. FOLLOWERS SHOULD NOT BECOME ARROGANT (V. 8)

8. Already you have all you want! Already you have become rich! You have become kings—and that without us! How I wish that you really had become kings so that we might be kings with you!

Whether some Corinthians were saying these things in words or just showing them by their attitude, Paul directly confronts their arrogant pride. In the competition among factions (1 Corinthians 1:12), members of each faction fancied that they were full of truth and sound doctrine, *rich* in Christian character and goodness. They thought they already *become kings* with Christ in his kingdom. And all this was *without us*: Paul, Apollos, and other teachers claimed no such exalted state.

Paul was not opposing any of their spiritual progress or victories. He wished they *had become kings* so he could share in their triumph. But the facts of their spiritual life belied their grandiose claims. To those who think they are perfect, Paul says perfection has not yet arrived (1 Corinthians 13:9-12).

It is true that Christians here on earth already are tasting some of the blessings of the age to come (Hebrews 6:5). But some of the Corinthian Christians seemed to think they had finished the whole banquet. We Christians today are in danger of a similar error if we suppose that here and now our faith gives us total freedom from all kinds of problems, weaknesses, and illnesses.

III. A MODEL OF FAITHFULNESS UNDER STRESS (1 CORINTHIANS 4:9-13)

A. APOSTLES MODEL LIFE UNDER A CROSS (V. 9)

9. For it seems to me that God has put us apostles on display at the end of the procession, like men condemned to die in the arena. We have been made a spectacle to the whole universe, to angels as well as to men.

In stark contrast to the life some of the Corinthian Christians were boasting about, the life of Paul and the rest of the apostles was life under a cross. There was nothing in it to elevate their social status or to give them anything to boast about. The apostles were like those prisoners who came *at the end* of an emperor's triumphal parade. Those prisoners were *condemned to die* in the arena, usually by lions, as the final *spectacle* of the evening.

B. APOSTLES AND CORINTHIANS CONTRASTED (V. 10)

10. We are fools for Christ, but you are so wise in Christ! We are weak, but you are strong! You are honored, we are dishonored!

So Paul continues the contrast between the claims of some Corinthian Christians and the lives of the apostles. We can almost hear Paul ask, "Isn't it a little strange that for Christ's sake we apostles are treated like *fools*, made to feel *weak* and *dishonored*, while you who are our converts are accepted in the world as *wise, strong,* and *honored?*"

Paul's point is not that Christians should intentionally act in foolish ways in order to invite ridicule, or try to justify foolish behavior because the Bible says we are to be *fools for Christ*. Rather, the point is that if we for Christ's sake are faithfully living under a cross, the world will almost inevitably think we are foolish and "not really with it."

We who are Christians living in developed countries need to ask ourselves this painful question: "Is it possible that we are respectable in the eyes of our world to the degree that we are *not* following the apostles' model of daily faithful living under a cross?"

C. Apostles Are Faithful Under Stress (vv. 11-13)

11. To this very hour we go hungry and thirsty, we are in rags, we are brutally treated, we are homeless. We work hard with our own hands. When we are cursed, we bless; when we are persecuted, we endure it; when we are slandered, we answer kindly. Up to this moment we have become the scum of the earth, the refuse of the world.

No doubt Paul was deeply hurt because some of the Corinthian Christians were looking down on him. They interpreted his gentleness and meekness as signs of weakness and inferiority (2 Corinthians 10:10, 11; 11:7-9). But Paul's meekness was really that of Christ (2 Corinthians 10:1-3). Paul warned that he, too, could be hard on them if he had to (1 Corinthians 4:18-21).

Paul's sorrow over their attitude expresses itself with great passion here. Certainly he had endured hunger, thirst, persecution, and manual labor, as well as other discomforts. Couldn't the Corinthians see that he did it for their sake and for the sake of the advancement of the gospel? (1 Corinthians 9:1-23).

Paul did not deny that his biography was full of what society would look down upon as "unfortunate" incidents, and even some ugly episodes (2 Corinthians 11:23-30). But he wanted the Corinthians to see also the grace with which God enabled the apostles to respond in all those problems: *we bless* (as Jesus commanded in Luke 6:28), *we endure* persecution, and we *answer kindly* even when *slandered.*

The true wisdom, power, and glory of the Christian life is not to deny, ignore, or, avoid suffering, but like Jesus to endure it faithfully under whatever stress the world may cause (Hebrews 5:7, 8; 12:2). Thus Christians can overcome evil with good (Romans 12:17, 21), even when they are called *the scum of the earth.*

Some Scum

We now regard the apostles as Christian heroes, as the specially empowered, inspired, and blessed agents of God. Many of their contemporaries, however, thought of them as weak and dishonored. They were cursed, slandered, and brutally treated. They were the "scum of the earth."

Such mistreatment has been seen often in the history of our faith. Those who have sought to translate the Bible into the language of the people have often been scorned and made scapegoats. John Wycliffe oversaw the rendering of our Bible into English, but he was hated and harassed. Upon his death in 1400, some of the opponents said in the English of that time that he was "The Devells Instrument, Churches Enemy, Peoples Confusion, Hereticks Idoll . . . Hatreds Sower, Lyes Forger, Flatteries Sinke: who at his death . . . breathed forth his wicked soule to the dark mansion of the black Devell."

What Do You Think?

Jesus said, "Do not call anyone on earth 'father'" (Matthew 23:9). Did Paul violate that command when he said, "In Christ Jesus I became your father through the gospel"? Why or why not?

In what ways are the duties of a Christian leader or teacher like those of a father? How can viewing the leader role as that of a parent help the leader? How can it help those who follow? Are there some leader-follower relationships that should not be viewed as parent-child relationships? Why or why not?

What Do You Think?

Paul told the Corinthians, "I urge you to imitate me." (See also 1 Corinthians 11:1) Is it proper for leaders in our church to offer that same exhortation? Why, or why not? What potential dangers does issuing such an exhortation hold for the leader who issues it? What potential dangers exist for the followers?

Why do you think more leaders—except for cult leaders—do not freely say, "Imitate me"?

How comfortable are you in encouraging others to imitate your example?

Option

Use the reproducible activity, "Imitate Me," on page 252 to make application of this lesson. Assure students they will not have to reveal anything they write in this activity if they do not want to.

THOUGHT TO REMEMBER

"His master replied, 'Well done, good and faithful servant! You have been faithful with a few things; I will put you in charge of many things. Come and share your master's happiness" (Matthew 25:21).

DAILY BIBLE READINGS

Monday, Mar. 6—Warning Against Relying on Human Wisdom (1 Corinthians 3:18-23)

Tuesday, Mar. 7—Servants of Christ (1 Corinthians 4:1-7)

Wednesday, Mar. 8—Faithfulness in Hard Times (1 Corinthians 4:8-13)

Thursday, Mar. 9—Fatherly Admonition (1 Corinthians 4: 14-21)

Friday, Mar. 10—Christian Conduct in Adversity (Romans 12:9-21)

Saturday, Mar. 11—Meet Trials With Steadfast Faith (James 1:1-8)

Sunday, Mar. 12—Encouragement for Christians (1 Thessalonians 5:1-11)

We may look at our missionaries as admirable and even heroic servants of our Lord, but they are not so regarded in all sections of our earth. In Muslim lands they often are scorned and opposed. This is also true in many areas of India and China.

It is true that in our day some have been murdered. But though regarded by misguided persons as "scum," they are indeed "fools for Christ" (v. 10). They are yet God's heralds and Jesus' shining servants. —J. G. V. B.

IV. AN APPEAL TO IMITATE FAITHFULNESS (1 CORINTHIANS 4:14-16)

A. AN APPEAL FROM LOVE (vv. 14, 15)

14. I am not writing this to shame you, but to warn you, as my dear children. Even though you have ten thousand guardians in Christ, you do not have many fathers, for in Christ Jesus I became your father through the gospel.

Paul knew his straightforward language would bring shame to some of the Corinthian Christians. That was not his purpose here, though it was in some parts of the letter (1 Corinthians 6:5; 15:34). Here Paul's primary purpose was to *warn* the Corinthians to change their views of leadership in the church. After all, was he not their spiritual father? It was he who had brought the *gospel* by which they were begotten to be born again.

B. AN APPEAL TO ACTION (v. 16)

16. Therefore I urge you to imitate me.

Our lesson ends with Paul's plea for the Corinthians to be followers of him, not because he wanted his party to win after all (1 Corinthians 1:12; 3:5, 6), but because he himself was faithfully imitating Christ's faithfulness to the Father (1 Corinthians 11:1). Imitation means a changed behavior: Paul wanted the Corinthians not merely to admire faithfulness under stress, but also to practice it in their own lives.

IMITATORS

Paul said, "Therefore I urge you to imitate me." In his reaction to scorn and insults, in his fortitude and faithfulness, Paul felt that he presented a worthy model.

We are constantly imitating others all of our lives. We learn our native language by making the same sounds we hear our parents and other adults making. We tend to imitate the dress and deportment of people whom we admire. In many of life's activities we are not ashamed to be "copycats." Often one will ask how he serves a tennis ball, or how he baits hooks so he can catch fish. We buy cookbooks so we can utilize the recipes others have created.

How important it is for us to be devoted to our Lord! We need to exhibit in our lives that humility, purity, compassion, and integrity we find in him. We may be much less comfortable than Paul seems to have been in urging others to imitate us. Is this because we doubt that our words, attitudes, and actions are really so much like those of Jesus that we dare to ask others to follow our example? Others, however, may be imitating us even when we don't know it. What a challenge this is to us every day! —J. G. V. B.

CONCLUSION

It is a beautiful and meaningful tradition at Lincoln Christian Seminary that each graduate during the graduation ceremony receives a diploma in the right hand and a new towel over the left arm. This ritual expresses the firm expectation that each graduate will prove to be a faithful servant of the Lord, his Word, and his people. Only by faithful service should success in ministry ultimately be evaluated.

Discovery Learning

This page contains an alternate lesson plan emphasizing learning activities. Classes desiring such student involvement will find these suggestions helpful. The next page is a reproducible activity page to further enhance discovery learning.

LEARNING GOALS

As a result of studying this lesson, a student will be able to:

1. Understand the difference between admonishing and shaming.

2. Describe the negative attitudes of poor followers of Christ and determine to avoid them in his or her Christian walk.

3. List specific characteristics of the ideal Christian leader as depicted by Paul.

INTO THE LESSON

Display the following sentence: "List as many stressful experiences in the life of Paul as you can recall." Give each class member a blank sheet of paper for this purpose. After a few moments, write the remembrances of the class on the board as they are shared. Then ask what Paul's usual reaction was in stressful times. (Answers should include faithfulness, rejoicing, contentment, and endurance.)

INTO THE WORD

Direct the students to read 1 Corinthians 4:11-13 and note Paul's struggles and stresses. Have them compare those with the list that the class compiled.

Go on to 1 Corinthians 4:14. Note Paul's purpose in sharing these things about himself: not to shame the readers, but to warn them, or to "admonish" them, as the *American Standard Version* has it. Have the class discuss the difference between the two. After hearing several answers, suggest that shaming is putting someone down, while admonishing is lifting him up. Shaming discredits and humiliates; admonishing corrects and encourages. Paul was sensitive to the need of the Corinthians to be corrected rather than put down.

Ask the class what tone of voice Paul would use if he were speaking the words of 1 Corinthians 4:8-13. (One commentator suggests that the words were "sanctified sarcasm.") Ask a capable reader to read these verses in a sarcastic tone. Point out that there is no place for selfish pride in Christian service. The pride and self-satisfaction of some in the church at Corinth needed correcting. To correct it, Paul told some of his troubles and how he reacted to them.

Then what did he tell the readers to do? Let students answer from verse 16. Ask, "Did this show that Paul himself had the kind of pride he was warning against?" Let

students answer, telling why or why not. Point out that Paul was not presenting himself alone as a model, but all the apostles (v. 9). Their reaction was the normal one for Christians.

Turn the students' attention back to verses 1 and 2. Have them find two models that were used to describe leaders ("servants"; stewards—i.e., "those who have been given a trust"). Point out that the Corinthians were dividing the church by their prideful loyalty to different leaders. Explain that a steward has important responsibilities, but still he is a servant answerable to his master.

INTO LIFE

Let students remain in their small groups to do this activity. Note again the mistake of some Christians in Corinth, taking pride in one leader over against another (v. 6). List some ways in which church members in our day make the same mistake. These thoughts may be included: choose a church because the preacher is eloquent, idolize a television evangelist while criticizing the minister of one's home church, act smug and self-satisfied about one's own spiritual growth.

Put the word *stewards* on the flip chart and ask the class to make an acrostic to list the characteristics of a Christian leader. (See the example below.)

S erving rather than "bossing"

T aking time for others

E ncouraging others in good works

W orking diligently for the Lord

A llowing God to work through them

R elying on God's direction

D esiring the best for God's people

S taying in touch with the Master in prayer

Afterwards, ask each student to write two sentences. First, "Paul's description of a Christian leader is important to me as a leader because. . . ." Second, "Paul's description of a Christian leader is important to me as a follower because. . . ."

Close with prayer.

Discover Your Leadership Style

There are many definitions for leadership floating around. The one I prefer is "leadership is having followers". Anyone who has followers—whether it be students in a classroom, an apprentice at work, or a toddler at home—is a leader. Paul also reduces Christian leadership down to its simplest form: servanthood. Most likely, you too are a leader or servant to someone. The question is, what kind of leader are you?

Secular leadership and spiritual leadership have many points of similarity, but there are some respects in which they are antithetical. In his book, *Spiritual Leadership,* Oswald Sanders lists several contrasting characteristics. The continuum will benefit you and the people you influence as you discover your leadership style by considering the contrasts between secular leadership and spiritual leadership. Place an X where you are now on each continuum.

SECULAR LEADERSHIP	SPIRITUAL LEADERSHIP
Confidence Is in Self	Confidence Is in God
Being Served by Others	Serving Others
Independent	Dependent on God
Originates Own Methods	Finds and Follows God's Methods
Motivated by Personal Considerations	Motivated by Love for God and Others
Knows People	Also Knows God
Enjoys Commanding Others	Delights in Obeying God

After your study of 1 Corinthians 4, go back to the leadership continuums above and draw a star on each one to represent Paul's leadership style. Commit yourself to imitating him in your leadership.

Imitate Me

Paul told the Corinthians to imitate his example (v. 16; cf. 11:1) Would you feel comfortable asking someone to imitate your example?

List below the positive characteristics in your life that you believe are worthy of imitation. Then list the negative traits you would be embarrassed to have someone imitate. Finally, list some characteristics that you are not comfortable with, but on which you are making significant progress in overcoming in your walk with the Lord.

Commit the last two categories to the Lord in prayer. If you have a prayer partner or a discipleship group with whom you feel comfortable sharing such things, ask them to pray for these things, too.

POSITIVE	NEGATIVE	GROWING

RESISTING TEMPTATION

LESSON 3

WHY TEACH THIS LESSON?

If we had our choice, nearly every one of us would choose a guide over a map. The guide is much more reliable. The same is true for examples over precepts. A good example is much clearer in showing us where to go. Even a bad example is useful in warning us where not to go.

This lesson gives your students both good examples and bad examples. In Israel's wilderness wanderings are the bad examples: immorality, grumbling, and testing the Lord. The good examples are much closer at hand. Every time they witness a baptism or partake of the Lord's Supper, they should be made aware once again of what God has provided to help us resist temptation. God's grace is what rescues us from having given in to temptation, and it is also what helps us not to give in.

INTRODUCTION

A. THE MASTER OF DECEIT

Several artists participated in a contest that required them to illustrate the concept of temptation. Most of them depicted scenes of decadence and evil. One drew a city scene with night clubs, bars, X-rated theaters, and sleazy characters lurking in the shadows. Another pictured the bright lights of Las Vegas.

The prize-winning canvas was different. Lovely wooded hillsides filled the frame. The picture radiated peace and serenity. A lone figure walked down a quiet lane in the woods. Branches arched overhead in a protective canopy. None of this seemed to suggest temptation—but ahead of the traveler was a fork in the road.

Most of the temptations that face us do not come with bright lights and warning signs. Satan, the great tempter, is a master of deceit. Often the key to resisting temptations is to recognize the importance of our simple, daily decisions.

B. LESSON BACKGROUND

Faithfully following Christ in an immoral city like Corinth was not easy. The believers faced many temptations. There were divisions in the church and hostility without. Moral questions of every sort abounded.

In 1 Corinthians 8–10, Paul addresses the question of idolatry, the worship of various pagan gods and goddesses. This was no small issue, since much of Corinthian social life centered around religious ceremonies and festivities associated with pagan shrines. Many real-life questions faced these Christians. Apparently different believers at Corinth answered these questions in different ways. Some argued that anything associated with the pagan shrines was untouchable. Others contended that a true believer knew the idols were false, and therefore he could eat the sacrificial meat without joining in worship of the god.

Paul cautions both sides about the dangers of arguing their case at the expense of others. True, he insists, the pagan gods are really nothing; therefore, one need not hesitate to eat the meat. However, not everyone can treat such matters so lightly. In deference to the weaknesses of other believers, every Christian needs to be very careful how he uses his freedom. Chapter 10 is a call to take seriously the dangers of idolatry and a call to follow the Lord without compromise.

DEVOTIONAL READING:
EPHESIANS 6:10-18
LESSON SCRIPTURE:
1 CORINTHIANS 10:1-17
PRINTED TEXT:
1 CORINTHIANS 10:1-17

Mar
19

LESSON AIMS

Today's lesson study is designed to help the student:

1. Recognize the danger and nature of the temptations faced in daily life.

2. Utilize the resources provided by the Lord to overcome temptation.

KEY VERSE:

No temptation has seized you except what is common to man. And God is faithful; he will not let you be tempted beyond what you can bear. But when you are tempted, he will also provide a way out so that you can stand up under it. —1 Corinthians 10:13

LESSON 3 NOTES

Visual 3 of the visuals packet calls attention to several main points of the Scripture text.

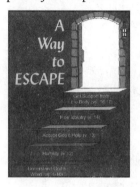

WHAT DO YOU THINK?

Paul's language here, "baptized into Moses," and "ate the same spiritual food and drank the same spiritual drink," reminds us of the Christian ordinances of baptism and the Lord's Supper. He makes the point that, even though Israel shared in these blessings, most of them were unfaithful.

To what extent do you think the same thing happens today, that Christians share in these ordinances but do not appreciate their significance and lapse into unfaithfulness? What should participation do for a Christian?

Do you think some Christians may actually feel that participation in these ordinances gives them license to do as they please? Why or why not?

I. RECOGNIZING THE DANGER (1 CORINTHIANS 10:1-5)

A. BLESSED OF GOD (VV. 1-4)

1. For I do not want you to be ignorant of the fact, brothers, that our forefathers were all under the cloud and that they all passed through the sea.

In the chapter that precedes our text, Paul has spoken of his own commitment to personal holiness. He has recalled the danger of failing in his own spiritual life while teaching others. Having voiced his own concern as a model for the concern that every believer should have, he now turns to an illustration from the Old Testament.

All is a key word in this section. It is repeated four times in verses 1-4. All of the Hebrews followed the same cloud out of Egypt (Exodus 13:21, 22). Everyone passed supernaturally through the Red Sea (Exodus 14:15-22). Whatever differences developed later could not be explained by different starts.

2. They were all baptized into Moses in the cloud and in the sea.

The cloud and sea through which they passed initiated them as followers of Moses. They all shared in this experience, and therefore all stood in the same relationship to Moses. Paul says *baptized* to make his readers think of their own lives. He is writing of Old Testament Jews, but he is thinking about the Corinthian Christians. They had been baptized into Christ (1:10-17; Acts 18:8) and into blessings shared with all other believers because of their relationship with Christ.

Christian baptism is a beautiful bond that unites believers. It is a common event with a common meaning that each individual can look back upon and remember how he or she started in the walk of faith. Though we have come from different backgrounds, lived different kinds of lives, and belonged to different social circles, we all began our Christian lives in the same way. All of our differences fade when compared to the one great fact that we all have in common—our relationship with Jesus.

3, 4. They all ate the same spiritual food and drank the same spiritual drink; for they drank from the spiritual rock that accompanied them, and that rock was Christ.

Spiritual probably means supernatural. Paul refers to the heavenly nourishment provided for Israel, the manna that sustained them (Exodus 16:1-18) and the miraculous supply of water (Exodus 17:1-7; Numbers 20:1-13) in the wilderness.

Paul presses the analogy a bit further in order to make the application obvious. It is not necessary to suppose Paul thought a literal rock actually accompanied the Hebrew encampment through the desert. He is using the *rock* as symbol of the divine provision that was never far from them.

That Rock was Christ emphasizes the truth that Christ is indeed the ultimate supply of all that every believer receives. Jesus claimed to give the living water that forever quenches the thirst of all who come to him (John 4:10-14; 7:37, 38). Paul here uses an Old Testament event as a symbol of what Christ does for those who place their trust in him. Just as all who followed Moses drank of the water that flowed from the *spiritual rock*, all who come to Christ drink of the "living water."

EXAMPLES

Paul mentions several Old Testament events in our lesson text. In verse 6 he says they are "examples," or "types" (Greek text: *tupos*). One of the principal examples was the Red Sea crossing as the Hebrews fled from Egypt. There they were "baptized into Moses in the cloud and in the sea" (v. 2).

This is a remarkable illustration of Christian baptism. They were covered by the cloud, which was overhead, and the sea water was a wall on each side. They thus passed across the sea as we, in baptism, are completely covered with water in our immersion into Jesus.

Further, they did this because of Moses' order, just as we are baptized at Jesus' command. They passed from an old life of slavery to a new life of freedom. So Paul, in Romans 6:16-18, says we have left sin's servitude to become the slaves of righteousness in Christ. Once they had been Egyptian slaves with no real identity, but now they had become a new people of God on the other side of the sea.

In the Exodus account we read that "Israel saw the Egyptians lying dead on the shore" (Exodus 14:30). The brutal taskmasters, the arrogant soldiers, the vicious chariot drivers, the proud archers, the mighty nobles and princes now were all pale, stiff, inert, in the final ignominy of death. So we think of our baptism as the time when we look at our former sins, follies, and misdeeds as dead. We are forgiven and cleansed and united with Jesus, our Lord. Israel's baptism "into Moses" testifies to us symbolically of our baptismal union with our Lord.   —J. G. V. B.

B. DISPLEASING TO GOD (v. 5)

5. Nevertheless, God was not pleased with most of them; their bodies were scattered over the desert.

One might mistakenly conclude that a people so blessed would all be destined for success. Starting together, however, does not guarantee finishing together. They were all blessed, but not all would see the promised land.

Most of them is an understatement. In fact, of the adults who left Egypt, only Joshua and Caleb actually completed the journey and entered the promised land. Early in the journey, Joshua and Caleb were no more blessed than the rest of Israel, but they were the only ones to receive the full blessing that all started out to obtain.

Scattered literally describes something strewn over the desert, scattered like the debris left in the path of a hurricane. It is a graphic description of the thousands of dead Hebrews left in the wake of God's judgment.

The ultimate verdict of Heaven and earth is found here. *God was not pleased.* A person can please almost everyone and be thought a success. But if he fails to please God, that person's life is an eternal failure. What a glorious blessing it will be to hear those wonderful words, "Well done, good and faithful servant" (Matthew 25:21).

The Corinthians had been blessed by God in many ways. They knew it. The danger was that they might begin to take their privileges and blessings for granted and assume that they were somehow made immune from spiritual failure. Nothing could have been farther from the truth.

If those in ancient Israel could fail when they had so much going for them, so can any of us fail if we do not take our calling seriously. This is the reason facing and resisting temptation is so important. Spiritual and moral success or failure hangs in balance.

II. HEEDING THE WARNINGS (1 CORINTHIANS 10:6-11)

A. EXAMPLES FROM THE PAST (v. 6A)

6a. Now these things occurred as examples.

Here Paul comes to his point. He has cited Old Testament examples because they have lessons for his readers. Many things in the Old Testament provide examples for believers. In this case, they are negative examples, things to be avoided.

B. PERILS OF THE PRESENT (vv. 6B-10)

6b. . . . to keep us from setting our hearts on evil things as they did.

Here we get to the purpose of the example previously cited. Paul begins a list of five sins of ancient Israel. All five are still very much alive in the world of his readers—and in ours!

WHAT DO YOU THINK?

Paul's warning about sexual immorality (v. 8) seems especially appropriate for our age. It appears to many that sexual temptation is much stronger today than it generally has been in the past. The widespread rejection of biblical standards of morality, highly publicized sexual escapades of prominent people, and the influence of television all contribute to increased immoral sexual behavior. But most of our comparisons are with a generation of just a few years back—generally not more than forty or fifty years.

Consider ancient Corinth. Immoral behavior was not just encouraged, it was considered religious. And most of the believers had come from a background in which immoral behavior was commonplace.

How much do you think the sexual temptation faced in our culture today is similar to that faced in Corinth? How would you have handled sexual temptation in ancient Corinth? How, if at all, is that different from the way you handle it today?

How to Say It:

Caleb. KAY-leb.

koinonia (Greek). coy-no-NEE-uh.

Joshua. JOSH-you-uh.

Sinai. SIGH-nye.

tupos (Greek). TOO-pahs.

The first sin is lust, *setting our hearts on evil things.* The original word means a strong desire of any sort, good or bad. In the New Testament, it usually refers to an evil desire—often to sexual desire. Here it more probably means the Hebrews' dissatisfaction with God's provision and their preference for the security of Egypt (Numbers 11:4-6).

7. Do not be idolaters, as some of them were; as it is written: "The people sat down to eat and drink and got up to indulge in pagan revelry."

The worship of man-made gods or physical representations of the living God was a common vice of Israel. It came to prominence at the foot of Sinai when Aaron made a golden calf (Exodus 32:1-6). It plagued Israel till the nation again went into captivity.

8. We should not commit sexual immorality, as some of them did—and in one day twenty-three thousand of them died.

Paul refers to an incident involving men of Israel and women of Moab (Numbers 25:1-9). Sexual immorality was a real problem in Corinth, also. Sexual activity was often a part of the pagan religious ceremonies. Pagans thought intimate relations in sacred places or with sacred people, priests or priestesses, guaranteed the fertility of one's land or flocks.

Sin is a powerful force in human life, and sexual temptation is a very real problem today. Abandonment of moral absolutes has undermined our society and has caused many to view immorality as natural. The spread of obscenity and near-pornographic television has served as aggressive advertisement for sexual sin. The temptation has always been present, but recently it has virtually saturated our society.

Jesus raised the standard of sexual conduct when he placed lustful looking on the same plane as immoral sexual activity (Matthew 5:27-30). No honest believer dare ignore his or her own vulnerability at this point. The failure of some well-known Christians and national leaders serves as a strong warning to us, just as does the example of the blessed but failing Israelites of old.

9. We should not test the Lord, as some of them did—and were killed by snakes.

The Israelites tested the Lord by complaining about his provision and challenging him to do better (Numbers 21:4-9).

10. And do not grumble, as some of them did—and were killed by the destroying angel.

Grumble means to voice an inner dissatisfaction. The people of Israel complained about Moses and Aaron, saying they had killed some people who had been swallowed by the earth (Numbers 16:41-50). The complaint was actually against the Lord. He chose and directed the human leaders, and he caused the earth to swallow the rebels (Numbers 16:1-35).

Note that two vices of ancient Israel were sins of the tongue: testing the Lord and grumbling. In the great catalog of sins that soil and smear the believer's life, sins of the tongue stand near the top. No wonder James gives the powerful warning that he does (James 3:1-12).

What Do You Think?

Certain temptations arise rarely in life. We may handle with ease the day-by-day temptations we face. Then suddenly we encounter one of those rare moments when a powerful temptation strikes—perhaps related to sex, money, or power—and we find ourselves shocked by how difficult it is to resist.

That is the reason Paul wrote, "Be careful that you don't fall." But how do you do that? What activities mark the person who is being "careful"? What activities mark the person who is careless?

(Consider Matthew 26:41 in your discussion.)

C. LESSONS FOR THE FUTURE (V. 11)

11. These things happened to them as examples and were written down as warnings for us, on whom the fulfillment of the ages has come.

The Bible is largely history, but it is history with a purpose. The record is purposefully selective. Not everything that happened was written down. What was written serves to show readers the ways of God.

Those *on whom the fulfillment of the ages has come* are those who live in the last period of world history. The term for *ages* refers periods of the world's time. *Fulfillment* indicates the goal or aim of history. That goal is the person and work of the Messiah. The Messiah has come, therefore the end has come upon those who are following him. The grand finale awaits his return.

III. SEEING THE ALTERNATIVE (1 CORINTHIANS 10:12, 13)

A. HUMAN WEAKNESS (VV. 12, 13A)

12. So, if you think you are standing firm, be careful that you don't fall!

This is a word to those who may think they are immune to temptation, that they have risen above the plane of mere mortals who are vulnerable to the behaviors just listed. Arrogance and pride can be among the deadliest of sins. This warning is especially important to those who know they have been blessed of God.

13a. No temptation has seized you except what is common to man.

Temptation is universal. All have faced it in the past and all will in the future. Our particular temptations have been here before. It is pointless to excuse ourselves by claiming to be different or in circumstances that are more difficult.

B. DIVINE FAITHFULNESS (V. 13B)

13b. And God is faithful; he will not let you be tempted beyond what you can bear. But when you are tempted, he will also provide a way out so that you can stand up under it.

Here is the great hope: not our ability, but God's. The God who saved us and who is with us promises to protect us. This protection does not mean freedom from temptation, but freedom from *irresistible* temptation. He pledges always to provide a way of escape. Temptation is inevitable, but giving in to it is not. Temptation can be overcome!

LOAD LIMITS

Paul assures us that God "will not let you be tempted beyond what you can bear," or, as Phillips renders the last part of this passage, "beyond your powers of endurance." Frequently as we drive along secondary roads in our country we come to bridges crossing small rivers or streams. Often a sign is posted just before one comes to the bridge. It says "Load Limit," then "Five," "Ten," or "Twenty Tons." The bridge can support only a certain weight, and so a truck driver is warned that he may wreck his truck and the bridge if his load is heavy.

In a similar manner God knows the load limit of each of us. Others might easily surmount troubles that vex us terribly. On the other hand, we may feel little stress in a situation someone else would quickly find intolerable. God, our Father, is well acquainted with each one of us. While we are all similar in general construction and organization, our fingerprints are different, our hair texture is different, and our whole convoluted mix of psychical and emotional makeup is distinctive. Bloodhounds can sniff out the unique odor of each person, though we do not perceive it.

God knows all of us completely, and he tempers our trials to our individual "breaking points." True, we sometimes falter, mistrust, complain, or despair. But we must cling to this assurance: our Father cares and knows and oversees. Stormy seas may rear angry surges, but our ship of life is buoyant as we trust his promises.

—J. G. V. B.

IV. DECIDING TO RESIST (1 CORINTHIANS 10:14-17)

A. AVOIDING THE SIN (VV. 14, 15)

14. Therefore, my dear friends, flee from idolatry.

Here is the conclusion. Idolatry is dangerous. Even the strongest believer must not trifle with it. Note the logical connection with the previous verse. God provides a way of escape. Use it!

OPTION

Use the reproducible activities on page 260 to help raise your students awareness of sin and their own vulnerability to its power.

WHAT DO YOU THINK?

Temptation can be a lonely thing. We wrestle with it in our innermost thoughts, our fleshly nature suggesting ways to justify sinful actions, and our spirits, prompted by God's Spirit, responding with biblical principles.

But Paul says temptation is a "common" thing. Hebrews 4:15 reminds us that temptation is not only common to man, but to Jesus, too. Why then does temptation seem so lonely? How can we draw strength from the fact that temptation is common to man?

Does this verse suggest that sharing our temptations openly with others might be helpful in dealing with them? Why or why not?

WHAT DO YOU THINK?

One might say Paul's advice in verse 14, "Flee from idolatry," is an application of the principle in verse 13, "God . . . will also provide a way out." The way out of temptation is to "flee"! (See also 6:18.)

From what kinds of situations can and should a Christian "flee"? How? Won't that offend the people you are with? Why or why not—and does it matter? From what situations is it not possible to flee? What do you do then?

Lord, I am no stranger to temptation. I have faced it and failed more times than I can count. I know I will face temptation again, even today. I ask you to give me eyes to see the path of escape that you have faithfully provided. Please give me the will to walk that path.

WHAT DO YOU THINK?

The lesson writer says the Lord's Supper "is more than just a reminder of what Christ did; it is also a renewal of our loyalty to him." How can one best use it to accomplish this purpose? What is the focus of your meditation during the Lord's Supper?

THOUGHT TO REMEMBER

Temptation is inevitable, but giving in to it is not. The secret of victory is God's faithfulness. Temptation can be overcome!

DAILY BIBLE READINGS

Monday, Mar. 13—God's Armor for Protection From Evil (Ephesians 6:10-18)

Tuesday, Mar. 14—Warning Against Overconfidence (1 Corinthians 10:1-13)

Wednesday, Mar. 15—Do Not Worship Idols (1 Timothy 6:9-19)

Thursday, Mar. 16—Pursue Righteousness (1 Timothy 6:9-19)

Friday, Mar. 17—Be Watchful and Firm in Faith (1 Peter 5:6-11)

Saturday, Mar. 18—God Helps Those Who Resist Evil (James 1:1-8)

Sunday, Mar. 19—Purity of Heart Is Blessed (Psalm 24:1-6)

15. I speak to sensible people; judge for yourselves what I say.

Paul's readers claimed to be wise. He exhorts them to act like it when they face temptation. Only the foolish toy with temptation. The wise flee like Joseph from the bedroom of Potiphar's wife (Genesis 39:11, 12). There may be times to think and times to talk; but when confronted with temptation, it is time to flee.

B. SEEKING THE LORD (vv. 16, 17)

16. Is not the cup of thanksgiving for which we give thanks a participation in the blood of Christ? And is not the bread that we break a participation in the body of Christ?

To keep the readers far from idolatry, Paul calls them to remember their commitment to Christ. When a believer partakes of the cup and the bread of the Lord's table, he is renewing his pledge of allegiance to Christ. It is a participation (a communion) with Christ. To take such a pledge seriously should be enough to cause us to take sin and temptation seriously. We would never want to do anything to dishonor Christ, his message, or his people.

This verse provides a good incentive for keeping the Lord's Supper central to the regular weekly gathering of the church. It is more than just a reminder of what Christ did; it is also a renewal of our loyalty to him.

17. Because there is one loaf, we, who are many, are one body, for we all partake of the one loaf.

The common experience of the Lord's Supper is a symbol of the common faith that joins believers together. This solidarity should cause us to honor and protect each other. We ought never harm another believer any more than we would harm ourselves.

FELLOWSHIP

The term *participation*, which occurs twice in verse 16 of our lesson, in the Greek text is *koinonia*. This is sometimes rendered "communion" (*King James Version*), or "sharing" (*New American Standard Bible*). Very often it is rendered "fellowship" in various contexts and various versions. The word *fellowship* is especially meaningful if we take it to mean "fellows on the same ship."

Anyone who has made an ocean crossing on a freighter has a keen realization of what such a condition is. One is out on a vast expanse of water in a relatively small ship. Perhaps there are about fifty-six persons on board—sixteen passengers and forty crew members. Some of these are mechanics. Others do the steering and map plotting. Others cook and serve meals, some make up beds and clean cabins. Passengers not only enjoy the trip, but are taught the use of life jackets and the locations of life-boats. There are many different tasks and life-styles, but all are on the same ship. They are going where it goes and are dependent on its safety and well-being.

So we are divergent in life's tasks and interests, but we are all united in being on that ship of destiny, the church Jesus purchased with his blood and sustains with his living Spirit. Our communion at the Lord's table shows us we are together on the ship of salvation.

—J. G. V. B.

CONCLUSION

A comic once declared, "I can resist anything except temptation." For many of us that is too true to be funny. But it need not be true. Resisting temptation is not "mission impossible."

Temptation can be resisted, but not because I am too strong to fall. It can be overcome because the God I serve is absolutely faithful. He promises to provide a way out. And he will!

Discovery Learning

*This page contains an alternate lesson plan emphasizing learning activities. Classes
desiring such student involvement will find these suggestions helpful. The next page
is a reproducible activity page to further enhance discovery learning.*

LEARNING GOALS

After this lesson the student will be able to:

1. Recite 1 Corinthians 10:13 from memory and be aware of the valuable resource that God makes available in times of temptation.

2. Apply the biblical warnings against idolatry to the types of temptation faced in modern times.

3. List some positive steps that can be taken when temptations arise.

INTO THE LESSON

Before class, prepare several envelopes as follows: Print the words of 1 Corinthians 10:13 in large type on a sheet of paper. (Do not include the book, chapter, and verse reference.) Then cut the paper into pieces that can be assembled like a jigsaw puzzle. Shuffle the pieces and put them into the envelope; then seal the envelope. Prepare one envelope for every two students you expect to be in class. Use the same Bible version for all envelopes.

As students arrive, put them in pairs and give each pair a sealed envelope. Challenge the pairs to unscramble the verse and write it on the outside of the envelope. Suggest that memorizing Scripture can be a strengthening force in their spiritual growth. Give a small prize to the couple who deciphers the verse first and can recite it by memory. Have all the students recite the verse together when everyone is finished.

Continue the session by asking people to share the answer to this question: "What was one of your biggest temptations when you were a grade-school child?" (Share your own answer first.) Answers may be something like this: "I was tempted to lie to my mother to escape punishment for things I did wrong." Allow as many to share as feel comfortable doing so.

INTO THE WORD

Lead into the Scripture by noting that people of all ages and from all stages in history faced temptations of a similar nature. In today's lesson we'll discover some of the basic temptations common to people down through the centuries. As Paul addresses the Christians at Corinth, he calls them to remember the history of the Israelites. Ask someone to read verses 1-5 aloud. Draw the students' attention to verses 6-11 and ask them to find the sins that Paul specifically cites. Write them on the board as members call them out (lust, idolatry, sexual immorality, testing God, grumbling). Ask, "Why should the behavior of the Israelites be of any importance to a New Testament church such as the one at Corinth?" (Verse 11 answers this well.) Point out that all of these sins existed in the church at Corinth. Ask, "Which of the sins seems to be of the most universal and timeless nature?" (Grumbling is the best answer.) Elaborate upon what a strong temptation it is.

Put this statement on the chalkboard or flip chart and ask the class to agree or disagree: "A Christian can be sure he will not give in to temptation." After some discussion, have someone read verse 12. Point out that pride is dangerous—ask someone to read Proverbs 16:18. Christians at Corinth seemed to think they could handle any temptation, but Paul warned that they needed to be on the alert.

Have the class repeat 1 Corinthians 10:13 from memory. Ask: What is the greatest assurance you get from this verse? (Answers may vary, but point out that the phrase *God is faithful* is the source of our greatest confidence.)

Have someone read verses 14-17 aloud; then take a minute or two to observe that the observance of the Lord's Supper is a rejection of idolatry—for the Corinthians as well as for us. One commits himself to Christ, by participating in the Lord's Supper. It would be dishonorable to dabble in the worship of idols—first-century idols or twentieth-century idols.

Discuss the types of "idols" that contemporary people "worship" today. "Do you think there is idolatry among Christians? Why or why not? How can we be sure to avoid—flee from—idolatry?"

INTO LIFE

Point out that Paul gives several positive actions to take in resisting temptation. Give each person an index card and ask that everyone write down the steps he or she discovered in this lesson. After a few moments, display the following steps on a piece of poster board or flip chart that you have prepared in advance:

- Study the Bible—Old and New Testament.
- Stay alert to the possibility of your own mistakes.
- Look for God's alternatives in tempting situations and rely on him to show you the way out.
- Flee temptations. Being in the wrong place at the wrong time is best remedied by grabbing your hat and running.

Close the session with a prayer circle, praying for strength to resist temptation.

Alert to Sin

The Bible warns us, "You may be sure that your sin will find you out" (Numbers 32:23). And there are certain sins that seem to find us more easily than others (Hebrews 12:1). Look up each Scripture reference and then complete the sentence by summarizing what the verse says about sin.

Romans 14:23   Sin is _____ .

James 4:17   Sin is _____ .

1 John 3:4   Sin is _____ .

1 John 5:17   Sin is _____ .

If the Shoe Fits

The Israelites would have approved of the first set of facts Paul chose to include in 1 Corinthians 10. In the first four verses, he describes four miraculous experiences of the Israelites while on their journey from Egypt to the promised land. They were "under the cloud" and drank from the "spiritual rock." These experiences would make any people proud of their heritage.

List four positive things that have helped to develop you to whatever level of spiritual maturity you now have.

In the next six verses, Paul lists four sins committed by these same people. They sacrificed to an idol, committed sexual immorality, tested the Lord's ability to provide, and grumbled incessantly. He serves notice to the Corinthians that they are not exempt from sin and its consequences. What happened to the Israelites can happen to the Corinthians. And what happened to the Corinthians can happen to you! Paul's purpose was not to ridicule, but to remind his readers of what happened in the past and to alert them to the danger of repeating the same sins.

Find a private place and write down at least four sins that Satan uses to tempt you. After you have done this self-examination, you'll want to look to God for alternatives to these tempting situations and rely on him to show you the way out (1 Corinthians 10:13).

Christians Living in Community
Unit 1: Responding to Challenges to Life in Community
(Lessons 1-4)

DEALING WITH CONFLICT

LESSON 4

WHY TEACH THIS LESSON?

If your class does not need a lesson of dealing with conflict, then it's the only one! Conflict is part of life. Some people attract it; others try to avoid it, but no one completely escapes it. Not even in the church.

Use this lesson to reassure your students that conflict is not necessarily a sign of failure. It happens to the best of us—even to Paul. Encourage them to deal with the conflict constructively, not defensively or in an effort to smooth over the conflict without resolving its source. Christ will be glorified only when we look our conflicts squarely in the eye and determine that no issue is important enough to allow it to drive a wedge between us and our Christian brothers and sisters.

INTRODUCTION

A. GREAT CHURCH FIGHTS

Conflict! Nobody likes it, so they say, but everyone faces it. It comes in all sizes and shapes. Like or not, we deal with it in the family, at work, and, sad to say, even in the church.

A deacon was giving a friend a tour of the church building. As he pointed out the organ and the stained glass windows, his friend always seemed to recall something nicer or more expensive in his church. Finally the deacon called attention to an old Bible displayed on the Communion table.

"That Bible is nearly two hundred years old," he noted with some pride.

Not to be outdone, his friend quickly responded, "Two hundred years old! That *is* something. But in our congregation, we have church fights older than that!"

I think I know that church. In fact, I have known congregations that have fought over everything from the translation of the Bible that should be used to the color of the carpet. I have heard of churches where members actually came to blows, and one where a deacon pulled a gun on another man in the midst of an argument over church matters. To be honest, church conflicts generally involve only a small number of people. But even that small number can exact an awful toll on the rest.

Nobody likes conflict, perhaps with the exception of a few depraved and disturbed individuals. Because of that, most of us are much better at ignoring it than dealing with it. Learning to deal constructively with conflict can be one of the most important lessons we ever learn in life.

B. LESSON BACKGROUND

Paul was no stranger to conflict. His faith was born in the midst of it. He was battling Christians when he was confronted by the Lord on the Damascus road and converted from a foe to a friend. Throughout his ministry for Christ, Paul seemed to attract opposition like a lightning rod in a thunderstorm. He was shouted at by mobs, stoned and left for dead, imprisoned, insulted, and attacked in countless ways.

No other conflict seemed to disturb Paul as much as the one he faced in Corinth. This one was in the church, and his opponents were fellow believers. The entire book of 2 Corinthians is Paul's defense and response to his critics.

DEVOTIONAL READING:
COLOSSIANS 3:8-17

LESSON SCRIPTURE:
2 CORINTHIANS 12,13

PRINTED TEXT:
2 CORINTHIANS 12:19-21;
13:5-13

Mar
26

LESSON AIMS

This lesson is designed to help the student:

1. Learn to approach conflict positively.

2. Develop good conflict management skills.

3. Desire to become a peacemaker rather than simply one who avoids conflict.

OPTION

Make copies of the "Case Study" on page 268. Use the activity to introduce the lesson; then come back to it after the Bible study to see how it should have been handled.

KEY VERSE:

Aim for perfection, listen to my appeal, be of one mind, live in peace. And the God of love and peace will be with you.

—2 Corinthians 13:11

LESSON 4 NOTES

WHAT DO YOU THINK?

Paul insisted he was not being defensive in his appeal to the Corinthians, but was looking out for their best interests. How common do you believe the problem of defensiveness is, and how does it work against church unity? Who do you think is most likely to be defensive in a church? Preacher? Elder? Teacher? A person with a secret? A struggling Christian? Some other? Why do you think so?

Caution: Think situation, not person. You might say you believe the preacher is generally most likely to become defensive, for example, even if your own preacher is very non-defensive. Think of the situation a person may be in, not the person himself.

WHAT DO YOU THINK?

Though we teach that everyone in the church should be working for the glory of God, and that no member should perform his or her tasks for the purpose of receiving human praise, still it seems inevitable that someone will be hurt or offended because their efforts were not properly recognized. Jealousy and conflict result when one member sees others being applauded while his contributions are seemingly taken for granted.

What can you do to soften the impact of jealousy in the church? How can you resist the tendency to become jealous? How can you encourage others so they do not begin to feel jealous of someone else?

Why the conflict? It was undoubtedly tied to the divisions in the congregation. The attacks on Paul were in part "turf battles" for control of the church. It was also partly theological or doctrinal, but it became very personal. Opponents said Paul wrote great letters, but was puny in appearance and contemptible in speech (10:10). Some thought it was degrading for him to work and support himself with his own hands (11:7-11).

Second Corinthians is loaded with tension and emotion as Paul seeks to deal with these problems from afar. He opens his heart, exposes his most personal motives, and calls upon those in conflict with one another and with himself to resolve the problems so the church can move on to its real business. In the process he provides some valuable lessons for anyone facing conflict.

I. CAUSES OF CONFLICTS (2 CORINTHIANS 12:19-21)

A. DEFENDING OURSELVES (V. 19)

19. Have you been thinking all along that we have been defending ourselves to you? We have been speaking in the sight of God as those in Christ; and everything we do, dear friends, is for your strengthening.

Paul's response to the critics at Corinth reveals both positive and negative factors involved in conflict. Often a major factor in unhealthy conflict is defensiveness. Paul insists that while he may have appeared to be defending himself, that was not his real interest. It was the Lord who would indict or acquit him.

Defend was a term used in law courts. *To you* implies that the readers were in the position of a judge or jury. But they were not the jury with which Paul was concerned. Any testimony he needed to give would be offered to God. His motive was to *strengthen* the readers, promoting their spiritual growth.

When one recognizes the Lord as his judge, he can be free to serve people honestly without concern about what others think.

B. FIGHTING DIRTY (VV. 20-21)

20. For I am afraid that when I come I may not find you as I want you to be, and you may not find me as you want me to be. I fear that there may be quarreling, jealousy, outbursts of anger, factions, slander, gossip, arrogance and disorder.

What a vivid description of the alternatives to selfless edification! This is exactly what happens when conflict and differences are not handled with loving care. Minor differences become major battles. Disappointments become disagreements. Disagreements escalate into division.

Paul acknowledges the potential for such. He knows it is possible that face to face he and some of his readers may discover differences. They may not be what he expects, and he may be something less than what they desire. In itself that need not be a problem. But where that leads can become a big problem!

Paul lists eight different (count them, eight!) evils that lead to wrongful conflict.

Quarreling describes expressions of conflict that lead to factions and divisions. Such strife is one of the "works of the flesh" (Galatians 5:19-21).

Jealousy is the desire to have what another has rather than finding satisfaction and contentment with one's present condition.

Outbursts of anger—losing one's temper.

Factions describes the kind of conflict that results in parties or competing groups.

Slander means speaking against someone.

Gossip is speaking badly about someone behind his back rather than to his face.

Arrogance, or pride, can be a cause of the attacks described in the previous terms, or it can result from believing that one has won a conflict. It is the opposite of love (1 Corinthians 13:4).

Disorder is the consequence of the previous behaviors. It is a state of confusion, or even anarchy. It is used in 1 Corinthians 14:33 in contrast to the word *peace*.

These eight terms describe bad conflict. While Paul doesn't say it here, the obvious solution to conflict is simply to do the opposite of the things listed here. Coming together rather than staying apart and talking to one another rather than about one another can work wonders in promoting healing and reconciliation.

RUINOUS REACTIONS

Jesus said, "Every kingdom divided against itself will be ruined" (Matthew 12:25). How true this is! Francisco Pizarro, the Spanish conquistador, landed on the coast of Peru in 1531 or 1532. His whole expeditionary force consisted of only 180 men. He was faced with an empire that was well organized. For hundreds of miles across the Andes this cohesive organization held sway with a remarkable system of roads and fortifications and many warriors. Pizarro faced a daunting task.

The secret of his military conquest was that this kingdom was in the throes of an internal conflict. The reigning monarch was fighting against powerful rivals. Pizarro allied himself with these forces and utilized their familiarity with roads and mountain passes to become victorious. Then he suppressed his native helpers and became master of the nation.

What a gruesome and graphic picture of spiritual "civil war" our printed text presents! Paul lists the internal difficulties he fears he may find among his Christian brothers in Corinth. He speaks of "quarreling, jealousy, outbursts of anger, factions, slander, gossip, arrogance and disorder" (v. 20). Alas, such disturbances are a great impediment to Christian growth and victory. We must try to replace all such disruptions with love, kindness, and works of compassion.   —J. G. V. B.

21. *I am afraid that when I come again my God will humble me before you, and I will be grieved over many who have sinned earlier and have not repented of the impurity, sexual sin and debauchery in which they have indulged.*

Paul is concerned that when he returns to Corinth he will find the problems of the past still unresolved. That would be humiliating to him and to those he would be forced to confront at that time. But confront he will if those guilty of known sins do not repent.

Impurity refers to the kinds of thinking, speech, and action that were called "dirty" or "indecent" before our society became tolerant of moral filth. *Sexual sin* is any sexual activity between persons who are not married to each other. *Debauchery* is unbridled passion or unrestrained lust. It is the vice of a person who shows no more shame than an animal in the satisfaction of its physical appetites.

A secret cause of conflict in the church is sometimes hidden guilt. Behind divisive behavior and quarreling is often an individual who wants to keep attention away from his vices. Unfortunately, a divided church can seldom bring constructive discipline to those who need it most.

II. HOW TO HANDLE CONFLICTS (2 CORINTHIANS 13:5-10)

In this section, Paul models five constructive attitudes and activities that can bring reconciliation out of what might otherwise be devastating conflict. Note the order in which they are presented.

A. EXAMINING OURSELVES (vv. 5, 6)
5. *Examine yourselves to see whether you are in the faith; test yourselves. Do you not realize that Christ Jesus is in you—unless, of course, you fail the test?*

Paul is addressing his critics in the conflicts at Corinth, but one can be assured that he has addressed the same instructions to himself. Self-examination is the first

WHAT DO YOU THINK?

Paul wanted the Corinthians, to whom he had presented Christ and before whom he had held himself up as an example (1 Corinthians 11:1), to know he had "not failed the test" (v. 6). At the same time, he seemed to care little whether from some people's perspective he "may seem to have failed" (v. 7). Paul was not concerned so much about how people perceived him as he was about how they perceived Christ as a result of his testimony.

In whose eyes does a Christian need to be seen as passing the test, and in whose eyes does it not matter? How can you keep from confusing the two—thus becoming more concerned about people's impression of you than about your Lord?

WHAT DO YOU THINK?

Paul noted that he continued to pray for the Corinthians, praying for their "perfection." What are some ways in which prayer can help us overcome or resolve conflict? Do you think it is more important to pray for yourself in a conflict—praying that your motives remain pure and that you do not lose your temper—or praying for the other person? Why? How are both important?

step in rightly handling any conflict. What have I done to contribute to the problem? Are my motives what they ought to be? Have I been guilty of the very things I am accusing or suspecting another of doing?

SELF-EXAMINATION

We all examine ourselves in many ways, and some of us submit to special regimens of self-testing. We all look at ourselves in mirrors to see if our hair is combed, and unusual irregularities of our complexion modified. Some undergo special self-inspection, as when women check their breasts for lumps and people with diabetes utilize machines to measure the glucose content of their blood. These are kinds of *physical* self-examination.

Mentally we read and reflect to check our knowledge of materials we need for communication and functioning in our crafts and occupations. The farmer checks his plans for crop sequences. The businessman, the physician, the architect, the engineer, and the teacher often check their recollection of what they have learned.

Paul urges us to examine ourselves spiritually to renew our awareness of Jesus' presence with us and in us. Is prayer a matter of weights or wings? Is the worship of God exciting and enthralling? Do we find challenge and change as we share with our fellow Christians? We know where we have been, but where are we *now*? Our *spiritual* weight and blood pressure are the true vital signs of our lives. —J. G. V. B.

6. And I trust that you will discover that we have not failed the test.

Paul is willing to stand on his own record. He has tested himself and is willing for his readers, including his critics, to test him. Integrity is of prime importance in dealing rightly with conflict. Double standards will not work.

B. PRAYING FOR OTHERS (V. 7)

7. Now we pray to God that you will not do anything wrong. Not that people will see that we have stood the test but that you will do what is right even though we may seem to have failed.

In the midst of conflict, it is easy to pray for "our side" to win. It is better to pray that all sides find and do God's will. Then good can come out of the battle. Samuel's farewell pledge needs affirming in every church conflict: "God forbid that I should sin against the Lord in ceasing to pray for you" (1 Samuel 12:23).

C. TELLING THE TRUTH (V. 8)

8. For we cannot do anything against the truth, but only for the truth.

Paul declares his devotion to the truth. He will, indeed can, do nothing but stand for the truth. If that creates a problem, then there will be a problem. But he will cling to truth.

How people conduct themselves in the face of conflict reveals much about their character. The temptation is to "fight fire with fire." Such a practice may double the damage.

FOR THE TRUTH

Paul asserts, "We cannot do anything against the truth, but only for the truth." Weymouth translates this, "For we have no power against the truth, but only for the truth."

In 1843, in Lexington, Kentucky, Alexander Campbell and Nathan L. Rice engaged in several days of debate. They considered the action, subjects, and purpose of Christian baptism, the function of creeds in the church, and the nature and activity of the Holy Spirit. In the course of this discussion, Mr. Campbell said some things about truth that are beautiful and powerful and very pertinent to Paul's words in our text.

"Truth, my friends, holy truth, stands upon the Rock of Ages. It lifts its head above the clouds—above the stars. . . . Its days are the years of God. Embodied in the Word of God, it came down from heaven and became incarnate. It is, therefore, immortal, and cannot be killed. It will survive all its foes, and stand erect when every idol falls. . . . It needs no fleshly wisdom, nor worldly policy, to give it power or gain it victory. It is itself redeeming, soul-redeeming, and disenthralling. . . . Light and fire, earth's purest elements, are but the shadows of its glory. The tongues of lambent flame that sat upon the heads of the apostles, were but indicative of its irradiating and consuming potency. But its language is that of love, of purity, and of peace."

William Cullen Bryant's poem "The Battle-Field" has a stanza that is expressive of the attitude toward truth that Paul exhibits and that Campbell's words exemplify:

Truth, crushed to earth, shall rise again:
Th'eternal years of God are hers;
But Error, wounded, writhes in pain,
And dies among her worshippers.

—J. G. V. B.

D. SEEKING THE BEST (v. 9)

9. We are glad whenever we are weak but you are strong; and our prayer is for your perfection.

Wishing the best for our adversaries is never easy. But it is right. And it is Christian. Jesus taught us to "love your enemies, and pray for those who persecute you" (Matthew 5:44). Paul recommends the advice found in Proverbs: "If your enemy is hungry, feed him; if he is thirsty, give him something to drink. In doing this, you will heap burning coals on his head. Do not be overcome by evil, but overcome evil with good" (Romans 12:20, 21; Proverbs 25:21, 22).

Perfection is from a word that means to make fit or complete. It was used in the sense of setting bones or reconciling parties. A form of the same word was used of the fishermen "mending" their nets (Matthew 4:21). Paul used the same word to speak of "restoring" a brother in difficulty (Galatians 6:1). Paul was wishing for the Corinthians to repair the damage done by their quarreling and to become completely fitted for Christian living and service.

E. CARING TO CONFRONT (v. 10)

10. This is why I write these things when I am absent, that when I come I may not have to be harsh in my use of authority—the authority the Lord gave me for building you up, not for tearing you down.

Paul was writing these things in the hope that the Corinthians would correct what was wrong and would resolve their conflicts so he would not have to speak sharply later, when he came to Corinth. He preferred to avoid confrontation, but confrontation was better than letting the conflicts continue and grow.

As an apostle, Paul had been given special power; but it was intended for *building you up*, not *tearing you down*. He was writing to build faith and right living and harmony in the church. Later he would be in Corinth and would speak with the same purpose. For that purpose he would speak a sharp rebuke if necessary, but he hoped he could speak praise instead.

Most of us will go out of our way to avoid confrontation. Lacking Paul's gift of special inspiration, we have the more reason to avoid sharpness if we can, to speak with Christian humility and respect for our brethren. But talking about opponents behind their backs adds fuel to a smoldering fire. If we really want reconciliation and peace, we may find that nothing works better than talking face to face with those who differ with us.

WHAT DO YOU THINK?

Here was a church to which Paul and Apollos had ministered, a church in which Peter also had wielded some influence (1 Corinthians 1:12). It was a church with spiritually gifted leaders. And yet it experienced an array of problems that went far beyond many of our church squabbles today.

If a church with all the advantages the church of Corinth had still had such problems, what hope is there for us? If strong teachers and gifted leaders do not ensure harmony [they didn't in Corinth], what does? What can you and your church do to promote harmony?

NOTE:

It is comforting to that, in spite of all its problems, Paul was not about to give up on the church at Corinth. We can conclude from this that our church also, whatever its failings, faults, and friction, is still precious to God and worthy of our continued faithfulness to it!

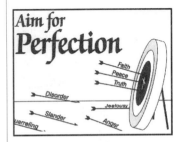

Visual 4 illustrates the message of verse 11: "Aim for Perfection."

PRAYER

I pray that I may be part of your solution and not one of the causes of conflict. Give me the grace to work for peace with those with whom I come into conflict. Lord, make me a peacemaker. In Jesus' name, amen.

THOUGHT TO REMEMBER

Peacemaking is hard work. It is dangerous work. It forces us to become involved in other people's problems. But most of all it makes us deal with our own shortcomings.

DAILY BIBLE READINGS

Monday, Mar. 20—Confronting Opponents in the Church (2 Corinthians 10:1-12)

Tuesday, Mar. 21—Boast Only of the Lord (2 Corinthians 10: 13-18)

Wednesday, Mar. 22—Refuting False Charges With the Truth (2 Corinthians 11:7-15)

Thursday, Mar. 23—Strength in Weakness (2 Corinthians 12: 1-10)

Friday, Mar. 24—Paul Justifies His Actions (2 Corinthians 12:11-18)

Saturday, Mar. 25—Admonition to End the Dissension (2 Corinthians 12:19—13:4)

Sunday, Mar. 26—Live in Peace With One Another (2 Corinthians 13:5-13)

No one has ever proposed a better method for dealing with conflict than that outlined by Jesus in Matthew 18:15-20. It is amazing to see how rarely Christians follow these directives.

III. HOW TO PREVENT CONFLICTS (2 CORINTHIANS 13:11-13)
A. STRIVING FOR PEACE (V. 11)
11. Finally, brothers, good-by. Aim for perfection, listen to my appeal, be of one mind, live in peace. And the God of love and peace will be with you.

Paul appeals to his readers to develop in their lives the qualities that contribute to peace and harmony. He issues five commands and then concludes with a promise.

The Greek word translated here as *good-by* is literally the imperative of a verb meaning *rejoice*. While it may be used as a simple parting salutation, it may also be understood as a command like the four that follow. If Paul meant it in that way, it is a call to turn attention to the positive, the joyous, and the blessed. The more we dwell on problems, the bigger they appear.

The second command, *aim for perfection,* is easily misunderstood. The term is not the usual word meaning complete or free of defect. Rather, the word is the same as in verse 9. It means to be fitted, mended, or restored.

Listen to my appeal is from a word that means to be encouraged or consoled. Forms of this word are used several times in 2 Corinthians (1:3, 4, 5, 6, 7; 7:4, 7, 13). It literally means to be called alongside. Paul is telling the Corinthians he is on their side. To accept his advice is not "giving in" or "losing" to an enemy. It is accepting the encouragement of a friend.

Be of one mind literally means to think the same thing. It calls for being harmonious and unified in word and deed as well as thought.

The fifth command, *live in peace,* calls for an end of quarreling. That does not mean there may be no differences of opinion; it means that Christians with minor differences work together harmoniously and happily.

B. LOVING THE FAMILY (VV. 12, 13)
12. Greet one another with a holy kiss.

The kiss of greeting was a part of Mediterranean culture, akin to a hearty handshake or a warm hug in ours. But the Christian kiss was not just a social formality. It was *holy,* different, set apart. It was an expression of Christian oneness and solidarity.

13. All the saints send their greetings.

Paul reminds his readers that they are part of a larger Christian community. Who they are and how they behave matters to others beyond their own borders. People we will never meet and never know by name have a stake in the peace and harmony of our fellowship.

CONCLUSION

Conflict is a natural part of human experience, even in the church. In fact, conflict can be a sign of health. It shows that people are close enough and care enough to take a stand. Sometimes what appears to be harmony is really apathy. It results because people are too far apart to come into contact, much less conflict. But conflict can destroy health unless it is well managed. It is important for all of us to deal with conflict in a way that will glorify the Lord and edify his people.

Dealing with conflict matters because our relationships in the church matter. Jesus said, "By this all men will know that you are my disciples, if you love one another" (John 13:35). He prayed that believers in him will all be one, one in him and the Father, so the world will believe that the Father sent him (John 17:21).

Restoring peace out of the midst of conflict is an answer to the Master's prayer!

Discovery Learning

This page contains an alternate lesson plan emphasizing learning activities. Classes desiring such student involvement will find these suggestions helpful. The next page is a reproducible activity page to further enhance discovery learning.

LEARNING GOALS

As a result of this lesson, students will:

1. Learn positive ways of dealing with conflict.

2. Be able to identify some of the underlying causes for conflict in the church.

3. Be able to become peacemakers in times of conflict within the church and family.

INTO THE LESSON

Call attention to the incomplete statements below. (Put them on a flip chart or on the chalkboard.) Ask each student to complete the sentences and to share responses with two or three people seated near by.

1. I usually deal with conflict by—

2. People get in conflict because—

3. The best way to deal with conflict is—

INTO THE WORD

Make the transition into the Bible study by pointing out that conflict is inevitable even in the church. Paul sent the church at Corinth a letter that had conflict as its main point. (Share further background information as needed.)

On the chalkboard make two columns. Label one *Conflict* and the other *Alternative*. Direct attention to 2 Corinthians 12:20 and ask the class to find eight expressions of conflicting behavior or attitudes that Paul mentions. List these in the first column. For each one, ask students to think of a behavior or attitude that would be less conflicting. List those in the column labeled *Alternative*. (Some possible answers: quarreling / discussion; jealousy / rejoicing; outbursts of anger / calm disagreement; factions / unity; slander / complimenting; gossip / silence; arrogance / humility; disorder / stability.) Use the lesson commentary to explain any unfamiliar words.

Looking at verses 20 and 21, ask the class what Paul was concerned about and why he delineated the shortcomings in such detail. (Paul was afraid he would come to Corinth and find the problems unresolved. Then he would be forced to confront those who were doing wrong. By writing the letter, he gave them opportunity to correct their attitude and behavior before his arrival. If he would come and find that no correction had been made, he would feel humiliated and grieved.) For an interesting discussion, ask, "How far do you think Paul would go to avoid direct confrontation?" (Opinions may vary, but it is wise to point out that Paul did not back away from cor-

recting Christian brothers face to face if they did not heed his letters.) Call attention to the fact that the sins mentioned in verse 21 all involve inappropriate sexual behavior or attitudes. In pagan Corinth, sexual immorality was considered normal and even had a part in some religious observances. Many of the Christians had been pagans, and some were slow to give up their immoral ways. Probably some church members tried to turn attention away from their own wrongdoing by being unduly critical of others. This contributed to the conflict in the church, the conflict that was so distressing to Paul.

On the chalkboard or a flip chart draw five steps. Tell the class that 2 Corinthians 13:5-10 suggests five constructive attitudes and activities that can bring about reconciliation instead of conflict. Write a descriptive phrase on each step as the class calls out suggestions based on these verses. (Suggestions: examine yourself, 13:5; pray for others, 13:7; be truthful, 13:8; wish your adversary well, 13:9; become mature, 13:9.)

Show that Paul was aware of the possibility of hurting people. Read verse 10 aloud. Ask how Paul might be hurtful. Observe that God wants us to edify one another and not destroy one another when we have conflict.

INTO LIFE

Distribute paper and pencils or pens. Ask the students to draw two horizontal lines across the paper, one about two inches from the top and the other about halfway between the first line and the bottom of the page. Give the following instructions:

In the first space, write the name of one person with whom you are experiencing conflict. in the next space, list as many of the negative traits we discussed (see verse 20) as you can identify in the situation. Next to each of these, write a positive counter measure.

In the third space, write a plan of action to incorporate the five constructive attitudes and activities that can bring about reconciliation that verses 5-10 suggest.

OPTION

Divide the class into two parts. Make a copy of the case history on the next page for each group. Assign one group to deal with the situation negatively, as the church at Corinth was doing. Have the other group deal with it as Paul advocated. Allow five or ten minutes, then let the groups share their responses.

Case Study

John, Frank, and several other elders believed that the minister should resign for the good of the church. They began talking to other influential people, and soon the church was buzzing and quarreling. Some concerned friends went to the minister and talked to him personally, but he adamantly refused to resign.

Before long, nearly everyone in the church was choosing sides. Long-time friends who found themselves on different sides of this issue quit speaking to one another.

Eventually, the minister did resign. He started a new church six miles from the one he left, and about 40% of the membership came with him.

What mistakes were made in the handling of this conflict?

How should the case have been handled?

On Your Side

Paul urged the Corinthians, "Listen to my appeal" (2 Corinthians 13:11). The word for "appeal" has a breadth of meaning in the New Testament, but the literal meaning is to "call alongside." One may be called alongside another to reprove him, to encourage him, to comfort him, or even to defend him in court! But one thing remains constant—the two are on the same side; they are not opponents. Look up the following Scriptures. Each uses a form of the word here (Greek, *parakaleo*). The translation is noted to the right of each reference.

How does the concept in each passage suggest a means of dealing with, or preventing, conflict?

Matthew 8:5—"asking for help"

John 14:16—"Counselor"

Acts 20:12—"comforted"

Romans 12:8—"encourage"

1 Corinthians 16:12—"urged"

2 Corinthians 8:17—"appeal"

1 Timothy 4:13—"preaching"

1 John 2:1—"one who speaks . . . in our defense"

BUILDING UP THE BODY

LESSON 5

WHY TEACH THIS LESSON?

It must be human nature, this tendency we have to evaluate differences. Everywhere we turn, our differences are rated, best, second-best, etc. It's what puts the thrill in competition and the pride in victory—a gold medal, a Super Bowl ring, an "A+" at the top of a paper.

But not all differences can be rated this way. The hand is different from the foot, but which is "better"? Use this lesson to encourage class members who may have devalued their own contribution to the body because of unfair comparisons with others more visibly gifted. Use it also to remind those with very visible gifts not to be arrogant. Point them all to God—the giver of every good and perfect gift.

INTRODUCTION

A. TO BE A STAR

My young cousin is a fan of Michael Jordan, the former star basketball player. The walls of his bedroom are covered with Michael Jordan posters. He quotes statistics of Jordan's performance.

My cousin is not alone. Michael Jordan has become a worldwide, multimillion-dollar phenomenon. The response of our youth is more than just appreciation for a good performance. There is also a burning desire to play as well as Jordan; or to be a star like Michael Jordan.

It is not bad to want to improve your performance in any endeavor. But it is unhealthy to despise your own abilities because they do not match the abilities of someone else. In the church, each one should be able to appreciate the value of his or her own distinctive contribution to the life and ministry of the congregation.

B. LESSON BACKGROUND

The church in Corinth apparently was beset with a problem of jealousy. If we read between the lines in 1 Corinthians 14, it seems evident that there was a widespread feeling within the congregation that speaking in tongues was the best spiritual gift a person could have. This idea resulted in a common desire for this gift, a feeling of superiority in tongues-speakers, and jealousy in others.

The apostle Paul responds to this problem with three lines of reasoning. In chapter 13 he argues that the attitude of love is more to be desired than any spiritual gift. In chapter 14 he argues that prophesying is more beneficial to the church than speaking in tongues. But laying the groundwork for these two arguments is chapter 12. Here Paul explains that a Christian should treasure and use whatever spiritual gift he or she has received from God, even if it is not speaking in tongues.

I. OUR DIVERSITY OF GIFTS (1 CORINTHIANS 12:4-11)

"Variety is the spice of life," we often say. Paul contends that a variety of spiritual gifts within a congregation is good for the church.

A. GOD'S MANNER OF DISTRIBUTION (VV. 4-7)

4. There are different kinds of gifts, but the same Spirit.

DEVOTIONAL READING:
EPHESIANS 4:4-16

LESSON SCRIPTURE:
1 CORINTHIANS 12

PRINTED TEXT:
1 CORINTHIANS 12:4-20, 26

Apr
2

LESSON AIMS

After this lesson, the students should:

1. Be able to explain why we Christians do not all have the same gifts and abilities.

2. Have some understanding of the special spiritual gifts used in the early church.

3. See the value in their own gifts.

KEY VERSE:

Now to each one the manifestation of the Spirit is given for the common good.
—1 Corinthians 12:7

Lesson 5 Notes

How to Say It

Corinth. COR-inth.
dunamis (Greek). DOO-nuh-
miss.

Option

The reproducible activity, "The Body Beautiful," on page 270 is designed to encourage your students to study the lesson text and to restate its principles in an imaginary letter to a friend.

What Do You Think?

Whatever your position on the existence of miraculous spiritual gifts, nearly everyone agrees that most of us do not have them. Without arguing about whether a few possess such gifts or not, how does Paul's discussion here apply to us who have no such miraculous gifts? What gifts do we have? How can they be used to promote the health of the body?

Do you think people today become as jealous about nonmiraculous gifts they see in others as the Corinthians did about miraculous gifts? Why or why not? How can we maintain peace among people of varying gifts?

The Corinthians did not need to be told that Christians do not all have the same spiritual gifts. They knew this, and some did not like it. Paul is emphasizing that variety in spiritual gifts is right and proper. The Holy Spirit is not only the source of spiritual gifts, but also the source of the diversity of gifts.

5. There are different kinds of service, but the same Lord.

A common literary device of Jewish literature is parallelism, in which a statement is immediately repeated in different words. Paul uses parallelism when he repeats the idea of "different kinds of gifts" (v. 4) by using the phrase *different kinds of service*.

Parallelism gives emphasis to an idea. Paul uses a third parallel sentence in the next verse, and this suggests that the Corinthian problem required an exceptionally strong emphasis upon the validity of diversity in spiritual gifts.

6. There are different kinds of working, but the same God works all of them in all men.

The triple parallel begun in verse 4 is completed with the phrase *different kinds of working*. The source of spiritual gifts is identified in verse 4 as the Holy Spirit, in verse 5 as the Lord (Jesus Christ), and in verse 6 as God (the Father). Similar linking of the Father, Son, and Spirit is seen in other New Testament passages such as Matthew 28:19 and 2 Corinthians 13:14. This supports the idea that there are three divine persons who live and work in perfect harmony as one God.

Ants and the Church

Some of the most unusual creatures in our world are those we call ants. Entomologists tell us some forty-five hundred species of ants have been identified. Ants always live in groups or colonies, so they are designated as social insects. Most species have groups called workers. These gather food, care for the young, and defend the colony. All eggs are laid by the queen, who makes this her sole occupation. Some species collect seeds of grain, which specialized ants with enlarged jaws crack for the other ants to eat.

Ants are mentioned twice in the Bible—in Proverbs 6:6-8 and 30:25. They are commended for their activity and for their provision for the future. One phrase in Proverbs 6:6 is apropos: "Consider its ways and be wise."

Christians are social creatures, too. As soon as the terms of pardon through Jesus' death and resurrection were proclaimed and people responded, they were gathered in a church. Our Christian faith expresses itself in the various functions that Jesus' disciples perform as members of this "colony of Heaven." So Paul says in verse 6 of our printed text, "There are different kinds of working, but the same God works all of them in all men." Just as ants are created by God to function in specific ways in the colony, so his Spirit enables Christians to function variously to accomplish his will through the church.

—J. G. V. B.

7. Now to each one the manifestation of the Spirit is given for the common good.

Paul's emphasis here is that spiritual gifts are intended to be used in ways that benefit others. This is a theme that is more fully developed in chapter 14.

Several spiritual gifts are named in the following verses. Many of us believe that these fulfilled their purpose in the infancy of the church, and therefore they are not needed by the church today. The following commentary will not only describe the nature of these gifts, but also point out why they are no longer necessary.

B. Examples of Spiritual Gifts (vv. 8-10)

8. To one there is given through the Spirit the message of wisdom, to another the message of knowledge by means of the same Spirit.

This verse illustrates one of the difficulties we have in trying to understand Paul's teaching regarding spiritual gifts. Paul does not explain what each one of these gifts enabled a person to do. For those gifts that are not explained elsewhere in the New

Testament, the best we can do is use the names themselves and devise a reasonable *guess* regarding the nature of each gift.

The *message of wisdom* may be an increase in one's ability to make wise and reasonable judgments. Many students connect this passage to James 1:5, which says, "If any of you lacks wisdom, he should ask God, who gives generously to all without finding fault." However, James seems to be referring to a blessing that is available to anyone who asks, while the spiritual gifts of 1 Corinthians 12 are distributed at the Spirit's will (v. 11)

It seems more likely that *message of wisdom* refers to an ability to receive some type of revelation from God. Revelation gifts were not uncommon in the early years of the church before the writing of the New Testament (Acts 2:17, 18; 11:27, 28; 13:1; 15:32; 21:8-10). Select individuals in the churches were used by the Holy Spirit to relay to their congregations whatever information God chose to give (1 Corinthians 14:29-31). It is reasonable to conclude that this method of divine guidance was used until the writings of the New Testament became available to the churches. Since that time, those writings provide all the inspired direction that mankind needs (2 Timothy 3:16, 17).

The *message of knowledge* sounds similar to the *message of wisdom*. It is grouped together with "revelation" and "prophesying" in 1 Corinthians 14:6 and with "prophecy" in 1 Corinthians 13:2. Without identifying the difference between the gifts of *wisdom* and *knowledge,* we conclude that both had to do with revelation.

9. To another faith by the same Spirit, to another the gifts of healing by that one Spirit.

All Christians have faith in Christ. Apparently *faith* here means something else, a special gift given to some Christians, not all of them. The clue to identifying this gift of faith may be in 1 Corinthians 13:2: "If I have a faith that can move mountains." The gift of faith may be the ability to perform miracles with nature, such as Jesus did when he changed water to wine, walked on the sea, and destroyed a fruitless tree. The disciples may have given this name to nature miracles because Jesus said anyone with a little faith would be able to move a mountain (Matthew 17:20).

Gifts of healing obviously refers to the ability to heal sickness, disease, or injury, and do it instantly. This divine power was often shown by Jesus and his apostles, as recorded in the four Gospels and the book of Acts. Apparently it was made available to select members of the early church. The plural *gifts* may be used because many kinds of sickness were healed.

Both nature miracles and healing miracles were used to show that the miracle workers were spokesmen for God, and thus to confirm the message they gave (Mark 16:20; Acts 8:6; Hebrews 2:3, 4). Such confirmation was needed in the early days of the church. Christians were presenting a new revelation from God, the New Covenant of Jesus Christ; but they did not yet have the written documentation. Miracles established the credibility of the Christian message. Soon that message was recorded in the New Testament. It seems reasonable to conclude that there was no need either of further revelation or of miracles in confirmation.

10. To another miraculous powers, to another prophecy, to another distinguishing between spirits, to another speaking in different kinds of tongues, and to still another the interpretation of tongues.

Miraculous powers obviously means an ability to perform some type of supernatural action, but it does not indicate what activity in particular. In the Greek text it is the word *dunamis* (power). Since this phrase immediately follows the references to nature miracles (*faith*) and healing miracles, it is likely that *miraculous powers* refers to something similar, a miraculous feat that impresses observers with its power. It was probably another gift for confirmation of the Christian message.

WHAT DO YOU THINK?

Whether or not the miraculous gifts have entirely ceased or not, the completion of the New Testament has certainly made some of them less necessary than in the first century. Consider the following gifts from 1 Corinthians 12. In what ways do you think the New Testament provides all Christians with at least some of the benefit that the spiritual gifts provided for a few in ancient Corinth?

Message of Wisdom
Message of Knowledge
Faith
Prophecy
Distinguishing Between Spirits
Speaking in Different Kinds of Tongues and the Interpretation of Tongues

(See Matthew 7:15-20; Galatians 1:8; 5:22-26; 2 Timothy 3:14-17; 1 John 4:1-3.)

Do you think this suggests a special role for people especially good (gifted, perhaps?) at Bible memorization? Why or why not? What about people with good communication skills? What other skills, combined with thorough Bible study, do you think might provide benefit to the body similar to that of the revelatory gifts of the New Testament?

WHAT DO YOU THINK?

We have a diversity of non-miraculous gifts to use in building up the church. Yet it seems these gifts are often as much a source for division and jealousy as they are for harmony and edification.

What kind of gifts seem to produce the most tension in your church? Why do you think this is? Does the church sometimes promote such problems—even if inadvertently—by putting certain people "up front" frequently? Or are those who become jealous of the "up-front" people more to blame? How can we use the gifts and talents of all the members—"up-front" people and "behind-the-scenes" people alike—and promote harmony at the same time?

The gift of *prophecy* is the ability and privilege of receiving direct revelation from God, with the duty of passing on the message received. Obviously it is similar to the message of wisdom and the message of knowledge; how it differs from them is not readily apparent.

Distinguishing between spirits probably is an ability to perceive something in the spiritual realm that is not usually observable. This could be an ability to recognize a false prophet or false teacher. Falsehood usually was exposed by comparing new ideas to the established teaching of the Old Testament and the apostles (2 Timothy 3:14-17; 1 John 4:1-3), but possibly this gift enabled a person to detect error immediately.

Another possibility is that *distinguishing between spirits,* called "discerning of spirits" in some translations, means an ability to know of a demon's presence. Without this gift a person could identify a demon-possessed individual by observing his behavior over a period of time, but with the gift he could instantly recognize a demon and drive him away (Mark 16:17, 20).

The gift of *speaking in different kinds of tongues* is an ability to speak in languages unknown to the speaker. Acts 2:4-11 lists fifteen languages spoken by the apostles when they spoke in tongues. It is possible that there was also a second category of the gift of *tongues,* that involved strange nonhuman sounds, but this has not been clearly demonstrated with a New Testament reference. The tongue that "no man understands" (1 Corinthians 14:2) could be a real human language unknown to anyone who was there. The reference in 1 Corinthians 13:1 to "the tongues of men and of angels" indicates that angels speak, but it does not indicate what kind of language they speak. Neither does it say that Paul actually did speak in their language. For our study it will be more profitable to focus on the gift of tongues that we know existed in the beginning of the church, rather than to deal with that about which we can only guess.

The ability to speak a foreign language without having studied and learned it probably was used by some other evangelists as it was used by the apostles. The apostles used their fifteen tongues on Pentecost to get the attention of the temple crowd, showing that something unusual was going on and "declaring the wonders of God." Peter explained that the Holy Spirit brought this gift of tongues (Acts 2:1-21).

The gift of *interpretation of tongues* probably is the instantaneous ability to translate something spoken in an unfamiliar language. Obviously this could be used along with speaking in tongues to convey the message to people who did not understand the languages being spoken. Both these gifts could be useful in a coastal city like Corinth, where people of many nations mingled—commercial travelers, sailors, pleasure seekers on vacation, worshipers at pagan shrines.

LIFE MANIFESTED

A principle of life is characteristic of much that we observe in our world. We hold in our hand an acorn. It does not seem much different from a brown marble. Yet within the acorn is a reality that the marble does not possess. If the hard acorn is placed in moist, warm soil, it gradually will soften, then break open. A tiny plant will emerge. Given sufficient time it will, on one end, climb through the dark soil up to light and air and sunshine. The other end will plunge deeper as roots, groping for the chemicals and nutrients it needs to sustain its life. Eventually there will be a little tree, and finally a great, stalwart oak. The life force will be made manifest.

When we become new creations in Jesus, the Spirit of life is placed within us. If we nurture our existence in him, this Spirit will be made manifest. It will be expressed in various gifts of the Spirit as the life in the acorn is expressed in the oak. These gifts are the manifestation of the Spirit within. —J. G. V. B.

The importance of every member in the church is illustrated by visual 5.

Who Is Needed in the CHURCH?

C. THE MASTER PLAN (V. 11)

11. All these are the work of one and the same Spirit, and he gives them to each one, just as he determines.

Paul brings his emphasis on the diversity of spiritual gifts to a grand conclusion. The selective distribution of spiritual gifts among the members of a congregation is not an unfortunate accident. It is a vital part of God's design. The Holy Spirit uses his wise judgment to spread the gifts throughout the church as he deems appropriate. We should not crave someone else's gift and let our own be unused. That would upset the balance intended by God.

This lesson can be readily applied to our modern-day church. We have little need for the gifts of revelation and confirmation that abounded in the first century, but we still profit from a host of nonmiraculous gifts. Some of them are named in Romans 12:6-8. These enable us to carry on the church's mission of evangelism and spiritual growth. Paul's principle of diversity in distribution is still applicable.

II. OUR UNITY AS A BODY (1 CORINTHIANS 12:12, 13)

"Do not let your left hand know what your right hand is doing" (Matthew 6:3). That is a hyperbole advising secret generosity; it is not literal advice for all the movements of a person. Neither does it state God's design for the church. Paul presents the concept of a body with all the parts working together in harmony for the good of the whole.

A. THROUGH OUR COMMON FAITH IN CHRIST (V. 12)

12. The body is a unit, though it is made up of many parts; and though all its parts are many, they form one body. So it is with Christ.

In faith we commit ourselves to Jesus Christ. This establishes a relationship not only with him, but also with others who have made a similar commitment. Just as the brain in a human body is the common point of reference for all the parts of that body, Christ is a significant point of contact for all believers.

B. THROUGH OUR COMMON EXPERIENCE WITH GOD'S SPIRIT (V. 13)

13. For we were all baptized by one Spirit into one body—whether Jews or Greeks, slave or free—and we were all given the one Spirit to drink.

The unity of Christians is evident not only in our commitment to the same Lord, but also in our common relationship with the Holy Spirit. All of us enjoy the Spirit's presence within our hearts as he gives us new life and helps us to fight off temptation, lust, and sinfulness (Romans 8:11-13; 1 Thessalonians 4:3-8). An awareness of this shared blessing attracts us to each other.

This verse also reminds us of the significance of baptism. Not only does it provide the occasion for the Holy Spirit to begin his sanctifying work in our lives (Acts 2:38); it also is a means by which the Holy Spirit incorporates the individual into the fellowship of the saints. Our shared experience of baptism should break down all barriers and foster a spirit of unity.

III. OUR NEED FOR DIVERSITY AND UNITY (1 CORINTHIANS 12:14-20, 26)

"Opposites attract," we often say regarding romantic relationships. Whether that is true or not, we can see that Paul is leading us to the conclusion that it is good for the church to have diversity in the midst of its unity.

A. FOR THE BENEFIT OF THE CHURCH (VV. 14-17)

14. Now the body is not made up of one part but of many.

WHAT DO YOU THINK?

We not only differ in regard to our talents or gifts, but in any church there are people who differ from the majority in economic status or educational accomplishments or family background. These differences can foster misunderstanding and jealousy. It is important, therefore, to make much of the tremendous blessings we hold in common. Malachi asks, "Have we not all one Father? Did not one God create us?" (Malachi 2:10).

Verse 13 stresses some of the common experiences all the Corinthian Christians shared. What are some others you might add for your church? To what extent should we emphasize our common experiences? How can we do that without devaluing the helpful diversity we have?

OPTION

Use the reproducible activity, "You're Important—I'm Important" on pager 276 to help your students apply the message of today's lesson to their lives.

THOUGHT TO REMEMBER

As we learn to appreciate the beauty and worth of the variety of gifts and abilities within the church, we enable ourselves to enjoy more fully the unity that is possible among co-laborers for the Lord.

PRAYER

Father, help us to properly value and use our own gifts and abilities while allowing others to do the same without any jealousy or interference from us.

WHAT DO YOU THINK?

Paul says "every part" of the body shares both the pain and the honor that comes to each individual member (v. 26). Do you see that in your church? Do you see it in yourself—that is, do you genuinely hurt when a fellow Christian suffers, and do you have heart-felt joy when another is honored? What are some practical ways in which Christians can share in each other's sorrows and gladness?

DAILY BIBLE READINGS

Monday, Mar. 27—Spiritual Gifts Given by God (1 Corinthians 12:1-6)

Tuesday, Mar. 28—Gifts Are for the Common Good (1 Corinthians 12:7-11)

Wednesday, Mar. 29—Many Members, One Body (1 Corinthians 12:12-20)

Thursday, Mar. 30—Members Need One Another (1 Corinthians 12:21-26)

Friday, Mar. 31—The Church Is Christ's Body (1 Corinthians 12:27-31)

Saturday, Apr. 1—Live in Unity of Faith (Ephesians 4:1-7)

Sunday, Apr. 2—Build Up the Body of Christ (Ephesians 4: 11-16)

Paul returns to his earlier emphasis on variety in a human body and in the church.

15, 16. If the foot should say, "Because I am not a hand, I do not belong to the body," it would not for that reason cease to be part of the body. And if the ear should say, "Because I am not an eye, I do not belong to the body," it would not for that reason cease to be part of the body.

Of course, body parts do not have the intellectual capacity to be jealous of one another. But this humorous picture well illustrates the jealousy that sometimes arises in the church over other people's gifts and abilities.

17. If the whole body were an eye, where would the sense of hearing be? If the whole body were an ear, where would the sense of smell be?

What an apt illustration of the way a church can become unbalanced if everyone seeks the same gifts! No one in his right mind wishes that all the parts of his physical body would perform the same function. If every body part were designed for vision, we would miss out on sounds, smells, tastes, and touch, not to mention the threat to continued existence when the internal organs would cease their normal functions and switch to vision. A healthy body requires diversity of functions.

B. FOR THE GLORY OF GOD (VV. 18-20)

18. But in fact God has arranged the parts in the body, every one of them, just as he wanted them to be.

Dissatisfaction with the distribution of gifts is in effect a criticism of God's judgment, whether it is intended or not. We will do well to accept gladly whatever gifts and abilities God has graciously given us, and to use them for his service and glory.

19, 20. If they were all one part, where would the body be? As it is, there are many parts, but one body.

Paul repeats his argument from verses 14-17, concluding with praise for diversity *and* unity.

C. FOR THE ENCOURAGEMENT OF EACH MEMBER (V. 26)

26. If one part suffers, every part suffers with it; if one part is honored, every part rejoices with it.

Try this experiment: smash your thumb with a hammer and see if only the thumb experiences feelings of pain and discomfort. Actually, none of us needs to perform this silly experiment, because we know from experience that a hurt in one part of the body is felt throughout the body.

This is the way it should be within the church. There should be such a union of purpose and love that we feel bonded to one another, that we care for one another, even to the point of sharing one another's sorrow and gladness. When this type of sympathy begins to occur naturally in a church, that is an indication that those Christians are beginning to achieve the balance between diversity and unity that Paul commended.

CONCLUSION

Some things in life are so different that you have to choose between the options. As we often say, "You can't have it both ways." But unity and diversity are not opposites of which one must exclude the other. As a musical quartet illustrates, diversity does not preclude harmony. Likewise, unity does not require an equal distribution of gifts and a strict conformity in activity. For a healthy church, diversity and unity are not opposites but complements of each other.

Discovery Learning

This page contains an alternate lesson plan emphasizing learning activities. Classes desiring such student involvement will find these suggestions helpful. The next page is a reproducible activity page to further enhance discovery learning.

LEARNING GOALS

Through today's lesson, the pupils will:

1. Understand the significance of spiritual gifts in the church.

2. Be able to contrast healthy and unhealthy views of the gifts others possess.

3. Desire to know their spiritual gifts.

INTO THE LESSON

Write these questions on the chalkboard before the class arrives:

What was the best gift you ever received?
What made it so very special to you?

When the class arrives, use the "neighbor nudge." Have each student share the answers to the questions with a nearby neighbor. Bring the class together again by saying that it is often the giver of the gift that makes it so special to the recipient. (Be sure to share your own gift and why it was special to you.) Explain that the church at Corinth was experiencing disunity because members were focusing on the gifts instead of the Giver.

INTO THE WORD

The apostle Paul approached the situation by calling the church's attention to the source of the diversity of gifts. Direct the students to 1 Corinthians 12:4-11 and ask them to be looking for the answer to this question: Whose idea was it to give such a diversity of gifts to the church? Have someone read the verses aloud. After the class has responded, explain that Paul's intent was to help the church focus on the fact that it was God's plan to meet the needs of the church by gifting its members with things that would be encouraging and build up the body. However, God's intent was being frustrated by the people in the church who had wrong attitudes.

Give each student a copy of the word search at the right. Instruct them to find four words that describe what Paul desired for the church (diversity, harmony, love, gifts) and four words that describe negative attitudes that threaten unity (covetous, envy, jealousy, pride).

After allowing time for individuals to complete the word search, share the answers and then go into the "Lesson Background" about what was going on at Corinth.

Continue the Scripture development, using the questions below as you interact with the students. Give specific verses to help them find answers.

1. What spiritual gifts are listed in verses 8-10? (Elaborate on the meaning of each.)

2. How would you define "spiritual gifts," based on this passage, Romans 12:4-8, and 1 Peter 4:10, 11?

3. Do you think the early church needed the spiritual gifts listed in 1 Corinthians 12 more than the church today does? Explain your answer. (See the lesson commentary, especially on verse 9.)

4. What is the significance of baptism as it relates to the body of Christ (v. 12)?

5. In what ways is the church like a human body? (vv. 14-20).

6. What attitudes promote a healthy church body?

INTO LIFE

Pass out construction paper and felt-tip markers. Ask each student to picture the part of the body that he or she is. For example, explain that you might be represented by a mouth because you are the teacher—but a mouth can also represent someone who invites others to come to church or shares the gospel with a friend. One who is a good listener may draw a huge ear; one who works in the kitchen may draw a hand; one who does much calling may draw a foot. Allow a few minutes for thinking and drawing; then ask students to hold up their papers and to look around the class at the papers of others. While they are doing this, draw a huge stick figure on the board. Check off the body parts that are illustrated by students' drawings.

Probably some cannot so quickly draw appropriate pictures. Tell them that does not mean they are any less important. Liver and spleen and sweat glands are not easily pictured, but the body needs every one of its parts. Each one of us can do something in the work of the church.

Close with a prayer of gratitude for the body of Christ as it is represented in your class.

```
O Z K C O V E T O U S
P R A S T U N P P C T
I Y R Y A C V E R F F
W S X M E O Y K I B I
A U L J G E O L D O G
B O G G E L Y O E R D
S L D I V E R S I T Y
H A R M O N Y S O O N
T E A S L D S A T P P
Q J O K E I S O N Y U
```

The Body Beautiful

The concept of the church as Christ's body is fundamental to the Christian's service to God. It is important that every person who becomes a Christian understand these principles early on.

Imagine, then, that a friend of your has just become a Christian. You decide to write to him or her to explain this concept, especially to point out how he or she fits into the body. Using 1 Corinthians 12:4-26 (and any additional Scriptures you want to add), write your letter. (You may need additional writing paper.) Be sure to answer the following questions in your letter:

1. In what ways is the church like the body of Christ?
2. What is a spiritual gift?
3. Why has God given different Christians different gifts?
4. How should the parts of the body relate to each other?
5. Why is each member important? Why is the new Christian to whom you're writing an important part of the body?
6. When the church is functioning as God intends for it to, what might we expect it to look like?

You're Important—I'm Important

As a part of Christ's body, you are important. Your gifts contribute to the health of the entire body. Thus, you should reject any feelings of inferiority; they are not based on truth. At the same time, every other member is also important. You should also reject any feelings of superiority.

As you seek to appreciate your own importance and the importance of others, consider these questions. Jot your thoughts below.

1. What are some ways in which God has equipped (gifted) you to assist others in Christ's body?

2. In what ways are you using your spiritual ability (gift) in the body?

3. Why is your gift valuable to the body? (Remember, 1 Corinthians 12 indicates that **every** member is valuable.)

4. List five people in your church who are using their spiritual gifts for the good of the body. Write each of them a note of appreciation and encouragement this week.

GROWING THROUGH WORSHIP

LESSON 6

WHY TEACH THIS LESSON?

Some adults feel the church needs to "get with it," to use a more contemporary style and less formality in worship. Others feel the worship service ought to be conducted by strict rules of procedure much as the Old Testament rituals were. Unfortunately, most of our evaluation is based on personal preference. If I like contemporary music, I think it should be used more in the worship service. If I don't, I think it has no place in the worship service. This lesson presents a better principle. The issue is not, "What do I like?" The issue is, "What will strengthen the church?"

Use this lesson to motivate your students to follow that principle even when it challenges their personal preference.

INTRODUCTION

A. ORDER IN THE COURT!

You have seen this scene on TV many times, from Perry Mason to Ben Matlock. The evidence weighs heavily against the defendant. The defense attorney appears to be running out of ideas. And then without warning he drops the bombshell, a piece of information that shocks the courtroom, implicates the prosecution witness, and clears his client. We know what happens next. Confusion and murmuring erupt in the courtroom, the judge pounds his gavel and demands, "Order in the court!"

It is a basic rule: if you want to carry on a meeting effectively, the participants must act in an orderly fashion. This is no less true in the church than in the courtroom. Paul wrote the fourteenth chapter of 1 Corinthians to straighten out a disorderly worship service, and at the same time to provide us with some helpful guidelines for an effective worship service today.

B. LESSON BACKGROUND

The previous lesson from 1 Corinthians 12 pointed out that the Christians at Corinth had been arguing about spiritual gifts. It seems there was a common desire to speak in tongues, and a spirit of superiority in those who did possess that ability. Chapter 14 implies that problems arose in the worship services. Apparently participants competed for opportunities to speak in tongues, often interrupting other tongues-speakers and even those who were delivering a message from God's Word. The result was a confusion that threatened to hinder the spiritual growth of the participants and drive away new prospects. Chapter 14 addresses this dangerous situation with concrete, practical rules for worship.

I. MATURE WORSHIP (1 CORINTHIANS 14:20-22)

"Grow up," we often say to someone who is speaking or acting in a manner that does not reflect mature thinking. This phrase well typifies Paul's message to the Corinthians.

DEVOTIONAL READING:
PSALM 95:1-7
LESSON SCRIPTURE:
1 CORINTHIANS 14:1-33A
PRINTED TEXT:
1 CORINTHIANS 14:20-33A

Apr
9

LESSON AIMS

When this lesson has been completed, the students should:

1. Have a desire to see that their own worship services are conducted in an orderly fashion.

2. Have an interest in participating in public worship in a way that benefits others.

3. Pay special attention to those portions of a worship service that present messages from the Word of God.

KEY VERSE:

When you come together, everyone has a hymn, or a word of instruction, a revelation, a tongue or an interpretation. All of these must be done for the strengthening of the church.
—1 Corinthians 14:26

A. A CALL FOR MATURE THINKING (V. 20)

20. Brothers, stop thinking like children. In regard to evil be infants, but in your thinking be adults.

Stop thinking like children. It is childish to compete in a worship service for the opportunity to speak, or to interrupt others when they are speaking. Boasting about your own spiritual gifts is immature. The apostle Paul challenges the Corinthians to act like mature adults in their church gatherings.

To reinforce his point, Paul says, *In regard to evil be infants.* Sometimes children are used in Scripture to illustrate characteristics that are appropriate for God's people. Jesus taught that the kingdom of Heaven belongs to those who approach God with a childlike spirit (Matthew 18:3). For example, they need the unconditional love and trust that children typically have for their parents. In a similar fashion, Paul says that when it comes to malicious and hurtful conduct toward others, childlike innocence and ignorance are appropriate. If the Christians of Corinth want to act like children, it should be in a positive manner, not in bickering and fighting.

WHAT DO YOU THINK?

Jesus urged us to be childlike in the kingdom (Matthew 18:1-4). Unfortunately, many times we insist on being childish instead. Paul confronted the same problem in Corinth. They were "thinking like children."

Perhaps he was referring to their elevation of one spiritual gift (speaking in tongues) over all the others. Perhaps it was their desire for something sensational (tongues would be more spectacular than prophecy). Or maybe it was a clamoring to be heard that destroyed the order that ought to have been maintained in their worship services.

What are some ways in which Christians today sometimes behave in a childish manner? How can childishness be overcome?

B. A MATURE VIEW OF TONGUES-SPEAKING (VV. 21, 22)

21. In the Law it is written: "Through men of strange tongues and through the lips of foreigners I will speak to this people, but even then they will not listen to me," says the Lord.

This quote from Isaiah 28:11 and 12 comes from a chapter that prophesies the conquest of the southern kingdom of Judah by the Babylonians. God's people had refused to listen to his Word as spoken by prophets like Isaiah, so God said he would one day get their attention by using foreign invaders. Listening to the foreign language of Babylon would not be a pleasant experience, for the occasion would represent humiliation and defeat.

Paul uses this Old Testament passage to lead up to the idea that it is inappropriate to speak to your own people in a manner that is foreign and unintelligible, for in biblical history that symbolizes distress and grief. One problem with tongues-speaking in a worship service is that it alienates those who do not understand.

22. Tongues, then, are a sign, not for believers but for unbelievers; prophecy, however, is for believers, not for unbelievers.

The mention of tongues as a *sign* relates to our earlier lesson in 1 Corinthians 12. In the beginning years of the church, supernatural spiritual gifts such as speaking in tongues, healing, and casting out demons were used by Christian evangelists as signs from God to indicate that they were spokesmen of God (Mark 16:20; Acts 8:6; Hebrews 2:3, 4). These "confirmation gifts" were needed when Christians were claiming a new revelation from God (the gospel of Jesus Christ), but did not yet have the written documentation that would later be provided by the New Testament writings.

Paul now reminds the Corinthians that confirmation signs such as speaking in tongues were designed for persuading non-Christians to listen to the gospel. They were not intended to be used among Christians.

In this chapter Paul challenges the Corinthian fascination with tongues-speaking by promoting the spiritual gift of *prophecy*. As we noted in our study of 1 Corinthians 12, this gift is the ability to receive direct revelation from God, with the responsibility for funneling that information to God's people. Apparently this revelation gift was given to select individuals in order that the churches would have a means of receiving divine guidance until the New Testament writings became available to them.

Paul says *tongues* are a sign for unbelievers, while prophesying is a sign for believers. This illustrates one difference between confirmation gifts and revelation gifts. The former were designed for use in evangelism. In the beginning years of the church they persuaded people to listen to this new religious group. The latter were intended to be used in the church for people who needed to be instructed in the beliefs and practices of the New Covenant. Paul's call for mature thinking among the Corinthians implies that it is time for them to move on from flashy confirmation gifts like speaking in tongues, and to give attention to the instruction of God being presented through the revelation gifts.

TONGUES

Paul says quite a bit about "tongues" in 1 Corinthians 14. His use of the term is much like ours when we speak of the French, Italian, and Swedish "tongues," or languages. Tongues were given to some of the early Christians for a sign to non-Christians. Some students think this gift was a supernatural ability to speak in tongues they had not learned, as the apostles did at Pentecost (Acts 2:1-11). Others believe the tongues at Corinth were an ecstatic form of utterance not in any known language.

However that may be, Paul was afraid an emphasis on "tongues" would obscure the common realities of Christian associations in love. So he began 1 Corinthians 13 with the warning, "I may be able to speak the languages of men and even of *angels*, but if I have no love, my speech is no more than a noisy gong or a clanging bell" (*Today's English Version*).

Ella Wheeler Wilcox looked in this direction when she discussed the "tongue" Jesus used:

The wise men ask, "What language did Christ speak?"
They cavil, argue, search, and little prove.
O Sages, leave your Syriac and your Greek!
Christ spoke the universal language—LOVE.   —J. G. V. B.

II. EDIFYING WORSHIP (1 CORINTHIANS 14:23-26)

A. THE BENEFITS OF PROPHESYING (VV. 23-25)

23. So if the whole church comes together and everyone speaks in tongues, and some who do not understand or some unbelievers come in, will they not say that you are out of your mind?

Some in Corinth thought it was great to stand before a congregation and speak prayer and praise in an unfamiliar language. Paul challenges them to step back and look at themselves from a different angle. Consider the view of those *who do not understand* what is said in tongues and the *unbelievers* (the non-Christians). The apostle suggests that this strange conduct will bring a negative reaction from visitors and will handicap the evangelistic mission of the church.

The truth of this statement should be evident to most of us who are working through this lesson. Those people today who often speak in tongues feel quite at ease with that practice, but many visitors think they are crazy.

24. But if an unbeliever or someone who does not understand comes in while everybody is prophesying, he will be convinced by all that he is a sinner and will be judged by all.

Here is the key advantage of *prophesying* over tongues-speaking in a meeting. Whatever message a prophet receives from God is presented to the assembly in their common language. Everyone, including the visitor, has a fair opportunity to understand the message and to respond appropriately. Unlike the incomprehensible sounds of tongues-speaking, prophesying presents God's message in a way that can persuade the hearer and convict him of his errors.

This passage reinforces the idea that confirmation gifts such as tongues-speaking and healing were especially helpful for evangelism in the marketplace. They caught attention and persuaded people that they were in the presence of a spokesman

OPTION

Use the activities on the reproducible page 284 for Bible study and application. The "Prophetic Puzzle" may be used to introduce the lesson; "Learning to Think Like Adults" will take your students deeper.

HOW TO SAY IT
Isaiah. Eye-ZAY-uh.
Syriac. SEER-ee-ack.

WHAT DO YOU THINK?

Paul's description of the convicted worshiper is very appealing: "He will fall down and worship God, exclaiming, 'God is really among you!'" When was the last time that happened in one of your church's worship services? Why is it not a more common occurrence? Have we tried to impress visitors with the wrong things—things we do, perhaps, instead of what God has done? The worshiper Paul describes was so affected by the power of the prophetic message—the Word of God. How can we make an impression that will produce a response similar to what Paul describes here? How much of the result depends on the preacher, and how much depends on the other worshipers? Why?

WHAT DO YOU THINK?

Verses 25 and 26 demonstrate two key components of worship. First, it should exalt God. Why else would a visitor exclaim, "God is truly among you"? Second, it should strengthen the church. Interestingly, no mention is made of how good the people in attendance are made to feel, or what kind of preferences are catered to in matters of style. Nothing is said of how emotional the preacher, or how dynamic, or how oratorical, or how entertaining.

If you were put in charge of planning your church's worship services for the next month, how would you incorporate the two components cited here?

from God. But in a worship service the need is for clear instruction from God's Word. This was provided by revelation gifts such as prophesying. Rather than contribute to the growth of the congregation and its guests, tongues-speaking gifts tended to befuddle. They belonged somewhere else.

25. And the secrets of his heart will be laid bare. So he will fall down and worship God, exclaiming, "God is really among you!"

This verse amplifies the idea in the previous verse. The heart of an unbeliever can be challenged if he is given a clear communication of God's Word, as was done in prophesying.

B. A CALL FOR EDIFICATION (V. 26)

26. What then shall we say, brothers? When you come together, everyone has a hymn, or a word of instruction, a revelation, a tongue or an interpretation. All of these must be done for the strengthening of the church.

Here is a key principle for evaluating everything that is done in a worship service: *All of these must be done for the strengthening of the church.* Everything must be aimed at helping people grow and develop.

The primary purpose of worship is to praise and glorify God. Our English word *worship* conveys this idea, being a shortened form of *worth-ship*. In worship we recognize the great worth of the Almighty.

Building people up is another goal of worship. Not only is God to be praised, but those who participate in the praising should be blessed by the experience. They should be built up in knowledge, in understanding, in faith, in devotion. This feature does not outweigh our primary purpose of giving glory to God, but it is so important that Paul uses it to measure the value of each activity in a worship service.

Paul names some activities that apparently were common in the worship services at Corinth. Our study of 1 Corinthians has already acquainted us with some of these items: a *tongue* (an unfamiliar language) a *revelation* (a prophecy), and *interpretation* (of an unfamiliar language). A *hymn* obviously refers to the use of music in worship. A *word of instruction* could refer to a prepared lesson or sermon, but perhaps it refers to another revelation gift. The same word is used in the list of revelation gifts in 1 Corinthians 14:6.

It is not Paul's purpose to make an exhaustive list of worship activities, as if anything left out of this list (such as the Lord's Supper or the offering) were somehow inappropriate. Nor is it Paul's purpose to require all of these items in our worship services today. We have already noted that we do not have the same need for the confirmation and revelation gifts today, now that the church is firmly established and the New Testament is available to guide us. Likewise, it is becoming apparent in this study that Paul saw little use for confirmation gifts such as tongues-speaking in the worship services of his own day.

In listing these activities, Paul illustrates his principle of strengthening the church. All activities used in a worship service, including tongues and the other items in this list, are proper only if they promote the spiritual growth of the assembly.

SIDEWALK SUPERINTENDENTS

In speaking about the worship activities of the church at Corinth, Paul sums up his ideal for all of them: "All of these must be done for the strengthening of the church." The word for *strengthening* here literally means "building up."

There is something fascinating about the erection of a building. Many people stop while shopping or walking to and from work to see "how it is coming along." Those who are just onlookers at the construction site are often called "sidewalk superintendents."

Paul indicates that the work and worship of God's people are for the purpose of "building up." They are for building up a structure of life and thought through which people are turned "from darkness to light, and from the power of Satan to God, so that they may receive forgiveness of sins and a place among those who are sanctified" (Acts 26:18).

It is our responsibility to help this structure of faith and obedience to take shape and to become a reality. Are we willing to be only "sidewalk superintendents"? Or will we take an active part in helping to build up the church?   —J. G. V. B.

III. ORDERLY WORSHIP (1 CORINTHIANS 14:27-33)

"What's the bottom line?" We say this when we want to bring a discussion to a succinct conclusion. After devoting three chapters to the misuse of spiritual gifts at Corinth, Paul concludes his discussion with a few simple rules for the orderly use of spiritual gifts in worship.

A. GUIDELINES FOR TONGUES-SPEAKING (vv. 27, 28)
27. If anyone speaks in a tongue, two—or at the most three—should speak, one at a time, and someone must interpret.

Here are three rules for tongues-speaking in a worship service. First, there should be a limit of no more than two or three expressions of tongues in a given service. Paul does not encourage everyone to participate.

Second, speaking in tongues should be done *one at a time*. Paul does not allow interruptions and competition among speakers. Nor does he allow simultaneous tongues-speaking, a choir of tongues. This would not help to win the visitor (as noted earlier).

Third, no one should speak in tongues unless there is someone present who can give a reliable interpretation of what is being said in the unfamiliar language. This is a logical implication from the principle enumerated in verse 26.

28. If there is no interpreter, the speaker should keep quiet in the church and speak to himself and God.

Paul has an interesting approach to the problem of tongues-speaking in the church. He has said enough to indicate that he does not believe tongues belong in a worship service. This spiritual gift is designed for evangelism outside the church. Even so, Paul does not command the Corinthians to stop speaking in tongues during public worship. Instead, he chooses to allow the practice, but under conditions that will minimize both its use and its negative impact.

Can this spirit of gracious concession still work among Christians who disagree sharply about modern-day tongues? Perhaps so. Many of us believe the confirmation and revelation gifts no longer are needed or given, but we need not make this issue a test of fellowship. We can maintain our position and challenge the views of others in a manner that does not alienate those who differ with us on this issue. It may be necessary to restrict a tongues-speaker according to the rules Paul gives, but this does not necessarily rule out fellowship in worship and service.

Those individuals who believe they have the ability to speak in tongues should follow Paul's instructions in this text. In keeping with the emphasis upon the principles of edification and order in worship, no individual should speak out in a tongue when doing so will be upsetting to the assembly.

The best advice for tongues-speaking in our time may be to minimize its use in public settings and leave it to the individual to determine what is appropriate in private devotion. This seems to fit the balance Paul strikes in this chapter, as he gives reasons why a tongues-speaker needs to *keep quiet in the church* and yet may *speak to himself and God*.

Visual 6 of the visuals packet illustrates the principle of verse 26.

WHAT DO YOU THINK?

Paul describes a worship service with as many as six different speakers (two or three speaking in tongues and two or three prophets). Do you think this suggests we should have more than one sermon in our worship services, or that there should be several speakers? Why or why not?

WHAT DO YOU THINK?

The lesson writer deals with the difficult matter of how to preserve fellowship and cooperation between those who practice tongues-speaking today and those who oppose such a practice. Do you agree or disagree with his conclusions? Why?

How would you respond if a person who disagrees with you on the issue of speaking in tongues were put in charge of planning the worship services at your church? Why?

THOUGHT TO REMEMBER

If we want our worship to please God, then we should do it according to his instructions.

Paul said that when the prophets speak, "the others should weigh carefully what is said." The lesson writer's explanation is at the right. Another explanation is that the "others" are the listeners. Those who are in attendance and hear the message should weigh carefully what is said in order to apply it to their own lives.

What do you think? Who are the "others" and what does it mean for them to "weigh carefully what is said"? How does that apply to our worship today?

PRAYER

Father, help us to worship you "in spirit and in truth," considering not only the attitude we bring to worship, but also the manner in which we worship. In Jesus' name. Amen.

DAILY BIBLE READINGS

Monday, Apr. 3—Worship God With Praise and Thanksgiving (Psalm 95:1-7)

Tuesday, Apr. 4—Use Spiritual Gifts to Edify Others (1 Corinthians 14:1-5)

Wednesday, Apr. 5—Unintelligible Speech Does Not Edify Anyone (1 Corinthians 14:6-12)

Thursday, Apr. 6—Speaking in Tongues Requires Interpretation (1 Corinthians 14:13-19)

Friday, Apr. 7—Be Mature in Using Spiritual Gifts (1 Corinthians 14:20-25)

Saturday, Apr. 8—Worshipers' Sharing Should Be Orderly (1 Corinthians 14:26-33

Sunday, Apr. 9—Meeting Regularly for Worship (Acts 2: 38-47)

B. GUIDELINES FOR PROPHESYING (VV. 29-31)

29. Two or three prophets should speak, and the others should weigh carefully what is said.

The Word of God belongs in a worship service. In 1 Timothy 4:13 Paul commends three ways to present God's Word to a congregation: the reading aloud of Scripture (without comment), preaching, and teaching. The gift of prophecy also served to bring the Word of God into a service, as those who received a message from God relayed that message to the assembly.

Still, Paul does not want too much of a good thing. He limits the use of the gift of prophesying with some of the rules given for the gift of tongues. This suggests a principle to be applied to all the activities we use in worship today. We should seek a reasonable balance between all of our worship activities and not let any one item take up so much time that it detracts from the edification of the assembly.

The others should weigh carefully what is said. This seems to say prophecies are to be evaluated. There were false prophets (Matthew 7:15; 2 Peter 2:1). They should be exposed. This could be done by comparing their words with the words of the Old Testament and the established teaching of the apostles (2 Peter 1:16-21; 1 John 4:1-3; Jude 3-5). The *others* may refer to other prophets, or perhaps it refers to the elders of the church, who must guard against false teaching (Acts 20:28-31).

30. And if a revelation comes to someone who is sitting down, the first speaker should stop.

It would not be good to interrupt rudely; but if a prophet receives a revelation from God, it is proper to ask the speaker to pause for a few moments when he gets to an appropriate breaking point. In such a case the speaker ought to yield.

31. For you can all prophesy in turn so that everyone may be instructed and encouraged.

The principles of orderly procedure and edification are the foundation for Paul's rules.

C. A CALL FOR ORDER (VV. 32, 33)

32. The spirits of prophets are subject to the control of prophets.

The gift of prophecy is not so compulsive that a prophet has no control of himself. One who is talking is able to stop, and one who receives a revelation is able to refrain from speaking until an appropriate opportunity.

33a. For God is not a God of disorder but of peace.

If two so-called prophets insist on talking at the same time, at least one of them is not really inspired by God. Perhaps neither one is. The source of prophecy and tongues and all spiritual gifts is One who always operates in a reasonable fashion. We should follow his lead. Whatever gifts and abilities he gives us, we should use them in an orderly manner.

CONCLUSION

One of Frank Sinatra's hits is the song "My Way." Many people like the idea of not allowing others to intimidate you. "Through it all, I did it my way."

This well describes the way many people approach worship. Some groups have replaced the simple elements of New Testament worship with rituals and traditions of their own devising. We seek to avoid that error and insist upon using the worship practices from the New Testament pattern: praying, preaching, singing, and the Lord's Supper. But sometimes we fail to consider how best to blend those practices together to glorify God and edify the worshipers. Often we settle for poorly planned services and mediocrity. As we criticize the Corinthian church for bringing disorder and confusion into worship, let us also evaluate what we ourselves do.

Discovery Learning

*This page contains an alternate lesson plan emphasizing learning activities. Classes
desiring such student involvement will find these suggestions helpful. The next page
is a reproducible activity page to further enhance discovery learning.*

LEARNING GOALS

After this lesson the pupils will be able to:

1. Enumerate things to be avoided when participating in a worship service.

2. Examine their church's worship service and suggest possible improvements.

3. Design a worship service that is orderly and inspirational.

INTO THE LESSON

Secure a worship tape of vocal music in Spanish or some language other than English. Or secure a tape of the Bible being read in another language. Have it playing as students arrive. As the session begins, tell the class there will be a short worship time listening to the tape. After a couple of minutes, turn the tape off. Ask the members to tell how they felt when they couldn't understand the language, but were being urged to worship.

Lead into the lesson by saying that speaking in tongues had become a problem in the worship services of the church at Corinth. First Corinthians 14 addresses this problem. In the process, it teaches us some lessons about our own worship.

INTO THE WORD

Divide the class into two groups. Assign each of the following sets of questions to one of the groups. Let groups share their conclusions after about ten minutes.

Group 1
- For whom is speaking in tongues intended? (v. 22)
- How would an unbeliever feel if he came into a worship service where everyone was speaking in tongues? (v. 23)
- What conditions were put upon the use of tongues in a worship service? (vv. 27, 28).

Group 2
- For whom is prophesying designed? (v. 22)
- How is the unbeliever affected by prophesying? (vv. 24, 25).

While the groups are at work, draw this chart on the board to record the answers found by each group. As the groups report, write their findings on this chart and discuss the conclusions reached.

OPTION

Make copies of the word puzzle on the next page and have your students complete the puzzles, using 1 Corinthians 14 as a guide.

INTO LIFE

Direct the class in enumerating all the things done in your church's worship service. Record them on the chalkboard. (For example: singing, praying, preaching.) Next, have the class look at verses 26-33 and discuss: "How does Paul say we should determine what is to be done in a worship service?" (The answer is that each activity strengthen, or edify, the church, v. 26.)

Let students sitting near each other form groups of two or three and discuss the activities in your church's worship service. (You have them listed on the board.) Let them rate each activity on a scale of 1 to 10 (10 being highest) as to how much each activity edifies the church.

Let each group record its ratings on a sheet of paper and tape it to the board. (No names need be attached.) Take a few moments to compare the opinions.

Ask the students if personal taste probably had a part in the ratings. Remind them of Paul's criterion: each activity should strengthen the church. Discuss with the class how you determine whether something edifies the church.

Some suggested answers: It's an activity modeled by the early church. The activity is well prepared and tastefully executed. The needs of people are considered. The content is biblically sound. The congregation is encouraged and built up through the activity. The activity glorifies God and makes him central. The activity is done in an orderly fashion and does not cause confusion. Allow the class to contribute.

Now ask the class for suggestions of activities that could be added to your current worship service. Each suggestion should include why or how it might edify the church if it were included in the worship service. List these ideas next to the list of current worship activities.

Return your class to the small groups formed earlier. Ask each group to draw from all the suggestions and evaluations to design a worship plan for an edifying service. If there is time, have each group share their plan with the class.

(If there are channels for making suggestions at your church, see about having one or more of these worship plans proposed for use in worship.)

Prophetic Puzzle

Complete the following puzzle with the names of worship activities practiced at Corinth and mentioned in 1 Corinthians 14.

1. Teaching, sermon
2. Gift of prophecy
3. (down) Foreign language
4. Use of music

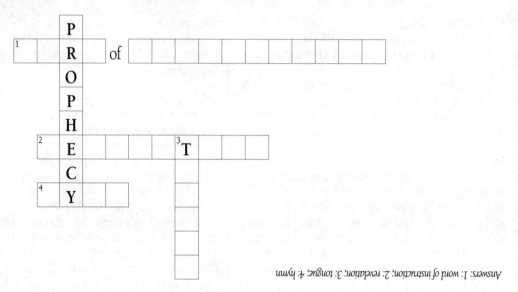

Answers: 1: word of instruction; 2: revelation; 3: tongue; 4: hymn

Learning to Think Like Adults

Read 1 Corinthians 14:20-33. Explore the passage for ways in which the Corinthians might have been thinking like children (that is, displaying immature attitudes). You may need to speculate a little. That's okay. List your ideas below in the left column Then look for adult ways of thinking Paul said they should have been practicing. Write your observations in the right column.

CHILDREN   ADULTS

Now look at your own attitudes and behavior. Are you guilty of some childish thinking or acting? List some ways below. Then suggest some mature behavior that should replace the childish behavior. Make this a matter of prayer this week.

CHILDISH   MATURE

BEING A
RESURRECTION PEOPLE

LESSON 7

WHY TEACH THIS LESSON?

A few years ago, a so-called theologian wrote a book that included one chapter he called "The Resurrection: Historically Probable; Theologically Insignificant." That author must not have read our lesson text for today! Indeed, the resurrection is the most significant fact in all of theology.

From every source—secular, commercial, and even religious, it seems—your students will be challenged to discount the importance of the resurrection. If they give in, their faith itself will be in jeopardy.

This lesson serves to bolster their confidence both in the resurrection and in their faith.

INTRODUCTION

A. PROVE IT

Missouri is well known as the "Show Me State." To some this suggests a stubborn spirit, unwilling to believe. But to others it seems like a sensible approach: if you want me to accept something as true, then give me a reason.

The Christian faith is grounded upon one astounding claim, that Jesus Christ rose from the dead after three days in a tomb. We are not asked to believe this without any evidence. On the contrary, the New Testament emphasizes the historical credibility of this event. From the disappearance of Jesus' body from a guarded tomb to the eyewitness testimony of people who saw Jesus alive, we are given good reasons to believe in the resurrection.

As we review the facts, let us reflect not only on the reasons we believe in Jesus' resurrection, but also on what difference this belief makes in our lives.

B. LESSON BACKGROUND

After his lengthy discussion of spiritual gifts in 1 Corinthians 12–14, Paul launches into a different subject. In 1 Corinthians 15 he addresses the false idea that Christians who have already died will remain dead and miss the future blessings of Heaven (1 Corinthians 15:12).

Paul begins chapter 15 by reminding the Corinthians of the gospel sermons they heard him preach in the past (vv. 1, 2). He then rehearses the three cardinal truths of the gospel: Christ's death, burial, and resurrection. The first two items receive only a brief mention (vv. 3, 4), but as a prelude to the theme of this chapter, the evidence of Christ's resurrection is summarized in several verses (5-8). At this point Paul is ready to take the fact of Christ's resurrection and demonstrate how it has relevance to our lives as Christians. He will not only clear up the doctrinal problem of the Corinthians regarding those who are dead, but he will also promote a sense of confidence and victory among those of us who are still alive.

But first, let us review the story of Christ's resurrection as presented in the twenty-fourth chapter of the Gospel of Luke.

DEVOTIONAL READING:
PHILIPPIANS 2:1-11

LESSON SCRIPTURE:
LUKE 24:1-11; 1 CORINTHIANS 15

PRINTED TEXT:
LUKE 24:1-11; 1 CORINTHIANS 15:12-17, 56-58

Apr
16

LESSON AIMS

When this lesson has been completed, the students should:

1. Experience a sense of excitement and joy in reflecting upon Christ's resurrection.

2. See the significance of Christ's resurrection to our religious faith and our eternal hope.

3. Have a spirit of confidence based on a knowledge of the victory Christ has already accomplished in our behalf.

KEY VERSE:

Stand firm. Let nothing move you. Always give yourselves fully to the work of the Lord, because you know that your labor in the Lord is not in vain.
—1 Corinthians 15:58

LESSON 7 NOTES

Display visual 7 as a reminder of the wonder and power of Christ's resurrection.

WHAT DO YOU THINK?

The women were looking for the living Lord among the dead—in a grave site. One might say the world is still looking for the living among the dead. They are looking for something—Someone—to fill the spiritual void in their lives, but they are looking at the material, the carnal, and the temporal. How can Christians point them to the living Lord?

Do you think it is true that, in some churches, a visitor might find himself looking for the living among the dead? If so, why? What would you suggest to correct the problem? Even if not, how can the problem be avoided?

I. FAITH IN CHRIST'S RESURRECTION (LUKE 24:1-11)

We who have been Christians for a long time may think it is easy for a person to believe in Jesus Christ. The Gospel of Luke reminds us that the beginning of faith can be a struggle.

A. THE EMPTY TOMB (vv. 1-3)

1. On the first day of the week, very early in the morning, the women took the spices they had prepared and went to the tomb.

Luke 23 describes the crucifixion of Jesus and tells of some women from Galilee who were loyal friends of Jesus. They followed Joseph of Arimathea to the tomb where he placed Jesus' body. Then they returned to their lodgings and prepared spices and ointments to embalm the body of Jesus. They could not return to the tomb on the day after the crucifixion because it was a Sabbath Day, and Jewish law would not permit them to attend to a burial on that day. They had to wait until Sunday, *the first day of the week.*

2. They found the stone rolled away from the tomb.

As they walked, the women were wondering whom they could find to move the heavy stone that Joseph of Arimathea had used to close the door of the tomb (Mark 16:3). The answer was provided by an angel who came with a great earthquake and moved the stone from its place (Matthew 28:2).

3. But when they entered, they did not find the body of the Lord Jesus.

The tomb presented perplexing clues for the women to consider. The stone was rolled away. The body of Jesus was gone, and in its place were the linens that had been wrapped around it when it was placed in the tomb Friday evening (John 20:6, 7).

B. THE WORD OF GOD (vv. 4-8)

4. While they were wondering about this, suddenly two men in clothes that gleamed like lightning stood beside them.

Matthew 28:5 confirms what the description in this verse suggests: the *two men in clothes that gleamed like lightning* were angels. Apparently they were not visible at first, but then they appeared.

5. In their fright the women bowed down with their faces to the ground, but the men said to them, "Why do you look for the living among the dead?

The women apparently came to the conclusion that these two men were angels. They reacted with the fear and awe that is common when angels appear. So did the shepherds of Bethlehem (Luke 2:9) and John on the island of Patmos (Revelation 22:8).

6. "He is not here; he has risen! Remember how he told you, while he was still with you in Galilee.

This is the first recorded announcement of Jesus' resurrection. As the angels pointed out, the news should have come as no surprise to anyone who had been a disciple of Jesus in Galilee. On at least three occasions he had predicted his death and resurrection (Matthew 16:21; 17:22, 23; 20:17-19).

Now consider the gentle rebuke given in the previous verse: "Why do you look for the living among the dead?" Had these women understood Jesus' teaching, they would not have been coming to his tomb to complete his burial. They would have been eagerly anticipating his return from the grave. The same rebuke was appropriate also for other disciples, and was delivered by Jesus himself in due time (Mark 16:14; Luke 24:25, 26).

7. "'The Son of Man must be delivered into the hands of sinful men, be crucified and on the third day be raised again.'"

Jesus' predictions of his death and resurrection were precise. He said he would be crucified in Jerusalem at the instigation of the Jewish religious leaders, and would rise on the third day following his death (Matthew 16:21; 17:22, 23; 20:17-19).

Sometimes we marvel that Jesus' disciples did not anticipate his resurrection, as if to say we would have done better. But Jesus often spoke in parables and figures of speech, and the disciples could easily have thought this talk of death and resurrection was some type of parable. They had always thought the Messiah would conquer and rule; they could not believe he would be killed by enemies. The angels were gracious in their rebuke, and we should not be too hard on the disciples.

8. Then they remembered his words.

Here we see illustrated a key step in the process of developing a faith in Jesus Christ. Faith begins with our focusing upon the Word of God. As Paul declares in Romans 10:17, "Faith comes from hearing the message, and the message is heard through the word of Christ."

Jesus had predicted his death and resurrection. When the angel directed the women back to his words, he was pointing them to the source of a true faith in the risen Savior. If we want to grow in our faith in Jesus Christ, we too need to focus upon the Word we have been given.

C. THE CHALLENGE OF FAITH (VV. 9-11)

9. When they came back from the tomb, they told all these things to the Eleven and to all the others.

The women reported their experience to a number of disciples of Jesus, including the apostles, who are now called *the Eleven* because Judas had hanged himself (Matthew 27:5).

10. It was Mary Magdalene, Joanna, Mary the mother of James, and the others with them who told this to the apostles.

Luke 8:2, 3 says many women in Galilee provided financial support and hospitality for Jesus during his ministry in that region. They began this after he healed them with his divine powers. Some of these women faithfully attended to him even after his death.

11. But they did not believe the women, because their words seemed to them like nonsense.

The men who had received the most training by Jesus were not prepared to accept the idea of his resurrection. For most of the disciples and apostles, faith did not come until they personally saw the risen Lord. At that point he rebuked them for their disbelief (Mark 16:14).

Is this to say there is little hope for modern man to be brought to faith in Jesus Christ, since we are twenty centuries removed from his personal appearances? Not at all. In the New Testament we have testimony from reliable eyewitnesses (1 Corinthians 15:5-8). Jesus anticipated that this testimony would lead many to believe in his resurrection, and he even promised a special blessing for those of us who arrive at faith without seeing the risen Lord (John 20:29-31).

WHO WON?

One of the world's decisive battles was fought on June 18, 1815, in Belgium, near a place named Waterloo. At one time during this conflict between the French, Prussians, Dutch, and British, fifty-seven thousand men lay dead, dying, or wounded within an area of three square miles. As everyone knows, the force under the Duke of Wellington defeated the famous Napoleon.

It is said, though I have not corroborated it, that an interesting incident occurred after the battle. A semaphore was set up to flash the news across the English Channel

WHAT DO YOU THINK?

Put yourself mentally into the place of Jesus' disciples. Feel their sense of expectancy, waiting for him to reveal himself as the Messiah. Share their perplexity because he did not. Experience the desperation that must have gripped them when Jesus was arrested and condemned to die. Identify with the heartbreak and desolation they knew after the crucifixion.

Now, some women have come claiming to have seen him alive! More and more evidence is mounting—is it true? Could he really be alive? Get caught up in the growing excitement as the reality of his resurrection becomes clearer.

Now why do you think the disciples were so energetic in their witness of the risen Lord? Do you sense the same excitement or energy in the modern church? If so, in what ways do you see it expressed? If not, why not? What do you think it will take to recover it?

We believe any inquirer who will, with an open mind, examine the evidence for the bodily resurrection of Jesus Christ will come to believe. We have a wide array of eyewitnesses who have testified to the event, including the skeptical Thomas and the scholarly Paul; the other apostles, who were all slow to believe; the several women who came to the tomb expecting it to be closed; and the remainder of the five hundred Paul mentioned in 1 Corinthians 15:6. Many of these witnesses endured suffering and death as a result of their testimony to a risen Christ. Second, the enemies of the gospel in the first century could not deny the resurrection or produce the body of Jesus. And the ingenious explanations advanced as alternatives to the actual resurrection do not take into account all the facts.

Then why do so many still not believe? Are their minds not open? Are we not providing them the evidence? Why? And what can we do to correct the situation? What can you do?

WHAT DO YOU THINK?

Based on verses 12-17 of our text, how would you answer a fellow church member who said, "I don't think it's really important whether Jesus rose from the dead or not. The important thing is that we live the way he taught us"?

to Britain. When the signal came, just two words were read between patches of drifting fog: "Wellington defeated." Anguish was intense in England. But that was not the full message. Two more words made it complete: "Wellington defeated the enemy."

So it was with Jesus' struggle with sin and death at Calvary. He was dead and laid in a tomb that was shut and sealed. But that was not the complete message. On the first day of the week, faithful women saw an angel of life and heard the message completed: "He has risen!" Jesus was not defeated! Instead, he had defeated the enemy.

—J. G. V. B.

II. HOPE FROM CHRIST'S RESURRECTION (1 CORINTHIANS 15:12-17)

Whether you are a twentieth-century modern thinker or a first-century disciple of Jesus, you are challenged to put your full confidence in the gospel of Jesus Christ. For those of us who come to faith, there is a great hope for the future.

A. THE BASIS FOR OUR PREACHING (VV. 12-15)

12. But if it is preached that Christ has been raised from the dead, how can some of you say that there is no resurrection of the dead?

This verse provides the first clue to the false idea that Paul is correcting in this chapter. Some at Corinth believe that a Christian who dies will remain in a state of death and not participate in the future blessings of Christ at his return. Their hope for the future lies in their remaining alive until the second coming.

Paul notes the fallacy of their thinking. On the one hand, these Christians apparently believe the fundamental truth that Christ rose from the grave on the third day. Yet, on the other hand, they say there is no such thing as resurrection from the dead. This is a contradiction, plain and simple.

13. If there is no resurrection of the dead, then not even Christ has been raised.

If there is no such thing as resurrection from the dead, then the logical conclusion is that Christ himself was not raised alive from the dead. This is in fact the view of many today who have adopted a "modern" approach to theology. They believe that the universe always operates by natural law without any breakthrough of supernatural activity. They discount the idea of creation, revelation, incarnation, miracles, and resurrection. In doing so they not only reject the concept of a future day of resurrection, but also the story of the resurrection of Christ from the grave.

14. And if Christ has not been raised, our preaching is useless and so is your faith.

The basic message we proclaim to the world is that Jesus Christ died for our sins and then rose from the grave (vv. 3-8). If that is not true, then it is a waste of time for us to preach the gospel. It would be foolish to pretend to deliver a serious message that you believe is nothing more than a religious fairy tale. To deny Christ's resurrection undermines our evangelistic witness and the whole vocation of preaching.

15. More than that, we are then found to be false witnesses about God, for we have testified about God that he raised Christ from the dead. But he did not raise him if in fact the dead are not raised.

Not only does a denial of Christ's resurrection make our preaching and witnessing a waste of time; it also calls into question our integrity. We are preaching a lie, if it is true that there are no resurrections from the dead. And we have spread this lie in the name of God and religion.

B. THE BASIS FOR OUR SALVATION (VV. 16, 17)

16. For if the dead are not raised, then Christ has not been raised either.

Paul repeats the logical implication he has drawn from the Corinthians' position; no resurrection of the dead, then no resurrection of Christ.

17. And if Christ has not been raised, your faith is futile; you are still in your sins.

You are still in your sins. This may be the most sobering statement Paul makes in his argument. If the resurrection of Christ is not a historical fact, then there was no forgiveness of sins accomplished at Calvary.

We understand that Christ died at Calvary as an atonement for our sins. That is to say he suffered on the cross in a way that was equivalent to the penalty we sinners deserved from God. So how does his resurrection relate to his work at Calvary? Some have reasoned that we would still be forgiven of our sins even if Christ had remained in the tomb, because forgiveness is based upon his death, not his resurrection. Our penalty has been paid and then some.

The problem with this idea is that the New Testament presents the resurrection of Christ as the crucial test of whether or not Christ accomplished what he set out to do at Calvary. Jesus claimed that his sacrificial death would be sufficient to appease God. He promised that God would raise him on the third day after his death as a public declaration that God had accepted his work in our behalf. Thus, if there is no resurrection on the third day, then God has not accepted Christ's death for our atonement. *If Christ has not been raised . . . you are still in your sins.*

But we celebrate the reality of our salvation because we believe in the reality of Christ's resurrection. As Paul proclaims in Romans 1:4, Jesus was "declared with power to be the Son of God by his resurrection from the dead."

"IF . . . NOT"

"If Christ has not been raised" has been called "the most potent negative supposition" that can be made about the Christian religion. The plan of redemption revolves around two great foci—the coming of Jesus into the world from the virgin's womb, and the coming of Jesus back into the world from the guarded tomb. Robert Browning speaks about Jesus' birth and resurrection together in a major poem, "Christmas-Eve and Easter-Day":

Earth breaks up, time drops away,
In flows Heaven, with its new day
Of endless life . . . .

Later Browning speaks of what Jesus' salvation means to us:

What is left for us, save, in growth
Of soul, to rise up, far past both,
From the gift looking to the giver,
And from the cistern to the river,
And from the finite to infinity,
And from man's dust to God's divinity?

In his poem he speaks of man's frustrations and failures, his doubts, denials, lapses, and losses. But beyond all these are God's great acts of redemption in his Son:

But, Easter-Day breaks! But Christ rises! Mercy every way is infinite,—and who can say?
—J. G. V. B.

III. VICTORY THROUGH CHRIST'S RESURRECTION (1 CORINTHIANS 15:56-58)

A. THE PROMISE OF VICTORY (vv. 56, 57)

Paul has demonstrated the fallacy of the idea that there will not be a day of resurrection in the future by showing its negative implication upon the resurrection of

---

WHAT DO YOU THINK?

Why do you think Paul concludes his discussion of the resurrection with an action step—"always give yourselves fully to the work of the Lord"? How is this an appropriate response to an appreciation of the resurrection?

How fully do you think he means? Attending every service? Doing a little volunteer work? Taking a vocational ministry? Just what do you think that means?

Do you think most Christians really give themselves fully to the Lord's work? Why or why not? Could a failure in this regard be one reason the world does not take our testimony of the Lord's resurrection seriously? Why or why not?

WHAT DO YOU THINK?

Much of what we do with our lives will not last. All the material elements in the world will one day perish (2 Peter 3:10). Whatever wealth we have accumulated will go to someone else. But our "labor in the Lord is not in vain." (See also 1 Corinthians 3:10-15.)

Why, then, does it seem we spend so much more time on the temporal things, working for material things, than we do in labor for the Lord? What do you think it would take to get more Christians to be active in the Lord's work?

PRAYER

Father, we thank you for the mighty work you displayed in raising up your Son Jesus Christ, and for the strength and hope that his resurrection brings to our daily lives. Amen.

THOUGHT TO REMEMBER

The resurrection of Christ is more than just an event in the past. It is the basis for our hope in the future.

DAILY BIBLE READINGS

Monday, Apr. 10—The First Easter (Luke 24:1-11)

Tuesday, Apr. 11—Paul's Witness to the Resurrection (1 Corinthians 15:1-11)

Wednesday, Apr. 12—Faith Is Futile Without the Resurrection (1 Corinthians 15:12-19)

Thursday, Apr. 13—We Are Made Alive in Christ (1 Corinthians 15:20-28)

Friday, Apr. 14—Resurrection of the Imperishable Body (1 Corinthians 15:35-44)

Saturday, Apr. 15—A Spiritual Inheritance (1 Corinthians 15:45-50)

Sunday, Apr. 16—Victory Through the Risen Christ (1 Corinthians 15:51-58)

Christ. Paul now concludes his argument by working in reverse. Our view regarding the resurrection of Christ likewise has an implication for the final resurrection. If Christ has been raised from the dead as he promised, then we have reason to believe that he will raise us from the dead as he promised.

56. The sting of death is sin, and the power of sin is the law.

Why does man die? Death is part of the curse that God placed upon creation when Adam and Eve first sinned (Genesis 2:17; 3:22-24). When the time came for us to take our place in God's creation, we did no better than Adam, for "all have sinned and fall short of the glory of God" (Romans 3:23). Our death is not just Adam's fault; it is something we deserve because we have chosen to sin. *The sting of death is sin* is another way of saying "the wages of sin is death" (Romans 6:23).

Why does sin produce such a severe penalty as death? Because *the power of sin is the law,* sin is a serious matter because it is a violation of the most serious law in the universe, the law of God. To disobey the will of the Creator is to deserve a severe penalty.

57. But thanks be to God! He gives us the victory through our Lord Jesus Christ.

No matter how depressing the reality of sin and death may seem, for the Christian there is great joy in our knowledge of the resurrection of Jesus Christ. Therein lies our hope for a deliverance from death in the future and an entrance into the eternal kingdom of God.

B. A LIFE OF VICTORY (V. 58)

58. Therefore, my dear brothers, stand firm. Let nothing move you. Always give yourselves fully to the work of the Lord, because you know that your labor in the Lord is not in vain.

Our resurrection hope is not just a dream for the future, but also a source of inspiration for the present. It motivates us to serve the Lord faithfully now as we await his ultimate gift of eternal life. It prompts us to face the joys and sorrows of life with a spirit of confidence and determination. It keeps within our hearts each day a spirit of rejoicing in the victory we have attained through our Lord Jesus Christ. It reassures us that our efforts in his behalf, however much they are opposed or ignored by the world, are significant after all.

CONCLUSION

One of the most loved portions of Handel's *Messiah* is the song "I Know That My Redeemer Liveth."

The words are taken from Job 19:25, 26 (*King James Version*): "I know that my Redeemer liveth, and that he shall stand at the latter day upon the earth: and though after my skin worms destroy this body, yet in my flesh shall I see God." The most amazing thing here is not what Handel was able to do with these words. The marvel is that Job ever said these words.

It is remarkable that, in the midst of his great suffering, Job could express such a positive statement about his future prospects. But even more remarkable is that Job had such a clear understanding of resurrection at this early stage of biblical history. Centuries before Christ would rise from the tomb, Job already spoke of his Redeemer being eternally alive. Long before Paul penned the words that would explain the significance of Christ's resurrection to us personally, Job expressed the idea that the hope for his future resurrection into the presence of God rested upon the fact that his Redeemer lived. What an inspiration and challenge this amazing man presents to us! May we join him in declaring with hope and confidence, "We know that our Redeemer lives."

Discovery Learning

This page contains an alternate lesson plan emphasizing learning activities. Classes desiring such student involvement will find these suggestions helpful. The next page is a reproducible activity page to further enhance discovery learning.

LEARNING GOALS

As a result of completing today's lesson, students will:

1. Be able to cite from the New Testament specific encounters that witness to the resurrection of Christ.

2. Be able to locate and refer others to biblical passages that declare the significance of Christ's resurrection to our Christian faith.

3. Defend their faith in Christ's resurrection.

INTO THE LESSON

Begin the session by asking, "What time do you normally have to get up in the morning?" Have people call out the times and jot them on the board. Call attention to who the early risers are. Then ask, "What time do you get up on your day off?" Comment that most of us enjoy sleeping a bit later on our day off, but that sometimes we have a special project that gets us out of bed even earlier on that day. Let students give examples of activities that may get them out of bed early on a holiday.

INTO THE WORD

Note that after Jesus' death, some women arose quite early to go to the tomb. Who were they? (v. 10). What was their purpose in going so early? (v. 1). State that we all know a great surprise awaited them: the body was gone. Ask who was there in its place, and what message the women received (vv. 4-8). Close this question and answer time by asking one final thing: Why did the apostles not believe the women when they returned with the good news? Point out that the Jews expected their Messiah to live and rule forever (Isaiah 9:6, 7). When Jesus died, they must have decided that he was not the Messiah after all.

Distribute paper and pencils to the students. Tell them that many others had unusual experiences relating to the resurrection of Christ. Ask them to list as many of these people and experiences as they can. When they finish, share these Scriptures with them and see if they can add to their lists. You may want to make photocopies of the matching game at the right. Let each student draw a line from each witness to the Scripture reference that tells of his experience.

Suggest that this information would be good to retain to share with skeptical friends who doubt the resurrection.

If you copy the matching game for the class, put the following exercise on the other side of the paper. Ask each student to complete each statement with information from 1 Corinthians 15:12-17 and 56-58.

1. Some in the church at Corinth were claiming that there is —

2. If it is true that no resurrection is possible, then —

3. If Christ was not raised from the dead, then Paul and the other apostles were —

4. If there is no resurrection of the dead, then people are still lost in —

5. The thing that gives death its terrible sting is —

6. Because we know the truth about the resurrection, we ought to give ourselves fully to —

Allow the students to share their answers.

Answers: 1—No resurrection of the dead. 2—Christ was not raised. 3—False witnesses. 4—Sin. 5—Sin. 6—The work of the Lord.

INTO LIFE

One week before presenting this lesson, appoint two people to work out a role play of this situation: Jack is a devout Christian who gives much of his money and time to the church. He is being attacked by his agnostic friend, Bill, for being overly committed and generous to a cause based on a dead hero and the myth of his resurrection. Have the two share the conversation that might transpire as Jack defends his faith. (Two women instead of two men may do this.)

Close by challenging each person to prepare his or her own defense of the resurrection.

Option: Use the activities from the reproducible page that follows to focus the students' attention on the significance of the resurrection and applying it to their lives.

Simon Peter	Acts 7:55, 56
Disciples going into country	Revelation 1:12-20
Eleven disciples	1 Corinthians 15:6
Seven disciples by Sea	Acts 9:3-6
Five hundred	1 Corinthians 15:7
James	John 21:1-23
Eleven disciples in Galilee	Matthew 28:16-20
Witnesses of ascension	Mark 16:12
Stephen at his martyrdom	Acts 1:3-9
Paul on road to Damascus	Luke 24:34
Apostle John	Mark 16:14

Focus on Christ's Resurrection

Jesus' resurrection is the central event of the Bible. That is the reason it is so important for Christians to know what they believe about the resurrection. This activity can be done with several others in your class or by yourself.

Prepare an outline for a speech or devotional about Jesus' resurrection. Try to include several main points, as well as some subpoints to support your main points. Choose from the following topics:

1. How Can I Be Sure of Jesus' Resurrection?
2. Why Is It Essential to Believe in Jesus' Resurrection?
3. What Practical Significance Does the Resurrection Have for My Life?

Use any passage of Scripture you want, but be sure to examine Luke 24:4-11; 1 Corinthians 15:1-17; 1 Peter 1:3-9.

Jesus' Resurrection and Me

What does Jesus' resurrection have to do with your life? How does it affect your thoughts, attitudes, choices, and conduct? How should it affect these? Reflect on how Jesus' victory over death affects your life and complete the following sentences:

If Jesus had not risen from the dead. . . .

Jesus' resurrection benefits my life right now by. . . .

If I were to focus on Jesus' resurrection each and every day, I could expect. . . .

Jesus' resurrection gives me this hope:

EXERCISING LIBERTY WISELY

LESSON 8

WHY TEACH THIS LESSON?

"It's a free country," we say, and usually what we mean by that is we are free to act as we please, even if the action we propose is not advisable. The fact of the matter is, our country does grant us more freedoms than we ought to exercise. It is legal to worship false gods (or no God at all), break promises (under certain conditions), and kill helpless babies (as long as they are still in the womb). Surely the Christian would know he or she is as free *not* to do such things as to do them!

Why, then, is it so hard for us to realize that our Christian liberty also frees us not to do certain things that are "legal." It was okay—legal, if you please—for Christians in Corinth to eat meat that had been part of a pagan sacrifice. But if, in so doing, they caused a fellow Christian to reverence the idol, they ought to have exercised their freedom not to eat.

Use this lesson to challenge your students to think beyond what is just okay, but to exercise their Christian liberty in such a way as to be a blessing to others.

INTRODUCTION

A. RESPONSIBLE FREEDOM

An old joke tells of a man just released from prison. He ran down the street, leaping for joy and yelling, "I'm free! I'm free!"

A little boy replied, "That's nothing, mister; I'm four!"

We hear about people released from imprisonment, slavery, or political tyranny; but most of us cannot identify with these situations. We can only imagine the excitement of being released from bondage. But when it comes to the freedom from sin and death that we enjoy through Jesus Christ, all of us Christians have personally experienced the excitement of being set free. Paul makes this freedom sound both exciting and challenging.

B. LESSON BACKGROUND

Apparently there was much disagreement in Corinth about the propriety of eating foods that had any association with the local idolatry. Some argued that it was simply a matter of conscience, while others contended that everyone should take the same position. In 1 Corinthians 8, Paul offers some insights on this subject.

But an even greater problem was the unloving way in which the Corinthians criticized those who reached ethical conclusions differing from their own. Corinth needed to learn the true nature of our liberty in Christ.

I. LIBERTY WITHOUT PRIDE (1 CORINTHIANS 8:1-3)

The spirit of pride and boasting was certainly a problem for the Corinthians in the area of spiritual gifts, as we noted in an earlier study. Now we discover that this attitude was present in other matters as well.

A. WITH A HUMBLE SPIRIT (VV. 1, 2)

1. Now about food sacrificed to idols: We know that we all possess knowledge. Knowledge puffs up, but love builds up.

DEVOTIONAL READING:
ROMANS 15:1-13
LESSON SCRIPTURE:
1 CORINTHIANS 8
PRINTED TEXT:
1 CORINTHIANS 8

Apr
23

LESSON AIMS

After this lesson the students should:

1. Evaluate their actions by New Testament teaching and make changes where appropriate.

2. Develop greater sensitivity to the impact of their actions upon other Christians.

3. Develop a spirit of conciliation that allows for differences among Christians who want to honor both God's Word and their conscience.

KEY VERSE:

Be careful, however, that the exercise of your freedom does not become a stumbling block to the weak.   —1 Corinthians 8:9

What Do You Think?

Paul says "knowledge puffs up." What kind of knowledge seems to you to puff certain Christians up today? Why do you think this happens? How should you respond to such people?

What kind of knowledge sometimes threatens to make you "puffed up"? How do you resist the temptation to be arrogant about what you know or achievements to your credit?

What Do You Think?

There is an increasing likelihood in our society that we are going to have contact with people who espouse a non-Christian religion. Many people from Oriental and Middle Eastern countries now live in our land. Their religions are similar to the idolatry practiced in Corinth in Paul's day—though not necessarily with the gross sexual rites performed in the first century.

Do you see anything in the advice Paul gave Christians who lived in a society full of such pagan worshipers that might help us to point our own pagan neighbors to Jesus Christ as the one Savior and Lord? If so, what?

We all possess knowledge. In 1 Corinthians, this is no compliment. The first chapter contrasts the so-called wisdom of the world with the simple truths of Jesus Christ. Though the gospel message appears as foolishness in the eyes of the world, Paul concludes that "the foolishness of God is wiser than man's wisdom" (1:25).

The second chapter contrasts Paul's simple preaching with the eloquence that many admire. Speaking of those who boast that they are wise and learned, chapter 3 calls them "infants in Christ," still limited to the "milk" of God's Word (3:1-3). Then Paul concludes by declaring, "If any one of you thinks he is wise by the standards of this age, he should become a 'fool' [that is, back away from the world's way of thinking] so that he may become wise. For the wisdom of this world is foolishness in God's sight (3:18, 19).

Then to say *we know that we all possess knowledge* is a bit of satire against those who are proud of their knowledge. Such an attitude *puffs up* a person and makes him arrogant.

The antidote for this prideful spirit is a dose of love and concern for others. As Paul declares quite eloquently in chapter 13, a spirit of love displaces arrogance and motivates us to relate to others in a gracious and considerate manner. Indeed, *love builds up;* it acts in a way that is beneficial to others.

2. The man who thinks he knows something does not yet know as he ought to know.

Paul repeats the conclusion that he reached in the first three chapters regarding the folly of man's pursuit of knowledge without a solid foundation in the Word of God.

Conceit

We all have been aware of people who are very "wise in their own eyes." It appears that such were some of Paul's critics and opponents. Some questioned his apostolic authority, and some denied essential doctrines of Christian faith. Perhaps worst of all was the way they affirmed their doubts and denials. They claimed to be more spiritual, more informed, more aware of mystic realities, than the ordinary Christian or even Paul himself.

They were like a group of balloons at a party. Colorful they were, and bouncing around in a splash of brightness. But there was nothing solid or sustaining about them. They were very unsubstantial—"puffed up," but not built up.

—J. G. V. B.

B. With a Devotion to God (v. 3)

3. But the man who loves God is known by God.

A genuine relationship with God is a far greater achievement than the world's knowledge and skills. God does not focus his attention upon those who excel in the eyes of the world, but upon those devoted to knowing him.

When dealing with bureaucracy and red tape, we sometimes say, "It's not what you know, but whom you know that counts." For a Christian who is seeking a real sense of satisfaction, the rule from this verse would be, "It's not whom you know, but who knows you."

II. LIBERTY WITHOUT GUILT (1 CORINTHIANS 8:4-8)

Two critics on TV refer to certain movies as their "guilty pleasures." They like these movies but are embarrassed to admit it because of their poor quality or objectionable content. The phrase "guilty pleasures" could well describe some of the things we Christians do. We think they are not really sinful, and yet we feel a little guilty. Paul shows us how to attain the clear conscience that we desire.

A. THROUGH KNOWING THE TRUTH (VV. 4-6)

4. So then, about eating food sacrificed to idols: We know that an idol is nothing at all in the world and that there is no God but one.

It was common practice to use only part of an animal as a sacrifice and then to sell the rest of the meat to the general public. In a pagan city like Corinth, virtually all of the meat sold in the marketplaces was first used in pagan sacrifices. Some in the church wondered if eating this "pagan meat" was proper.

Also troubling to Christians was the practice of blessing a meal with a prayer to a pagan deity. Though Christians would not say such a prayer in their own homes, they could not eat with non-Christian neighbors or participate in community meals without sitting through these pagan blessings. Was it better to withdraw further from the world and forfeit some opportunities for evangelism, or to sit through the prayers without an "amen" and appear to condone pagan activity?

The first thing Paul does to resolve this issue is to look for guidance in the basic truths of our faith. We know that our God is the only true deity. When dealing with difficult moral issues, the best place to begin is with the relevant truths we are given in God's Word. Not every ethical question is specifically answered in the Bible with clear rules to be followed, but when we have to make a judgment call, we can assume that the Bible will lay down general principles that will point us in the right direction.

5, 6. For even if there are so-called gods, whether in heaven or on earth (as indeed there are many "gods" and many "lords"), yet for us there is but one God, the Father, from whom all things came and for whom we live; and there is but one Lord, Jesus Christ, through whom all things came and through whom we live.

Residents of the Roman Empire recognized at least one hundred pagan gods and goddesses—and this is mild compared to the claims of Hinduism, which speaks of millions of deities. Nevertheless, as verse 4 declares, none of these so-called gods has any reality.

How do you know who is the real God in the midst of so many claimants? A key question is whether a particular "god" is created or uncreated. With this thought in mind, we can understand why Paul said it was disastrous for mankind to worship and serve "created things rather than the Creator" (Romans 1:25).

This matter of identifying God is so significant that Paul often links God to the work of creation. In this verse he refers to *God, the Father, from whom all things came,* and his Son *Jesus Christ, through whom all things came.* This basic truth indicates that pagan deities are not real entities.

So how does this information relate to the issue of meats sacrificed to pagan idols? Since pagan deities are not real, it is reasonable to conclude that they cannot contaminate the meat and make it inedible for Christians. This is Paul's own conclusion in 1 Timothy 4:4, where he says, "Everything God created is good, and nothing is to be rejected if it is received with thanksgiving." Those Christians in Corinth who felt free to eat meats purchased in the marketplace had made a proper judgment.

CONCEPTS

There were many so-called gods in the first century: Isis and Osiris of Egypt; the Persian deity Mithra; and many local divinities such as Athena, patron goddess of Athens, and Aphrodite or Venus, worshiped in Corinth. Then there was the God of the Jews.

Paul went back to the absolute essentials when he said that, after all, there was but one real God and one true Lord. Devotion to our heavenly Father and dedication to Jesus, his Son, is the vital reality of our faith as Christians.

WHAT DO YOU THINK?

When making a decision about participating in a certain activity, we may ask, "Is what I am about to do consistent with the Word of God?" (See the comments on verse 8.) This requires, of course, that we be thoroughly familiar with the moral principles of the Word of God.

Do you think most Christians have an adequate understanding of the moral precepts in the Bible to use this test? Why or why not? What can be done to equip new Christians and others who need help to deepen their understanding? What would help you deepen your own understanding?

WHAT DO YOU THINK?

When making a decision about participating in a certain activity, we may ask, "Does this in any way violate my conscience?"

Do you see any difference between this question and the one about whether the issue violates a principle of Scripture? If so, what? Why do you think a person's conscience might bother him or her about an issue that has no Scriptural prohibition? It might mean the conscience is overly sensitive, or it could be that one's Bible understanding is weak. How can you tell which is right? What is the proper response when you don't know which is the case?

WHAT DO YOU THINK?

A third test when making a decision about participating in a certain activity is, "Might this in any way violate the conscience of others who may see me participate?"

How important do you think it is to use this test? Would you recommend it as a general rule or only if you know someone will likely take offense? Why?

Paul makes the point that refraining from an acceptable activity is sometimes the right choice for the sake of another. Do you think there are times when refraining is not the right choice—even if a weaker brother is involved? That is, are there times when participating may help the weaker brother to become strong, to correct his wrong perception, rather than simply embolden him to violate his conscience? If so, name some examples. How would this strengthening take place?

HOW TO SAY IT

Aphrodite. AF-ruh-DITE-ee.

Apollos. Uh-PAW-lus.

Aquila. Uh-KWILL-uh or ACK-wih-luh.

Athena. Uh-THEE-nuh (th as in thin).

Isis. EYE-sis.

Mithra. MITH-ruh.

Osiris. Oh-SIGH-rus.

Priscilla Prih-SILL-uh.

Often in athletic contests the great need is seen to "get back to the fundamentals." In football all depends on blocking, tackling, running with, throwing, catching and holding onto the ball. In baseball it lies in hitting, catching, running, and throwing. In basketball it is in dribbling, passing, shooting, and rebounding. These are the continually repeated actions on which all the patterns and developments of the games rest.

Whatever matters there are of meeting place, time of gathering, symbolic acts performed, and speakers heard, the real question is, "Who is the real, true, living God, the Creator and Sustainer of all things? Who is the One above all others who has the right to claim our loyalty and trust?" The answer: God the Father, and our Lord Jesus Christ.

—J. G. V. B.

B. BY HEEDING OUR CONSCIENCE (vv. 7, 8)

7. But not everyone knows this. Some people are still so accustomed to idols that when they eat such food they think of it as having been sacrificed to an idol, and since their conscience is weak, it is defiled.

There was nothing wrong with the meat at Corinth, but not every Christian could eat it in good conscience. Some felt that they were doing wrong. Their feelings were wrong, their *conscience* was *weak;* nevertheless, that is how they felt. So Paul had to address the issue of what to do when your conscience is wrong.

God has given to every person a conscience that produces inner feelings when we make moral decisions. When we make bad decisions, our conscience should make us feel guilty. When we make good decisions, it should make us feel good. But reading the conscience is not always easy. When we play around with sin, we can so harden our hearts that we cannot clearly hear the warning signals of the conscience. And then there is the problem illustrated by some in Corinth. Sometimes we interfere with the working of the conscience by bringing in ideas and rules devised by man's imagination rather than the Word of God. The idea that a pagan idol could somehow contaminate meat was wrong. Those who accepted this idea were causing their conscience to accuse them wrongfully.

There is reason to be concerned when someone's conscience is *weak* and not operating properly. But it is worse when such a person goes ahead and does the thing for which he feels guilty. That person becomes *defiled* or spiritually corrupted.

When dealing with the same issue in Romans 14, Paul advises his readers not to violate their conscience when it gives a warning, even if their conscience is wrong. "The man who has doubts is condemned if he eats, because his eating is not from faith; and everything that does not come from faith is sin" (Romans 14:23).

8. But food does not bring us near to God; we are no worse if we do not eat, and no better if we do.

The question of pagan meats turned out to be a false issue. It was commendable that the members of the church were concerned about doing right. It was unfortunate that not everyone was able to find the best answer, and that some violated their conscience.

How can we determine whether or not to proceed with an activity we are considering? There seem to be two key tests. First, is what we are about to do consistent with the Word of God? This does not mean an activity must be approved by name in the Bible (though when that happens it is quite helpful). Since much of what we do is not specifically mentioned in Scripture, we need to consider whether there is some biblical truth or principle that seems to contradict the activity in question. If there is not, then we can reasonably assume that the action is consistent with God's Word.

The second test is to consider whether or not our conscience is setting off any alarms. This is a good thing for us. The conscience can provide a ready safeguard if we miss something in our consideration of biblical principles. But this chapter has also shown that the conscience can unnecessarily restrict us when we have weakened it. Nevertheless, if our conscience says no, then we should proceed no further.

Of course, you and I do not often have to determine whether or not to eat meat sacrificed to idols (and even if we did, we now know the correct answer). But consider some of the activities that we do have occasion to wonder about. Is it proper for a Christian to use tobacco or drink alcoholic beverages? Does it matter whether I choose caffeine or no caffeine, sugar or diet, salt or no salt, regular or low fat? Can a Christian listen to popular music (including rock and rap!) and enjoy modern dances? Can I watch movies and TV programs with all their wickedness as long as I do not consent to the immoral things that are said and done on the screen?

The apostle Paul's tests are just as valid with these issues as they were with pagan meats. We know that some of these activities look questionable in light of biblical principles, such as our responsibility to take good care of our bodies (1 Corinthians 6:12-20), and the challenge for us to devote our minds to things that are good and true (Philippians 4:8). The test of conscience also snags some of these activities. We ought to be suspicious when we are doing something that we would not want the rest of the church members to know about.

III. LIBERTY WITHOUT OFFENSE (1 CORINTHIANS 8:9-13)

Those who reasoned through the meat issue correctly may be thinking at this point that they are in the clear. But it is not necessarily so. A person with a "strong" conscience must take care not to hurt his friend who has a "weak" conscience.

A. BY NOT MISLEADING OTHERS (VV. 9, 10)

9. Be careful, however, that the exercise of your freedom does not become a stumbling block to the weak.

A *stumbling block* is just what it sounds like, an object lying in someone's path that causes him to trip. Paul's fuller discussion of the idea of a stumbling block is found in Romans 14. The warning he gives there is similar to that given in this verse: "Make up your mind not to put a stumbling block or obstacle in your brother's way" (Romans 14:13).

10. For if anyone with a weak conscience sees you who have this knowledge eating in an idol's temple, won't he be emboldened to eat what has been sacrificed to idols?

Paul's warning about *eating in an idol's temple* does not necessarily mean that some Christians were participating in pagan worship services. In Corinth and other pagan cities, civic and social functions often were held in rooms or porches of pagan temples. The temples served as public shelters for any community meeting.

Some of the Christians who mistakenly thought pagan meats are bad were eating those meats anyway because they saw the more mature Christians doing it. These weaker Christians were trying to rethink their position, but their conscience was still telling them they were doing wrong. Thus, they ended up violating their conscience, contrary to Paul's teaching above—and the example of stronger Christians caused them to do it.

The stumbling block warning is usually given to strong Christians, not to those who are weak. A weaker Christian rarely becomes a stumbling block, for a mature Christian is not likely to follow the example of one less experienced. However, an immature Christian does often follow the lead of those he considers more advanced, and therefore the stronger needs to consider where he is leading his friend.

B. BY CONSIDERING CHRIST'S CAUSE (VV. 11, 12)

11. So this weak brother, for whom Christ died, is destroyed by your knowledge.

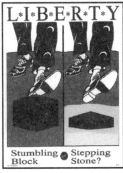

L*I*B*E*R*T*Y

Stumbling ● Stepping
Block ● Stone?

Visual 8 of the visuals packet suggests two ways of exercising Christian liberty. Display it as you come to verse 9.

WHAT DO YOU THINK?

This lesson came about because of a disagreement among the believers in Corinth. Disagreements in the church may be inevitable. What general principles can you suggest from this passage that will help us learn to disagree in a gracious and tactful manner? Perhaps the example of the Christian couple Priscilla and Aquila, in the way they dealt with the inadequately informed Apollos, may also help. See Acts 18:24-28.

PRAYER

Father, help us to be faithful to the teaching of your Word and the guidance of our conscience, and to be gracious toward those with whom we disagree. In Jesus' name we pray. Amen.

THOUGHT TO REMEMBER

It is hard to praise a person for being right on an issue when his manner of being right is all wrong.

DAILY BIBLE READINGS

Monday, Apr. 17—Avoid Disputes Over Opinions (Romans 14:1-9)

Tuesday, Apr. 18—Refrain From Passing Judgment (Romans 14:10-18)

Wednesday, Apr. 19—Seek Peace and Mutuality (Romans 14:19-23)

Thursday, Apr. 20—Bear With the Weak (Romans 15:1-6)

Friday, Apr. 21—Receive One Another in Christ (Romans 15: 7-13)

Saturday, Apr. 22—Love, Not Knowledge, Aids Christian Growth (1 Corinthians 8:1-6)

Sunday, Apr. 23—Use One's Christian Liberty With Care (1 Corinthians 8:7-13)

If the weaker Christian is getting mixed signals from his conscience, one might be inclined to say, "Well, that is his problem." But Paul recommends a more considerate view. Considering how precious this individual is to Christ, we ought to be very concerned about what he does to hurt himself, even if it is his fault.

12. When you sin against your brothers in this way and wound their weak conscience, you sin against Christ.

The weaker Christian sins when he disregards his conscience (Romans 14:22, 23). But likewise, the stronger Christian is wrong when he encourages his friend to violate his conscience (Romans 14:22, 23). One who is committed to Christ does not want to do anything that displeases his Lord.

C. BY BEING WILLING TO ADAPT (v. 13)

13. Therefore, if what I eat causes my brother to fall into sin, I will never eat meat again, so that I will not cause him to fall.

Paul's personal resolution for dealing with the stumbling block issue is plain: stop doing whatever is leading a fellow Christian into sin.

This is a difficult idea for most of us. It does not seem fair for a weaker Christian, who is thinking wrong on an issue, to dictate what mature Christians can do. But consider the following observations.

For one thing, weaker Christians do not have the right to require that other Christians make concessions to them. Weaker Christians are instructed in Romans 14:2-6 not to make an issue out of differences of opinion and conscience. If the mature make any concessions, it should be done voluntarily, as Paul illustrates in this verse.

Furthermore, the stumbling block principle seems to refer only to those situations where the weaker Christian actually follows our example in opposition to his conscience. It does not encompass those who simply choose to criticize our actions. We do not lead them to violate their conscience, and so what we do is not a true stumbling block. Their criticism violates Paul's instructions to keep such judgment to themselves (Romans 14:3-6).

While a mature Christian need not concern himself about the unjustified sniping of others, he does want to do whatever he can within reason to keep from encouraging someone else to sin.

CONCLUSION

Numbers 12:3 (*King James Version*) says that "Moses was very meek, above all the men which were upon the face of the earth." In the western world we often think of meekness as a characteristic of someone who is weak and unwilling to stand up for himself and for his convictions. Not so with Moses.

Moses was indeed a man of power and determination. He stood before Pharaoh and faced him down in a duel of wits and nerve. He stood before the people of Israel and served as their leader and judge. He stood before the presence of God on Mount Sinai and received from God the law that he would later be responsible for enforcing in Israel. Moses was anything but weak and passive, and yet he was considered the meekest man on earth.

Moses had developed a style of conduct and leadership that allowed him to carry out his responsibilities and stand for his convictions in a way that impressed others favorably.

This is the impression we desire to leave with other Christians when we are discussing our differences of opinion. Our goal should be not only to be correct in our doctrinal and ethical thinking, but also to be considerate in the way we address our truth to others.

Discovery Learning

This page contains an alternate lesson plan emphasizing learning activities. Classes desiring such student involvement will find these suggestions helpful. The next page is a reproducible activity page to further enhance discovery learning.

INTO THE LESSON

Write the following sentence on the chalkboard:

Love God and do as you please.

Explain that these words were written by Augustine, one of the great early church fathers. Ask the students whether they agree or disagree. After hearing their opinions, tell them that 1 Corinthians 8 deals with the issue of using liberty wisely, which is closely akin to the words on the board. Ask them to be watching for verses that apply to the above statement.

INTO THE WORD

Tell about the issue of meat offered to idols and the problem it created at Corinth. (See the "Lesson Background.") Give each class member a sheet of paper that has been divided into two columns with suggested Scriptures on each. Label one column "love" and the other "knowledge." Ask people to write phrases in each column to describe the actions and results pointed out in the suggested verses.

KNOWLEDGE
v. 1 Puffs up.
v. 2 Is incomplete at best.
v. 4 An idol is nothing.
v. 4 There is only one God.
v. 11 Weaker brother can be destroyed by it.

LOVE
v. 1 Builds up.
v. 3 God knows the one who loves.
v. 11 Refuses to ruin the weaker brother.
v. 12 Cares more about the weaker brother than about exercising his own freedom.

After the paper study is completed, share answers and then point out that the Corinthians had focused on knowledge and forgotten love.

Suggest that other passages reinforce the emphasis upon loving others. Let these verses be read aloud: Ephesians 4:15; John 13:35; Romans 13:10; Ephesians 4:1, 2; Matthew 22:39.

Return to the agree/disagree statement and ask what ideas students have now. Remember Matthew 22:37-39.

If we love God we will keep his commandments, and that will be what pleases us (1 John 5:3). Chief among his commandments is that we love one another.

Use the word *conscience* to make an acrostic. Let students make short statements about the conscience. Some possible ideas are:

C alls out to us when we do wrong
O nly contains what it is taught
N ot always to be your guide
S eeks the good of the individual
C an be ineffective if wrongly taught
I t can be used by the Holy Spirit
E xhorts us to do right
N ot the same in all individuals
C an be silenced if ignored
E nergizes, encourages.

Remind the class that being "right" is not the only thing we have to think about. A Christian's love should control his behavior.

Use the following diagram to summarize the lesson:

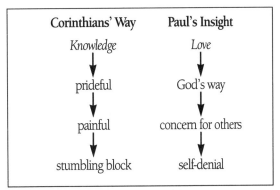

Corinthians' Way	Paul's Insight
Knowledge	*Love*
↓	↓
prideful	God's way
↓	↓
painful	concern for others
↓	↓
stumbling block	self-denial

Discuss: Why must the stronger believer defer to the weaker? Is there ever a limit to this deferring? (The stronger defers to keep the weaker from falling and to help him grow and mature. The limit comes when the weaker demands pampering and makes unreasonable demands.)

INTO LIFE

Draw several square blocks on the board and ask the class to suggest some issues in the 90s that might be considered stumbling blocks. Close with prayer focusing on growing in love.

In Opinions, Liberty

Look at the practices named below. These are practices on which not all Christians agree. Some are specifically addressed in Scripture; some are not. Read each one and try to determine whether it is directly addressed in Scripture. If so, write an "S" (for Scripture) in front of it. If it is not, write an "O" (for Opinion) in front of it.

If you indicate the practice is addressed in Scripture, try to identify where it is mentioned. Write the reference if you know it or can find it.

___ Baptism by immersion

___ Clapping hands in a worship service

___ Drinking alcoholic beverages

___ Gambling

___ Having a Sunday evening worship service

___ Having elders and deacons in a church

___ Praying with eyes open

___ Singing rock music in a worship service

___ Speaking in tongues

___ Using drama in a worship service

___ Watching movies

___ Women working outside the home

___ Baptism of infants

___ Dancing

___ Drinking caffeinated beverages

___ Having a Saturday evening worship service

___ Having a Wednesday prayer meeting

___ Listening to rock music

___ Raising hands in a worship service

___ Smoking

___ Taking the Lord's Supper every Sunday

___ Using musical instruments in a worship service

___ Women serving the Lord's Supper

Compare your results with another person. Do you agree on every point? Why or why not? How will you respond to differences? What if the other person cites Scripture on a certain point, but you feel it is misapplied? Is that a problem? If so, describe the nature of the problem. If not, why not?

In All Things Love

How would you respond to someone who has a different view from your own? Consider the following situations:

If the issue is clearly explained in Scripture, how do you respond to someone who does not agree with you? How do you uphold the Scriptures without becoming unloving toward the other person? Are there some Scripturally addressed issues you would treat differently from others? If so, why? How?

If the issue is not directly addressed in Scripture, but you believe the pertinent principles are clearly described in Scripture, do you respond differently from the situation above? Why or why not? How do you show love while still disagreeing?

If the issue is not really addressed in Scripture, but is basically a matter of personal preference, how do you show love to someone whose preferences are different from your own?

CARING FOR ONE ANOTHER

LESSON 9

WHY TEACH THIS LESSON?

If you polled your class for pain and suffering, you might be surprised at the depth of pain some of your students are carrying. Some are estranged from their parents or from prodigal children. Some have endured abuse at the hands of those who should have loved them. Others have chronic illness or are on the brink of financial ruin.

Add to this the fact that our faith puts us out of step with society, and there is potential for enormous suffering. Encourage your students to look to their brothers and sisters in Christ to find relief. And encourage them to be sources of relief, comforting others with the comfort they have received from God (v. 4).

INTRODUCTION

A. YOU CAN'T HIDE

Suffering and sorrow are woven into the fabric of life. We can close our eyes to the news of disasters and famines, of criminal assault and unfortunate accidents. We can avoid those sections of town where we are likely to encounter poverty. Yet, suffering still finds us as it touches those we love and cherish, or takes its toll on our own physical health. We need to learn how to deal properly with suffering.

B. LESSON BACKGROUND

Paul's first letter to Corinth must have been difficult for him to write. We often refer to it as "the sorrowful epistle" because the Corinthians were made sorrowful by its rebukes (2 Corinthians 7:8-11).

Paul's second letter to Corinth is more uplifting. According to Titus's first-hand report, things still are not perfect in the church, but they are improving. Especially encouraging to the apostle is the news that his friends in Corinth still love him despite his criticisms (2 Corinthians 7: 6, 7).

In light of all this, it is appropriate that 2 Corinthians deals with the theme of comfort. After agonizing within himself at having to write such a stern first letter, Paul enjoys the comfort of hearing good news from Titus. After being called to task in the first letter for their childish behavior (see 1 Corinthians 3:1), the Corinthians need a letter to comfort them with words of kindness and love. Chapter 1 not only describes the nature of comfort; it also brings comfort both to Paul and to his friends in Corinth.

I. COMFORT FROM SUFFERING (2 CORINTHIANS 1:3-7)

We readily echo the words of Hebrews 12:11: "No discipline [suffering] seems pleasant at the time, but painful." But the second half of the verse is harder to appreciate: "Later on, however, it produces a harvest of righteousness and peace for those who have been trained by it." The following verses from 2 Corinthians likewise emphasize the benefits that derive from suffering.

A. AS A GIFT FROM GOD (VV. 3, 4)

3. Praise be to the God and Father of our Lord Jesus Christ, the Father of compassion and the God of all comfort.

DEVOTIONAL READING:
GALATIANS 6:1-10
LESSON SCRIPTURE:
2 CORINTHIANS 1:1-14
PRINTED TEXT:
2 CORINTHIANS 1:3-14

LESSONS AIMS

After this lesson the students should:

1. Suggest some reasons God allows good people to suffer.

2. See the need to be a care-provider for Christian friends when they are suffering.

3. Determine to pray when others ask for prayer for their needs.

Apr
30

KEY VERSE:

Praise be to the God and Father of our Lord Jesus Christ . . . who comforts us in all our troubles, so that we can comfort those in any trouble with the comfort we ourselves have received from God.
—2 Corinthians 1:3,4

LESSON 9 NOTES

A positive aspect of personal suffering is carried by visual 9 of the visuals packet. It illustrates verses 3 and 4 of the text.

There are many qualities of God that deserve our praise: his power, wisdom, holiness, faithfulness, justice, love, and so forth. Each one has relevance to our lives; each one contributes to our well-being. We especially enjoy celebrating God's mercy, comfort, and compassion.

To have *compassion* is to feel sad when others are grieving, to wish for relief. But there is more. As illustrated in the life of Jesus, compassion involves more than just feeling. Compassion leads one to do something to alleviate the hurt. Often the Gospels note that Jesus was "filled with compassion" as he looked at the people who surrounded him, and then he would heal them or feed them with bread and fish. God does not simply watch us suffer, but he acts in our behalf.

4. . . . who comforts us in all our troubles, so that we can comfort those in any trouble with the comfort we ourselves have received from God.

The Greek word translated *comfort* literally means to be called to one's side to help and support him. This brings to mind those occasions when we visit a friend in the hospital or speak to a family at a funeral home. The important thing is not what we say, but the fact that we are there, that we care enough to be around, and wait, and listen. This picture does not exhaust the full meaning of how God *comforts us,* but it is true that his caring presence is often felt by those who trust in him.

Why do we have to put up with *our troubles?* Why do God's people have to suffer? One answer is given in Hebrews 12. Suffering is a tool used by God to discipline his children. The hardships of life toughen us and force us to grow in faith and perseverance. Discipline is never pleasant at the time, but as we mature we learn to appreciate the correction of our earthly parents and our heavenly Father.

Verse 4 of our text suggests another reason why God's people sometimes suffer. We learn how to deal with pain and grief through the aid of Christian friends and the ever-present peace of God. Then God expects us to take what we have learned and share it with others, *so that we can comfort those in any trouble with the comfort we ourselves have received from God.*

WHAT DO YOU THINK?

Paul describes God as "the Father of compassion and the God of all comfort" (2 Corinthians 1:3). The word compassion *means to "feel with" another. The word for* comfort *carries the idea of being "called alongside" another to give aid.*

What emotional support does picturing God as "feeling with us" our pain and "calling us to his side" provide for you? How can we comfort others with the same sort of comfort? Cite some specific examples.

OPTION

Use the reproducible activity, "Getting a Grip on Suffering" on page 308 to lead your students in a study of why God may sometimes allow suffering.

TRUE COMFORT

We find the word *comfort,* in some form, five times in the third and fourth verses of 2 Corinthians. These verses are dear to us because we face many times of grief, anxiety, and loss. "The comfort we ourselves have received from God" is a reality blessed and beautiful. This is what the following poem expresses:

The furrow on the brow of care,
The mind near yielding to despair;
The hollow gulf of lonely days
The future holds, in all its ways;
The sense of emptiness and grief,
The constant weight, with scant relief—

To these, what balm sweet comfort brings,
To soothe our wounds, and give us wings
With which to rise o'er darksome things;
To change the bitter and the sour
With sense of purpose and of power.
The love of God, the grace of Christ
Have blessed sad lives, and have sufficed
To tinge with glory all the gloom,
When his way and his Word have room.
　　　　　　　　　　　—James G. Van Buren

　　　　　　　　　　　　　　　—J. G. V. B.

B. AS A SHARING WITH CHRIST (V. 5)

5. For just as the sufferings of Christ flow over into our lives, so also through Christ our comfort overflows.

In Philippians 3:10 Paul makes the strange statement that he wants to know Christ, "and the power of his resurrection, and the fellowship of sharing in his sufferings." This is not an irrational impulse to seek out harassment and persecution. Paul simply wants to be an active part of the Christian experience. Jesus had taught his disciples, "If they have persecuted me, they will persecute you also" (John 15:20). We are not to look for trouble; but we are to expect it, knowing that it is a common experience for us who are committed to Christ to have *the sufferings of Christ flow over into our lives.*

The good news in all of this is that our sharing with Christ in suffering brings with it a sharing in the peace and comfort that he abundantly supplies to his friends. Restating his earlier emphasis upon God as the source of compassion and comfort, Paul declares that *through Christ our comfort overflows.*

C. AS A BLESSING FOR OTHERS (VV. 6, 7)

6. If we are distressed, it is for your comfort and salvation; if we are comforted, it is for your comfort, which produces in you patient endurance of the same sufferings we suffer.

This is another way of expressing the idea from verse 4: Christians are expected to use their sufferings to help them help others who are suffering. Our insights can used to help our friends be strong and remain faithful to God as they are hurting.

Consider how Paul uses this concept to help himself in times of trouble. He says, *If we are distressed, it is for your comfort and salvation.* Apparently he toughens his mind and emotions in the midst of suffering by telling himself that this is a part of his training for helping his friends. We can benefit by following Paul's example, by developing a positive attitude that will lessen the pain we are feeling.

7. And our hope for you is firm, because we know that just as you share in our sufferings, so also you share in our comfort.

And our hope for you is firm. Paul is serious about this mutual sharing of suffering and comfort. These are not simply nice-sounding words, but Paul is practicing what he is preaching by writing this letter of consolation as a follow-up to his "sorrowful letter." He does care about the feelings of his friends in Corinth.

How serious are we about bringing comfort and relief to our Christian friends who are hurting? Are we listening as needs are expressed in our fellowship gatherings, and then remembering to pray? Are we taking the time to call our friends and check up on their progress, or to visit in their homes, in the hospital, and at the funeral home? Are we contributing funds and physical assistance when needed? When we do these things, we are truly serving as agents of comfort for our brothers and sisters, just as "the Father of compassion and . . . comfort" has done for us.

II. DELIVERANCE BY PRAYER (2 CORINTHIANS 1:8-11)

Paul has been through hurt, time and time again. He preached for the church at Corinth for a year and a half (Acts 18:11), and doubtless he had told about some of his difficulties. Now Paul gives a brief reminder of his own hardships, and of the relief that God always provided.

A. PAUL'S EARLIER TROUBLES (VV. 8, 9)

8. We do not want you to be uninformed, brothers, about the hardships we suffered in the province of Asia. We were under great pressure, far beyond our ability to endure, so that we despaired even of life.

WHAT DO YOU THINK?

One reason we encounter suffering is that it is a means by which God disciplines and trains us. Unfortunately, the natural tendency during sufferings is to complain and to give in to an attitude of mourning. How can one keep a positive attitude during times of trouble so that they produce a "harvest of righteousness and peace" (Hebrews 12:11)? What kind of preparation must one have before times of trouble so that they produce this result? (See Hebrews 12:1-13.)

How has suffering produced growth in your life? How were you able to grow from and not give in to the trouble?

WHAT DO YOU THINK?

Another reason we encounter suffering is that it equips us to appreciate and minister to the sufferings of others. If nothing else, having been through similar troubles gives us credibility when we speak to someone who is suffering. We can also recall our own feelings while we were dealing with the troubles and be sensitive to those feelings in another, remember the kind of advice we received that came across as mere platitudes, and the Scriptures that especially helped us. And we are better able to pray for them.

Which of these aspects do you find most beneficial in trying to help another who is suffering? Why? Which is most beneficial in someone who attempts to comfort you? Why?

Do you think looking at troubles as equipping us to minister to others might help us to endure the trouble itself, or is that a realization that dawns on us later? Why do you think so?

OPTION

Use the reproducible activity, "Suffering and You" on page 308 to lead your students in a study of how to respond to suffering.

Across the Aegean Sea from Corinth is the Roman province called Asia, where Paul recently was the focus of a city-wide riot (Acts 19:23-41). He may have faced other dangers (1 Corinthians 15:32). In 2 Corinthians 11:24-27 he lists some more of his troubles: "Five times I received from the Jews the forty lashes minus one. Three times I was beaten with rods, once was I stoned, three times I was shipwrecked, I spent a night and a day in the open sea, I have been constantly on the move. I have been in danger from rivers, in danger from bandits, in danger from my own countrymen, in danger from Gentiles; in danger in the city, in danger in the country, in danger at sea, in danger from false brothers. I have labored and toiled and have gone without sleep; I have known hunger and thirst and have often gone without food; I have been cold and naked." With a history like this, we understand why Paul says he sometimes felt tremendous *pressure*.

9. Indeed, in our hearts we felt the sentence of death. But this happened that we might not rely on ourselves but on God, who raises the dead.

In our day Paul might say, "I felt like I was on death row." As he declares in the previous verse, there were times when things got so tough that he "despaired even of life." He thought he actually was about to die.

Why did this great servant of God have to live through such anxiety that he feared for his life? So that he and his companions might learn not to trust in themselves, *but on God, who raises the dead.* We human beings are by nature self-reliant, thinking we can handle any situation that comes our way. God uses trials and tribulations to humble us and force us to look beyond ourselves and seek out his divine assistance. When we reach the end of our rope, we finally realize what we should have been doing all along: that is, looking to God for strength and guidance and deliverance.

SENTENCE OF DEATH

Paul is telling the Corinthians about his problems and perplexities. These were not just physical dangers, but also emotional and mental tensions. In his heart, he said, he "felt the sentence of death" (v. 9).

How many times we find ourselves in similar situations! We go to a hospital for tests to determine if we have cancer or some other deadly disease. Often we become very despondent even before we learn the results. We feel in our hearts a "sentence of death." Sometimes this feeling comes when someone we love is wheeled into an operating room for major surgery. We are apprehensive and anxious. Sometimes we are concerned as friends or relatives are coming on a long highway through sleet, snow, fog, or heavy thunderstorms.

How exhilarating it is when all our dire forebodings are found to be in error. So it is with Paul. He has faced death, and God has delivered him (v. 10).

May our trust in God grow as we realize that whatever the "sentence of death" seems to be, there is one who can repeal the sentence and give us, as he gave Paul, new hope, new help, and new horizons of benefit and blessing.

—J. G. V. B.

B. GOD'S GRACIOUS RESPONSE (v. 10)

10. He has delivered us from such a deadly peril, and he will deliver us. On him we have set our hope that he will continue to deliver us.

Past, present, and future. Paul has already experienced God's ability to help him through difficult times. He feels that he is enjoying a little bit of God's comfort in his current situation (of which we know little). And he believes there will yet be other occasions for the hand of God to assist him in times of trouble. What a well-rounded picture of the work of God!

The value of reflecting upon past comfort is well expressed by Johnson Oatman, Jr. in the words of his hymn "Count Your Blessings":

> When upon life's billows you are tempest-tossed,
> When you are discouraged, thinking all is lost,
> Count your many blessings, name them one by one,
> And it will surprise you what the Lord hath done.

When we proceed with this exercise, we do find a reason for encouragement, a reason for believing that God does care for us as individuals. We develop a confidence that God will continue to deliver us.

Of course, we know there came a day when life ended for Paul. Church tradition says that he was beheaded during the persecution of Nero. Does this mean Paul's hope in God's future deliverance finally played out? Not at all. Even in death there is deliverance for God's people: he takes us home to live with him eternally. (See Psalm 23:6).

C. CORINTH'S SUPPORTIVE PRAYER (v. 11)

11. . . . as you help us by your prayers. Then many will give thanks on our behalf for the gracious favor granted us in answer to the prayers of many.

Why did God grant Paul the compassion, comfort, and deliverance that he experienced during his troubles? Partly because of the prayers of Paul's friends in Corinth. Paul tells the Corinthians of the report he had received from Titus regarding "your longing for me, your deep sorrow, your ardent concern for me" (2 Corinthians 7:7). Paul credits the prayers of this church (along with the prayers of other friends) for bringing the relief he is now enjoying.

This serves as a reminder of how important prayer is in times of trouble, prayer not only for ourselves, but also for those we care about. We hear the needs of our friends as they are mentioned in public prayers in our church gatherings, and we give our silent assent. But do we remember to follow up with the same concerns in our private prayers throughout the week? When our assemblies are dismissed, we do well to take our prayer lists home and mention some of our church concerns throughout the week. If we do this, we will not only grow in a spirit of compassion and comfort, but will also be agents that bring relief from God for our friends.

III. JOY IN FRIENDS (2 CORINTHIANS 1:12-14)

"A friend in need is a friend indeed." In times of trouble we begin to see who our real friends are. We also see the great value in developing friendships, as we observe our friends ministering to our needs. It is fitting to close our study with a word of appreciation for friends.

A. AN HONEST RELATIONSHIP (vv. 12, 13)

12. Now this is our boast: Our conscience testifies that we have conducted ourselves in the world, and especially in our relations with you, in the holiness and sincerity that are from God. We have done so not according to worldly wisdom but according to God's grace.

Paul has treated his friends at Corinth with *holiness* and *sincerity*. Paul declares that he has been fair and played by the rules of God. He has never been deceitful, but has always spoken with *sincerity*. This statement is in harmony with the testimony of *our conscience*: that is, Paul can say this with a clear conscience.

Paul's behavior is in contrast to the way people of the world often treat their acquaintances, as they operate by the rules of *worldly wisdom*. Such worldly aphorisms

WHAT DO YOU THINK?

Many churches publish a weekly prayer list. One wonders, however, just how much prayer is actually offered for the people listed. What can you do to make a prayer list a more effective tool for encouraging prayer?

WHAT DO YOU THINK?

Paul said he had a clear conscience because he had conducted himself "in the holiness and sincerity that are from God." We have seen too many examples of prominent Christian leaders conducting themselves by a much lower standard—to the shame of the church and the detriment of the gospel.

What temptations are present to draw church leaders away from this standard? What can you do to encourage holiness and sincerity in your leaders?

WHAT DO YOU THINK?

Paul contrasted "worldly wisdom" to "God's grace" in verse 12. We might have expected him to say "God's wisdom" in parallel with the "world's wisdom," and consistent with his argument in 1 Corinthians 1–3. What significance do you see in his choice of the word grace instead of wisdom? What does that suggest to you about how we today can resist following the ways of "worldly wisdom"?

PRAYER

Father, continue to grant us your comfort and peace when we are feeling the hurts that life brings our way, and then remind us to share that divine comfort with our friends when they are in need. In Jesus' name. Amen.

THOUGHT TO REMEMBER

If it is truly "more blessed to give than to receive" (Acts 20:35), then we who have received comfort from the hand of God should be giving it away as much as we can.

WHAT DO YOU THINK?

Paul expected to "boast" of the Corinthians "in the day of Christ." Apparently, he had great expectations for them!

Too often, it seems that we today do not look for the best in or expect the best from our fellow Christians. Why do you think that is? How can we develop the habit of doing that?

DAILY BIBLE READINGS

Monday, Apr. 24—Sharing Both Suffering and Comfort (2 Corinthians 1:1-7)

Tuesday, Apr. 25—A Request for Prayer (2 Corinthians 1:8-14)

Wednesday, Apr. 26—Thankfulness for Faithful Christians (Romans 1:8-15)

Thursday, Apr. 27—Give Support to One Another (Galatians 6:1-5)

Friday, Apr. 28—Persevere in Doing Good (Galatians 6:6-10)

Saturday, Apr. 29—Be Kind to One Another (Ephesians 4:25-32)

Sunday, Apr. 30—Active Caring for a Friend (Mark 2:1-5)

as "do unto others before they have a chance to stick it to you" are far removed from the way Paul treated his friends.

SINCERE PREACHING

Paul asserts he has conducted his Christian work among the Corinthians "in the holiness and sincerity that are from God."

Our English word *sincere* seems to be derived from two Latin words: *sin*, meaning *without*, and *cera*, meaning *wax*. The background of this term is explained in at least two ways. Some say it refers to honey on the Roman market. Sometimes a large amount of wax was mixed with the honey, so pure honey was labeled "without wax."

A second explanation is that sometimes pottery was cracked before sale. The cracks would be filled with wax and touched up so they would not show. Pottery "without wax" was undamaged.

Many times something is presented as "gospel preaching" when it is not "without wax." The Christian gospel is not a plea for democracy, or a more just social order, or the liberation of women, or kindness to children. Such concerns have a valid place in Christian thinking, but the good news of God is that Christ died for our sins and rose again from the grave (1 Corinthians 15:3, 4), and that eternal life is for those who believe in him (John 20:31). To proclaim this is to preach in *sincerity that is from God.*

—J. G. V. B.

13a. For we do not write you anything you cannot read or understand.

The Christians at Corinth know Paul so well that they themselves can testify to the truth of what he says in verse 12. They can recall what they observed during his ministry with them. Also they have his letters, by which they can judge what kind of attitude he has.

B. A MUTUAL RESPECT (v. 14)

13b, 14. And I hope that, as you have understood us in part, you will come to understand fully that you can boast of us just as we will boast of you in the day of the Lord Jesus.

In their zeal for their favorites, some of the Corinthians belittle or criticize Paul. He says he should not have to defend himself to them. On the contrary, they should be proud of him and of what he has done in their behalf. The fact that he led them to Christ is evidence that he is a good minister of the Master (2 Corinthians 3:1-3). *In the day of the Lord Jesus,* the day when Christ comes to claim his own, Paul's *boast* will be in those—like the Corinthians—whom he has led to Christ. In anticipation of that day, he rejoices in them even now. Part of them likewise rejoice in him. Paul longs for all of them to rejoice in him in the same way. The mark of a good friendship is that each friend finds joy in the other and speaks well of him. The key is mutual respect.

CONCLUSION

There are times of sorrow in which words are meaningless. We are not of a mind to comprehend what is being said. Sometimes the best thing a friend can do for us is to give us a hug and hold us tight while we deal with our emotions.

Knowing how much we benefit from the comfort of a friend, we should be quick to comfort our friends, especially those in our church fellowship. The church is an ideal setting for mutual care. It is composed of people who share with us a love for Christ and the doctrinal truths and moral values given in his Word. These are people whom we value greatly. They deserve our concern when they are suffering, and we in turn can expect the same from them. To borrow a phrase from 2 Corinthians 1:5, the church should be a place where "comfort overflows."

Discovery Learning

This page contains an alternate lesson plan emphasizing learning activities. Classes desiring such student involvement will find these suggestions helpful. The next page is a reproducible activity page to further enhance discovery learning.

LEARNING GOALS

After studying today's lesson, students will be able to:

1. Cite specific Scripture that deals with the problem of why good people suffer.

2. Feel compassion for those who suffer.

3. Commit themselves to intercessory prayer with the use of a prayer list.

INTO THE LESSON

Make copies of this exercise and give one to each pupil. Introduce it by saying that it is helpful to be thoughtful when we are comforting people in their suffering.

Imagine that the sixteen-year-old son of a faithful Christian elder and his wife was killed in a head-on collision with a drunken driver. The drunken driver escaped unhurt. You are going to see the family at the funeral home and want to say something helpful to them. Which of these statements will be most appropriate? Check one and explain why you chose it.

____ The Lord gives and the Lord takes away.
____ What a senseless loss of life! Killed by a drunk!
____ Just remember Romans 8:28.
____ Your boy is with the Lord. Heaven is a much better place for him.
____ Give a hug and say, "You're in my prayers."
____ I know you'll be a good example to all of us through this time of pain.

Let the students form pairs and compare choices. Explain that the best way is generally to give a hug and offer the best help you can—intercessory prayer. The other statements are pat answers that give little consolation.

Among other things the text of this lesson helps us understand why good people suffer, and how a Christian's suffering can be relieved. (Share the "Lesson Background" in full with the class.)

Option: Use the reproducible activity, "Getting a Grip on Suffering," on the next page.

INTO THE WORD

Ask someone to read 2 Corinthians 1:1-9 aloud while the rest of the class listens for some reasons that Paul cites as an explanation of why there is suffering in the world, even the good person's world. (Verse 4 tells us that we are troubled and have suffering so we can comfort others with the same kind of comfort that God gives us. We can be more sympathetic. Verses 5 and 7 indicate that suffering brings us great comfort from the Lord. Times of suffering draw us closer to God. Verse 9 tells us that suffering causes us to rely more upon God and less upon ourselves.)

Note that James 1:2-4 says trials strengthen our character. Add that 1 Peter 1:6, 7 indicates that suffering or persecution proves and refines our faith so it will bring us honor when Jesus comes again. Hebrews 12 adds that suffering provides discipline (training) for righteousness.

Paul illustrates what he is saying by citing several experiences from his own life. Ask the students to read verses 8 and 9 silently and then answer this question: "Why do you think Paul shared so personally with the Corinthians?" (One answer is so they would know they were not alone, that even great men of faith were not spared the experience of suffering.)

Note that Paul's suffering brought growth: he learned to depend on God rather than himself. Verse 9 indicates this.

Remind the class that some eager evangelists lead people to believe that wealth and health are blessings that always come with being a good Christian. Paul's life and the life of Jesus certainly show us that this is not always true. In John 16:33 we find Jesus explaining that his followers will have trouble and suffering in this world, but that he has overcome the world. If our Lord experienced suffering, how are we to ask to be excused from it? It brings many blessings.

Option: Use the reproducible activity, "Suffering and You," on the next page.

Conclude the study by referring to verse 11 and asking, "What part could the Corinthians play in helping Paul and others through times of suffering?" (Their prayer support was vital.)

INTO LIFE

Author Richard Foster tells us that intercessory prayer is a way of loving others and a sacred obligation. Ask the students to share some ways that they have found effective in helping them to be faithful in prayer for others. Prepare these suggestions on a flip chart:

1. Keep a prayer list.
2. Have a set time to pray for others.
3. Send up flash prayers all day.
4. Pray specifically.
5. Drop a note telling the person that he or she is in your prayers.

Getting a Grip on Suffering

Problems, suffering, and pressure plague everyone to some degree. They were not a part of God's original design for humans—and they won't be a part of life after Jesus returns. Until then, however, a good portion of our time is spent trying to deal with problems. The Scriptures have a lot to say about handling difficulties. Below are several passages. Look up at least two of them and summarize what they say about how we should handle problems.

2 Corinthians 1:3-11

2 Corinthians 4:7-11, 16-18

Hebrews 12:1-13

James 1:2-23

1 Peter 1:3-9

1 Peter 4:12-19

> Summarize at least two of the passages listed at the left in this space:

Suffering and You

Complete the following statements:

1. When I encounter problems, I usually. . . . (Check ✓ as many as apply.)
   ___ a. get angry with God.
   ___ b. get angry with others.
   ___ c. get angry with myself.
   ___ d. feel sorry for myself.
   ___ e. become depressed.
   ___ f. try to fix the problem.
   ___ g. deny that I have a problem.
   ___ h. look on the bright side.
   ___ i. stuff my feelings inside and avoid dealing with them.
   ___ j. allow myself the freedom to feel sad but allow the sadness to motivate me to seek God.
   ___ k. become "religious"—say spiritual words even though I don't really understand.
   ___ l. become confused.
   ___ m. feel sad.
   ___ n. hide from others to keep from getting hurt further.

2. When I encounter problems, God wants me to. . . .

3. God can use the personal pain of my problems to help me in these ways. . . .

4. Complete this prayer:
   God, I realize this life has problems, and I can't escape them. Help me. . . .

LIVING IN
CHRISTIAN FREEDOM

LESSON 10

WHY TEACH THIS LESSON?

Paul addresses so many different issues and problems in 1 Corinthians, we may be a little surprised that he spends two chapters on the one issue of the exercise of Christian freedom. We saw part of his treatment in lesson 8, in which his focus was on relationships within the church.

One gets the impression that his application in chapter 9 is closer to the heart of the apostle. On one hand, it provides a defense for his own behavior. But the greater issue is evangelism. Paul was a man with a mission. If it were humanly possible, he would deliver the gospel to every person on the planet. Nothing would stand in his way—not even his personal "rights."

In a culture that values individual rights and liberties above all else, Paul's example stands out like a brilliant light in the darkness. Challenge your students with his example. The need for people to hear the gospel remains much more important than whether we enjoy every right and privilege to which we might lay just claim.

INTRODUCTION

A. TESTED BY FREEDOM

"For seventy years we were tested by persecution. Now we are being tested by freedom."

That is the way a thoughtful Russian citizen summarized the situation of Christians in the former Soviet Union several months after the collapse of Communism. It is great to be free from heavy-handed control on every aspect of living. But many persons are not prepared for the continuing responsibility for their own decisions and provisions. Becoming free was one thing, but long-term living as free persons with others equally free is proving to be something else, and much more demanding.

So it is also with the liberty we enjoy in Christ Jesus. At immeasurable cost to himself Jesus offers freedom from sin and its slavery. As Christians we have chosen that freedom. Now we live as responsible persons in that freedom.

Our springtime Bible lessons on "Christians Living in Community" include two sessions dealing with our experience as free Christians. Lesson 8 urged the wise use of liberty so as to help, rather than hurt, others in the church. Now we are taught to use Christian freedom helpfully toward folk who are not yet Christians. This is geared to evangelism. Our Key Verse says it: "Though I am free and belong to no man, I make myself a slave to everyone, to win as many as possible" (1 Corinthians 9:19).

B. LESSON BACKGROUND

Today's lesson from 1 Corinthians 9 is built directly on the text studied two weeks ago from the preceding chapter. In chapter 8 Paul dealt with the relationship among Christians, asking, "Should I eat meat that may have been dedicated to an

DEVOTIONAL READING:
GALATIANS 5:13-26
LESSON SCRIPTURE:
1 CORINTHIANS 9
PRINTED TEXT:
1 CORINTHIANS 9:1-7,19-27

LESSON AIMS

This study should equip the student to:

1. Name several ways in which the apostle Paul voluntarily surrendered his own rights and preferences in order to win others to Christ.

2. Name adjustments he or she can make in order to present Christ more effectively to people who are different from himself or herself.

May
7

KEY VERSE:

Though I am free and belong to no man, I make myself a slave to everyone, to win as many as possible. —1 Corinthians 9:19

LESSON 10 NOTES

HOW TO SAY IT

Barnabas. BAR-nuh-bus.
Cephas. SEE-fus.
Cilicia. Sih-LISH-ee-uh.
Isthmian. ISS-mee-un.
Joses. JOE-sis.
Sibelius. Suh-BAL-yus or Suh-BAY-lee-us.
Wycliffe. WICK-liff or WICK-luff.

WHAT DO YOU THINK?

There is no New Testament command that requires us to be present at every service of worship or Bible study our church offers. Hebrews 10:25 cautions against neglecting our assembling, but it can hardly be taken as a command to attend every meeting. Do you think, then, that attending worship services and Bible studies is a matter of Christian liberty, like eating meat sacrificed to idols was in Corinth? That is, are we free either to attend or not at will? Why or why not? How is the situation similar or different from the meats issue?

One of Paul's concerns in the meats issue was the example that was set for weaker Christians. Which example, of attending or not attending, is more likely to set a negative example for a weaker Christian. Why?

idol?" Since an idol is nothing but a figment of pagan imagination, Paul said, a Christian may normally regard such meat as any other, to be accepted with thanks to God who made all things. But some Christians still think of idols as real beings and link the eating of "their" meat with worshiping them. These brothers could be misled by a believer's eating the food in question. In such a case, Paul said, he would do without such food entirely. He would go hungry before he would influence another Christian to violate his conscience.

Some folk in Corinth were questioning Paul's apostleship, thinking him weak and spineless (2 Corinthians 10–12). If he were really an apostle, they said, he would know his rights and would stand up for them. Today's text answers that argument plainly. In it Paul shifts his viewpoint from that of a brother yielding to the welfare of others in the church to that of an apostle surrendering certain of his rights for the sake of winning unbelievers to Christ.

I. THE RIGHTS OF AN APOSTLE (1 CORINTHIANS 9:1-7)

Paul's respect for the conscience of the "weak" brother did not include any surrender of his apostleship or permanent cancellation of his rights. He would remain free to make each decision on the merits of the issue at hand.

A. PAUL WAS AN APOSTLE (vv. 1-3)

1, 2. Am I not free? Am I not an apostle? Have I not seen Jesus our Lord? Are you not the result of my work in the Lord? Even though I may not be an apostle to others, surely I am to you! For you are the seal of my apostleship in the Lord.

To be an apostle, one had to be an eyewitness of the risen Lord (Acts 1:21, 22). Jesus appeared to Saul on the road to Damascus and appointed him as apostle to the Gentiles (Acts 9:3-8; 22:6-11; 26:12-18). In pursuit of that apostleship Paul had come to Corinth, converting both Jews and Gentiles to Christ (Acts 18:1-11). Now they themselves were the *seal*—the mark of genuineness—of his apostleship. So by qualification, by appointment, and by accomplishment (see especially 2 Corinthians 12:11, 12), he was fully an apostle, entitled to all the rights and privileges, as well as the powers and responsibilities, of the office. So he was perfectly *free*, either to enjoy or to forgo the benefits that went with it. Likewise any mature Christian ought to be stable and confident, free and flexible, choosing the way of humble service in likeness to his Lord.

CONCERNING CRITICISM

It is helpful to know that even an inspired apostle such as Paul had many who were critical of him. We remember that many heroic servants of our Lord have been subjected to vilification and even to execution. John Wycliffe was treated severely, and his body was exhumed and burned after his death in 1384. In a letter to the Duke of Lancaster in 1381, he said, "I believe that in the end the truth will conquer."

William Lloyd Garrison led the abolition movement in New England. His newspaper office was wrecked and burned by his adversaries. He did not retreat or relent, but wrote in defiance, "I am in earnest—I will not equivocate—I will not excuse—I will not retreat a single inch; and I will be heard."

John Sibelius (1865-1957), the famous Finnish composer, once said, "Pay no attention to what the critics say; no statue has ever been put up to a critic." First we need to be sure our motives are honest and our efforts in line with the will of God and the truth and spirit of Jesus. Then we can be firm as Paul was, and unyielding in our continued work for our Lord, however severe the criticism against us may be.

—J. G. V. B.

3. This is my defense to those who sit in judgment on me.

What follows is Paul's defense to those who questioned his apostleship because he had voluntarily given up certain of his rights.

B. APOSTLES WERE SUPPORTED (VV. 4-7)

4. Don't we have the right to food and drink?

The apostles' *right to food and drink* included the thankful enjoyment of such food and beverage as were set before them, without asking "questions of conscience" until and unless such enjoyment posed a problem for observers who still worried about spiritual pollution in the food (1 Corinthians 10:23-30).

Now Paul turned to the apostles' right to receive material support, including meals and lodging, from the people they served. Jesus had directed the twelve apostles to accept the hospitality of their hearers in the cities to which they went (Matthew 10:9-15). He said the laborer is worthy of his wages (Luke 10:7).

Paul had not exercised his right to "live of the gospel," however, when he labored in Corinth; and he still refused to claim it from the Corinthians, lest he "hinder the gospel" (v. 12). For a part of his time in their city he earned his living at tent making, and part of the time he accepted support from Christians elsewhere (Acts 18:1-7; 2 Corinthians 11:8).

5. Don't we have the right to take a believing wife along with us, as do the other apostles and the Lord's brothers and Cephas?

It seems that other apostles were accompanied by their wives, as faithful helpers, when they traveled among the churches. Both husband and wife were supported. *Cephas* (Simon Peter) is named specifically.

The Lord's brothers—sons of Joseph and Mary—are named in Mark 6:3 as James, Joses, Judas, and Simon. James became a leader in the church at Jerusalem (Galatians 1:19); he and Judas are known as the writers of New Testament letters James and Jude. They seem to have been accompanied by their wives in evangelistic travels.

Evidently Paul was not married (1 Corinthians 7:8). If Barnabas had a wife, she did not travel with him.

6. Or is it only I and Barnabas who must work for a living?

Paul and Barnabas supported themselves by other labors while they preached, but that did not mean they did not have a right to be sustained by the people they taught. They simply chose not to exercise that right. No one could ever say they were using the gospel as a means of easy living.

7. Who serves as a soldier at his own expense? Who plants a vineyard and does not eat of its grapes? Who tends a flock and does not drink of the milk?

The basic right to receive one's living from his employment extends far beyond the work of an apostle. In a military campaign the soldier's expenses are paid by those who send him. The farmer lives on the products of his land and his labor. The herdsman makes his living from the animals he raises and feeds.

Verses 8-18 expand the argument. Quoted is Deuteronomy 25:4 with its provision that even an animal should be allowed to eat a little while he works. That is applied to God's concern for the persons who labor in his cause.

II. WINNING TO CHRIST AND WINNING IN CHRIST (1 CORINTHIANS 9:19-27)

A. PAUL ADAPTED IN ORDER TO WIN OTHERS (VV. 19-23)

19. Though I am free and belong to no man, I make myself a slave to everyone, to win as many as possible.

WHAT DO YOU THINK?

Some people take Paul's example of not receiving support from the people with whom he ministered as evidence for their belief that no ministers or other church workers should be paid for their labors. However, 1 Corinthians 9:7-14 seems to argue forcefully that Christian workers do have the right to support.

Considering how some religious leaders have abused their prerogative of soliciting financial support, do you think there are times when it would be prudent for Christian workers to forgo financial support? If so, when—under what conditions? If not, why not?

Who should determine whether a Christian worker should be paid: the worker, or those who will pay? Why?

WHAT DO YOU THINK?

The word compromise *is generally viewed in an unfavorable way in the church. Of course, when it comes to the truth, we dare not compromise, nor can we compromise on clear standards of morality. Stealing, lying, adultery, homosexuality, and the like are sins, and we cannot regard them as anything less. But in contrast to these matters, there are countless areas of personal opinion and individual liberty in which we can work out a compromise with other people. How can we distinguish between legitimate and unacceptable compromise?*

Paul's desire to bring all persons to the knowledge of Christ is the message carried by visual 10.

OPTION

The reproducible activity on page 316, "All Things to All Men" will help your students apply to real-life situations the principles expressed here.

Much more than daily upkeep was included in Paul's personal adjustments for the sake of winning others to Christ. It became an all-inclusive principle of his behavior.

As one born into Roman citizenship at Tarsus of Cilicia (Acts 21:39; 22:28), Paul enjoyed special privileges and protections, including the right to a hearing before being punished on any accusation (Acts 22:24-26). As a Christian, Paul cherished his freedom from the burdensome strictures of Jewish ceremonial law (Galatians 5:1). Especially he appreciated his liberation from the guilt and power of sin through the sacrifice of Christ. He knew, though, that liberty from outer controls could result in slavery to one's own passions and prejudices—an ever-present and all-inclusive servitude. "You, my brothers, were called to be free," he wrote. "But do use your freedom to indulge the sinful nature, but serve one another in love" (Galatians 5:13). The truest and most lasting freedom is the way of service, self-chosen and motivated by love. Martin Luther is quoted in a paraphrase of the verse before us: "A Christian man is the most free of all, and subject to none; a Christian man is the most dutiful servant of all, and subject to every one."

Paul's love-motivation reached in two directions—to Christ and to the people before him. Love of the Lord made him obedient to Jesus' Great Commission (Matthew 28:18-20; Acts 26:19, 20), and love of the people made him desire their salvation more than his own comfort or safety.

20. To the Jews I became like a Jew, to win the Jews. To those under the law I became like one under the law (though I myself am not under the law), so as to win those under the law.

Here is specific application of the principle just stated. Paul approached the Jewish people sympathetically, respecting their traditions. In each city to which he went, he addressed himself first to the Jews in their synagogues, using their Scriptures to establish the fact that Jesus was indeed their promised Messiah. When he asked Timothy, the son of a Jewish mother and Gentile father, to be his helper, he made a concession to Jewish sensibilities by having Timothy circumcised (Acts 16:1-3). To avoid offending zealous Jews, Paul participated in the ceremonial vows of certain Jews in the temple at Jerusalem (Acts 21:17-26). Yet he made it abundantly clear that his salvation did not depend on his being a Jew and keeping the law.

21. To those not having the law I became like one not having the law (though I am not free from God's law but am under Christ's law), so as to win those not having the law.

Heathen Gentiles would not be won by citing the law and the prophets. So what did Paul do? He approached them in terms they understood. He showed the futility of their idols, and he spoke of God, who created the world they knew. He named Jesus, risen from the dead, as the revealer of God (Acts 17:16-34). He made it clear that the Gentiles' salvation did not depend on their following the ceremonial law of the Jews. The way of salvation to Jew and Gentile alike lay in Jesus (Acts 15:11).

Christ's law was not negotiable. It could not be compromised. How could one bring converts to him if in the effort he condoned in Jew or Gentile the attitudes and actions that Jesus opposed? The law of Christ, seen in his life, his teaching, and his cleansing grace, provided the unchangeable core of Paul's commitment. All else was negotiable.

22. To the weak I became weak, to win the weak. I have become all things to all men so that by all possible means I might save some.

The *weak* are described in 1 Corinthians 8:7-13 and Romans 14:16—15:3 as those Christians whose faith was not vigorous enough to disregard the dedication of meats to lifeless images. Paul was willing to follow the "weak" ones' scrupulous practices if in doing so he could win them to Christ—and then teach them not to demand the same compliance on the part of others.

That by all possible means I might save some. This was the uncompromising purpose for which Paul would compromise on most other matters. What, then, among *our* rights, privileges, and preferences is so important that it must be protected at the cost of hindering another in his approach to Christ?

23. I do all this for the sake of the gospel, that I may share in its blessings.

The gospel was the cause for which Paul would compromise almost anything else.

Sharing works in two directions. Paul would give to others, including the Corinthians, the gospel that had come to him. Paul would receive, along with others, the blessings available in the gospel. His motivation was two-directional. He would sacrifice his ease and self-interests both for the sake of others, to save them; and for his own sake, to fulfill his own salvation. Apostle though he was, he had his own salvation to "work out . . . with fear and trembling" (Philippians 2:12).

B. PAUL CONTENDED FOR THE CROWN OF LIFE (VV. 24-27)

24. Do you not know that in a race all the runners run, but only one gets the prize? Run in such a way as to get the prize.

In several of his epistles Paul compared the Christian experience with an athletic contest, with its demand for discipline, observance of rules, strenuous participation, patient continuance, and rewards for successful completion (Philippians 3:13, 14; 2 Timothy 2:5; 4:7, 8; Hebrews 12:1, 2).

The famous Isthmian Games were held near Corinth every two years; Paul's readers knew them well. They would surely scoff at the silly suggestions of modern lottery and sweepstakes promoters—or even certain evangelists—indicating that "all you have to do is enter" to win fabulous rewards. It is simply not so!

The *prize* Paul mentioned here has been called the "umpire's award," given to the contestant who was judged to have observed all the rules and finished first in any race. And there was only one winner in any race.

In Christ the winner's circle is not limited to one, but neither is it gained by all who enter the race. Consider Paul's vivid description of winning: "I have fought the good fight, I have finished the race, I have kept the faith. Now there is in store for me the crown of righteousness, which the Lord, the righteous Judge, will award to me on that day—and not only to me, but also to all who have longed for his appearing" (2 Timothy 4:7, 8). The reward is for those who love Christ and finish the course.

25. Everyone who competes in the games goes into strict training. They do it to get a crown that will not last; but we do it to get a crown that will last forever.

Rigid self-discipline in persistent training is the price of successful accomplishment on any meaningful level. It demands purposeful, total direction, not trading off one virtue for another self-indulgence, nor a general program of virtue for an occasional binge. But for the Christian the rewards are immeasurably greater than the efforts (2 Corinthians 4:17, 18).

A crown that will not last—a circlet of green herbs or of pine—was worn by a winner in the Isthmian Games. It didn't last long. For the Christian, by contrast, is the "crown of righteousness" (2 Timothy 4:8), the "crown of life" (James 1:12; Revelation 2:10), the "crown of glory that will never fade away" (1 Peter 5:4).

26. Therefore I do not run like a man running aimlessly; I do not fight like a man beating the air.

WHAT DO YOU THINK?

Paul frequently used athletic metaphors to illustrate spiritual truth. What are some valuable spiritual lessons that athletic events illustrate for us today? What other kind of metaphors might illustrate the same concepts for those who are not athletically minded?

OPTION

Use the reproducible activity on page 316, "A Crown That Will Last Forever" to help your students to compare the commitment of an athlete with that of a Christian.

WHAT DO YOU THINK?

How literally do you think Paul's example of "beating" his body (v. 27) should be followed. There have been people who took it quite literally, actually abusing their bodies in the name of holiness. While nearly everyone agrees that is an extreme application and one to be avoided, do you think we are generally concerned enough about avoiding the other extreme? That is, shouldn't we practice some degree of physical discipline in order to maintain spiritual health? What is the relationship between physical and spiritual health? (See 1 Corinthians 6:19, 20.)

One Christian university made headlines a few years ago when it issued a policy that said it would expel overweight people. Is that taking Paul too literally? Why or why not?

PRAYER

Thank you, our God and Father, for Jesus, who willingly surrendered his glory and his life to save us. Thank you for Paul and others who freely gave of themselves to bring the saving gospel to us. Thank you for the freedom in which we live, to follow in their path for the sake of others. May we follow it well, for Jesus' sake. Amen.

THOUGHT TO REMEMBER

"You, my brothers were called to be free. But do not use your freedom to indulge the sinful nature; rather, serve one another in love" (Galatians 5:13).

DAILY BIBLE READINGS

Monday, May 1—Live by the Spirit (Galatians 5:13-21)

Tuesday, May 2—Fruit of the Spirit (Galatians 5:22-26)

Wednesday, May 3—Rights of an Apostle (1 Corinthians 9:1-7)

Thursday, May 4—Refusing to Claim One's Rights (1 Corinthians 9:8-18)

Friday, May 5—Free to Adapt for Christ's Sake (1 Corinthians 9:19-27)

Saturday, May 6—The Lord's Spirit Gives Freedom (2 Corinthians 3:12-18)

Sunday, May 7—Christ Frees Us From Condemnation (Romans 8:1-11)

The direction of verse 25 finds substance in Paul's example, cited here. The course of his life was not wavering and aimless; he looked straight ahead and pressed toward his chosen goal (Philippians 3:13, 14). Or if you change the figure from the racetrack to the boxing ring, his blows were directed, every one toward its mark to defeat the enemy, Satan. Or if you accept the Lord's figure of the workman putting his hand to the plow, Paul was not looking back (Luke 9:62).

27. No, I beat my body and make it my slave so that after I have preached to others, I myself will not be disqualified for the prize.

The human body can become a spoiled tyrant. Its appetite for food, for ease and comfort, for sexual satisfaction, or for pride in its own power and appearance can become insatiable.

Paul would not have his body bossing him around. He treated it severely, he said, showing it who was boss and keeping it under subjection to his God-serving purposes. He refused to be a slave to his bodily demands. Instead, he made his body the obedient servant to his spiritual will.

There was necessity in this. As a preacher of the Word he had been like a herald at the Isthmian games, announcing the contests, summoning and instructing the competitors, and declaring the winners. What shame, then, if he himself should be disqualified and expelled for violating the rules he declared to others!

GETTING SERIOUS

Paul uses the athletic efforts of the Greeks and Romans to illustrate the intensity with which we should discipline ourselves for Christian activity. Athletes go "into strict training." This they do for a fast-fading laurel crown, whereas we are looking forward to an everlasting reward.

Often we use the expression "get serious." In basketball, baseball, or football, all kidding or "fooling around" is held down when the "big game" is near. The coach says, "Let's get serious."

We may live through a period when eating is a wild delight and a frenzy of calorie-disregarding adventure. But one day we look in astonishment at the numbers on a scale, and say, "I must get serious about losing weight."

The apostle is urging us to regard our Christian life with a sense of its supreme significance. We are living in a world in which there is real sin. People are hurt, humiliated, and harassed. There is a real death to be faced and an endless eternity to be entered. It is indeed important to get serious about our way and our work in Christ.

—J. G. V. B.

CONCLUSION

The apostle Paul was not original in his exercise of freedom to forfeit his own rights, comforts, and interests for the sake of those he had come to serve. Because he was following another who had gone the same way before him, he could recommend that others follow him. "Follow my example," he said, "as I follow the example of Christ" (1 Corinthians 11:1). Hear again his description of the one he had chosen to follow: "Your attitude should be the same as that of Christ Jesus: Who, being in very nature God, did not consider equality with God something to be grasped, but made himself nothing, taking the very nature of a servant, being made in human likeness. And being found in appearance as a man, he humbled himself and became obedient to death—even death on a cross!" (Philippians 2:5-8).

In response to this kind of self-sacrifice to save others, God himself supplies the ultimate glory to Christ, to Paul, and to those who follow in the way of their leading.

Discovery Learning

This page contains an alternate lesson plan emphasizing learning activities. Classes desiring such student involvement will find these suggestions helpful. The next page is a reproducible activity page to further enhance discovery learning.

LEARNING GOALS

As a result of this lesson, students will:

1. Become aware of specific things that tend to limit Christian freedom.

2. Learn to practice some growth techniques that help Christians mature and be faithful.

3. Learn to limit their freedom because of their responsibility to others.

INTO THE LESSON

To open the session share this statement by a Russian citizen: "For seventy years we were tested by persecution. Now we are being tested by freedom." Divide the class in half and tell one half to give specific ways in which persecution tests people. *(For example, persecution tempts one to protect oneself by denying one's faith.)* Assign the other half to list specific ways in which people are tested by freedom. *(For example, freedom tempts one to drift away and be distracted by all of the opportunities available.)* Make two columns on the board, labeling one PERSECUTION and the other FREEDOM. Record the answers of the class in the appropriate columns.

Lead into the lesson background by saying that Paul seems to be declaring his freedom but not using it. (Use the "Lesson Background" material in the commentary.)

INTO THE WORD

Type the following questions on index cards and distribute them to class members. Allow their answers to be the springboard for the lesson development.

1. Read 1 Corinthians 9:1-3. What were some things that Paul would not surrender in spite of all criticism? Where did the Corinthians fit into the picture? *(Possible answers: his apostleship, his freedom to make personal choices. The Corinthians were the "seal" or living proof of his apostleship.)*

2. What were some things to which Paul had a right but had voluntarily given up the right? Read 1 Corinthians 9:4-7. *(Answers: his right of choosing what to eat and drink, his right to have a wife, his right to be paid for his preaching.)* What is your opinion of the choices Paul made? For example, do you think he might have been more effective if he had not taken time for his tent-making? Explain.

3. What was Paul's supreme motivation whenever he had to choose whether or not to exercise a particular free-dom? Read 1 Corinthians 9:19-22. *(Best answer: A love that made him care for the lost and want to convert them at whatever cost to his own personal freedoms.)*

4. In what specific ways did Paul accommodate himself to Jews, to Gentiles, and to the weak? Read 1 Corinthians 9:20-22.

5. How did Paul regard the role of personal discipline and self-mastery? Read 1 Corinthians 9:24-27. *(Possible answers: Personal discipline and self-mastery make a more effective servant, and that was what Paul was intent upon. His deepest desire was to convert others to Christ. In the illustration of the games, only one person wins the prize, but in Christ all are winners if they keep on doing their best.)*

INTO LIFE

Point out that our freedom in Christ does not excuse us from disciplining ourselves in order to be more effective in winning others. Put the following verses on the chalkboard, or photocopy them. Ask the class to study the verses and find techniques that are effective in keeping Christians faithful for a lifetime as well as useful in reaching the lost: Matthew 16:24. *(Self-denial, personal sacrifice, obedience to Christ.)* Colossians 4:2, 3. *(Devoted prayer and supplication for open doors for the gospel.)* Colossians 4:6. *(Grant grace to others and be ready with your Christian witness.)* Philippians 2:5-15. *(Have the mind of Christ, be willing to submit to others, don't complain, etc.)* Ask the class for other suggestions.

Explain that curtailing one's freedom by voluntary self-discipline is different from accepting unreasonable limits. Paul would not accept the notion that all Christians must keep the Old Testament law (Galatians 5:1). See whether class members can mention traditions or opinions that would limit our freedom unreasonably. We must not violate Bible teaching in order to be agreeable with those around us.

OPTION

The reproducible activities on the next page are also designed to lead your students to make application of this lesson.

Close with prayer focusing upon reaching the lost with love. Encourage the students to be specific in asking God to use them in reaching the people for whom they pray.

All Things to All Men

Paul said he would adapt himself to find common ground with anyone for the sake of sharing the gospel with that person. Of course, there are limits: ". . . though I am not free from God's law but am under Christ's law" (1 Corinthians 9:21). Consider the following situations. How far should a Christian go to be "all things to all men" to win people to the Lord? Use another sheet of paper or the back of this one for your answers.

1. Frank has a co-worker, Dave, who often heads for a bar after work. He has invited Frank to go along, but Frank has refused. Frank has invited Dave to church and has tried to share his faith with Dave, but without success. Frank has prayed for an open door. Today, Dave repeats the invitation to "hit the bar together." What would you do if you were in Frank's situation?

2. Bob and Mary are faithful members of the church and regularly tithe their income. They have looked forward to the purchase of a new luxury automobile for some time, but just as they were about to make their purchase, the church issued a financial challenge.

In order to reach more people for the Lord, the church is planning to build a new and larger facility. It will be expensive, so the people have been asked to pray and consider what they can do to support this new venture for the sake of the gospel.

"We have a right to have this new car," Bob told Mary. "We've never been stingy with the Lord's work. We already give more than many people even after they 'dig a little deeper.' But if we support this building, we'll have to put off the purchase of our car."

If you were Mary, how would you answer?

3. Hank is a Christian businessman. He enjoys some indoor sports, but he has never been much of an "outdoorsman." His neighbor, Fred, is loves to go fishing. In fact, he often goes on Sunday morning.

Hank has recently begun to feel he needs to do more to try to reach Fred with the gospel. He wonders if, in order to be "all things to all men," he should learn to like fishing—or just pretend he likes fishing—in order to establish some common ground with Fred.

If Hank came to you for advice, what would you tell him?

A Crown That Will Last Forever

Olympic athletes are known for their dedication to their sport. "They do it," Paul says, "to get a crown that will not last." While today's gold medals last longer than the laurel or pine wreaths that crowned the winners of the Isthmian games and the ancient Olympics, they still don't compare with the "crown of life" that awaits the Christian.

Compare the Olympic athlete's expression of commitment with your own expression of commitment to the Lord, using the table below.

ATHLETE	CHRISTIAN
Strict discipline while training	
Starts at an early age	
Constantly trying to improve	
Does not participate in many activities in order to spend more time in practice	

Christians Living in Community

Unit 3: Ministering as a Christian Community
(Lessons 10-13)

WORKING FOR
RECONCILIATION

LESSON 11

WHY TEACH THIS LESSON?

When thinking of "Christians Living in Community," perhaps no theme is more important than that of reconciliation. Humans become estranged from one another from time to time and need to be reconciled. Even Christians.

Some in your class are feeling alienated. Perhaps a family argument has left them not speaking to a relative. Perhaps a slight by a neighbor has left a lingering hurt. Perhaps a division has even developed within the church body and created tensions. Besides such obvious divisions is the sometimes overlooked separation that exists between Christians and non-Christians.

Just as Christ is the answer to our being reconciled to God, so he is to our being reconciled to each other. Encourage your students to receive and to promote reconciliation on both fronts.

INTRODUCTION

A. IRRECONCILABLE DIFFERENCES

It is a sad commentary on our society that the reason of "irreconcilable differences" is so often that which excuses a divorce and the dissolution of a family. Neither party is willing to move, to change, to adapt to the needs of the other; and reconciliation is thus rendered impossible.

It should really come as no surprise, however, since God is not included in so many modern marriages. To accomplish reconciliation in its full and scriptural sense is, in fact, possible to none other than God himself. Let us consider.

The word Paul uses for *reconcile* means to change something or someone thoroughly, to make an adjustment that brings into agreement those who have been at odds, to restore to friendship or harmony those who have become enemies.

Since God is unchanging, he cannot be adjusted to bring him into conformity to any other. The adjustment must come the other way. It's a little like the reconciliation that is frequently necessary between my bank's monthly statement of my checking account and the figures I keep for myself. Very seldom do I find the bank in error. A careful search finds, instead, some error of mine that needs to be corrected. Likewise, God is not in error. Reconciliation brings us into harmony with his truth, goodness, and mercy.

God is not our enemy. His love is constant. If we are uncomfortable with him, it is because we, like Adam (Genesis 3:7-10), have sinned and thus desire to run and hide, building a wall of resentment between God and us. The enmity is on our part. The initiative and the provision for reconciliation are from him. He offers the hand of friendship and the encircling arm of support; it is ours to acknowledge and accept.

B. LESSON BACKGROUND

First Corinthians, including last week's lesson text, was written from Ephesus during Paul's third missionary journey. It included plain words concerning serious

DEVOTIONAL READING:
1 JOHN 4:7-21
LESSON SCRIPTURE:
2 CORINTHIANS 5
PRINTED TEXT:
2 CORINTHIANS 5:11-21

LESSON AIMS

This lesson should equip the student to:

1. Show how Jesus has brought about the student's own reconciliation to God.

2. Indicate specific changes that have taken place with his being made new in Christ.

3. Accept some definite responsibility in the work of reconciling sinners to God.

May
14

KEY VERSE:

God . . . reconciled us to himself through Christ, and gave us the ministry of reconciliation.
—2 Corinthians 5:18

LESSON 11 NOTES

HOW TO SAY IT

Jaipur. JYE-pur.
Macedonia. Mass-uh-DOE-nyuh
    or Mass-uh-DOE-nee-uh.

WHAT DO YOU THINK?

We who have experienced the love and grace of God still retain a sense of reverential fear toward him, an appreciation of his power and holiness. In fact, contemplation of the ultimate fate of the unsaved should fill us with a certain amount of terror, which can be an aid in developing an urgency in our efforts to win unsaved family members and friends.

Balancing the church's message between pictures of judgment and of grace is difficult. Too much emphasis on the negative can become manipulative, producing an emotional response without adequate teaching. Focusing too much on the positive can fail to paint the picture of need or urgency.

Do you think the church you attend speaks and teaches often enough on the theme of judgment on those who reject Christ? Why or why not?

problems; also plain answers to those who challenged Paul's apostleship. How would it be received? When should Paul go again to Corinth to face the issues in person? Titus went to Corinth to learn the answers to those questions.

Restless with waiting, Paul left Ephesus on his way toward Corinth. Titus met him in Macedonia. The news he brought from Corinth was generally good, though some problems with false teachers and opposers still remained. Still in Macedonia, approximately three months after he wrote 1 Corinthians, Paul wrote the second epistle and sent it to Corinth.

Appropriately for its mission to mend the relationship between Paul and the Corinthian church, this letter contains more autobiographical material than any other of Paul's writings. Its early chapters deal with his afflictions, his commitment, his dangers and difficulties, including Corinthian challenges to his apostleship. Chapter 5 begins with a cheerful acceptance of his own mortality and the coming judgment. In this awareness he continued to minister, and he advised the church to continue its ministry. That ministry included an outreach to all the world with the message of God's reconciliation through his Son Jesus.

I. RECONCILING CORINTHIANS TO PAUL (2 CORINTHIANS 5:11-15)

The apostle turned his attention to some "housekeeping chores," seeking to improve relationships between his readers and himself.

A. SUPPLYING AN ANSWER (VV. 11, 12)

11. Since, then, we know what it is to fear the Lord, we try to persuade men. What we are is plain to God, and I hope it is also plain to your conscience.

Aware of God's power, holiness, and knowledge of all things, Paul was moved by awe for the Almighty. Having bowed humbly before God, he was not afraid of men. And the people in Corinth who questioned Paul's apostleship needed to learn some things they didn't know. The ones with whom he had worked most closely knew already, down deep in their *consciences*, what sort of ministry Paul was rendering.

Persuade. Paul's word indicates "bringing about a change of mind by the influence of reason or moral considerations" (W. E. Vine, *New Testament Words*). The use of political pressure to win compliance is not the apostle's way.

12. We are not trying to commend ourselves to you again, but are giving you an opportunity to take pride in us, so that you can answer those who take pride in what is seen rather than in what is in the heart.

Among those who would be reading his letter, Paul saw no need for a continuing campaign of self-justification. He hoped, however, to provide them with grounds for some legitimate pride in him. Thus they could answer false teachers who scoffed at them for taking seriously an apostle who was not imposing in physical appearance or show of human authority. Even in Corinth some might boast of having seen Jesus in the flesh, or having associated with the apostle Peter. They might boast a more imposing presence, or dress, or life-style. They might be proud of being "above" doing manual labor.

Among ourselves there is always a temptation to judge a preacher by the size of the church he serves, or to judge a stranger by his physical appearance, or to judge a church by the size of its budget or its building. It is less easy to find our satisfaction in the inner realities of faith, love, and character, as Jesus urged: "Stop judging by mere appearances, and make a right judgment" (John 7:24).

EXTERIORIZATION

Remember the small town in the old west, as recreated on movie sets? The stores on the dusty main street appear to be two or three stories high, but they are only one story. The added stories are just false fronts. This is seen in an even more exaggerated form in the Indian city of Jaipur, where the rose-red buildings on the main street seem to be several stories high, but they are just facades on top of one-story structures.

This is called *exteriorization,* giving attention to appearance instead of to reality. Another example is applying rouge to cheeks so they *appear* flushed with healthy blood when they're not. Sometimes people wear clothes that seem to have pockets, but do not. It is possible to talk about books one really has never read, or to buy academic degrees from "mail order" colleges that offer no courses, but only sell empty titles.

We must not aim at looking good without being good, or "take pride in what is seen rather than in what is in the heart." Jesus had nothing but scorn for the religious leaders who "for a pretense" made long prayers. They were like tombs, whitewashed on the outside, but inside they were full of dead men's bones (Matthew 23:14, 27, 28). We need a zeal that is real, a genuine devotion, not just a pumped-up emotion.

—J. G. V. B.

B. "THINKING OF YOU" (v. 13)

13. If we are out of our mind, it is for the sake of God; if we are in our right mind, it is for you.

Paul's extreme zeal for Christ, with his lack of ambition for himself, made some suspect him of being out of touch with reality. His trances, visions, and revelations caused critics to call him mad (Acts 26:24, 25). Paul was quite willing to be thought a fool for Christ's sake (1 Corinthians 4:10). In presenting the gospel, however, he spoke and wrote plainly with sober reasoning. He avoided flowery rhetoric or sensationalism, lest some should be won to Paul's artistry rather than to God's truth (1 Corinthians 2:1-5). For the sake of his hearers he kept his message simple. How wealthy Paul could have become if he had thought more of himself and less of those to whom God sent him!

C. CONTROLLED BY CHRIST'S LOVE (vv. 14, 15)

14. For Christ's love compels us, because we are convinced that one died for all, and therefore all died.

Christ's love came to bear on Paul from several different directions. (1) Christ loved Paul and gave himself for Paul's redemption—as also for us all. (2) Paul loved Christ, and that love became within him the dominant motivation for all he was and all he did. (3) Christ supplied to Paul a capacity to love others in a way he could not have attained otherwise. (4) Christ supplied to the brethren a capacity to love one another (1 Corinthians 12:31—13:13)—including Paul—in a way that held the body of Christ together in spite of all difficulties.

The constraining or controlling power of Christ's love was like walls alongside a road, preventing the traveler from wandering off his course, or like a vise holding a piece of work from coming apart as it was being fashioned.

Christ's love was expressed most prominently in his self-sacrifice on the cross, where he died willingly for all mankind. As believers participate in that death—dramatized and realized in Christian baptism (Romans 6:1-11)—they become dead, not only to sin and its guilt, but also to the selfish ambition that would prevent their following Christ. Christianity is indeed a matter of death and life—first in Christ, who died and conquered death; then in the believer who dies to self that he may live to God in Christ. The natural person, self-centered and self-serving, is transformed into the selfless, self-sacrificing, and self-giving image of Jesus. This is indeed no less radical than death and resurrection. It was this death/resurrection experience that motivated Paul's behavior, which was beyond comprehension to those who had never outgrown the "first law of [earthly] nature"—self-protection and self-preservation.

WHAT DO YOU THINK?

Paul said Christ's love compelled him to action. Christ's love for us should compel us, also, to holy and righteous living, to serving the Lord in some expression of our spiritual gifts, and to maintaining healthy relationships within the church.

Why doesn't Christ's love seem to be a more significant factor in the lives of many Christians? That is, why are these things just named not more in evidence in the lives of many Christians? Do they not really appreciate what Jesus has done for them?

Do your own actions show evidence that you are compelled by Christ's love? Why or why not?

OPTION

Use the reproducible activity, "Ambassadors for Christ" on page 324 to explore and apply the concept of verses 18-20.

The following suggestions may help your students complete the "Diplomat" column in that activity:

Residence: among the people to whom he is sent.
Message: terms of peace.
Goal: reconciliation.
Responsibility: to deliver the message. (The diplomat can not guarantee a response.)

WHAT DO YOU THINK?

Many people see in Jesus of Nazareth nothing more than a carpenter/teacher of ancient times around whose personality and teachings a great religion eventually developed. Others try to fit Jesus into a preconceived mold in order to give divine authority to their personal agenda, whether it be one of pacifism or organized labor or an anti-establishment viewpoint or various other causes. But these are examples of regarding Jesus "from a worldly point of view." They fall short of the eternal nature of his lordship.

Do you think Christians sometimes regard Jesus "from a worldly point of view"? Do they try to fit Jesus into their own agendas for their own lives or for the church? Why or why not? How can we be sure to regard Jesus from a spiritual point of view and conform the rest of our thinking to that view?

OPTION

Use the reproducible activity, "What's New?" on page 324 to explore the concept of being a "new creation" in Christ.

One's newness in Christ is the theme of visual 11 of the visuals packet.

IN CHRIST ...

A New Purpose
A New Perspective
A New Person!

LOVE'S COMPULSION

There are many kinds of love that compel people to act in certain ways. The love of golf causes people to arise at dawn and drive for miles to get on the course in good season. The love of money and gambling drives people to spend countless hours at slot machines in smoke-filled casinos. The love of gardening impels many to spend long periods of time on their knees cultivating the soil.

A mother's love for her children causes her to be available to bandage cuts, kiss bruises, wipe away tears, and help with play times. The love of learning about antiquity drives archaeologists to live for months in desert areas to discover ancient pottery, artifacts, and writings.

Should it then be considered strange if those who love Jesus and trust in him feel obligated to go into all the world in an effort to lead others to know him too? "For Christ's love compels us."

—J. G. V. B.

15. And he died for all, that those who live should no longer live for themselves but for him who died for them and was raised again.

The central fact of the gospel, received as the basis of faith, is here repeated for emphasis: Christ *died for all*. The resurrection life has a new center and purpose—Christ rather than self. Christ's self-giving not only makes the new life possible; it establishes the standard and the energy for its development. The believer is able to serve others, not alone for their sakes, but especially for Christ's sake. So one result of Christ's death and resurrection is finally to remake believers into the kind of extreme—"mad"—persons Paul was!

II. RECONCILING MEN TO GOD (2 CORINTHIANS 5:16-21)

There was sober method, or purpose, in Paul's "madness." It was to convey to every living person the message of God's reconciliation of mankind to himself. Since it was manifestly impossible for Paul to do it by himself, he would enlist the entire church—including the reconciled brethren at Corinth—in the effort.

A. NEW VIEWPOINT OF A NEWLY CREATED ONE (VV. 16, 17)

16. So from now on we regard no one from a worldly point of view. Though we once regarded Christ in this way, we do so no longer.

The worldly person evaluates all things—including all persons—by material standards. What does he look like? What does he wear? How wealthy is he? How influential? Of what abilities or accomplishments can he boast? That is the way Paul's critics were looking at him.

Such thinking belongs to the pre-Christian person. It is to be rejected because of Christ. In him, all judgment is to be made from the spiritual or eternal viewpoint, and every person is to be known as one for whom Christ died.

Paul confessed that he had once judged Jesus himself by worldly standards, looking for a conquering Messiah/King. From that viewpoint he had resisted and opposed Jesus as a false pretender.

After his conversion, Paul recognized Jesus for his eternal qualities. His emphasis is on God's Son who surrendered Heaven's glory for earth's sorrows; who gave himself in death for our redemption, who broke the bonds of death for our resurrection, and who will come again in glory to claim his own.

17. Therefore, if anyone is in Christ, he is a new creation; the old has gone, the new has come!

In Christ one is united with him through faith in him and commitment to him. Thus one becomes *a new creation*. God, who created all things in the beginning, creates believers anew in Christ. They become different in every important way, including the way they look at and evaluate people; including themselves. As a new creation I am committed to new purposes. As new creations my Christian friends are endowed with new possibilities and prospects, to be evaluated for their eternal worth.

Among the *old* things that have *gone* is the old habit of judging according to outward appearances, along with old sins and their guilt, old grudges, old self-centeredness, old isolation and alienation. Among the new things of the new creation are new affections growing from God's love; new purposes, seeking first the kingdom of God; new aspirations and hopes, leading to Heaven; and new Christ-centered activities suitable to the new nature.

B. NEW MISSION OF RECONCILIATION (VV. 18-20)

18. All this is from God, who reconciled us to himself through Christ and gave us the ministry of reconciliation:

God is the supplier of the new creation, just as he first supplied the creation of the world. In the matter of reconciliation, he takes and maintains the lead in repairing broken relationships. Paul and his readers, like all other believers, had been estranged from God and had been brought back by God's ministry through Jesus. Now God was making them his agents, charged with carrying to others the reconciling gospel they had received. Here is the mission of the church as a ministering community. The saved are engaged in the salvation of others.

19. That God was reconciling the world to himself in Christ, not counting men's sins against them. And he has committed to us the message of reconciliation.

Let no reader fail to understand what Paul meant by "the ministry of reconciliation" (v. 18). Paul now specifies, repeats, and explains. It is indeed a staggering declaration, and it may not be accepted on the first presentation. The ministry of reconciliation began with the act of God in visiting earth in the person of Jesus of Nazareth, to attract and win rebellious mankind to himself by his self-sacrifice. In this, God removed from all mankind the penalty for their sins by paying it himself. He made redemption available to all who will accept it and so become reconciled, or adjusted, to him. Then God moved to win as many as possible to that salvation. He charged the reconciled ones to carry the *message of reconciliation* to the persons around them.

Committed is a serious word, describing a responsibility. It speaks of a commission, and it demands devotion in carrying it out. The *us* to whom the commission is committed are the ones who have received God's merciful ministry of reconciliation.

GOD'S INITIATIVES

Paul was very much aware of the fact that *God* had initiated the whole of what one Bible scholar called "The Scheme of Redemption." Paul tells us, "All this is from God" (v. 18). It was God who caused the babe of Bethlehem to be born, he who impelled his words and his ways, and who made clear his will in Gethsemane's garden. He it was who sustained Jesus on the cross and raised him from the guarded tomb to everlasting life. God it was who initiated all the main acts in the drama of human salvation from sin.

When there is a labor-management dispute and a strike, unless someone is willing to present some ameliorating or softening proposal, both sides will remain aloof and alienated. Occasionally family members become disaffected because of something one or another has done or not done. When a mutual relative has died, one may say, "Aunt Rachel promised me I could have her cherry chest of drawers, and that Ida

WHAT DO YOU THINK?

Since we have become new creatures in Christ, our newness should be evident. No longer can acquisition of wealth and enjoyment of pleasure be the Christian's major aims. Bringing glory to God, serving others in the name of Jesus Christ, growing in knowledge of the Word and in effectiveness in prayer must now receive priority. Greed, selfishness, and jealousy must give way to love, compassion, and generosity (Colossians 3:5-17). The Christian should demonstrate a new approach to the use of his money, now recognizing that he is simply a steward of what God owns.

Unfortunately, many recent polls have revealed a startling sameness between Christians and non-Christians in these areas. Why do you think this newness is not more in evidence in the lives of professing Christians? What can make it so?

If a new employee began working with you, would he or she see a difference between you and non-Christian employees? If so, what? If not, why not?

PRAYER

How greatly you have blessed us, O God, in giving us a place in your embassy to mankind! Give us grace, we pray, to be faithful in delivering your message to those about us. May our lives never be such as to deny the truth of what we say. In Jesus' name, amen.

WHAT DO YOU THINK?

Since God is our Creator, he has the prerogative to make the rules as to how he wants us to live. If we deviate in any way from those rules, we in effect take a stand against our Creator. We become his enemies in need of reconciliation. (See also James 4:4.)

Many people think of themselves as autonomous, answerable only to themselves for the way they live. As such, they don't see themselves as enemies of God—just not "religious fanatics."

How can a Christian present the biblical position that those outside of Christ are actually enemies of God in need of reconciliation without offending such a person to the point he or she will not listen to the message of reconciliation?

THOUGHT TO REMEMBER

Be reconciled to God!

DAILY BIBLE READINGS

Monday, May 8—One Who Loves Knows God (1 John 4:1-7)

Tuesday, May 9—We Love Because God Loves Us (1 John 4:13-21)

Wednesday, May 10—God's Spirit Sustains Us (2 Corinthians 5:1-5)

Thursday, May 11—Aim to Please God (2 Corinthians 5:6-10)

Friday, May 12—Christ's Love Controls Us (2 Corinthians 5:11-15)

Saturday, May 13—The Ministry of Reconciliation (2 Corinthians 5:16-21)

Sunday, May 14—Seek Reconciliation Before Worshiping (Matthew 5:21-26)

Mae just went in there and took it. I'll never forgive her for such a selfish action!" This may provoke a "family feud" that goes on for years.

In all such instances someone must take the initiative if there is to be a reconciliation. God took the initiative in an effort to woo man back to himself. Jesus' coming and his loving life, sacrificial death, mighty resurrection, and empowerment of his church show us the initiative God has taken. Now the opportunity and challenge to us is, "Be reconciled to God" (verse 20).   —J. G. V. B.

20. We are therefore Christ's ambassadors, as though God were making his appeal through us. We implore you on Christ's behalf: Be reconciled to God.

An *ambassador* is a person who has received and must convey a message authorized by another. He does not speak in his own name, act in his own way, or communicate his own ideas. God's original ambassadors—the apostles and their companions—were commissioned, directed, and empowered by the Holy Spirit. We do not stand in that same level of authorization; but as a faithful messenger of the King, any one of us can deliver the same reconciling word. It is God's appeal, coming through the mouth of any faithful messenger, and it ought to be respected for its divine source.

"We implore you on Christ's behalf: Be reconciled to God." Yield to God's plea for conformity to him! Cease your resentment and resistance to the Almighty! Cease making gods, or any god, with your own hands or your own imagination. Adjust your fickle self to the reality of the unchanging Creator. Yield to the divine purpose for which Christ died.

That is the message and ministry of the Lord's church.

C. THE MEANS OF RECONCILIATION (V. 21)

How will earth-bound, sin-stained mortals ever become worthy to carry God's ministry of reconciliation to their fellow men? Simply by becoming themselves reconciled to him as he has provided.

21. God made him who had no sin to be sin for us, so that in him we might become the righteousness of God.

A double transformation is involved in our salvation-cleansing. God's one and only Son became something that he was not, in order that we might become something that we were not! By nature he was the embodiment of righteousness. At the conclusion of his earthly life span, exposed to the same kinds of temptations that beset and upset all of us, he could not be rightly charged with any fault in word or deed (John 8:46; Hebrews 4:15). Yet for our sakes he went to a criminal's death as the very embodiment of sin.

Our sins were attributed to the sinless One in order that his righteousness might be attributed to us. The ultimate result is even more than that. It is more than having good things made available to us or credited to our account; it is shaping us into the image and character of God. We become something we were not. We are born anew from above. And that is an experience abundantly worth sharing!

CONCLUSION

All this about the old being gone and the new having come is a bit extreme, isn't it? What living person is a candidate for that kind of transformation? And where is the living demonstration that it actually takes place? Certainly not in me?

Yes, in you! As for demonstration, the text before us provides it in the apostle Paul! It can happen. It has happened. It does happen. It will happen. But not without the permission of the person involved. And that is where you come in. Yes, you!

Discovery Learning

This page contains an alternate lesson plan emphasizing learning activities. Classes desiring such student involvement will find these suggestions helpful. The next page is a reproducible activity page to further enhance discovery learning.

LEARNING GOALS

As a result of this lesson students will be able to:

1. Define, understand, and illustrate the meaning of reconciliation.

2. Describe the changes that occur when a person becomes reconciled to God.

3. Be purposeful and committed to the ministry of reconciling the lost to God.

INTO THE LESSON

Tape a length of butcher paper or shelf paper to the chalkboard and letter on it these words:

"Reconciliation in everyday life is needed in the following situations: warring tribes, quarreling children—"

Ask class members as they arrive to add other situations. (Provide magic markers for this purpose.)

Lead into the Scripture by saying that sinful mankind needs to be reconciled to a righteous and holy God. This is the greatest reconciliation of all, and it will lead to reconciliation in everyday life situations as well. Today's text concentrates on the importance and significance of being reconciled and leading others to be reconciled, also.

INTO THE WORD

Briefly present the information included in the "Lesson Background" section. Then have someone who has been assigned in advance read 2 Corinthians 5:11-21 to the class. Tell the students to be looking for answers to the following questions as the passage is read. Develop the lesson in response to the answers discovered by the class.

1. What was Paul's motivation for talking so much about himself in the second letter to the church at Corinth? (*To give the Corinthians ammunition to counteract the statements of false teachers who laughed at Paul as a leader.*)

2. Apparently some thought Paul was overly zealous, to the point of madness. What was his explanation for his behavior? (*In verse 13 Paul makes it clear that he had two motives—to serve God and to help the Corinthians.*)

3. What in Paul's experiences might have led people to think he was out of touch with reality? (*Have students read Acts 26:24, 25. Remind them of Paul's visions and trances; Acts 9:3-9; 22:17-21.*)

4. What one thing compelled all of Paul's life? (*Verses 14-16; point out that it was the love of Christ, who died for all.*)

5. What does it mean to be "in Christ"? (*We become new creations and that old things are gone, v. 17.*)

6. Whose responsibility is it to share the good news that God has reconciled sinful people to himself through Jesus Christ? (*Verses 18-20 suggest that every reconciled person should be helping others to be reconciled. This responsibility is not merely for missionaries, ministers, and other "hired help." See Acts 8:1, 4.*)

INTO LIFE

Pass out blank sheets of paper and ask the class members to make two columns. Label one OLD SELF and the other NEW SELF. Then direct students to list as many characteristics as they can of each to show the contrast between life without Christ and life in Christ. (*Some typical examples follow: OLD SELF—selfish, self-righteous, egotistical. NEW SELF; self-giving, declared righteous in Christ, humble.*)

After students share their ideas, ask, "Do all of these changes into a new creation occur instantly, or in a lifelong process?" Point out that we become new creations instantly when we become Christians (v. 17). However, we then are newborn babes in Christ. We need to grow and mature (1 Corinthians 3:1; 1 Peter 2:2). This involves changes in our attitudes and our actions that may continue as long as we live. Have each person write this statement on the bottom of the sheet of paper and complete it as he wishes: "One attitude or action that I will ask God to help me change is _____." Allow five minutes of silence for meditation as people prepare their statements.

Go on to explain that sometimes Christians fail to grow because they do not realize that they need any change. All of us have blind spots about ourselves. Have the class assist you in listing some often overlooked attitudes and behaviors in the lives of Christians. (*Some ideas: bias or prejudice about races or ethnic groups, negativism that results in grumbling and complaining, hateful attitudes toward those with whom we disagree.*) Suggest that each one pray daily for needed change in his or her own life.

Observe that one "blind spot" many of us have is that we fail to appreciate the need to be involved in reconciling others to the Lord. Read verse 18 aloud, pointing out that God both "reconciled us" and "gave us the ministry of reconciliation." In your closing prayer, ask for increased commitment on behalf of all the class members to this ministry.

Ambassadors for Christ

To appreciate the Christian's role as an ambassador for Christ (2 Corinthians 5:18-20), consider the role of the diplomatic ambassador in government service. Then compare the role of the Christian witness. The following chart will help you.

	DIPLOMAT	*CHRISTIAN*
Represents (speaks for)	President (government, country)	
Residence		
Message		
Goal		
Responsibility		

What's New?

Paul says in Christ, we are a "new creation." What's new about it? Look up the following Scriptures to explore what is "new" in Christ.

Romans 6:4 _____   Romans 7:6 _____

2 Corinthians 3:6 _____   Ephesians 4:23 _____

Colossians 3:10 _____   1 Peter 1:3 _____

1 John 2:8 _____   Revelation 2:17 _____

Revelation 5:9_____   Revelation 21:1 _____

Revelation 21:5_____

As you can see, some of the new is available to us right now, but there are more new things yet to come! How does this affect the message of reconciliation we have for people of the old way? What will you do this week to share the message of the new with someone?

Christians Living in Community

Unit 3. Ministering as a Christian Community
(Lessons 10-13)

SHARING BLESSINGS WITH OTHERS

LESSON 12

WHY TEACH THIS LESSON?

Financial stewardship is an important aspect of our Christian life. Paul addresses the issue in both of the Corinthian letters. It was a "grace" in which he wanted the Corinthian Christians to excel.

Grace is a good word for this service. It is rooted in the grace of God and expresses one's appreciation for that grace. "Thanks be to God for his indescribable gift!" (2 Corinthians 9:15). It is an expression of grace as well. As such, it cannot be demanded or compelled, but must flow freely from the giver. As Jesus said, "Freely you have received, freely give" (Matthew 10:8).

Use this lesson to challenge the members of your class to "excel in this grace" also (2 Corinthians 8:7).

INTRODUCTION

A. FUND RAISING BY MAIL

As a sometime contributor to "good causes," I find my mailbox loaded with letters of appeal from all manner of agencies—Christian, social, moral, educational, and political. I have attempted to reduce the volume by asking for financial statements from the fund raisers; then actively discouraging all but those in whom I have the greatest interest. Fewer than half responded to my request for financial reports. The reports of those who did showed an average of about eighty percent of income finding its way past the costs of fund raising and administration to program accomplishment.

That does not measure up to the level of Paul's fund raising among Gentile Christians in Europe and "Asia" for the relief of poverty among Jewish Christians in Judea. Paul differed from modern fund raisers in many ways. He never named an amount of money expected or called it "voluntary dues." Instead, the gift was to be as God had prospered the Christian being approached. The amount or the proportion was to be determined freely and deliberately by the donor. Paul was very careful that the moneys be handled by dependable persons chosen from among the givers. No breath of scandal must be allowed to dishonor Christ in this raising, handling, and delivering of funds. Oh that the cause of Christ would always be so respected! The eighth and ninth chapters of 2 Corinthians provide a model for Christian fund-raising letters.

B. IN DEBT TO THE TEACHER

Those who are taught worthwhile truths owe something to their teachers. So says the apostle in a passage dealing with Christians' responsibilities to one another: "Anyone who receives instruction in the word must share all good things with his instructor" (Galatians 6:6).

Paul applied that principle plainly to the Gentile Christians' obligation toward the Jewish pioneers from whom they had received the gospel of Christ. To the

DEVOTIONAL READING:
MATTHEW 25:31-46
LESSON SCRIPTURE:
2 CORINTHIANS 8,9
PRINTED TEXT:
2 CORINTHIANS 9:1-15

LESSON AIMS

This study should enable the student to:

1. Name Paul's two main purposes in raising funds among Gentile Christians to help the poor saints in Judea.

2. Cite some benefits to the contributor of such funds.

3. Review his own pattern of contributing financially to the cause of Christ.

KEY VERSE:

Whoever sows sparingly will also reap sparingly, and whoever sows generously will also reap generously. —2 Corinthians 9:6

May
21

LESSON 12 NOTES

WHAT DO YOU THINK?

The lesson writer observes that Paul "was anxious to establish a strong bond of unity among Christians from . . . diverse backgrounds." This was one reason he put so much emphasis on the collection for the Christians in Judea.

Do you feel a bond with the missionaries whom you and your church support? Why or why not? What would help you to feel more connected with the recipients of your missionary giving?

Romans Paul wrote, "I am on my way to Jerusalem in the service of the saints there. For Macedonia and Achaia were pleased to make a contribution for the poor among the saints in Jerusalem. They were pleased to do it, and indeed they owe it to them. For if the Gentiles have shared in the Jews' spiritual blessings, they owe it to the Jews to share with them their material blessings" (Romans 15:25-27).

That clarifies one important reason Paul pushed the project. He was a Jew carrying the gospel to Gentiles. He was anxious to establish a strong bond of unity among Christians from the two diverse backgrounds. Nothing would serve that purpose better than for the Gentiles to express real appreciation and concern for their Jewish brothers and sisters. The second obvious reason was that the Christians in Jerusalem had exhausted their resources in seeing the church through its difficult infancy, and they were in real need.

Acts 2:41-47 and 4:32-37 reveal that the earliest Christians left homes and employment to receive daily teaching from the apostles. Many who had traveled from distant places to Jerusalem for the great Feast of Pentecost remained there, supported by their fellow believers in Judea, who even sold their fields and houses to provide for those in need. The Judean Christians so drained their resources that when a general famine occurred some years later, the disciples at Antioch recognized the special need at Jerusalem, and moved immediately to send financial help, "each according to his ability" (Acts 11:27-30).

A longer-term, more substantial collection for Jewish Christian relief became a major project of Paul's third missionary journey. He promoted it among the churches of Galatia, and while in Ephesus he sent directions for the gathering of gifts in Corinth and the surrounding country, Achaia (1 Corinthians 16:1-3). Titus became his emissary to develop the project in Macedonia, where it was eminently successful, and also in Achaia (2 Corinthians 8). The relatively poor churches in Macedonia had responded to Paul's appeal with exemplary generosity and Paul was now sending Titus and two other trustworthy messengers to help the churches in Achaia to gather their funds in preparation for Paul's arrival.

For us, the events offer a marvelous study in Christian generosity.

I. PLANNED GENEROSITY (2 CORINTHIANS 9:1-5)

A. GOOD BEGINNING (VV. 1, 2)

1. There is no need for me to write to you about this service to the saints.

The Corinthians were aware of the need in Judea; they had already pledged their help. Thus, Paul has *no need* to introduce the problem. He is writing to confirm their plans, not to initiate them.

2. For I know your eagerness to help, and I have been boasting about it to the Macedonians, telling them that since last year you in Achaia were ready to give; and your enthusiasm has stirred most of them to action.

The people of Achaia seem to have been naturally excitable and enthusiastic. On Paul's first presentation of the need in Judea, made more than a year earlier, they had responded with immediate plans for generous participation. Paul had spoken of this to the folk in Macedonia, and they had been motivated to a surprisingly generous response. But in the meantime the churches in Achaia had lagged in fulfillment of their plan. Now they needed prodding. They needed to act as the Macedonians had acted. Plans and promises must be followed by performance.

B. HELP ON THE WAY (VV. 3-5)

3. But I am sending the brothers in order that our boasting about you in this matter should not prove hollow, but that you may be ready, as I said you would be.

OPTION

The reproducible activity, "Generous Giving," on page 332 offers students an enjoyable means to study the Bible passage for today's lesson.

Paul was sending a blue ribbon committee to help the Achaian Christians complete their benevolent project. The three messengers are introduced in 2 Corinthians 8:16-23. Best known was Titus, Paul's partner in the project. The others, "representatives of the churches" (v. 23), are not named, but one had already "proved . . . in many ways that he is zealous" (v. 22) in his association with the apostle. The third was apparently known to Paul only by a generally excellent reputation with "all the churches" (v. 18). Paul was being careful to provide things honest in the sight of all men. It was almost as if he foresaw and shuddered at the damage done to the cause of Christ by fiscal irresponsibility on the part of some prominent evangelists in our day.

The Achaian Christians must be *ready* with their offering, as Paul had said they would be.

4. For if any Macedonians come with me and find you unprepared, we—not to say anything about you—would be ashamed of having been so confident.

Paul was in Macedonia at the time of this writing. Sopater of Berea, and Aristarchus and Secundus of Thessalonica, all in Macedonia, would be named to travel with the party delivering the collection to Jerusalem (Acts 20:4). They or other Macedonians might come with Paul to Corinth. They had heard Paul's glowing report of the good start made there a year ago. If the visitors were to find the project stalled in Achaia, Paul would be humiliated. That humiliation would be shared by the Christians in Corinth.

5. So I thought it necessary to urge the brothers to visit you in advance and finish the arrangements for the generous gift you had promised. Then it will be ready as a generous gift, not as one grudgingly given.

Here the apostle spells out the assignment given to Titus and his two companions, to help the Achaian churches overcome their present stalemate. *Generous gift* here is usually rendered "blessing." It is an expression of generous goodwill. Made up freely beforehand, the gift would be a happy expression of love to the Jewish Christians.

II. JOYOUS GIVING (2 CORINTHIANS 9:6-9)

There follows a description of giving that brings pleasure to God and man because it reflects the nature of God himself.

A. GOD'S PLEASURE (VV. 6, 7)

6. Remember this: Whoever sows sparingly will also reap sparingly, and whoever sows generously will also reap generously.

In Galatians 6:7 we are reminded that a person reaps *what* he sows; here we note that one reaps *as* he sows, stingily or generously.

Generously repeats the "blessing" theme of the previous verse: "in a manner of blessing." One should dispense liberally as he has been blessed and expects to receive blessing. Both in sowing seed and in bestowing gifts, one accepts the possibility of losing what he has distributed. But he acts in faith, expecting God to bring from it something far more valuable.

7. Each man should give what he has decided in his heart to give, not reluctantly or under compulsion, for God loves a cheerful giver.

Christian giving is voluntary. Each person must make up his own mind and act accordingly. Paul would not recommend schemes and gimmicks designed to act like novocaine injected into purses to reduce the pain of coin extraction. Deliberate acts of love are much preferred.

Not reluctantly; literally, "not from grief." Not *under compulsion*—compelled by either the giver's need to give or the recipients' need for the money. Either of these

WHAT DO YOU THINK?

Paul's discussion on giving here is in the context of raising a special offering to assist the poor Christians in Judea. None of the funds collected in this offering would be used for the Corinthians' own local ministry needs. Do you think it is proper to apply the principles here to one's regular weekly giving to the Lord's work, most of which is used locally, or only to parallel situations of collecting for a special need? Why?

Visual 12 of the visuals packet illustrates the praise that results from generous giving.

HOW TO SAY IT
Achaia. Uh-KAY-yuh.
Achaian. Uh-KAY-yun.
Aristarchus. Air-iss-TAR-cuss.
Berea. Beh-REE-uh.
Galatia. Guh-LAY-shuh.
Macedonia. Mass-uh-DOE-nyuh
   or Mass-uh-DOE-nee-uh.
Secundus. Se-KUN-dus.
Sopater. SO-pah-ter or SOP-a-ter.

would provide sufficient reason to give, but would rob the act of its proper joy, "The cheerful giver God loves." The sentence is so arranged in the Greek for emphasis.

God's pleasure is in those who are enough like himself to give unsparingly because of love.

CHEERFUL GIVING

There are many types of giving about which we need to be gracious and glad. One is the matter of giving *in*. We may have some aim we feel determined to accomplish. We "hold on" even though circumstances make the outcome we desire most unlikely. Finally we have to give in to reality: our wishes are not going to be realized. It is important to do this without whining or complaining or blaming others, to be *cheerful* when giving *in*.

There is also the matter of giving *up*. There are times when we have to give up our wish to have certain pews chosen for a building, or a certain mission liberally supported, or a certain minister called. We need to be able to give *up* without bitterness or moodiness—to give up cheerfully.

We often come to the place where we must give *away* money, or effort, or valued earthly treasures. This we should do ungrudgingly; not morosely, but with good cheer and goodwill.

As we become advanced in years we sometimes discover occasions in our work for God when we just give *out*. "The spirit is willing, but the flesh is weak." We must not let this discourage or defeat us. We must do what we can with joy, and with joy pass the baton in the relay race of life to fresher and younger runners, urging them on to stronger endeavors with glad hands and happy hearts.   —J. G. V. B.

B. GOD'S EXAMPLE (VV. 8, 9)
8. And God is able to make all grace abound to you, so that in all things at all times, having all that you need, you will abound in every good work.

God's abundant, overflowing *grace,* providing all things good and necessary, acts in at least three ways to encourage Christian generosity. (1) It provides the perfect example. (2) It promises a more than adequate reward to the generous giver. (3) It assures a continual supply from which the generous one can draw for continued generosity. When the windows of Heaven are opened to provide overflowing supply (Malachi 3:10), it includes, but is definitely not limited to, things material. God's abundant grace is given to be shared.

ABOUT ABOUNDING

It is interesting to visit the Hershey chocolate factory in Hershey, Pennsylvania, where candy bars, cocoa, and other chocolate goodies are manufactured. As one tours the factory, one sees chocolate bars on conveyor belts as they go to be packaged for shipment to outlets everywhere. One may have seen a box of two of such bars from which one or two bars would be "fished out" to be handed over the counter to the purchaser. But here are thousands and thousands of such bars, a veritable river of chocolate bars flowing in an unceasing stream before one's eyes. This is *abundance* objectified.

Likewise God's grace or kindness and his empowering blessings flow to us in an avalanche of goodness, mercy, and bounty. God is able to do all this when *our* surrender of heart and life enables him to fulfill his will in and through us.
                                                                                    —J. G. V. B.

9. As it is written: "He has scattered abroad his gifts to the poor; his righteousness endures forever."

The quotation is from Psalm 112:9. The entire psalm speaks of prosperity for the person who fears the Lord. Scripture everywhere indicates God's special care for those who cannot take care of themselves. In this psalm is particular reference to the *godly* poor; hence it is appropriate to Paul's present purpose. Because the recipients are God's people, they have a special claim to the Lord's favors; and because the donors are God's people, they have a special motivation to serve as the channels of divine care.

III. PROVISION AND PRAISE (2 CORINTHIANS 9:10-14)

The apostle's appeal approaches its climax in describing the Gentiles' generosity as a means of bringing praise to God, the provider of all things to all mankind.

A. GOD SUPPLIES (VV. 10, 11)

10. Now he who supplies seed to the sower and bread for food will also supply and increase your store of seed and will enlarge the harvest of your righteousness.

Here is reference to the seedtime and harvest mentioned in verse 6. God *supplies seed* in the manner of a wealthy patron providing for a public program. The portion of grain that goes into the ground as seed, and that which is retained to make bread, and the sprouting and growing that bring a bountiful harvest, all come from God. This is not wishful thinking or even a prayer, but a promise that generous giving will be answered with more generous supply. The divine Provider will multiply your goodness with blessings not limited to things material.

11. You will be made rich in every way so that you can be generous on every occasion, and through us your generosity will result in thanksgiving to God.

The generous person will be made able to continue to give generously—perhaps in ways other than material.

B. GOD IS PRAISED (VV. 12-14)

12. This service that you perform is not only supplying the needs of God's people but is also overflowing in many expressions of thanks to God.

Where there was lack of material supply in Judea, the offering would serve to fill it. But the spiritual benefit would be even greater; it would overflow in thankful praises to God. Jesus' judgment scene of Matthew 25:31-46 comes to mind. Those who supply the hunger of the needy will discover that they have inherited an overflow forever with their Lord. The Christian's ultimate goal, not only in offerings but in all else, is brought into focus. "Seek first his kingdom"; his glory above all!

13. Because of the service by which you have proved yourselves, men will praise God for the obedience that accompanies your confession of the gospel of Christ, and for your generosity in sharing with them and with everyone else.

The Achaian Christians' offering will prove to their fellow believers in Judea that the Gentiles' obedience to *the gospel of Christ* is deeper and more meaningful than mere words. They will praise God again for the gospel's power to change lives. They will praise him, too, for the benefit that has now come to themselves because of the gospel for which they have made such great sacrifices. And they will praise him because such benefit is available not only to them but to all nations.

14. And in their prayers for you their hearts will go out to you, because of the surpassing grace God has given you.

The Judeans' prayer response will include not only thanks and praise, but also petitions on behalf of the Gentile Christians, who have now become objects of friendly affection. Paul has written of "the grace of our Lord Jesus Christ" in surrendering the riches of Heaven for the poverty of earth (2 Corinthians 8:9), and

WHAT DO YOU THINK?

Paul promised the Corinthians, "You will be made rich in every way . . ." (v. 11). This sounds a lot like the TV preachers who promise health, wealth, and happiness to those who support their TV "ministries." Do you think Paul would endorse these modern claims? Why or why not? In what ways do you think Paul's approach and appeal are different from that of the televangelists of today?

WHAT DO YOU THINK?

It is significant that Paul concludes his extensive discussion of Christian giving with the exclamation, "Thanks be to God for his indescribable gift!" Considering what God has given us, we should feel ashamed if we give less than the best we can give. We should be so awed by God's grace and love that we respond with thanksgiving and give generously of all we have.

Yet, most Christians do not give very much to the Lord's work. Even with a number of faithful saints who give 10% or more, the overall average is somewhere between 1.5% and 3%, depending on which poll you take as reliable.

How can Christians be inspired to respond to the indescribable gift of God and be generous? What inspires, or what would inspire, you to give generously to the Lord's work?

OPTION

The reproducible activity, "Guidelines for Giving," on page 332 will help your students apply the message of today's lesson.

PRAYER

Thank you, our heavenly Father, for the undeserved gifts by which you have provided life and all that makes life meaningful— especially the gift of your Son. In his name we plead for the grace that would make us most like yourself— the grace of a generous spirit, to share our blessings with others. Amen.

THOUGHT TO REMEMBER

"It is more blessed to give than to receive" (Acts 20:35)

DAILY BIBLE READINGS

Monday, May 15—Works of Compassion Are Blessed (Matthew 25:31-41)

Tuesday, May 16—Give Freely to Help Others (2 Corinthians 8:1-7)

Wednesday, May 17—Give in Proportion to One's Means (2 Corinthians 8:8-15)

Thursday, May 18— Responsible Accounting in the Church (2 Corinthians 8:16-24)

Friday, May 19—Be Ready With One's Gifts (2 Corinthians 9:1-5)

Saturday, May 20—Share With Cheerfulness (2 Corinthians 9:6-10)

Sunday, May 21—Enriched by Generosity (2 Corinthians 9:11-15)

he has spoken of generous giving as a "grace" (8:6). It is indeed an attractive and lovable quality in anyone—especially as it reflects the boundless self-giving of Christ. Something more than ordinary gratitude for material relief would be needed to break down the "barrier, the dividing wall" between Jew and Gentile; but Paul was confident that in Christ that something was present (see Ephesians 2:14).

IV. GOD'S MATCHLESS GIFT (2 CORINTHIANS 9:15)

The final verse of our text concludes the message with a triumphant doxology. **15. Thanks be to God for his indescribable gift!**

Language fails us when we try to describe the gift of salvation in God's Son! John's comes close in John 3:16. But how, then, shall one express appropriate gratitude for that precious Gift? Material payment is impossible, and to suggest it is almost an insult to the Almighty. Thanksgiving becomes a lifelong project, and ceaseless hymns of thanks are both an obligation and a privilege. God's *indescribable gift* becomes the pattern and motivation for the kind of giving Paul urged upon the Corinthians. The exercise of generosity in Jesus' name becomes in itself an appropriate expression of thanks to God for his gift.

There is something fascinating about the singular *gift*—not *gifts*. Paul had spoken of God's supplying food continually in abundant measure (v. 10), but seed and food and every other material provision—even physical life itself— are but loans, to be called in at a time of final accounting. Only Jesus is totally and eternally God's *gift* to mankind, to be enjoyed by grateful recipients forever. In the light of that gift, what believer could refuse to share his blessings with others?

GOD'S GIFT

Accustomed as we are to giving and receiving gifts, we can think of none to compare with God's gift of his Son as our Example, Redeemer, Savior, and Master. His gift meets our greatest needs; it is absolutely vital to us. Such a gift is characteristic of the God of love and wisdom.

Paul is unable to express how significant God's gift of his Son is to us. Our text describes God's Gift as "indescribable."

Have you seen a gift so great that it left the recipient speechless? Some couple is leaving a local church where they have served selflessly for a couple of decades. They are given an expense-paid trip to Bible lands, or a new car, or a travel trailer. Such a gift may well render the recipients voiceless.

Still, such a gift is worth less than the decades of loving service it recognizes. God's great gift was not given in recognition of our "good" service; it was given while we were yet sinners. Then how much more should God's wonderful gift of his Son overwhelm our comprehension and still our utterance!   —J. G. V. B.

CONCLUSION

Acts 21:17 and 24:17 make it clear that Paul and his companions were successful in bringing the Gentile Christians' gifts to Jerusalem, and that they were well received. So Paul was blessed in the fulfillment of that mission. The poor among the saints in Judea were benefited by the money, but how long did it last? Certainly not past the destruction of Jerusalem ten years later. The comfort that came from knowing the care of their brothers and sisters was longer lasting.

The choicest blessings were reserved, however, for those who gave—with greatest pleasure and liberality. Theirs was a special fellowship with God, the giver of all; with Christ, who gave of his very self; and with the grateful recipients of the benefit. They enjoyed especially the approval of their Lord (Matthew 25:34).

Discovery Learning

This page contains an alternate lesson plan emphasizing learning activities. Classes desiring such student involvement will find these suggestions helpful. The next page is a reproducible activity page to further enhance discovery learning.

LEARNING GOALS

As a result of this lesson, students will be able to:

1. Cite several different motives for giving generously to others.

2. Examine their life-styles and determine what would have to change if they were to become more generous givers.

INTO THE LESSON

Begin by saying, "We've all received fund-raising letters or been involved in some campaign or another designed to raise money for some cause. Sometimes, we've probably been a little embarrassed by the approach of the fund-raisers. Paul also raised funds. He did it to support the poor Christians in Judea. Let's imagine Paul was a Madison Avenue type and was designing a fund-raising strategy, and he has asked for our help."

Ask the class to work in teams of three or four each to write a fund-raising campaign. Encourage humorous satire. After about five minutes, let each group share its results.

Move into the Bible study by saying, "Now let's see how Paul *really* approached the matter of raising funds. His method can teach us a lot about how God wants us to respond to needs in the body."

INTO THE WORD

Share the thoughts in the section entitled "In Debt to the Teacher," which is included in the introduction to this lesson. This explains why the Jerusalem church needed special gifts from other churches.

Ask the class why it is necessary to encourage Christians to give generously. Some possible answers: People are basically selfish; times are difficult and money is in short supply; some people have tunnel vision and need to have their vision expanded; some fail to see any connection between giving to others and what Christ has given to them. Show that Paul was not reticent about talking about generous gifts. Have everyone read 2 Corinthians 9:1-15 silently, looking for five special encouragements that Paul gave the Corinthians.

(1. Their giving stirred the Macedonians to action. 2. Their giving would meet special needs. 3. Their giving would glorify God. 4. Their giving would bless them personally. 5. Their giving would unite God's people.)

After these answers are found ask: Why did Paul send messengers to Corinth before the gift was to be ready?

(The advance messengers would assure the readiness of the gift, assure its generosity, and keep all parties involved from being humiliated.)

Have each person turn to a neighbor and discuss honestly: "How do you feel when you are reminded that you need to give generously to the church? How much do you resent sermons and lessons about money?" Point out that Paul was very tactful in his letter. He praised rather than harangued the readers about their promise to give. Go on to explain that giving is an integral part of being a Christian. Refer the class to 2 Corinthians 9:6-11 and ask people to enumerate the blessings that come to the generous giver. *(Some answers are a generous return, the love of God for his cheerfulness in giving, the continued blessing of God so that he can continue to give.)*

Photocopy the following Scripture references, leaving a blank space after each reference so the student can write a brief summary similar to the one printed here.

Romans 15:25-27: Paul praised the churches' contribution, but said they owed it to the church at Jerusalem.

Proverbs 11:24, 25: Generosity is rewarding.

Malachi 3:10: You can't outgive God.

Matthew 25:31-46: Giving to others is giving to Christ.

Acts 4:34-37: Early disciples sold their property to meet the needs of others.

Matthew 6:24: You must choose between serving God and materialism.

Matthew 6:19, 20: Store up your treasures in Heaven, not on earth.

Summarize the Scripture study by saying that giving to others frees us from the tyranny of loving money and meets the needs of others as well.

INTO LIFE

Divide the class into four groups and assign each of the following sentences to be completed by one of the groups:

1. If most Christians were to grow in their giving, these things would have to change:

2. Some wrong motives for generous giving are—

3. Some ways that we can teach our children or grandchildren to be generous are—

4. A generous one-time gift to a missionary from this Sunday school class should total—

Have one person from each group share the group's sentence completion with the class.

Conclude the class session with prayer.

Generous Giving

Read 2 Corinthians 9:1-15 (NIV) and complete the following puzzle. If you fill in each row of boxes correctly, the vertical column outlined in bold lines will spell out a trait that should characterize all Christians.

1. "God is able to make all _____ abound to you" (v. 8).
2. Paul had bragged to these people about the Corinthians' eagerness to help (v. 2).
3. The Corinthians' _____ stirred the people of #2 to action (v.2).
4. Paul urged these to visit Corinth in advance to finish the arrangements (v.5).
5. "Whoever sows _____ will also reap _____ (v. 6).
6. "You will be made rich . . . so you can be generous on every _____ (v. 11).
7. One should not give "reluctantly" or "under _____" (v. 7).
8. "Thanks be to God for his indescribable _____!" (v. 15).
9. "Each man should give what he has decided in his _____ to give" (v. 7).
10. "In their _____ for you, their hearts will go out to you because of the surpassing grace God has given" (v. 14).

Answers: 1. grace; 2. Macedonians; 3. enthusiasm; 4. brothers; 5. sparingly; 6. occasion; 7. compulsion; 8. gift; 9. heart; 10. prayers.

Guidelines for Giving

Read the following verses. For each one, choose one word that should describe the Christian's giving.

1. 2 Corinthians 9:5, 6 _____

2. 2 Corinthians 9:7 _____

3. 2 Corinthians 9:7 _____

4. 1 Corinthians 16:2 _____

5. 1 Corinthians 16:2 _____

Do these words describe you? Pray for increasing grace in this area of your relationship with the Lord.

Suggested answers: 1. generous; 2. intentional; 3. cheerful; 4. regular; 5. proportionate.

Copyright ©1994. The STANDARD PUBLISHING Company, Cincinnati, Ohio. Permission is granted to reproduce this page for ministry purposes only. Not for resale.

Christians Living in Community

Unit 3. Ministering as a Christian Community
(Lessons 10-13)

EXPRESSING LOVE TO ALL

LESSON 13

WHY TEACH THIS LESSON?

Here is another very familiar text, and one that requires careful handling in order to have anything new and fresh to offer your students. Dispensing new information is probably not going to be one of your goals. Challenging and encouraging application surely is. For while we know love is "the most excellent way" (1 Corinthians 12:31); we continue to wrestle with acting on what we know.

One of our problems is the world's misrepresentation of love. Cheap imitations are available everywhere. Use this lesson to challenge your students to discern between the world's concept of love and that of 1 Corinthians 13, to reject the world's way, and to love "with actions and in truth" (1 John 3:18).

INTRODUCTION

A. GETTING THE IDEA

He was a loving and lovable Christian gentleman, preaching and living faithfully what he found in Christ Jesus. Now he was fervently recommending that pattern to a friend who seemed more interested in establishing his own superiority over his neighbors. Finally the friend exploded in exasperation. "Love! Is that all you can talk about? The way you tell it, love is the be-all and end-all of Christianity!"

Here it was the preacher's turn to explode, but in delight he said, "Praise the Lord! You're beginning to get the idea!"

Readers of 1 Corinthians 13 might come to think of the apostle Paul the way the impatient friend thought about our preacher—that he seemed to consider love as the be-all and end-all of Christianity. But Paul did not invent the idea. Jesus quoted two commandments as supremely important—to love God with your whole being, and to love your neighbor as yourself. He added, "All the Law and the Prophets hang on these two commandments" (Matthew 22:34-40). On the night before his crucifixion Jesus expounded the same idea to his apostles: "If you obey my commands, you will remain in my love"; and "My command is this: Love each other as I have loved you" (John 15:9-17).

John, the "beloved apostle," wrote extensively on the same theme, saying, "Whoever does not love does not know God, because God is love" (1 John 4:7-21). Peter also wrote, "Love one another deeply, from the heart" (1 Peter 1:22). Paul summarized the subject in Romans 13:8-10: "Let no debt remain outstanding, except the continuing debt to love one another. . . . Love is the fulfillment of the law."

Godly love—an unselfish seeking of another's good, without regard to the other's worthiness—is exemplified nowhere else so grandly as in God's gift of his only Son for our sins (John 3:16). It is not the kind of romantic passion into which one "falls," nor the friendliness that graces society, or even the warmth of family ties. Classical Greek literature had words for these, but those would not serve the Christian purpose. But in the Greek translation of the Old Testament was another word, hardly used in earlier Greek literature, into which the translators had poured the meaning of divine love and its human reflections. That word—*agape*—is the one the New Testament writers preferred in describing God's love and the love exemplified by his people. It is the word Paul used in our text for today.

DEVOTIONAL READING:
JOHN 15:9-17

LESSON SCRIPTURE:
1 CORINTHIANS 13

PRINTED TEXT:
1 CORINTHIANS 13

LESSON AIMS

This lesson should equip the student to:

1. Distinguish between "gifts of the Spirit" and the fruit of the Spirit that validates all gifts.

2. Report what Christian love does in terms of attitudes and actions.

3. Choose and activate a specific expression of love, as needed in his or her own life.

KEY VERSE:

And now these three remain: faith, hope and love. But the greatest of these is love.
—1 Corinthians 13:13

May
28

LESSON 13 NOTES

WHAT DO YOU THINK?

One reason it is difficult to talk about Christian love in our society is that the word love *is used in so many different ways—many of which have nothing to do with the biblical concept of love. Love is used to express attachment to a certain kind of food, or a specific form of recreation or a particular possession. It is employed to describe an emotional attraction or physical act between two persons, without any mutual commitment. Even in the church, we say we* love *one another, but the shallowness of what we feel is often demonstrated by selfish squabbling.*

What is wrong with these uses of the word love? *Why do they fail to communicate the depth of the biblical concept? (See verses 4-8.) What makes the biblical concept clearest to you? How might you share that understanding with another?*

B. SHOWING THE WAY

Chapters 12—14 of 1 Corinthians deal with the subject of spiritual gifts, which seemed important to the church at Corinth. Paul and other apostles conveyed special powers of the Holy Spirit for special purposes with the laying on of their hands (compare Acts 8:14-20). Nine different special gifts are named in 1 Corinthians 12:8-10: wisdom, knowledge, faith (special measures and kinds of general abilities), healing, miraculous powers, prophecy, distinguishing between spirits (supernatural endowments), various kinds of tongues (vocal utterances), and interpretation of tongues. Verses 28 and 29 mention persons who employed some of these powers.

Chapter 14 picks up the same theme, as it deals especially with the gifts of prophecy (conveying messages by revelation from God) and tongues (speaking in words other than the languages normally learned). Paul preferred prophecy as more helpful to the church.

Bridging between chapters 12 and 14 is the biblical gem before us, dealing with love, not as a separate spiritual gift, but as a first fruit of the Spirit (Galatians 5:22). Hence it is the proper endowment of every believer and is necessary to validate every gift. It offers the "most excellent way" (12:31) to exercise whatever abilities one may possess, and it is to be "followed" in choosing and pursuing any course (14:1). Thus the bridge-chapter is anchored firmly at both ends in the discussion of spiritual gifts.

I. LOVE IS ESSENTIAL (1 CORINTHIANS 13:1-3)

The first three verses of the chapter cite three extreme hypothetical circumstances to declare the futility of even the most remarkable accomplishments—in speech, in spiritual prowess, and in good works—without love.

A. NOISY TALK (v. 1)

1. If I speak in the tongues of men and of angels, but have not love, I am only a resounding gong or a clanging cymbal.

The gift of speaking in "other" or "unknown" languages was prized in Corinth, so it is mentioned first. On the Day of Pentecost the apostles were heard in the native languages of at least fifteen different groups (Acts 2:4-12). But now Paul insists that even if he should become eloquent in every language employed by mankind or by heavenly messengers, but without love, his speech would be mere noise. A *gong* is known for its loud reverberation, and *cymbals* for their clang. Separated from the orchestra, they generate only noise without meaning. So also tongues-speaking for its own sake.

B. EMPTY ACCOMPLISHMENTS (v. 2)

2. If I have the gift of prophecy and can fathom all mysteries and all knowledge, and if I have a faith that can move mountains, but have not love, I am nothing.

The gift of prophecy, to speak by inspiration, sometimes foretelling the future, was found in such first-century Christians as Agabus (Acts 11:27, 28; 21:10, 11). It was also claimed by other persons who were not at all pleasing to Christ (Matthew 7:15-23).

To know and understand secrets of God not yet revealed to others was a spiritual gift mentioned in 1 Corinthians 12:8. But to have such gifts even to the fullest extent (notice how the *alls* are piled up), in the absence of motivating love, would leave the possessor without value.

Mountain-removing *faith* is obviously not the same as saving faith or justifying faith in Christ. It is instead a power to work miracles. "Remover of mountains" was, we are told, an expression by which rabbis referred to a notably great teacher. Paul was evidently familiar with Jesus' similar expression (Matthew 17:20), but no such alteration of landscape is recorded among biblical miracles. In any case, the utmost of miraculous powers, exercised without love, would be *nothing*.

LOVE'S EXCELLENCE

The apostle Paul insists one may have *all* knowledge, but be nothing without love. A recent publication (1992) of *The Anchor Bible Dictionary* consists of six volumes written by nearly a thousand authors. It contains almost seven million words. All this Bible-related material might be understood, yet without love it would be meaningless.

Someone has said that love is like a digit placed before a series of zeros. It is possible to have nine zeros in a row, but this would add up to nothing. It is when the numeral 1 is placed before the first zero that it becomes a billion. Love is the one thing that, when placed first in our lives, transforms all our endeavors and makes significant what otherwise would be a string of nothingness.   —J. G. V. B.

C. UNPROFITABLE ALMSGIVING (v. 3)

3. If I give all I possess to the poor and surrender my body to the flames, but have not love, I gain nothing.

Generosity in giving is elsewhere recommended to the Corinthians as a grace-gift to be cultivated along with their other accomplishments (2 Corinthians 8:6, 7).

Loveless speech is not hard to imagine. Loveless mastery of spiritual powers is a bit more difficult. But what about loveless giving—especially giving all a person has, or is? Yet if one were to indulge in the utmost generosity for the sake of displaying his piety or gaining merit for himself, his purpose would be defeated automatically. No matter how the recipient might benefit, the giver would gain nothing!

Scripture provides no clear example of one giving his body to be burned. We may think of young Isaac going to the altar (Genesis 22:7-9), and of Daniel's three companions yielding to the fiery furnace (Daniel 3:16-23), but we cannot improve on the idea that the ultimate giving is still of no benefit to the loveless giver. Experience shows that some apparently generous and helpful actions may result from pride, ambition, or vainglory. Without love, the user of impressive speech will produce nothing, the man of impressive performance will be nothing, and the giver of impressive donations will gain nothing. So says the Spirit!

II. LOVE SERVES OTHERS (1 CORINTHIANS 13:4-7)

What is this love on which the apostle insists? A definition in descriptive and abstract terms may still not be helpful to the practical common mind. So Paul speaks again in personal terms, saying what love does and what love avoids. He seems to invite the reader to supply a name— Jesus, Paul, Mother, or my teacher—as the embodiment of love. Could you use your own name? The testing ground is at home and in the work place, and the testing time is every day.

A. LOVE OPPOSES SELFISHNESS (vv. 4-6)

4. Love is patient, love is kind. It does not envy, it does not boast, it is not proud.

Immediately evident is the total contrast and conflict between Christian love and the self-indulgent, self-promoting pride of the pagan world, ancient or modern. What love does is what God has done, for God is love (1 John 4:8), and "the Lord is compassionate and gracious, slow to anger, abounding in love" (Psalm 103:8).

To match the passive endurance of patience with continuing active kindness is one of the notable achievements of our loving God and his loving children.

WHAT DO YOU THINK?

Love is "not rude" (v. 5) One could almost say, however, that rudeness has become an art form today. On many television shows a common "humorous" device is the rude remarks family members make to one another. People who regularly watch such shows may copy such rudeness in their own conversation. There is a place for humorous teasing of one another in the home and in the church, but this rudeness goes beyond mere teasing with its disrespectful and discourteous character. Our love should lead us to speak respectfully to and about one another.

Why do you think rudeness has become so popular today? What can a Christian do to avoid being caught up in an imitation of this worldly trait?

The excellence of Christian love is emphasized by visual 13 of the visuals packet. It is designed to be cut apart into 9 pictures suitable for framing and/or presentation. Allow the class to give them, as expressions of love, to people who are shut in.

HOW TO SAY IT

Agabus. AG-uh-bus.
agape (Greek). uh-GAH-pay.

WHAT DO YOU THINK?

Real love "keeps no record of wrongs"; it will not allow us to hold onto bitter memories of slights we have suffered and injuries that have been inflicted on us. It looks beyond the injury to the reasons why it was inflicted. It responds with compassion.

But what if the hurtful behavior continues? How does love continue to put up with hurtful actions—or does it? Does keeping no record of wrongs mean excusing rude behavior? Why or why not?

WHAT DO YOU THINK?

Commenting on v. 7, the lesson writer states that "love accepts the risk of giving another the benefit of the doubt." How does one practice this quality when he hears an unconfirmed report that a friend has committed some act of unkindness or infidelity?

How does one practice it when the report is confirmed as true?

Another situation in which this quality is important is when two people disagree on some matter of importance. How do you grant someone the benefit of the doubt even when you believe that person is in error?

Add the mind-set of love, free from envy, even of another's fame as a tongues-speaker. That enables a person genuinely to rejoice with others in their good fortune as well as to grieve with them in their woe (Romans 12:15).

Consider the communication of love, totally free from boasting and inflated pride, the foolish puffery of "tooting one's own horn." Paul has already warned the Corinthians that knowledge puffs up, but love builds up (1 Corinthians 8:1).

LOVE'S KINDNESS

"What is the real good?"
I asked in musing mood.
Order, said the law court;
Knowledge, said the school;
Truth, said the wise man;
Pleasure, said the fool;
Love, said a maiden;
Beauty, said the page;
Freedom, said the dreamer;
Home, said the sage;
Fame, said the soldier;
Equity, the seer;—

Spake my heart full sadly,
"The answer is not here."
Then, within my bosom
Softly this I heard:
"Each heart holds the secret;
Kindness is the word."
          —John Boyle O'Reilly

5. It is not rude, it is not self-seeking, it is not easily angered, it keeps no record of wrongs.

Love does not indulge in boorish disregard for other people's feelings or preferences. It is courteous, and so can feed the spirit as well as the body of the recipient.

Love does not pursue selfish advantage, but considers the welfare of others as important as its own (Philippians 2:4). It will never make merchandise out of mountain-moving faith.

It does not respond in anger to neglect, wrong, insult, or abuse.

Love does not have a long memory to keep account of evils suffered, and does not dwell on the wickedness of the world around it. It thinks on what is good and godly (Philippians 4:8).

6. Love does not delight in evil but rejoices with the truth.

Evil and *truth* are directly contrasted here, in deeds as well as in words. The apostle John rejoiced when he found his beloved "children" walking in truth (3 John 3, 4). In every respect love finds its pleasure in contemplating what is right and good, rather than what is wrong and wicked.

Here is a warning against enjoying in others the kind of behavior one would not indulge in himself. The dominant fare in popular entertainment invites one to enjoy evil! And the unloving spirit is sorely tempted to delight in the moral decline and fall of folk who excel us in wealth or prominence. Love chooses its sources of pleasure.

B. LOVE "HANGS IN THERE" (V. 7)

7. It always protects, always trusts, always hopes, always perseveres.

Love keeps on keeping on, never setting a limit beyond which it refuses to go, either in bearing its own burdens or helping another to bear his or hers (Galatians 6:2-5). In protecting, trusting, hoping, and persevering, love cannot set limits on the times, places, and persons of its involvement. It is available to all.

Love accepts the risk of giving another the benefit of the doubt. Love is not skeptical, cynical, fault-finding. It looks forward expectantly to the fulfillment of all God's promises. It protects both the lover and the loved ones from the erosion of spirit that plagues the doubter. Love is a survivor because it helps others to survive.

III. LOVE IS FOREVER (1 CORINTHIANS 13:8-12)

Love is an ingredient necessary to every spiritual gift before it can serve God's purposes, and love works. Moreover, it will keep on working after all the spectacular gifts have served their purposes and have vanished.

A. "GIFTS" WILL VANISH (VV. 8, 9)

8. Love never fails. But where there are prophecies, they will cease; where there are tongues, they will be stilled; where there is knowledge, it will pass away.

Never fails. Literally, it never falls away, like the petals of a withered flower. Love is constantly renewed and always fresh.

True prophecies will be dependably fulfilled, but the special gifts of *prophecy* will be abolished, or rendered inactive, when they have served their purpose. Similarly, tongues-speaking by a special gift will fall silent when it is no longer needed. And the gift of *knowledge,* or wisdom by special revelation, will be abolished (the same original word as the one applied to prophecy). All these are transitory, having been conveyed by the laying on of the apostles' hands, and designed for the infancy of the church.

LOVE'S ENDURANCE

Paul tells us that tongues shall cease. This we may believe is true of the tongues that were a gift of the Spirit in apostolic times. But even languages known and spoken by entire populations may become extinct. The language of the ancient inhabitants of Crete has so far vanished that the written material on buildings and monuments is only partially understood. The writings of the Mayan cultures of Central America are only now being partially and painfully restored. It is not so with love.

Human love has lightened peoples' lives in every age. Christian love has endured wherever it has been expressed. It passes from life to life—blessing, helping, lifting, brightening all who give and all who receive it.   —J. G. V. B.

9. For we know in part and we prophesy in part.

Unlike the *fruit* of the Spirit—notably love, which is the possession of every member in the body of Christ—the spectacular *gifts* of the Spirit were bestowed on individual members here and there. Moreover, no one person was given the whole revelation of God's truth. To each was given a facet of knowledge, a piece of revelation, a part of understanding.

B. WHAT IS COMPLETE WILL LAST (VV. 10-12)

10. But when perfection comes, the imperfect disappears.

Perfection—what is complete, whole, mature in Christianity will leave no need for what is found in bits and pieces. If by *perfection,* or "that which is perfect" (*King James*), we mean the visible presence of Christ, we are talking of his appearance for the final judgment. If we mean fullness of the revealed Word, we are talking of the completed New Testament Scriptures, at the end of the first Christian century. If we

OPTION

The reproducible activity, "How's Your Love Quotient?" on page 340 will help your students apply the message of verses 4-8.

WHAT DO YOU THINK?

Scholars have long debated the meaning of perfection in verse 10. This translation implies it is a state, a level of maturity. The language of verse 11 seems to support that idea. The King James translation, "that which is perfect," makes it sound substantive. Some have suggested the completed New Testament is "that which is perfect." Others insist it must refer to the second coming, when we will all "know fully, even as [we are] fully known" (verse 12).

What do you think? What is the "perfect" or "perfection" Paul anticipates? How does your understanding of this term affect your application of the principle he is teaching?

OPTION

The reproducible activity, "The Chicken or the Egg?" on page 340 poses a challenging question about love and maturity. Copy the page or simply toss the question out for discussion.

THOUGHT TO REMEMBER

"Let us not love with words or tongue but with actions and in truth" (1 John 3:18).

WHAT DO YOU THINK?

"Love . . . will blossom increasingly in Heaven, whereas faith will merge into realization, and hope will ripen into fulfillment." Thus the lesson writer explains the message of verse 13.

But doesn't the text say all three qualities remain? Do you see a contradiction in explaining the superiority of love by suggesting it alone will remain in Heaven and the other two will cease? Why or why not? If so, how then would you describe love's superiority over faith and hope?

PRAYER

Open my eyes, God, to see; and open my heart to understand the instructions of love that are to be found in your being and in your Book. Thank you for every demonstration of divine love. Help me to be like my loving Lord. Amen.

DAILY BIBLE READINGS

Monday, May 22—Jesus' Commandment: Love One Another (John 15:9-17)

Tuesday, May 23—The Way of Love (1 Corinthians 13:1-7)

Wednesday, May 24—Love Is Above All Spiritual Gifts (1 Corinthians 13:8-13)

Thursday, May 25—Empowered by Christ's Love (Ephesians 3:14-20)

Friday, May 26—Love Your Enemies (Matthew 5:43-48)

Saturday, May 27—Love Your Neighbor (Luke 10:29-37)

Sunday, May 28—Love Shows No Partiality (James 2:1-8)

are talking of maturity in the church, it may relate to the inclusion of Jew and Gentile—all kinds of persons—in the body of Christ (Galatians 3:26-29). If we are speaking of mature Christian character, we must refer to Ephesians 4:11-16 and becoming "mature, attaining to the whole measure of the fullness of Christ." The coming of the perfect, the mature, the complete, leaves no need for the gifts of prophecy, tongues, and knowledge. Each one *disappears*—again we see the word that is used of prophecy and knowledge in verse 8.

11. When I was a child, I talked like a child, I thought like a child, I reasoned like a child. When I became a man, I put childish ways behind me.

It is natural and right for a child to be childlike in all things, including speech, understanding, and patterns of thinking. So there was a time in the church for spectacular patterns of speech, and for exciting displays of knowledge, and for being tremendously impressed with signs and wonders. But the mature church becomes increasingly focused on the person of Christ and the prospect of his coming in glorious judgment. So also does the mature Christian.

12. Now we see but a poor reflection as in a mirror; then we shall see face to face. Now I know in part; then I shall know fully, even as I am fully known.

Now we are invited to turn from the earthbound present to Heaven's boundless future. Our present acquaintance with Heaven is mediated through human language. It is imperfect, as even the best image mediated through a mirror is only an imperfect reflection of the reality. What we learn of God's infinite glory must be perceived, moreover, through the limits of the finite mind! It is like trying to solve a riddle. No wonder we look for something better, when we shall see our Lord as he is (1 John 3:2), and we shall know the things of eternity as fully as the eternal God knows us now. Love is our lasting link with that blessed forever.

IV. LOVE IS SUPREME (1 CORINTHIANS 13:13)

13. And now these three remain: faith, hope and love. But the greatest of these is love.

Christian love is built on *faith* in God's love as revealed in the gospel. That faith is quieter and more lasting than the faith that empowered miracles. Love's activity looks with confident *hope* to the fulfillment of God's promises. You can't have one of the trio without the others.

Some distinction must be made, however, among the elements in the cluster; and *love* is the one supremely valuable. Love, rather than faith or hope, is the quality of God. Love gives; faith and hope receive. Love keeps faith and hope from becoming selfish; it motivates and purifies their finest expressions. Love, moreover, will blossom increasingly in Heaven, whereas faith will merge into realization, and hope will ripen into fulfillment.

CONCLUSION

The chapter before us is remarkable in many ways including this: it does not contain any plain exhortation! It is filled with practical implications, but nowhere does it say clearly, "Do this" or "Don't do that"! The opening verse of chapter 14, however, supplies the need: "Follow the way of love and eagerly desire spiritual gifts." Love is wholly constructive. It does not set aside anything of value. But when love becomes the most important feature on the agenda, it adds value to every good thing. And it gets better as it goes. "You . . . have been taught by God to love each other. And in fact, you do love all the brothers. . . . Yet we urge you, brothers, to do so more and more" (1 Thessalonians 4:9, 10). And the outreach of love does not stop at the church door: "Therefore, as we have opportunity, let us do good to all people, especially to those who belong to the family of believers" (Galatians 6:10).

Discovery Learning

This page contains an alternate lesson plan emphasizing learning activities. Classes desiring such student involvement will find these suggestions helpful. The next page is a reproducible activity page to further enhance discovery learning.

LEARNING GOALS

After this lesson students will be able to:

1. Define and differentiate among several different kinds of love, and especially understand the love described in this text.

2. Evaluate their depth of *agape* based upon the characteristics found in 1 Corinthians 13.

3. List things that they sometimes substitute for the giving of love.

INTO THE LESSON

Collect magazines and bring them to class. Distribute them so that each person has two or three from which to choose. Ask students to search through the magazines and tear out things that are often used as love substitutes in personal relationships. Have each person find two or three things. (For example, a picture of a diamond ring, an expensive car, and a pet.)

Allow a few people to share their findings and explanations for choosing those particular things. Explain that God intended us to love people and use things, but that some people have reversed that. Lead into the Scripture by saying that the church at Corinth had become enamored, not of material things, but of abilities given to them. In doing so they had ignored the most excellent way, love.

INTO THE WORD

Point out that there is great danger in studying this familiar passage. It is so familiar that much of its meaning is sometimes overlooked. Begin by having the entire chapter read aloud antiphonally by the class and you. You read verses 1, 3, 5, 7, 9, 11, and have the class read the alternating verses. Conclude by having everyone read verse 13. At the end, direct the students to close their Bibles and answer the following questions without looking at the text.

1. Name seven positive characteristics of love according to this chapter? (Patient, kind, rejoices with truth, always protects, always trusts, always hopes, always perseveres.)

2. What are some things love does *not* do? (Envy, boast, be proud, be rude, be self-seeking, be easily angered, keep a record of wrongs, rejoice in evil, fail.)

3. Recall all the heroic and admirable things Paul listed as being desirable behavior but of no value unless accompanied by love. (Speaking in tongues, gifts of prophecy and knowledge, faith, give away everything, give body to be burned.)

Read the answers aloud and have people check their written responses. Ask if anyone got every answer correct by memory. Point out that we forget very easily and need to refresh ourselves periodically and also delve ever deeper into the meaning of the passage. To this end, discuss these questions:

1. Why will some spiritual gifts cease to be given? (*They pass from the scene when they are no longer needed. For example, speaking in tongues was needed as a sign of authenticity in the early church; but when the authentic message was recorded in the New Testament, such signs were no longer needed.*)

2. Why will love always continue? (*It is the greatest commandment of all, Matthew 22:34-40; it is one of God's outstanding attributes, 1 John 4:8, 16. We need to be like him always.*)

3. Why does love need to be patient and long-suffering in our work place? (*When frustrations and failures come at work, the Christian's response should be different from the pagan's.*)

INTO LIFE

Type the description of love in 1 Corinthians 13:4-7, using a separate sentence for each characteristic and leaving a blank for the word *love* or its pronoun. For example:

_____ is patient.
_____ is kind.
_____ does not envy.

Make copies of this list and pass them out to the class. Ask each person to write his or her name in each blank. Now comes the tough part. Ask them to look over the list and write "G," "S," or "N" next to each statement. "G" means generally; this is usually a true statement. "S" is for sometimes; it is sometimes true, but too often it is not. "N" means not usually; this is generally not a true statement.

Lead a time of preparatory prayer, using words similar to these: Father, we want to grow in the kind of love we have been studying. Help us not to be blind to our shortcomings, but to see them so as to ask your grace in overcoming them.

Option: Use the reproducible activity, "How's Your Love Quotient?" on the next page to do a similar evaluation.

After everyone has had time to mark his or her paper, direct everyone to choose one characteristic in which he or she rated an "N" and ask God for help in growing in that area.

How's Your Love Quotient?

Circle your present level of excellence in giving love through these particular characteristics. (Ten is the highest.)

Patient .... 1 ......2 ......3 ......4 ......5 ......6 ......7 ......8 ......9 10
Kind .... 1 ......2 ......3 ......4 ......5 ......6 ......7 ......8 ......9 10
Does Not Envy .... 1 ......2 ......3 ......4 ......5 ......6 ......7 ......8 ......9 10
Does Not Boast .... 1 ......2 ......3 ......4 ......5 ......6 ......7 ......8 ......9 10
Is Not Proud .... 1 ......2 ......3 ......4 ......5 ......6 ......7 ......8 ......9 10
Is Not Rude .... 1 ......2 ......3 ......4 ......5 ......6 ......7 ......8 ......9 10
Is Not Self-seeking .... 1 ......2 ......3 ......4 ......5 ......6 ......7 ......8 ......9 10
Is Not Easily Angered .... 1 ......2 ......3 ......4 ......5 ......6 ......7 ......8 ......9 10
Keeps No Record of Wrong .... 1 ......2 ......3 ......4 ......5 ......6 ......7 ......8 ......9 10
Rejoices With Truth, not Evil .... 1 ......2 ......3 ......4 ......5 ......6 ......7 ......8 ......9 10
Always Protects .... 1 ......2 ......3 ......4 ......5 ......6 ......7 ......8 ......9 10
Always Trusts .... 1 ......2 ......3 ......4 ......5 ......6 ......7 ......8 ......9 10
Always Hopes .... 1 ......2 ......3 ......4 ......5 ......6 ......7 ......8 ......9 10
Always Perseveres .... 1 ......2 ......3 ......4 ......5 ......6 ......7 ......8 ......9 10
Never Fails .... 1 ......2 ......3 ......4 ......5 ......6 ......7 ......8 ......9 10

Choose the area in which you rated yourself the lowest and commit that part of your character to prayer that God will help you to grow in his love.

The Chicken or the Egg?

Whatever Paul means by the coming of "perfection," or of "that which is perfect," it is clear that love is a mature attitude. Whatever is not of love, then, is not mature.

But which comes first? Does one have to be mature to practice love, or does one practice love in order to become mature? In the space below, write about a situation, real or hypothetical, that illustrates your understanding.

Summer Quarter, 1995

Theme: A Nation Turns From God
(1 and 2 Kings, Amos, Hosea, Micah, Isaiah)

Special Features

Lessons

Unit 1. The Price of Power

Unit 2. The Approaching Judgment

Unit 3. The Judgment Arrives

About these lessons

The lessons of the Summer quarter span two centuries of the history of Israel, from the death of Solomon to the fall of the northern kingdom in 722/721 B.C. The violation of Israel's covenant with God, injustice, and the oppression of the poor and weak by the rich and powerful characterize these times. This period witnessed the ministries of many of God's prophets, among whom were Elijah, Elisha, Amos, Hosea, Micah, and Isaiah. Some of the actions and pronouncements of these prophets are presented in this study.

Jun 4
Jun 11
Jun 18
Jun 25
Jul 2
Jul 9
Jul 16
Jul 23
Jul 30
Aug 6
Aug 13
Aug 20
Aug 27

"History Is Bunk!"

by John W. Wade

History is bunk!" Henry Ford once exclaimed. Ironically, even as he made that statement he was making history by introducing the assembly line technique that revolutionized automobile production.

Many people share Mr. Ford's evaluation of history. Perhaps one reason so many feel this way is that history is often taught as an endless series of persons, places, events, and dates that really don't have much meaning. History does have meaning, however. A sizable part of the Old Testament is given over to history—it deals with persons, places, events, and dates. The divinely inspired writers, while they recorded historical facts, saw beyond these data to give us a glimpse of what they meant. Beyond the ongoing collision of events that comprise human experience, these writers saw the hand of God interwoven and involved in them. In Israel's prosperity they saw God extending blessings; in the disaster that befell the nation, they saw him exacting justice from an erring people.

If God had abandoned his world, if he had ceased to intervene in human events, we might be justified in concluding that history is nothing more than an academic exercise of interest to only a few scholars. At the very heart of our Christian faith, however, is the belief that God has not abandoned the world, that instead he cares about us and is involved in our activities. Therefore, we of all people ought to be interested in history.

The Old Testament gives us ample opportunity to see God at work. We can see how he blessed those who were righteous. We can also begin to understand the intricate pattern of events that he used to bring judgment upon his people when they fell into sin and rejected him. We study this history in order to know how to use the blessings he gives us. We also study history in order to avoid the types of mistakes that brought the Hebrew people to repeated disasters. If we fail to study history, we are, as George Santayana once remarked, doomed to repeat it. The tragic fact is that ancient Israel failed to learn important lessons from her history, and that failure led to her dismal end.

The lessons of this quarter, beginning with the division of the kingdom in 931 B.C. and concluding with the fall of the northern kingdom in 722/721 B.C., chronologically follow the lessons of the September-November, 1994, quarter (pages 11-120). That quarter's lessons began with the conquest of the promised land and ended with Israel at the peak of its glory during the reigns of David and Solomon.

JUNE

UNIT 1: THE PRICE OF POWER

The title for this quarter's lessons is "A Nation Turns From God." Unit 1, "The Price of Power," gives us an opportunity to see the dangers of power when it is used unwisely or maliciously.

Lesson 1 introduces us to Rehoboam, who was thrust into a position of power at the death of his father, Solomon. It was a critical time in the life of the nation, and a change in leadership, as it often does, brought things to a head. Solomon's building extravagances had created problems for the people, who were demanding a change. The problems were compounded by the fact that young Rehoboam had not been adequately prepared for the heavy burdens he had to assume. When he took bad advice from his young advisors, the kingdom was divided, a division that was never mended.

Lesson 2 deals with Elijah's dramatic confrontation with the false prophets of Baal on Mount Carmel. When Jeroboam, the first king of the northern kingdom, erected golden calves as elements of worship at Dan and Bethel, he opened the door to out-and-out apostasy. That apostasy was not long in coming. Solomon had already set a bad example of marrying foreign wives and allowing them to bring their pagan religions with them. In marrying Jezebel, daughter of the king of Sidon, Ahab was following a precedent already established. Jezebel was a follower of Baal with missionary zeal. She quickly began a campaign to convert Ahab and Israel to her faith. She had remarkable success until God sent Elijah to confront her and her false prophets.

Lesson 3 shows how a false religion leads to moral corruption. Ahab was thwarted in his effort to secure the vineyard of Naboth; but Jezebel, who knew no moral restraints, did not hesitate to use perjury and murder to gain the vineyard. Once more it was Elijah who stepped forward and announced God's judgment. The lesson reminds us that God, who is no respecter of persons, will not let sin in high places go unpunished.

Lesson 4, the final lesson of this unit, sounds a happier note. In the days of Elisha, successor of Elijah, the city of Samaria was besieged by the Syrians and reduced to the level of dire want. The king, seeking a scapegoat for his problems, tried to blame Elisha. The prophet, however, informed him that the siege would soon be lifted. The king didn't believe this report, and so it was left to four lepers, who ventured into the Syrian camp, to bring back the good news that the enemy had fled. This lesson may suggest to us that God uses all kinds of people to deliver his good news.

UNIT 2: THE APPROACHING JUDGMENT

JULY

The second unit of the quarter calls our attention to the fact that ominous clouds were beginning to darken Israel's future. The events discussed in this unit all take place in the eighth century B.C.

Lesson 5 relates Amos's pronouncement of God's judgment on both Judah and Israel for their rejection of him and of his laws. Amos reminded the people of the blessings that God had showered on them in the past, but he assured them that God would just as surely shower judgment upon them if they did not change their ways.

Lesson 6 also centers on Amos. The recipients of the prophet's message recorded in chapters 4 and 5 were the people of the northern kingdom. They were regularly involved in worship, but their efforts were nothing more than vain gestures that covered their corrupt hearts. Their worship was unacceptable to God because it did not translate into lives of justice and mercy. The application of this lesson to our own times is obvious.

Lesson 7 introduces us to Hosea, who also delivered God's warnings and entreaties of repentance to the people of the northern kingdom. In the view of many Bible students, Hosea used the tragedy of his own marriage as an object lesson to illustrate how Israel had rejected God. Out of the depths of his own sorrow, he cried out for the people to repent and turn back to God. This lesson can be used to remind us that even personal tragedy can be used of God as a means of conveying his love for his wayward people.

Lesson 8 focuses on Hosea's picture of God as a loving parent, tenderly rearing his child, Israel. But Israel rebelled, turning away from God in pursuit of selfish interests. Yet God didn't give up, but continued to reach out to his erring child. While this lesson is directed to the people as a nation, it can touch the heart of parents who have been disappointed by their children.

Lesson 9, the final lesson of Unit 2, introduces us to Micah, whose messages were addressed to both Israel and Judah. This lesson carries Micah's denunciation of the dishonest priests and false prophets who were lining their own pockets, even as they misled the people. He also took aim at the political leaders who perverted justice and resorted to violence for their own gain. Many of the problems that he addressed seem so contemporary that we can almost believe we are studying the morning's newspaper as we discuss them.

AUGUST

UNIT 3: THE JUDGMENT ARRIVES

The final unit of the quarter, "The Judgment Arrives," emphasizes the inevitable result of Israel's rebellious course of action. Three of these lessons are based on passages from Isaiah, the greatest of the eighth-century prophets.

Lesson 10 highlights Isaiah's dramatic call to his ministry to Judah. In a vision that brought him into the presence of a holy God, he was overwhelmed, and confessed his own unworthiness. After receiving forgiveness of sins, he was sent on a mission to his people. Like Amos, Hosea, and Micah, Isaiah pleaded with his people to stop their evil doing and return to God, but the people would not hear.

Lesson 11 deals with Judah's confrontation by enemies to the north. In this crisis Isaiah was sent to stubborn King Ahaz with a message of hope. A sign was given to the king, carrying the assurance that this hope would be realized. This sign had far-reaching implications, for it also tells us of the virgin-born Son, who would bring hope to the whole world.

Lesson 12 is full of woes, for it emphasizes Isaiah's pronouncement of woe on the people of Judah for their sins. He singled out the rich who enhanced their wealth at the expense of the poor, those who became inflamed with wine, those who perverted justice, and those who set their own standards of morality.

Lesson 13, the final lesson of the quarter, paints the tragic picture of the end of a nation that shunned the messengers God had sent. The irony of the destruction of the northern kingdom is that it came at the hands of Assyria, a nation even more wicked than Israel. Among other things, this lesson illustrates that God requires much from those to whom he has given much.

CONCLUSION

To help your students gain a better understanding of these lessons, prepare a large, historical time line of this period and display it in your classroom. Such a time line may be found in most Bible dictionaries. This series of lessons should convince your students that history is indeed bunk, but only to those who refuse to study it.

SPECIAL NOTE

Visual 1 of the visuals packet provides such a time line, noting the kings and prophets of both kingdoms. It extends beyond the time of these lessons, all the way to the Babylonian captivity of Judah and the return. It will be most effective if you cut it apart and make a continuous line from it. (You will want to wait until after lesson 8, however, as the visual for that lesson is printed on the back. Until then, it can be used if you keep in mind the three segments should be viewed as a continuous line.)

Visual 14 is a map of the divided kingdom. Its display will also assist your students in getting some perspective for these lessons.

WHEN POWER IS MISUSED

LESSON 1

WHY TEACH THIS LESSON?

If you were expecting something "light" for the summer quarter's lessons, this first lesson may come as something of a surprise. Our lesson writer has "quit preachin' and gone to meddlin'" right from the start. It points out a flaw that is displayed by many of us when we look for advice. We often do not want an objective evaluation so much as we want endorsement for our own plan—however misguided that plan may be.

Thus, we see ourselves in Rehoboam, son of Solomon, and first king of Judah—a mere remnant of the great empire built by his father and grandfather. By his own choice of bad advice, that empire had been divided, and he got the "little half."

Guide your students past the foolish decision and its fateful consequences. Help them to discover *why* the choice was faulty. In so doing, you will have given them a valuable tool for evaluating advice they receive so that they can make wiser and happier choices.

INTRODUCTION

A. BECOMING A MAN

A couple of generations ago when a young boy was given his first pair of long trousers, he felt that he had become a man, or at least was well on his way to becoming a man. Jeremy and his younger sister, Ruth, had been reared in a Christian home, and each morning before they left for school they would pray a brief prayer that God would help them and bless them that day. But on the day that Jeremy wore his long trousers for the first time, he refused to pray with his sister. "After all," he said, "I am a man now, and I don't need God's help."

After school that day Jeremy flew his kite. As he did so, the string broke and the kite fell into a tree. He climbed up into the tree to retrieve it, but as he reached out for it he slipped and fell to the limb below, where his foot became wedged in a fork. Try as he might, he couldn't free himself. Becoming frightened, he began to cry. Just then Ruth appeared and asked what was the matter. "Oh, Ruthie, I need help. Pray for me," he said.

"I thought you said this morning that you didn't need God's help," she said.

"That was this morning," he replied. "But I need him now." And so they prayed. Their prayer was soon answered when a neighbor saw Jeremy's plight and helped him out of the tree.

When Rehoboam became the new king of Israel, he was like Jeremy with his first pair of long trousers. He was a man now, and he didn't need God's advice or help. Unlike Jeremy, he didn't learn his folly until it was too late.

B. LESSON BACKGROUND

The forty-year reign of Solomon had come to an end, and the powerful king now "rested with his fathers" (1 Kings 11:42, 43). In his stead reigned his son Rehoboam, who began his rule in 931 B.C. at the age of forty-one. We are told that his mother was Naamah, who was an Ammonite, but we know little else about his childhood or youth (1 Kings 14:21).

LESSON SCRIPTURE:
1 KINGS 11:26—12:24

PRINTED TEXT:
1 KINGS 12:6-11, 16, 17

DEVOTIONAL READING:
PSALM 14

LESSON AIMS

As a result of studying this lesson the students should:

1. Understand the events that led to the division of the kingdom of Israel.

2. Be willing to listen to people who believe they have grievances.

3. Resolve to heed sound advice when they receive it.

VISUALS FOR THESE LESSONS

The Adult Visuals/Learning Resources *packet contains classroom-size visuals designed for use with the lessons in the Summer quarter. The packet is available from your supplier. Order no. 492.*

KEY VERSE:

They replied, "If today you will be a servant to these people and serve them and give them a favorable answer, they will always be your servants." —1 Kings 12:7

What Do You Think?

(Use This Question If you Have a Young or Middle Adult Class)

We generally expect that an older person has a measure of wisdom born of experience. Whether a person succeeds or fails at some endeavor, it is to be hoped that he or she learns something valuable that can be passed on to those who come along later. On the negative side, some older people may not have stayed in touch; their experience may be so dated that it does not include prevailing factors of today's world.

When you need advice, from whom do you seek it: someone older with the wisdom born of experience, or from someone your own age? Why? For what kinds of advice do you look to someone older? For what kinds of advice do you look to someone your own age—or even younger?

(Use This Question If you Have an Older Adult Class)

We are not surprised that Rehoboam failed because he rejected the advice of his elders! We generally expect that an older person has a measure of wisdom born of experience. Still, there are areas in which it is difficult to stay in touch; our experience soon becomes so dated that it does not include prevailing factors of today's world.

On what kinds of matters do you think you could give good advice to a younger person? Why? What matters would be better referred to a younger person? Why?

Rehoboam inherited a substantial kingdom that stretched from the Euphrates River in the northeast to Egypt in the southwest. This kingdom had been built by the military conquests of David and the political alliances forged by Solomon. The strategic location of Israel had allowed Solomon to control a number of trade routes, which brought considerable wealth to his kingdom. With this wealth he had carried out large building programs that included the temple, his own palace, and numerous military fortifications. Thus Rehoboam fell heir to a rich and powerful kingdom, but it was also a kingdom that had some serious problems. One was that the people had been heavily taxed to maintain Solomon's program. A more serious problem was that Solomon, as a result of his many foreign marriages, had allowed the worship of pagan gods to enter his kingdom.

The immediate background of our lesson text is found in verses 1-5 of 1 Kings 12. The time for Rehoboam's coronation had come, and Shechem was chosen as the place for it. This is surprising because Solomon had firmly established Jerusalem as his capital. It may have been that Shechem, which is located about thirty miles north of Jerusalem near Mount Gerizim, was chosen to attempt to conciliate the northern tribes, who were showing signs of discontent.

When the people assembled at Shechem for the coronation, they used the occasion to air their grievances. Their spokesman was Jeroboam, who had earlier opposed Solomon and had been forced to flee to Egypt to save his life. With the death of Solomon, Jeroboam felt it safe to return to Israel and had become the leader of the people. They were willing to serve the new king, but their condition was that he relieve the heavy tax burden that Solomon had laid upon them. Faced by such a request, Rehoboam asked for three days to consider a reply.

I. GOOD ADVICE REJECTED (1 KINGS 12:6-8A)

A. CONSULTATION WITH THE ELDERS (V. 6)

6. Then King Rehoboam consulted the elders who had served his father Solomon during his lifetime. "How would you advise me to answer these people?" he asked.

Rehoboam wisely turned to the older men who had counseled Solomon during his reign. Although they had not been able to prevent Solomon from making some foolish decisions, at least they had a good understanding of the conditions that had led to the present crisis.

B. THE OLD MEN'S ADVICE (V. 7)

7. They replied, "If today you will be a servant to these people and serve them and give them a favorable answer, they will always be your servants."

The senior advisers, who had watched Solomon develop his extravagant programs, urged Rehoboam to listen to the complaints of the people. They counseled him to be a *servant* to the people. The demands of the people were reasonable, and these older counselors felt that it would be wise and to Rehoboam's long-term good if, on this one occasion, he gave in to their wishes. These men realized that the people had been under a heavy burden, and to gain their support Rehoboam needed to give them some relief.

Ancient monarchs ruled with a heavy hand, and the thought of becoming a servant to his people undoubtedly did not appeal to Rehoboam, even if it involved putting their interests ahead of his own personal desires on this one occasion only. Rehoboam had grown up in the household of Solomon, a fabulously wealthy and mighty potentate. He was only beginning to enjoy his position with all its rights and privileges. He was not inclined to relinquish his hold on any of them, and he was unable to see that to make a concession to his suffering people at the beginning of his reign would have increased their loyalty to him for many years into the future.

C. REJECTION OF ADVICE (V. 8A)

8a. But Rehoboam rejected the advice the elders gave him.

The advice the older counselors had given Rehoboam just did not seem reasonable to the young king. It is hard for the world to realize that the bonds of love are stronger than the heaviest steel chains. Yet millions of Christians through the centuries have learned the truth of this, and it is still true today. That isn't what Rehoboam wanted to hear. Most of us, when we get advice that we don't like, are inclined to reject it. That is exactly what Rehoboam did.

AGE DISCRIMINATION

Senior citizens sometimes are discriminated against, particularly in vocational settings. Otherwise-qualified job applicants may be rejected in favor of younger candidates. Though retirement may not be mandatory at age sixty-five, many employees who are near that age frequently are removed from service by the subtle offer of monetary concessions they can hardly refuse.

Older doesn't always mean *wiser,* but older people do possess awareness and understanding that come only by virtue of experience. Many in the current "youth culture" discount such wisdom. They stereotype anyone past age forty as "out of touch" with things as they are in the nineties.

Even so, a few companies are recognizing the value of counsel from retired executives, and have put them "on retainer" for occasional business advice. Rehoboam was not that smart. "He rejected the advice the elders gave him" in favor of the *unwisdom* of the young men in his peer group.

Not all of the ideas of young people are bad; nor is all advice from older folk necessarily wise. Maturity and wisdom are not exclusively linked to chronological age. But youth demonstrate wisdom when they seek counsel from their elders.

—R. W. B.

II. BAD ADVICE ACCEPTED (1 KINGS 12:8B-11)

A. CONSULTATION WITH THE YOUNG MEN (VV. 8B, 9)

8b, 9. … and consulted the young men who had grown up with him and were serving him. He asked them, "What is your advice? How should we answer these people who say to me, 'Lighten the yoke your father put on us'?"

The "elders" had been counselors of Solomon. One almost gets the feeling that Rehoboam had sought their advice just out of courtesy to them, already knowing what they would advise. Then, having gone through the motions of listening to them, he could turn to his own friends. They had been his constant companions as he grew up, and they knew exactly what he wanted to hear. Courtiers and sycophants know how to answer their superiors, for their jobs and sometimes even their lives depend upon their answers. And so they gave him the answer he wanted.

In speaking to the two different groups, Rehoboam addressed them differently. To the old men he asked, "How would you advise *me* to answer these people?" On the other hand, he identified with the young men when he asked, "How should *we* answer these people?"

B. THE YOUNG MEN'S ADVICE (VV. 10, 11)

10, 11. The young men who had grown up with him replied, "Tell these people who have said to you, 'Your father put a heavy yoke on us, but make our yoke lighter'—tell them, 'My little finger is thicker than my father's waist. My father laid on you a heavy yoke; I will make it even heavier. My father scourged you with whips; I will scourge you with scorpions.'"

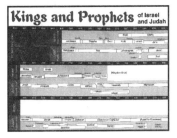

Kings and Prophets of Israel and Judah

Display visuals 1 and 14 throughout the quarter. Visual 1 (above) shows the kings and prophets of Israel and Judah. Visual 14 (not shown) is a map of the divided kingdom.

WHAT DO YOU THINK?

Rehoboam asked for advice until he heard what pleased him. The magnitude of the issue before him should have caused him, instead, to give careful consideration to the possible outcomes of following the advice he received. What was the upside potential if the prescribed course of action succeeded? What were the downside risks if it failed? What was the potential personal cost of following it or not following it?

Why do you think he failed to consider these factors, fairly and objectively? What was driving his decision-making process? How can we be sure to include such objectivity in our own decision-making and not simply choose the advice that sounds good to us?

WHAT DO YOU THINK?

Rehoboam was being crowned king of all Israel. Power and wealth were within his grasp. Perhaps he had looked forward to this day for a long time. Now was his opportunity to make his mark, and to enjoy the privileges of power. But he was being asked to make concessions, and he did not want to do that. Looking back, we can see that he made the wrong choice. But what about contemporary situations? How does one determine whether to "give in" and when to "take charge"? Consider this issue for a variety of "leaders":

A political leader

A parent

A church leader

A business leader (manager or foreman)

OPTION

Use the reproducible page 352 to help your students examine their own leadership roles in the light of today's lesson.

WHAT DO YOU THINK?

Our lesson text focuses on the response of the northern tribes, who broke away from Rehoboam's kingdom because the king promised a heavier yoke and scourging with scorpions. What about the people in Judah, who would remain under Rehoboam's heavy hand? How do you suppose they took the news of the king's answer? Why didn't they also rebel?

What lessons do you think this might suggest for people today who are led by bad leaders?

The answer that the young men proposed revealed a complete lack of understanding of the situation and a complete lack of compassion for the burdens that the people had had to bear under Solomon. Their response smacks of the isolation and arrogance that are so often displayed by those of privilege who live out of touch with the common people. Their contempt for the people can be felt in their words, and the complete lack of concern that their answer reveals could only serve to fan the spark of anger that had been just a smoldering ember during Solomon's reign.

The young men's answer rejected the requests of the people as almost an act of rebellion. In their view the best way to put down a rebellion was not by making concessions to the rebels but by dealing with them with a heavy hand. Every tyrant in history has thought like this. If the people thought Solomon's yoke was heavy, then add to it. If Solomon's overseers had beaten them with whips (and perhaps they had), then scourge them with scorpions. This may be a figure of speech simply meaning a more severe beating. Some commentators think it refers to a whip that had barbed points on it that would bite into the skin like the sting of a scorpion.

The verses that follow tell us that Rehoboam accepted the advice of these young men, and when the people, led by Jeroboam, returned after three days, the king gave them his decision. He "answered the people harshly" (v. 13). It should not surprise us that the people, already in a sullen mood, reacted violently to the king's speech.

III. TRAGIC RESULTS (1 KINGS 12:16, 17)

A. REBELLION OF THE NORTHERN TRIBES (V. 16)

16. When all Israel saw that the king refused to listen to them, they answered the king: "What share do we have in David, what part in Jesse's son? To your tents, O Israel! Look after your own house, O David!" So the Israelites went home.

If there was anything praiseworthy in Rehoboam's answer to the people's request, it could only be that he gave them an honest answer. Unlike some modern politicians, who lie to the people or coat their threatening words with honey, the king gave it to them straight out.

They answered the king. We are not told explicitly, but probably the leaders of the northern tribes consulted among themselves after the king announced his decision. *All Israel* was in agreement when the northern tribes responded to Rehoboam. It seems apparent that tribal jealousies had simmered beneath the surface as far back as the time of the judges. Following the death of King Saul, civil war raged between the house of Saul and the house of David. For seven and one-half years David reigned as king over the tribe of Judah. The elders of the northern tribes then came to David and agreed to recognize him as king over their tribes as well. Now that unity was threatened. If we have trouble understanding how God's people could divide, we need only to look to the area that was once Yugoslavia. Ethnic and religious differences have completely shattered that country. For that matter, we need look no further than to some of our churches where Christian brothers and sisters have divided over lesser matters.

What share do we have in David? The people of the north proclaimed that they were not part of David's tribe. The implication of this statement and the parallel statement that follows it—*what part in Jesse's son*—is that they were receiving nothing from David's son, so why should they give anything to him? Thus the northern tribes harshly rejected the ruling house that David had founded. In less than two generations his heirs squandered the trust and goodwill that he had built up in the nation

Look after your own house, O David! Their meaning was, "Rule the house of Judah, Rehoboam, and don't interfere in our affairs."

To your tents, O Israel. This may have simply been a call for the people to return to their homes, but it may have had a more ominous meaning—a call to take the field in their tents to prepare for battle.

"HONESTY!"

Politicians in general are not characterized as honest ("Honest Abe" Lincoln being the notable exception). If their platform and plans will require higher taxes, or any other unpopular development that might cost them votes, most of their speeches and debates will avoid mention of those topics.

Rehoboam, of course, had a distinct advantage: he was not required to run for office. Had it been necessary for him to do so, the electorate never would have voted for him. He certainly was no politician. He deliberately antagonized and alienated most of Israel. True, he didn't skirt the issues, but his intentions were more than wrong—they were ungodly.

We can't even give Rehoboam "points" for honesty. Some folk still try to justify their sinful intentions by confessing them: "I won't promise to be in worship Sunday," one might say, "because, frankly I probably won't be there." Or, "I may forgive, but I'll never forget."

Honesty may be the best policy, but it won't cover a multitude of sins.

—R. W. B.

B. REDUCED KINGDOM IN THE SOUTH (v. 17)

17. But as for the Israelites who were living in the towns of Judah, Rehoboam still ruled over them.

Left to be ruled by Rehoboam were the tribe of Judah and those persons of other Israelite tribes who had settled in the territory of Judah. It appears that the tribe of Benjamin also accepted him, for when Rehoboam prepared to go to war against the northern tribes, the tribe of Benjamin stood with him (v. 21).

A great tragedy had befallen the people of God. Yet even this tragedy was within God's oversight. Because Solomon had allowed the people to drift away from God and into idolatry, God took the northern tribes away from Solomon's son. God's prophet had previously announced to Jeroboam this division of the kingdom (1 Kings 11:28-39). Even though Rehoboam acted out of his own free will in dealing harshly with the people, God used that action to accomplish his purpose.

CONCLUSION

A. HEEDING SOUND ADVICE

How often heartache and disaster come when persons fail to follow sound advice! A young person has been flooded with good advice about avoiding drugs, but he fails to heed that advice and soon finds himself trapped in addiction. A young woman is swept off her feet by a dashing, handsome young man. Against the advice of her parents and friends she marries him, only to awaken from her dream to find that he is lazy and unfaithful. A scam artist appears on the scene with a surefire get-rich-quick scheme. The entranced victim flies in the the face of common sense and good advice and takes the bait, only to find himself poorer for it.

Why is it that so many people, like Rehoboam, fail to take the good advice that is offered them? There are several reasons.

Often good advice goes contrary to what we want to do; it requires us to make some sacrifice, take on some burdensome duty, or give up some cherished pleasure. All of us are guilty on occasion of taking the easy way out and ignoring what we know to be sound advice.

WHAT DO YOU THINK?

In conflict situations the persons involved may concede, contend, compromise, or collaborate. If we consider that collaboration is the win-win resolution that gives all parties what they desire, then that is the option that should be pursued first. In this case the people wanted relief from the burden of supporting the king's many ambitions. Rehoboam wanted to be regarded as a powerful ruler, and he wanted to reign in no less splendor than his father, Solomon.

Do you think it would have been possible for Rehoboam and the people to collaborate and come up with a win-win solution? Why or why not?

Think of the last conflict in which you were involved. Did you concede, contend, compromise, or collaborate? If you could do it over again, which would you choose? Why?

WHAT DO YOU THINK?

Rehoboam first ignored the people's response and then he attempted to force compliance. Do you think he could have sent a peace envoy to work things out and have saved the kingdom? Why or why not?

If you had been one of the rebels, how would you have responded if a messenger from Rehoboam had come with the king's apologies and suggested you negotiate terms of peace? Why?

How do you respond to apologies you really receive after a conflict has become heated? How can you improve on that?

Prayer

Almighty God, who watches over the destinies of men and of nations, we come to you humbly acknowledging our complete dependence on you. Teach us to avoid the folly of Rehoboam by learning to walk humbly with you and to obey your commandments. In Jesus' name we pray. Amen.

Thought to Remember

Pride goes before a fall.

Daily Bible Readings

Monday, May 29—A Wise Person Seeks God's Help (Psalm 14)

Tuesday, May 30—Prophecy That Jeroboam Will Succeed Solomon (1 Kings 11:26-40)

Wednesday, May 31—Israel's Appeal for a Lightened Load (1 Kings 12:1-5)

Thursday, June 1—King Rehoboam Rejects the People's Appeal (1 Kings 12:6-11)

Friday, June 2—Israel Withdraws Allegiance From Rehoboam (1 Kings 12:12-17)

Saturday, June 3—Jeroboam Is Made King Over Israel (1 Kings 12:18-24)

Sunday, June 4—A Wise Person Uses Good Judgment (Proverbs 16:16-25)

Sometimes we are persuaded by our friends not to take good advice. We may do what we know is wrong or foolish because we are afraid of offending our friends or we are afraid of being different.

At times we may question the motives of those who give us good advice. We may be led to believe that they are seeking to control our lives or deny us our freedom. How often young people believe that parents or teachers lay down restrictions because these people actually dislike them or want to do them harm!

We may fail to follow good advice because we fear we don't have the resources or courage to see the matter through. Lack of self-confidence may cause us to follow the path of least resistance, which means we don't follow the best advice available.

Many of the problems we face in our society are extremely complex, forcing us to rely on experts to provide the answers we need. On certain issues, however, Christians are, or should be, experts. Science cannot provide answers to moral issues, nor can psychology, nor sociology, nor medicine. We must turn to the Bible to find those answers. To do that, we must know the Bible, and to know the Bible, we must study it diligently.

B. "Pride Goes Before Destruction"

Perhaps the most frequent reason we fail to take good advice is that it goes against our pride. It is ironic that these words of Solomon, "Pride goes before destruction" (Proverbs 16:18), should find their embodiment in the life of his son Rehoboam. While the Scriptures do not provide any details about the life of this young prince as he was growing up, we can imagine what it must have been like. With his many wives and concubines, Solomon must have had many sons. Undoubtedly, this led to all kinds of conflicts and bitterness as each son struggled to gain a favorable position in that competition. We have no idea why Rehoboam was chosen from among all these sons to become the next king.

One virtue Rehoboam did not learn as he grew up was humility. When Solomon came to the throne, he at least did so humbly, acknowledging that he was "only a little child" (1 Kings 3:7). Not Rehoboam! He had been born to the purple, and in no way was he willing to become a servant to his people. That arrogance almost cost him his life. Soon after the incident recorded in our text, Rehoboam sent Adoram, the head taskmaster, to the rebels, perhaps to collect taxes or to round up workers for the king's service. Thus the king would let the people know that he gave no heed to their words. This added insult to injury, and the people took out their wrath on Adoram, stoning him to death. When Rehoboam learned what had happened, he realized that his own life was in jeopardy. Quickly he got into his chariot and sped back to the safety of Jerusalem.

Pride had cost Rehoboam much of his kingdom and had almost cost him his life. Yet, instead of repenting of his arrogance and trying to make amends for the damage he had done, he sought to gather his forces and launch an attack against the rebelling tribes. Before Rehoboam could carry out this plan, God sent his messenger to stop him.

How often we behave like Rehoboam! Pride leads a person to take an unwise course. Even when it becomes obvious that such a course can end only in disaster, one's pride keeps him from admitting his folly and making proper amends.

Pride causes us all to go astray from God. If we continue in such a course, the disaster that will ultimately befall us will be worse than any we can imagine in this life. The kingdom of God is reserved for those who will humble themselves before him (Matthew 18:3, 4). Let us cast off our pride, humble ourselves before God, and submit to the lordship of Christ. In so doing, blessings will attend our way, and it will lead us to eternal life.

Discovery Learning

This page contains an alternate lesson plan emphasizing learning activities. Classes desiring such student involvement will find these suggestions helpful. The next page is a reproducible activity page to further enhance discovery learning.

LEARNING GOALS

This study will enable the students to:

1. Analyze Rehoboam's use of power as recorded in 1 Kings 12.

2. Understand that individuals in positions of power are to use that power to serve others, not themselves.

INTO THE LESSON

Begin the session by giving each class member a three-by-five card. Write the following on your chalkboard:

An individual in a position of power who used that power to serve others.

An individual in a position of power who used that power to serve self.

Say to the class, "Today we are considering the use of power. I'd like for each of you to jot down the name of a person who fits the first category on the chalkboard, and another person who fits the second category."

Allow about sixty seconds for your students to think of individuals. Then ask volunteers to tell whom they selected for each category. Have them indicate how each person they named demonstrated the particular use of power.

Lead into the Bible study by saying, "Power is a fact of life. Certain individuals are in positions of power. That power can be used for good or evil, to benefit others or to promote one's selfish interests. In this lesson we will learn about a king who was presented with the option of using his power to serve others or to serve himself. Let's see what we can learn about the appropriate use of power."

INTO THE WORD

Present a brief lecture to establish the background of today's study. Use the thoughts included in the "Lesson Background" section on pages 345 and 346 for this. The lecture should last only about three or four minutes.

Have a class member whom you have asked ahead of time to read 1 Kings 12:1-20 aloud to the class at this point. Then have the class form groups of four to six people. Appoint a leader for each group, and give each leader a copy of the following questions so each group may discuss them. Allow the groups about fifteen minutes to discuss the questions. Then have the groups reassemble as a class.

1. What did the people request of Rehoboam?

2. What different kinds of advice did Rehoboam receive regarding this issue?

3. Put yourself in Rehoboam's place. You have received conflicting advice from the elders and from the young men, and you must make a decision. The following four questions seem to be logical ones to consider. Discuss them in your group.

• What are the pros for the advice from the elders?
• What are the cons for the advice from the elders?
• What are the pros for the advice from the young men?
• What are the cons for the advice from the young men?

4. What were the consequences of Rehoboam's choice?

When the class reassembles, ask, "What were the most important observations made in your group?" Allow for comments. Then ask, "From this incident, what do we learn about the use of power?"

Rehoboam failed miserably in his first test as a leader. Ask the class to give reasons for his failure.

OPTION

Have a volunteer read 1 Kings 12:1-20 aloud to the class. Present a brief lecture on the background of the lesson, as suggested in the first paragraph of the "Into the Word" section. Then have the class break into groups of four students each. Provide each group with a pen and several sheets of paper. Give the following assignment: "Put yourself in Rehoboam's place in this narrative. Write a brief journal entry revealing your thoughts and concerns at each of these points: (1) vv. 1-5; (2) vv. 6-8a; (3) vv. 8b-11; (4) vv. 12-20."

Allow about twenty minutes. Then ask each group to read its journal entries to the rest of the class.

INTO LIFE

Conclude this lesson by leading your class in discussing these questions:

1. On the basis of the incident in the lesson text, what qualities do you think a person in authority should have to be a successful leader?

2. In seeking advice, what is the danger of going only to people in our "own crowd"?

3. How can we decide from whom to seek advice?

Option: Use the reproducible activity page that follows to help your students apply this lesson to situations in which they exercise power or authority.

The Use and Abuse of Power

Power may be used to serve oneself or others. In the space below, give one historical example of a person who fits each category. (You may wish to use the other spaces to note the examples given by others in your group.)

SERVING SELF   SERVING OTHERS

_____   _____

_____   _____

_____   _____

Think of specific areas in your life (church, work, family, etc.) where you have been given a degree of power. Write those areas on the line below indicating how you are presently using that power. For example, if you are a leader in your church and you feel you are doing well at serving others in that position, write "Church" on the line below near the word *Others*. If you are a leader at work and feel perhaps you have been using that position mostly to enhance yourself, write "Work" near the word *Self.* Add as many labels to the line as you can. (Write diagonally across the line to get more labels on the line.)

Self _____ **Others**

The most powerful man ever to walk the earth was described by Paul as "being in very nature God [yet he] did not consider equality with God something to be grasped, but made himself nothing, taking the very nature of a servant." Even though Jesus Christ had much more power available to him that did Rehoboam, he did not act out of selfish ambition.

How would following the example of Jesus affect your use of power in the areas you listed above. Be specific.

	AREA	WHAT I WOULD CHANGE:
1.		
2.		
3.		
4.		
5.		

THE DANGER OF FALSE RELIGION

LESSON 2

Jun
11

WHY TEACH THIS LESSON?

"Desperate times demand desperate measures." Such is the wisdom of the world, but it is not the wisdom of God. "Desperate times demand measures of faith." The world may see these measures of faith as "desperate," but as we saw last quarter, "the foolishness of God is wiser than man's wisdom" (1 Corinthians 1:25).

Thus we see Elijah, alone on Mt. Carmel against hundreds of hostile false prophets. They must have thought Elijah's position desperate indeed. By human standards, it surely was. But God answered in fire and made his will known.

Use this lesson to challenge your students to take a stand, even when it seems desperate—to trust in God, even when he seems absent—to make a difference, for the glory of God.

INTRODUCTION

A. "HERE I STAND"

In 1517 Martin Luther nailed his famous "Ninety-five Theses" to the door of the Castle Church in Wittenberg. This document attacked many of the corruptions of the Roman Catholic Church. The controversy it ignited continued to grow until it shook both the Roman Church and the Holy Roman Empire to their foundations. By January of 1521, Leo X had made the church's response clear by excommunicating Luther. On behalf of the empire, Emperor Charles V summoned Luther to appear before the Imperial Diet to be held in Worms that April. The emperor demanded that Luther recant his teachings or face the consequences. The consequences, Luther knew, could very well be the same that John Hus had received a century earlier. This Bohemian reformer, haled before the Council of Constance, had refused to recant his beliefs and was burned at the stake.

Standing before the Diet, Luther refused to recant his writings, and boldly proclaimed: "Unless I am convinced by the testimony of Scripture or by evident reason (for I trust neither in popes nor in councils alone, since it is obvious that they have often erred and contradicted themselves) I am convicted by the Scripture which I have mentioned and my conscience is captive to the Word of God. Therefore I cannot and will not recant, since it is difficult, unprofitable and dangerous indeed to do anything against one's conscience. Here I stand! I can do no other! God help me!"*

In the same way, Elijah, in challenging the false prophets of Baal, placed his life in jeopardy. But, in the face of a life-and-death choice, he did not flinch. Like Luther, he said, "Here I stand! I can do no other! God help me!"

B. LESSON BACKGROUND

Ahab, the son of Omri, became the king of the northern kingdom about 875 B.C. Omri had been a wicked king, but Ahab outdid his father: "Ahab son of Omri did more evil in the eyes of the Lord than any of those before him" (1 Kings 16:30). To compound his wickedness, Ahab married Jezebel, the daughter of the king of

DEVOTIONAL READING:

DEUTERONOMY 6:5-15

LESSON SCRIPTURE:

1 KINGS 18

PRINTED TEXT:

1 KINGS 18:30-39

LESSON AIMS

As a result of studying this lesson, the students should:

1. Have a high regard for the influence one person can have on others.

2. Appreciate the uncompromising courage of Elijah in the face of those who promoted the worship of false gods.

3. Have courage to obey God when they are faced with a choice between good and evil.

*NOTE:

Historians are divided on whether or not Luther said the words, "Here I stand. I can do no other." Actual records of the Diet do not include them, but they are found in some e early printed reports of the event. What is clear is that Luther did take the stand, compelled by the belief that he could do no other. (The rest of the quote is from a newspaper report cited in The Reformation, Hans J. Hillerbrand, ed., ©1964 by SCM Press Ltd and Harper & Row, Inc., reprinted in 1978 by Baker Book House, page 91.)

KEY VERSE:

"How long will you waver between two opinions? If the Lord is God, follow him."

—1 Kings 18:21

LESSON 2 NOTES

HOW TO SAY IT

Asherah. Uh-SHEER-uh.
Baal. BAY-ul.
Diet. DEE-ut.
Jehu. JEE-hew or JAY-hew.
Jezebel. JEZ-uh-bell.
Omri. AHM-rye or AHM-ree.
Sinai. SYE-nay-eye or SYE-nye.
Worms. VORMZ.

OPTION

The reproducible activity, "The Pattern of God's Spokesman," on page 360 will lead your students in a Bible study of this and some related texts.

WHAT DO YOU THINK?

The Israelites were lured away from God by the appeal of Baal worship. While idol worship, as such, holds little threat to one's commitment to God in our day, many activities or things can become idols if we allow them to compete with God for our devotion. It may be a car, a house, a boat, a job, a hobby, or even a friendship. A good test might be to ask, "Is this interest contributing to God's will in my life, or is it crowding him out?"

What do you think is the biggest idol in your community? How much is the church affected? What does the church need to do to take an Elijah's stand against this idolatry? What can you do to take such a stand?

Sidon. Jezebel imported into Israel the worship of Baal, along with many priests to serve this false god. As a result, God, using Elijah as his spokesman, proclaimed a prolonged drought upon the land (1 Kings 17:1).

After the land suffered three and one-half years (Luke 4:25), God sent Elijah back to speak to Ahab. When they met, Ahab charged Elijah with being the troubler of Israel, but Elijah returned the charge, labeling Ahab as the real troubler of the nation. Elijah then challenged the prophets of Baal and the prophets of Asherah—a supposed female deity often associated with Baal—to a contest on Mount Carmel (1 Kings 18:7-19).

Each side was to prepare an altar and offer a bullock as a sacrifice. The prophets of Baal were to call upon their god to send down fire and consume the sacrifice. Elijah would make the same request of Jehovah. Whichever one answered the prayer by fire would be recognized as the true God.

The prophets of Baal cried out to their god from morning until noon. When no answer came, they cried out louder, leaped about the altar frantically, and even cut themselves, but Baal did not answer. It is at this point that our lesson text begins.

I. GOD'S ALTAR REPAIRED (1 KINGS 18:30-32)

A. INVITATION TO THE PEOPLE (V. 30)

30. Then Elijah said to all the people, "Come here to me." They came to him, and he repaired the altar of the LORD, which was in ruins.

The prophets of Baal had had their chance to demonstrate the power of their god, but they had failed, and understandably so. The god they worshiped was one of their own imagining. He could not respond because he simply did not exist outside of the minds of those who proclaimed him a god.

Now it was Elijah's turn. The people who were witnessing this contest probably had been standing around the altar to Baal, waiting for something to happen. Elijah called them to come near to him so they could watch carefully as he repaired the altar to Jehovah. Elijah encouraged them to watch so that they could be credible witnesses of the event later on.

Elijah began to repair the altar that had either fallen into disrepair or been deliberately destroyed by Ahab's forces (1 Kings 19:10). This involved assembling the stones that had been used in its initial construction.

B. CONSTRUCTION OF THE ALTAR (VV. 31, 32)

31, 32. Elijah took twelve stones, one for each of the tribes descended from Jacob, to whom the word of the LORD had come, saying, "Your name shall be Israel." With the stones he built an altar in the name of the LORD, and he dug a trench around it large enough to hold two seahs of seed.

The stones that Elijah used were probably not shaped stones but merely rough stones one might pick up on a mountain ridge. Of those available, he chose only twelve. In this action he may have been giving a reminder of the essential unity of God's people, even though the tribes had been divided into two separate kingdoms. He also reminded them that God had spoken to their father Jacob and had given him a new name—*Israel* (Genesis 32:28).

After building the altar, Elijah *dug a trench* around it. This action must have surprised the crowd, for they would have had no idea what purpose it could serve. *Two seahs of seed.* The seah was a dry measure equal to about a third of a bushel. One normally describes a trench by its depth, so the meaning may be that this trench was as deep as the measure containing two seahs of grain. Thus it would not have been a very deep trench, but it would have been adequate to hold the excess water that was to be poured over the sacrifice.

II. A SACRIFICE PREPARED (1 KINGS 18:33-35)

A. CAREFUL ARRANGEMENT (V. 33A)

33a. He arranged the wood, cut the bull into pieces and laid it on the wood.

In preparing the sacrifice, Elijah apparently followed the instructions set forth in Leviticus 1:3-9. In following the procedure set forth in the law, Elijah may have been visually reminding the people that they were still subject to the law of Jehovah. Normally, the next step would be to kindle a fire under the sacrifice; what Elijah did, however, was unheard of and obviously unexpected.

B. CONVINCING PRECAUTIONS (VV. 33B-35)

33b-35. Then he said to them, "Fill four large jars with water and pour it on the offering and on the wood." "Do it again," he said, and they did it again. "Do it a third time," he ordered, and they did it the third time. The water ran down around the altar and even filled the trench.

Fill four large jars with water. Since a drought lasting three and one-half years had preceded this incident, one might wonder where this water was obtained. We are not told, and so we can only conclude that the water came from a nearby spring that was supplied by an aquifer ample enough to keep flowing in spite of the drought.

Some ancient altars were constructed with holes beneath them so that concealed priests could ignite the wood, leading the worshipers to believe that their god had started the fire. Elijah took precautions against any charge of fraud. First, he called for the people to come near to him, and he built the altar right before their eyes so that they could know there were no secret hiding places beneath it (v. 30). Then, by drenching the sacrifice, the wood, and the altar, he completely excluded any possibility of being charged with deception.

Three times he called for four jars of water to be brought—thus twelve jars in all were poured on the sacrifice and the wood. As a consequence, the altar and everything on and around it were thoroughly soaked, and the excess water filled the trench that had been dug around it.

THE WORK OF A PROPHET

Wise employers make certain that workers know what is expected of them. Written job descriptions make for fewer misunderstandings and better efficiency.

Who would have guessed that a prophet of God would be required to build altars and slaughter cattle? Elijah either did that work or supervised it; he could have balked at all that menial labor. He might have said, "Why can't I just pray for fire to consume these animal sacrifices lying whole on the ground? Lord, can't you prove your existence and power without all this human effort?"

It seems that God most often chooses to work through human agency. Elijah set the stage for a dramatic demonstration of divine power. Such assistance was part of his *unwritten* job description, and it is part of ours, too.

What can you do to help God's miracles of love and grace happen?

The hymn writer Frances R. Havergal said it well:

Take my hands, and let them move
At the impulse of thy love.

—R. W. B.

III. ELIJAH'S PRAYER AND ITS ANSWER (1 KINGS 18:36-38)

A. REQUEST OF GOD'S PROPHET (VV. 36, 37)

36. At the time of sacrifice, the prophet Elijah stepped forward and prayed: "O LORD, God of Abraham, Isaac and Israel, let it be known today that you are God

---

WHAT DO YOU THINK?

Some believers are choosing to go head-to-head with the powers of darkness in the courts, in legislative bodies, and even in the marketplace. How might these be compared to Elijah and the stand he took on Mt. Carmel? How would you compare their victories with the victories won by those who focus on simply sharing the gospel? In what ways are both needed today?

Visual 2 illustrates the superiority of following God's Word over the ways of the world—the point Elijah was making on Mt. Carmel.

WHAT DO YOU THINK?

Elijah prayed that God would act in a way that would prove that he was God's servant. Have you ever prayed to be recognized as God's servant? Why or why not? How would God be glorified today if more of his people were as concerned as Elijah with being recognized as servants of the true God? What would be different about the church and society if this were more common?

WHAT DO YOU THINK?

Not only the sacrifice, but also the wood, the stone altar, and the water were consumed when the fire of the Lord fell on them. No one could argue that Elijah had accomplished this by some clever trick. The fact that the people came near to Elijah while he constructed the altar gave assurance that there could not have been an accomplice hidden under the altar to ignite the sacrifice at the proper moment. The fact that the wood was water-soaked made the outcome even more convincing. There could be no excuse for disbelief that day.

What evidence can we produce today that will be convincing to people about their need to follow the Lord? How do the facts concerning the resurrection give us similar "convincing proofs" (Acts 1:3) for people today?

in Israel and that I am your servant and have done all these things at your command.

The Hebrew text at the beginning of this verse may literally be translated, "At the offering of the sacrifice," without any time reference. The words *the time of* were supplied by the translators. However, the translators may be correct in supposing that Elijah offered this sacrifice "at the time of sacrifice," when the second of two daily sacrifices was being offered in the temple in Jerusalem, probably about three o'clock in the afternoon.

Elijah addressed God as *Lord,* Jehovah or Yahweh, the distinct name for God. This would remind the people of the covenant they had made with Jehovah when they came out of Egypt. It is he who had guided them and watched over them from the time of *Abraham, Isaac and Israel* (Jacob) right down to their own time. *Let it be known.* The prophet then asked that God in a dramatic way demonstrate to the people not only that he was God but that he, Elijah, was God's spokesman.

37. Answer me, O LORD, answer me, so these people will know that you, O LORD, are God, and that you are turning their hearts back again."

The object of the miracle about to be performed was to convince the people that Jehovah was indeed the true God. But more than that, it was to turn their hearts back to him. The language anticipates the people's conversion from Baal to Jehovah, and also indicates that hearts were already being turned even while Elijah was praying.

B. REVELATION OF GOD'S POWER (V. 38)

38. Then the fire of the LORD fell and burned up the sacrifice, the wood, the stones and the soil, and also licked up the water in the trench.

Zap! In a split second God demonstrated his power. A flash of fire fell, and everything was consumed—the sacrifice, the wood, the stones, the dust, and even the water in the trench about the altar. Right before their eyes everything vanished. This was no sleight-of-hand magic; it was God's might revealed. Some commentators have suggested that this was a bolt of lightning. If so, it would have been out of a perfectly clear sky, a miracle indeed. That it was a cloudless sky is evident when later even a cloud the size of a man's hand could attract attention (1 Kings 18:44). It is interesting that some who hesitate to accept the miraculous will offer explanations that also require the miraculous.

IV. THE PEOPLE'S RESPONSE (1 KINGS 18:39)

A. ACKNOWLEDGMENT OF THE MIRACLE (V. 39A)

39a. When all the people saw this, they fell prostrate.

The people immediately fell on their faces, acknowledging the miracle. In our culture we do not often assume the prone position, but in the culture of ancient Israel such a posture indicated fear, reverence, awe, and worship. It is likely that the people felt all of these emotions. They did not need an involved theological explanation for them to understand that God had intervened. He had not only revealed his own mighty power, but he had also accredited Elijah's claim that he was God's messenger.

B. AFFIRMATION OF JEHOVAH (V. 39B)

39b. ... and cried, "The LORD—he is God! The LORD—he is God!"

Before this experience on Mount Carmel, the hearts of many of these people were divided. They were attempting to give allegiance both to Jehovah and to Baal. They did not want to break away from the worship of Jehovah, neither did they want to give up the sensuousness of the Baal worship. When Elijah arrived on

Mount Carmel this day, he indicated that such a division of allegiance should not exist and challenged the people to make a choice between the two (1 Kings 18:21). Some today may think they can be a part of Christ's body, receive the blessings he bestows, and still participate in all the pleasures the world offers. It cannot be! We too must make a choice. Jesus must be Lord of all, or not at all.

In affirming that Jehovah is God, the people were saying that he is more than just one god among many, more even than the chief god. He is the *only* God! No longer would they go limping between Jehovah and Baal.

Now they were ready to do the bidding of God and his spokesman, Elijah. The prophet's first order was that the prophets of Baal be executed. Without hesitation the people carried out that order.

SEEING IS BELIEVING?

Wouldn't it have been exciting to live in an era when God often revealed his presence and power by supernatural phenomena? Wouldn't faith have come easier in those days?

When Elijah's contemporaries saw fire from heaven consume the altar and everything on and around it—sure, they believed that Jehovah is God. Why not? Baal offered no such sensational evidence of existence or might. Seeing is believing!

But Jesus was frustrated by people who demanded to see before they would believe: "Why does this generation ask for a miraculous sign? I tell you the truth, no sign will be given to it" (Mark 8:12).

Remember also what the risen Christ told Thomas: "Because you have seen me, you have believed; blessed are those who have not seen and yet have believed" (John 20:29). Christian faith is the "evidence of things *not seen*" (Hebrews 11:1, *King James Version*).

Daily sunrises, sowing/reaping cycles, childbirth, the spiritual transformation of those who are "born again"—for most of us these will have to suffice for sensational evidence of God in this era. Yet, we know it is true: "The Lord—he is God! The Lord—he is God!   —R. W. B.

CONCLUSION

A. THE INDISPENSABLE MAN

In a very real sense, no person is indispensable. Even those who may seem to be so for a time eventually retire or die, and life somehow goes on without them. If nothing else, this fact should keep us humble.

Yet, in another sense, some people have been indispensable if a certain course was to be followed or if a certain goal was to be attained. Such a person was Elijah. The people of Israel were in a sorry state. For some time they had followed a zigzag course, claiming loyalty to God on the one hand and trying to serve Baal on the other. The faithful followers of God had become a small minority in the nation— seven thousand, we are told (1 Kings 19:18). The path the nation was following was leading to certain destruction. Then, without any prior notice, Elijah appeared on the scene. Sent by God to salvage what he could of the nation while there was still time, Elijah followed a course that was both stern and uncompromising. The times called for such a leader.

When Elijah confronted the people, he gave them a simple, clear-cut choice— Jehovah or Baal. The people were hesitant to make a decision until God revealed himself dramatically on Mount Carmel. When they finally saw the truth, they turned their anger against the false prophets of Baal. Later, Elijah was sent to anoint Jehu who would eventually become king and in the process wipe out the house of Ahab, including the wicked Jezebel.

WHAT DO YOU THINK?

The people's response was dramatic. "They fell prostrate and cried, 'The LORD—he is God! The LORD—he is God!'" How can we demonstrate our belief in and loyalty to God today? (See Deuteronomy 6:5, 14, 17; John 14:21, 23.)

OPTION

The second half of the reproducible activity, "The Pattern of God's Spokesman," on page 360 is designed to apply the message of this lesson.

PRAYER

O Jehovah, you alone are God. Let us never forget that you are a jealous God, demanding our complete allegiance. Help us to understand that we cannot serve you while seeking what the world has to offer. We confess that there have been times when our loyalty has been divided. Forgive us, we pray. From this day forward, may our decision to serve you be followed by full commitment to your way and to your will. In Jesus' name, amen.

THOUGHT TO REMEMBER

"The Lord—he is God."

DAILY BIBLE READINGS

Monday, June 5—Third Year of Israel's Drought (1 Kings 18:1-6)

Tuesday, June 6—Obadiah Carries Elijah's Message to Ahab (1 Kings 18:7-16)

Wednesday, June 7—Command to Gather at Mount Carmel (1 Kings 18:17-21)

Thursday, June 8—Baal's Prophets Fail the Test (1 Kings 18:22-29)

Friday, June 9—Elijah Prepares the Burnt Offering (1 Kings 18:30-35)

Saturday, June 10—God's Fire Consumes Elijah's Offering (1 Kings 18:36-40)

Sunday, June 11—God Ends the Drought (1 Kings 18:41-46)

No doubt, God in his own way would have accomplished his purpose for Israel even if Elijah had not been on the scene. Yet Elijah was there, and because he was willing to be used of God, judgment was brought upon the house of Ahab. In this sense, Elijah was indispensable. Each of us can have a part in the fulfilling of God's ultimate plans for mankind. To do so we must be willing to submit ourselves to him, study his Word and pray for his guidance, and then as did Elijah, have the faith and courage to do the work that is set before us.

B. THE DANGER OF COMPROMISE

Jehovah God is a jealous God. He is not willing to accept a half-way commitment. He made this clear when he gave the law to Moses on Mount Sinai (Exodus 20:4, 5). Unfortunately, the Israelites forgot this, and thought they could serve both Baal and Jehovah. It seems obvious that the fathers failed to teach their children as instructed in Deuteronomy 6:4-12): "Hear, O Israel: The Lord our God, the Lord is one."

Because their fathers had not taught well, the Israelites were not very well prepared to resist the allurement of pagan deities when it came. The worship of pagan gods had been a problem to the Israelites as early as the time of the judges. King Solomon allowed his foreign wives to bring the worship of false gods with them when they came to Jerusalem. When Jezebel became Ahab's queen in the northern kingdom, things took a decided turn for the worse. Not only did she bring the worship of Baal with her, she imported numerous priests to assist her. She was not content to carry out her own worship in private. She seems to have had an evangelistic zeal to convert all of Israel to Baalism. She even set about to kill the true prophets of God. No wonder God sent a bold and forceful prophet to deal with the situation!

People often become involved in religious compromise when they are swept along by what is happening around them. It is likely that worshiping Baal became the "in" thing in ancient Israel. They may not have had popularity polls to determine what was the latest rage, but even in that society word got around. Add to this the pressures that came from friends and family who were into Baalism, and the result was that many people were swept along with the tide without really being aware of where they were going or what they were doing.

Does all this sound familiar? It should, for things haven't changed much in the nearly three thousand years that have passed since the time of Ahab and Elijah. Oh, of course, we moderns don't bow down before idols, but many are guilty of more subtle forms of idolatry—the all-consuming pursuit of possessions, popularity, and pleasure—to name just a few. Television and the movies have been allowed to erode our nation's long-standing moral standards and family values. Almost inundated by a sea of clever advertising, people today lust for things. To acquire these things, many will either drown their futures in debt or resort to shady business practices that bankrupt their ethical standards. The tragedy is that while their situations are developing, many are unaware of what is happening to them.

The loss of our standards has not come overnight. That loss has occurred gradually, a little bit here and a little bit there. We justify these compromises by speaking in glowing terms of the importance of tolerating other people's views. We insist on personal freedom and the right of choice, even as these things are destroying the very fabric of our society. If we are to stem this tide that is sweeping our nation, we must return to standards that are clear and absolute. Only the Bible provides these standards. In our homes and in our congregations we must turn to careful and thorough study of the Bible if we are to save our land.

Discovery Learning

This page contains an alternate lesson plan emphasizing learning activities. Classes desiring such student involvement will find these suggestions helpful. The next page is a reproducible activity page to further enhance discovery learning.

LEARNING GOALS

In this session you will seek to lead your class members to:

1. Conclude that God insists that we follow him wholeheartedly.

2. Identify specific beliefs and values that compete with wholehearted devotion to God.

3. Reject all "rivals" to God and worship him alone.

INTO THE LESSON

Write this statement on the chalkboard:

You can't have it both ways.

Point out that in some situations in life a person may be presented with more than one option, but accepting one excludes the others. For example, a single man may be attracted to two women, but he can marry only one. Ask your class to mention some other situations in which the choice of one option automatically excludes another option. (*If students have difficulty coming up with ideas, suggest one of these to get them started: having a diet of rich foods and losing weight; saving money and buying everything you see.*)

Allow two minutes for discussion. Then lead into the Bible study by saying, "The most important area of life in which this principle applies (point to the statement on the chalkboard) is in our spiritual life, specifically in our choice of the God to whom we will give our allegiance. At the time of the incident in today's lesson, Israel's loyalty was divided. The prophet Elijah informed them, however, that they could not continue that pattern. They could serve but one God. Our lesson text tells of an incident that guided them in their choice."

INTO THE WORD

If your class is large enough, read 1 Kings 18:1-40 as a narrative. In the week before class ask various class members to read the words spoken by these in the text: God, Elijah, Obadiah, Ahab, at least two for the prophets of Baal, and at least two for the people. Another person should read the narrative portions.

After the Scripture reading, have your class form groups of six to discuss the questions below. Give each group a copy of the questions and appoint a leader for each group. Allow the groups twenty minutes for their Scripture exploration.

1. How were the Israelites in Elijah's day trying to "have it both ways"?

2. How did Elijah emphasize that they couldn't have it both ways?

3. Why was Elijah so dramatic in his confrontation with the prophets of Baal?

4. What does each passage below say about a person's dividing his loyalty between Jehovah and any other god?

Exodus 34:14-16
Deuteronomy 6:13-15
Deuteronomy 13:6-11
Joshua 24:14, 15, 19, 20, 23
Matthew 6:24
Luke 14:26, 27, 33

After time has expired, bring the groups together. Ask, "Which passage in question 4 do you think is the most powerful in teaching that we must worship God alone?" Allow for comments.

OPTION

Have your class participate in the narrative reading as described above. Then have them form groups of four. Provide each group with paper and a pen, and appoint a leader. Ask each group to write what it considers to be the three most important questions about this passage (1 Kings 18:1-40). Allow about ten minutes for this. Then exchange questions with another group. Then have each group discuss the questions given them.

INTO LIFE

Say to the class, "A tendency of humans is to combine different forms of belief or practice from two or more religious faiths to create a religious system of one's own liking. This is called 'syncretism.'

"The Israelites in today's passage had been practicing syncretism of sorts—mixing worship of God with worship of Baal. Let's consider how Christians today might be tempted to practice syncretism."

Lead your class in discussing these questions:

1. How have others' beliefs and values invaded the church today?

2. Why might Christians today be tempted to mix and match beliefs and values from the Bible with beliefs and values from other sources?

3. What can you do to keep from compromising your faith in God with other beliefs and values?

4. What will you do to remain wholeheartedly committed to worshiping God alone?

The Pattern of God's Spokesman

The incident on Mt. Carmel was not the only challenge Elijah faced. Each time he followed much of the same pattern:
1. The challenge, speaking clearly the word (judgment) of the Lord
2. A threat or rebuke to the prophet for his challenge
3. A description of the decisive struggle
4. A description of how God intervenes
5. A confirmation of the prophets' authority

See if you can find all five of these points in the following passages.

	DROUGHT	MT. CARMEL	JEZEBEL'S THREAT	AHAZIAH'S DEATH BED
1. The Challenge	1 Kings 17:1	1 Kings 18:21	1 Kings 19:1	2 Kings 1:3, 4
2. Threats/ Rebuke	1 Kings 18:17, 18	1 Kings 18:21	1 Kings 19:2	2 Kings 1:9, 11
3. The Decisive Struggle	1 Kings 18:41	1 Kings 18:22-24	1 Kings 19:9-14	2 Kings 1:10, 12
4. God's Intervention	1 Kings 18:43-45	1 Kings 18:38	1 Kings 19:11, 12	2 Kings 1:10, 12
5. Confirmation	1 Kings 18:46	1 Kings 18:39	1 Kings 19:15-18	2 Kings 1:13-17

How many of these same situations can you identify in your own world? Complete the following chart, answering first for your church and then for yourself. (It may be that not every point will apply. Simply fill in the answers where it does.) Compare your answers in column 1 with others in your class.

	YOUR CHURCH	YOU
1. The Challenge	_____	_____
2. Threats	_____	_____
3. The Struggle	_____	_____
4. God's Intervention	_____	_____
5. Confirmation	_____	_____

A Nation Turns From God

Unit 1: The Price of Power
(Lessons 1-4)

WHEN JUSTICE IS CORRUPTED

LESSON 3

WHY TEACH THIS LESSON?

Today's lesson is one of a buyer turned seller. Ahab wanted to buy a vineyard. When the owner refused to sell, Ahab himself became the seller. He "sold [himself] to do evil in the eyes of the Lord" (1 Kings 21:20). He got the vineyard, but what he lost in the bargain made the gain of no consequence. "What good will it be for a man if he gains the whole world, yet forfeits his soul?" (Matthew 16:26).

Use this lesson to challenge your students to the higher plane that Naboth exemplifies, putting value in God's Word and God's will more than in material wealth. Challenge them to take a stand, like that of Elijah, against corruption wherever they find it.

INTRODUCTION

A. NO ELIJAH

During the California gold rush of 1849, thousands of people streamed into that state hoping to strike it rich. Some actually did find gold, and when they did, they went to the land office to register their claims. In one area an unscrupulous mining company made a deal with the local surveyor and the clerk who recorded the claims. When a prospector registered a claim, they would survey it and record the claim incorrectly. Then they would record the correct claim information in the name of the mining company. When the unsuspecting prospector later tried to sell his claim, he found that the company already had a deed to it. When this happened, there was no Elijah to greet the crooked mining officials when they showed up to take possession of the claim.

B. LESSON BACKGROUND

Last week's lesson was about Elijah's tremendous victory over the false prophets of Baal. God's prophet had little time to celebrate that victory, however. First Kings 19 records the ensuing events.

As soon as word got back to Queen Jezebel about what had happened, she vowed to even the score by killing Elijah. As soon as he heard this, he ran for his life, not stopping until he reached the Judean wilderness south of Beersheba. Fearful, disappointed, and exhausted, he cried out for God to let him die; but God wasn't through with him yet.

After Elijah had eaten and rested, he then proceeded farther southward in the Sinai peninsula, to the area of Mount Horeb. There God spoke to him. Elijah was instructed to stand upon the mountain while God passed by. Subsequently there was a series of natural phenomena: a great wind, an earthquake, and fire. But God was in none of these. Instead, he revealed himself in a "still small voice" (1 Kings 19:12). God ordered Elijah to visit Syria and anoint Hazael king over that country. Then he was to anoint Jehu, a military leader, to be king over Israel. Next, he was to find Elisha and anoint him to be his successor as God's prophet.

DEVOTIONAL READING:
MICAH 6:6-13

LESSON SCRIPTURE:
1 KINGS 21

PRINTED TEXT:
1 KINGS 21:1-4, 15-20

LESSON AIMS

As a result of this lesson, a student should:

1. Be aware of the corrupting effect of power.

2. Have increased concern for justice in our time.

3. Be able to suggest ways that he or she can work for justice in our times.

KEY VERSE:

You have sold yourself to do evil in the eyes of the LORD.
—1 Kings 21:20

HOW TO SAY IT

Beersheba. Beer-SHE-buh.
Elisha. Ee-LYE-shuh.
Hazael. HAZ-uh-el or
    Haz-ZAY-el.
Jehu. JEE-hew or JAY-hew.
Jezebel. JEZ-uh-bel.
Jezreel. JEZ-reel.
Jezreelite. JEZ-reel-ite.
Naboth. NAY-both
    (short "o" as in "odd").
Thyatira. THIGH-uh-TIE-ruh.

WHAT DO YOU THINK?

From a strictly financial perspective, Naboth had good reason to accept King Ahab's offer for his vineyard. But the value Naboth placed on his vineyard could not be measured tangibly. This parcel was part of his family's portion when the Israelites first settled the land. Having been passed down from generation to generation of his descendants, the land was his inheritance. He considered that it would dishonor God and his family to sell the land.

What issues should similarly take precedence over financial matters for the Christian? Are there some business deals that a Christian should refuse even though it would be financially profitable? Why or why not?

OPTION

Use the reproducible activity, "Not for Sale," to enhance your students' understanding of Naboth's refusal to sell the land. The activity is found on page 368.

Elijah next appears in the biblical record when God sends him to confront Ahab in Naboth's vineyard, where that wicked king had gone to take possession of it.

I. AHAB'S DESIRE FOR NABOTH'S VINEYARD (1 KINGS 21:1-4)

A. AHAB'S OFFER (VV. 1, 2)

1. Some time later there was an incident involving a vineyard belonging to Naboth the Jezreelite. The vineyard was in Jezreel, close to the palace of Ahab king of Samaria.

Some time later refers to a series of events recorded in 1 Kings 20. Ben-Hadad, king of Syria, invaded Israel and besieged Samaria. With God's help, Ahab and his forces were able to defeat the Syrian forces and lift the siege. In a later conflict God enabled Ahab's outnumbered army to shatter completely Ben-Hadad's forces, causing the Syrian king to plead for mercy. Because he agreed to spare Ben-Hadad in spite of the fact that God had condemned the Syrians to utter destruction, Ahab came under God's condemnation. An unnamed prophet brought the message of condemnation to Ahab: "It is your life for his life, your people for his people" (1 Kings 20:42). Ahab then returned to Samaria "sullen and angry" (v. 43).

We are not told how much time later. It was not immediate since the king had returned to Samaria after the prophet's rebuke, and this event occurred in Jezreel.

2. Ahab said to Naboth, "Let me have your vineyard to use for a vegetable garden, since it is close to my palace. In exchange I will give you a better vineyard or, if you prefer, I will pay you whatever it is worth."

Ahab's capital was at Samaria, but he maintained another palace in Jezreel, which was located about twenty miles north of Samaria. Naboth owned a vineyard next to Ahab's palace there. We are not told how large the plot of ground was, but if it was within the walls of the city, it could not have been large. Ahab wanted the plot for a kitchen garden where herbs could be grown for the royal table. He made Naboth what seemed to him a reasonable offer. He promised Naboth a better vineyard than the one he had, or if he preferred, he would buy it outright from him.

B. NABOTH'S REFUSAL (V. 3)

3. But Naboth replied, "The LORD forbid that I should give you the inheritance of my fathers."

Naboth was a man of both courage and integrity. He had the courage to reject an offer from the king, and the courage to confess his faith in God before King Ahab, who worshiped Baal (1 Kings 16:31). The source of his courage was his faith in God, and his integrity is seen in his adherence to the laws God had given that governed the sale and transfer of land. The ancient law of the land bound property to a family (see Leviticus 25:23; Numbers 36:7). Naboth refused to sell his property to the king because he felt it was wrong for him to do so.

HERITAGE NOT FOR SALE

A certain widow has been left with more real estate than she knows what to do with—at least, more than she can use. Her house has two stories, with several add-on ells. There are out-buildings, also, and multiple acres of land.

Well situated in a resort area, the property would bring a sizable price. But it is not for sale. Too many memories live there. That is where she and her groom settled in a honeymoon cottage. They constructed the current residence practically with their bare hands, room by room by room. They enjoyed nearly forty years of married life in that spot. The place is not for sale—at any price.

We understand the widow's feelings, and we understand Naboth's, too. His vineyard was property inherited from cherished ancestors. It is likely that they sacrificed to provide it, and had worked endless hours to develop and maintain it. Such an inheritance is much more than a mere piece of real estate; it is an invaluable heritage, a link to past generations, a repository of blessed memories. What price tag could begin to reflect its worth?

Some treasures are simply not for sale. —R. W. B.

C. AHAB'S DISAPPOINTMENT (V. 4)

4. So Ahab went home, sullen and angry because Naboth the Jezreelite had said, "I will not give you the inheritance of my fathers." He lay on his bed sulking and refused to eat.

Even though Ahab had strayed far from Jehovah, he still respected the ancient laws enough that he would not use force to take the vineyard from Naboth. We know people in our times who, while abandoning the Christian faith, still have considerable respect for the ethical standards that that faith requires. The problem is that under pressure those standards give way because they are not based upon a solid foundation.

At Naboth's refusal, Ahab showed his immaturity by going home (probably to his palace in Samaria) and pouting like a spoiled child. This was no small pout, for he lay on his bed and refused to eat. Before we are too harsh on Ahab for his childishness, however, we need to take a look at some of our own actions. At times we are guilty of getting "out of sorts" over matters even more trivial than the disappointment that caused Ahab's pout. Have we ever acted childishly when we haven't got our way in some matter in the church, or when we haven't received the recognition that we felt due us?

II. AHAB'S JUDGMENT (1 KINGS 21:15-20)

In verses 5 through 14 we learn the outcome of Ahab's effort to secure the vineyard. When Jezebel learned the reason for her husband's sour disposition, she went into action. First she chided him for being such a weakling. When it became obvious that Ahab would not take action, Jezebel said, "Get up and eat! Cheer up. I'll get you the vineyard of Naboth the Jezreelite" (v. 7).

Unconcerned about breaking any Israelite laws, Jezebel began to unfold a shameless plan that would accomplish her goal. She sent letters in Ahab's name to the leaders of Jezreel, instructing them to proclaim a fast and to set Naboth in a prominent place among the people. To proclaim a fast was to create the impression that the city was somehow disgraced. To set Naboth in a "prominent place" was to bring him into the court of justice, as if he were the cause of the problem. Then the city leaders were to bring in two false witnesses who would testify that Naboth was guilty of blasphemy. The penalty for blasphemy was death by stoning (Leviticus 24:10-16), and this penalty was carried out once the guilty verdict was brought in against poor Naboth.

A. THE VINEYARD AVAILABLE (V. 15)

15. As soon as Jezebel heard that Naboth had been stoned to death, she said to Ahab, "Get up and take possession of the vineyard of Naboth the Jezreelite that he refused to sell you. He is no longer alive, but dead."

When the wicked deed was completed, Jezebel informed Ahab that the vineyard was his. She seemed to gloat over the fact that Naboth, who was too foolish to sell the plot of land to the king, ended up paying for it with his life. Second Kings 9:26 seems to indicate that not only was Naboth killed, but his sons as well. With any possible heirs out of the way, there would be no one to challenge Ahab's control of the vineyard. As so often happens, one sin leads to another.

Visual 3 illustrates Ahab's covetousness—and ours.

WHAT DO YOU THINK?

God's spokesman in Ahab's day was Elijah, and he did not shrink from exposing evil and prodding conscience. Jesus has called his followers to be "the light of the world" (Matthew 5:14), to reveal or expose the deeds of evil. The charge of the watchman (Ezekiel 33:7-9) is still on us.

How do you think we should go about that task? Of course, it requires the positive, consistent witness of a life lived in obedience and reverence to God. Is that enough? Ought Christians to picket, boycott, demonstrate, launch petition drives etc., in exposing evil? Why or why not?

Do you think the Lord raises up individuals, like Elijah, to challenge the forces of evil today, or is that the work of the church as a body? Why do you think so?

WHAT DO YOU THINK?

Ahab referred to Elijah as his enemy. Apparently it was easier to blame the preacher than to repent of his own sin. Sermons and lessons on sin sometimes evoke a similar reaction today. Why is that a common response? How can a Christian be sure to respond appropriately to lessons and sermons that expose their own sin?

Wise Solomon said, "Faithful are the wounds of a friend; but the kisses of an enemy are deceitful" (Proverbs 27:6, KJV). How can you be sure to speak as a faithful friend, even when exposing sin in a friend's life, and not as an enemy?

B. POSSESSION AT LAST! (V. 16)

16. When Ahab heard that Naboth was dead, he got up and went down to take possession of Naboth's vineyard.

We can imagine that Ahab went down to the garden like some child who had just got a toy that had previously been denied him. It is likely that a sizable entourage accompanied the king as he marched triumphantly down to the vineyard to claim his victory. A self-centered person such as Ahab would want to enjoy his victory in the presence of others. By possessing the property he would be demonstrating to his subjects that he was indeed king.

C. PRONOUNCEMENT OF JUDGMENT (VV. 17-19)

17, 18. Then the word of the LORD came to Elijah the Tishbite: "Go down to meet Ahab king of Israel, who rules in Samaria. He is now in Naboth's vineyard, where he has gone to take possession of it.

We don't know where Elijah was when all this was happening. It is likely that he was in hiding, for he still feared the wrath of Jezebel. However, he could not have been far from Jezreel, because he was able to reach the vineyard only shortly after Ahab, coming, presumably, from Samaria, arrived there. Since Elijah traveled by foot, he must have been only a few miles away.

19. Say to him, 'This is what the LORD says: Have you not murdered a man and seized his property?' Then say to him, 'This is what the LORD says: In the place where dogs licked up Naboth's blood, dogs will lick up your blood—yes, yours!'"

The message that Elijah was to deliver was short and to the point. Ahab was guilty of two sins—he had committed murder and he had taken property illegally. Both of these were serious crimes, and it is clear that God intended to deal with them. The punishment God pronounced would fit the crime. The dogs would lick the blood of Ahab just as they had licked the blood of Naboth. This judgment was fulfilled later, after Ahab was mortally wounded in battle. His blood flowed out into his chariot, and when the chariot was washed, the blood was licked up by dogs (1 Kings 22:34-38).

D. CONFRONTATION OF PROPHET AND KING (V. 20)

20. Ahab said to Elijah, "So you have found me, my enemy!"

"I have found you," he answered, "because you have sold yourself to do evil in the eyes of the LORD."

At the moment of Ahab's celebration, suddenly Elijah appeared. At that moment the possession he had longed for and sulked about turned to ashes instantly. Ahab didn't need to ask why Elijah was there. He knew! His previous confrontations with Elijah had ended disastrously, and there was no reason to believe that this one would end any differently. Ahab's immediate response was to blame Elijah for his troubles. He tried to make it seem that Elijah was his enemy carrying out a personal vendetta against him. It is always easier to blame the messenger than it is to accept the message. Ahab refused to recognize the prophet as God's spokesman; instead, he viewed Elijah as an enemy trying to do him in. Actually, Elijah was the best friend Ahab had, one who tried to steer him aright; but Ahab refused to recognize that truth.

Elijah would not allow Ahab's personal attack to turn him aside from the message he had come to deliver. Ahab had sold himself to do evil, and for that reason anyone who opposed him was his enemy. How cheaply this wicked king had sold himself! For a vineyard, which couldn't have been more than a few square yards, he had sold his integrity, and worse, his eternal destiny. Even if we grant that Ahab was not directly involved in the murder of Naboth and the corruption of the officials who carried it out, nevertheless, he was willing to accept the fruits of the evil deeds of Jezebel.

The verses that follow the lesson text tell that the words of judgment had a profound impact upon Ahab. He "tore his clothes, put on sackcloth and fasted. He lay in sackcloth and went about meekly" (v. 27). The arrogant king, who had entered the garden so triumphantly to claim his ill-gotten possession, now left it in abject humility. This clearly was not just a public display that Ahab put on to impress those about him. It is obvious that his repentance was sincere, for God delayed part of the announced punishment (vv. 28, 29). The house of Ahab would not fall in Ahab's days, but in the days of his son.

ACCESSORIES TO SIN

Indicted in the infamous Watergate case were more suspects than those who actually burglarized the offices of the Democratic party's headquarters. Several public officials, who were merely accessories to the crime, were convicted. They had knowledge of it and consented to it, if only by silence. Even the president is not above the law that implicates accessories in such cases.

Jezebel wrote the letters that "put out a contract" on Naboth. But she signed Ahab's name and affixed Ahab's seal to the letters. So Ahab became a consenting, if unwitting, partner in the assassination of his neighbor. Jezebel engineered the crime, and verse 23 following indicates the judgment that would fall on her. Ahab's hands, however, were not clean in this sordid affair. He was guilty as an accessory.

Is it possible that we too may be unwitting and silent accessories to sin? The church at Thyatira was rebuked by Jesus for tolerating "that woman Jezebel . . . [who] misleads my servants into sexual immorality" (Revelation 2:20). The church is obligated to confront Christians with the errors of their ways, to call them to repentance, and to attempt to reclaim them by speaking the truth in love.

—R. W. B.

CONCLUSION

A. ABOVE THE LAW

Many years ago a European nobleman, in order to impress some visiting noblemen, pointed out a man working in the courtyard below them. Then he took a gun and deliberately shot and killed the man. Some of the guests were appalled and insisted that when the king heard about it, he would have the nobleman brought to trial. The man snorted at the idea. "I'm too powerful for the king. He can't touch me!"

When the king heard about the incident, he was furious. There was nothing much that he could do, however, for he lacked the military strength to challenge the wicked nobleman. Then he had an idea. He issued an order that gave an automatic pardon to anyone who killed the nobleman. The man knew that he was almost universally hated, and he became so fearful for his life that he was afraid to leave his castle. Soon he was afraid of even his own servants, and before long his fear and isolation killed him.

Ahab was rather like this nobleman, thinking that he could live above the law. And he was above the law as far as his subjects were concerned. What he did not realize was that he would not be tried before a jury of his subjects but by the divine judge. There was no way that he could escape that court.

In our own times we have seen men and women, both in government service and in private life, who have acted as if they were above the law. They have stolen from the public till with apparent impunity, or they have flouted the standards of

WHAT DO YOU THINK?

We have all heard the statement, "Every person has his price." When we look at Ahab, we might tend to believe it is true. But then there is Naboth, who reassures us it is false.

The Bible contains a number of examples of persons who maintained their faith and integrity, who held to their moral principles, in the face of strong temptation to do otherwise. Joseph, Moses, and Daniel and his three friends immediately come to mind. They would not sell their moral integrity.

Do you think the church is raising up a generation who will able to make the tough choices required to maintain integrity? Why or why not? What needs to be included in the teaching and examples set for young people to equip them for moral integrity?

PRAYER

Almighty God, we come to you concerned about the corruption we see on every hand. Keep us from becoming disheartened in our struggle against evil. Show us how we can use the tools we have to make a consistent witness for truth. In Jesus' name we pray. Amen.

THOUGHT TO REMEMBER

One who has sold himself to do evil knows few restraints.

DAILY BIBLE READINGS

Monday, June 12—God Requires Justice and Faithfulness (Micah 6:6-13)

Tuesday, June 13—Naboth Refuses to Sell His Vineyard (1 Kings 21:1-7)

Wednesday, June 14—Jezebel Causes Naboth's Death (1 Kings 21:8-14)

Thursday, June 15—Ahab Seizes Naboth's Vineyard (1 Kings 21:15-19)

Friday, June 16—Elijah Judges Ahab and Jezebel (1 Kings 21:20-24)

Saturday, June 17—Ahab's Repentance Brings Temporary Reprieve (1 Kings 21:25-29)

Sunday, June 18—Evildoers Do Not Reverence God (Psalm 36)

---

decency and morality before a shocked public. And they have got away with it—almost!

We may have no modern Elijahs to confront these arrogant evildoers in their wickedness, but God in Heaven holds high the sword of justice, and in his own time he will wield it with might.

B. SOULS AT A BARGAIN BASEMENT PRICE

Facing Ahab in the ill-gotten vineyard, Elijah accused the king of having sold himself to work evil. He had sold himself as a slave to Satan. And how cheaply he had sold himself! For a few square feet of land that he wanted for an herb garden, he had mortgaged his soul.

What about us? Have we ever entered into such an arrangement with Satan for some worthless trinket, for a fleeting moment in the spotlight, for a few minutes of pleasure? Yes, all of us at one time or another have mortgaged our souls to Satan at a bargain basement price. Thank God for Jesus, who paid the price of our redemption.

C. THE POWER BEHIND THE THRONE

Of the two, Ahab and Jezebel, Jezebel was clearly the more strong-willed. Brought up in the idolatrous culture of Phoenicia, she was not hindered by the ethical standards that every now and then seemed to hold Ahab in check. If she had ever had a conscience, it had long since been seared into total insensitivity. It didn't bother her a bit to forge letters to the public officials in Jezreel and seal them with Ahab's seal. She didn't hesitate to corrupt these officials nor to bribe some wicked men to perjure themselves. And if she ever had the slightest twinge of conscience about sending an innocent man and his sons to death, she never showed it.

Even though Ahab was a moral weakling, he cannot be let off the hook so easily. Far too often in our own times we have excused people of heinous behavior by allowing them to blame it on their neglected childhood or their inadequate education or their poverty. God did not excuse Ahab just because he had a wicked wife. God knew that Ahab had the power to say no at every step he took that drew him closer to moral disaster. That he didn't say no made him as guilty as Jezebel.

D. JUSTICE CORRUPTED

Lord Acton once observed that "absolute power corrupts absolutely." The reign of Ahab illustrates that axiom very well. When Ahab couldn't get what he wanted, Jezebel took matters in her own hands and, using the power of the throne, caused the courts of Jezreel to convict and execute an innocent man.

With the collapse of the Soviet Union and its satellites, we have been shocked at reports of the corruption and the abuse of power that existed in the countries behind the Iron Curtain. Even with all the checks and balances that are built into our system of government to protect us from this abuse of power, we have not been able to escape corruption. Every branch of our government—executive, legislative, and judicial—has suffered from the corroding effects of greed and a lust for power.

We today may not have a call from God to right the wrongs of our society in the manner that Elijah did. But we do have in our hands powerful weapons that we can wield against the corruption we see about us—the freedoms of speech, press, and religion. Further, we have the power of the ballot box. Certainly we have a mandate from God to use this power to provide the best leadership possible for our nation.

Discovery Learning

This page contains an alternate lesson plan emphasizing learning activities. Classes desiring such student involvement will find these suggestions helpful. The next page is a reproducible activity page to further enhance discovery learning.

LEARNING GOALS

As a result of this session, your class members will be able to do the following:

1. Determine God's attitude toward injustice.

2. Explore how Christians can promote justice in our nation.

INTO THE LESSON

Make copies of the statements below and distribute them to your students.

1. Christians in our nation aren't very concerned about justice.

2. Christians have a responsibility to take a stand against injustice.

3. Generally speaking, our national leaders are more concerned with personal gain than standing up for justice.

4. Generally speaking, Christians in our nation are more concerned with personal gain than standing up for justice.

5. There is very little that Christians can do to rid our nation of injustice.

Have students read each statement and put a plus sign (+) in front of the statement they agree with the most, and a minus sign (-) in front of the statement they disagree with the most. Allow about ninety seconds for students to decide. Then read each statement aloud and ask how many put a plus sign, and how many put a minus sign, for each. Ask why they selected the ones they did.

Help your class see the connection between this activity and today's Bible passage by saying, "In our study today we will consider a king who mocked justice, and we will see God's response. Let's look for some principles that God wants us to apply today."

INTO THE WORD

Have your students form three groups. If you have more than twenty students, form six groups and give some of the groups duplicate assignments.

Using the four questions below, each group is to prepare an imaginary interview of the biblical person assigned to it. When the groups have done that, each group is to present its interview for the rest of the class.

Select a leader for each group to keep things moving. Each group will need to select one person to be the interviewer and one person to play the part of the assigned biblical character when the group's interview is presented to the class. In their groups the students are to read 1 Kings 21:1-24 and then write answers they think their assigned person might have given to each question. The biblical characters to be assigned are Ahab, Jezebel, and Elijah. Here are the interview questions:

1. From your perspective, what happened to Naboth? Why did it happen?

2. From your viewpoint, what were the results?

3. As you look at it, how just was the situation?

4. What do you think God's opinion of the situation is?

Following the interviews, lead the class in discussing these questions: 1. What is justice? 2. Why does God demand that we deal justly and fairly with one another?

OPTION

Have a volunteer (or several volunteers) read 1 Kings 21:1-24 aloud to the class. Then lead the class in a discussion of these questions:

1. Was anything wrong with Ahab's original request of Naboth? (See verses 1-3.) Explain.

2. Jezebel plotted the injustice done to Naboth. Why was Ahab also condemned for it?

3. Based upon verses 17-24, how does God regard the perversion of justice?

4. How do these passages speak to the situation in 1 Kings 21; Jeremiah 22:3-5, 11-17; Micah 6:8?

5. Why does God demand that we deal justly and fairly with one another?

INTO LIFE

Read Micah 6:6-8 to your class. Say, "It is clear from this passage and others we have considered that God abhors the unjust treatment of human beings. For a nation to please God, it must stand for justice. Its leaders must promote justice in its laws. Its courts must dispense justice. Its citizens must deal fairly with one another."

Our nation is committed to the just treatment of all its citizens. But we are not perfect in that regard. Have your students gather in their previous groups. Ask them to write some newspaper headlines one might read if existing injustices were removed from our society. Let the groups share their headlines with the class.

Ask, "What can Christians do to promote justice in our nation?" Allow discussion. Then close with prayer, asking God to help us be just in all our dealings.

Not for Sale

Even though Ahab offered Naboth a choice of money or compensation in kind, Naboth refused to sell his vineyard. He did so based on God's laws found recorded in the books of Moses. Because the land and soil were so important to Israel's economy, there were many carefully defined regulations relative to their use.

Below are listed several important passages that summarize Israel's civil law regarding the ownership and use of the land. Find each of these passages and summarize in your own words both the law and its purpose.

SABBATH (EXODUS 23:10-12)

JUBILEE (LEVITICUS 25:1-24)

REDEMPTION OF PROPERTY (LEVITICUS 25:25-34; RUTH 4:1-8)

PERMANENT PROPERTY BOUNDARIES (DEUTERONOMY 19:14)

Faithful Stewards

The key principle at work in Israel's laws about selling property was the ownership of God. God owned the land, not the human owners. The same truth guides Christians in their stewardship of what God has given them. How does God's ownership of everything apply to decisions regarding the following?

USE OF LEISURE TIME

ACQUISITION OF MATERIAL WEALTH

USE OF MONEY AFTER GIVING A TITHE TO THE LORD

A Nation Turns From God

Unit 1: The Price of Power
(Lessons 1-4)

A DAY OF GOOD NEWS

LESSON 4

WHY TEACH THIS LESSON?

Good drama is often characterized by a solid plot combined with one or more good sub-plots. That is, along with the main action of the story, something else, equally interesting, is also developing.

By that criterion, today's lesson text would make for a good novel or motion picture. Along with the obvious lesson, at least one other "sub-plot" emerges that also teaches a good lesson. The obvious reason for teaching the lesson is to expose your students to the challenge of the four lepers: "This is a day of good news. . . . Let's go at once and report this." We have the best news of all, that Jesus Christ died for our sins, was buried, and rose again on the third day. Let's go and report this to all who will listen.

There's another good reason to teach this lesson, which is seen in the sub-plot. In the king's aide, we see skeptical modern man. "Impossible!" he scoffs at the promises of God. But the promises of God—even the ones that sound too good to be true—prove to be true indeed! This lesson is a good reminder of that fact.

INTRODUCTION

A. GOOD NEWS

In late 1814 a large British force entered the Gulf of Mexico and headed toward New Orleans. Their objective was to capture that city, a major port for Americans living in what was then the West, and close off their shipping and receiving of supplies via the Mississippi River. The force landed and proceeded toward New Orleans, but they were met by an American army led by General Andrew Jackson. A fierce battle ensued. The Americans, fighting from behind a makeshift fortress built of bales of cotton, inflicted severe losses upon the British, repulsing the attack.

Ironically, this battle need never have been fought. The Treaty of Ghent, signed two weeks before the battle, had already ended the War of 1812. Because neither the telegraph nor the radio had been invented yet, the good news of the war's end did not reach New Orleans in time to prevent the battle.

As Christians we have good news for those locked in deadly battle with Satan. That good news is that Christ died to give men and women the victory over the powers of evil. What if we don't deliver that good news? Or what if we deliver it too late? Our lesson today touches on the subject of good news and how we should deal with it.

B. LESSON BACKGROUND

Upon the completion of his earthly ministry the prophet Elijah was taken up into Heaven, and his prophetic mantle fell on Elisha. Elisha continued the ministry that Elijah had conducted in the kingdom of Israel. War between Israel and Aram (Syria) had broken out once again. The Arameans (Syrians) under Ben-Hadad had besieged Samaria, the capital of Israel. This siege had reduced the people to starvation, causing some of them even to resort to cannibalism (2 Kings 6:24-29). Learning of this, Jehoram, who was king of Israel, rent his garments and donned sackcloth as a sign of contrition. Blaming Elisha for the horrible conditions that

DEVOTIONAL READING:
1 THESSALONIANS 5:8-18

LESSON SCRIPTURE:
2 KINGS 6:24—7:20

PRINTED TEXT:
2 KINGS 7:1-9

Jun
25

LESSON AIMS

As a result of studying this lesson, each student should:

1. Understand that God works in the affairs of nations.

2. Share the good news of salvation in Christ with someone who does not know it.

KEY VERSE:

"This is a day of good news. . . . Let's go at once and report this to the royal palace."

—2 Kings 7:9

LESSON 4 NOTES

WHAT DO YOU THINK?

Elisha's prophecy that flour and barley would be readily available in Samaria the next day must have seemed preposterous. The only apparent reason for believing it was confidence in Elisha as a prophet of God.

Which of God's promises for today do you think the world finds hardest to believe? Why? Do you ever find yourself wondering if they can really be true? If so, what do you do to reassure yourself the promises of God are reliable?

What can you do to convince people that God's promises can be trusted?

OPTION

Introduce the ministry of Elisha with the reproducible activity, "Forerunners," page 376. The following Scriptures will help your students complete the center column of that activity:

1. Matthew 14:13-21; 15:29-38 (multiplied food)

2. Luke 7:11-15 (raised widow's son to life)

3. John 2:1-10 (changed one substance into another)

4. Matthew 14:13-21; 15:29-38 (multiplied food)

5. Matthew 8:1-4 (healed a leper); Matthew 8:5-13 (healed without being present)

6. Matthew 14:22-32 (miraculous buoyancy)

existed, the king ordered the execution of the prophet and sent one of his court officers to carry it out. Relenting, it seems, from his hasty decision, the king himself came to Elisha's home (vv. 30-33). Today's lesson begins at this point.

I. ELISHA'S PROPHECIES (2 KINGS 7:1, 2)

A. PLENTY BY TOMORROW (V. 1)

1. Elisha said, "Hear the word of the LORD. This is what the LORD says: About this time tomorrow, a seah of flour will sell for a shekel and two seahs of barley for a shekel at the gate of Samaria."

Even as Elisha spoke up, his life hung in the balance. The man whom the king had sent to kill Elisha was still there, and the king had not revoked his order to the man. The prophet's fate depended on how the king responded to his words. Elisha made it clear that the words he uttered were not his own, but the *word of the Lord*.

The message was one of hope and deliverance. Tomorrow, food would be available for the starving city. A *seah* seems to have been nearly two gallons. In this period the *shekel* was not a coin, but a measure of weight, probably of silver. It is impossible to give an exact value for it. Most commentators indicate that a shekel was a high price to pay for a seah of flour, but it would be much less than the prices then current during the siege (see 2 Kings 6:25). The point is that food would be available this same time the next day. The famine would have ended. Elisha's obvious meaning was that the siege of the city was soon to be lifted. It was a common practice for business transactions to take place *at the gate*.

B. PROPHECY REJECTED (V. 2A)

2a. The officer on whose arm the king was leaning said to the man of God, "Look, even if the LORD should open the floodgates of the heavens, could this happen?"

The officer on whose arm the king was leaning was probably the king's personal aide. The king did not immediately reply to Elisha, so this officer spoke up. "Even if God opened the windows of Heaven," he insisted, "this could not happen!" Thus the officer expressed his disbelief in Elisha's prediction and in the power of God.

C. FURTHER PREDICTION (V. 2B)

2b. "You will see it with your own eyes," answered Elisha, "but you will not eat any of it!"

Elisha's prediction about the coming availability of food was precise. His prediction about what would befall this officer, however, is vague, perhaps deliberately so. If the officer would see the lifting of the siege but not eat any of the food that would become available, then obviously Elisha was predicting his death. Verses 17-20 of this chapter tell us of the outcome of this prophecy. After it was discovered that the Arameans had fled, the king appointed the officer to be in charge of the gate. At the news that there was food outside the walls of the city, the hungry people inside the city panicked and stampeded through the gate, trampling the officer to death.

WINDOWS IN HEAVEN

"When God shuts a door, he often opens a window." If the death of a loved one slams life's door in your face, God opens a window of comfort. When a door of opportunity closes, God opens a window of hope. Just as doors sometimes swing shut on today's dreams, God's window lets in the light of tomorrow's possibilities.

God seemed to have closed the door on his people in Samaria when the Arameans besieged the city. The gates were literally shut against enemy attacks. Inside, famine had reduced some citizens to cannibalism. Most were convinced that they would starve to death.

Then God opened a window of hope! Through his prophet Elisha, an imminent miracle was announced. The siege would end; food would once more be available.

The king's aide was cynical. "In your dreams!" he seemed to say. He had lost all hope. By God's miracle, however, the windows of Heaven did open, and the blessings of deliverance poured forth. It was as if the unwitting prophecy of the sarcastic aide was being fulfilled.

Faith, hope and *love* are the names of God's windows in Heaven. His light of life dispels disappointment, doubt, and despair.   —R. W. B.

II. FOUR LEPERS' DECISION (2 KINGS 7:3, 4)

A. FACING THE FUTURE (v. 3)

3. Now there were four men with leprosy at the entrance of the city gate. They said to each other, "Why stay here until we die?

The law prohibited lepers from living inside a city (Leviticus 13:45, 46; Numbers 5:1-4). So they would gather about the city gate, where, presumably, their friends inside the city would bring food for them. Because of the siege of Samaria and the accompanying famine, the plight of these four lepers was worse than usual.

B. DECISION TO ACT (v. 4)

4. "If we say, 'We'll go into the city'—the famine is there, and we will die. And if we stay here, we will die. So let's go over to the camp of the Arameans and surrender. If they spare us, we live; if they kill us, then we die."

The lepers' choices were limited. Even if they could sneak into the city, what good would it do? The famine was there, no less than on the outside of the city, and they would die there. Or they could remain where they were and die from starvation. Their third option, and the one they chose, was to leave the gate and surrender to the Aramean army, which surrounded the city. They probably believed that the Arameans would kill them. If that happened, at least they would not suffer a long, lingering death. There was even the outside chance that the Arameans might spare them. If the Arameans had heard about the healing of Naaman (2 Kings 5:8-14), perhaps they might remember it and extend them mercy.

NOTHING TO LOSE

A young couple and their baby were trapped by a mountain blizzard miles from civilization. Their car was immobilized, and they took shelter in a small cave. After several hours, this courageous father made a decision. "We can all stay here and die, or I can try to make it down the mountain for help." Struggling through blinding snow in freezing temperatures, this young hero trudged more than fifty miles to a ranger station. Rescuers soon found the mother and child, alive and without serious injury.

Their story is inspiring. The husband/father told how he came to his hard decision. "There was nothing to lose. I decided not to let my family die without trying to save us."

The lepers at the gate of Samaria made a similar decision. "We have nothing to lose, and perhaps we'll live," they reasoned as they ventured into the enemy camp. They too survived, along with all Israel, rescued by God.

We who follow Christ in this life know we have nothing to lose—and everything to gain. We know that our physical lives must end, but we trust Christ, who promises, "Whoever lives and believes in me will never die" (John 11:26). We stake our eternal destiny on that truth.   —R. W. B.

III. THE LEPERS' DISCOVERY (2 KINGS 7:5-8)

A. EMPTY CAMP (v. 5)

5. At dusk they got up and went to the camp of the Arameans. When they reached the edge of the camp, not a man was there.

WHAT DO YOU THINK?

One who scoffed at Elisha's prophecy was told he would see it come to pass but would not personally benefit from it. In that, he typifies unbelievers today who scoff at the faith of Christians and miss out on blessings that believers in Christ enjoy. Of all the blessings that an unbeliever could see believers enjoying, if he would only notice, what one do you most appreciate? Why? How might you convince an unbeliever that it really is a blessing, and that it is available in Christ Jesus?

WHAT DO YOU THINK?

The four lepers decided they had nothing to lose by going to the enemy camp. They would die anyway if they stayed in or around Samaria. Do you think the "nothing to lose" argument is a valid one to use with non-Christians? That is, is it right to suggest one has nothing to lose by considering the claims of the gospel and much to lose if they do not? Or is that too negative an approach? Give reasons for your position.

WHAT DO YOU THINK?

God caused the Arameans to be overcome with a fear that, except for what the Lord put in their minds, was unfounded. At the same time, once the Arameans had fled, the people of Samaria were hiding in fear of a danger that no longer existed. How similar are their situations to cases today when people withdraw from a situation because of fears that are unfounded? How are they different? How can you face down the fears that arise in your life? What promises of God are particularly helpful?

WHAT DO YOU THINK?

"Finders keepers." "We have been poor all our lives; we deserve this now." "God must have meant for us to have it." "We took the risk. . . . " With any of these statements the lepers might have justified hoarding the wealth left by the Arameans. Instead, they realized that, by not sharing, they were "not doing right" (v. 9).

How does that compare with the way people justify selfishness today? "I work hard for my money, . . ." "I sacrificed to go to college so I could get this job . . . ," "God has rewarded me with wealth, and I am going to enjoy it." What is the proper response to being blessed by God? How common is this response?

How appropriate has your own response to God's blessings been?

At dusk. The lepers may have waited until after sunset to avoid being seen deserting to the enemy and consequently being shot by archers on the walls of the city.

The edge of the camp. This was the most advanced part of the Aramean forces, the part nearest the city of Samaria. The lepers would have come to it first. Imagine their surprise and joy when, expecting mistreatment or even death, they found the camp abandoned!

B. EXPLANATION (VV. 6, 7)

6. For the Lord had caused the Arameans to hear the sound of chariots and horses and a great army, so that they said to one another, "Look, the king of Israel has hired the Hittite and Egyptian kings to attack us!"

Clearly this was a miracle. As darkness approached (v. 7), the Lord caused the sound of a mighty advancing army to fall on the ears of the Aramean forces, an army they did not want to meet in combat. The Arameans' first thought was that the king of Israel had hired Hittite and Egyptian mercenaries to come to his rescue. The Hittites were located north of Aram. Both the Hittites and the Egyptians had centuries of experience in chariot warfare, and were considered skilled in the use of this weapon. Pharaoh of Egypt had used chariots in an attempt to prevent the Israelites from escaping (Exodus 14:7, 9, 17).

7. So they got up and fled in the dusk and abandoned their tents and their horses and donkeys. They left the camp as it was and ran for their lives.

This chaotic rout of the Aramean army occurred also in the twilight. It seems, therefore, that not long before the lepers entered the camp on the side nearest the city, the Arameans had fled the camp, going out the opposite side. In their haste the Arameans even left their animals tethered where they were (v. 10). The animals would not have had saddles or bridles on, and to equip them for riding would have taken more time than the frightened men dared take. They *ran for their lives.*

C. FOOD AND TREASURE (V. 8)

8. The men who had leprosy reached the edge of the camp and entered one of the tents. They ate and drank, and carried away silver, gold and clothes, and went off and hid them. They returned and entered another tent and took some things from it and hid them also.

When the four lepers entered the camp, the only sign of life they saw in the gathering darkness was the animals—they neither saw nor heard any soldier. When it became obvious that the Arameans had abandoned the camp, the men satisfied their immediate need—food. After they had eaten their fill, they began to look over the wealth that had been left behind. For years, perhaps, these men had lived in abject poverty. Now they were surrounded by tents in which were all kinds of treasure. Since they could not carry with them all the wealth they found, they *hid* it, probably in the ground. Their plan, no doubt, was to come back later and retrieve it.

IV. SHARING GOOD NEWS (2 KINGS 7:9)

9. Then they said to each other, "We're not doing right. This is a day of good news and we are keeping it to ourselves. If we wait until daylight, punishment will overtake us. Let's go at once and report this to the royal palace."

It may be, as some suggest, that the lepers' consciences were pricked when they stopped to realize that they were keeping this good news to themselves, all the while people inside the city were starving. It also seems that they were concerned about what would happen to them if they didn't share this good news. *Punishment will overtake us.* This suggests that the lepers began to think that if they kept quiet about this good news and spent the whole night gratifying only themselves, they would be found out when the morning came and would suffer for what they had done.

In some respects we who are Christians are like these lepers. We have come upon a vast treasure—the wonderful news that Christ saves sinful men. We should, of course, rejoice in that fact. At the same time, however, we have a moral obligation to share it with others. More than that, we have a divine mandate to do so. The lepers knew that they would be punished if they didn't do what was right. Dare we neglect the Lord's mandate?

Once the men realized the situation they were in, they returned to the city with the good news. They called out to the gatekeepers and told them what they had found in the enemy camp. The gatekeepers shouted the news inside the city, and so the news reached the palace.

At first, the king was skeptical, fearing that the Arameans were setting an ambush for him. So he sent out scouts, who picked up the Arameans' trail—"they found the whole road strewn with the clothing and equipment the Arameans had thrown away in their headlong flight" all the way to the Jordan River. When they returned, then, they confirmed the word of the lepers. Word quickly swept through the city, and the people rushed out to gather the food and wealth the Arameans had left behind. In the process two of Elisha's prophecies were fulfilled. A measure of fine flour did sell for a shekel, and two measures of barley for a shekel (v. 16). Further, the officer who had ridiculed Elisha's prophecy was trampled under foot by the people as they rushed out of the gate (v. 20).

GO AND TELL

What a relief finally to hear some good news! Communism No Longer a Threat! Spiritual Revival in Russia! Israelis and Arabs Come to the Peace Table! Divorce Rate Declines!

Such headlines are good news, indeed. To suppress word of these positive happenings and trends would be unthinkable. Good news is for sharing.

The lepers who discovered that the Aramean camp was deserted had some mighty good news to share. Even in the middle of the night, they knew that the mystifying departure of the enemy troops must be reported. Motivated by both privilege and obligation, they returned to Samaria and told the gatekeepers, who told the king, who told advisers—and so the news spread quickly.

Christians have incredibly good news to share—the gospel of Jesus Christ. It is a privilege to report that God has delivered mankind from sin and death. It also is an obligation to tell the lost of God's love, and of his plan for our redemption. Like the friends of Jesus who first discovered the empty tomb, let us "go and tell" that he is risen, that he can save, that he is Lord!   —R. W. B.

CONCLUSION

A. JUST SUPPOSE

Just suppose that the four lepers had remained in the Aramean camp, gathering up the treasures the fleeing enemy had left behind. Just suppose they had worked throughout the night on this self-aggrandizing mission and had waited until the next day to report to those trapped in the city what they had found.

The four might have got away with it—at least for a while. Since no one had seen them, there would have been no reason for accusing them of wrongdoing. However, there may have been serious consequences for the people within the city had the men not reported the good news. For some inside the city on the verge of

Visual 4 illustrates the message of verse 9 and demonstrates the contemporary need of Christians to share the good news they possess.

WHAT DO YOU THINK?

The lepers realized that their discovery was too wonderful to keep to themselves. People who could be saved by this news were dying. They also realized that they could be punished if it was discovered later that they withheld this news.

How does this compare with our knowledge of the gospel? Should the same motives drive us to share the good news? In what ways should our motives be the same, and in what ways should they be different?

OPTION

Use the reproducible activity, "Great Things He Has Done," page 376 to apply this lesson to the lives of your students.

PRAYER

Dear Father, help us not to forget those who are needy. May we share our physical blessings with them, but more important, may we share the good news of salvation with those all about us. Give us a passion for lost souls. Give us the courage to seek them out. Show us how to share with them the greatest news of all—that you loved us so much that you gave your Son to die for us. In his name we pray. Amen.

THOUGHT TO REMEMBER

"Woe to me if I do not preach the gospel!" (1 Corinthians 9:16).

DAILY BIBLE READINGS

Monday, June 19—A Prayer for God's Help (Psalm 86:1-7)

Tuesday, June 20—God Does Wondrous Things (Psalm 86: 8-17)

Wednesday, June 21—Aram's Siege Brings Famine in Samaria (2 Kings 6:24-29)

Thursday, June 22—Elisha's Assurance of Imminent Relief (2 Kings 6:30—7:2)

Friday, June 23—Lepers Find the Aramean Camp Abandoned (2 Kings 7:3-8)

Saturday, June 24—The Lepers Report the Good News (2 Kings 7:9-15)

Sunday, June 25—Relief From Siege and Famine (2 Kings 7: 16-20)

starvation, the delay of even a few hours might have brought death. Others may have been driven to violence by their hunger, and may have robbed or even killed to get food.

What about the lepers themselves? Suppose they had worn some of the expensive garments they had taken from the Arameans' tents. Wouldn't someone have begun to ask questions? It isn't likely that lepers ordinarily wore new, expensive clothing. Suppose they had tried to spend some of the gold or silver they had hidden away. Wouldn't this have raised further questions? The simple fact is that they couldn't have enjoyed the fruits of their venture very long before someone would have become suspicious and found out the truth.

"Be sure that your sin will find you out" (Numbers 32:23). How often this is true, even with the person who thinks he has committed the perfect crime! But does one ever really get away with it? Even if one goes to his grave without being caught, he has to live with his own conscience. That can be a more severe judge than any earthly judge. Suppose, however, that one has so dulled his conscience that he never feels its pangs—and some have done that! The grave does not end it all. Beyond this life one must face the divine Judge, who not only knows all the facts, but who will deal with them according to his eternal laws.

B. "NO MAN IS AN ISLAND"

John Donne once observed that "no man is an island . . . every man is part of the main." In an age that stresses individualism to the point of selfishness, many seem to have forgotten that fact. Certainly, every one of us is an individual, and each person must bear individual responsibility for his or her actions. No one can repent for another person's sins, and no one can stand before God in another's stead.

Our individual responsibilities notwithstanding, we have responsibilities that go beyond our own immediate concern. We owe a great debt to our parents, who brought us into this world and sustained us through our fragile years. We owe thanks to those who across the centuries have sacrificed and worked that we may enjoy the blessings of freedom and affluence. Most of all, we owe a debt to our Savior, who left his heavenly home to bring us salvation.

What have we done to pay back some of this debt we owe? Too often we're like the four lepers. We become so busy stashing away treasure for ourselves that we forget others who need what we are hiding away. These men finally came to their senses and thought about the people in the besieged city, who needed some of the things they were hiding. Let us be alert to the needs of others and do what we can for them.

C. THE BEST NEWS

For those starving survivors trapped in Samaria, there could have been no better news than the news the lepers brought them—food was available. We who are Christians have better news—the best news: Christ died to save sinful men. All about us people are starving spiritually. Jesus Christ, who is the bread of life, alone can satisfy their souls' hunger. Are we hesitating to take this good news to them? Or are we too busy seeking and hiding away the treasures that never can completely satisfy? Could it be that we are not quite sure in our own mind that the Bread of Life will sustain?

Someone has observed that we ought to share the good news of the gospel with all the intensity of one starving beggar telling another starving beggar where bread can be found. Let's do as the lepers did. Let's "go at once" to the starving people and let them know that this is a day of good news.

Discovery Learning

This page contains an alternate lesson plan emphasizing learning activities. Classes desiring such student involvement will find these suggestions helpful. The next page is a reproducible activity page to further enhance discovery learning.

LEARNING GOALS

In this session your students will be led to do the following:

1. Analyze the decision of the four lepers in 2 Kings 7 who shared their newly acquired provisions.

2. Become more aware of the needs of others and more willing to meet those needs.

INTO THE LESSON

Write the following incomplete statement on the chalkboard before class begins:

Most people would be more generous if—

Begin this session by asking your class members to pair off. Give each pair a pen and a sheet of paper and ask them to complete the sentence in at least five ways. Allow two minutes for the pairs to complete this activity.

After two minutes call time. Ask for volunteers to share several of their completions and discuss these as necessary. Then make the transition into the lesson by saying, "Our study today will introduce us to four men who chose to be generous rather than hoard the much-needed supplies that came into their possession."

OPTION

Bring to class several pages of newspaper comics, a page for every three persons whom you anticipate will be in class. Have the class form groups of three. Distribute one page of comics to each group. (It may be necessary for you to ask several class members to bring a page of comics so you will have enough.)

Ask half of the groups to look for cartoon strips that illustrate selfishness or acquiring things. Ask the other half to look for comic strips that illustrate generosity. Allow several minutes for the groups to do their searching. Then ask for volunteers to share the illustrations they found.

INTO THE WORD

In order for your students to gain the full significance of the events recorded in the Scripture text assigned for this lesson, it is necessary that they understand the historical background of the passage. This may be found in 2 Kings 6:24-33. Present a brief lecture (three to five minutes in length) based on these verses. Refer also to the comments included in the "Lesson Background" section of the lesson commentary. After you have established the background, ask a volunteer (whom you contacted during the week before class) to read 2 Kings 7:1-9 aloud to the class. Then lead your class in discussing the following questions based on the text (2 Kings 7:1-9).

1. Elisha prophesied that within a day the siege of Samaria would be lifted (v. 1). The king's officer who scoffed at the prediction would see it but would not eat of the food that would become available (v. 2). What was Elisha's meaning? (See verses 17-20.)

2. What was the condition of the four men at the city gate? (v. 3)

3. What options were available to the four men? (v. 4)

4. What change in these men's situation took place? (vv. 5-8).

5. What was their response to their incredible find? (v. 9)

6. What arguments might these men have used for not sharing the news of their find? (See "What Do You Think?" on page 372.)

7. What principles do we need to learn from these four men?

INTO LIFE

Point out to the class that the four men refused to keep their good news to themselves, and they refused to hoard the provisions God had given them. They were willing to sacrifice for the good of others.

Lead your class members in discussing the following questions to help them make personal application of the principles we have seen illustrated by the four men in the lesson text.

1. What do we have that we could share with others? (Time, skills, material resources.)

2. How generous does God want us to be with what we have?

3. What causes us sometimes to be less than generous with our resources?

4. How can we develop a more generous heart?

5. The good news that every Christian has to share is the gospel of Christ. What one step can we take this coming week to share the news of salvation with someone who needs to hear it?

Forerunners

Just as there are similarities between Elijah's ministry and that of John the Baptist (an emphasis on public condemnation of sin and preaching judgment), so there are similarities between Elisha and Jesus (an emphasis on miracles demonstrating God's grace).

In the chart below are listed several miracles performed by Elisha. In the space provided indicate similar acts performed by Jesus and what these deeds tell us about God.

	SIMILAR MIRACLE FROM LIFE OF JESUS	WHAT DO WE LEARN ABOUT GOD
2 Kings 4:1-7		
2 Kings 4:18-37		
2 Kings 4:38-41		
2 Kings 4:42-44		
2 Kings 5:1-19		
2 Kings 6:1-7		

Great Things He Has Done!

Gehazi was Elisha's servant. On one occasion, the king told Gehazi, "Tell me all about the great things Elisha has done" (2 Kings 8:4). We are servants of Jesus. How would you respond if someone asked you, "Tell me about all the great things Jesus has done for you"?

A Nation Turns From God

Unit 2: The Approaching Judgment

(Lessons 5-9)

CONDEMNATION FOR NATIONAL WRONGDOING

LESSON 5

WHY TEACH THIS LESSON?

One good reason to teach this lesson, and several of the ones to follow, is to remind your class there is nothing "minor" about the message of the "minor prophets." The name refers to the length of the books, shorter than those of the "major prophets" (Isaiah, Jeremiah, Ezekiel, and Daniel).

As for their message, we could call these the "contemporary prophets," for they sound as if they are commenting on our own times. The sins they condemn in the people of their day are the same sins we see around us in our own.

Our lesson text for today, from the book of Amos, is no exception. The greed and government corruption sound like a news report on a Christian radio station. Amos could be talking to our own government leaders, or to the business leaders of our community, or even to the leaders of our church! This lesson challenges your students to measure themselves by the divine plumb line to be sure they are living and leading by God's standards.

INTRODUCTION

A. AN AVALANCHE OF SIN

Several years ago in the Alps a heavy snowfall accumulated high on a mountainside. Something disturbed the snow near the top of the mountain, and it started to slide. Soon a mighty avalanche thundered down the slope, carrying rocks and trees with it. The snow and the debris swept across a narrow valley, blocking a small stream. This barrier effectively dammed the stream, and water began to build up behind the barrier. Before long a sizable lake had formed. After a while the water burst through the dam, and a mighty flood swept down the valley to the village below. There it destroyed everything before it, including houses, barns, and bridges.

The situation in Judah and Israel was rather like this. Like the heavy snowfall, their sins has been growing and accumulating. God delayed his judgment for a time, but eventually his justice would prevail. It came first upon Israel, the northern kingdom. Like a mighty avalanche, Assyria swept down upon that nation and destroyed it. Judgment was delayed awhile for Judah, but finally that nation came to feel God's wrath at the hands of the Babylonians.

Through Amos and other prophets, God gave the people a chance to repent and turn back before it was too late. But they were so entrapped in their sins that they did not heed the word of the Lord. Would Amos get a better hearing among us today if he should come back with the same message?

B. LESSON BACKGROUND

Both Israel and Judah were enjoying prosperity and freedom from external threats. Egypt was in a period of decline, Assyria was also in a temporary decline, and Babylon had not yet come on the scene as a major power.

DEVOTIONAL READING:
PSALM 82
LESSON SCRIPTURE:
AMOS 1:1—3:2
PRINTED TEXT:
AMOS 2:4-8; 3:1, 2

Jul 2

LESSON AIMS

As a result of studying this lesson, each student should:

1. Understand that the actions of a nation have consequences.

2. Understand that the actions of a nation are determined by the actions of its citizens.

3. Appreciate the importance of having absolute standards to govern human conduct.

4. Be able to point out ways in which our nation is guilty of violating God's laws.

KEY VERSE:

"You only have I chosen of all the families of the earth; therefore I will punish you for all your sins."
—Amos 3:2

LESSON 5 NOTES

HOW TO SAY IT

Ammon. AM-mun.
Assyria. Uh-SEAR-ee-uh.
Canaanites. KAY-nan-ites.
Jeroboam. Jair-uh-BO-um.
Sinai. SYE-nay-eye or SYE-nye.
Tekoa. Tee-KOE-uh.

WHAT DO YOU THINK?

Amos began his sermon to Is-rael by announcing judgment on alien nations. His Israelite listen-ers must have been caught some-what by surprise when he suddenly turned to address their own sins.

How effective do you think that approach is today? What method do you think is most effective for helping people to see and own up to their own sin? Why? What is most effective for you?

Both Israel and Judah squandered the wealth that this respite brought them. The rich were becoming richer at the expense of the poor, who were becoming poorer. Not only did the rich often gain their wealth underhandedly, they fre-quently wasted it on luxuries and riotous living. Both nations were on their way to becoming prodigals, storing up for themselves God's righteous indignation.

God sent a warning before he sent judgment. His messenger was Amos, a shep-herd from the remote village of Tekoa, about six or seven miles south of Bethlehem. Amos had no special training for the ministry to which he was called (Amos 7:14), yet he was a most powerful proclaimer of God's message. Although he was a native of Judah, his prophetic ministry was to the northern kingdom. While we cannot precisely date his ministry, we know it occurred when Jeroboam II was king of Is-rael and Uzziah was king of Judah, about 750 B.C. or a bit earlier.

I. JUDGMENT UPON JUDAH (AMOS 2:4, 5)
A. THEIR SINS WERE MULTIPLIED (V. 4A)
4a. This is what the LORD says: "For three sins of Judah, even for four, I will not turn back my wrath.

The book of Amos opens with denunciations directed at Israel's neighbors: Damascus, Gaza, Tyre, Edom, Ammon, and Moab. No doubt his audience, the citi-zens of the northern kingdom, greeted these denunciations with loud amens, be-cause all of the people mentioned were their enemies. Then Amos turned his attention to Judah, the southern kingdom. He probably got some strong amens for this, too, because Israel and Judah had often been at odds.

B. THEY DESPISED THE LAW (V. 4B)
4b. "Because they have rejected the law of the LORD and have not kept his decrees, because they have been led astray by false gods, the gods their ancestors followed.

The denunciation of Israel's other neighbors came because of their cruel and vio-lent acts committed in war, including acts against Israel. But while Judah may have been guilty of similar violence, her condemnation was on a different basis. She was denounced because she had *rejected the law of the Lord:* that is, she had broken the covenant God had made with his people at Mount Sinai. The audience must have taken special delight in this denunciation, because Judah had always claimed that she was the defender of the covenant while Israel was accused of being the covenant breaker. We can almost savor their delight as they heard Judah being de-nounced by one of her own citizens.

Not only had the people of Judah broken the covenant, but they had done so by chasing after *false gods.*

THREE OR FOUR NATIONAL SINS

Headlines on grocery-store scandal sheets are sometimes amusing (for example, "Two-Headed Two-Year-Old Quarrels Alone"), often disgusting, usually ridiculous, and almost always fictitious. Thinking people rarely take them seriously. Television counterparts to such yellow journalism may be a bit more credible, but still cater to the public appetite for sensationalism.

"Investigative reporting" seems to delight in digging up dirt about dignitaries. Wouldn't it be a surprise if any of them featured the *Sins of Our Nation*? Headline: *Four Vilest Sins of America.* The hard part would be deciding which national disgrace is the worst.

When God condemned Judah and Israel for their sins, he was specific; retribution was certain. God didn't have to manufacture sensationalized accounts; Amos spoke the tragic truth, listing three or four sins that God hated.

What sins of America does God hate most? Adultery? Pornography? Homosexuality? Pride? Apathy? Greed? Prostitution? Abortion? Humanism? Materialism? Satanism? Would only three or four make the top of his list? "Sin is a disgrace to any people" (Proverbs 14:34).   —R. W. B.

C. A JUDGMENT OF FIRE UPON JUDAH (V. 5)

5. "I will send fire upon Judah that will consume the fortresses of Jerusalem."

Although Judah's sins were different, she would receive the same punishment that the other nations received: God would *send fire upon Judah.* God would punish other nations at the hands of Assyria. Judah would also suffer the wrath of Assyria; but her final punishment, including the destruction of Jerusalem, would come at the hands of the Babylonians nearly two hundred years after Amos spoke these words.

II. JUDGMENT UPON ISRAEL (AMOS 2:6-8)

A. THEIR SINS WERE MULTIPLIED (V. 6A)

6a. This is what the LORD says: "For three sins of Israel, even for four, I will not turn back my wrath.

Up to now, Amos's pronouncements of judgment upon Israel's neighbors were welcome news. People of Israel readily agreed that those neighbors deserved God's punishment. But now they found themselves the subject of Amos's pronouncements. One cannot help but feel the prophet had carefully chosen this approach in order to capture and hold the attention of his audience, to set them up for the real thrust of his message. Israel's sins that Amos enumerated were not sins of violence and atrocities in war. Israel may on occasion have been guilty of these, but Amos spoke of social sins of Israelite against Israelite, neighbor against neighbor.

B. THEY WERE UNJUST (V. 6B)

6b. "They sell the righteous for silver, and the needy for a pair of sandals.

The greed of some knew few limits. The righteous, sometimes because they were righteous and refused to cheat or take advantage of others, fell into debt and were being sold into slavery. The law allowed a debtor to serve his creditor, but he was to serve as a hired servant, not as a slave (Leviticus 25:39-43). Some commentators believe that the creditors were able to enslave their fellow citizens by bribing the judges. The bribe is *silver* or *a pair of sandals.* Others suggest that the greed of the creditor is the point here, that he would sell a debtor into slavery for such a trivial sum as a piece of silver or a pair of shoes. Whichever interpretation we accept, it is obvious that this sin must have been fairly common, otherwise Amos would not have used it as his first charge against the people.

C. THEY WERE GREEDY (V. 7A)

7a. "They trample on the heads of the poor as upon the dust of the ground and deny justice to the oppressed.

The rich were taking advantage of the poor in every way they could. Like the modern executive who climbs the corporate ladder on the backs of his contemporaries, the greedy trampled the poor in their pursuit of wealth, oblivious to their plight. Such greed seems to arise in every generation. We see the same sin today in our society. Men use all kinds of devious ways, some legal and some not so legal, to acquire wealth and position. But legal or not, this greed is immoral.

They *deny justice to the oppressed.* Of course they did! It was they who oppressed the poor. To grant them justice would be to cite themselves for their sins. Thus, they prevented the down-and-outers from taking the steps they needed to take in order to relieve their poverty.

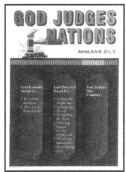

Visual 5 notes God's judgment on Israel and Judah and challenges us to think about his response to abuses in our own country.

While Amos directed his message against the sins of whole nations, it is clear that the sins of individuals affect all of society and become the sins of nations. Samuel illustrated it in confronting Saul, as did Nathan in singling out David's sin.

When people take seriously the application of spiritual truth in their lives, it makes a difference in the direction of the nation. Many credit John Wesley's preaching in the 1700s with preventing a social upheaval in England comparable to the French Revolution in 1789. Christians so affected the pagan empire of Rome that its emperor declared himself a Christian barely three centuries after a Roman governor crucified Jesus.

How much do you think individual Christians today affect their society? Why? What would make the impact of individual Christians stronger?

WHAT DO YOU THINK?

In the judgment against Judah and again in the judgment against Israel, part of the problem was improper worship (vv. 4, 8). What does this suggest to you about the importance of the church's witness to society? About the individual Christian's witness? How can you enhance each one?

OPTION

The reproducible page 384 has an activity, "How Do We Measure Up?" that helps students compare Amos's message to Israel with the needs of our own country.

D. THEY ENGAGED IN SEXUAL SINS (V. 7B)

7b. "Father and son use the same girl and so profane my holy name.

An incestuous relationship in which a father married his son's widow or a son married his father's widow was forbidden by the law (Leviticus 18:1-18). But that may not be the situation here. Both father and son may have been going to the same concubine or prostitute. If this was the case, the father was setting a terrible example for his son. To *profane my holy name* may suggest that they were going to a sacred prostitute in a pagan temple. Thus they were guilty of a double sin: violating God's laws against sexual immorality and becoming involved in worshiping a pagan god. We who live in a sex-saturated society know very well how destructive such activity can be.

PROFANITY

My mother heard me swear at a dog when I was still in diapers. She said she had no idea where I learned the word; no one in our household used such language.

As far as I know, that incident was my only experiment with cussing. Early on I was taught never to "take the name of the Lord thy God in vain."

Even people who profess few religious convictions know the Third Commandment. On the other hand, God's name is spoken profanely more and more in movies and television shows. What most folk don't understand are the far-reaching implications of the prohibition against profanity. God's name is profaned in more ways than just by swearing. Taking God's name in vain also means wearing his name (professing to be his child) while disgracing him with a sinful life-style. Israel had profaned the holy name of God with sexual immorality, as well as by other transgressions.

Does anyone really believe that America is a Christian nation anymore? Our culture's profanity belies the name. We must confess with Isaiah, "Woe to me! . . . I live among a people of unclean lips" (Isaiah 6:5).

—R. W. B.

E. THEY BECAME DRUNK (V. 8)

8. "They lie down beside every altar on garments taken in pledge. In the house of their god they drink wine taken as fines."

The *garments* were the large outer garments that were worn as cloaks during the day and used as bedding at night. A person in dire poverty might give up his cloak as a pledge against a loan; but according to the law, it was to be returned to him at night so that he would not be without bedding (Exodus 22:26, 27; Deuteronomy 24:12, 13). In this action the rich were violating the law and oppressing the poor. They were using the cloaks as bedding as they worshiped *in the house of their god*, presumably one of the altars that had been set up at Dan and Bethel. Since the only divinely authorized altar was in Jerusalem, their worship was improper at these altars. They were further condemned because they were engaged in drunken debauchery even as they worshiped. This kind of worship under these circumstances was more akin to the Baal worship of the Canaanites than the worship of Jehovah God. The *wine taken as fines* may refer to unjust fines levied by corrupt judges.

III. JUDGMENT UPON ISRAEL AND JUDAH TOGETHER (AMOS 3:1, 2)

A. GOD'S WORD WAS SPOKEN AGAINST THEM (V. 1)

1. Hear this word the LORD has spoken against you, O people of Israel—against the whole family I brought up out of Egypt.

Amos attempted to get their attention by pointing out that his message was not his own, but had come from God. It carried authority far beyond anything that mere men could utter. It is worth remembering that God's authority is still found in his Word, the Scriptures, which carry far greater weight than the words of human wisdom. This message was not just against the citizens of the northern kingdom, but against the *whole family,* that is, Judah as well as Israel.

Hundreds of years earlier, God had established his covenant with his people, the descendants of Jacob. But they forgot so easily. One way of reminding them of who they were was to remind them of their history and how God had worked mightily on their behalf. Their miraculous escape from enslavement in Egypt is a recurring theme in the Old Testament. It was indelibly imprinted upon their memories, and again and again it served to unite the people and to carry them through difficult times.

B. THEY HAD BEEN GREATLY BLESSED (V. 2)

2. *"You only have I chosen of all the families of the earth; therefore I will punish you for all your sins."*

God knew all the families of the earth, but he knew only Israel as his own. They had been selected to be the channel through which God would send his Son. They had not been selected because they were more deserving than others. Their selection is an example of God's grace that is poured out, not on the basis of merit, but because he in his infinite wisdom knows what is best.

But there is a flip side to the coin. "From everyone who has been given much, much will be demanded" (Luke 12:48). Because the Israelites had received so much from God, he would in turn require much from them. Amos had denounced the sins of the nations surrounding Israel; but they had often sinned in ignorance, not having the blessings of the light that came from God's revelation. The Israelites, however, had sinned in spite of the light they had and the blessings they had received.

If God made greater moral demands upon the Israelites because he gave them greater blessings, how will he deal with us who have received even greater blessings? In material things we have been blessed beyond the wildest imagination of even King Solomon. But our spiritual blessings have been infinitely greater. We have been privileged to receive further revelation in the New Testament, revelation that points us to our Lord and Savior.

TOUGH LOVE

Conscientious parents discipline their children out of love. And though kids don't believe it, the punishment often is harder on the parent than on the child. Some children have kids of their own before they understand that "tough love" is tough on both generations of the family. Genuine parental love, however, is not permissive. Father and mother must rear sons and daughters with the "iron hand" of authority in the "velvet glove" of tenderness.

God loves his children—all of his children, all of the time. He loved Israel before they were a nation, when they were slaves in Egypt. He loved Israel, even when they complained during their wilderness wanderings. He loved Israel when they prospered in Canaan. And he loved them still when they disobeyed and disgraced him. In these latter cases, as today's text illustrates, God demonstrated his love with disciplinary punishment.

Nothing can separate us from the love of God (Romans 8:38, 39), not even ungodly behavior. But as all children of loving parents must suffer certain consequences of rebelling against authority, so we, the children of God, also must expect just retribution for wrongdoing. God is not a doting grandparent. He brings us to repentance when we sin. That is tough love.

—R. W. B.

WHAT DO YOU THINK?

What specific connections do you see between social sins and social unrest? Do you think the violent problems of a society reflect its lack of attention to the needs of its poorest and most despised? Why or why not? What solutions can you suggest for such societal problems?

OPTION

The lower portion of the reproducible page, "How Do I Measure Up?" provides an opportunity to apply the message of Amos to your students' lives. See page 384.

THOUGHT TO REMEMBER

"Righteousness exalts a nation: but sin is a disgrace to any people" (Proverbs 14:34).

DAILY BIBLE READINGS

Monday, June 26—God Wants Justice in the World (Psalm 82)

Tuesday, June 27—Amos Announces God's Judgment on Syria (Amos 1:1-5)

Wednesday, June 28—Judgment on Philistia, Tyre, and Edom (Amos 1:6-12)

Thursday, June 29—Judgment on the Ammonites and Moab (Amos 1:13—2:3)

Friday, June 30—Unexpected Judgment on Judah and Israel (Amos 2:4-8)

Saturday, July 1—God's Mercy Has Been Ignored (Amos 2:9-13)

Sunday, July 2—Punishment for Abusing God's Favor (Amos 2:14—3:2)

CONCLUSION

A. AMOS, OUR CONTEMPORARY

In today's lesson text and in other passages from Amos, it is quite clear that one purpose of his ministry was to arouse the people to the social injustices found in Israel in his day. It was a society in which the rich were getting richer while the poor were becoming poorer. Worse still, the rich gained their wealth, not by hard work and frugality, but by using illegal methods to exact their toll from the poor. Further, they used their ill-gotten wealth, not in a responsible way, but to secure luxuries and to make a public display. For example, they lived in "houses adorned with ivory" (Amos 3:15) and lay upon "beds inlaid with ivory" (Amos 6:4). Since ivory was imported and very expensive, its use spoke of great extravagance even as the poor went without food. Archaeologists working at the site of ancient Samaria have found ivory plaques that apparently adorned the walls of the houses of the rich, and they have found ivory works that were inlaid in furniture, giving ample evidence of the truthfulness of Amos's charges.

Persons who use material wealth in an irresponsible fashion are likely to be careless in other areas of their lives. Such was the case in ancient Israel. Amos accused them of sexual immorality, of drunkenness, and of going through the motions of meaningless worship.

Does not this all sound embarrassingly contemporary? To read the prophet's listing of the evils of his day is almost like reading the daily newspaper. Because Israel refused to heed Amos's call to repentance, she fell within a generation after the prophet delivered his message. We are foolish indeed if we do not observe Israel's tragic fate and learn from it.

B. SEEKING A PLUMB LINE

A theme runs through the book of Amos that expresses the authority with which he spoke. Again and again we read such expressions as "This is what the Lord says," "Hear this word the Lord has spoken," "This is what the Sovereign Lord says," and "The Lord Almighty declares." Amos spoke with conviction and without compromise because he spoke with divine authority. The standard he held the people to was not his own, but God's. In one vision he saw the Lord with a plumb line in the midst of the people, measuring them with his standard (Amos 7:7, 8).

Many in our society seem to have rejected all absolute standards. It is almost as if we were back in the times of the judges when "everyone did as he saw fit" (Judges 21:25). Because God's standards are no longer widely recognized, our elected leaders disregard the Word of God, our legislative bodies pass laws that violate its teachings, and our judges ignore it. Even our citizens, when they vote on referendums, often ignore what the Bible teaches.

Rather pessimistic, you may say. Yes, but certainly not hopeless. So long as we have the Bible as our guide and so long as God continues to intervene in the affairs of man, no situation is hopeless. Further, we do not have to wait until God calls us from tending sheep in Tekoa as he did with Amos. We do not need some new revelation to give us direction. The Bible provides us with all the direction and all the motivation that we need.

But if we are to do God's bidding, we must know what his will for us is. His standards are clearly laid out for us in the Bible. But we must study the Bible if it is to become the standard that we follow. We must share our understanding of the Bible with others. We have a special obligation to pass it on to our children. While the church offers us vehicles for Christian education—Sunday school, Vacation Bible School, Christian camps, and other methods—yet the greater responsibility rests on us as parents and grandparents to get the job done.

Discovery Learning

This page contains an alternate lesson plan emphasizing learning activities. Classes desiring such student involvement will find these suggestions helpful. The next page is a reproducible activity page to further enhance discovery learning.

LEARNING GOALS

This lesson should help your students do the following:

1. Identify some of the sins for which God would judge Judah and Israel as noted in Amos 2 and 3.

2. Consider what their own role is for helping their nation turn to God.

3. Commit themselves to influence their nation to turn to righteousness.

INTO THE LESSON

Write the following words on the chalkboard:

*nation to is sin a people righteousness
but exalts any a disgrace*

Have students work in groups of three to unscramble the words. Allow two minutes, then ask for the unscrambled sentence.

It is "Righteousness exalts a nation, but sin is a disgrace to any people" (Proverbs 14:34).

Lead into the Bible study by saying, "God has always demanded righteousness from nations. Today we will examine God's warning to the nations of Israel and Judah."

INTO THE WORD

Have the class form groups of four to six. Have one group complete Assignment One below, another complete Assignment Two. *All other* groups should complete Assignment Three.

ASSIGNMENT ONE

Read Amos 2:4-8; 3:1, 2. Use the helps provided to study the background of the book of Amos. Who was Amos? When did he minister? What prompted him to write this book? What are the main points of his book? Be prepared to report your observation.

ASSIGNMENT TWO

Using the commentaries provided, research Amos 2:4-8 and 3:1, 2. For what sins would Israel be punished? Prepare a brief commentary to read to the rest of the class.

ASSIGNMENT THREE

Read Amos 2:4-8; 3:1, 2. Discuss what God is looking for in a nation and how our own nation measures up.

Provide the group doing Assignment One with **Bible dictionaries** or **encyclopedias, Bible handbooks** such as Halley's or Eerdmans', perhaps the *New International Study Bible.* The group doing Assignment Two will need several **commentaries on Amos.** The groups doing Assignment Three will need copies of the **reproducible page** that follows.

Allow twenty-five minutes for the projects, then let the groups report.

OPTION

Divide the class into groups of four to six. Have them complete the chart on the reproducible page. Discuss these questions:

1. How will God deal with Judah (2:5)? With Israel (3:1, 2)?

2. According to Amos, what is the solution for Israel's problem? See Amos 5:6, 14, 15.

INTO LIFE

Lead your class in discussing these questions:

1. How can our church make a difference in helping our nation turn toward righteousness?

2. How can *you* make a difference in helping this nation turn toward righteousness?

Allow ten minutes for talk. For the first question, develop a list on the chalkboard as answers are called out. Comment briefly on each answer as needed. For the second, you may want to sit down and discuss the answers in more of a low key. Some of the answers may be rather personal.

Distribute paper and pencils. Ask each student to write a prayer, asking God to help him or her to make a difference.

OPTION

Distribute paper and pencils. Have students look up 2 Chronicles 7:14 and rewrite it in their own words. Discuss these questions:

1. What would happen to our nation if a significant number of Christians were to repent of their sins and pray fervently for the nation?

2. What is one thing you will do to help turn our nation back to God?

Ask each student to write a prayer, asking God to help him or her to make a difference.

How Do We Measure Up?

Read Amos 2:4-8; 3:1, 2. Discuss the questions below with your group and use the space provided to record your answers.

	WHAT IS GOD LOOKING FOR IN A NATION?	*HOW DOES OUR NATION MEASURE UP IN THIS REGARD?*
Amos 2:4	_____	_____
	_____	_____
Amos 2:6	_____	_____
	_____	_____
Amos 2:7	_____	_____
	_____	_____
Amos 2:8	_____	_____
	_____	_____
Amos 2:12	_____	_____
	_____	_____
Amos 3:2	_____	_____
	_____	_____

Choose one shortcoming above and discuss with your group what you could do to help our nation to act more justly in this area.

How Do I Measure Up?

The course of the nation is set by the course of individuals in that nation. Look at the expectations for the nation you listed above. How do you personally measure up to the standard? Pick one area in which you need personal improvement. Make it a matter of prayer this week to conform more closely to God's expectation.

A CALL FOR JUSTICE AND RIGHTEOUSNESS

LESSON 6

WHY TEACH THIS LESSON?

Someone has said, "There's no such thing as a good habit." We may debate that point, but there is truth to the concept that the statement attempts to illuminate.

The Scriptures tell us that we are to be self-controlled (Galatians 5:23; Titus 1:8), not habit-controlled. Even a good habit makes a poor master. Thus, even activities that are good, if they become habits, often lose an essential quality that makes them "good."

Most Christians would agree that regular worship is a good practice. Even Jesus had the custom (some might say habit) of weekly worship in the synagogue (Luke 4:16). But if our worship is just a habit, then we have not worshiped at all!

This was Amos's point in our lesson text for today. The Israelites believed their worship habits put them in good stead with God, in spite of how they lived their lives the rest of the time. Amos told them, and he tells you and your students, such worship *habits* are not pleasing to God.

INTRODUCTION

A. HAY AND WORSHIP

A church in a large city erected a new sanctuary that was impressive both for its size and for its strikingly modern architecture. When the building was dedicated, Christians from the surrounding area were invited to share in the service. A farmer and his family accepted the invitation and attended the meeting. After the service the wife commented to her husband, "Wasn't the huge organ exciting? The sound just sent shivers down my spine."

"I didn't notice," replied the husband.

"Wasn't the choir lovely? Such singing we don't get in our church!" she said.

"I guess it was all right," responded he.

"And what a powerful sermon!"

"I didn't catch much of it."

"For goodness sakes, Pa, didn't you pay attention to anything?"

"Not really. I was too busy trying to figure how many bales of hay I could store in a building like that."

We must admit that at times we are as preoccupied with the things of the world as that farmer was. That was one of the problems that Amos had to deal with as he brought God's message to the people of Israel.

B. LESSON BACKGROUND

Amos, a native of the southern kingdom, was called by God to bring a message of judgment upon the northern kingdom. As he entered into this ministry, he had at least three barriers to overcome.

First, he was a southerner who had to face the national prejudices of the citizens of the northern kingdom. After the kingdom had divided in 931 B.C. at the beginning of

DEVOTIONAL READING:
Amos 5:6-15
LESSON SCRIPTURE:
Amos 4, 5
PRINTED TEXT:
Amos 4:4, 5; 5:18-24

Jul
9

LESSON AIMS

As a result of studying this lesson, each student should:

1. Understand the social and religious situation in Amos's day.

2. Understand that the day of the Lord is a day of judgment for the wicked, but a day of blessings for the righteous.

3. Appreciate the importance of sincere worship that leads to righteous lives.

4. Be able to point out problems we face today in our worship.

KEY VERSE:

But let justice roll on like a river, righteousness like a never-failing stream!   —Amos 5:24

HOW TO SAY IT

Gilgal. GIL-gal.
Jeroboam. Jair-uh-BO-um.
Rehoboam. Re-ho-BO-um.

WHAT DO YOU THINK?

Amos used sarcasm to make his point to the Israelites. The word sarcasm *comes from two Greek words that literally mean "flesh tearing." It is often used to cut down a person, sometimes maliciously.*

What dangers do you see in using sarcasm when teaching people? What guidelines would you suggest for using sarcasm to be sure it does not "tear the flesh" in an unhealthy manner?

Rehoboam's reign, the two nations had experienced a stormy relationship that often led to open hostilities. Although relations between the two states were better than they had been, yet ethnic and national bitterness lasts a long time. We in our times have seen it in such places as Northern Ireland and the area that was formerly Yugoslavia.

Second, Jeroboam II was king of Israel when Amos began his ministry about 760 B.C. Under this strong king, Israel, or at least the wealthy merchant class, was enjoying unprecedented prosperity. For Amos to appear at this time and bring a message of doom was certain to antagonize his hearers.

Finally, Amos had no formal preparation for the prophetic ministry to which he had been called. He readily acknowledged that he was but a humble shepherd and one who "took care of sycamore-fig trees" (Amos 7:14). Ordinarily when God calls a person to a ministry, he calls one who is prepared. But we need to realize that one can become prepared through other than the normal channels, and this certainly was the case with Amos. During those long and lonely hours as he watched over his flock, the word of the Lord came to him in ways that we may not understand. But there was no doubt in Amos's heart about the authenticity of the message that he brought.

I. AMOS'S IRONIC CRITICISM (AMOS 4:4, 5)

A. COME TO WORSHIP AND SIN (V. 4A)

4a. "Go to Bethel and sin; go to Gilgal and sin yet more.

In the verses before this, Amos prophesies that the people of Samaria will be defeated and taken captive like fish taken on hooks. Now he uses irony to drive home his point. He encourages them to continue their sin at Bethel and Gilgal. More than a century and a half earlier, Jeroboam I had set up a place of worship at Bethel, about a dozen miles north of Jerusalem, where he erected a golden calf (1 Kings 12:28, 29). He did this to prevent the people from going to Jerusalem to worship, knowing that he would have trouble maintaining their loyalty if they went to Judah to worship.

Gilgal was located just west of the Jordan River. It was here that the twelve stones were set up as a memorial to the Israelites' crossing of the Jordan (Joshua 4:19-24). Apparently Gilgal, like Bethel, had become a center for worship. One can sense the biting sarcasm in Amos's voice as he urges the people to continue their false worship, thus piling up their sins.

B. BRING SACRIFICES (VV. 4B, 5)

4b, 5. "Bring your sacrifices every morning, your tithes every three years. Burn leavened bread as a thank offering and brag about your freewill offerings—boast about them, you Israelites, for this is what you love to do," declares the Sovereign LORD.

Every morning the Israelites brought their sacrifices. *Every three years* is "every three days" in some versions (e.g., *New American Standard Bible*). Some commentators suggest that Amos means the people were paying their tithes more often than the law required. The *thank offering* and the *freewill offerings* were offerings that went beyond the minimum. The people were doing more than was prescribed by the law. Yet the thanksgiving offering was *with leaven*, a clear violation of the law. The people were making these offerings in an apparently generous fashion, yet they were doing it their way, not God's way. *Boast about them* seems to mean that they were making a public display of their worship, calling attention to their generosity. Jesus spoke in a similar fashion about the hypocrites who sounded a trumpet before them as they gave their alms (Matthew 6:2).

The people were going through the motions of worship, but their efforts were not acceptable to God. All their empty worship would not avert God's judgment, which Amos describes in the verses that follow. God had sent famine, drought, pestilence, and war upon them, yet they had not repented. Now even worse suffering would be their lot.

They came under God's condemnation for at least three reasons. First, the legitimate place of worship was Jerusalem, not Bethel or Gilgal. Second, they had a golden calf as the center of their worship, a clear violation of the Second Commandment, which forbade the worship of images. In the third place, while they went through the motions of worship, they failed to display righteousness in their lives.

LOST IN THE WRITING

Sarcasm can be an effective figure of speech—*speech* being the key word here. Tone and inflection must be heard to identify sarcasm immediately and accurately. Written down, sarcastic comments lack that sound, and thus can be misunderstood. That is why good writers who create sarcastic dialogue add clues such as ". . . he said sarcastically," or ". . . she said with a sneer in her voice."

Israel couldn't miss the sarcasm in Amos's voice as he spoke for God. But in print, the tone and inflection are lost, so readers can become confused. God, of course, would never literally instruct people to sin—not in Bethel or Gilgal or anywhere else. The prophet is speaking sarcastically to point out Israel's foolishly presumptuous behavior.

Amos was rebuking the Israelites for presuming upon God's grace, for thinking that religious ceremonies could atone for their sin. What he, and God, really wanted them to do is expressed in Amos 5:5, 6: "Do not seek Bethel, do not go to Gilgal . . . Seek the Lord and live."

Careful Bible study considers the context of each passage, and requires readers to "tune in" to the tone of the rhetoric for correct interpretation and understanding.

—R. W. B.

II. THE DAY OF THE LORD (AMOS 5:18-20)

A. THE DAY OF THE LORD IS DARK (V. 18)

18. Woe to you who long for the day of the LORD! Why do you long for the day of the LORD? That day will be darkness, not light.

Many in Israel longed for *the day of the Lord*. They thought Jehovah then would lead his people in triumph over their enemies. Because they were people of the covenant, they thought the day of the Lord would be a day of light, of victory for Israel. They must have been shocked when Amos announced that it would be just the opposite, a day of darkness, not of light.

B. DANGERS OF THE DAY OF THE LORD (V. 19)

19. It will be as though a man fled from a lion only to meet a bear, as though he entered his house and rested his hand on the wall only to have a snake bite him.

Amos illustrates his point by examples from life. A man fleeing from a lion thinks he has escaped, but just at that moment he comes face to face with a bear, which some believe was a greater threat than a lion. Or a man has worked all day in the fields where he has faced all kinds of dangers. At last he enters his own home, expecting to find safety, only to be bitten by a snake.

C. NATURE OF THE DAY REAFFIRMED (V. 20)

20. Will not the day of the LORD be darkness, not light—pitch-dark, without a ray of brightness?

When Amos announced that the day of the Lord would be darkness, no doubt there were mutterings of unbelief and rejection, not only because it was a new idea,

WHAT DO YOU THINK?

The "day of the Lord" would come for Amos's audience in Samaria in 722 or 721 B.C., when Assyria would take the northern tribes into captivity. This dark day was not at all what the people were expecting.

The "day of the Lord" for which we wait is the second coming of Christ. We do not know when that day will come, but we do know some of what to expect: resurrection (1 Corinthians 15:52), judgment (2 Peter 3:7), and an end to the physical world we know today (2 Peter 3:10, 11).

How do you feel about the "day of the Lord"? Does it give you comfort or fear? Why?

See also John 5:24-30; 1 Thessalonians 4:13-18.

OPTION

Use the reproducible activity, "Great Expectations," on page 392 to discuss "the day of the Lord."

WHAT DO YOU THINK?

God was not pleased with Israel's worship because their lifestyles contradicted their worship. Their worship did not arise from a sense that God was holy and worthy of praise. It seemed, rather, that they looked on worship as a talisman; they did it to prevent bad things from happening to them.

Do you see the same attitudes infecting the church today? What should characterize a person who worships God from the heart, who worships "in spirit and truth"?

WHAT DO YOU THINK?

The people of Israel were going through rituals of worship, but that did not keep them from mistreating each other. How might the observance of the Lord's Supper help to prevent us from the same error? What attitudes need to be present in the Lord's Supper to prevent its being mere ritual, and a hedge against mistreating our brothers and sisters in Christ?

See 1 Corinthians 10:16, 17; 11:20, 21; Matthew 5:23, 24.

Visual 6 illustrates the message of verse 24. The photo was taken at Tell Dan, in Israel.

but because it contradicted what the hearers wanted to believe. Amos assures them that their ears were not deceiving them: he really had said the day of the Lord would be darkness. Indeed, it would be *pitch-dark, without a ray of brightness* in it. In the verses that follow, Amos once again denounces their empty and hypocritical worship, assuring them that these acts will not save them from God's judgment.

FROM FRYING PAN TO FIRE

Sometimes a preacher escapes problems in a congregation by moving to serve another church. Often, however, he finds difficulties in the new place that equal or surpass those he left behind. Running is rarely the best way to resolve conflict. Changing schools, changing climates, changing marriage partners—all of these involve a risk that the latter situation will be worse than the former. (That explains why the rate of divorce among those who have been married more than once is higher than among those who are married to their first mates.)

Millions gamble away happiness by choosing what seems to be greener grass, only to find they have jumped from the frying pan into the fire. Those familiar metaphors may not mix well, but the meaning is clear enough.

Amos warned the people of Israel that they were deluding themselves if they thought "the day of the Lord" would bring them happiness and light. The unholy and disobedient cannot hope to be delivered from frustration, boredom, fear, and despair when the world ends. They will be held accountable for their wickedness, and thus be condemned to destruction that lasts forever. The "frying pan" of earth's trials is but a light affliction compared to divine punishment of the ungodly (Revelation 21:7, 8).   —R. W. B.

III. EMPTY WORSHIP NOT ENOUGH (AMOS 5:21-24)

A. GOD HATES THEIR FEAST DAYS (V. 21)

21. "I hate, I despise your religious feasts; I cannot stand your assemblies.

The *religious feasts* were the great annual feasts—Passover, Pentecost, and Tabernacles—and some more frequently observed days such as Sabbaths and New Moon festivals. The people were not neglecting these feast days, but their practices did not meet God's approval because the people's lives did not demonstrate the righteousness that true worship should produce. God was not pleased with their worship *assemblies*.

B. OFFERINGS NOT ACCEPTABLE (V. 22)

22. Even though you bring me burnt offerings and grain offerings, I will not accept them. Though you bring choice fellowship offerings, I will have no regard for them.

God also refused to accept their offerings. *Burnt offerings* involved the burning of various animals on the altar. Such offerings symbolized the consecration of the worshiper. *Grain offerings* were offerings of flour or meal and oil, not animal flesh. The *fellowship offerings* were offerings in which certain parts of a sacrificed animal were burned on the altar, while other parts were eaten by the priests and worshipers in a common meal.

All of these offerings were presented, but they were not acceptable to God because they were not offered with the right motives or with the proper spirit.

C. MUSIC NOT ACCEPTABLE (V. 23)

23. Away with the noise of your songs! I will not listen to the music of your harps.

Music was important in the praise of God in the Old Testament. The book of Psalms is ready testimony to this fact, for it was a hymnbook for Jewish worship. While we do not have a detailed description of music used in worship, it is generally agreed that singing to the accompaniment of stringed instruments, like *harps* or lyres, was a part of that worship.

In the previous verse, Amos proclaimed God's rejection of the people's sacrifices. In this verse he adds God's rejection of their praise. The reason was not that the people sang off key or used the wrong kind of music. God rejected their songs because they did not present them in the right spirit.

D. AN APPEAL FOR RIGHTEOUSNESS (V. 24)

24. But let justice roll on like a river, righteousness like a never-failing stream!

Some commentators take this to mean that Amos is calling for God's judgment to overwhelm the sinful people like a disastrous flood. Others understand this to be Amos's call for the people to repent, to turn from their worldliness and wickedness to righteousness. This latter interpretation seems best to fit the situation here. The prophet is calling for the people to remove the barriers and take away the hindrances and let justice cover the land as an overwhelming flood.

The people of Israel were people of the covenant. They had agreed to serve God fully, but they had failed in that commitment. Would we call a businessman honest if he cheated once or twice a month? Of course not! What would we think of a husband who boasted of faithfulness to his marriage covenant and yet occasionally committed adultery? Obviously, the man is an adulterer. Just so with the Israelites. They worshiped regularly, but in their daily living and even in their worship they violated the requirements of the covenant. Protest as they might, they were covenant breakers.

MEANINGLESS WORSHIP

Jesus said, "Woe to you, teachers of the law and Pharisees, you hypocrites! You give a tenth of your spices—mint, dill and cummin" (Matthew 23:23). Did Jesus condemn tithing? These religious leaders were meticulous about giving a tenth of everything, even their kitchen spices, in temple offerings.

Christ did not rebuke them for their faithful stewardship. Rather, he told them not to neglect such giving. Jesus was indignant because in the course of tithing, *justice, mercy* and *faith* were being ignored. He said, "You should have practiced the latter, without neglecting the former."

During the prophetic ministry of Amos, Israel made some similar mistakes. Despite their flagrant disobedience, they continued to fast and feast and sacrifice and sing praises to Jehovah. God didn't condemn their worship activities *per se*; he rebuked them for idolatry and other sins of affluence. Rituals and ceremonies are fraudulent and meaningless without righteousness in attitude and behavior.

James defined "pure religion" in terms of benevolence and morality (James 1:27). He also insisted that faith be accompanied by works (James 2:14-26). We can be certain that philanthropy without morality is not acceptable. Christianity involves the whole person, both heart and hand.   —R. W. B.

CONCLUSION

A. "IN SPIRIT AND TRUTH"

In his conversation with the Samaritan woman at the well, Jesus stated that "a time is coming and has now come when the true worshipers will worship the Father in spirit and truth" (John 4:23). At least two things are suggested in this passage. First of all, to worship "in spirit" means to worship in harmony with God, who is spirit. To worship in spirit, one's worship must be free of hypocrisy. To pretend to worship God while allowing oneself to be in bondage to Satan would be a clear violation of this principle. Further, to go through the motions of worship in order to impress others comes under this condemnation. Jesus had strong words

WHAT DO YOU THINK?

The best source of right living is right worship. As we are confronted by God's Word and the revelation of his love in Jesus, we are impelled to go forth and live for him. As we realize that Jesus died for us when we were not worthy (Romans 5:8), we are moved to seek what is right for all those for whom Jesus has such love.

On that basis, how can our worship services become instrumental in making "justice roll on like a river, [and] righteousness like a never-failing stream"? Do you think the key lies in impacting individuals one by one, or corporately, as a body? Why?

OPTION

Use the reproducible activity, "God's Expectations," on page 392 to focus on true worship.

WHAT DO YOU THINK?

How can we strengthen the connection between what we do and say in worship and how we serve God during the week? Think of the following worship activities and make at least one suggestion for each one for strengthening the connection between that activity and your daily life:

Singing
Scripture Reading
Sermon
Invitation
The Lord's Supper
Offering
"Special Music"

PRAYER

Dear God and Father, as we approach you in worship, let us never forget that you are high and holy. Teach us to worship in spirit and truth, and may our lives reflect the fact that we have been in your presence in our worship. In Jesus' name we pray. Amen.

THOUGHT TO REMEMBER

"The true worshipers will worship the Father in spirit and truth" (John 4:23).

DAILY BIBLE READINGS

Monday, July 3—Israel's Vain Piety Will Be Punished (Amos 4:1-5)

Tuesday, July 4—God's Warnings Have Been Ignored (Amos 4:6-11)

Wednesday, July 5—God's Punishment Is at Hand (Amos 4:12—5:3)

Thursday, July 6—There Is Still Time for Repentance (Amos 5:4-9)

Friday, July 7—Warning and Call to Seek God (Amos 5:10-15)

Saturday, July 8—The Day of the Lord: Judgment (Amos 5: 16-20)

Sunday, July 9—God Wants Justice and Righteousness (Amos 5:21-27)

for those who took all kinds of measures to make their religious devotion more obvious to their fellowmen (Matthew 23:5-7).

The second basic principle of worship is that it must be "in truth." This means that it must be as God asks. Since God ruled out all forms of idolatry, the use of any figure or symbol that even suggested idolatry was wrong. Jeroboam, when he led the northern tribes to separate from the southern tribes, erected golden calves to be used in worship at Dan and Bethel. He probably argued that this was not idolatry because the images actually represented God, and the people were worshiping God, not the images. Clearly this violated the Second Commandment. In actual practice, many people did not distinguish between worshiping God through the image and actually worshiping the image. As a result, many people were led astray even as they intended to worship in truth.

Amos condemned the people's worship because it violated both of these principles. They were going through the motions of worship, but their actions revealed that their worship was empty and meaningless. Even as they worshiped, they were plotting ways to cheat their neighbors and pervert the judicial process to their own advantage. In addition, they had erected sanctuaries in various places when the law established only one. They had added both plans and practices that were not authorized by the law. As the years passed, these innovations had come to be accepted as normal. No one questioned them. It is little wonder that the people were shocked when Amos harshly criticized them.

B. OUR SOLEMN ASSEMBLIES

Suppose Amos were to visit one of our worship services. What criticisms might he level at us? First of all, he would need to recognize that we no longer live under the law, that the detailed regulations that covered worship in the tabernacle and the temple do not apply to us. Other than to stipulate that true worship must be "in spirit and truth," the New Testament gives us few specific directions. From the examples of worship that we read about in the New Testament, we learn that the apostles' teaching, fellowship, the breaking of bread or the Lord's Supper, and prayers were elements of that worship (Acts 2:42). Other passages teach the singing of "psalms, hymns and spiritual songs" (Ephesians 5:19; Colossians 3:16). It seems proper to include them in our meetings for worship. The New Testament leaves us free to incorporate other elements if they do not violate the principles of "in spirit and truth."

Today if one visits from congregation to congregation and from one culture to another, he finds a great variety of activities included in worship services. Some involve formal and exacting rituals; others are more spontaneous and informal. It is easy for us to become critical of any worship service that does not conform to our own accustomed practices. Today we hear much argument about the choice of music used in worship. Some prefer the majestic music of the classics and the stately lyrics of the traditional hymns. Others would adapt the beat, the volume, and repetitive lyrics of contemporary music to our worship. Controversies over worship have raged across the centuries, and so it should not surprise us that we still have these arguments with us.

The real issue is the bottom line. What happens when the last amen is said and we leave the sanctuary to face the world outside? That's what Amos's message is all about. God hated the feast days and the noise of the people's songs because justice and righteousness did not prevail in their lives after they left the sanctuary. Since much of what we do in worship is subjective and cannot be readily measured, the most effective test of our worship is what happens in our lives.

Do our lives pass the test?

Discovery Learning

*This page contains an alternate lesson plan emphasizing learning activities. Classes
desiring such student involvement will find these suggestions helpful. The next page
is a reproducible activity page to further enhance discovery learning.*

LEARNING GOALS

As a result of this lesson your students should:

1. Identify a correlation between worshiping God and living righteously.

2. Evaluate the quality of their own worship.

INTO THE LESSON

Before class, write these headings on the chalkboard:

God accepts worship that—
God doesn't accept worship that—

When class begins, have the class form groups of four. Provide each group with a sheet of paper and a pencil. Assign half of the groups to brainstorm answers to the first heading above, and half to do the same for the second heading. Allow two minutes. Then ask those who brainstormed the first heading to report their suggestions as you write them on the chalkboard. Then do the same for those who brainstormed the second heading.

Connect this activity with today's passage by saying, "The nation of Israel in Amos's time was very religious. They had a high level of worship activity. And yet God was totally disgusted with their worship. Let's discover why."

INTO THE WORD

Review the background of Amos in a brief lecture. Utilize the material in the introductions for today's lesson and last week's lesson.

Ask a volunteer to read Amos 4:4, 5; 5:18-24. Then lead your class in discussing these questions:

1. In Amos 4:4, 5 God speaks sarcastically to Israel. What is the point of his sarcastic words?

2. Reread Amos 5:18-20. What will the "day of the Lord" hold for Israel?

3. How did the Israelites worship God? (5:21-23)

4. Why were these acts of worship unacceptable? (5:21-24; 2:6, 7; 4:1; 5:7, 11, 12; 8:4-6).

5. What would it require for the nation of Israel to "let justice roll on like a river" (v. 24)?

6. Why isn't it enough to participate in worship activities? What else does God require? (See Isaiah 1:10-20; 58:1-11; Hosea 6:6; Micah 6:6-8.)

OPTION

Use the reproducible activity page that follows in addition to or instead of the study questions above.

INTO LIFE

Point out that acceptable worship involves a number of aspects, including these:

1. It must be based upon truth about God.

2. It must be practiced according to God's instruction.

3. It must be done with the right attitude and motive.

4. It must result in righteous living.

Write those four principles on the chalkboard. Then have your class form at least four groups with groups no larger than six.

Assign one of the principles to each group. Ask the groups to create questions that they can ask themselves to see if they are practicing that principle of worship. Here is an example for each of the four principles: (1) Am I worshiping God as the Bible describes him, or am I worshiping him as I want him to be? (2) Am I more interested in worshiping God in a way that makes me feel good than I am in following his instructions for worship? (3) When I worship God, are my thoughts and desires focused on pleasing him? (4) When I worship God, does it lead me to be kinder to those around me?

Appoint a discussion leader and provide each group with paper, a pencil, a sheet of poster board, and a felt-tip marker. Encourage them to have a recorder for the group, who will write down the questions they create. After they have compiled their list, they are to write the questions on the poster board large enough to be seen by the class.

After ten minutes, ask each group's leader to present its poster board to the class and read the questions out loud. Suggest to the class that they write these questions on paper and place them in their Bibles for periodic review.

OPTION

Suggest the four principles of acceptable worship under "Into Life." Then have the class form groups of four to six. Provide each group with paper and a pencil. Say to the class, "I'd like you to work in your groups to write a letter to an imaginary new Christian. You are trying to teach and encourage him to develop a life of worship, but you want to make sure he is worshiping God in an acceptable way. Be sure to utilize some of the Scriptures we have studied today, as well as others you think might apply."

Allow the groups twelve to fifteen minutes to compose their letters. When time has expired, bring the groups together and let a spokesperson for each group read their letter to the class.

Great Expectations

"Woe to you who long for the day of the Lord!"

In this text Amos refers to a time when God will clearly show his power over the world. Israel looked forward to this time because they expected to be exalted as God's own people.

How does Amos describe this day in 5:18-20? (See also Amos 8:9; Isaiah 2:11, 17, 20.)

How is that similar to and how is that different from the "day of the Lord" for which we wait? (See 2 Peter 3:1-14.)

God's Expectations

One area that specifically displeased the Lord was Israel's worship. Read the following passages and discuss these questions with your group.

- Amos 5:21-27
- Romans 10:16-21
- James 1:22-25
- Micah 6:8

What was missing in Israel's worship?

How can we be sure we are worshiping the Lord "in spirit and truth"—being the kind of "worshipers the Father seeks?" (John 4:23)

A Nation Turns From God

Unit 2: The Approaching Judgment
(Lessons 5-9)

A PROPHET WHO LIVED HIS MESSAGE

LESSON 7

WHY TEACH THIS LESSON?

This is a good lesson for people who think they have God all figured out. His method of working with Hosea, involving the prophet's personal life with his message, challenges the understanding. God is sometimes a God of surprises. This lesson reminds us we need to be open to his ways, even when they are not exactly as we might have expected.

The message itself provides marvelous reassurance for those who have strayed. What could be more vile than selling one's body in prostitution? God viewed Israel's apostasy in the very same light. Yet he was willing to restore his love to Israel if they would but repent. Whatever is our guilt, God will restore us to fellowship with him if we will just repent.

INTRODUCTION

A. RESTORED TREASURE

Browsing in a cluttered second-hand store, a London art dealer found a dingy painting in a battered frame. His trained eye could see a gleam of greatness through the grime. He bought the picture for thirty-five shillings and took it to his studio, where he used all his expertise to clean it without damaging the paint. Then he took it to an expert for evaluation. It was a genuine work of the famous Rubens! Now it was worth thousands of pounds.

People too can become dingy and apparently worthless, and so can nations. But the expert eye of God can see value behind the dirt, and the expert hand of God can clear away the grime to reveal hidden beauty. In this lesson we see a dingy nation in need of cleansing, and we see a dingy person presented as a symbol of that nation.

B. LESSON BACKGROUND

Hosea began his ministry when Jeroboam II was king of Israel, which Hosea sometimes calls Ephraim. It was a time of prosperity for the rich, but they built their prosperity by cheating the poor. With such prosperity came greed, corruption, drunkenness, and sexual sins, as we have seen in our studies from Amos. A unique feature of Hosea's work is the way he illustrated his teaching in his life and his family.

I. THE PROPHET'S WIFE (HOSEA 1:2, 3)

A. THE LORD'S COMMAND (V. 2)

2. **When the LORD began to speak through Hosea, the LORD said to him, "Go, take to yourself an adulterous wife and children of unfaithfulness, because the land is guilty of the vilest adultery in departing from the LORD."**

The Lord had not been giving messages by Hosea before: this was the beginning of his speaking *through* Hosea. He began with a command, and it sounds as if he ordered Hosea to marry a woman who had committed adultery and who had children by her adultery. The *King James* translation is even more graphic: "a wife of

DEVOTIONAL READING:
ROMANS 5:1-11

LESSON SCRIPTURE:
HOSEA 1:1—3:5

PRINTED TEXT:
HOSEA 1:2-9; 3:1-5

Jul
16

LESSON AIMS

As a result of studying this lesson, each student should:

1. Appreciate God's love for Israel, and for us.

2. Consider his or her own love and compare it with God's love.

3. Be able to give, receive, and respond to love in his or her own life.

KEY VERSE:

I will betroth you in righteousness and justice, in love and compassion. —Hosea 2:19

whoredoms," that is, a prostitute. Some students think that was exactly what the command meant. Imagine how Hosea felt if it was.

It seems strange, however, that a holy God would give such a command to a good man called to be his spokesman. Many students therefore wonder if the command should be understood in some other way.

The nation of Israel is frequently represented as married to Jehovah. Any worship of another god is considered *adultery*. That explains the phrase, *the land is guilty of the vilest adultery in departing from the Lord.* The adulterous woman Hosea is called to marry may then be an idol worshiper, guilty of spiritual adultery or prostitution. Or it may simply be that, because the nation as a whole was far gone in great adultery, any woman of that nation could be called an adulterous woman even if she herself were pure.

WHAT DO YOU THINK?

The lesson writer suggests three possibilities for explaining the command for Hosea to marry an "adulterous woman": (1) One who had committed adultery, possibly even a prostitute; (2) an idol worshiper; (3) a resident of an idol-worshiping land. One other has also been suggested. God may have directed Hosea to a particular woman (Gomer) whom he foreknew would commit adultery. Thus Hosea would experience what God experienced in Israel's unfaithfulness.

Which explanation do you think best explains the situation? Why? What application can we draw form that?

SIGNS AND SYMBOLS

Good teachers know the value of illustrations, audiovisual aids, analogies, and examples. The Master Teacher was fond of telling parables to get his point across. He also used fish and fig trees, vines and branches, lambs and children to underscore his truths. Christ pointed to the temple as a type of himself; he used coins to teach about taxes and authority. His most memorable symbols, of course, are the bread and fruit of the vine that represent his body and blood.

Pictures, symbols, and allegories are rhetorical devices used by most prophets to clarify and give impact to God's message. Rarely, however, has the messenger himself been required to become a living illustration of prophecy. Hosea was such a messenger. His marriage and family became the dramatic portrayal of God's relationship with Israel. Hosea acted out the role of God; Gomer played the part of Israel; and their children stood for Jehovah's reactions to his nation's unfaithfulness.

We remember only thirteen percent of what we only hear, but at least half of what we hear and see. Maximum retention is possible of lessons that we *hear, see,* and *participate in.* God's message through Hosea was so urgent that all available media enhanced the communication process. Significant lessons require dramatic symbols.

—R. W. B.

B. THE PROPHET'S OBEDIENCE (V. 3)

3. So he married Gomer daughter of Diblaim, and she conceived and bore him a son.

Whatever the command meant, it seems clear that Hosea understood it perfectly and obeyed it exactly. About Gomer and her father we know only what we learn from this book.

WHAT DO YOU THINK?

With Hosea God worked in unusual ways to make his will known. The same might be said of Jesus. His methods and purposes were not understood by the religious experts of his time.

What caution does this suggest for those who think they have God "figured out"? How can we maintain a sense of awe and expectancy about God's involvement in our lives and truly let him lead rather than plan our own way and attribute our own plans to God?

In view of the uncertainties noted in verse 2, we can see various possibilities in verse 3. We may suppose Hosea walked down the street and took the first prostitute he met, or that he saw many prostitutes and chose the one he liked best. We may suppose he ignored the literal prostitutes and chose a worshiper of false gods, or he chose a worshiper of the true God out of a nation that worshiped false gods. We may suppose that God specifically directed Hosea to a particular woman. That is not stated in the text, but neither is it denied. We may even suppose that Hosea was already in love with Gomer, but had been delaying marriage for some reason. Two things are quite clear: Hosea took a wife, and in due time she *bore him a son.*

II. THE PROPHET'S CHILDREN (HOSEA 1:4-9)

A. JEZREEL (VV. 4, 5)

4. Then the LORD said to Hosea, "Call him Jezreel, because I will soon punish the house of Jehu for the massacre at Jezreel, and I will put an end to the kingdom of Israel.

The house of Jehu was then the ruling family of Israel. The king was Jeroboam II (Hosea 1:1). About sixty years before he became king, his great-grandfather, Jehu, had destroyed the former ruling family in a bloody massacre beginning near the city of Jezreel (2 Kings 9:14—10:7). Many students think that coup was *the massacre at Jezreel* that God was going to avenge. However, God himself had authorized that massacre before it began and had approved it after it was done (2 Kings 9:1-10; 10:30). Can we think he was going to avenge it now by punishing the descendants of Jehu? Perhaps there was some later bloodshed, some unjust bloodshed, either in the city of Jezreel or in the plain of the same name. For that unjust killing the Lord promised vengeance. That promise was not fulfilled in the time of King Jeroboam, but in the time of the next king. Jeroboam's son Zechariah ruled only half a year before he was killed by a rebel who then took the throne (2 Kings 15:8-10). Thus the rule of Jehu's house came to an end.

The last part of verse 4 looks even farther into the future. About forty years after the end of Jehu's house came the end of *the kingdom of Israel* (2 Kings 17:1-6).

5. "In that day I will break Israel's bow in the Valley of Jezreel."

Israel's bow means the nation's military power. Second Kings 17:1-6 tells how it was broken. The king of Assyria invaded the country with an overwhelming army. In the light of this prophecy, we can suppose the army of Israel was crushed in a decisive battle *in the Valley of Jezreel.* King Hoshea was taken captive. Then the Assyrians besieged the capital city, Samaria, and starved out the people who had taken refuge there.

So the name *Jezreel* came into the prophecy at two points. First, bloodshed at Jezreel was to be avenged when Jehu's family would lose the kingdom. Second, the valley of Jezreel would be the scene of the decisive battle in the campaign that would end the kingdom of Israel.

The meaning of the name *Jezreel* supplies yet another link with the prophecy of Hosea. It means "God will scatter." Wondering people would ask, "Why did you name the boy 'God will scatter'?" Hosea would reply, "Because that is what God will do if the people of Israel don't straighten up and do right. God will take them from their homes and scatter them in foreign lands." (See Hosea 9:17; 2 Kings 17:6.)

B. LO-RUHAMAH (VV. 6, 7)

6. Gomer conceived again and gave birth to a daughter. Then the LORD said to Hosea, "Call her Lo-Ruhamah, for I will no longer show love to the house of Israel, that I should at all forgive them.

Lo-Ruhamah is literally translated, "She received no mercy." What a name to give a little girl! People would be sure to ask about it. Then Hosea could reply, "She is like Israel. For many years Israel did receive mercy in spite of many sins, but the time of mercy is coming to an end. Soon God will withdraw his mercy from our people. Then everybody will say of Israel, 'Lo-Ruhamah: she received no mercy.'"

7. "Yet I will show love to the house of Judah; and I will save them—not by bow, sword or battle, or by horses and horsemen, but by the LORD their God."

The former empire of David and Solomon had long since been divided between Israel, to the north, and *Judah,* to the south. God would continue to have mercy on Judah. The hordes of Assyria would attack it too, but God would save her. He would do it by his own power, not by Judah's military strength. Second Kings 19:32-36 tells how this prophecy was fulfilled. The angel of the Lord killed 185,000 of the Assyrian troops in a single night. The rest quickly went home, leaving Judah in peace.

WHAT DO YOU THINK?

Instead of thanking the Lord for their blessings, the people of Israel looked to other gods (Hosea 3:1). Just listen any day to the credit that is given to "Mother Nature," or "my lucky stars," or even "the weather man" and you'll know the practice continues even in our own day.

We know God gives the sunshine and rain (Matthew 5:45), along with "every good gift and every perfect gift" (James 1:17). We know our physical and mental abilities are gifts from the Lord (1 Corinthians 4:7). Why do you think we are so slow to give credit where credit is due? How can we cultivate a greater sense of gratitude to God for his blessings?

WHAT DO YOU THINK?

The house of Jehu had committed some atrocity, identified here as "the massacre at Jezreel." It must have seemed that they had got away with it, but God said he was going to exact vengeance against them after all.

What caution does this suggest for people who use circumstances to determine God's will? What are some better ways for determining the will of God in specific situations?

Visual 7 illustrates Hosea's message that a faithful marriage relationship illustrates faithfulness to God.

WHAT DO YOU THINK?

Hosea's story is fascinating because of the depth of love he showed in rescuing a woman that most people would call worthless. But the best part of that fascinating story is that it pictures God's love for us. In our selfish and self-destructive sinning we have rejected not only God's way, but the Father himself. The marvel is that God still loves us. And Jesus told his disciples to love one another as he loved them. Obeying that word is a clear indication that we belong to him (John 13:34, 35).

How can we develop that kind of love for people, especially people whose standard of decency and morality are very much different from our own?

KNOWING YOUR OWN STRENGTH

Did you ever try to loosen lug nuts (when changing a tire) that had been tightened by someone who didn't know his own strength? Pneumatic torque wrenches have complicated that problem. The power added to human strength by well-engineered tools is amazing.

Knowing one's strength is important; knowing the source of one's strength is *more important*. Before David challenged Goliath, he told King Saul, "The Lord who delivered me from the paw of the lion and from the paw of the bear will deliver me from the hand of this Philistine" (1 Samuel 17:37). David knew where his help came from. Well might he sing, "My help comes from the Lord, the Maker of heaven and earth" (Psalm 121:2).

God's people must be reminded from whom our strength comes. God told Hosea that Judah would be saved, "not . . . by bow, sword or by battle, or by horses and horsemen" (Hosea 1:7). God told Zerubbabel, "Not by might nor by power, but by my Spirit" (Zechariah 4:6). The *enemies* of God's people also should know.

We who are Christians need to know our own weakness and the source of our strength. Paul knew. He wrote, "I can do everything through [Christ] who gives me strength" (Philippians 4:13).   —R. W. B.

C. LO-AMMI (VV. 8, 9)

8. After she had weaned Lo-Ruhamah, Gomer had another son.

In those days a baby might be breast-fed for three years before being weaned, so Lo-Ruhamah may have been four years old when her baby brother was born.

9. Then the LORD said, "Call him Lo-Ammi, for you are not my people, and I am not your God.

Lo-Ammi means "not my people." It was another name that would surely arouse interest and bring questions. "Why do you call your son 'not my people'?" "Because that is what the Lord God Almighty is saying to all of us. For centuries we have been his people, blessed with his special care and protection. But we have not acted like people of the Lord. We have been disobedient for a long time. Now our sins have piled up so high that the Lord is about to disown us. No longer will he protect us and provide for us. He will leave us to depend on our own resources, and we shall be destroyed."

Still the prophecy of doom was followed by a prophecy of restoration. Israel again would be innumerable; in the very place where God disowned her, he would claim her again, "for great shall be the day of Jezreel," the day when Israel would be planted again in her own land, the day when the valley of Jezreel would not be a place of conflict and defeat, but a fruitful field for peaceful production (vv. 10, 11).

III. LOVING RESTORATION (HOSEA 3:1-5)

A. RESTORING A FALLEN WOMAN (VV. 1-3)

1. The LORD said to me, "Go, show your love to your wife again, though she is loved by another and is an adulteress. Love her as the LORD loves the Israelites, though they turn to other gods and love the sacred raisin cakes."

The Lord sent his prophet to "love a woman." Our text takes that woman to be Gomer; thus, the translation, *Go, show your love to your wife again*. However, the Hebrew text is vague enough to allow a different understanding. If *show your love* is a reference to sexual intimacy, as many commentators and lexicographers believe it is, then it would be natural to understand Gomer to be the woman in question. It is supposed that she left Hosea to live in adultery, but that her paramours failed her, and so she finally became a prostitute and a slave. Hosea was then sent to buy her back out of her slavery (v. 2).

However, not all students agree that the woman was Gomer. Her name does not appear in this text from the third chapter, neither is the woman necessarily said to be Hosea's wife. (The Hebrew word may be translated simply *woman* and not *wife*.) But whether this depraved woman was Gomer or some other, the message of the text is the same: *The Lord sent his prophet to give loving care to an adulteress*. Most men would scorn such a woman, but Hosea was told to *love* her (the word does not have to refer to sexual intimacy) and help her, to redeem her from her slavery. Thus he would picture the way *the Lord loves the Israelites*. Their devotion to other gods was adultery in a spiritual sense. It was going to bring misery and slavery; but God's love would continue, and he would lift Israel out of misery and bondage.

2. So I bought her for fifteen shekels of silver and about a homer and a lethek of barley.

Fifteen shekels would be about six ounces *of silver*. The *barley* measures about ten bushels by our standards. Exodus 21:32 indicates that a slave was worth thirty shekels of silver. Some students conclude that Hosea paid that price, but paid half of it in produce instead of silver.

3. Then I told her, "You are to live with me many days; you must not be a prostitute or be intimate with any man, and I will live with you."

The relationship of this woman with Hosea is as disputed as her identity. Some would understand her to be restored to the role of Hosea's wife, living with him and him with her. This would picture Israel's being taken from idolatry and restored to her relationship with the Lord.

Others see a different relationship, that whether the woman was Gomer or not, she was not now to live with Hosea as his wife. She was to live with him for *many days*. She was not allowed to engage in prostitution. She was not to *be intimate with any man*—neither with Hosea nor with anyone else. Hosea likewise would abstain from sexual relations with her. This temporary arrangement (*live with me many days*) pictures the temporary bondage to Assyria, as explained in the verses that follow.

B. APPLICATION TO ISRAEL (VV. 4, 5)

4. For the Israelites will live many days without king or prince, without sacrifice or sacred stones, without ephod or idol.

As the woman had left her husband for another man or for other men, so Israel had left the Lord for false gods. As the woman had become enslaved, so Israel had found herself enslaved by the many sins that go with false worship. As the woman was freed from her slavery but left without any sex life at all, so Israel was going to be freed from her present enslavement by being deported to foreign lands, but she would be without any national life or religious life at all. Scattered in foreign lands the people of Israel would no longer be a nation, so they would have no *king* or *prince*. They could not get together to offer *sacrifice* either to the Lord or to imaginary gods. They would have no *sacred stones*, the high places of pagan worship, and no *ephod* such as the priest wore when he conducted the proper worship of Jehovah. They would no longer worship an *idol*, but neither would they be able to worship the Lord in the way prescribed by his law. This condition would continue for *many days*, for a long time.

This prophecy of scattering was fulfilled when the Assyrians overran Israel and took her people to other countries, as we have noted earlier in this lesson (Hosea 1:5, 6; 2 Kings 17:1-6). God saved Judah from the Assyrians (Hosea 1:7), but in later years Judah also sank so deep in sin that God abandoned her as well. Then the Babylonians destroyed Jerusalem and took most of the surviving people of Judah into captivity (2 Kings 25:8-12). It was about 722 B.C. when Israel fell to

WHAT DO YOU THINK?

Hosea prophesied in a time when the law of the Lord and the law of the land were the same. Thus, he could call for a return to the Lord as a matter of legal propriety.

In our country, church and state are separate. We cannot appeal to the law of the land to urge biblically right behavior in many cases. How, then, can we uphold biblical standards of morality as the right way to behave?

HOW TO SAY IT

Assyria. Uh-SEAR-ee-uh.
Diblaim. DIB-lay-im or Dib-LAY-im.
Ephraim. EE-fray-im.
Gomer. GO-mer.
Hosea. Ho-ZAY-uh or Ho-ZEE-uh.
Hoshea. Ho-SHE-uh.
Jehu. JEE-hew or JAY-hew.
Jeroboam. Jair-uh-BO-um.
Jezreel. JEZ-reel.
lethek. LETH-ek.
Lo-ammi. Lo-AM-my or Lo-AM-me.
Lo-Ruhamah. Lo-roo-HAY-muh or Lo-roo-HAH-muh.
Zechariah. Zeck-uh-RYE-uh.

WHAT DO YOU THINK?

Hosea prophesied a restoration that finds its fulfillment in the Messiah, Jesus Christ. As such, it includes us. Read 1 Peter 2:9-12 (noting especially verse 10). What does Peter's application suggest to you as the proper response to the message of Hosea?

PRAYER

Dear God, teach us the paths of righteousness that we may walk in them. Make us aware of our own weakness that we may walk humbly. Teach us to show mercy and understanding to all those about us. In Jesus' name we pray. Amen.

THOUGHT TO REMEMBER

There, but for the grace of God, go I.

DAILY BIBLE READINGS

Monday, July 10—Peace With God Through Christ (Romans 5:1-11)

Tuesday, July 11—God's Call to Hosea (Hosea 1:1-5)

Wednesday, July 12—Israel Compared With Hosea's Unfaithful Wife (Hosea 1:6—2:1)

Thursday, July 13—Public Shame and Hardship for Israel (Hosea 2:2-13)

Friday, July 14—God Will Woo Israel Back (Hosea 2:14-23)

Saturday, July 15—God Will Restore Israel (Hosea 3:1-5)

Sunday, July 16—Praise for God's Steadfast Love (Psalm 115:1-13)

Assyria. It was about 586 B.C. when the Babylonians destroyed Jerusalem, and it was about fifty years later when the Jews were allowed to go back home (Ezra 1:1-4). They were indeed many days without a national life or a national religion. Those days added up to about 186 years.

5. *Afterward the Israelites will return and seek the LORD their God and David their king. They will come trembling to the LORD and to his blessings in the last days.*

The children of Israel would be deprived of nation and religion for a long time, but not forever. They would *return*. Again they would give their allegiance to *the Lord their God, and David their king*. The books of Ezra and Nehemiah record how people of Judah came back from captivity in Babylon. No doubt many of the scattered Israelites joined them in the years that followed. But Hosea's prophecy looks far beyond that. David would not be back in person, but with the New Testament to guide us, we know that the Israel of God includes not only people of Israel and Judah, but also people of all nations who give their allegiance to the Son of David, Jesus Christ. With reverence and awe, the people of this real Israel *come trembling to the Lord and to his blessings* now and forever.

TWICE OWNED BY GOD

The women's movement in the last two or three decades has made a change in male/female relationships. Much of that change has been positive progress, affirming the personhood and rights of women. Most men no longer consider wives to be their personal property. Most wives have made it clear: "You don't own me!"

Gomer was in a different situation, as well as in a different culture. She was not only Hosea's wife, but Hosea had actually bought her back from the slavery of prostitution. At God's command, the prophet had married her, then redeemed her from unfaithfulness. So Gomer belonged to Hosea by virtue of both the marriage covenant and the price of her redemption.

Israel belonged to God by virtue of both covenant and deliverance. Christians, too, are twice-owned: God made us; then he bought us. We are like the toy sailboat made by a boy, who later lost it. When finally he spied the boat in a pawnshop window, he bought it back. When we were lost in sin, God purchased our redemption with the blood of his only begotten Son.

None of us can say to God, "You don't own me!" "You were bought at a price. Therefore honor God with your body" (1 Corinthians 6:20).

—R. W. B.

CONCLUSION

In recent political campaigns in the United States, much has been said about family values. Everyone seems to agree that we need to emphasize such values, but who knows exactly what they are? In a democracy, should we vote on what is good, and accept the majority opinion? No, in a diverse culture such as ours, that would result only in confusion.

God knows what is good, and he shares his knowledge with us. "He has showed you, O man, what is good. And what does the Lord require of you? To act justly and to love mercy and to walk humbly with your God" (Micah 6:8).

Obeying God's Word is good for a family, and equally good for an individual or a nation. Justice, mercy, humility before God—these are right, and they will bring good results. Greed, mistreatment of others, ignoring God—these are wrong, and they will be punished. But God is as merciful as he wants us to be. If we leave our wicked ways and obey him, he is ready to forgive and restore, for he loves us. Hosea strongly reaffirms the ringing call of Amos: "Let justice roll on like a river, righteousness like a never-failing stream!" (Amos 5:24).

Discovery Learning

This page contains an alternate lesson plan emphasizing learning activities. Classes desiring such student involvement will find these suggestions helpful. The next page is a reproducible activity page to further enhance discovery learning.

LEARNING GOALS

In this lesson your students will do the following:

1. See how Hosea and his family illustrated God's relationship with Israel.

2. Determine what is involved for Christians and the church to live faithfully to God in the 1990s.

INTO THE LESSON

Before class, write the word *Betrayed* on the chalkboard. Ask students to form groups of four or five. Provide each group with paper and a pen. Ask them to list five situations in which a person might feel betrayed. (Some examples may include a spouse having an affair; a friend gossiping about him; a teen running away from parents.)

Allow two to three minutes for groups to complete their discussions. Then ask each group to report the situations they listed. Write these on the chalkboard.

Lead students in exploring the feelings of betrayal by discussing these questions:

1. What kind of emotions tend to accompany being betrayed?

2. How does being betrayed tend to affect our ability to function?

After several minutes of discussion, make this transition into today's Scripture study: "I doubt that anyone can make it through life without feeling betrayed. People let us down. They hurt us.

"God himself has experienced constant betrayal. Our lesson today includes a vivid, real-life illustration of how God has been betrayed. We will consider the fact that we too can betray God. And we will explore what it means to live faithfully to him in our generation."

INTO THE WORD

Present a brief lecture on the background of Hosea. Use the information in the "Introduction" as well as a Bible handbook or commentary or study Bible.

Ask students to form their groups again. Provide each group with a copy of the questions in the box in the next column. Provide each group with a sheet of poster board and felt-tip markers.

Before they discuss the questions, assign to each group one of these references: Hosea 2:8, 13; Hosea 4:1, 2; Hosea 8:1-4; Hosea 10:4, 12, 13. (If you have more than four groups, two or more groups will be assigned the

same passage. If you have fewer than four groups, don't worry about covering all the passages.)

Read Hosea 1:1-9 and 3:1-5, and discuss these questions:

1. In what way was Hosea betrayed? How might that have affected him?

2. In what ways was God betrayed? How might that have affected him?

3. How had the nation of Israel been unfaithful to God? Read your assigned passage in Hosea to discuss this question.

4. Using poster board and felt-tip markers, create a stick figure cartoon to illustrate how Israel had been unfaithful. Base your cartoon on your assigned passage. Your cartoon can have as many frames as you desire.

Allow groups twenty minutes to complete their assignments. Then bring the groups together. Ask each one to present its cartoon with a brief explanation.

Following the cartoon displays, lead your students in discussing these questions:

1. How did Hosea serve as a living illustration?

2. Though Israel would be punished, what hope did God give the nation in 1:10, 11 and 3:4, 5?

INTO LIFE

Help your students see the implications of Hosea for their lives by asking, "In what ways might we live unfaithfully to God without realizing it?" Allow for discussion.

Provide each student with a sheet of paper and a pencil. Ask students to write a brief essay. They are to work on this individually. They can choose one of these two topics:

• What it Means for the Christian to Be Faithful to God in the 1990s.

• What it Means for the Church to Be Faithful to God in the 1990s.

Tell your class that they will have five minutes to write their brief essays. When time has expired, ask volunteers to read their essays to the class.

Close with students in their small groups. Ask them to pray that God will help them be faithful.

OPTION

Use the reproducible activity page that follows to provide a means of applying the lesson.

Amazing Love

"The proof of God's amazing love is this: that it was while we were sinners that Christ died for us" (Romans 5:7, 8, *Phillips*).

The book of Hosea provides for us several graphic images of the love of God for his people—even those who have strayed far from his will. In each of the following passages Hosea presents a different image of our loving God. Read each of these passages carefully. Then list some specific ways you have experienced each aspect of God's love in your life.

Hosea 2:14, 15
Tender
Love

Hosea 2:19, 20
Faithful
Love

Hosea 3:1, 2
Redeeming
Love

Hosea 11:1, 3, 4
Nurturing
Love

Hosea 14:5-7
Protecting
Love

A Nation Turns From God

Unit 2: The Approaching Judgment
(Lessons 5-9)

GOD'S LOVE FOR ISRAEL

LESSON 8

WHY TEACH THIS LESSON?

They say repetition is helpful for learning. If so, then your students should by now be getting a good understanding of the fact that God warned his people to repent or face the penalty for their sin. This is the fourth consecutive lesson that has focused on a prophet's warning Israel to repent or be destroyed as a nation.

In spite of their similarity, each lesson has had some unique feature about it. Last week we saw God's relationship with Israel compared to that of a patient husband and a wayward wife. This week we see it compared to a parent and child. This is perhaps the most tender of all the pictures we will see. Just as a loving parent does not want to punish a child but must in order to preserve discipline, even so we see God not wanting to punish his people, but compelled by his holy nature to do so.

Focus on this tender aspect of God's nature. Urge your students to feel the pain in God's voice when he cries, "How can I give you up, Ephraim? How can I hand you over...?" (Hosea 11:8). Short of Calvary, it may be the clearest picture of what our sin does to our holy God. Surely it will motivate us to live in purity rather than to grieve our God!

INTRODUCTION

A. CONDEMNATION AND FORGIVENESS

Dwight L. Moody, that popular evangelist of the last century, brought thousands of people under conviction before God by his thunderous denunciation of sin and sinners. But Moody's message was not entirely of judgment and doom. He also offered God's love and forgiveness. On one occasion the governor asked him to deliver a pardon to a prisoner then in the state prison. Moody was delighted to carry out the assignment. At a chapel service he preached a powerful sermon about the righteous judgment of God, but in his conclusion he told of God's forgiveness. Then just before the benediction, he called the fortunate prisoner forward and presented him with the pardon.

Hosea's ministry was rather like this. Much of his message was one of condemnation for Israel's sins and of God's judgment upon the nation. But he also brought a message of hope and restoration to the people.

B. LESSON BACKGROUND

Last week's lesson provided the historical background for the ministry of Hosea. He began his ministry when Israel was enjoying great prosperity, but accompanying this prosperity was a great falling away from God's laws. It became the prophet's painful duty to bring a message of condemnation for the sins of the people. His burden was made the more painful by the tragedy of his own marriage, which typified God's relationship with Israel.

He had to speak of the punishment that would come to Israel through Assyria. This violent nation would soon take Syria, which was to the north of Israel. Then in 722 B.C. it would capture Israel's capital, Samaria, and take many of the citizens away into bondage. But God gave Hosea the prophetic vision to see beyond these disasters. He could see a God who would not give up on Ephraim (Israel), who

---

DEVOTIONAL READING:
PSALM 103:6-14

LESSON SCRIPTURE:
HOSEA 11

PRINTED TEXT:
HOSEA 11:1-9

LESSON AIMS

As a result of studying this lesson, each student should:

1. Appreciate the tenderness of God's love for Israel.

2. Realize God still exercises such love for mankind.

3. Be better able to extend unconditional love to others.

Jul
23

KEY VERSE:

I will heal their waywardness and love them freely, for my anger has turned away from them.
—Hosea 14:4

LESSON 8 NOTES

would not execute the fierceness of his anger upon his people. Once the people had turned from their idolatry, God would restore them.

I. THE RICHNESS OF GOD'S LOVE (HOSEA 11:1-4)

A. GOD'S LOVE FOR ISRAEL IN EGYPT (V. 1)

1. "When Israel was a child, I loved him, and out of Egypt I called my son.

God remembered Israel even while they were trapped in the agony of the Egyptian bondage. *Israel was a child:* that is, they were just in the early stages of their development as God's people. But they were children in another sense. They were completely helpless to deliver themselves from their Egyptian tyrants. God did not love them because they had done anything to deserve his love. Indeed, like a true parent, he loved them precisely because they were helpless and unworthy. *Out of Egypt I called my son.* This reminds us of the words of Moses before Pharaoh: "This is what the Lord says, 'Israel is my firstborn son'" (Exodus 4:22).

We often take our blessings for granted, forgetting what they cost our forefathers. We enjoy our Thanksgiving turkey with scarcely a thought about the suffering the early Pilgrims bore. We celebrate our freedom without even thinking of how it was hammered out on the bitter anvil of Valley Forge and sustained by the bloodshed at Gettysburg.

B. THE REJECTION OF GOD'S LOVE (V. 2)

2. "But the more I called Israel, the further they went from me. They sacrificed to the Baals and they burned incense to images.

God made numerous calls to his people through Moses, the judges, kings like David, and the prophets. God had not made just one call to the people, while they were in bondage in Egypt, but had continued through a variety of spokesmen to remind them again and again of the covenant he had made with them on Mount Sinai. These frequent reminders were necessary because the people soon forgot. But do we? We sing, "Tell me the story often, For I forget so soon"; and this is appropriate because we do indeed forget so soon.

They sacrificed to the Baals. When the Israelites entered the promised land, they came into contact with the Canaanites, who were followers of Baal. Thus from the beginning they were tempted by this false god. *Baals* is plural because he was worshiped under different forms in different places. The worship of Baal often involved sexual orgies, and even infant sacrifice.

The people *burned incense to images,* indicating their commitment to a pagan god represented by an idol. While burning incense was not as vile as some of the other acts of worship, it was plainly condemned by God.

C. GOD AS A LOVING PARENT (VV. 3, 4)

3. "It was I who taught Ephraim to walk, taking them by the arms; but they did not realize it was I who healed them.

Ephraim was the name of one of the more powerful tribes of the northern kingdom and was sometimes used to signify the whole northern kingdom. The picture is of a parent teaching a child to walk. God as a parent had been beside Israel to guide and protect him as he took his first steps. *Taking them by the arms* pictures God holding their arms to guide and protect them during their first halting and unsteady steps. The *Revised Standard Version* has "I took them up in my arms," suggesting an even more tender and loving God who embraced them and comforted them when they fell and hurt themselves.

They did not realize it was I who healed them. This was the tragedy of the situation. Even though God had comforted them when they had been hurt and healed their

---

WHAT DO YOU THINK?

It seems Israel quickly and repeatedly forgot the blessings they had received from God, or at least the responsibility that went along with the blessings. The lesson writer suggests we have the same problem. How can we keep from forgetting God's blessings as Israel did?

Obviously, the Lord's Supper (Jesus instituted it "in remembrance") and God's Word are good reminders for us. What other reminders can you suggest? How can we take full advantage of the reminders we have?

The message of verse 3 is illustrated by visual 8.

bruises when they had fallen, yet they had not acknowledged their benefactor. Such behavior is unnatural, for a small child will normally turn to his parents when he is hurting or discouraged. This is a theme God's spokesmen often used—that Israel's rejection of God was unnatural.

4. "I led them with cords of human kindness, with ties of love; I lifted the yoke from their neck and bent down to feed them.

Hosea now changes the figure. He picks up a picture he used earlier (10:11) and portrays Israel as a stubborn young calf. Anyone who has worked with young calves knows that they can be about as stubborn as any animal, and their strength makes them hard to control. Sometimes about the only way to handle such an animal when it sets its heels is with a firm tug on a strong rope about its neck. On occasion God had to resort to such not-so-gentle treatment. Even then, however, he used *cords of human kindness*. He bound them with *ties of love*.

A parent might use a soft harness and leash to guide and protect a child. We would hardly expect a loving parent to use a heavy, abrasive rope for this purpose. Jesus said, "I, when I am lifted up from the earth, will draw all men to myself" (John 12:32). Ultimately, love is far more powerful than threats and violence.

I lifted the yoke from their neck. God is now depicted as a farmer who removes the heavy wooden yoke from the neck of the oxen at the end of a busy day. This yoke may specifically refer to the Egyptian bondage, but it may also include several other occasions when the people were subjugated by their neighbors. Each time God had removed this heavy burden.

I . . . bent down to feed them. The picture of a parent patiently feeding his or her child adds another gentle touch to this view of God.

UNGRATEFUL KIDS

Most parents are thrilled when their children take first steps. Lots of hugging and picture-taking usually accompany the event. Such moments make happy memories.

Have your kids ever thanked you for teaching them to walk? Probably not. Parental help and support is taken for granted by children. And parents don't expect to be thanked by toddlers for acts of love and caring. Our reward comes in seeing the children develop skills and make achievements.

Gratitude doesn't come naturally for children. It is a learned response that grows out of experience and example. Ephraim behaved as ingrates, but they were old enough to know better. They had experienced the love, care, protection, and encouragement of Father Jehovah for centuries. Gratitude should have expressed itself in Israel's obedience and faithfulness. They should have matured enough to live lives that said, "Thank You, God."

Now, we are a new generation of God's children. He has given every skill, talent, and resource. He has helped us with every accomplishment. Have we acknowledged his support and guidance? Do our work, worship, and service say, "Thank You, Lord"?
—R. W. B.

II. GOD'S CONTINUED LOVE (HOSEA 11:5-9)

A. PUNISHMENT FOR REJECTING GOD'S LOVE (vv. 5, 6)

5. "Will they not return to Egypt and will not Assyria rule over them because they refuse to repent?

From speaking of God's love and concern for his people, Hosea turns abruptly to speak of his judgment, which would soon fall upon those people. Assyria posed a growing threat to Israel. *Egypt* becomes a symbol for bondage, much like what they had experienced in Egypt before the Exodus. In that sense, they would *return to Egypt* (the question in the text is written in such a way as to suggest an affirmative answer). Literally, they would fall under the heavy hand of *Assyria*. As

---

HOW TO SAY IT

Admah. AD-muh.
Assyria. Uh-SEAR-ee-uh.
Baal. BAY-ul.
Baalism. BAY-uh-lism.
Canaanites. KAY-nan-ites.
Ephraim. EE-fray-im.
Gomorrah. Guh-MOR-uh.
Hoshea. Ho-SHE-uh.
Sinai. SYE-nay-eye or SYE-nye.
Sodom. SOD-um.
Syria. SEAR-ee-uh.
Zeboiim. Ze-BOY-im.

WHAT DO YOU THINK?

When we look at the material blessings we enjoy, we can hardly deny that they are more than we deserve. Those of us who put our faith in God are convinced that he is the source of our blessings. Our forefathers held that same conviction, and it is reflected in many patriotic songs and writings. But many of our contemporaries refuse to acknowledge God's hand in the affairs of our nation.

To what extent do you think this situation parallels that of ancient Israel—blessed by God but refusing to recognize it? What demands does that put on those who do recognize God's blessings?

Do you think our nation can expect a similar fate to Israel's? Why or why not?

devastating as the Egyptian bondage had been, the Assyrian conquest would be worse. This disaster would come upon them because they *refuse to repent*.

6. "Swords will flash in their cities, will destroy the bars of their gates and put an end to their plans.

The fate of Israel would be even more painful than the Egyptian bondage, for the Assyrians would bring war to the land with all its death and suffering. In such times the people normally fled to the *cities,* hoping to find protection behind their walls and *gates.* Sometimes this was a wise action, but it did not work against the Assyrians. Archaeologists have provided convincing evidence of the efficiency of the Assyrian war machine. Using battering rams and siege towers, they were able to overwhelm even the best fortified cities. Once a breach was made in a city wall, the Assyrian soldiers would rush in and finish their bloody task with *swords*.

The reason for this terrible judgment upon Israel was that they had followed *their* own *plans*. The leaders and the people had followed false prophets. Some of this bad advice had led the people to turn to Baal and other pagan gods. This bad advice may also have referred to the activities of King Hoshea, who reigned from about 732 to 722 B.C. He sought assistance from the pharaoh of Egypt against the Assyrians. When the Assyrians learned of this, they increased the pressure on Israel, captured Hoshea, and laid siege to Samaria, its capital (2 Kings 17:1-6).

B. ISRAEL'S PRONENESS TO BACKSLIDING (v. 7)

7. "My people are determined to turn from me. Even if they call to the Most High, he will by no means exalt them.

The Hebrew text poses some difficulties in this verse. As a result, different versions have widely varying readings. Regardless of the version we choose to follow, the verse makes certain points. First of all, God has not rejected his people. He still refers to them as *my people*. The second point is that their rejection of God is not just an occasional departure from his teaching. Rather, it reflects a deeply ingrained tendency to backslide. Their apostasy took two forms. It was sometimes theological: that is, they turned from Jehovah to pagan deities. It was often moral, in that they turned from the ethical teachings of the covenant to worldly behavior.

DOGS AND HOGS

Dogs have long enjoyed a reputation of being "man's best friend." Cat-lovers have argued otherwise. In recent years, many folk have found *hogs* to be quite friendly pets. Regardless of your preference, most animals have one or two obnoxious habits. The apostle Peter quotes these proverbs: "A dog returns to its vomit," and, "A sow that is washed goes back to her wallowing in the mud" (2 Peter 2:22).

God was grieved at Israel's bent to backsliding. He had delivered them, protected them, and provided for them. Yet they repeatedly turned to other gods. Such unfaithfulness breaks the heart of the Lord.

The dog and hog proverbs illustrate the human tendency to regress to old habits. "You can take the hog out of the mud," Peter could have said, "but you can't take the mud out of the hog." Though animals can hardly be held accountable for instinctive behavior, humans have conscience and power to choose. Christ not only can take us out of sin, but he also *can take sin out of us*. When saved people choose to disobey, "they are worse off at the end than they were at the beginning" (2 Peter 2:20).

—R. W. B.

C. GOD'S MERCY TOWARD ISRAEL (vv. 8, 9)

8. "How can I give you up, Ephraim? How can I hand you over, Israel? How can I treat you like Admah? How can I make you like Zeboiim? My heart is changed within me; all my compassion is aroused.

WHAT DO YOU THINK?

The Israelites were said to be "determined to turn from [God]." That determination usually manifested itself in idolatry. How have you seen the same determination manifest itself in our culture? In your church? In your own life?

What can you do about it?

OPTION

Use the reproducible activity, "Determined to Turn," on page 408 to explore Israel's, and our, determination to stray from God.

The previous verses brought a message of judgment. Now the prophet brings words of mercy. He shows that God's judgment is not dealt out whimsically or from a desire to see the people suffer. Rather, he shows God deliberating between his justice on one hand and his mercy on the other. God's love is a holy love that requires satisfaction when it is violated. Yet it is also a compassionate love that seeks to salvage the fallen Ephraim. The people deserved to be punished, and yet God did not desire to turn them over to their enemies. In a sense God faced and still faces a dilemma that can be solved only through the sacrificial death of his Son (Romans 3:24-26).

Admah and *Zeboiim* were cities that had been located near Sodom and Gomorrah, probably at the southern end of the Dead Sea. They had suffered the same fate as these two infamous cities (Deuteronomy 29:23). Down through the centuries these cities have become a symbol of God's righteous judgment. Ephraim deserved a similar judgment, but the nation could still be spared if it heeded the prophet.

My heart is changed within me; all my compassion is aroused. Even as God contemplated the punishment that Ephraim rightly deserved, his compassion stirred within him. The word *changed* seems to be an attempt on the part of the translators to avoid the word *repent* (as in the *King James Version*), so that the reader will not think of this as being the same thing as human repentance. On more than one occasion, the Scriptures use this term of God. For example, when God looked upon the earth in the time of Noah, we are told that it *repented* (*King James Version*) or *grieved* (*New International Version*) the Lord that he had made man (Genesis 6:6). It does not imply any moral change on God's part; it is an attempt to express in human language God's actions.

9. "I will not carry out my fierce anger, nor will I turn and devastate Ephraim. For I am God, and not man—the Holy One among you. I will not come in wrath.

God would indeed punish his wayward children, but he would not utterly destroy them. God is not human: he would not go too far, as an angry man might do. *I will not come in wrath* and destroy the nation. Although God's punishment would fall upon Ephraim, it would be tempered by his mercy. The following verses explain that their punishment, exile at the hands of the Assyrians, would eventually be followed by their restoration.

ANTHROPOCENTRICITY

"God created man in his own image" (Genesis 1:27), and we tend to think of God in *our* own image. Though we know he is spirit, we generally think of him as having human characteristics: hands, ears, feet, and face.

Many of our ideas about God are *anthropocentric*—centered in what we know about human traits. For example, divine mercy is difficult to understand because our idea of justice is drawn from humanity's imperfect examples.

In light of Israel's gross unfaithfulness, we might think that God's response would be angry vengeance, death and destruction. Yet God says, "I will not . . . devastate Ephraim. For I am God, and not man" (Hosea 11:9).

Aren't we glad that God is God? We are quick to condemn and slow to forgive, but he "looks beyond our fault and sees our need." "The Lord . . . is patient with you, not wanting anyone to perish, but everyone to come to repentance" (2 Peter 3:9).

—R. W. B.

CONCLUSION

A. ASSURED MERCY

The people of Israel had a unique relationship with God. In a very real sense they were the "chosen people," chosen as a means of bringing God's plan of

---

WHAT DO YOU THINK?

Try to understand God's dilemma: he has to punish sin and destroy evil, yet he loves people and wants them to be free to choose and to respond to him by their own wish, not by compulsion. What kind of emotional impact do you think that has on God? To what extent ought we to share the same emotions when considering the lost in the world? To what extent should we share it when we ourselves stumble and sin?

Of course, Jesus' death ultimately resolves that dilemma. If we really appreciated the depth of God's love that Jesus' death portrays, what kind of behavior would characterize us? Does it?

WHAT DO YOU THINK?

God had a right to be angry with Israel. Yet he said, "I will not carry out my fierce anger. . . . For I am God, and not a man." The obvious implication of that statement is that we, if we would act like God, must be able and willing to forego our right to exact justice on those who wrong us—at least some of the time. What practical applications would you make of that? When should we carry out our anger and when should we not? How can we still the anger in us? How can we respond in love to someone who hurts us without treating the sin too lightly?

OPTION

Use the reproducible activity, "Determined to Return," on page 408 to apply this lesson to life.

PRAYER

Almighty God, help us learn from these ancient prophets how to walk humbly with you in obedience to your commandments. Let us never forget that you are a righteous God who demands that we become holy. Let us also never forget that you are a merciful God who will forgive us and restore us and set our feet on the right pathway if we but turn to you. In Jesus' name we pray. Amen.

THOUGHT TO REMEMBER

"The Lord disciplines those he loves" (Hebrews 12:6).

DAILY BIBLE READINGS

Monday, July 17—Mercy for Those Who Love God (Psalm 103:6-14)

Tuesday, July 18—Punishment for Israel's Unfaithfulness (Hosea 10:9-15)

Wednesday, July 19—God's Love Has Been Rejected (Hosea 11:1-7)

Thursday, July 20—God's Anger Is Restrained by Compassion (Hosea 11:8-12)

Friday, July 21—Israel Urged to Return to God (Hosea 14)

Saturday, July 22—A Prayer for God's Forgiveness (Psalm 79:8-13)

Sunday, July 23—God Forgives and Restores (Psalm 130)

---

salvation to the entire human race. The Israelites had not been chosen because they had special qualifications that others lacked. Trapped in grinding slavery in Egypt, they seemed to have little chance of ever making any significant contribution to the world. Yet God in his marvelous grace led them out of that bondage into a land that they could claim as their own. Step by halting step he led them to independence and prosperity.

That progress had not been easy. Again and again the people had strayed from Jehovah, seeking other gods and abandoning the paths of righteousness he had set before them. Hosea wrote as Israel stood poised on the brink of national catastrophe. The instrument of that disaster, the Assyrians, were already threatening. Hosea did not draw back from announcing this impending doom. Yet even as he brought God's word of judgment, he also offered hope, hope based upon God's love for his people.

We sometimes speak of our country as being a Christian nation, but no nation today can claim the special relationship that Israel enjoyed with God. It is true that for most of our history we have been guided by, or at least we have paid lip service to, Christian values. But in a proper sense only individuals can be Christians, not nations. We must gratefully acknowledge that God has richly blessed our nation, in part at least because we have followed Christian principles.

Suppose God were to send Hosea to our country today. What kind of a message would he bring? Certainly he would be appalled because he would see so many parallels between his time and ours: crime rampant not only in the highways but in high places, sexual promiscuity openly flaunted, homes shattered, and personal morality considered out of date. His message would assuredly reverberate with the somber sounds of judgment.

Yet there would also be words of mercy—the unflagging love of a husband for an adulterous wife, the love of God the Father for his erring child. Make no mistake. Our nation rapidly approaches the precipice of moral disaster. If we are to be spared God's wrath, we must turn from our worldly ways, cease our backsliding, and turn once more to God. When we do return to him we can do so with the assurance that his mercy is still available.

B. HOLD IT STEADY

Beside his shop my grandfather had a big grindstone that was turned by a crank. My cousin and I would occasionally try to sharpen our knives on the stone. But try as we might, we never could get a sharp edge on our knives. Granddad offered good advice: "Boys, if you want a keen edge on your blade, you have to hold it steady against the stone."

That was good advice for sharpening a knife, and it is also good advice for maintaining our proper relationship with God. In a way God's commandments are like a grindstone. When properly used, they can bring our lives to a keen moral edge. To accomplish this desired end, we have to hold our lives steady against God's laws. This is not an easy task, and sometimes it is even painful. If one does not use a grindstone properly, he can ruin a knife. In the same way, if we misunderstand God's laws or misapply them, we can do serious damage to our lives. If we are not willing to work at it, our lives will never have the keen, cutting edge that they must have if we are to be pleasing to God. But by God's grace, we can become morally keen and useful if we hold our lives steady against his commandments.

That is the only way our nation can be spared. Good laws will help, of course, and we must work for good laws. But in the end, only a dedicated citizenry whose lives are honed to a keen edge can save our nation.

Discovery Learning

This page contains an alternate lesson plan emphasizing learning activities. Classes desiring such student involvement will find these suggestions helpful. The next page is a reproducible activity page to further enhance discovery learning.

LEARNING GOALS

As your students participate in this lesson, they will:

1. Explore the nature of God's love to unfaithful Israel.
2. Celebrate God's love for them.

INTO THE LESSON

Write the following sentence on the chalkboard before class:

If it weren't for God's love—

Give a sheet of paper and a pencil to each student. Ask each student to write at least three ways of completing the sentence.

Ask your class to form groups of four to six. In their groups they should allow volunteers to share how they completed the sentence.

Allow several minutes. Then say, "We often take God's love for granted. According to the Bible, however, God doesn't owe us his love. In fact, if we got what we deserve, we would be in a terrible condition. We can be thankful that God has not treated us as we deserve. In our study today we will see this illustrated in the nation of Israel."

INTO THE WORD

Present a brief lecture to review last week's Scripture text and to set the background for today's passage. You will find helpful information in the "Introduction" to this week's commentary.

Your students should remain in their groups. They are to study the specified passages in Hosea and discuss the questions below.

1. Read Hosea 11:1-9. How had God shown his love to Israel? (vv. 1, 3, 4) Note: Israel is also called Ephraim.
2. How had Israel been unfaithful to God? (vv. 2, 7)
3. What would happen to Israel because the people refused to repent? (vv. 5, 6)
4. Verses 8 and 9 indicate that though God would punish Israel, God still had compassion on his people. Paraphrase these two verses as a group.
5. Read Hosea 14:1-4. God wanted Israel to return to him, but with more than empty words. What would it take for Israel to return to God according to verse 2? According to verse 3?

Allow students about fifteen minutes for discussion. Then bring the groups together. Ask the class: "What did Israel deserve from God?" Allow for discussion. (The clear teaching of Scripture is that Israel deserved severe punishment and rejection from God.) Then say, "God wanted to overwhelm Israel with goodness and kindness even though Israel needed punishment. So he determined to soften the punishment and give Israel a chance to return. This is passionately expressed in Hosea 11:8, 9, which each group paraphrased."

Ask each group to read their paraphrase. Then read Psalm 103:1-12. Ask, "What phrases from this passage are illustrated in Hosea?" Allow for comments.

OPTIONS

Have students continue in the groups they began in. Give the groups a choice of how to explore Hosea 11:1-9. The options are:

1. Discuss the questions above.
2. Read Hosea 11:1-9. As a group prepare a pantomime to depict the passage. Be prepared to present the pantomime to the class.
3. Create a mural to depict what is said in Hosea 11:1-9. The mural should contain several scenes that are expressed in the passage.

Provide groups doing number 1 with a copy of the questions, and groups doing number 3 with newsprint, pencils, and felt-tip markers.

Allow fifteen to twenty minutes for groups to complete. Then bring the groups together and allow each group to present its work to the class.

INTO LIFE

Lead your class in celebrating God's amazing love. Provide each student with a hymnal. Ask students to look for hymns that focus on God's love. They may look in the topical index, perhaps under God's love or Christ's love.

Ask them to note phrases that especially help them appreciate God's love. After about three minutes, ask students to read from some of the hymns they found moving. If the class knows the song, ask a talented member to lead in singing it.

Close with a praise time. Ask the class to worship God by completing this sentence, spoken to God: "Father, your love is—"

OPTION

Use the reproducible page that follows, especially the second activity, to make application of the lesson.

Determined to Turn

God said Israel was determined to turn from him (Hosea 11:7). Read the passages listed below to find out what Israel had done to turn from God. Then, in the space provided, list ways in which we sometimes express similar unfaithfulness.

<table>
<tr><td align="center">WHAT HAD ISRAEL DONE?</td><td align="center">WHAT HAVE WE DONE?</td></tr>
<tr><td>Hosea 2:8 _____</td><td>_____</td></tr>
<tr><td>_____</td><td>_____</td></tr>
<tr><td>Hosea 2:13 _____</td><td>_____</td></tr>
<tr><td>_____</td><td>_____</td></tr>
<tr><td>Hosea 4:1, 2 _____</td><td>_____</td></tr>
<tr><td>_____</td><td>_____</td></tr>
<tr><td>Hosea 8:1-4 _____</td><td>_____</td></tr>
<tr><td>_____</td><td>_____</td></tr>
<tr><td>Hosea 10:4, 13 _____</td><td>_____</td></tr>
<tr><td>_____</td><td>_____</td></tr>
</table>

Determined to Return!

"Sow for yourselves righteousness, reap the fruit of unfailing love, and break up your unplowed ground; for it is time to seek the Lord." (Hosea 10:12)

Unplowed ground is soil is too hard to receive seed. Every spring farmers plow their ground to loosen the soil to allow the seeds they will be planting to sprout and grow. It is essential that we maintain our hearts as well-cultivated ground—ground that is receptive to the word of God.

What are some ways that you can keep your heart soft and receptive to God's love? List them below. If you are working with a group, share your ideas with others in the group.

GREEDY LEADERS DENOUNCED

LESSON 9

WHY TEACH THIS LESSON?

One of the troubling features of modern life is the absence of heroes. The modern media seem to have made it their business to expose the flaws in every public figure. The bigger the leader and the bigger the flaw, the better!

Fallible leadership is nothing new. Our lesson today shows it goes back at least twenty-seven centuries! Thus, the lesson challenges those of us who would be leaders. Dare we think we are immune to the temptations that have wasted so many leaders before us? And it challenges the rest of us to demand the best of our leaders.

INTRODUCTION

A. A NINETEENTH-CENTURY MICAH

In 1825 Alexander Campbell wrote a biting satire he called the *Third Epistle of Peter,* which he directed against the clergy of his day. It reminds us so much of Micah's writing that it bears repeating.

"In all of your gettings get money! Now, therefore, when ye go forth on your ministerial journey, go where there are silver and gold, and where each man will pay according to his measure. For verily I say ye must get your reward. . . .

"And when ye shall have fleeced your flock, and shall know of another call, and if the flock be greater, or rather if the fleece be greater, then greater be also unto you the call. . . .

"And the more that the people give you the more will they honor you; for they shall believe that 'in giving to you they are giving to the Lord'; for behold their sight shall be taken from them, and they shall be blind as bats, and 'shall know not what they do.'. . .

"And ye shall wax richer and richer, and grow greater and greater, and you shall be lifted up in your own sight, and exalted in the eyes of the multitude; and *lucre* shall be no longer *filthy* in your sight. And verily ye shall have your reward. . . ."

As they say on television, "Only the names have been changed." If these charges were true one hundred seventy years ago in Campbell's day and true twenty-seven hundred years ago in Micah's day, what assurance do we have that we don't still have the problem today?

B. LESSON BACKGROUND

Micah, whose ministry was carried on in the latter part of the eighth century B.C. was a contemporary of Hosea and Isaiah. We know little about him personally except that he came from the town of Moresheth, about twenty miles southwest of Jerusalem.

When he began his ministry during the reign of Jotham, both Judah and Israel were enjoying prosperity; but that was soon to end. Already Assyria, the great power from the northeast, was beginning to make itself felt. Soon Syria fell, and then in 722

DEVOTIONAL READING:
MICAH 2:1-7

LESSON SCRIPTURE:
MICAH 1—3

PRINTED TEXT:
MICAH 3:5-12

LESSON AIMS

As a result of studying this lesson, each student should:

1. Understand the problems created by corrupt leaders.

2. Have a growing commitment to personal integrity.

3. Be able to suggest one or more ways in which he or she can help improve the dedication of leaders both in the church and in society.

Jul
30

KEY VERSE:

Then they will cry out to the LORD, but he will not answer them. At that time he will hide his face from them because of the evil they have done.   —Micah 3:4

LESSON 9 NOTES

B.C. Samaria, the capital of the northern kingdom, was captured and thousands of its citizens were carried off into captivity. Before Micah's ministry ended, Judah also was to feel the wrath of the Assyrian marauders. Sennacherib, who ruled Assyria from 705 B.C. to 681 B.C., boasted about taking forty-six towns and walled cities in Judah.

Micah, although he grew up in a rural area, was quite aware of the evils that beset the society of Judah. His message echoes the messages of Amos and Hosea that we have already studied. He spoke out against corrupt leaders, greedy priests, and injustices that oppressed the poor. He foretold the judgment that God would bring upon Judah through the Babylonians, but he also looked forward to the time when God would heal his people and restore their land.

I. THE FALSE PROPHETS (MICAH 3:5-7)

A. THEY LEAD PEOPLE ASTRAY (V. 5A)

5a. This is what the LORD says: "As for the prophets who lead my people astray.

In the previous verses Micah has already condemned the "heads of Jacob" and the "princes of the house of Israel" for oppressing the people. Now he turns to the religious leaders, the prophets and priests. These should have had an even greater responsibility to protect the people. Where there is good money, counterfeit money often arises. In the same way, because there are true prophets, false prophets appear. Since there were true prophets like Micah and Isaiah, others, not sent by God nor inspired by his Holy Spirit, tried to cash in on prophetic work. The result was that the people were led into error. When the blind lead the blind, both are likely to fall into the ditch.

B. THEY ARE GREEDY (V. 5B)

5b. "If one feeds them, they proclaim 'peace'; if he does not, they prepare to wage war against him.

The false prophets had a price tag on their services. They expected to be fed when they brought their prophecies. They remind us of the false teacher that Paul mentions in Philippians 3:18, 19: "For, as I have often told you before and now say again even with tears, many live as enemies of the cross of Christ. Their destiny is destruction, their God is their stomach, and their glory is in their shame. Their mind is on earthly things."

Their message was designed to keep the bribes coming. These false prophets would not challenge their hearers or suggest there was any need to repent. They catered to the same kind of clientele that Paul described in 2 Timothy 4:3, 4, people who "will not put up with sound doctrine. Instead, to suit their own desires, they will gather around them a great number of teachers to say what their itching ears want to hear. They will turn their ears away from the truth and turn aside to myths." One of the myths these false prophets offered was that of *peace*, even as the Assyrian enemy was preparing to invade the land. Instead of warning the people of impending danger, they gave them the false assurance that the peace and prosperity that they were enjoying would continue. It is bad to warn of danger when none exists, but it is much worse not to warn of danger when it is impending.

They prepare to wage war against any who refuse to pay the bribes. This may mean that they actually threatened them with physical violence. It is more likely, however, that they would prophesy evil against those who refused to pay. In a culture that held prophets in high regard, this was a frightening threat.

C. THEY WILL BE CONFOUNDED (VV. 6, 7)

6. "Therefore night will come over you, without visions, and darkness, without divination. The sun will set for the prophets, and the day will go dark for them.

WHAT DO YOU THINK?

How common today is the problem Micah condemned in his day—that of leaders or speakers who are more concerned with feathering their own nests than with delivering God's message? How can you tell whether a leader is genuinely concerned with God's business or is merely pretending for personal gain? What should you do when you believe you have spotted an imposter?

WHAT DO YOU THINK?

Micah pronounced God's judgment on the prophets who preached for profit. Paul leveled his condemnation on the hearers who encouraged the teachers to say "what their itching ears want to hear" (2 Timothy 4:3, 4). Who is to blame when leaders and speakers say only what people want to hear—the speakers or the listeners? What responsibility falls on preachers, elders, and congregations to be sure what is preached and taught is according to God's Word? What is their responsibility when they believe that truth is being compromised?

God's message was of coming judgment; but this was an unpopular message. These so-called prophets gave instead a message that people liked and would pay for, a message of continuing prosperity. Such prophets would be *without visions:* that is, they would not receive any revelation from God. The sun would go down; *darkness* would fall upon them; they would be ignorant of the truth.

7. "The seers will be ashamed and the diviners disgraced. They will all cover their faces because there is no answer from God."

God gives *no answer* to mercenary prophets who care more for money than for truth. In time their lies will prove to be lies, and then they will be *ashamed* and *disgraced.* In shame they will *cover their faces* and speak no more.

1-900-HIS WORD

"Psychic Hotlines" seem to be the newest craze in telephone scams. Just call that 900 number, and you can connect yourself to some phony fortuneteller who, with a very sexy voice, will supposedly predict your future.

Imagine the devastating blow to a caller's self-esteem, if, when he dialed a sexy psychic, he was put "on hold," or if no one answered at all!

Micah pronounced God's judgment on mercenary seers, proclaiming that they would receive no answer from God. Divine truth and wisdom are not to be commercialized. God's supernatural gifts cannot be bought, nor are they to be sold. Simon, the sorcerer of Samaria, had to learn that lesson, too (Acts 8:9-24).

Prophesying for money is selfish and shameful. Truly, "The love of money is a root of all kinds of evil" (1 Timothy 6:10). Basic greed is behind every contract a sinner signs with Satan. God's servants are not immune to such temptations. Nor are Christians above the seduction of psychics. The lure of knowing the future is most enticing.

But all of the future we need to know is revealed in the Scriptures. God prophesies through his Word—and it doesn't cost two dollars a minute!   —R. W. B.

II. THE TRUE PROPHET (MICAH 3:8-12)

A. HE PROCLAIMS HIS AUTHORITY (V. 8)

8. But as for me, I am filled with power, with the Spirit of the LORD, and with justice and might, to declare to Jacob his transgression, to Israel his sin.

Micah contrasts his ministry with that of the false prophets. First of all, he presents the basis for his authority. His prophecies are not rooted in his imagination, nor do they come out of his desire to make money by pleasing the crowd. Rather, he is full of *power, with the Spirit of the Lord.* He does not tell us how God's revelation came to him, whether it came as an audible voice, as a vision, in a dream, or in some other form; but he leaves no doubt that his word did come from God. This Spirit-filled quality makes the Bible unique among all the literature in the world. All Scripture is given by inspiration, or, as Paul expresses it, "All Scripture is God-breathed" (2 Timothy 3:16).

The second point Micah makes is that the message he delivered came *with justice.* Unlike others who claimed prophetic powers, he did not tailor his message to fit the whims of his hearers. His prophetic blessings were not available to the highest bidders. Instead, he fearlessly pointed out to *Jacob his transgression,* and *to Israel his sin.* As a faithful servant of the Lord, he could not protect his beloved countrymen from the harsh words of condemnation that he had to deliver. He was no politician seeking some kind of a popular consensus; he was a fearless spokesman delivering God's indictment without compromise.

POWER AND LIGHT COMPANY

One of the most impressive technological innovations in modern missionary enterprise is the solar-energy pack, developed to bring electric power for projected visual

OPTION

Use the reproducible activity, "Misleading Leaders," on page 416 to explore the problem of corrupt leaders.

WHAT DO YOU THINK?

When an election is near, there is often a lot of "mudslinging" instead of clear and sober discussion of facts and issues. On the other hand, many candidates refuse to be held accountable for immoral behavior, calling it "not relevant to the issues." To what standard should a Christian hold contenders for political office? How relevant are moral issues for secular offices? Why?

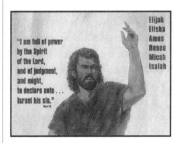

Visual 9 illustrates the message of verse 8 and applies it to all the prophets studied this quarter—not just to Micah.

aids to primitive villages in third-world countries. Here's the way it works: A missionary carries a battery pack on his back as he travels on foot or by cycle to an out-back bush community to share the gospel. As he goes, sunlight generates energy through small solar panels to charge the batteries. When the missionary arrives in the village, he hangs a sheet, connects a projector to the battery pack, and shows a movie about Jesus. Thousands of unreached peoples have received the good news by this ingenious and effective method.

Prophets need power and light. Genuine spokesmen for God are energized and enlightened by his Spirit. The truth and courage of forthtellers comes from above. Micah had it; the mercenary "clergy" of his day did not.

Christians have received the Son-light of Jesus Christ. Even without a special gift of prophecy, we are empowered to declare "good news to the poor . . . to proclaim freedom to the captives . . . to proclaim the year of the Lord's favor, and the day of vengeance of our God" (Isaiah 61:1, 2).   —R. W. B.

B. HE CONDEMNS THE RULERS (VV. 9, 10)

9. Hear this, you leaders of the house of Jacob, you rulers of the house of Israel, who despise justice and distort all that is right.

Micah next turns his attention to the rulers of Judah, who are called *leaders of the house of Jacob, and rulers of the house of Israel.* During the time of the divided kingdom, the north part usually was called Israel and the south part was called Judah. However, in this case it seems that the southern kingdom is called Israel and Jacob, which is Israel's other name. Possibly this prophecy was given after the northern kingdom was destroyed. The south part then was all that was left of Israel.

Justice may be perverted in several ways. Illegal actions can be carried out so secretly that no one ever discovers them. Or laws may be passed that make certain actions legal even when they are obviously immoral. Or some activities may be practiced so long that they become accepted without challenge even though they are unjust. It is likely that all of these factors were at work in ancient Judah. They became starkly visible only when Micah focused God's spotlight on them. Some of the evils this spotlight revealed were idolatry (1:7; 5:13), covetousness (2:2), witchcraft (5:12), using dishonest scales and false weights (6:11), violence, and lying (6:12).

10. . . . who build Zion with bloodshed, and Jerusalem with wickedness.

Zion is Jerusalem. When Micah says it was built *with bloodshed*, he may mean this literally. We recall how Jezebel and Ahab plotted the death of Naboth so they could seize his vineyard (1 Kings 21:1-19). Perhaps some of the kings of Judah were guilty of similar atrocities in Jerusalem. On the other hand, Micah often uses forceful language to drive home a point, and so he may be using the expression in a figurative sense to indicate that the rich built the city by extortion and deceit. The rulers may have levied taxes on the people, confiscating their very livelihood, reducing them to beggars, and shortening their life-span. In either case, the activities of the rulers came under Micah's scathing denunciation.

C. HE CONDEMNS THE JUDGES, PRIESTS, AND PROPHETS (V. 11)

11. Her leaders judge for a bribe, her priests teach for a price, and her prophets tell fortunes for money. Yet they lean upon the LORD and say, "Is not the LORD among us? No disaster will come upon us."

Not only were the rulers corrupt; so were the judges, priests, and prophets. In ancient Judah, when the judges dispensed justice, they were looked upon as representatives of God. Yet they were perverting this high honor by taking bribes. The law specifically forbade such practices: "Do not accept a bribe, for a bribe blinds those who see and twists the words of the righteous" (Exodus 23:8).

WHAT DO YOU THINK?

Micah condemned the leaders for distorting "all that is right." Distorting the right and making evil appear good is as old as the Garden of Eden. Jesus faced essentially the same temptation in the desert. The example of Jesus, of course, is better than that of Eve. Easily we see that he used Scripture to correct the picture.

In what ways do the news media, popular advertisements, and entertainment media portray evil as good? What can you do to correct the picture?

WHAT DO YOU THINK?

When we see a need to change great numbers of people and to turn a bad situation around, political action often seems appealing. In some situations it may help. But Jesus did not organize a political party or start a referendum drive. He sent out disciples to make more disciples. Why do you think we are so eager to try political measures instead of Jesus' method? Do you think some people have concluded disciple-making won't work? How can true revival be brought to our country—spiritual revival, not political revival?

The *priests* also came under Micah's indictment. The priests were not condemned because they were paid for their services. Jesus makes it clear that teachers may be compensated for their teaching (Luke 10:7). Paul agrees (1 Timothy 5: 17, 18). The problem was that these priests were perverting their teachings to please the people, hoping thereby to be rewarded. Paul foresaw a similar practice among Christians (2 Timothy 4:3, 4). The priests were looked to as interpreters of the law, and it is likely they collaborated with the corrupt judges to subvert justice.

Nor do the *prophets* escape Micah's condemnation. Faithful prophets often stood outside the system, serving as God's independent spokesmen against the establishment that broke God's laws. They were often rejected and mistreated, endangering their lives to be faithful spokesmen for God. We think immediately of Elijah, or Micaiah, or Amos, or Jeremiah, who prophesied a century after Micah. But many who claimed to be prophets were victims of the same contagion that afflicted other leaders—greed. They divined *for money.*

These leaders would never admit that they had done wrong. Indeed, they did just the opposite! They arrogantly insisted that the Lord was with them, blessing them in their activities. They were quite certain that the punishment Micah was predicting would not fall on them.

MINISTERIAL MERCENARIES

Jim Bakker went to prison after he was convicted of misappropriating supporters' contributions. Even so, gospel hawkers of every description continue to crowd the airwaves.

The contemporary situation is hardly different from the circumstances surrounding Micah's prophecy. Israel's judges, priests, and prophets sold their ministries to the highest bidder. Their greed doomed Jerusalem, and the entire nation, to defeat and destruction. And their sin was compounded by their presumption upon God's grace. They actually thought Jehovah would continue to bless them, despite their shameless materialism.

Not all ministerial mercenaries have radio or TV programs. The love of money can motivate the poor as well as the rich. Each of us needs to examine his personal attitudes toward material resources. All Christians are ministers in some capacity, and Christian service never is to be for sale. "You cannot serve both God and Money" (Matthew 6:24). —R. W. B.

D. HE PRONOUNCES DOOM UPON JERUSALEM (V. 12)
12. Therefore because of you, Zion will be plowed like a field, Jerusalem will become a heap of rubble, the temple hill a mound overgrown with thickets.

Micah and his generation saw the destruction of north Israel by the Assyrians, and they should have learned their lesson. But they didn't. Even when Jerusalem was besieged by the Assyrians and saved by divine intervention (2 Kings 19:35), they still didn't learn. Micah's prophecy was fulfilled a century later when the Babylonians brought destruction to Jerusalem.

Plowed like a field. The destruction of the city would be so complete that a peasant might plant crops where it had been. *The temple hill* refers to Mount Moriah, upon which the temple was built. It would become covered with trees and underbrush.

CONCLUSION
A. WE NEED A MODERN MICAH

Reading the book of Micah reminds us that corrupt leadership, whether political or religious, is not only a modern phenomenon. Indeed, it is nearly as old as the

WHAT DO YOU THINK?

In the face of the present passion for personal gain and material wealth, how can we help the next generation to set proper values?

Some factors we might consider are good leadership in our churches, personal example, and prayer. How important are each of these? What others would you suggest? How can we be sure we have each of the factors in place?

OPTION

Use the reproducible activity, "Godly Leaders," on page 416 to further your discussion of having godly leadership.

HOW TO SAY IT
Assyrian. Uh-SEAR-ee-un.
Micah. MY-kuh.
Sennacherib. Sen-NACK-er-ib.

PRAYER

O gracious God, give us wisdom as we select our leaders. Help us prepare men and women and boys and girls for positions of leadership. Teach us to lead with humility and to follow our faithful leaders with grace. In all of these things may your name be glorified. In the name of the Servant of servants we pray. Amen.

THOUGHT TO REMEMBER

"The greatest among you will be your servant" (Matthew 23:11).

DAILY BIBLE READINGS

Monday, July 24—Judgment for Israel's Sins (Micah 1:1-7)

Tuesday, July 25—Lamentation for the Judgment on Israel (Micah 1:8-16)

Wednesday, July 26—Woe to Those Who Oppress Others (Micah 2:1-5)

Thursday, July 27—Israel's Moral Uncleanness (Micah 2: 6-11)

Friday, July 28—Restoration After Punishment for Evil Deeds (Micah 2:12—3:4)

Saturday, July 29—Evil Rulers and Lying Prophets Denounced (Micah 3:5-12)

Sunday, July 30—Retribution for Wickedness Is Certain (Psalm 37:1-15)

human race. But the time since World War II seems to have experienced more than its share of scandals among its leaders. We have seen local leaders proved guilty of serious immoralities and convicted of crimes against the public. Nor have our congressmen and senators been immune to these problems. For that matter, even some of the residents of the White House have not lived lives above reproach. Even more stunning to church members has been the moral failure of many religious leaders. As one scandal has followed another, it has become painfully apparent that no religious group is immune from this problem.

Are our times worse than earlier days? Not if we understand anything about the ministry of Micah, who devoted much of his effort to condemning the same failings that trouble us today. If these problems have always existed, why do our times seem so much worse? For one thing, the modern media, for all of their faults, have made it more difficult to conceal our misdeeds. At times the media seem to revel in exposing human imperfections, and the profit motive is often all too obvious in their actions. And yet their searchlight on our foibles makes us painfully aware of the serious task we have before us.

We would do well to examine reasons for so many moral failures. We must certainly recognize that greed is a significant factor. Materialism permeates every aspect of our society. Our very social structure is largely defined by possessions. We categorize people as lower, middle, or upper class, not on the basis of moral character, but almost entirely on what they possess.

We live in a sex-saturated society. On every hand—on television, in the movies, in the printed media—sex is served up and exploited. In such an atmosphere it should not surprise us that sexual purity is so hard to maintain. Short of living on some remote mountain top completely isolated from the rest of the world, there is little we can do to avoid all these pervasive influences. But we can avoid some of them and protect our families from some of them by controlling the switch on the TV, censoring what we read, and avoiding persons and places where contamination is rampant.

In all of this we must not overlook the part that ego plays. Positions of leadership feed our egos and give us power over other people. To enhance our power over others, we are often tempted to take moral shortcuts. Sins of sex and greed are easier to detect in others and in our own lives than is the lust for power. Some religious leaders seem especially blind to this sin as they labor in the vineyard of the Lord. Like the religious leaders in Micah's day, they say, "Is not the Lord among us?"

B. LIKE PRIEST, LIKE PEOPLE

It is certainly true that leaders shape the people they lead, whether the leaders are secular or religious. Leaders set the standards and become the models for their followers. For this reason, leaders bear a very great responsibility for their words and their actions.

But in a situation where leaders are selected by a democratic process, we might reverse this and say instead, *like people, like priest*. After all, we do elect our leaders, and often they are but reflections of ourselves, including our weaknesses. Most of the time we deserve the leaders we get.

In our churches, too, we have a voice in selecting our leaders. In other words, we deserve the leaders we get. If some of our well-known leaders have been careless or worse about their finances or their personal lives, we must bear some of the responsibility because we supported them. Let us, then, use great care and seek divine guidance in selecting those who will lead us and those whom we will follow.

Discovery Learning

This page contains an alternate lesson plan emphasizing learning activities. Classes
desiring such student involvement will find these suggestions helpful. The next page
is a reproducible activity page to further enhance discovery learning.

LEARNING GOALS

Through this lesson your students will:

1. Pinpoint evidence of corruption among the leaders during Micah's time.

2. Emphasize the necessity of righteousness, truth, and integrity for leaders.

3. Commit themselves to be people who live in righteousness, truth, and integrity.

INTO THE LESSON

Give each student a copy of the statements below.

1. A church or nation will not rise above the level of its leaders.

2. Most churches or nations deserve the leaders they select.

3. Corrupt leaders usually lead their people into corruption.

4. Leaders should be expected to live with higher integrity than others.

5. Being in leadership makes it more difficult to live with integrity than not being in leadership.

Give a copy of the statements and a pencil to each student. Ask class members to read each statement and write *A* in front of each statement with which they agree and *D* in front of the statements with which they disagree.

After about three minutes, take a tally on each statement. For each one ask volunteers to explain why they chose their opinions. Allow for brief discussion on the most controversial ones.

Say to your class, "We have been focusing on the nation of Israel in recent weeks. Unfortunately, the nation failed to follow God's instructions and brought God's displeasure. Judah, the southern part of what had been the empire of Israel, made many of the same mistakes as Israel to the north. In our lesson today, we will see that God pinned a lot of the responsibility for Judah's dismal spiritual condition on the leaders."

INTO THE WORD

Prepare your class for their Scripture study by briefly lecturing on the background of Micah. Zero in on the "Introduction" in the commentary on page 409.

Ask a volunteer to read Micah 3:1-12. Then involve your students in a large-group discussion of these questions:

1. What complaints are made against the leaders (national and spiritual) of Israel?

2. What will happen to the leaders, according to verse 4? Verse 6? Verse 7?

3. What will happen to the city (Zion) because of the leaders? See verse 12.

4. Spiritual leaders were tempted to tell people what they wanted to hear rather than what God wanted them to hear. Compare these passages: Micah 3:5; Jeremiah 6:13, 14; 23:17, 22; 2 Timothy 4:1-4. What does each passage say about corrupt teachers or teaching that tells people what they want to hear, not what God wants them to be told?

INTO LIFE

Help students connect the Scripture with the issues of today. Have students discuss the questions below in groups of six:

1. Righteousness. Integrity. Truth. God requires these of both political and spiritual leaders. In what ways have we witnessed corruption in leadership in the past several decades?

2. Are people becoming more tolerant of corruption in leadership? Support your answer.

3. In what ways may churches today be tempted to tell people what they want to hear rather than what God wants them to hear?

4. We ought to be as good as we want our leaders to be. Discuss these questions:

• In what ways are you tempted to compromise regarding truth or righteousness?

• How can you build a life of integrity?

Allow ten to fifteen minutes for discussion. Then give a sheet of paper to each class member. Ask each one to write a personal prayer committing himself to live in righteousness, truth, and integrity.

OPTION

Have students form groups of six. Ask each group to think of a situation in which Christians might be tempted to compromise regarding truth or righteousness. (Examples may include: reporting income on tax forms; church publicity committee preparing a newspaper ad that promises people more than the church can deliver.) Each group is to develop a skit to illustrate the situation.

Allow each group to perform its skit. Following each one ask, "How would the situation have been approached if the people had been committed to integrity?"

Conclude by asking students to write prayers as described in the activity above.

Misleading Leaders

Micah spoke out clearly against leaders (both religious and political) who were more concerned with themselves than their followers.

Read the following passages and indicate in the space provided what the Bible says about corrupt teachers—especially about their motivation to mislead.

Micah 3:5, 9-11 _____

_____

Jeremiah 6:13, 14 _____

_____

Jeremiah 23:17, 22 _____

_____

Matthew 6:24 _____

_____

Luke 22:3-6 _____

_____

Philippians 3:18, 19 _____

_____

2 Timothy 4:1-4 _____

_____

Godly Leaders

Now read Isaiah 8:13 and 1 Peter 3:8-17. How should the motivations of a godly leader differ from those you saw in the passages above? Focus on specific ways you can judge whether or not a leader is godly.

Spend some time praying for your leaders—that they might fear God and not men.

ISAIAH'S CALL AND MESSAGE

LESSON 10

WHY TEACH THIS LESSON?

"Worship" is big business these days. More than one company has seen sales rise as churches clamor for the latest in worship techniques: slides and projectors, dramatic scripts and costumes, tape players and tapes, video projectors. . . . All these make for a very moving experience in contemporary worship assemblies. Even traditional worship services can be extravagant, with expansive pipe organs, hand bells, beautifully robed choirs. . . . Again, the result may be a very powerful experience—but is it, is either of them, worship?

Whatever style of worship your church employs, remind your students that it is not the style or the trappings of the service that make for true worship. True worship only happens when we can say, as a result, "I saw the Lord seated on a throne, high and exalted." True worship produces a response, "Here am I; send me." This lesson challenges our worship *forms* and demands we fill them with *substance*.

INTRODUCTION

A. OPENING THE LINES OF COMMUNICATION

A severe thunderstorm swept across the city, knocking out the power for many of its residents. Even before the storm had completely subsided, a utility truck carrying several workers pulled up to a corner and stopped. Lightning had knocked out a transformer on a pole at the corner, and the men had come to repair it.

One man climbed the pole, inspected the transformer, and began to shout instructions to the men below. But the noise of the traffic made it impossible for him to be heard. Finally he climbed back down, put on a headset, and climbed the pole again. One of the other men also put on a headset. What they were using was a special radio system that allowed them to communicate. The man on the pole began to give instructions, and soon with a rope he was pulling up the things he needed to repair the transformer.

It was somewhat like this for Isaiah. God wanted to instruct him and prepare him for service, but because of the busy world about him with all of its sin, he did not hear the instructions. Only after he was cleansed was he prepared to hear the Lord and obey him. All of us are like Isaiah. We live in a society that is drowning in sin, and we have been corrupted by our surroundings. To serve the Lord we must first hear his call.

B. LESSON BACKGROUND

The prophet Isaiah lived in the second half of the eighth century B.C., a contemporary of Hosea and Micah. His long ministry, conducted in Judah, the southern kingdom, fell in the reigns of four kings—Uzziah, Jotham, Ahaz, and Hezekiah. Isaiah was called to minister in difficult times. Judah had enjoyed considerable prosperity during the reign of Uzziah, in part because of the decline of Assyria's power, but that was about to end. In the tumultuous times that followed, Assyria once more moved westward, capturing Damascus, Syria's capital, and then Samaria, Israel's capital. Soon the Assyrian hordes were at the gates of Jerusalem, and only God's divine intervention spared that city (2 Kings 19).

DEVOTIONAL READING:

ISAIAH 55:6-11

LESSON SCRIPTURE:

ISAIAH 6; 1

PRINTED TEXT:

ISAIAH 6:1-8; 1:14-17

LESSON AIMS

As a result of studying this lesson, each student should:

1. Have an understanding of the circumstances surrounding Isaiah's call.

2. Appreciate Isaiah's sense of total inadequacy in the presence of God's holiness.

3. Realize that we must be cleansed before we can be at our best in God's service.

4. Be able to enumerate ways he or she can serve in the Lord's kingdom.

Aug
6

KEY VERSE:

Then I heard the voice of the Lord saying, "Whom shall I send? And who will go for us?"

And I said, "Here am I. Send me!"   —Isaiah 6:8

LESSON 10 NOTES

Visual 10 illustrates Isaiah's call and challenges us to a right response to the holiness of God.

WHAT DO YOU THINK?

Isaiah's vision of God was an awesome experience. How we would like to approach that sense of awe in our worship services today! What factors make it difficult for you to sense the holiness and majesty of God in the worship service? What can be done before, during, or after the worship service to negate those factors and enhance the awe and majesty of experiencing the presence of God?

WHAT DO YOU THINK?

Can you imagine the drama of Isaiah being interrupted to announce a picnic? Do you think we lose a sense of awe and reverence in our effort to be friendly, make announcements, and report on the sick? How can we all be aware of God's holiness and yet have a warm and friendly service?

We know little about Isaiah's personal life. His father was Amoz (not to be confused with Amos the prophet), and he had a wife who bore him two sons. His name means "Jehovah saves." Tradition has it that he was a member of the royal family, or at least a noble family. This is borne out by the fact that he had ready access to the royal court.

Many acclaim Isaiah as the greatest of the writing prophets. His elevated literary style, his sweeping vision of God's acting in history, his eloquent denunciation of Judah's sins, and most of all his messianic prophecies give him a just claim to this title.

I. VISION IN THE TEMPLE (ISAIAH 6:1-4)

A. THE VISION OF THE LORD (v. 1)

1. In the year that King Uzziah died, I saw the Lord seated on a throne, high and exalted, and the train of his robe filled the temple.

The reign of Uzziah, sometimes called Azariah, was long and prosperous. Although near the end of his reign he was smitten by leprosy because he tried to offer incense in the temple contrary to the law, he was on the whole a good king. His death was perhaps in 736 B.C. Isaiah's vision occurred *in the year that King Uzziah died*, whether before or after his death we are not told. Many commentators believe this was Isaiah's initial call to the prophetic ministry. Others, seeing that his call is in chapter 6, believe that his prophetic ministry had begun earlier and that this call was to a new and more specific ministry. They argue that the death of Uzziah marked the beginning of new and more serious threats to Judah, requiring a new commission for the prophet.

I saw the Lord. Since no man has seen God at any time (John 1:18), we take this to mean a vision of God. Probably Isaiah had gone to the temple to worship when the vision occurred.

In this vision Isaiah saw God *on a throne,* indicating his power and authority. Presumably he appeared as a human being, dressed in a flowing robe—but much larger than an ordinary human. The word used for *Lord* in this verse is *Adonay,* which seems to stress his might and sovereignty, rather than *Yahweh,* the personal name of Israel's God, which is used in verses 3 and 5. *The train,* that is, the skirt, *of his robe* was so expansive that it *filled the temple.* This imagery—the elevated throne and the flowing robe—obviously presents a picture of an earthly king of that day, but on a larger scale.

B. THE VISION OF THE SERAPHS (vv. 2, 3)

2. Above him were seraphs, each with six wings: With two wings they covered their faces, with two they covered their feet, and with two they were flying.

Seraphs (*seraphim* in some versions) are mentioned only here in the Scriptures. Mention of *faces* and *feet* suggests a human form, but each one had six *wings.* With four of these he humbly shielded himself from the divine glory; with the other two he flew, hovering in the air over the outspread robe.

We know little about the seraphs. Even the origin of the name is disputed by some scholars, although many hold that it means fiery or burning. Perhaps they were bright and shining. From this passage we can conclude that their function was to praise God and act as his servants and messengers.

3. And they were calling to one another: "Holy, holy, holy is the LORD Almighty; the whole earth is full of his glory."

Across the ages men have assigned many different attributes to God. For some he is the creator and sustainer of the universe. For others he is all wisdom and all knowledge. Some see him as a stern and demanding judge, while others view him as a loving and merciful Father. Jehovah God is all of these, but he is more. He is *holy!* No description of God is complete unless it makes reference to his holiness. When ascribed to man, holiness conveys the idea of being set apart, especially set apart or dedicated to God. It also includes the idea of a degree of moral purity. This idea of holiness, however, is inadequate when it is applied to God. God is holy in the sense that he is completely separate from and exalted above his creation. Our language is inadequate to express all that is involved in God's holiness, nor do we have the intellectual capacity to understand it even if we could somehow express it.

Holy, holy, holy. The repetition is for emphasis. Some commentators suggest that the seraphs were arranged as a heavenly choir. As one of the seraphs led, the others responded antiphonally.

C. THE IMPACT OF THE PRAISE (V. 4)

4. At the sound of their voices the doorposts and thresholds shook and the temple was filled with smoke.

The volume and the tone of the chorus reverberated so thunderously that they shook *the doorposts and thresholds.* It must have been like a mighty church organ whose deep bass notes make the whole building vibrate. *The temple was filled with smoke,* indicating the divine presence (Exodus 19:18; 20:18).

II. CALL TO SERVICE (ISAIAH 6:5-8)

A. ISAIAH'S UNWORTHINESS (V. 5)

5. "Woe to me!" I cried. "I am ruined! For I am a man of unclean lips, and I live among a people of unclean lips, and my eyes have seen the King, the LORD Almighty."

It may surprise us that Isaiah was so completely overwhelmed by this experience. If he already had uttered the strong condemnations recorded in the first five chapters, then he had been the Lord's faithful spokesman, carrying out his proper duty. Why should he feel undone?

First of all, we need to recognize that any mere mortal ushered into the presence of Almighty God will be utterly overwhelmed (Exodus 33:20).

Further, Isaiah was honest enough to recognize that even though he had faithfully delivered God's message of judgment, yet he had not completely escaped the sins he had condemned. No matter how carefully one makes his way through a coal mine, he is certain to pick up some coal dust on his clothing or shoes. So it is with a sinful society. Even a righteous man like Isaiah was bound to suffer some contamination just by living in such a society. We today face a similar problem, and we must honestly face up to it.

Like anyone who sincerely seeks to minister to a people, Isaiah identified with his people. His own lips, like those of his people, were unclean, suggesting that their utterances betrayed the corruption within. In sharing with his people, Isaiah indicated his willingness to share their punishment with them. This is the mark of a true shepherd.

YOU ARE WHAT YOU SAY

Sam (twenty-five) was trying to make conversation with cousin Andrew (nine) at a family reunion. "Whatta ya say, Andrew?" said Sam in friendly greeting. Without hesitation, Andrew replied with Pavlovian predictability: "Thank you!" He obviously had been coached repeatedly in the social grace of gratitude, coached with the parental prompt, "What do you say, Andrew?" So his learned response was triggered even by a rhetorical version of the question.

HOW TO SAY IT

Adonay. A-doe-nay (short "A" as in "bat").
Ahaz. AY-haz.
Amoz. AY-mahz.
Assyria. Uh-SEAR-ee-uh.
Azariah. Az-uh-RYE-uh.
Hezekiah. Hez-ih-KYE-uh.
Isaiah. Eye-ZAY-uh.
Jotham. JO-tham.
seraphim. SAIR-uh-fim.
seraphs. SAIR-ufs.
Uzziah. Uh-ZYE-uh.

WHAT DO YOU THINK?

Isaiah felt very unworthy and aware of his sin as he recognized the awesome holiness of God. Does that suggest that true worship requires us to sense our sinfulness? How does today's emphasis on "positive thinking" relate to true worship?

WHAT DO YOU THINK?

One of the features of Isaiah's vision was the cleansing that took place when he confessed his unworthiness (vv. 6, 7). Long ago Jesus died to atone for our sins; today "if we confess our sins, he is faithful and just to forgive us our sins, and to cleanse us from all unrighteousness" (1 John 1:9). How can that promise be used to enhance our worship times? How does the Lord's Supper utilize that same principle to enrich our worship?

The conversation starter, *Whatta ya say?* may be more significant than it appears. It means everything from "How do you feel?" to "What do you think?" to "Where do you stand?" It is an invitation to share at least part of your character and personality. What you say reveals who you are.

When Isaiah bemoaned his and the nation's "unclean lips," he was confessing more than specific sins of speech, like lying and profanity. *Lips* stood for life. "Woe to me," he might have said, "for we are people of unclean thoughts, unclean habits, and unclean behavior."

Speech can reveal character. That is why James taught that the tongue "corrupts the whole person" (James 3:6). *Conversation* in the *King James Version* of the Bible meant *life-style,* not just dialogue. So, "Be careful, little lips, what you say."

—R. W. B.

B. HIS CLEANSING (VV. 6, 7)

6, 7. Then one of the seraphs flew to me with a live coal in his hand, which he had taken with tongs from the altar. With it he touched my mouth and said, "See, this has touched your lips; your guilt is taken away and your sin atoned for."

Isaiah stood before the throne of God as a penitent sinner, confessing his guilt. He made no attempt to plead his case or to claim extenuating circumstances. In the presence of Almighty God no defense was possible. All he could ask for was mercy; but before he could even ask for it, God took action. *One of the seraphs* took *tongs,* lifted a *live coal* from the altar, and flew to Isaiah. Then he touched it to his lips, symbolically purging him from sin. Fire can have purifying power. It can be used to burn away infected flesh, cauterizing a wound so that it can heal. Here the sin-infected lips were figuratively burned away, that they might be healed and once more become useful. Such a dramatic figure would leave no doubt in Isaiah's mind that he was cleansed, no longer having to carry about a burden of guilt.

C. HIS RESPONSE (V. 8)

8. Then I heard the voice of the Lord saying, "Whom shall I send? And who will go for us?" And I said, "Here am I. Send me!"

Up to this point, the Lord had not uttered a word. Now as the prophet stood before him, cleansed of his sins, he heard his voice for the first time. *Whom shall I send? And who will go for us?* God's call to service was quite general. God called for a messenger, but neither his destination nor his specific duties were mentioned.

In a sense, this is the way everyone who becomes a Christian is called. We are called to service, and only later may we learn the specific nature of that service. Isaiah didn't hesitate an instant in responding to the call. He didn't ask any questions about what God wanted him to do, nor did he insist upon any conditions before he would accept the call. He responded out of a joy that came from a deep sense of gratitude because God had cleansed him from sin.

III. DEMAND FOR REFORM (ISAIAH 1:14-17)

Some believe that these words were uttered early in Isaiah's ministry, before he received his special call recorded in chapter 6. Others believe that they came after his call and were typical of the message he was to carry to his people. If this is the case, we can readily understand why God warned him that the people would close their eyes and ears to the message (Isaiah 6:9, 10). After all, it was a message of condemnation and judgment, not of pious and pleasant platitudes.

WHAT DO YOU THINK?

Isaiah's "worship" experience concluded with a call to service, which he accepted. For what kind of response does our worship call? For what kind of response should it call? How can we be sure we properly respond to the Lord's call in worship?

Do God's demands on Israel to "stop doing wrong" and "learn to do right" (verses 16, 17) in order for their worship to be accepted suggest anything about a proper response to worship? If so, what, and how can we be sure our worship calls for such a response?

WHAT DO YOU THINK?

No one can miss the emotion present in Isaiah's experience. At the same time, emotional worship may sometimes bring impulsive responses that are ill-considered and inappropriate. How can we merge thoughtful resolution with grateful exuberance? To express emotion freely without being controlled by emotion?

What demands does seeking a balance between emotion and thoughtfulness make on the ones who plan our worship times? What demands does it make on all who worship?

A. EMPTY WORSHIP REJECTED (VV. 14, 15)

14, 15. *Your New Moon festivals and your appointed feasts my soul hates. They have become a burden to me; I am weary of bearing them. When you spread out your hands in prayer, I will hide my eyes from you; even if you offer many prayers, I will not listen. Your hands are full of blood.*

Isaiah condemned his people because, while they were going through the motions of worshiping Jehovah, they were not really worshiping him. That was the problem—they were just going through the motions. Their lives did not prove that their worship was sincere.

In the previous verses Isaiah has indicated God's dissatisfaction with the people's sacrifices, burning of incense, New Moons, Sabbaths, and convocations. In this verse, he concentrates on the *New Moon festivals* and *appointed feasts.* The festival of the new moon came on the first day of each lunar month. Special sacrifices and feasting accompanied this day. (See 1 Chronicles 23:30, 31.) The appointed feasts were the regular annual religious observances such as Passover, Pentecost, Tabernacles, and the Day of Atonement. The people were observing these, and so it must have come as a shock to hear their actions denounced in such strong terms.

God refused even to hear prayers that were offered hypocritically and perfunctorily. Sometimes people become so alienated from him that he will not answer their prayers (Proverbs 1:28).

"CHURCHIANITY"

Church Growth is the buzz word of preference among Christians in this last decade of the century. Congregations are pulling out all the stops to coax greater numbers into highly mortgaged sanctuaries. Telemarketing, direct mail, sensational programming, entertainment spectaculars, "visitor friendly" formats, and culture-accommodating schedules—all are accepted means to the end that more and more warm bodies fill the pews. This caution is valid: "What people are won *by* is what they are won *to.*"

Big crowds of worshipers are one worthy goal for a church. But genuine conversion of sinners to authentic Christianity must be our first priority. The nation of Judah appeared to be faithful in attendance at temple rituals and ceremonies. God rejected their formal worship, though, because their hearts were empty of sincere faith, and their hands were full of guilty blood.

Is it possible that many modern worshipers are practicing *churchianity* instead of *Christianity?* Many simply go through the motions of church attendance without applying the gospel to daily living. Could you be guilty, too? The instruction of the apostle Paul is well taken: "A man ought to examine himself" (1 Corinthians 11:28).

—R. W. B.

B. WORSHIPERS MUST BE CLEANSED (V. 16)

16. *Wash and make yourselves clean. Take your evil deeds out of my sight! Stop doing wrong.*

Their first step, if they would become pleasing to God, was to turn away from their evil ways. There was no way they could cover over their sins or hide them. They had to repent and quit doing them. This included not only their empty worship services, but also acts of violence such as mentioned in verse 15: "Your hands are full of blood." God stands always ready to welcome the wayward sinner to him, but repentance must always come first. Repentance involves a sincere sorrow for past sins, but it also requires a resolve to turn away from those sins.

WHAT DO YOU THINK?

Because of the people's sin, God rejected their worship. He said, "Even if you offer many prayers, I will not listen." Paul prayed for the removal of the "thorn in his flesh," but God did not remove it. Instead, he said, "My grace is sufficient for you" (2 Corinthians 12:7-9).

How can you tell whether God is not answering your prayers because of sin in your life and when his answer is, "My grace is sufficient for you"? How should you respond to unanswered (or "no" answered) prayer?

OPTION

Use the reproducible activity page 424 to guide your students through an examination of "Worship That Is Not Worthy," such as Israel and Judah practiced in Isaiah's day, and a look at "Worship That Pleases God" and how it is a natural result of holy living.

PRAYER

Almighty God, as we come before you, let us never forget that you are high and holy and exalted. Let us never approach you casually or hypocritically. Open our hearts and our ears to your call to service. May we, like Isaiah, respond readily when that call comes. In the name of the Servant of servants we pray. Amen.

THOUGHT TO REMEMBER

"Here am I; send me" (Isaiah 6:8).

DAILY BIBLE READINGS

Monday, July 31—Isaiah's Call and Plea of Unworthiness (Isaiah 6:1-5)

Tuesday, Aug. 1—A Forgiven Isaiah Accepts His Call (Isaiah 6:6-13)

Wednesday, Aug. 2—God's Message to Judah Through Isaiah (Isaiah 1:1-6)

Thursday, Aug. 3—Judah's Desolate Condition (Isaiah 1:7-11)

Friday, Aug. 4—Superficial Religion Is Offensive to God (Isaiah 1:12-17)

Saturday, Aug. 5—God Expects Justice and Righteousness (Isaiah 1:18-23)

Sunday, Aug. 6—Sinful Rebellion Must Be Punished (Isaiah 1:24-31)

C. THEY MUST REFORM THEIR LIVES (v. 17)

17. Learn to do right! Seek justice, encourage the oppressed. Defend the cause of the fatherless, plead the case of the widow.

Now come the positive requirements. To be pleasing to God, one must not only refrain from evil activities; he must also be involved in doing good. The specific things that Isaiah mentions give a clue about some of the more serious problems besetting the society of his day. To *seek judgment* is to give justice in the courts, where bribery and shady deals seem to have been prevalent. The *oppressed* were the poverty-stricken who were taken advantage of by the rich. The *fatherless* and the *widow*, because they lack men to protect them, seem always to be ready victims of oppression. Isaiah's words echo those of his contemporary, Micah, who wrote that the Lord requires his people "to act justly and to love mercy and to walk humbly with your God" (Micah 6:8).

DON'TS AND DOS

A nearby church has developed a sad situation: these folk are trying to live in a vacuum of negativism. They are well-versed in what they are against—graded Sunday school, church dinners, a trained ministry, etc. Their mistake is not in opposing what they consider to be extra biblical practices; but their negative emphasis has produced a melancholy, lifeless, shrinking congregation of legalistic, sour-spirited drudges. They know all the *don'ts* of their persuasion, but they are not accentuating the positive *dos* of Christian discipleship.

Isaiah issued a two-pronged exhortation to Judah: "Stop doing wrong, learn to do right!" There's both a *don't* and a *do*. Paul wrote the same admonition: "Hate what is evil; cling to what is good" (Romans 12:9).

Giving up bad habits is fine, but *good* practices must replace them. The Scriptures tell us what we should do as well as what we should not do. Righteousness is demonstrated by active good works as much as by abstinence from wickedness. Christianity is not neutrality; it is taking a stand for positive convictions, acting rightly toward God and toward all of our neighbors. "Anyone, then, who knows the good he ought to do and doesn't do it, sins" (James 4:17).

—R. W. B.

CONCLUSION

Once Isaiah had been confronted by God and purged of his sins, he was ready to be used of God. Thus prepared, he did not hesitate when God asked for a volunteer. He did not even raise any questions about the kind of service God was calling him to. Then when God began to explain to him that his mission was to carry a message of judgment to his people, a message the people would reject, he did not begin to make excuses or try to back out of his commitment.

Every day God throws out similar invitations to us. He challenges us when we first become Christians. We are not called into a life of ease but to a life of service. At that point we may not be adequately prepared to serve, and so he calls us to study and prepare ourselves so that we can serve more effectively.

This lesson gives us an opportunity to examine our lives to see how we are responding to God's call to cleansing and to service. Some need to be challenged to make that initial commitment to serve. Others, already serving faithfully, need to be challenged to step out and prepare themselves so that they can serve even more effectively.

In either situation, today's Scripture makes it clear that cleansing must precede commitment. Without that cleansing, our service will become exactly like that of the Israelites whom Isaiah condemned—empty and hypocritical, a kind of service that wearies God.

Discovery Learning

This page contains an alternate lesson plan emphasizing learning activities. Classes desiring such student involvement will find these suggestions helpful. The next page is a reproducible activity page to further enhance discovery learning.

LEARNING GOALS

In this session your students will do the following:

1. Grasp that God is holy.

2. Explain a connection between worshiping God, seeking cleansing from God, and being committed to God's calling to mission.

3. Determine to be people who are saturated with worshiping a holy God.

INTO THE LESSON

Begin by asking your class to sing the hymn, "Holy, Holy, Holy." Have hymnals available for the class to sing all four stanzas.

After singing, lead the class to discuss these questions:

1. What does it mean that God is holy?

2. How important do you think God's holiness is to Christians today?

INTO THE WORD

Lead into the Bible study by presenting a brief background of Isaiah, using information in the "Introduction" to the commentary on pages 417 and 418.

Then point out that God's holiness has two primary aspects. First, God is holy in that he is separate and exalted above everything else. Nothing can compare to him. Second, God is holy in a moral sense. That means that he is separate from sin or error or flaw.

Everything God is and does is holy. His love is a holy love. His wrath is a holy wrath. His wisdom is a holy wisdom. Nothing in God and nothing he does is unholy.

Have your class form at least three groups of not more than six. Give each group one of the assignments below. (If you have more than three groups, give duplicate assignments as needed.) Allow about twenty-five minutes for discussion.

ASSIGNMENT ONE

Focus on worship as a response to God's holiness. Read Isaiah 6:1-8. Then discuss these questions:

1. How is God's holiness shown in verses 1-4?

2. What in this passage suggests that worshiping God is serious business?

3. Compare Isaiah 6:1-8 with Revelation 4:1-11; Isaiah 57:15; and Psalm 96:9. Based on these passages, what do you learn about God's holiness? What do you learn about how to worship?

4. God is holy. Based on your study, what difference should that make in our lives?

ASSIGNMENT TWO

Focus on personal cleansing as a response to God's holiness. Read Isaiah 6:1-8 and discuss these questions:

1. What convicted Isaiah of his uncleanness?

2. How did he react to his uncleanness?

3. How was he symbolically cleansed?

4. Compare Isaiah 6:1-8 with Psalm 51:1-4, 10-17; Hebrews 10:19-22; and James 4:7-10. According to these passages, how are we cleansed? What role does worship play in cleansing us?

5. God is holy. Based on your study, what difference should that make in our lives?

ASSIGNMENT THREE

Focus on participation in God's mission as a response to his holiness. Read Isaiah 6:1-8. Then discuss:

1. To what mission did God call Isaiah?

2. How may the following have contributed to Isaiah's willingness to accept God's mission?

• Seeing God in his holiness

• Coming to grips with his own uncleanness

• Having his sins taken away

3. Being involved in God's mission is a natural companion of true worship of God. How do Isaiah 6:1-8; Matthew 28:16-20; and Acts 13:1-4 support that statement?

4. God is holy. Based on your study, what difference should that make in our lives?

After groups have completed their study, bring them together and let each group report. (If time is short, have each group report just its final answer.)

INTO LIFE

Conclude by reading Isaiah 6:1-8 and Revelation 4:1-11. Have students sing "Holy, Holy, Holy" again, very meditatively. Then ask them to pray silently about how they can grow in worship.

OPTION

Use the reproducible page that follows. Use "Worship That Is Not Worthy" for your Bible study ("Into the Word") and "Worship That Pleases God" for application ("Into Life"). Close with prayer, thanking God for revealing himself to you in his Word.

Worship That Is Not Worthy

Isaiah condemned the people for participating in evil practices and allowing injustice while continuing their ritual forms of worship. The problem was not in the rituals of worship, but in the hearts of the people. Read the following passages from the prophets and, in the space provided, indicate in each instance what it was about the worship of the people of both Israel and Judah that was unacceptable to God.

Isaiah 1:12-17 _____

_____

Isaiah 66:3, 4 _____

_____

Jeremiah 7:21-26 _____

_____

Hosea 6:6 _____

_____

Amos 5:21-24 _____

_____

Micah 6:6-8 _____

_____

Worship That Pleases God

Now read Colossians 3:1-17 and describe how worship that is pleasing to God is a natural result of holy living.

Too many times when we talk of worship, our focus is on the form or style. We lose sight of its holy object. Someone has said that we have nothing to gain by scrutinizing worship but we have much to gain by gazing upon the Lord. What would you change about your worship services that would allow you to focus more on the Lord himself?

Read Psalm 27:8 and 17:15 and meditate on God. Then spend some time in prayer thanking the Lord for revealing himself to you in his Word.

WHEN A NATION IS IN DANGER

LESSON 11

WHY TEACH THIS LESSON?

We live in troubling times. National security does not seem to be at stake as it did during the cold war, but certainly we have concerns about terrorist attacks and other isolated incidents. Even more, however, we are troubled by internal problems. Crime, drugs, and gangs plague our cities. Moral decay all around us threatens the very fiber of our nation. These issues are every bit as disconcerting as the idea of a growing Soviet nuisance seemed thirty years ago.

The adults in your class—especially parents and grandparents—think about these issues often. What is the solution? Where can they find refuge? How can they protect their children? Today's lesson provides answers. We may be tempted to find human solutions—legislation, secular counselors, "better" schools. These, in fact, may be necessary, just as a doctor sometimes must treat the symptoms before he can treat the cause of a disease. Still, the real solution is spiritual. If we stop at treating the symptoms, the disease is sure to return.

"Immanuel," God with us. That's the answer. Encourage your class to draw their strength from him.

INTRODUCTION

A. HE HOLDS THE FUTURE

A train filled with vacationers lost its brakes as it came down a long mountain grade. The passengers at first were not aware of any problem, but soon the increasing speed showed that something was wrong. Some began to scream and others to cry as they realized the danger. During all the noise and commotion, one little lad sat calmly, apparently quite unaware of the danger. Ahead was an especially sharp curve, and those who knew about it began to cry out all the louder. But then the train slowed and made the turn safely.

After the crisis had passed, a lady asked the boy, "Weren't you afraid the train was going to wreck?"

"No, ma'am, I wasn't afraid," he replied.

"But the train could have wrecked and all of us could have been killed," said the lady.

"No, ma'am, the train wasn't going to wreck. My daddy's the engineer, and he can take care of everything." This lad could view the future with calm assurance because he knew who was in charge.

When Isaiah came to visit King Ahaz, the king was as frightened as the tourists on that train, and for good reason. Aram (Syria) and Israel were about to gang up on him, and he knew that Judah could never withstand their onslaught. Isaiah assured him that Judah would be saved from these two enemies, but Ahaz still was fearful. He refused even to ask for a sign that would give him assurance. Isaiah gave him a sign anyway, because he knew the future; and more importantly, he knew who was in charge of the future.

DEVOTIONAL READING:
PSALM 125:1-5

LESSON SCRIPTURE:
ISAIAH 7; 2 KINGS 16

PRINTED TEXT:
ISAIAH 7:2-6, 10-17

LESSON AIMS

As a result of studying this lesson, each student should:

1. Understand the political situation in the time of King Ahaz.

2. Appreciate Isaiah's courage in criticizing the king.

3. Trust in God rather than in political and military alliances.

4. Be able to share his or her faith that God controls history.

Aug
13

KEY VERSE:

Be careful, keep calm and don't be afraid.   —Isaiah 7:4

LESSON 11 NOTES

Visual 11 shows an archeological rubbing depicting Pharaoh Thutmosis III in a chariot. Quoting Psalm 20:7, it illustrates Isaiah's message to Ahaz, to trust God and not in an army or her chariots. Ironically, Thutmosis III may well be the Pharaoh of the Exodus, the last king to enslave the Israelites. Now Ahaz was inviting a new king to enslave God's people.

Many of us today face the future with concern and fear. Unfortunately, we have no modern-day Isaiahs to reassure us. But even if we don't know what the future holds, at least we know who holds the future, and that ought to bring assurance enough.

B. LESSON BACKGROUND

Last week's lesson introduced us to Isaiah and his dramatic call to the prophetic ministry. Things did not go well for Judah after that call. King Uzziah was succeeded by his son, Jotham. Jotham tried to serve Jehovah; "the people, however, continued their corrupt practices" (2 Chronicles 27:1, 2). Also, the nation was threatened by the rising Assyrian power to the north. Jotham died about 732 B.C., leaving the throne to his son, Ahaz, who soon proved to be a bad king. Aram and Israel wanted him to join them in a coalition against Assyria. When he refused, they turned on him and sought to depose him. Ahaz knew little Judah did not have the strength to fend them off, and he became quite fearful. It was at this point that Isaiah came to him with reassuring words from Jehovah.

I. ISAIAH REASSURES AHAZ (ISAIAH 7:2-6)

A. AHAZ AND THE PEOPLE TROUBLED (V. 2)

2. Now the house of David was told, "Aram has allied itself with Ephraim"; so the hearts of Ahaz and his people were shaken, as the trees of the forest are shaken by the wind.

The *house of David* included King Ahaz, who "did not do what was right in the eyes of the Lord." Among other sins, he made "cast idols for worshiping the Baals," offered incense to pagan gods, and even "sacrificed his sons in the fire" (2 Chronicles 28:1-3). As a result of these sins, he was delivered into the hands of Syria and then Israel, both of whom defeated his troops with great slaughter. Judah was so seriously weakened by these defeats that she was easy prey for the Philistines and the Edomites (2 Chronicles 28:5-19)

Now the news that frightened Ahaz was that *Aram* and *Ephraim,* that is, Syria and Israel, were coming again. They had joined forces to attack Jerusalem, depose Ahaz, and install a king who would join them in the struggle against Assyria. Ahaz and his people were so frightened that their hearts were shaking like trees in the wind.

B. ISAIAH SENT TO MEET AHAZ (V. 3)

3. Then the LORD said to Isaiah, "Go out, you and your son Shear-Jashub, to meet Ahaz at the end of the aqueduct of the Upper Pool, on the road to the Washerman's Field.

At this critical moment God spoke to Isaiah, sending him to meet the king. Accompanying Isaiah was his son whose unusual name meant "a remnant will return." This was seen as a message of hope: at least some of the people would survive the coming crisis.

Ahaz was out examining the defenses of the city when Isaiah found him. Probably he was hoping to protect Jerusalem's water supply when the city was besieged.

C. ISAIAH ENCOURAGES AHAZ (V. 4)

4. "Say to him, 'Be careful, keep calm and don't be afraid. Do not lose heart because of these two smoldering stubs of firewood—because of the fierce anger of Rezin and Aram and of the son of Remaliah.

Isaiah's message to the king was to be calm in the face of this threat. If he would put his trust in God, he would have nothing to fear. Trusting God was not easy for

Ahaz. Already he had suffered at the hands of Syria and Israel, sent by God to punish him for his evil ways. He had not repented, but had continued in his wickedness. In sending Isaiah, God was giving him another chance. *Rezin* was the king of Syria, and *the son of Remaliah* was Pekah, who had murdered his predecessor to become the king of Israel. These two firebrands need not be feared; they were only smoking embers about to be extinguished.

"I SHALL NOT BE MOVED"

Ship travel is the ultimate luxury. Thirty years ago, a transatlantic crossing took a full week—seven days of leisure, only occasionally interrupted by rough waters. Our tour director organized a passenger talent show, so four of us formed a quartet. We sang in the ship's theater, just in front of a stage curtain. We happened to be in the midst of a storm, and the curtain was visibly swinging and swaying with the pitch and roll of the vessel. Our song selection was appropriate: "I Shall Not Be Moved."

King Ahaz needed the message of that song. The refrain says, "Just like a tree that's planted by the waters, I shall not be moved." The hearts of Ahaz and Judah were "*moved . . . as the trees of the wood are moved* with the wind" (Isaiah 7:2, *King James Version*). But Isaiah communicated God's encouragement: "Keep calm and don't be afraid." The winds of war are disturbing, but not always destructive.

Storms of fear and trouble can bend our branches, but never uproot our faith if we plant it by the living water Jesus gives. There our roots grow deep and strong. We continue to produce fruit of the Spirit, never withering and always prospering (Psalm 1:3). We shall not be moved!

—R. W. B.

D. JUDAH'S ENEMIES' PLANS (vv. 5, 6)

5, 6. "'Aram, Ephraim and Remaliah's son have plotted your ruin, saying, "Let us invade Judah; let us tear it apart and divide it among ourselves, and make the son of Tabeel king over it."'"

The earlier defeat of Judah by Syria and Israel gave Ahaz good reason to fear another attack. In that first victory the two allies had not been able to take Jerusalem, but now they seemed determined to breach the wall and take the city. Then their plan was to depose Ahaz and replace him with the *son of Tabeel*, who would cooperate with them. We know nothing more about this man.

II. THE LORD SPEAKS TO AHAZ (ISAIAH 7:10-13)

A. AHAZ TOLD TO ASK FOR A SIGN (vv. 10, 11)

10, 11. Again the LORD spoke to Ahaz, "Ask the LORD your God for a sign, whether in the deepest depths or in the highest heights."

God did not speak to Ahaz directly, but through his prophet, Isaiah. He had already told Ahaz that the coalition against him would fail (vv. 7-9), but the king was not willing to trust God's assurance. Perhaps a few days or even weeks elapsed between verses 7-9 and verses 10 and 11. Since Ahaz had rejected the first message, Isaiah returned, this time encouraging him to ask for a sign that the message was true. Sometimes asking for a sign can be wrong. For example, the Pharisees asked Jesus for a sign, but he rejected their request because he knew they had hardened their hearts against believing in him (Matthew 12:38, 39). A dozen signs wouldn't have changed their minds. On the other hand, when Gideon asked for a sign for reassurance, God answered his request because he knew that Gideon's heart was right (Judges 6:36-40).

Ahaz was given a wide choice of possible signs. He could ask for something from the depths or something from the heights. Obviously, anything between

WHAT DO YOU THINK?

Isaiah took God's message to a government official. In that, he represents many of us who wish our government leaders would hear our input about values and morality. What do you think a Christian can do today to influence the decision makers in our nation's capital? In state government? In local government?

WHAT DO YOU THINK?

God's signs are not always miraculous. Jesus' birth from a virgin certainly was a tremendous miracle, a sign that he is truly the Son of God. But many signs are not miracles. Circumcision was a sign of God's covenant with Abraham (Genesis 17:11). The Sabbath also was a sign of the covenant (Exodus 31:12, 13). Today, the lives of Christians are signs to our generation that God is still at work in the world (1 Peter 2:12). If an unbeliever followed the "sign" of your life this past week, what direction would he or she be heading? How does thinking of yourself as a sign to unbelievers affect your decisions about what to do?

would be equally appropriate. The signs that God gives are not always miraculous, but in this situation he seemed ready to offer a miraculous sign.

B. AHAZ REFUSES TO ASK (VV. 12, 13)

12, 13. But Ahaz said, "I will not ask; I will not put the Lord to the test."

Then Isaiah said, "Hear now, you house of David! Is it not enough to try the patience of men? Will you try the patience of my God also?

Ahaz refused to ask because he had decided to seek help from Assyria instead of God. Trying to appear pious, he said asking a sign would be tempting God, testing him. That was forbidden (Deuteronomy 6:16). Of course, Ahaz should have trusted God without a sign; but it would not be wrong to ask for a sign when God invited him to do so.

The Lord's reply was addressed to the *house of David:* not only Ahaz, but his whole family, even future generations of that family. Isaiah's patience was about exhausted. He had grown weary of Ahaz's arrogance and obstinacy, and he made it clear that even God was getting tired of it.

I.D.

Most of us have become accustomed to showing proof of personal identity every time we write a check. We are surprised when it is not required. I have been patronizing the same dry cleaners for fifteen years, and they still insist on seeing my driver's license when I write a check. It's routine; obviously a store policy with no exceptions.

Business loss due to bad checks has made I.D. proof a necessity in our corrupt society. But Ahaz should have trusted God with or without a sign, and so should we. Over the centuries, Jehovah has established unimpeachable credibility with his people. Jesus condemned some who demanded evidence of God's presence and power: "A wicked and adulterous generation asks for a miraculous sign" (Matthew 12:39).

Some Christians still "put out a fleece," as Gideon did (Judges 6:36-40), to determine God's will, to see if God's guidance is really his. It is like asking the King of the universe for I.D., proof of identity and integrity. Isaiah would chide, "Will you try the patience of my God also?" And he would exhort, "Trust in the Lord forever" (Isaiah 26:4). The only I.D. God needs is, "I am who I am" (Exodus 3:14).

—R. W. B.

III. THE SIGN TO BE GIVEN (ISAIAH 7:14-17)

A. A VIRGIN SHALL BEAR A SON (VV. 14, 15)

14. Therefore the Lord himself will give you a sign: The virgin will be with child and will give birth to a son, and will call him Immanuel.

This verse has sparked a great deal of controversy. Space in this book does not allow a discussion of the arguments, and neither does time in a Sunday school session. We shall try merely to state the two main opinions as briefly as possible.

Opinion one: This birth was to be a sign to Ahaz. Therefore it must occur during his lifetime. The Hebrew word translated *virgin* may mean a young woman who is not a virgin. Isaiah was saying that some young woman known to Ahaz would soon conceive, bear a son, and name him Immanuel. However, in the same words Isaiah was also foretelling the virgin birth of Jesus. This is clear in Matthew 1:18-23.

Opinion two: The word translated *virgin* does mean virgin. This is shown by the quotation of it in Matthew 1:18-23. Verse 13 of our text shows that Isaiah turned from Ahaz to address the house of David. The virgin birth was not to be a sign to Ahaz, but to the house of David seven hundred years later. The prophecy of Isaiah 7:14 is fulfilled only in Jesus. No one else has been born of a virgin; no one else can so fittingly be called Immanuel, God with us.

15. He will eat curds and honey when he knows enough to reject the wrong and choose the right.

If we choose the first of the two opinions cited above, of course, we take verse 15 to mean the child soon to be born. Armies of Syria and Israel would steal the harvests in Judah so there would be no bread, but a farmer could hide a cow or a few goats to provide milk and *curds* (cottage cheese) for his son. Honey would be taken from wild bees.

If we think verse 14 refers to Jesus only, verse 15 is not so simple. Possibly it means Jesus would live on simple fare because he would be in a poor family. Possibly only verse 14 refers to Jesus, while verse 15 refers to a child of Ahaz's time, but not some particular child. *He will eat curds and honey*: any child of that time in Judah will have that limited diet.

B. JUDAH WILL BE SPARED (vv. 16, 17)

16. But before the boy knows enough to reject the wrong and choose the right, the land of the two kings you dread will be laid waste.

Now we come to the reassuring message for King Ahaz, and it is the same whether we have been thinking of a particular child soon to be born, or just any child born in those days, or of Jesus to be born much later. The message is that the kings of Israel and Syria will both be removed. That will happen soon, within the few years required for a child to grow old enough to know good from bad.

17. The LORD will bring on you and on your people and on the house of your father a time unlike any since Ephraim broke away from Judah—he will bring the king of Assyria."

Even though Ahaz refused to trust and obey, the Lord was going to save Judah from Israel and Syria. That is the promise of verse 17. But there was worse to come. The days ahead would be more troublesome than any time had been in the two hundred years since the big kingdom of Solomon was divided into *Ephraim*, or Israel, in the north, and *Judah* in the south. That trouble would come with *the king of Assyria*, from whom Ahaz was asking help.

That was exactly what happened. Ahaz went on with his plan to seek help from Assyria. He paid heavily for help, but got none (2 Chronicles 28:16-21). And a few decades later, the Assyrians invaded Judah with terrible results (2 Kings 18:13-16). But again the Lord came to the rescue (2 Kings 19:35, 36).

GOOD NEWS/BAD NEWS

We are all familiar with "good news/bad news" jokes. The question incorporated in the joke usually is, "Which do you want to hear first, the good news or the bad news?"

Quite often, good news is tainted by negative implications. We are somewhat conditioned, it seems, when we hear announcements that make us glad, to listen for "the other shoe to drop." Phrases such as, *"on the other hand,"* or *"the other side of the coin"* or even a simple *"but"* are clues that not-so-good news will follow.

Prophets foretold both good and bad futures. Isaiah predicted for Ahaz that both Israel and Syria would soon lose their kings, and thus no longer be a threat to Judah. That was good news to Ahaz. With his next breath, however, Isaiah warned that the king of Assyria would bring incomparable grief to Judah, due to their sin and rebellion.

I prefer to receive my good news last, as in Romans 6:23: "For the wages of sin is death; *but the gift of God is eternal life in Jesus Christ our Lord.*"

—R. W. B.

WHAT DO YOU THINK?

Ahaz had counted on Assyria for help. Isaiah said Assyria would become the worst thing to happen to Judah since the division of the kingdom! Have you also found the object of misguided affection sometimes to be its own punishment? If so describe the event. What have you learned from the experience?

OPTION

The reproducible activity page (page 432) will help your students apply the message of today's lesson.

PRAYER

Almighty God, we come before you recognizing that in your hands you hold the destinies of men and of nations. We feel the need of your presence when life comes crashing down around us; but may we also realize our needs when all seems to be going well. Show us how to understand and accept the guidance you give us through the Scriptures. Let us find assurance in the words of our Savior that he will be with us to the end of time. In the name of Immanuel we pray. Amen.

THOUGHT TO REMEMBER

Immanuel, God with us.

DAILY BIBLE READINGS

Monday, Aug. 7—*Isaiah Advises Ahaz to Trust God (Isaiah 7:1-9)*

Tuesday, Aug. 8—*A Sign for the Fearful King (Isaiah 7:10-17)*

Wednesday, Aug. 9—*Ahaz's Actions Will Bring Hard Times (Isaiah 7:18-25)*

Thursday, Aug. 10—*Ahaz Turns Away From God (2 Kings 16:1-6)*

Friday, Aug. 11—*Ahaz Buys Help From Assyria (2 Kings 16: 7-11)*

Saturday, Aug. 12—*Ahaz's New Altar (2 Kings 16:12-18)*

Sunday, Aug. 13—*God Will Judge Unrighteousness (Psalm 75)*

CONCLUSION

A. GOD STILL SPEAKS

The same holy God who confronted Isaiah in the temple is seen in today's lesson confronting King Ahaz. Two aspects of this confrontation are different. First, in this confrontation God did not speak to Ahaz in a vision as he had spoken to Isaiah. Instead, he spoke through Isaiah. In the second place, Ahaz did not respond in the same way that Isaiah had. Isaiah was overwhelmed by the experience, readily confessing his own sinfulness and the sinfulness of the people. Once he was cleansed he was ready to serve God. On the other hand, Ahaz never acknowledged his sin and never experienced a cleansing, nor did he offer himself for service.

Not many of us feel as pious as Isaiah, nor do many of us believe we are as wicked as Ahaz. We certainly do not expect to experience a vision in which we are brought directly into the presence of Jehovah. Nor is it likely that we will be confronted by an inspired prophet like Isaiah. Yet we cannot escape being confronted regularly by God. That confrontation comes through his holy Word. As we read and study the Bible, we read of his standards that should govern our conduct, or we draw guidance from reading about a historical situation in which God intervened.

As we read the Bible reverently and expectantly, we find guidance for our lives. Most of us do not live on a heroic plane, nor are we great leaders whose decisions affect the lives of thousands. But whether we live in a king's palace or are homeless, God expects us to live in accordance with his will. Finding his will in our complicated times may be difficult, yet we must seek it diligently. Once we have found it, we must follow it courageously. A holy God can demand nothing less.

B. WE NEED AN ISAIAH

For many decades now we have suffered through tumultuous times both in our personal lives and as a nation. To protect the security of our nation, our leaders have resorted to huge expenditures for armaments and have entered numerous military alliances. We may debate about which decisions were wise, but we know for certain that they have not brought the security we hoped for.

In Ahaz's day, he made most of the decisions for his country. The citizens could do little more than try to live with these decisions. But it is different for us who live in a democracy. We choose our leaders and we have a hand in the decisions that they make. We must accept some of the responsibility for these decisions. Since we don't have an Isaiah to give us direction as we make decisions, let us learn to make them prayerfully, intelligently, and in the light of God's Word.

C. IMMANUEL

Immanuel! It is not likely that Isaiah understood the full implications of this name when he spoke to King Ahaz. Of course, he knew that it meant "God with us," and in a sense that was true in Isaiah's time. In spite of Ahaz's sinful behavior, God had not abandoned his people. He would deliver them from the threat of Judah's neighbors to the north.

Only as we read Matthew 1:20-23 do we begin to plumb the depth of meaning conveyed in Isaiah 7:14. This verse and other passages in Isaiah gave assurance that God in his own good time would intersect history in a new and dramatic fashion. In Isaiah's day God spoke through the prophets; but seven hundred years after Isaiah lived, God spoke with finality through his Son, who was born of a virgin. It is unfortunate that we seldom think of this except at Christmastime. We need to be reminded every day that God is still with us, that he will provide us light for our darkest times.

Discovery Learning

This page contains an alternate lesson plan emphasizing learning activities. Classes desiring such student involvement will find these suggestions helpful. The next page is a reproducible activity page to further enhance discovery learning.

LEARNING GOALS

In this lesson your students will do the following:

1. Explore the issue of reliance on human resources vs. reliance on God.

2. Pinpoint their own tendencies to rely on human resources instead of God.

3. Seek to rely on God for security.

INTO THE LESSON

Bring a number of magazines to class. As the class session begins, ask students to form groups of four. In these groups they are to browse through magazines and cut out pictures that suggest reliance upon something other than God. For example, they might select a picture of someone drinking alcohol, or someone with a fancy new car. As they select pictures they should discuss how each picture symbolizes reliance upon a human resource.

Allow about five minutes. Then bring the groups together and ask volunteers to display their pictures and briefly explain what they represent.

Lead into the Scripture study by saying, "The Bible instructs us to trust in God, not human resources. In fact, many of the Scriptures are focused upon this very issue. In our lesson today we will observe a king who was challenged to trust God, not military might."

OPTION

Write the following sentences on the chalkboard:

Sometimes it is easier for people to trust in _____ than to trust in God.

Sometimes it is easier for nations to trust in _____ than to trust in God.

Sometimes it is easier for churches to trust in _____ than to trust in God.

Have your class form groups of three or four. Provide paper and pencils for each. Ask one third of the groups to work on the first sentence, one third to work on the second, and one third to work on the third. Ask each group to think of three to five ways to fill in the blank in its sentence.

Allow about two minutes. Then ask each group to report its answers to the rest of the class.

INTO THE WORD

Ask a volunteer to read Isaiah 7:2-17. Explain the background of this passage, using the commentary in this book. Then have the students continue in their groups to discuss these questions:

1. What was Ahaz's predicament?

2. How did the king and people of Judah react to the predicament?

3. What encouragement did Isaiah bring to Ahaz?

4. How did God emphasize that he is in control?

5. Did Ahaz put his trust in God? What evidence supports your answer?

6. How do these two passages relate to Ahaz's situation: Psalm 20:7 and 33:17, 18?

OPTION

Ask a volunteer to read Isaiah 7:2-17. Then present a brief lecture on the background and on the passage. The lecture should take no more than ten minutes and should cover the main ideas of the text.

Then have the class members meet again in the groups they formed earlier. In their groups they are to write a poem about relying on the Lord, based upon Isaiah 7:2-17. Students need not worry about the quality of the poem. They can be serious or humorous. They may or may not want their poems to rhyme.

Allow fifteen to twenty minutes for the groups to work on their poetry. Then ask each group to present its poem to the rest of the class.

INTO LIFE

Lead your class in discussing these questions:

1. What is the difference between *using* a human resource and *relying upon* it?

2. What clues can we look for to tell us if we are relying on human resources instead of on God?

3. How does God teach us to rely upon him instead of his resources?

4. What are you personally tempted to rely upon instead of God?

Allow time for this final portion of the lesson. Write on the chalkboard the words of Zechariah 4:6, "'Not by might nor by power, but by my Spirit,' says the Lord Almighty." Point out that this verse teaches that God accomplishes his will, not through human strength or human efforts, but through his Holy Spirit.

Close your session by asking students to meet in their groups again and to pray that they will learn to rely upon God, as individuals and as a church.

A Lesson From Ahaz, Faithless King of Judah

Second Kings 16:1-20 (along with 2 Chronicles 28) tells of the reign of King Ahaz and provides the setting for the prophecy given in Isaiah 7. Israel and Syria had joined forces against Judah because they were under Assyria's control and wanted to rebel. By besieging Jerusalem, Israel and Syria hoped to force Judah to join their revolt. But the plan backfired when King Ahaz unexpectedly asked Assyria to come to his aid.

With this background in mind, read 2 Kings 16:8-18 and answer the following questions.

What did Ahaz reveal about the object of his faith when he took the gold and silver from the temple and paid it in tribute to the Assyrian king?

If Ahaz had put his faith in God, what do you think he would have done instead?

Think of a difficult time in your life (a serious conflict with another church member, the death of someone close you prayed for, the loss of a job, etc.). In what ways did your response to that difficult time reflect a search for other gods (a desire to put your trust in other people or things)?

In what ways did your response display a determined faith in God?

When the Heat Is On

The heat was on for Ahaz, and his faith quickly reached the boiling point and evaporated. Let the thermometer at the right to indicate a measuring device for your faith. List the items below on the "temperature" scale: the most difficult item should be at the top and the easiest at the bottom. Arrange the others relatively in between. Then color the thermometer to indicate the "temperature" you think your faith can withstand.

Martyrdom
Loss of spouse (death)
Loss of spouse (divorce)
Loss of entire family
Death of a child
Sexual temptation
Rejection of Christian values by one of your children

Loss of material wealth
Dramatic increase in material wealth
Loss of job
Promotion to top position
Unanswered prayer
Being wronged by a fellow church member
Being convicted of a crime you did not commit

What can you do to raise the boiling point of your faith?

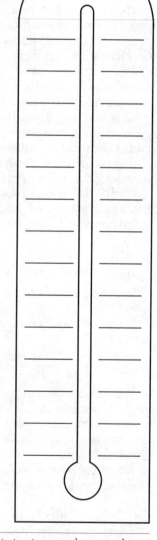

A Nation Turns From God
Unit 3: The Judgment Arrives
(Lessons 10-13)

JUDGMENT COMES ON ISRAEL

LESSON 12

WHY TEACH THIS LESSON?

George Orwell's *1984* made some frightening predictions for our time. Fortunately, most of the predictions did not materialize. But at least one of them did. He described a method of communication called "newspeak." Essentially, newspeak enabled oppressive government officials to say one thing and mean another.

We hear the same thing today. By changing the terminology, bad things are made to sound good and good things bad. Who would have thought "virgin" would be a name to be shunned, or that the label "bad" would be coveted?

Let Isaiah's message speak to your students in "oldspeak." He will remind them that sin is still sin, and judgment is still judgment.

INTRODUCTION

A. WOE AND WHOA

Isaiah uses the word *woe* a number of times in today's lesson text. In each case he is pronouncing God's judgment on a particular sin of the people. In verse 8 he condemns their greed for real estate. In verse 11 he condemns their drunkenness. In verse 18 he speaks out against those who have allowed themselves to become enmeshed in sin. In verse 20 woe is pronounced upon those who set up their own standards of right and wrong. Their spiritual arrogance is denounced in verse 21. In verse 22 their indulgence in strong drink is again condemned.

Years ago when we still worked our farms with horses, we yelled the word *whoa* when we wanted them to stop. Horses that were well trained would stop immediately when they heard that command. When Isaiah condemned a particular sin of his people with a strong *woe*, he also intended to convey the idea of *whoa*, stop it. It's a pity that the Israelites were not as well trained as our horses.

B. LESSON BACKGROUND

Scholars differ about the exact date when the oracles that serve as today's lesson text were proclaimed. Some hold that they come early in Isaiah's ministry, before his call recorded in chapter 6. In this case the prophet was addressing the conditions that existed during the reign of Uzziah. It is plain that sin was rampant among the people even while that good king was promoting true worship and righteous living. If, on the other hand, these oracles were uttered after his special call, then they dealt with the conditions that occurred during the reign of Jotham or Ahaz, or somewhere after about 740 B.C.

In either event, it was a time of prosperity for Judah, perhaps the most prosperous time since the days of Solomon. Prosperity, unfortunately, breeds certain kinds of sins, and these were plainly evident in that society. But the international scene was soon to change. Assyria, under Tiglath-Pileser, regained the power it had lost and began to extend its influence over Syria, Israel, and Judah. Syria and Israel formed an alliance to resist Assyria and tried to force Judah to join the alliance. When King Ahaz refused, the two threatened to replace him with a puppet of their own choosing. In desperation, Ahaz appealed to Tiglath-Pileser for help. As a result, he was forced to pay tribute to the Assyrians.

DEVOTIONAL READING:
PSALM 2

LESSON SCRIPTURE:
ISAIAH 9:8—10:4; 5:1-30

PRINTED TEXT:
ISAIAH 5:8-12, 18-23

LESSON AIMS

As a result of studying this lesson, each student should:

1. Understand the social and political situation in the time of Isaiah.

2. Recognize that some of the moral evils that Isaiah dealt with are similar to those that we must deal with today.

3. Appreciate the dangers of strong drink.

4. Be able to mention a specific way of applying the lesson to his or her own situation.

KEY VERSE:

Take your evil deeds out of my sight! Stop doing wrong, learn to do right! Seek justice, encourage the oppressed. Defend the cause of the fatherless, plead the case of the widow. —Isaiah 1:16, 17

Aug
20

LESSON 12 NOTES

All of this was still on the horizon when Isaiah addressed some of the serious evils of his nation. He clearly saw that moral decay in Judah was the reason for the disaster about to befall her. But it didn't have to happen. If they would only repent, this catastrophe could be avoided.

I. DANGER OF COVETOUSNESS (ISAIAH 5:8-10)

A. THE RESULTS OF GREED (V. 8)

8. Woe to you who add house to house and join field to field till no space is left and you live alone in the land.

Woe is a strong word. It is more than a slap on the wrist or an expression of mild disapproval. It suggests divine condemnation. Greed drove the rich to accumulate houses and land. Micah, writing near the same time, condemns the same sin (Micah 2:2). By joining *house to house* a rich man would acquire a whole row of houses along a street; and by laying *field to field* he would add land to what he already had. As a result, poor people were reduced to the level of impoverished peasants. The Mosaic law required that the title to land revert to the original owners in the jubilee year, but the rich had ways to subvert this law. A rich man attempted to *live alone in the land,* owning all the property he could see. In his greed he seized poor people's houses and lands with injustice and violence (Micah 2:2). His own gain was more important to him than the very livelihood of the poor people.

B. THE PUNISHMENT OF GREED (VV. 9, 10)

9. The LORD Almighty has declared in my hearing: "Surely the great houses will become desolate, the fine mansions left without occupants.

Isaiah made sure the greedy ones would understand that the message of doom came from the *Lord of hosts* and was not the prophet's own idea. God spoke in his ear in such a way that he could not misunderstand. The rich would not be able to enjoy their ill-gotten gain. The houses would be left desolate, the inhabitants gone. Apparently this desolation would result from the war that was about to fall upon the land.

10. "A ten-acre vineyard will produce only a bath of wine, a homer of seed only an ephah of grain."

An acre was the amount of land a yoke of oxen could plow in a day. A *bath* probably was about five and a half gallons. Such a pitiful yield from such a large vineyard would indicate an almost total crop failure. The exact volume of a *homer* is disputed, with estimates ranging from six and a half bushels to about fourteen bushels. An *ephah* was a tenth of a homer. The desolation of the land was obvious when a farmer got back only a tenth of the seed he planted. Whether these crop failures came as a result of bad weather, ravenous insects, or invading armies, Isaiah does not tell us. The point that Isaiah was making was that God would see to it that greed did not pay.

II. DANGER OF STRONG DRINK (ISAIAH 5:11, 12)

A. STRONG DRINK INFLAMES (V. 11)

11. Woe to those who rise early in the morning to run after their drinks, who stay up late at night till they are inflamed with wine.

The second woe is pronounced upon those who drink to an excess. Their pursuit of strong drink was carried out with all the enthusiasm and energy generally reserved for more worthy causes. *Those who rise early in the morning* ordinarily do so because they are hard-working, industrious people. These did so because they were hard-drinking. Further, their drinking bouts continued all day long and into the

---

WHAT DO YOU THINK?

Isaiah warned about the results of a degenerate life-style supported by greed and injustice. These will still bring disaster in our time as well. God has built in certain laws of cause and effect, and with all our sophistication we cannot evade them. Gravity pulls downward, fire destroys, and greed also has results that we cannot escape.

Are rich people more affected by these effects? If so, why and how? To what extent are "poor" people affected?

By the standards of Isaiah's day, virtually every one of us is rich beyond measure. How should that affect our appreciation and application of his message?

OPTION

The reproducible activity page at the end of this lesson (page 440) will lead your students through a Bible study of this passage to discover six sins condemned by Isaiah, as well as New Testament solutions to these sins.

evening. Obviously, these people had to be rich to be able to engage in such pro-longed debaucheries. Such behavior on the part of those who have to work daily for a living would soon leave them in poverty.

WHY ASK WHY?

Isn't it surprising that society has become so smoke-conscious? Public smoking seems on its way to being banned everywhere—even in baseball stadiums! Thousands give up cigarettes each year, and thousands more push for anti-smoking statutes to reduce the hazard of inhaling "second-hand smoke." Frankly, it is surprising to see so many making such good sense!

Now, a logical question occurs to thinking people: Why isn't similar good sense being demonstrated in regard to alcohol? Why no warning labels on beer cans and liquor bottles? Has no one determined that imbibing alcohol can be dangerous to one's health?

Obviously, distillers and brewers have a strong lobby in Washington. And media marketers are reluctant to forfeit the billions of dollars of advertising revenue realized from beer and wine ads. But there's another bottom line to this question. *People like to drink.* They like to depress their inhibitions and dull their pain. Never mind the jeopardy to health, home, jobs, relationships, and eternal salvation. If inebriation feels good, drinkers will consider those risks worth taking, if they give it any consideration at all. Jeremiah was right: "The heart is deceitful . . . and beyond cure" (Jeremiah 17:9).

—R. W. B.

B. STRONG DRINK DOMINATES FEASTS (V. 12)

12. They have harps and lyres at their banquets, tambourines and flutes and wine, but they have no regard for the deeds of the LORD, no respect for the work of his hands.

The strains of various musical instruments enhanced their drunken revelries. The variety of instruments used gives an indication of their wealth. There is a good deal of confusion about musical instruments mentioned in the Old Testament. The *harps and lyres* mentioned in this verse are probably very similar, much like the modern lyre, a stringed instrument that can be held in the hand. The *tambourine* was a small percussion instrument. The *flute* was probably a wind instrument like the modern flute. The impression one gets is that professional musicians were employed to perform at these feasts, a further indication that only the rich were involved in these drinking orgies. Whether other entertainers were present we are not told. Perhaps these feasts were not as sophisticated as our modern night clubs, but the parallels are obvious.

These people, consumed by their drinking, gave little thought to the *deeds of the Lord.* They were not interested in how God had called the Israelites to become his own people and how he had blessed them across the centuries. Assuredly, they gave no thought to how their own wealth came from him. The wine had dulled their senses so they could not discern God's work in history, and it had destroyed their gratitude for all he had done for them. Isaiah's message still confronts a similar problem in our society today.

III. DANGERS OF SIN (ISAIAH 5:18-23)

A. SIN BECOMES A BURDEN (V. 18)

Verses 13-17 announce the judgment that is about to fall upon those who have blatantly ignored God. Verse 13 tells of the coming captivity of the people. The tragedy is that many of those who would suffer as a result of this captivity were innocent of the excesses that brought it on. But that is often the case. One of the

WHAT DO YOU THINK?

From Isaiah's condemnation, one might think being rich is itself a sin. Jesus' warning might be cited to support the idea: "It is easier for a camel to go through the eye of a needle than for a rich man to enter the kingdom of God" (Matthew 19:24).

What do you think? Is it possible to be both rich and godly? Why are so many "good" people corrupted by wealth? How can one avoid such corruption?

WHAT DO YOU THINK?

The costs of alcohol consumption are high—purchase costs, health-care costs, time lost from work, families disrupted, lives lost by accidents and violence. Why do you think it remains so popular and so protected from any moral criticism? What appeals can be made to people who try to justify drinking to see the harm it causes?

HOW TO SAY IT
Ahaz. AY-haz.
Assyria. Uh-SEAR-ee-uh.
Assyrians. Uh-SEAR-ee-unz.
Isaiah. Eye-ZAY-uh.
Jotham. JO-tham.
Tiglath-Pileser. TIG-lath-Pih-LEE-zer.
Uzziah. Uh-ZYE-uh.

Visual 12 illustrates the message of verse 20.

terrible aspects of sin is that the innocent often have to suffer along with the guilty. We see this in the current AIDS epidemic. Little children and others who have not been guilty of violating God's laws have to suffer along with the guilty.

Verse 14 states that the grave will be enlarged, indicating that multitudes will die as a result of this captivity. Verses 15 and 16 inform us that the proud will be humbled and that God will be exalted. In verse 17 we learn that the land will become desolate, fit only for a pasture, where the "lambs will feed among the ruins of the rich."

18. Woe to those who draw sin along with cords of deceit, and wickedness as with cart ropes.

In this third woe, Isaiah uses a striking figure to make his point. The exact meaning of this figure may not be clear, but the point the prophet is making is evident enough. He indicates that the people had willfully engaged in a sinful life-style. With a thrust of sarcasm, he points out that their sins had become a heavy cart that they unwittingly pulled behind them. They had willingly accepted the yoke of sin without looking back to see what they were hitched to. Truly, "the way of the unfaithful is hard" (Proverbs 13:15).

B. Sin Leads to Arrogance (v. 19)
19. . . . to those who say, "Let God hurry, let him hasten his work so we may see it. Let it approach, let the plan of the Holy One of Israel come, so we may know it."

Those who reject the word of the Lord often do so with brazen arrogance, or at least they put up a bold front that reflects a defiant attitude. In effect, they were saying, "OK, so God is at work in history. But right now we don't see any evidence of his work. Let him show us, and then we will believe." They remind us of Jesus' enemies who said, "Come down from the cross, if you are the Son of God" (Matthew 27:40). But unbelief was so deeply ingrained in their hearts that no demonstration, regardless of how dramatic it might be, would convince them.

This attitude is not that of blatant atheism. It is, rather, the attitude of persons who believe in a God who is so remote that he doesn't make any difference in their lives. These ancient skeptics have their modern counterparts. Surveys indicate that few people in our society boldly deny the existence of God. When asked, they may affirm that they believe in God, but then they proceed to live as if he didn't exist. At least they live that way until they face a crisis in their lives. That crisis came in ancient Judah, and we are foolish to suppose that we can forever avoid crises in our lives.

C. Sin Has Its Own Standards (vv. 20, 21)
20. Woe to those who call evil good and good evil, who put darkness for light and light for darkness, who put bitter for sweet and sweet for bitter.

When people who have known the will of God fall into sin, they experience a sense of guilt because they know they are doing wrong. Unwilling to mend their ways, they seek a means of relieving the irritation that a guilty conscience brings. One way to do this is to confuse the issue by changing definitions. If they can make bad look good, then the wrong they are doing appears to be right. Those who approve of homosexuality now refer to it as "an alternate life-style," as if changing terms will somehow change the way God looks at it. To avoid the burden of guilt that comes from destroying life still in the womb, some no longer talk about aborting babies. Rather, the procedure is merely a "termination of a pregnancy," and all sense of guilt is removed. Isaiah does not hesitate to pronounce a woe upon this moral sleight of hand.

CONFUSED VALUES

Thousands of babies are killed each day by abortion. In spite of God's clear prohibition of murder, this slaughter is considered by many to reflect a good "choice" by mothers with unwanted pregnancies. Condoms are freely distributed by some schools to protect sexually active students. Contrary to biblical standards of morality, this is viewed as a good approach to curbing teenage pregnancies and sexually transmitted diseases. Homosexuals are allowed to join our armed forces, and even the ministry of some churches. This is seen as a good interpretation of the "equal rights" guaranteed by the Constitution.

Prayer, Bible reading, and Christmas nativity scenes are banned from public schools in America, for such expressions of religion are viewed by some as politically wrong. Sexual abstinence and morality are not taught, because such lessons are considered by liberal educators to be socially inhibitory. Homemaking careers are viewed by feminists as less than fulfilling (at least), and a bad choice by modern women who,they say, should find "meaningful employment" outside the home instead.

This confused culture needs to hear the warning of Isaiah: "Woe to those who call evil good and good evil." Values are so confused today that many people have little idea of what is right and what is wrong. What will prevent God's wrath from being kindled against America, just as it was against Judah?

—R. W. B.

21. Woe to those who are wise in their own eyes and clever in their own sight.

Those who subvert God's laws often develop a proud complacency that blinds them to their moral condition. They set their own standards, and since they are able to meet these human standards, they feel quite comfortable. They proclaim woe to those who dare threaten their comfort. Such persons are likely to be labeled as "narrow-minded," "legalists," "bigots," or even "hypocrites." But that's not the way Isaiah sees it. His woe is reserved for the moral compromisers whose complacency ought to be disturbed.

Wisdom and prudence are often extolled in the Old Testament as virtues. The question is by what standard or by whose standard are wisdom and prudence determined. Some had created their own standards, and by these standards they appeared quite wise. Upon such persons Isaiah pronounces a forceful woe. One of Satan's tricks is to convince us that we are better than we really are, and we often fall for the bait. Self-deceit is a dangerous weakness, because when we are self-deceived, we stubbornly refuse to listen to advice from others.

D. SIN PERVERTS JUSTICE (VV. 22, 23)

22, 23. Woe to those who are heroes at drinking wine and champions at mixing drinks, who acquit the guilty for a bribe, but deny justice to the innocent.

This is the sixth of Isaiah's woes. At first glance it may seem that he is simply repeating the woe he had earlier pronounced against strong drink. The word here translated *heroes* was often used to describe those who had proven themselves outstanding in military combat. Here it is used in a less positive sense to describe those who were champions in drinking bouts.

They are singled out here for the prophet's condemnation, not just because they could drink everyone else under the table, but because their drinking led to serious injustices in society. They were guilty of using their positions in the courts to gain bribes, which in turn were spent on strong drink. It was bad enough to spend on strong drink the money one had earned by hard work. It was far worse to pervert justice in order to finance one's drinking habit. In the process the wicked were winning court decisions while the righteous were denied justice.

WHAT DO YOU THINK?

The liquor traffic is legal almost everywhere, and so is abortion. Gambling is becoming legal in more and more places, and even prostitution is legal in some. While we might understand the passion that led Carrie Nation to go into saloons and smash the furniture with a hatchet, or some anti-abortion activists to bomb abortion clinics, Christians are taught to live within the law (Romans 13:1-7). We cannot justify illegal violence against legal wrongs. But what can be done? What can individuals and churches do to make God's Word known on such matters and to curb the benefits accrued to people who "have no regard for the deeds of the Lord, no respect for the work of his hands"?

WHAT DO YOU THINK?

Stewardship is being faithful managers of whatever God has put in our charge. It encompasses all of life all through the year. We contribute a share of our incomes to the church because the church is Christ's body, doing his work in the world. But it is no less important to use the rest of our incomes in ways that he approves. "Where your treasure is, there your heart will be also" (Matthew 6:21).

How might such an understanding of stewardship have prevented the abuses in Isaiah's day? What do you think a true appreciation for stewardship would do for our own culture? How can you make a difference in a positive way in this regard?

PRAYER

Bountiful Father, we give you thanks for the many things you have entrusted to us. Help us to avoid the temptations of greed. We pray for those who have become trapped in the throes of alcohol and other drugs. Show us how to help them. Keep us from the same snares. In our Master's precious name we pray. Amen.

THOUGHT TO REMEMBER

"Wine is a mocker and beer a brawler; whosoever is led astray by them is not wise" (Proverbs 20:1).

DAILY BIBLE READINGS

Monday, Aug. 14—Punishment for Proud and Corrupt Leaders (Isaiah 9:8-17)

Tuesday, Aug. 15—Moral Decay and Injustice Are Judged (Isaiah 9:18—10:4)

Wednesday, Aug. 16—Israel and Judah as a Vineyard (Isaiah 5:1-7)

Thursday, Aug. 17—Judgment on Greed and Selfish Indulgence (Isaiah 5:8-12)

Friday, Aug. 18—God's Judgment Is Just (Isaiah 5:13-17)

Saturday, Aug. 19—Judgment on Arrogant Immorality (Isaiah 5:18-22)

Sunday, Aug. 20—Destruction Awaits the Wicked (Isaiah 5:24-30)

CONCLUSION

A. THE TIMES THEY ARE *NOT* A-CHANGIN'

Many things were different in Isaiah's day. Most of us would not feel comfortable about these differences. We take for granted so many of our physical comforts—heating and air conditioning, electric lights, a rich variety of plentiful foods, household conveniences. We enjoy our comfortable cars and the good highways on which they ride. And what about the electronic magic that makes communication so excellent and so easy?

Yet, in spite of these differences, some things haven't changed; or, if they have changed, it is for the worse. We speak of the excessive use of alcoholic beverages that in Isaiah's day inflamed the hearts of the imbibers and today still produces the same results. The situation in many respects is worse today. Alcoholic beverages are more readily available than they were twenty-seven hundred years ago. Further, our beverages are available with a much higher alcoholic content than that of ancient wine, resulting in much more potent drinks.

Our government spends billions of dollars a year fighting the so-called hard drugs—marijuana, heroin, cocaine. Yet alcohol creates more havoc in the form of broken homes, crime, ruined health, and death than all the hard drugs combined. The hard drugs we attempt to stamp out; alcohol we license and make legal. Obviously, our logic isn't any better than it was in Isaiah's day.

Even though the cost of alcohol is high, it has gained general acceptance in our society. The outcry against liquor that once sounded forth from our pulpits has largely been muted. Churches that once led the crusade against strong drink now champion other causes. The International Sunday School Lessons years ago designated one lesson a quarter as a temperance lesson. Of course many lessons, such as today's, still point out the dangers of strong drink, but the topic is no longer given specific emphasis each quarter. No doubt many factors have contributed to this change of emphasis, but certainly the advertising campaign carried on by the liquor interests has been one of these factors. Because alcoholic beverages have become so generally acceptable, Christians need to become more involved in warning against alcohol's dangers and providing help for those who have become its victims.

B. GREED, ANCIENT AND MODERN

The sin of greed is most pervasive. It ignores the boundaries of time, culture, and socio-economic classes. It engulfed the society of ancient Judah when Isaiah lived, and it has penetrated every level of our society. The prophet pronounced woe upon those who joined "house to house" and laid "field to field," thus gaining a real-estate monopoly. Isaiah did not condemn them because they were rich, but because they used this monopoly to oppress the poor.

We have seen similar things in our own times. The scandals that have rocked the savings and loan institutions and our banks came about because of greed. Junk bonds and stock market manipulations are other symptoms of the epidemic of greed that has swept across our land. We are bombarded continuously by advertisements that stimulate our desire for things and more things. So clever are these enticements that all of us are affected to some degree. Even if we do not succumb to these blandishments, we become more tolerant of them, muting the objections we ought to be raising against this blatant materialism.

God created a world that is rich in resources, resources he intends us to use and enjoy. But he intends us to use them wisely, frugally, and unselfishly. Only then can we experience the joy that comes from responsible stewardship of all these good things.

Discovery Learning

This page contains an alternate lesson plan emphasizing learning activities. Classes desiring such student involvement will find these suggestions helpful. The next page is a reproducible activity page to further enhance discovery learning.

LEARNING GOALS

Focus on leading your students to do the following through this session:

1. Identify sins for which God condemned his people in Isaiah 5.

2. Compare and contrast the positive and negative approaches we might take toward the sin of our world.

INTO THE LESSON

Ask two volunteers to participate in a role play, assuming a role and making up their conversation and activity spontaneously.

Give a copy of the following instructions to each of the volunteers:

The role play will involve two Christians discussing a radio preacher.

The first Christian complains that the preacher is too negative. He is always harping on sin. This person suggests that the preacher needs to take a more positive approach.

The second Christian disagrees. He believes society is under God's judgment and needs to be warned. And many Christians are lukewarm and need to be shaken from complacency.

Give both players about a minute to think through their roles. Then ask them to play it out. Allow about three minutes; then cut off the role play. Be sure to thank both players.

Ask the rest of the class, "Which points did you agree with the most?" Allow for discussion.

Relate this activity to the Bible study by saying, "A positive approach usually is welcome. That makes it difficult for us to understand why God was frequently negative in dealing with the sins of his people. Today we will consider another message from one of God's prophets, and it was a message of condemnation. God used this approach for a reason, and he put it in Scripture for a reason, too. Let's try to figure out why God focused so much on condemnation."

INTO THE WORD

Read Isaiah 5:8-12, 18-23.

Briefly summarize the background for today's passage. Then pass out copies of the outline below to your students, one per person. You can find this outline (without the answers included here) on the next page.

WHAT IS CONDEMNED?	WHAT IS THE SOLUTION?
Isaiah 5:8-10 (*exploiting others*)	1 Tim. 6:6-10
Isaiah 5:11-17 (*being drunk*)	Eph. 5:15-20
Isaiah 5:18, 19 (*blasphemy*)	James 3:2-13
Isaiah 5:20 (*confusing moral standards*)	1 Thess. 5:21, 22
Isaiah 5:21 (*being conceited*)	James 4:6-10
Isaiah 5:22, 23 (*perverting justice*)	Amos 5:24

Ask your class members to form groups of four and fill in the column under "What is condemned?" They should not discuss the solution unless they are finished before the other groups. Allow about eight minutes for the groups to complete the first column. (Note: they can finish the second column at home. This will encourage them to dig deeper into the lesson on their own.)

Ask the groups for their observations in the first column. Write these on the chalkboard. Then ask the question, "Why did God take the negative approach when dealing with his wayward people?" Allow for discussion.

INTO LIFE

Write these three situations on the chalkboard:

1. *A person with a serious illness.*
2. *A person on a sinking ship.*
3. *A person in a house on fire.*

Ask these questions for each situation:

1. *What hope would a person in this situation want to hear?*
2. *What bad news would the person have to agree with before receiving hope?*

Then say, "The gospel is good news. It has a strongly positive message. But the positive message cannot be received until a person has accepted the bad news that we deserve God's wrath unless we are forgiven in Christ."

Then lead a discussion of these questions:

1. In what ways should we be negative in dealing with the world?

2. In what ways should we be positive?

3. What should be our attitude when we have to deal negatively with the world? Why?

4. What negative message from God do you personally need to pay attention to?

5. What positive message from God do you need to cling to?

Encourage students to complete the chart, dealing with the solutions, at home. Close with prayer.

Condemn Sin

In Isaiah 5:8-23 God condemns six sins. List those sins in the chart below and then look at the passages in the right-hand column for the solutions.

WHAT IS CONDEMNED?	WHAT IS THE SOLUTION?
Isaiah 5:8-10 greed	1 Timothy 6:6-10 godliness with contentment bring nothing in & take nothing out. food & clothing. Some eager for money have wandered from faith & many griefs
Isaiah 5:11-17	Ephesians 5:15-20 Don't get drunk on wine but be filled with spirit speak, sing & make music giving thanks to the Lord.
Isaiah 5:18, 19	James 3:2-13 both good & bad should not come out of our mouth. humility
Isaiah 5:20	1 Thessalonians 5:21, 22 Test everything hold on to what is good. Avoid every kind of evil.
Isaiah 5:21	James 4:6-10 He gives us more grace. God opposes the proud & gives grace to the humble submit resist the devil.
Isaiah 5:22, 23	Amos 5:24 Let justice roll on like a river righteousness like a never-failing stream

Enjoy Life

In light of the exercise above, explain the meaning of the following passage of Scripture. Use the box below to record your answer. If you are working on this in a group, discuss your insights with others in the group.

"The earth and every good thing in it belongs to the Lord and is yours to enjoy"
(1 Corinthians 10:26, *The Living Bible*).

THE END OF A NATION

LESSON 13

WHY TEACH THIS LESSON?

Many of us who are parents have used the 1-2-3 warning before stern discipline. It lets the child know he or she is headed in the wrong direction and allows her to change "voluntarily" without further retribution.

Some parents, however, have subverted the process and nullified its effectiveness You hear them calling after a wayward child: "I said, 'Come back here!' Now I mean it. One . . . two . . . Come on now. One . . . two . . . two and a-half!" The child knows they will never get to "three," so he never takes the warning seriously.

This lesson lets us know God's warnings are indeed to be taken seriously. Throughout this quarter's lessons, we have heard him warn his people Israel to return. "One . . . two. . . ." Today he gets to "three." Israel had refused his warnings, so the Assyrians were allowed to conquer Samaria and deport its citizens to other lands.

The application is clear. Though he no longer deals with his people in a political way—at least, not in the same sense as he dealt with the nation of Israel—he still warns us to follow his ways and that judgment is sure to follow if we do not. Use this lesson as a reminder that, "unless [we] repent, [we] too will all perish" (Luke 13:3, 5).

INTRODUCTION

A. NEGLECT BRINGS DISASTER

Several years ago Joe bought a new car. With it came a manual that explained how the car should be cared for to keep it in good running condition. But Joe was more interested in driving his new car than he was in maintaining it, and so he ignored the manual. He didn't worry about keeping the tires properly inflated, he didn't check the radiator coolant, and he didn't change the oil regularly. The car ran well for a while, but eventually little things began to go wrong. Joe had repairs made to keep his car running, but he still paid little attention to proper maintenance. He ignored friends who kept telling him that he would ruin the engine if he didn't change the oil. Then one day it happened. The engine blew up, throwing a rod through the side of the block. Joe no longer had a car to drive, and he had no one but himself to blame.

This sounds rather like the situation in ancient Israel. God had placed them in the land of promise and given them instructions about what they were to do so they could continue to enjoy its blessings. But they had ignored these instructions. Again and again God had sent his spokesmen to warn them of the dangers they faced if they didn't change their ways. But they rejected these messengers and continued on their reckless way. Then it happened. As a result of moral decay within and Assyrian aggression from without, the nation was swept away—and it had only itself to blame.

B. LESSON BACKGROUND

During the reigns of Jeroboam II of the northern kingdom and Uzziah of the southern kingdom, Israel and Judah had enjoyed great prosperity. In part this

DEVOTIONAL READING:
DEUTERONOMY 8:11-20
LESSON SCRIPTURE:
2 KINGS 17:1-23
PRINTED TEXT:
2 KINGS 17:6-14

LESSON AIMS

As a result of studying this lesson, each student should:

1. Understand the political situation at the time Israel fell.

2. Understand how Israel sinned against God.

3. Appreciate the fact that disobedience to God's commandments has dire consequences.

4. Be able to point out sins in our nation that can lead to our downfall.

KEY VERSE:

The LORD warned Israel and Judah through all his prophets and seers: "Turn from your evil ways. Observe my commands and decrees." —2 Kings 17:13

Aug
27

LESSON 13 NOTES

HOW TO SAY IT

Assyria. Uh-SEAR-ee-uh.
Ben-Hadad. Ben-HAY-dad.
Canaanite. KAY-nun-ite.
Gozan. GO-zun.
Habor. HAY-bor.
Halah. HAY-luh.
Hoshea. Ho-SHE-uh.
Jeroboam. Jair-o-BO-um.
Nineveh. NIN-uh-vuh.
Omri. AHM-rye or AHM-ree.
Pekah. PEE-kuh.
Sargon. SAR-gon.
Shalmaneser. SHALL-man-
    EE-zer.
Tiglath-Pileser. TIG-lath-
    Pih-LEE-zer.
Uzziah. Uh-ZYE-uh.

OPTION

The reproducible activity page, 448, contains a Bible study activity, "The Downfall of the Redeemed," that will help your students explore today's text.

Display visual 13 throughout the lesson period. It illustrates verses 7, 13, and 14.

prosperity came because the power of Assyria had declined. But all this was to change when Tiglath-Pileser came to the throne of Assyria in 745 B.C. Once he gained firm control over his kingdom, he turned his attention to the west, forcing Syria, Israel, and Judah to pay him tribute.

In 731 B.C. Hoshea assassinated Pekah, the king of Israel, and made himself king. At first he paid tribute to Shalmaneser, who had succeeded Tiglath-Pileser as king of Assyria. But when Hoshea later withheld the tribute, Shalmaneser marched against Israel, determined to punish her. Apparently he ravaged the countryside, and then in 725 laid siege to Samaria, the capital. After three years Samaria fell. Some records indicate that by this time Shalmaneser had been succeeded by Sargon II, who takes credit for the capture of Israel's capital. The fall of Samaria brought an end to Israel, which never again appears as a nation separate from Judah.

I. ISRAEL FALLS TO ASSYRIA (2 KINGS 17:6)

A. SAMARIA IS CAPTURED (V. 6A)

6a. In the ninth year of Hoshea, the king of Assyria captured Samaria.

Samaria was located in the hill country of central Palestine, about forty miles north of Jerusalem. The city, built by Omri about 880 B.C., was situated on a readily defended height, which is apparently the reason that Omri chose to make it his capital. On one occasion Ben-Hadad, king of Syria, besieged the city and was able to bring the people almost to the point of starvation (2 Kings 6:24, 25). Yet he was not able to breach the walls or enter the city. The Assyrians had perfected the art of warfare. Few cities could stand against them when they brought their battering rams and their siege towers into play. Yet Samaria was able to hold out for three years, attesting to its formidable defenses. But after three years it fell in 722 B.C., probably because its food supplies were exhausted.

B. THE CAPTIVES ARE DEPORTED (V. 6B)

6b. . . . and deported the Israelites to Assyria. He settled them in Halah, in Gozan on the Habor River and in the towns of the Medes.

When the Assyrians captured a city, it was not unusual for them to put to death all the able-bodied men, often subjecting them to terrible cruelty in the process. While some may have been killed at Samaria, apparently many of the inhabitants were spared and sent back to Assyria. In the Assyrian records that have been recovered, King Sargon II boasts of deporting 27,290 prisoners. The deportees were sent to several different places. Halah has been identified with a town northeast of Nineveh. Some translations indicate that Habor was a river that ran through the area of Gozan and emptied into the Euphrates River. The Medes lived in an area north and east of the Tigris River in what is now Iran.

This deportation served two purposes. First, it provided the Assyrians with a good supply of slaves. Further, it is quite likely that those who were selected for deportation were the most capable people, those who might lead a revolt in the future. By depriving the Israelites of their natural leaders and by settling foreigners among those who remained, the Assyrians were trying to prevent another uprising.

II. REASONS FOR ISRAEL'S FALL (2 KINGS 17:7-12)

A. THEY HAD SINNED AGAINST GOD (V. 7)

7. All this took place because the Israelites had sinned against the LORD their God, who had brought them up out of Egypt from under the power of Pharaoh king of Egypt. They worshiped other gods.

The first six verses in this chapter tell of the destruction that came upon the nation of Israel. This verse introduces an explanation of why it happened. The *Israelites had sinned* against God, though they owed him their gratitude and obedience because he had delivered them out of Egypt. The nation that God had formed and called *out of Egypt* was now going back into bondage and would lose her identity. The cycle that we see in the book of Judges—Israel falling into sin, God sending punishment upon them, the people repenting, and then God restoring them to favor—would not be repeated this time. Their great sin, one that had been repeated time and again, was that they had turned to the worship of *other gods*.

PARADISE LOST

Eve and Adam were removed from God's garden because they sinned against the Lord. They ate forbidden fruit, so they lost paradise. They were separated from God by their disobedience, and they were punished by pain, sorrow, toil, and ultimately death.

The nation of Israel was removed from God's promised land because "the Israelites had sinned against the Lord their God." These "chosen people" were rebellious and disobedient. So God allowed them to be defeated by enemies who displaced them to foreign lands and strange cultures.

Sin hasn't changed. It still separates us from God, but "we were reconciled to him through the death of his Son" (Romans 5:10). So Christians again possess the promise of paradise. "To him who overcomes, I will give the right to eat from the tree of life, which is in the paradise of God" (Revelation 2:7).

What we must learn from the experiences of Adam and Israel is that God's promise is *conditional*. "Be faithful, even to the point of death, and I will give you the crown of life" (Revelation 2:10).

—R. W. B.

B. THEY HAD FOLLOWED PAGAN LAWS (v. 8)

8. . . . and followed the practices of the nations the LORD had driven out before them, as well as the practices that the kings of Israel had introduced.

It is not possible for one to separate his religion from his daily life. When the Israelites abandoned Jehovah to worship various pagan gods, they also became involved in immoralities that Jehovah considered abominations—human sacrifice, for example, and sexual orgies. These activities of pagan worship were reflected in everyday matters. Human sacrifice devalued human life, increasing the likelihood of violent crimes, and sexual orgies undermined the sanctity of marriage and family life.

From Canaanite neighbors they learned to follow *the practices* of the pagans. God had ordered them to drive the Canaanites out of the land, but they had never completely carried out this order. The Canaanites who remained infected the Israelites with their false religion. But this was not the only source of infection. On occasion their own kings, Ahab, for example, imported pagan religion and encouraged the people to become involved in it.

C. THEY HAD WORSHIPED PAGAN GODS (vv. 9-12)

9. The Israelites secretly did things against the LORD their God that were not right. From watchtower to fortified city they built themselves high places in all their towns.

A *watchtower* was any one of the many towers built in fields and vineyards to help the owners guard their crops against thieves. The *fortified city* was a town with

WHAT DO YOU THINK?

When the people of Israel came to the promised land, they were told to drive out or destroy the depraved pagans who lived there. They failed to do that, and eventually adopted many of the abominable practices of those same pagans. Israel itself was destroyed because it fell into the pagan style of worship and life.

What about us? We cannot wipe out the pagans in our culture. What can we do to prevent the infiltration of pagan attitudes and behavior in the church? How well do you think we are doing at that? What form of punishment do you think the church will experience if it fails as Israel did?

WHAT DO YOU THINK?

Compare the Great Commission with Israel's order to exterminate the pagans from the land. How are they similar? How are they different? What will happen to the unsaved if we fail in our commission? What will happen to us?

WHAT DO YOU THINK?

King Jeroboam I introduced idolatry in a sneaky way. Calling Israel to worship golden calves, he said, "It is too much for you to go up to Jerusalem. Here are your gods, O Israel, who brought you up out of Egypt" (1 Kings 12:28). In other words, he tried to pretend the calves represented a more convenient way to worship Jehovah. But they violated his Second Commandment (Exodus 20:4, 5). Centuries later the people were still pretending to honor Jehovah even while they were pagan in worship and life-style.

In what ways are Christians sometimes guilty of pretending to worship God, but actually violating his commands? What time-honored practices, or practices that "everybody" seems to be doing, might actually be violations of the Lord's commands?

a massive stone wall. The historian is saying that *high places* were built all over the country, from the most remote rural area to the big city. These high places were places of worship on hilltops and artificial mounds. It seems that false worship in these places was open and blatant, so it is hard to see what is meant by saying they *secretly did things against the Lord*. Possibly some people pretended to worship Jehovah, but secretly worshiped other gods. Some students think did secretly means covered or hid. Possibly it means the worship of Jehovah was buried and lost in the mass of words or things that were *not right*—the ceremonies of pagan worship. Or could the meaning be that the people of Israel secretly committed other crimes in addition to building high places for false worship?

10. They set up sacred stones and Asherah poles on every high hill and under every spreading tree.

The making of an image to be worshiped was strictly forbidden by the Second Commandment, which is so clear and specific that there was no reason for anyone to misunderstand it. The people had so compromised their faith that they had no trouble violating such a plain commandment. If we find this hard to understand, we need only to look at our own times. The Scriptures have some quite specific teachings about homosexuality, and yet some church groups have completely ignored these teachings.

The *sacred stones* were stone obelisks that undoubtedly had some significance in idolatrous worship. *Asherah* was the Canaanite fertility goddess. Her symbol was often a trunk of a tree, hence the reference to *poles*. The fact that she was the fertility goddess gives a clue to the licentious sex acts that went on in the name of worship.

11, 12. At every high place they burned incense, as the nations whom the LORD had driven out before them had done. They did wicked things that provoked the LORD to anger. They worshiped idols, though the LORD had said, "You shall not do this."

Burning *incense* symbolized prayer, and so in this act they were praying to false gods just as the pagans had done before them. Because of their wickedness, the pagans had been *driven out*. Now the Israelites were guilty of the same offense, and as a result they would soon have to suffer the same punishment. *Wicked things* may refer to the sexual activities involved in the worship, or perhaps to human sacrifice. Both of these were abominations to the Lord. Involvement in idolatry disobeyed God's direct commands against it, making their offense all the more wicked.

III. ISRAEL HAD BEEN WARNED (2 KINGS 17:13, 14)

A. PROPHETS AND SEERS HAD WARNED THEM (v. 13)

13. The LORD warned Israel and Judah through all his prophets and seers: "Turn from your evil ways. Observe my commands and decrees, in accordance with the entire Law that I commanded your fathers to obey and that I delivered to you through my servants the prophets."

Incorporated in the law of Moses were prohibitions that should have kept the people from the idolatry into which they had fallen. But God's warnings did not stop with these prohibitions. Again and again he sent his spokesmen to bring further warnings. The term *prophets* covers a great variety of people who spoke for God, including Abram and Aaron. Specifically, we think of the writing prophets such as Isaiah, Jeremiah, and the so-called minor prophets. Some of these whom we have studied this quarter directed their messages specifically at some of the sins that were dragging Israel down to destruction. The term *seer* is sometimes used synonymously with *prophet*; however, it carries the idea of one who sees

WHAT DO YOU THINK?

God warned Israel and Judah through prophets and through adverse political and economic conditions. Besides the Bible itself, what "messengers" do you think God sends us today to call us to repentance? How can we know whom to believe? (See 2 Corinthians 12:7-10; Romans 8:28; Hebrews 1:1-4.)

beyond what a person can ordinarily see. God gave the power to see not only the future, but also a deeper meaning in ordinary events.

God had sent these special messengers over a period of many years. He was unwilling to give his people up at their first offense, but patiently and lovingly tried to bring them back to him. God is "patient with you, not wanting anyone to perish, but everyone to come to repentance" (2 Peter 3:9).

B. THEY HAD REJECTED THE WARNINGS (v. 14)

14. But they would not listen and were as stiff-necked as their fathers, who did not trust in the LORD their God.

The people of Israel certainly had heard the messages the Lord had sent, but they *would not listen* in the sense that they would not heed the messages God had sent. When Isaiah was called to speak to God's people, God warned him that his preaching would "make the heart of this people calloused; make their ears dull and close their eyes" (Isaiah 6:10). The very message that could save them would only harden their hearts. They were *stiff-necked*, like stubborn oxen that refused to be turned from the wrong way. They *did not trust in the Lord.* They were like many today who say they believe in God, but their lives clearly show that they do not trust him to provide direction for their lives.

MULISH HERITAGE

"Like father, like son!" Children have proved through the ages that offspring inherit not only physical characteristics, but temperament and personality, too.

No one knows for certain if stubbornness is a genetic or learned trait, but often stubborn parents have at least one stubborn child. And when an "immovable object" lives under the same roof with an "irresistible force," troubled times are inevitable.

The stubbornness of mules is legendary. Some people are so mulish one might think of them as evidence of a new theory of evolution. Apparently several generations of both Judah and Israel were like that. They "hardened their necks" and refused to believe in Jehovah. They were stubbornly wicked. In fact, they acted both stubbornly and stupidly.

A case could be made for stubbornness when it is channeled for righteous causes. Tenacity can be a good quality when rightly used.

But stiff-necked sinners cannot be justified. When personal pride and wanton selfishness preclude repentance, stubbornness is totally detrimental and self-destructive. God wants us to give in to goodness and receive his grace; "he is patient, . . . not wanting anyone to perish" (2 Peter 3:9).

—R. W. B.

CONCLUSION

A. WHILE THERE IS STILL TIME

Nearly four centuries ago a few hardy venturers left the shores of England to find homes in the New World. Many came out of deep religious conviction, hoping to find the freedom to worship God that they felt was denied them in their native land. They hoped to build a "city built on a hill" that would serve as a model to the whole world. The Old Testament law, tempered by the teachings of the New Testament, served as their constitution and their guide for daily living.

Not all who came to the New World shared this Puritan faith. Some came in search of gold or wealth in other forms. Some came with religious convictions that differed from the convictions of the Puritans. Some arrived in chains, victims of the horrible slave system. Yet, regardless of how they came or what they believed when they came, they were all in one way or another influenced by the Puritans.

WHAT DO YOU THINK?

We say we believe in God and Jesus, but several studies have indicated that there doesn't seem to be much difference between the way Christians act and the way non-Christians act. That is a serious indictment, for Jesus said a tree is known by its fruit (Matthew 12:33). Are we affected by our culture more than by our Lord? If we say, "Jesus is Lord," that means we run everything by his teaching; moment by moment we do what he wants.

If we trust God, what evidence should our lives give to verify our trust?

OPTION

The reproducible activity page, 448, contains an application activity, "These Things Happened as Examples." You can use it by making copies or simply by reading the passage cited and asking the students to complete the statements.

WHAT DO YOU THINK?

Destroyed by Assyria, Israel ceased to exist as a nation. For her, there were no more second chances. Someday that will be true for the whole world. As long as Jesus has not returned, there is still time—but not for everyone. Every day some are dying and going unprepared to face judgment.

What specifically is your church doing to win the lost? What priority does your church give to evangelism and missions? What share do they have of our money, our prayer, our concern? What are you doing to win your lost friends and neighbors?

PRAYER

Dear God, use these lessons from ancient Israel to open our eyes to the dangers that our nation faces. Give us the wisdom to bring your Word to bear on the moral problems that we face. Teach us that your mercy is still available to those who repent and turn to you. In the name of our Savior we pray. Amen.

THOUGHT TO REMEMBER

Time was limited for Israel. Time is limited for people who do not know Jesus as Lord. Time is limited for the church to be about the Father's business.

DAILY BIBLE READINGS

Monday, Aug. 21—A Warning to Keep God's Commands (Deuteronomy 8:11-20)

Tuesday, Aug. 22—Israel Falls, the People Are Deported (2 Kings 17:1-6)

Wednesday, Aug. 23—Israel's Sins Caused Its Fall (2 Kings 17: 7-12)

Thursday, Aug. 24—Israel Scorned God and Worshiped Idols (2 Kings 17:13-18)

Friday, Aug. 25—Jeroboam's Leadership Started Israel's Decline (2 Kings 17:19-23)

Saturday, Aug. 26—The Land Resettled With Other Peoples (2 Kings 17:24-28)

Sunday, Aug. 27—The End of the Nation Israel (2 Kings 17: 29-34)

It is popular today to sneer at the Puritans, rejecting them as narrow-minded bigots whose main purpose in life was to keep people from enjoying themselves. Or they are simply ignored in our history texts, or their contributions are greatly minimized. Of course, not all of their actions can be justified. Their intolerance of dissent is a black mark on their record, and so is the hanging of a number of alleged witches. Nevertheless, their stern ethic made a lasting impact on American history. Their commitment to God and their dedication to hard work, combined with the rich natural resources God had placed in the land, allowed America eventually to become the richest country in the world.

But America faced some of the same problems that ancient Israel encountered. With wealth came temptations that over the years gradually eroded the firm convictions of these stalwart pioneers. The Pilgrims were not able to pass on their convictions to their children and their children's children. If they were to return today, they would surely be shocked to see what has happened to their dreams of building the kingdom of God on earth. On every hand they would see crime, drug abuse, political corruption, adultery, abortion, and religious apathy. No doubt they would tremble as they contemplated the wrath of God that certainly will fall upon such a nation if it continues to sink deeper into wrongdoing.

All of us to some extent have been beneficiaries of these Pilgrim fathers. In the Old Testament they found guidelines that helped shape their theology. We too can learn from ancient Israel and Judah. They were God's chosen people; yet when they departed from his ways, he did not withhold his judgment from them. We also have been richly blessed by God, and someday he will call for an accounting. God is still on his throne, and he still demands righteousness of a nation.

We have an obligation to speak out against the evils we see about us. We need to enlist others to join us in that mission. Most of all, we must impart to our children the faith that can yet save us.

B. PROPHETS AND SEERS

When God gave Moses the law on Mount Sinai, he did not leave the people without further guidance. After they entered the promised land, it was not long before they began to go astray. God sent judges to deliver them from their enemies and bring them back to him. He used great heroes like Samuel and David to provide guidance for his people. Then came prophets and seers. In the exercise of their office these men were both foretellers and forthtellers. In some cases God gave them the vision to pull aside the curtains and catch a glimpse of the future. With this divine insight they could bring warnings of impending doom that threatened the nation if the people did not change their ways. As forthtellers they told of God's righteousness and his requirements that the people live up to his law. This quarter we have studied the lives and messages of several of these prophets. Even after twenty-five hundred years or more, their messages strike a responsive chord in our hearts. They brought God's condemnation of wrong in their societies, a judgment that is still needed today.

We do not have prophets and seers in the same sense that they did in those days. No one today can proclaim Holy Spirit inspired messages as they did. But we no longer need such inspired messengers because we have God's inspired Word, the holy Scriptures. That puts a responsibility on each one of us. If the Bible is to speak to us today, we must read it and study it and heed it. Each one of these steps takes effort on our part. That's the reason it is important that students in your class be regular in their attendance and participate in the learning activities.

Discovery Learning

*This page contains an alternate lesson plan emphasizing learning activities. Classes
desiring such student involvement will find these suggestions helpful. The next page
is a reproducible activity page to further enhance discovery learning.*

LEARNING GOALS

By the end of this lesson each student will be able to:

1. Determine a correlation between obedience and God's blessing, and between rebellion and God's punishment for a nation.

2. Evaluate where his own nation is on a continuum between God's blessing and God's punishment.

3. Suggest principles to help our nation turn to God and receive his favor.

INTO THE LESSON

Write these two sentences on the chalkboard and call attention to them:

*Obeying God brings his blessing.
Rebellion against God brings punishment.*

Ask your students to brainstorm examples that illustrate both of these principles. The examples can be from Scripture, from other history, or common examples from life.

Then say to the class, "This is the final lesson in this quarter. In the history of nations and their leaders, we have observed a strong correlation between rebelling against God and receiving God's judgment. The opposite is also true. Nations that seek God and obey him receive his blessing. Today we will see God's judgment against his northern kingdom, Israel."

INTO THE WORD

Explain the background to today's text. Then ask a volunteer to read 2 Kings 17:6-20. Have your class form groups of six to discuss the questions below (make a copy of the questions for each group):

1. Why was Israel (also called Samaria) punished, according to:
   verses 7-13
   verses 14, 15
   verses 16, 17
   verses 18-20
2. How was Israel punished?
3. How had God tried to prevent this punishment?
4. What does this passage teach you about human nature?
5. What does it teach you about God?
6. According to Jeremiah 18:7-11, how can a wicked nation prevent punishment from God?

OPTIONS

Option 1: Explain the passage background and ask a volunteer to read 2 Kings 17:6-20. Have class members form groups of six.

In their groups they are to imagine they are prosecuting attorneys in a courtroom trial of the nation of Israel. They are seeking to prove that Israel is guilty and should be punished. Based upon 2 Kings 17:6-20 they should prepare a closing argument to present to the jury.

Appoint a leader for each group and provide paper and pens. Give the groups twenty minutes to compile their arguments. They should appoint someone from the group to present the closing argument to the rest of the class, who will serve as the jury.

Then have the class read Jeremiah 18:7-11. Ask, "Based on this passage, how can a wicked nation prevent God's punishment?" Allow discussion.

Option 2: Use the first activity on the reproducible page that follows, "The Downfall of the Redeemed," to study 2 Kings 17:7-17 and discover reasons God allowed the nation of Israel to fall. Then have the class read Jeremiah 18:7-11. Ask, "Based on this passage, how can a wicked nation prevent God's punishment?" Allow discussion.

INTO LIFE

Write the following on the chalkboard:

Blessing 1   2   3   4   5   6   7   8   9   10 *Punishment*

Provide pen and paper for each student. Ask each to write the scale on his paper. Then ask him to circle the number that best represents where he thinks our nation is in relation to God's blessing or punishment.

Take a tally and try to get an average score. Explain that this obviously is only an opinion, and only God knows where our nation is in relation to his favor or rejection.

Have class members form their small groups again. Then ask the groups to discuss and identify what they believe are the three most important things our nation needs to change in order to gain God's continual blessing. After five minutes, ask the groups to report their conclusions.

Ask each class member to write down what he thinks are the three most important things for him to do individually to help our nation gain God's blessing. He can write these on the paper he received earlier.

Close in small group prayer, asking students to pray that they and their country will live righteously for God.

The Downfall of the Redeemed

2 Kings 17 recites the reasons God brought about the downfall of his covenant people. In the spaces following the Scripture references below describe both what specific sins brought about this disaster and what similar activities we find our nation guilty of today.

TEXT	WHAT HAD ISRAEL DONE?	WHAT HAVE WE DONE?
2 Kings 17:7	Had sinned against Lord Worshiped other Gods	
2 Kings 17:7, 12, 17	worshiped idols Sacrificed sons & daughters practiced divination & sorcery	
2 Kings 17:8-11, 15-17	followed practices of other nations Secretly did things against God burned Incense	
2 Kings 17:13-15	were stiff-necked rejected his decrees & covenant	
2 Kings 17:13-16	bowed down to all starry hosts & they worshiped Baal.	
2 Kings 17:9, 15-17	Did evil in the eyes of the Lord	

These Things Occurred as Examples

Have someone in your group read 1 Corinthians 10:1-12 which is a warning to us from Israel's history. Then discuss with your group the meaning of the command "do not be idolaters."

In order to better apply these lessons of history to each member of the group, have each person take the following personal inventory:

• I couldn't live without _____.

• When my mind is idle, it automatically turns to _____.

• If I could have anything in the world I would choose _____.

• I know God wants me to _____ but I can't.